CARIBBEAN

FODOR'S TRAVEL GUIDES

are compiled, researched and edited by an international team of travel writers, field correspondents, and editors. The series, which now almost covers the globe, was founded by Eugene Fodor in 1936.

OFFICES
New York & London

Fodor's Caribbean:

Fodor's Editor: Andrew Beresky
Contributing Editors: Janet E. Bigham, Nancy B. Clarke, Sally Cummings, Barbara A. Currie, Claire Devener, Margaret Enos, Anita Gates, Adrienne Henzel, Brian Hickey, J.P. MacBean, David P. Schulz, Kay Showker, David Swindell, Tony Tedeschi
Maps and Plans: Pictograph, Xhardez
Drawings: Michael Kaplan

FODOR'S

CARIBBEAN

1986

FODOR'S TRAVEL GUIDES
New York

The following Fodor's Guides are current; most are also available in a British
edition published by Hodder & Stoughton.

Country and Area Guides

Australia, New Zealand
  & The South Pacific
Austria
Bahamas
Belgium & Luxembourg
Bermuda
Brazil
Canada
Canada's Maritime
  Provinces
Caribbean
Central America
Eastern Europe
Egypt
Europe
France
Germany
Great Britain
Greece
Holland
India, Nepal &
    Sri Lanka
Ireland
Israel
Italy
Japan
Jordan & The Holy Land
Kenya
Korea
Mexico
North Africa
People's Republic of
  China
Portugal
Scandanavia
Scotland
South America
Southeast Asia

Soviet Union
Spain
Switzerland
Turkey
Yugoslavia

City Guides

Amsterdam
Beijing, Guangzhou,
  Shanghai
Boston
Chicago
Dallas–Fort Worth
Greater Miami & The
  Gold Coast
Hong Kong
Houston
Lisbon
London
Los Angeles
Madrid
Mexico City &
    Acapulco
Munich
New Orleans
New York City
Paris
Philadelphia
Rome
San Diego
San Francisco
Stockholm, Copenhagen,
  Oslo, Helsinki &
  Reykjavik
Sydney
Tokyo
Toronto
Vienna
Washington, D.C.

U.S.A. Guides

Alaska
Arizona
California
Cape Cod
Colorado
Far West
Florida
Hawaii
New England
New Mexico
Pacific North Coast
South
Texas
U.S.A.

Budget Travel

American Cities (30)
Britain
Canada
Caribbean
Europe
France
Germany
Hawaii
Italy
Japan
London
Mexico
Spain

Fun Guides

Acapulco
Bahamas
London
Montreal
Puerto Rico
San Francisco
St. Martin/Sint Maarten
Waikiki

CONTENTS

A CAPSULE VIEW OF THE ISLANDS

Anguilla 1; Antigua 1; Aruba 1; Barbados 1; Bonaire 2; British Virgin Islands 2; Cayman Islands 2; Curaçao 3; Dominica 4; Dominican Republic 4; Grenada 4; Guadeloupe 5; Haiti 5; Jamaica 5; Martinique 6; Montserrat 6; Nevis 6; Puerto Rico 7; Saba 7; St. Barthelemy 7; St. Eustatius 7; St. Kitts 8; St. Lucia 8; St. Martin/Sint Maarten 8; St. Vincent and the Grenadines 8; Trinidad and Tobago 9; The Turks and Caicos Islands 9; U.S. Virgin Islands 9

FACTS AT YOUR FINGERTIPS

Planning Your Trip 10; How to Get There by Air 10; How to Get There by Sea 11; Yachting 16; Passports and Visas 16; Travel Agents and Tour Operators 16; Tourist Information Services 17; Tips for British Visitors 19; When to Go 20; Packing 21; What Will It Cost? 21; Seasonal Events 21; Money 22; Traveling with Pets 22; Hotels and Other Accommodations 22; Time-Sharing 23; Dining Out 23; Tipping 23; Time Zone 23; Electric Current 24; Senior-citizen and Student Discounts 24; Hints to Handicapped Travelers 24; Health 24; Airport Departure Taxes 25; Customs 25

CONTENTS

CONTENTS

FOREWORD

Mention the Caribbean Islands and the phrase conjures up images of white-sand beaches, bright sunshine, tall palm trees gently swaying in balmy breezes, cool fruity rum punches, and a pervading feeling of quiet leisure. That's true, but the Islands also have another face. There's the challenge of sport fishing, the thrill of discovering undersea flora and fauna, hiking through tropical rain forests, dancing to throbbing island rhythms at the newest disco, and tempting fate in the casinos. The Caribbean is also synonymous with excitement.

The contributors to *Fodor's Caribbean* have combed beaches, browsed shops, found quiet island retreats, and stayed at properties that ranged from cottage colonies to highrise palaces. We have picked and savored indigenous island fruits and vegetables; lingered over spicy West Indian dishes; sampled the coconut coolers made with island rums; and discovered soups thick with seafood and vegetables.

These islands are also for music, which ranges from tantalizing drum rhythms to precise quadrilles; for their history, which runs the gamut from Indian chieftains to pirate and royal kings; and for their variety of ethnic cultures, brought over and still somewhat maintained from almost every country you can name.

We have listened to the pure French, Dutch, and Spanish spoken on some islands, the lilting Creole patois in the French West Indies, and the Dutch dialect called Papiamento in the Netherlands Antilles. We have even found places where West Indian English has overtones of an Irish brogue or a Scottish burr.

There have been days for sailing, snorkeling, swimming, shelling, and scuba diving to see the wonders of the coral reefs and marine gardens that hug the ocean floor. Hiking on trails through rain forests, climbing to volcanic peaks, and swimming in mountain pools beneath cascading waterfalls have added to our Caribbean pleasures. Even when it rains in the Caribbean, the islands are full of historic places, museums, and shops that will captivate you.

Fodor's Caribbean guide has been prepared to help you to choose the island that is best for you. All descriptions, whether favorable or adverse, are based on the editors' personal experiences. Although we make last-minute checks just before going to press, much of the information is still perishable because the Caribbean changes from island to island, almost day to day. We cannot, therefore, be responsible for the sudden closing of a restaurant, change of management of a hotel, or the moods of chefs and hotel personnel.

We welcome your comments on our exploration of each Caribbean island and all it has to offer. We are always on hand to take another look at a restaurant, hotel, or sightseeing attraction if the situation warrants. Send your letters to **Fodor's Travel Guides,** 2 Park Ave., New York, NY 10016, or to our offices at 9-10 Market Place, London W1N 7AG, England.

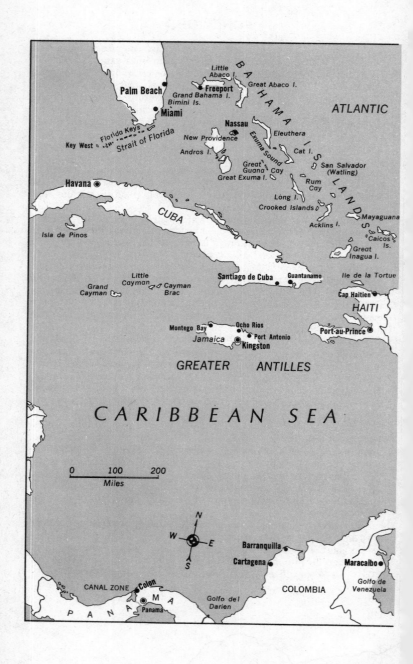

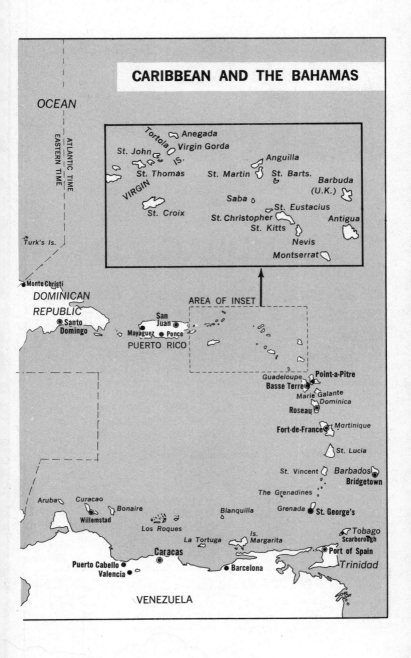

CARIBBEAN AND THE BAHAMAS

A CAPSULE VIEW OF THE ISLANDS

We know just how hard choosing a vacation island can be. People say, "What's your favorite place?" The answer has to be, "For what?" And even then, we're not sure that what we like on vacation is perfect for you. All the places covered in this guide have sun—and trade winds; many have mountains; some have deserts; all have plenty of deep blue sea. Although Cuba is in the Caribbean, it is not a likely vacation destination for many Americans and thus has been excluded from this guide.

For your preliminary planning, we present a summary of highlights on each island to help you decide which island or island grouping is best for you.

Anguilla. One of the best-kept secrets in the Caribbean, Anguilla is a beach-comber's delight where tourism is just beginning. Accommodations—cottages, villas, apartments, informal guesthouses, and elegant hotels—are small and special and the government is doing its best to keep them that way. Day-trippers from St. Martin are discovering there's no mass tourism here, no casinos, no cruise ships, no shops. But for those who want it, peace, quiet, and the simple unspoiled beauty of nearly deserted, dazzling white beaches, clear turquoise water with colorful undersea gardens, and halcyon days can easily be found. Anguilla may not be for everyone, but this island is impossible to beat for those looking to get away from it all.

Antigua. Thoroughly British, with a long colonial history, Antigua and sparsely populated Barbuda gained independence in 1981. The two major draw-ing cards are the many white-sand beaches—reputedly 365 in all—and the history acquired when Admiral Lord Nelson dropped anchor here two hundred years ago and the island became headquarters for the British Royal Navy's Caribbean fleet. Restoration of Nelson's Dockyard at English Harbour is a major tourist attraction, while the capital city of St. John's is a popular port of call with cruise ships. A new airport terminal speeds the handling of jumbo jets full of tourists from the U.S. and Canada, as well as Britain and, to a lesser extent, continental Europe. Resorts and hotel facilities range from the surpris-ingly inexpensive to the ultraluxurious and from huge and lively to remote and exclusive. There are two gambling casinos, major evening entertainment, and international sporting events. Winter season is still the busiest, although year-round holiday and long-weekend hops are gaining popularity. With such a range of accommodations, there is something for almost every age, income, and inter-est group.

Aruba. Glorious white-sand beaches on the Caribbean, the charming Dutch capital of Oranjestad, a rugged Atlantic coast with thundering waves, and an arid interior marked by cactus, aloe, and rock formations describe the four faces of Aruba. As part of the Netherlands Antilles, the island has a political climate as calm and constant as its year-round 82-degree weather and gentle trade winds. Independence, however, is in the offing. Tourism has been developing steadily since the early 1960s, so that today more than a dozen hotels are lined up along the island's seven-mile stretch of beach. Swimming, snorkeling, sailing, deep-sea fishing, scuba diving, international cuisine, and five lively casinos attract honeymooners, some families, and visitors of all ages. Americans predominate, but tourists from Venezuela, the Netherlands, and other parts of South America and Europe are frequently seen too. Winter (December to April) is high season, but the beaches are uncrowded even then. Summer and fall are off-season, less expensive and just as delightful.

Barbados. Easternmost of all the Caribbean islands, Barbados has been a "tourist destination" since the 18th century, when it lured visitors from the

1

faraway British Isles to its coast to enjoy sunbleached beaches, lush rolling hills, and what was considered the healthiest climate in the West Indies.

Modern Barbados offers more variety in both accommodation and recreation within its 166 square miles than other Caribbean islands many times its size. Visitors will find golf, horse racing, polo, and a cornucopia of aquatic offerings, including a professional windsurfing school. Its "platinum coast" to the west has one of the region's finest stretches of white-sand beach and, after the sun goes down, some of the finest calypso and steel-band entertainment in the islands.

Add to that a population known for its cheerful outlook on life and congenial treatment of visitors, plus one of the most stable political scenes in the Caribbean, and you have a nation that's a model for other islands searching to preserve their culture and progress economically.

Barbados is the favorite vacation spot of Americans, Canadians, and Europeans of better-than-average means, who appreciate its genteel ambience and friendly people—as well as the superb quality of the Mt. Gay rum it produces in quantity. With the exception of casinos, this island has it all.

Bonaire. The second-largest, but least populated, of the Dutch "ABC" islands of the Netherlands Antilles, Bonaire is a haven for scuba divers, bird watchers, and photographers who come to enjoy this "desert" island's unique protected terrestrial and marine environments.

The surrounding Caribbean and thriving coral reef system immediately offshore from the Bonaire Marine Park, a five-year-old project whose strict conservation regulations were enacted to preserve the island's underwater attractions for divers and snorkelers in future generations. Onshore, the entire northern part of Bonaire comprises 13,500 acres of wilderness sanctuary known as Washington/Slagbaai National Park, whose Gotto Meer flamingo preserve and stark, desert vistas are scenes unexpected on a Caribbean island.

Bonaire is internationally known for its successful solar saltworks on the island's southern tip.

This is an island that has no off-season in terms of climate. With scant rainfall and year-round sunshine, the only variation is the wind velocity of the southeasterly trade winds, at their peak in summer months. Bonaire is a vacation island for those with simple needs ashore and a fascination with nature above and below the sea's surface. But visitors won't have to sacrifice any amenities. Bonaire is easily accessible by jet from the U.S., and its few hotels include two modern and well-appointed resorts.

British Virgin Islands. The water is the message in the B.V.I. and sailing is the medium by which the message is delivered. About half the visitors at any given time are on chartered yachts, which can be chartered with crew or "bareboat" (without). There are more than 50 islands, most accessible by yacht. Only about a dozen have any inhabitants at all. The beaches are among the most beautiful in the world, and many are accessible only by boat. Most of the 12,000 inhabitants live on Tortola and Virgin Gorda.

Places to stay range from small inns and guesthouses to some of the most expensive resorts in the Caribbean. Most of the resorts are built along beaches on Tortola, Virgin Gorda, Peter Island, Anegada, and Jost Van Dyke. "The Baths" on Virgin Gorda is a dramatic beach with huge boulders that form a grotto. Norman Island is said to be the Treasure Island of Robert Louis Stevenson's novel.

Political, economic, and social conditions are very stable in this British territory. The government has been very careful at reigning in development.

High season is December 16–April 15. It is difficult to get rooms at this time and they should be reserved well in advance. Weather is very dependable year-round, with not much variation in temperature. August is the hottest month. If there are tropical storms, they will come in late August or early September.

Sailing and water sports are the reasons to vacation here.

Cayman Islands. Less than a decade ago, this trio of tiny islands in the Western Caribbean was called "the islands time forgot." Now, with its reputation for excellence as a scuba-diving destination and offshore banking center, this British Crown Colony can no longer claim that it offers a turtle's pace.

Comprising less than 100 square miles, Grand Cayman, Cayman Brac, and Little Cayman are neither dramatic nor exciting above water compared to their closest neighbor, Jamaica. But their underwater attractions of thriving coral reefs, exciting sheer drop-offs, crystal-clear water, and a menagerie of marine creatures have made them one of the top four diving destinations in the world, and the fastest-growing saltwater sport fishing center in the Caribbean for Atlantic blue marlin.

The three "s's," sun, sea, and sand—including a fine strand called Seven Mile Beach on Grand Cayman's west coast—are the primary natural attractions of these islands. Golf and gambling are nonexistent. The fourth "s" is stability—the Caymans remain one of the most politically docile and predictably safe of all Caribbean destinations and the Caymanians themselves, among the most hospitable people you'll find on any islands.

From a variety of hotels and quality condominiums to a wide range of restaurants, Grand Cayman offers something for almost everyone whose entertainment needs are as simple as year-round sunshine and calm seas. It is also one of the most popular ports of call for over a dozen cruise ships each year, hosting at least three each week year-round.

Cayman Brac, the most beautiful island of the trio, is a tiny speck located 80 miles northeast of Grand Cayman. Its backbone is a limestone bluff which rises to a height of 140 ft. on the eastern end, the island's most dramatic panorama. Its 1,700 residents share space with 140 species of migratory birds and 11 species of wild orchids. This, too, is a haven for divers and fisherman.

Little Cayman, seven miles north, remains an unspoiled tropical wilderness of 12 square miles, and is a refuge for serious bonefishermen and light-tackle enthusiasts who pursue small tarpon in its landlocked brackish lake. Its north-coast Bloody Bay and Jackson Point area shelter some of the finest dive sites in the Caribbean, but facilities are lacking to reach them regularly.

Although weather wise the Caymans are an ideal year-round destination, they are expensive in winter months and prices drop as much as 50% between mid-April and December 1.

Curaçao. Combine the cultures of Holland, South America, Portugal, and Africa and you have the hospitable potpourri that's Curaçao. Blessed with year-round temperatures of 80°, freshened by continual trade winds, Curaçao. has an excellent, dependable climate. With only 20 inches of rainfall annually, the island, 38 miles long and 7 miles wide, is arid—but excellent for weary sun seekers. Curaçao is relaxed.

Its beaches often are small in size, but there are 38 delightful coves to explore with clear, pristine water and fine coral reefs. For those who prefer gambling to snorkeling, there are four casinos.

Curaçao's population of 160,000 is governed by a democratic parliament. The country enjoys an autonomous relationship with the Netherlands and is politically stable. It is the largest of the six Netherland Antilles islands; Willemstad is the seat of all Antilles government. Most residents speak four languages: Dutch, Papiamento, Spanish, and English. The Shell oil refinery, built in 1915, has contributed to the island's present prosperity.

Tourism is the island's number-two industry. The people of Curaçao are congenial and extend themselves toward visitors. Politeness and hospitality are the order of the day. Because of Curaço's proximity to South America's coast, Venezuelans have been the most frequent visitors in the past, but with the weakening bolivar, the influx from Venezuela has tapered off somewhat and now more Americans, Dutch, and other Latin Americans are discovering Curaçao. Modern-day treasure hunters find Curaçao's duty-free shopping enticing.

Carnival time is the busiest time for tourism (20,000 visitors) and accommodations are at a premium for a week before the Shrove Tuesday finale of celebration. Plan ahead if you plan to visit Curaçao during its biggest fiesta of the year. Remember, too, Carnival is for dancing, not for an "R & R" vacation. During the rest of the year, the scene is laid back and, with only seven major hotels, relatively quiet.

Summer hotel rates start in mid-April and are in effect until mid-December. They are generally about 15% lower than winter rates.

Dominica. A mountainous treasure house of flora and fauna, Dominica offers a natural alternative to the sand-sun-surf lure of many Caribbean islands. Several species of plants and animals are unique to the island. Bountiful rainfall in the interior gives rise to the legend of the 365 rivers on the island and enables the country to export commercial agricultural crops abroad and garden crops and water to Caribbean neighbors. Independent and politically stable since 1978, the island has attracted foreign investment for upgrading roads that ring the island without endangering the pristine beauty of the mountains and rain forest in the interior.

While tourism is heavier in winter months than in summer, the unique attractions of the island draw visitors all year round and some hotels and guesthouses don't bother with seasonal rates. Tourists are as likely to be daytrippers or overnighters from nearby islands as they are to be long-term visitors. Most still come from the U.S. and Canada, but a good percentage are from France and other continental countries because of the proximity of Martinique and Guadeloupe.

Hotels are smallish—none more than 50 rooms and most much smaller—and nightlife is on the quiet side, although there is some entertainment and dancing in the capital city of Roseau. The major attractions, however, are natural beauty, mountains, waterfalls, and freshwater ponds and pools fed by both hot and cold springs.

Dominican Republic. Founded by Christopher Columbus, in 1492, the Dominican Republic shares the island of Hispaniola with Haiti. As the birthplace of western civilization in the New World, it should be a required visit for anyone who lives in the Western Hemisphere. A treasure trove of 16th-century Spanish colonial relics, Santo Domingo contains the Alcazar, a splendid palace built for Columbus's son, Diego; the restored commercial area called the Atarazana; the Cathedral of Santa María la Menor, the oldest in the New World and the final resting place for the great navigator; and much, much more of historical significance. Not a place to rest solely on its history, the Dominican Republic has wonderful in-town hotels in Santo Domingo and beautiful coastal resorts at La Romana, Samana, and its newest resort area, Puerto Plata. The best months to visit are December through April, although prices are right year-round due to a very favorable exchange rate. Water sports abound here, as do golf, tennis, horseback riding, and baseball, which is the national spectator sport. The country is a favorite among Canadians as well as Americans and is very popular with families and couples, both younger and older.

Grenada. Grenada is at the very beginning of a new phase in tourism development. Despite its spectacular beauty, 45 white-sand beaches, wonderful cuisine, and friendly populace, tourism here languished after a Communist government took control in 1979. Following a coup and the subsequent U.S. invasion in October 1983, a constitutional government based on popular vote was restored to the island. Tourists are very welcome and hotel rooms are being built, but accommodations are still limited. As a result, visitors to Grenada find themselves very much a part of local life, eating in the same restaurants, dancing in the same places, shopping in the same stores as local people. The traveler to whom this appeals will be very happy in Grenada. Sailing, swimming, and snorkeling are major pastimes here, and the deep-sea fishing is excellent. Some of the hotels have tennis courts, but bring your own gear. Golf is almost nonexistent. With the opening of its new airport, Grenada is able to accept direct wide-body flights, undoubtedly marking a turning point for the island; bolstered by millions of dollars in U.S. aid and investment, tourism is sure to become a bigger industry each year. Right now, the "high" or winter season (December 15–April 15) is almost indistinguishable from the "low" or summer season (April 16–December 14)—the dozen or so small, first-class hotels are more or less full, and the atmosphere is lively but relaxed. The U.S. invasion may have been controversial at home, but in Grenada it is referred to as "the rescue operation" and it has made the U.S. very popular indeed. Tucked under Uncle Sam's wing as it is, Grenada is one of the safest of Caribbean islands to visit. For now, it's an unspoiled gem for people who truly love islands.

Guadeloupe. Somewhat less popular among U.S. visitors than its sister islands of St. Barts, St. Martin, or even Martinique, Guadeloupe is nonetheless a multifaceted island where natural beauty abounds, fine hotels offer excellent accommodations, and there's a gourmet restaurant to please every palate and pocketbook. Nature lovers find the 74,000-acre Natural Park absorbing; night-owls are caught up in activities from dusk to dawn. Shoppers delight at bargains on French luxury products; gamblers test their skills at the two casinos. Sailors can dock at one of the largest and most modern marinas in the Caribbean; golfers are offered a fine 18-hole championship golf course. Scuba enthusiasts thrill at the underwater pleasures at one of the world's ten best diving sites; and sun seekers discover beaches galore. A knowledge of French will add to your vacation pleasure, but even if you don't "parler," you won't have any trouble enjoying the good life here.

Haiti. The first black republic in the New World, Haiti today is a fascinating blend of African and French cultures, complete with pulsating rhythms, voo-doo, indigenous paintings, and foods that are French, Creole, and West Indian. Although English is spoken in the large hotels, French is the language of the land. Port-au-Prince, Haiti's capital, throbs with music and personality. Its old Iron Market is a landmark, with dozens of stalls displaying wares and echoing the sounds of the marketeers. Cap-Haitien's remarkable Citadelle in the north is a five-hour drive from Port-au-Prince, or just 40 minutes away if you choose to fly. Accommodations range from small hotels with lots of character to chic retreats with comparable prices. Good restaurants, nightly entertainment at the major resorts, and two casinos keep things swinging until the early hours. The season is December 16–April 15, with the hottest months July–September. Since hotel rates for the most part are quoted on a year-round basis or vary only slightly out of season, you can go at any time. The country is least crowded in the shoulder seasons, April–June or September–December, but these are the times you're most likely to have rain, although even then the rain seldom lasts for long spells. The political climate is stable, the government having been controlled by the Duvalier family dictatorship for more than 25 years. Haiti is a very poor country with one of the lowest per-capita incomes in the world. It is not overdeveloped for tourism, although there are some very posh hotels. The best beaches are in the Plage area just north of Port-au-Prince, west of Cap-Haitien, around Jacmel and Grand Gonâve. About half the tourists visiting the country each year are Americans, the rest mostly Canadian and European, with French and Germans predominating.

Jamaica. This island is the third largest in the Caribbean. It floats in the tropics about equidistant from Miami and the Panama Canal. It has the geography of a subcontinent, with such distinctive variations in climate, character, and scenery that the island is like many countries in one. Jamaica's resort capital is Montego Bay. But its real capital is fast-paced Kingston. They're about as different as Miami, Florida and Washington, D.C. More than a half-million visitors arrive every year. Most settle in for days of sun on the 146-mile north coast during the peak winter season (December 16–April 15), when prices are the highest. However, many holiday-seekers—and lots of honeymooners—arrive during the off-peak summer season (April 16–December 15) when prices are lowest, but the sun still shines. The island's economy is almost entirely dependent on tourists, although it has a substantial and controversial subeconomy focused on "ganja" (marijuana). While it flirted with Castro-style communism in the 1970s it now has a pro-western government and a freewheeling democracy. The island's biggest draw—largely for residents of the northeastern U.S. and Canada—is sun at beautiful resorts that have virtually every type of water sports and serve distinctive Jamaican and continental cuisine. The island is beginning to attract more and more Europeans. Jamaica also gave birth to reggae music, and many come solely to dance in its discos, attend reggae concerts like Sunsplash, or just see what's happening. Because such a variety of accommodations is available, the island appeals to visitors of all ages. Some pay barely $300 for a week, including air fare, and stay at no-frills inns, guesthouses, or campsites. The '80s would-be "hippies" hang out on seven miles of beach at Negril, which is starting to emerge as the new "in" spot. Those of fame and fortune pay three or four times more for a week or more of pampered service in the island's luxury hotels and villas in the more established resorts of Montego Bay, Ocho Rios, and Port Antonio. They combine their lazy days by the sea with dress-up dinners at night. Celebrities have long favored the island. It is so large, so scenic, and so sophisticated that it offers visitors just about everything except gambling casinos.

Martinique. American visitors with a strong dollar in hand will find that Martinique now offers some of the Caribbean's best values. It's popular with the French and other Europeans who tend to mass exodus to the sun at Christmas, Easter, and in the months of July and August when island accommodations are priced 30–50% lower. This bit of France in the tropics is well equipped for tourism with modern hotels, country inns, and small guesthouses; nice beaches and adequate sports facilities; a unique and varied landscape; good shopping and excellent restaurants. U.S. travelers may be happier with a good French phrase book and/or dictionary; but *les Martiniquais* are helpful and friendly and abound with *joie de vivre*—and that means good time in any language.

Montserrat. Although you won't find much evidence of the island's original Irish settlers, who arrived from St. Kitts in 1632, Montserrat deserves its label "the Emerald Isle of the Caribbean." Its mere 39½ square miles offer lush, rolling volcanic vistas; the island wears a thick cloak of rain-forest vegetation around the base of its mountainous interior. There are still Irish surnames here, and you'll detect a kind of West Indian brogue spoken by the country's 12,500 people, but in all other respects, this British Crown Colony in the Leeward chain is strictly West Indian. It's also one of the most fertile producers of tropical fruits and vegetables in the Caribbean, and home of the succulent "mountain chicken."

In the past five years, Montserrat's tourism industry hasn't grown much, and the trickle of visitors into Blackburne Airport is far less than neighboring island Antigua welcomes each season. But those who have discovered Montserrat (Americans, Canadians, and English) apparently find it difficult to go anyplace else because of the warmth of the climate and of the people who live there, and the special tranquility it offers. Golf, swimming, sightseeing, and hiking are the main outdoors activities on this otherwise quiet island.

Nevis. The island of Nevis floats in the warm waters of the eastern Carribbean at the very heart of an arc of islands that sweeps from Puerto Rico to South America. Fully independent since 1983, it is still part of the British commonwealth and its people, mostly farmers, are extremely proud of their past and present connections with the United Kingdom. English is their language. The island is popular with the British, and many have put down roots. American and Canadian tourists also find the island to their liking and return season after season to pretend they have been transported back to the gracious days of the Empire when Nevis was renowned for its glamorous social life.

You can see the major tourist attractions of historic interest in a few hours—after that you're on your own to swim on a golden-sand beach, snorkel in coral reefs, ride a horse through the fields of sugar estates, stroll through a rain forest, or just watch the sun through palm fronds.

Nevis has been wed historically to St. Kitts (two miles north) for hundreds of years, and today the two islands (one nation) are joined in a political partnership that has given new vigor to the health of its democratic government.

Until late in the term of the previous government, both islands had been reluctant to encourage tourism. However, the new government is dedicated to expanding agricultural output, increasing exports, and diversifying the industrial base. In the course of diversification, tourism is getting a shot in the arm—but slowly and cautiously. Nevis and St. Kitts intend to preserve their charm, serenity and unspoiled natural beauty.

Nevis may never be the place where tourists find glitzy discos and high-rise hotels. Instead, it will remain, at least for the foreseeable future, a place where the owners of small inns sit with their guests on the verandas of restored plantations, sipping rum punch and discussing such weighty matters as the sunset.

Puerto Rico.

Puerto Rico is the hub of the northern Caribbean, a busy American commonwealth with a Spanish flavor. Most people equate Puerto Rico with San Juan, whose palm-fringed shoreline and fashionable Condado area are filled with glittering high-rise hotels and casinos that provide entertainment until dawn. Puerto Rico also brings to mind Old San Juan's old-world colonial flavor, with its many shops and fine restaurants to reward the weary. Puerto Rico is not only a tourist playground; in fact, tourism is not its first, or even its second industry. Delving into Puerto Rico's rich history and exploring its countryside offer memorable diversions. The ample night life and sporting facilities of all types are simply the icing on the cake. To experience Puerto Rico fully, you should get out on the island—visit the chain of government-sponsored country inns known as the *paradores;* see the sun set off a quiet southwestern beach; revel in the coolness of a rain forest; venture into parts of the island that tourists seldom tread.

High season in Puerto Rico is from mid-December to mid-April, when San Juan and the resorts are at their most crowded. The tourist seasons don't really affect much of the country outside San Juan. April and November are the driest parts of the off-season and consequently may be best for those seeking a Puerto Rico bargain.

Puerto Rich attracts tourists from all walks of life—from honeymooners and vacationing college students taking advantage of airfare and package-deal bargains, to luxury cruise-ship passengers of all ages.

Saba.

A tiny, lush, green Dutch island that rises dramatically from the blue sea. There are only a few towns and country lanes to explore; one "wandering beach" that comes and goes; and just a handful of spots for overnighting and dining. Most people make a day trip here from St. Maarten, but divers are discovering Saba's off-shore delights; writers and artists are inspired by her magic; retired Americans—even celebrities—are finding the peace and privacy they've been seeking. Saba is a step back through the centuries to another world untouched by "tourism" as we know it today.

St. Barthélemy.

Tiny, unspoiled St. Barts, as it is affectionately called, seems far away from everything, but in reality is easily accessible. This eight-square-mile island is packed with enchantment. It's reminiscent of the French Riviera as it once was—long, uncrowded beaches, small protected coves, flowering meadows, rugged hills, and rocky promontories speckled with charming little hotels, villas, and bungalows. There's fine French cuisine and friendly people who have managed to keep their traditional Norman culture and language intact over 300 years. Travelers here are worldly sophisticates and just plain sunseekers from many lands who come for St. Bart's very special, "get away from it all" feeling.

St. Eustatius.

Statia, as she is called, is a secret refuge for world-weary minds and bodies in search of total relaxation. If you can be satisfied with good books, fine food, and stimulating conversation, then you'll be happy here. You'll meet serious students of archeology and history and many repeat U.S. customers who come to this unhurried and relatively unknown little island to get away from group tours, organized outings, and boisterous night life. Hike, bike, swim, roam the ruins, sun, snorkel, hunt for blue beads by day and land crabs by night, enjoy nature, get immersed in history, and get to know your fellow guests and the Statians, who have a very special way of making you feel right at home.

St. Kitts. In 1493, Christopher Columbus discovered this island in the eastern Caribbean and named it St. Christopher after his patron saint. The British came along later and quickly shortened that to St. Kitts.

On September 19, 1983 St. Kitts and Nevis, its sister island two miles to the south, changed their 360-year affiliation with the United Kingdom and became one unified nation—but within the commonwealth.

St. Kitts is an oval-shaped land mass with a narrow neck of land extending like the handle of a cricket bat from the southeastern end. (Nevis roughly resembles a cricket ball.) The central part of the main body consists of a rugged mountain range, whose highest point is Mount Liamuiga (formerly Mount Misery). The island was formed from a volcanic eruption, so most of its beaches consist of black, volcanic sand. White sandy beaches, however, can be found along the peninsula of Frigate Bay and Salt Pond, extending toward Nevis.

One of the most appealing features of St. Kitts is its accommodations. It has a predominance of small hotels, inns, cottages, and guesthouses. Giant, bustling, high-rise hotels are nowhere to be found.

Until late in the term of the previous government, both St. Kitts and Nevis had been reluctant to encourage the construction of hotels or boost tourism in any other way. However, the new government is dedicated to expanding agricultural output, increasing exports, and diversifying industries. Tourism is getting a shot in the arm—but slowly and cautiously. St. Kitts' deep-water harbor has recently been completed, giving a boost to trade and tourism by allowing cruise ships and other large vessels to call. Golden Rock Airport, the major international airport of the islands, has plans to expand its facilities.

Presently, an 850-acre site is being developed into an integrated complex of small hotels, condominiums, and private villas. Known as Frigate Bay Resort, the area is isolated and peaceful, yet only minutes away from Basseterre, the capital, and the small airport. Strict architectural and environmental controls are in effect to preserve the landscape.

The opening of the Royal St. Kitts Hotel at Frigate Bay may have been the turning point for the island, for it included the first casino for gambling. Others are planned, but hang, for the time being, in limbo. On the other hand, most visitors—Europeans, Americans, and Canadians—visit and revisit the island to enjoy the island's peace and quiet, continental and local cuisine, and limitless water sports.

St. Lucia. St. Lucia is a tropical island paradise 21 miles south of Martinique that offers superb beaches, sailing, snorkeling, a beautifully landscaped golf course, and a selection of hotels ranging from folksy West Indian guesthouses with a couple of rooms to 200-room international resorts. The months from December to April are especially busy here; considerable savings are available during the low season, June through October. In the eyes of many people, St. Lucia has achieved a nice balance between the lush, natural beauty and unencumbered lifestyles of the West Indies and its development as a leading tourist spot. British, Italian, French, German, American, and Caribbean travelers come here to bask, dine, and dance, and the island's success can well be measured by the large number of people who come back every year to this garden getaway.

St. Martin/Sint Maarten. This half-Dutch, half-French island has become the Caribbean's most popular year-round playground. It's easy to get to and vacation packages are numerous; U.S. dollars and credit cards are accepted everywhere; the friendly population speaks English; and the wide variety of accommodations, beautiful beaches, water-sports facilities, excellent shopping, restaurants, and lively night life is quite astounding. It's one destination which can honestly boast something to offer every type of traveler.

St. Vincent and the Grenadines. The richly cultivated mainland of an exotic group of islands 100 miles west of Barbados, St. Vincent is one of the

Carribbean's best-kept secrets since the location of Captain Kidd's treasure. Eighteen miles long and 11 miles wide, St. Vincent is volcanic in origin and offers tropically adorned solitude amid a folksy West Indies culture.

St. Vincent draws an international crowd—Europeans, Canadians, Americans, as well as Caribbeans—who know a good thing when they see it. Yachters have known about St. Vincent and its Grenadines for ages. Scuba divers and sun worshippers alike are only recently discovering the quiet charms of this island.

December through May are the busiest months in St. Vincent, though the crowded, hectic atmosphere found in many other Caribbean vacation spots does not apply here. The food is an island delight: creamy thick soups, an abundance of seafood, fresh fish, locally grown vegetables, and added touches such as freshly baked bread and homemade ice cream.

An array of historic and colorful sites, including the oldest botanical gardens in the Western Hemisphere, romantic, secluded beaches, and a warm, responsive people are just some of the offerings of this island in the sun.

There are over 100 islands and cays making up the Grenadines, sprinkled south of St. Vincent from Young Island, 200 yards from the mainland, to Petit St. Vincent, just under 40 miles to the south. The main islands of the Grenadines are Bequia, Mustique, Canouan, Mayreau, Union, Palm Island, and Petit St. Vincent. Each island has its own distinct character and each draws a dedicated band of sun-and-fun seekers from Europe, the U.S., Canada, and the Caribbean. Accommodations range from lush, secluded resorts to inexpensive, cozy inns and guesthouses. Boating, swimming, and the gamut of water sports, combined with superb West Indian cuisine and plenty of steel-band "jump-up" fun, make the Grenadines a paradise on earth.

Trinidad and Tobago. Trinidad is a land of vibrant rhythm, songs, *fetes* and festivals where steel bands, calypso, and limbo came to life and the spirit of Carnival pervades year-round. The population is a fascinating blend of colors, creeds, and cultures reflecting African, European, Indian, and Oriental heritages. Rich in history, natural resources, and natural beauty, Trinidad is a place where hospitality is a way of life and the joy of living is infectious.

Tobago, Trinidad's little sister, is just a short air hop away, but as Trinidad sizzles, Tobago sleeps. This is a place to unwind—to enjoy long, lazy sun-filled days, scenery as colorful beneath the sea as it is above, sparkling blue water and pristine white beaches. Off the sea lanes of cruise ships and untouched by mass tourism, this is the fabled island of Robinson Crusoe and the Swiss Family Robinson—names that evoke a mental image of the tropics just discovered, still unspoiled. Tobago is just about as close as you can get to this romantic picture.

The Turks and Caicos Islands. Southeast of The Bahamas, these quiet islands form a tropical string through the Atlantic and along the fringes of the Caribbean. Although there are dozens of cays, there are just five islands equipped to handle tourists. Any of them (Grand Turk, North Caicos, South Caicos, Pine Cay, and Providenciales) are ideal for the traveler in search of beauty and seclusion. There are a few tennis courts, but the main attraction here is the water. Extensive beaches, exceptional underwater life, sport fishing, scuba diving, snorkeling, and simply sunbathing are about all there is here—but you couldn't ask for more. Accommodations are in small and special hotels and inns.

U.S. Virgin Islands. Of the three major islands, St. Thomas is most developed with an active cruise-ship port and sprawling resorts; St. Croix, though physically larger, moves to a more relaxed beat; St. John is a pristine jewel that scores high on natural beauty, but low on night life or even daytime action anywhere but on the beach. On all three islands high season is mid-December through mid-April; best off-season months are June, July, and November. August, September, and October can be uncomfortably muggy and wet. As a territory of the United States, the islands are politically stable, and since tourism is the number-one industry visitors are generally treated with care and attention. Duty-free shopping, beaches, water sports in general, and sailing in particular attract more than one million visitors annually from throughout the world.

FACTS AT YOUR FINGERTIPS

 PLANNING YOUR TRIP. If you don't want to bother with reservations on your own, a travel agent won't cost you a cent, except for such specific charges as long-distance calls and telegrams. Travel agents get their fees from the airlines, cruise lines or hotels they book for you. A travel agent can also be of help if you prefer package-tour vacations, which keep your own planning to an absolute minimum. If you prefer the convenience of standardized accommodations, remember that the major hotel chains publish free directories of their hotels and reservations numbers, enabling you to plan where to stay and reserve a room ahead of time. Facilities at resort destinations in the Caribbean, of course, will be more elaborate than what you'd find in a big city, where these same chains cater primarily to business travelers.

Plan to board the pets and discontinue paper and milk deliveries. Ask a kindly neighbor to keep an eye on your house, and keep your mail, or have it held at the post office. Look into the purchase of travel insurance (including trip cancellation and baggage insurance) and make certain your auto, fire, and other insurance policies are up-to-date. Today, most people who travel use credit cards for important expenses such as gas, repairs, lodging, and some meals. Consider converting the greater portion of your trip money into traveler's checks. Arrange to have your lawn mowed at the usual times, and leave that kindly neighbor your itinerary (insofar as possible), car license number, and a key to your home. Since some hotels and attractions give discounts to senior citizens, be sure to have some sort of identification along if you qualify. Usually AARP or NRTA membership is best. (See below at the end of the *Hotels and Other Accommodations* section.)

 HOW TO GET THERE BY AIR. Air fares are in a constant state of flux, and our best advice is to consult a travel agent and let him or her make your reservations and find the cheapest fares for you. Agents are familiar with the latest changes in fare structures as well as with the rules governing various discount plans. Among those rules: booking (usually) 21 days in advance, minimum-stay requirements, maximum stay, the amount that (sometimes) must be paid in advance for land arrangements. Lowest prices overall will, of course, prevail during the off-season periods, usually late spring, summer, and early fall.

Generally, on regularly scheduled flights to the Caribbean, you have the option, in descending order of cost, of first-class, club or business class, and APEX. Budget tickets, for which you choose the week you will fly but give the airline the option of determining on which flight, are often available. Budget travelers with fixed schedules will want to meet the requirements for APEX or Super-APEX (the latter are slightly cheaper than APEX but with additional restrictions).

Because of the availability of inexpensive air fares, charter service has generally decreased in recent years, but some charters are still available. Again, a travel agent will be able to recommend which charter operators are reliable. Sometimes it is also worth investigating package tours even if you do not wish to use the tours' other services (hotels, meals, etc.). Since a packager block-books seats on regularly scheduled flights—thereby guaranteeing the airline a virtually full flight—the price of a package can be lower than the cost when air fare is booked independently.

If you have the flexibility, you *can* sometimes benefit from last-minute sales that tour operators have in order to fill a plane; but do try to find out whether the tour operator is reputable and whether you are tied to a precise round trip or whether you will have to wait to return until the operator has a spare seat.

Among the major airlines serving the region are *American, Eastern, Delta,* and *Pan Am* from the U.S.; *Air Canada* from Canada; and *Air France, British Airways, Lufthansa* and *KLM* from Europe. In addition, many smaller airlines, including *Air Jamaica, ALM, BWIA, Dominicana* and *Prinair,* provide services within the Caribbean and between the Caribbean and the U.S.

 HOW TO GET THERE BY SEA. Cruising the Caribbean is perhaps the most relaxed and convenient way to tour this beautiful part of the world.

A cruise offers all the benefits of island hopping without the inconvenience. For example, a cruise passenger packs and unpacks only once and is not bound by flight schedules, tour-bus schedules and the "non-schedules" of fellow travelers.

Cruise ships usually call at several Caribbean ports on a single voyage. Thus, a cruise passenger experiences and savors the mix of nationalities and cultures of the Caribbean, as well as the variety of sightseeing opportunities, the geographic and topographic characteristics, and the ambience of each of the islands. A cruise passenger tries out each island on his or her cruise itinerary and has the opportunity to select favorites for in-depth discovery on a later visit.

As a vacation, a cruise offers total peace of mind. All important decisions are made long before boarding the ship. For example, the itinerary is set in advance, and the costs are known ahead of time and are all-inclusive. There is no additional charge for accommodations, entertainment, or recreational activities. All meals are included and—surprise!—there are no prices on the menu. A cruise ship is a floating Caribbean resort; each passenger gets to know the cruise staff and sits back and relaxes while he or she enjoys the consistency of service and experience.

When to Go on a Cruise. Caribbean cruising is excellent any time of the year. The waters are calm, and the prevailing breezes keep temperatures steady year-round. Tropical storms are most likely in September, October, and November, but modern navigational equipment warns cruise ships of impending foul weather, and the lines will vary their itineraries to avoid a storm, if necessary.

Vacation times are the periods during which ships are likely to be at their fullest and, therefore, higher priced. Excellent cruise bargains are available during post-vacation periods, such as fall to mid-December, spring, and the first few weeks after Christmas—New Year's. Christmas sailings are usually quite full and are priced at a premium.

Questions about Cruising. Most potential cruise vacationers have basic questions about cruising the Caribbean: What cruise ship is right for me? How do I select an itinerary I'll enjoy? How do I select a cabin that will be comfortable and affordable? What should I wear? What should I know about tipping? What will the weather be like? How should I choose a shore excursion? These are all important questions to be answered to make your cruise the complete Caribbean vacation. So even before you visit a travel agent to make arrangements, do your homework. The travel sections of the Sunday newspapers can give you some idea of what is available, at what price, and when, but read the fine print—those banner prices don't always apply.

To get some idea of which ships are sailing where and when, contact the *Caribbean Tourism Association,* 20 East 46th Street, New York, NY 10017, which has information about cruise lines that operate to its member nations. These lines are Royal Caribbean, Princess Cruises, Carnival Cruise Line, Commodore Cruise Line, Paquet, Home Line, Royal Viking, Sun Line, Sitmar, Costa Line, Holland America and Cunard. Don't be disappointed if some of the liners change their ports of call at the last minute, which they sometimes do, but be assured that CTA's listing will be as up-to-date as possible. CLIA *(Cruise Lines International Association)* has published a pamphlet entitled "Answers to the Most Asked Questions about Cruising," which is available by writing *CLIA,* Pier 35, Suite 200, San Francisco, 94133, or 17 Battery Place, Suite 631, New York, NY 10004. In this case, you must enclose a stamped, self-addressed envelope with your request. Their information is a good primer for all ships at sea but doesn't center on the Caribbean specifically. Our observations in that area follow:

How to Choose a Cabin. Write the cruise line directly or ask your travel agent for a ship's plan. This elaborate layout, with all cabin numbers noted, may seem overwhelming at first, but closer inspection will show you all facilities available on all decks (the higher the deck, the higher the prices). Outside cabins have dramatic portholes to add to the flavor, but even if they aren't sealed shut, most provide no more than a view of the surrounding deck. Inside cabins are less expensive, but check the plan—you don't want to be over the kitchen, over the engine room, or next to the elevators if you want quiet. Then check on the facilities offered—they're part of the plan as well. Look over the less-expensive cabins which have upper and lower berths, those which have bathtubs in addition to showers, and the luxury suites, which can still provide all the accoutrements of a voyage across the sea.

Tipping. Even though some of the liners advertise a no-tipping policy, be aware that most of the ship's service personnel depend on tips for their livelihood. There is no hard-and-fast rule about who gets what, but if you think of services rendered on board as you would at resort hotels, bars, and restaurants, you'll come close. The personnel who should be tipped are the cabin steward, the dining-room waiter, the maître d'hôtel, the wine steward, and the bartender (who should be tipped with each bar check as you travel). Gratuities to other ship's personnel are always given the night before the voyage ends.

How to Choose a Table. Once you have selected your table, you will have it for the length of the cruise. The maître d' will assist you, especially if you're traveling alone. On most ships there are two sittings for dinner, so decide whether first (usually about 6:00 P.M.) or second (approximately 8:30) suits you.

Shore Excursions. Tour options will be posted on the bulletin board near the purser's office a day before arrival at your port of call. Rates vary for different tours offered, so your best bet is to read ahead (see individual island chapters) to determine just what's right for you. If the ship is in port for a full day you might choose to rent a car and explore on your own (see *How to Get Around* section in each island chapter for approximate rates and requirements).

Weather and What to Wear. The bonus that comes with cruise travel is that you can carry as much as you like on board. No matter who says what, dinner jackets for men and long dresses for women are still *in* and are especially appropriate at the captain's dinner and the captain's cocktail party. When the ship is in port, dress is less formal. Bring bathing suits, cover-ups, and comfortable resort wear, including rubber-soled shoes or sneakers for shore excursions. Just imagine yourself packing for a resort hotel, and you'll be right on target.

Fly-and-Cruise. Several cruise lines offer this option, but be aware that the air fare is built into the rate, so the cost for the *total* package will be higher. Embarking from Miami and San Juan will assure warm weather instantly, so checking on this option is a good idea. In most cases, the air-plus-cruise rate will be lower than round-trip airfare to the ship's pier, even though accommodations may cost more.

Life at Sea. No matter how early you rise, you'll find a list of the day's activities that has been slipped under your cabin door. The options are endless and vary each day. For example, you may find jazz or classical concerts; dance classes; yoga sessions; bingo games; language lessons; films on the islands you'll be visiting; arts-and-crafts sessions; and afternoon movies as part of the daily schedule. But usually the highlight each day is one tournament or another (backgammon, bridge, or Ping-Pong among them) in which passengers compete for prizes.

No matter what the event in which you choose to participate, be assured that there is always a ship's photographer on hand. He snaps away all day and the results appear on rotating bulletin boards the following morning. You may be surprised to see that you were unwittingly "caught" here or there. Part of the morning fun is spinning the rack and then ordering copies of the photos, which will be ready in twenty-four hours. The charge may be high, but well worth it for the candid souvenir.

How to Choose Your Ship. Over the years the cruise lines have made every attempt to attract potential passengers. They have done so by heralding their cuisine, their staff, their entertainment; they have even gone so far as to offer cruises for singles. The ships are as different as the ports of call they schedule. Perhaps the following will help you make a decision. (British residents should refer to *Tips for British Visitors* in this chapter.)

Bahama Cruise Line, 61 Broadway, New York, NY 10006. The *Veracruz* (704 passengers, 10,600 tons, 487 feet) and the *Bermuda Star* (713 passengers,

23,395 tons, 617 feet) each feature shops, casino, swimming pool, standard sports facilities, children's counselors seasonally, and pizza parlor. The crews are made up of German and English officers with an international hotel staff. The company describes the atmosphere of both ships as casual, friendly and unpretentious. The *Veracruz* sails from Tampa to the Mexican Caribbean (the Yucatán) and Key West, while the *Bermuda Star* sails from New Orleans to the same destinations.

Carnival Cruise Lines, 3915 Biscayne Boulevard, Miami, FL 33137. The *Carnivale* (950 passengers, 27,250 tons, 640 feet), the *Festivale* (1,148 passengers, 38,175 tons, 760 feet), the *Mardi Gras* (906 passengers, 27,250 tons, 650 feet) and the *Holiday* (1,452 passengers, 45,912 tons) feature shops, full casinos, several swimming pools each, standard sports facilities, children's playrooms, and children's counselors seasonally. The crew—consisting of 550 each on the *Carnivale* and the *Mardi Gras* and 580 on the *Festivale*—is composed of Italian officers and an international hotel staff. Carnival Cruise Lines describes itself as the "Fun Ships" company. The large ships have the size and space to provide a wide variety of activity and entertainment possibilities. The emphasis is on fun, casual attire, and an unstuffy atmosphere. The ships are among the few that offer double, queen-, and king-sized beds, as well as twin beds. The ships depart from Miami, with the *Carnivale* and *Festivale* sailing to the eastern Caribbean and the *Mardi Gras* to the western Caribbean. The new *Holiday* sails year-round from Miami to St. Martin and St. Thomas.

Commodore Cruise Line, 1007 North America Way, Miami, FL 33132. The *Boheme* (448 passengers, 11,000 tons, 450 feet) has the usual complement of shops, a mini-casino, sports activities, and it also has golf (driving practice), a soda bar, a children's playroom, children's counselors seasonally, and a swimming pool. The 220 officers and crew are international. The *Boheme* bills itself as the "Happy Ship," with a casual atmosphere and a loyal passenger following. It is well-known for its theme cruises, such as Mayfest, Easterfest, Oktoberfest, and country-and-western sailings; elegant dining and good value. It sails weekly from St. Petersburg to Port Antonio, Key West, and Cozumel. The *Caribe-I* (900 passengers, 23,000 tons, 610 feet) also has the usual complement of shops, a Las Vegas-style casino, a 600-capacity dining room, three elevators, 11 public rooms (including bars), a 250-seat theater, two pools, and an outdoor bar on pool deck. *Caribe-I* is Commodore's second "Happy Ship" and offers the same sort of theme cruises as its sister ship *Boheme*. Officers and crew are international and the ship features quality food service. *Caribe-I* sails weekly from Miami on seven-day cruises to St. Thomas, San Juan, Cap-Haitien and Puerto Plata.

Costa Cruises, 1 Biscayne Tower, Miami, FL 33131. The *Carla C* (748 passengers, 20,500 tons, 600 feet) and the *Daphne* (406 passengers, 16,300 tons, 532 feet), have shops, casinos, and two swimming pools each and provide the standard amenities. The new 1,000-passenger luxury liner *CostaRiviera* was set to debut with seven-day cruises in December 1985. The Costa ships convey an exuberant Mediterranean spirit, a casual atmosphere, and good value for the price. The ships sail from San Juan and Ft. Lauderdale to such destinations as Curaçao, La Guaira, Guadeloupe, St. Martin, Martinique, Barbados, St. Lucia, Antigua, and St. Thomas.

Fantasy Cruises, 1052 Biscayne Blvd., Miami, FL 33132. The *Amerikanis* (700 passengers, 16,485 tons, 576 feet) features shops, a casino, two swimming pools, nightclub, ballroom, lounge, four bars, two restaurants, beauty salon, barbershop, cinema, gym/sauna, children's playroom, and television in every cabin. Departures are from Miami to Nassau.

Clipper Cruise Line, 771 Bonhomme Ave., St. Louis, MO 63105. The 100-passenger "ultra-yachts" *Newport Clipper* and *Nantucket Clipper* combine the comfort of a deluxe cruise liner with the intimacy and exclusivity of a private yacht. All-American crew and cuisine complement the relaxed, country-club atmosphere aboard, as the shallow-drafted vessels explore the secluded bays and harbors of the Caribbean. Both ships cruise through the American and British Virgin Islands.

Cunard Line/NAC, 555 Fifth Avenue, New York, NY 10017. The *Queen Elizabeth 2* (1,815 passengers, 67,139 tons, 963 feet) is one of the great ships of Caribbean cruising. This large, luxurious vessel offers a wide range of amenities and services, only a few of which are shops, four swimming pools, a casino, a nursery, a children's playroom, a teen room, year-round children's counselors, the Golden Door health spa, computer center, golf facilities, lectures by famous personalities, accommodations for the handicapped, and a kosher dining room. The crew of 930 is all-British on the *QE2*. Cunard, more than 140 years old, is a cruise line steeped in tradition. The company lays claim to developing the "floating resort" concept. The *QE2* makes periodic sailings to the Caribbean. The *Vistafjord* (736 passengers, 24,492 tons, 628 feet) and the *Sajafjord* (589 passengers, 25,000 tons, 625 feet) feature indoor and outdoor pools, Golden Door health spa, library, beauty salon, barbershop, gift shop, casino, theater, grand ballroom, ship-to-shore phones in each cabin, and luxury suites with outside balconies. The ships include a theatre-in-the-round nightclub and a complete sports deck. Crews are Norwegian and the hotel staff is European. The *Vistafjord* sails from Ft. Lauderdale to such ports as Cozumel, Grand Cayman, Montego Bay, St. Kitts, Nevis, Aruba, Grenada and Barbados, while the *Sajafjord* sails from San Juan to Barbados on its way to South America.

Holland America Westours, 300 Elliot Ave. West, Seattle, WA 98119. The *Rotterdam* (1,114 passengers, 38,000 tons, 748 feet) and the *Nieuw Amsterdam* (1,214 passengers, 33,390 tons) have shops, swimming pools (inside and outside on the *Rotterdam*), casinos, sports activities, children's counselors seasonally, ramps for wheelchairs, and golf-practice facilities. In addition, the *Rotterdam* offers a children's playroom, a teen room and a tennis practice room, among other amenities. The crews are composed of Dutch officers and Indonesian hotel staff. The company describes itself as providing "gracious service, warm Dutch hospitality, and a relaxed holiday atmosphere . . . A tradition for more than 100 years." The outgoing Indonesian crew offers friendly, comfortable service. As with most ships, there are some formal evenings, but casual attire rules during daytime activities. The ships feature periodic sailings from Ft. Lauderdale and Tampa to St. Martin, St. Thomas, Cozumel, Jamaica, Grand Cayman.

Home Lines, One World Trade Center, New York, NY 10048. The *Atlantic* (1,055 passengers, 30,000 tons, 671 feet), one of the newest ships of the Caribbean fleet, and the *Oceanic* (875 passengers, 39,241 tons, 774 feet) offer shops, sports activities (including golf practice), casinos, television, inside and outside swimming pools, and children's counselors seasonally. In addition, the *Oceanic* has deck tennis, a soda bar, a teen room, and a retractable glass dome over its outside pool. The officers and crew are Italian, and conviviality and spirit are hallmarks of a Home Lines cruise. Italian cuisine and elegant service are the rule, and the ships enjoy a loyal following in the Northeast. Both ships sail from New York to various destinations in the Caribbean, including St. Thomas, Martinique, Barbados, Aruba, and St. Martin.

Norwegian Caribbean Lines, One Biscayne Tower, Miami, FL 33131. The *Norway* (1,778 passengers, 70,202 tons, 1,035 feet) is the former *France,* one of the most luxurious of the venerable transatlantic liners. The *Norway* has successfully made the transition to a cruise ship and boasts extensive facilities and elaborate entertainment. Among its amenities are shops, sports activities (including golf practice), a casino, two outside and one inside swimming pools, television in all cabins, accommodations for the handicapped, a children's playroom and children's counselors seasonally, an outdoor café, and a soda bar. The *Skyward* (725 passengers, 16,264 tons, 525 feet), the *Southward* (752 passengers, 16,600 tons, 536 feet), the *Starward* (758 passengers, 16,000 tons, 525 feet), and the *Sunward II* (674 passengers, 14,100 tons, 485 feet) provide shops, casinos, outside swimming pools (plus an inside pool on the *Starward*), children's counselors seasonally, and other amenities. The eight-hundred-person crew on the *Norway* is made up of Norwegian officers and Caribbean, Korean, and European hotel staff. The crews of the other four vessels, each numbering approximately three hundred, are composed of Norwegian officers and Caribbean and Korean hotel staffs. Norwegian Caribbean bills itself as "America's Favorite Cruise Line," and truly its presence, innovations, and recognition as a leader in the field support its claim. The ships provide plenty of excitement and activity and yet a relaxed atmosphere. They sail from Miami on seven-night cruises to various ports in the Caribbean. NCL's "Dive-In" snorkeling program is available on all ships.

Paquet Cruises, 1007 North America Way, Miami, FL 33132. The *Mermoz* (550 passengers, 13,800 tons, 530 feet), and the newcomer to the fleet, the

Rhapsody (850 passengers, 24,500 tons, 642 feet), offer shops, casinos, swimming pools, children's counselors seasonally, and sports activities. The 230-person crew on the *Mermoz* is French and Indonesian, and the 430-member crew on the *Rhapsody* is French and international. The flavor aboard the ships is definitely French, with French and Continental cuisine prepared by Paquet's own French chefs and complimentary dinner wines. The *Mermoz* sails from San Juan to Curacao, Grenada, St. Vincent, Guadeloupe, Antigua, and St. Thomas, while the *Rhapsody* sails from Ft. Lauderdale to San Juan, St. Thomas, and St. John.

Princess Cruises, 2029 Century Park East, Los Angeles, CA 90067. The *Sun Princess* (686 passengers, 17,400 tons, 535 feet), one of the "Love Boats," offers shops, a casino, a swimming pool, children's counselors when twenty-five or more children are aboard, and other amenities. *Princess* has become known during almost twenty years in the cruise business for its excellent service, yet easygoing atmosphere. It has also introduced enrichment programs and lectures aboard its cruises and enjoys great popularity on the West Coast, particularly. It is well-known too, for charging only ten percent above the regular fare for single passengers who do not wish to share a cabin. The *Sun Princess's* crew of 379 is made up of British officers, Italian dining room staff and international hotel staff. The *Sun Princess* sails for such destinations as Barbados, Martinique, St. Martin, St. Thomas, Curaçao, and Palm Island.

Royal Caribbean Cruise Line, 903 South America Way, Miami, FL 33132. The *Song of America* (1,414 passengers, 37,584 tons, 705 feet), one of the sleek newcomers to the Caribbean fleet, the *Nordic Prince* (1,038 passengers, 23,000 tons, 637 feet), and the *Sun Viking* (728 passengers, 18,556 tons, 563 feet) offer shops, slot machines, swimming pools (two on the *Song of America*), sports activities, and other amenities, including the famous Viking Crown Lounge aboard each ship, which affords spectacular views ten stories above the sea. The crews of 400 on the *Nordic Prince,* 500 on the *Song of America,* and 320 on the *Sun Viking* are made up of Norwegian officers and international hotel staffs. The ships are noted for their informality, with casual attire by day and suits and ties at most dinners, but feel free to leave the tux at home, please. Theme nights, such as Pirate's Night, the Masquerade, Gay Nineties Night, and Roaring Twenties Night, are part of the fun. Royal Caribbean offers seven-, eight-, ten-, and fourteen-day cruises year-round from Miami. Island calls include Jamaica, Curaçao, Barbados, Martinique, St. Maarten, Puerto Rico, St. Thomas, Cozumel, Caracas, Antigua, St. Croix, Key West, the Yucatán, and Grand Cayman.

Royal Viking Line, One Embarcadero Center, San Francisco, CA 94111. The *Royal Viking Sea,* the *Royal Viking Sky,* and the *Royal Viking Star* (725 passengers, 28,000 tons, 676 feet) are built for luxury cruising and feature shops, sports facilities, children's counselors seasonally, swimming pools, and other amenities. The crews—more than 420 on each vessel—consist of Norwegian officers and European hotel staffs. The ratio of crew to passengers is exceptionally high, and the cruise company emphasizes service and elegance. The ships are Norwegian in spirit and style, but shipboard life is international in appeal. Food, drink, and decor are geared to the best in global taste. The ships make periodic cruises to the Caribbean in connection with trans-Panama Canal voyages, longer trips from more exotic locations, and special Caribbean and holiday cruises. Calls are to such destinations as St. Thomas, Puerto Rico, Curaçao, Colombia, Dominican Republic, Jamaica, and Grand Cayman Island.

Scandinavian World Cruises, 1290 South America Way, Miami FL 33132. The *Scandinavian Star* (525 passengers, 10,513 tons) sails from Tampa to Cozumel on three-night cruises that are among the lowest-priced cruises available in the Caribbean.

Sitmar Cruises, 10100 Santa Monica Boulevard, Los Angeles, CA 90067. The *Fairwind* and the *Fairsea* (925 passengers, 25,000 tons, 608 feet) offer suites as well as comfortable cabins, excellent children's facilities including a pizza parlor, three outside swimming pools on each ship, shops, and casinos. Sitmar, based in Los Angeles, has a solid reputation for good quality and friendly service, with particular emphasis on family cruising. The crews are composed of Italian officers and Italian and Portuguese service staffs. Fifty-four chefs and their assistants for each ship prepare seven-course menus for each meal. Sitmar ships offer Caribbean cruises to such ports as St. Thomas, Puerto Rico, Antigua, Barbados, St. Johns, St. Croix, Martinique, Jamaica, and Curaçao.

Sun Line Cruises, One Rockefeller Plaza, New York, NY 10020. The *Stella Solaris* (620 passengers, 18,000 tons, 550 feet) features boutiques, slot machines, pools, and sports activities (including trapshooting). The officers and staff are Greek, and with charm and conviviality, they emphasize luxury service, with such touches as chocolates on each pillow at night. The *Stella Solaris* sails to various Caribbean islands, usually in connection with cruises to Rio de Janiero.

YACHTING. Chartering your own yacht, either with or without crew, has become a very popular way to find uninhabited isles and cays and to visit the major tourist destinations. Yachts and motor cruisers of all sizes are available for rental on a week-long or longer basis, and rates vary according to size and season. You won't be able to cruise through the entire Caribbean, but you have options in the north and the south which will afford the opportunity to tie up at as many places in those areas as possible.

Should you choose to set out on your own, your rental firm will direct you to nearest markets for stocking up; should you rent a boat with captain and crew, provisions will be provided. In either case, there will be navigational maps on board so that you can chart and change your course as you go. The Caribbean has hundreds of marinas available, many at resort hotels, where you can not only refuel, but also enjoy a special dining-and-entertainment evening ashore.

The British Virgin Islands have become the yachting capital of the Caribbean. Tortola, the capital of the chain, teems with yachtsmen and has hotels geared for the seafarers. Sailing out from the B.V.I. will quickly acquaint you with the northern waters. In the southern Caribbean, St. Vincent and St. Lucia are prime rental points. Others throughout the islands are Antigua, Jamaica, St. Martin, and the United States Virgin Islands.

Write for information well ahead of time; then, after you've made your choice, make reservations as soon as possible, especially if you plan to travel during the winter season. Explore every possibility through:

Caribbean Sailing Yachts, Ltd., Box 491, Tenafly, NJ 07670 (telephone: 800–631–1593); *Nicholson Yacht Charters,* 9 Chauncy Street, Cambridge, MA 02138 (telephone: 617–661–0181); *Stevens Yachts of Annapolis,* Box 129, Stevensville, MD 21666 (telephone: 800–638–7044); *Tortola Yacht Charters,* 5825 Sunset Dr. S., Miami, FL 33143 (telephone: 800–243–2455); *The Moorings, Ltd.,* 1305 U.S. 19 South, Suite 402, Clearwater FL 33546. (telephone: 800–535–7289).

(British residents should refer to *Tips for British Travelers* in this chapter.)

PASSPORTS AND VISAS. Entry requirements for each island differ; they are detailed in the appropriate sections of this book. Generally speaking, you will need proof of citizenship (we recommend a passport, but for U.S. and Canadian citizens most Caribbean islands will accept a birth certificate or a voter-registration card) and possibly a visa or tourist card. Some also require that you have return or ongoing airline tickets upon arrival and may ask you to demonstrate that you have sufficient funds to sustain your visit.

Visas are obtained through embassies or consulates; tourist cards are issued by travel agents or airlines for a small fee.

TRAVEL AGENTS AND TOUR OPERATORS. The critical issues in choosing a travel agent are how knowledgeable that person is about travel and how reliable his or her bookings are, regardless of whether you are looking for a package tour or planning to travel independently. The cost will be essentially the same whether you go to a major tour operator, such as *American Express* or *Thomas Cook,* or to the small travel agency around the corner. In Europe there may be a small general service charge or a fee per reservation; in the U.S., only out-of-the-ordinary telephone or telex charges are ever paid by you.

The importance of a travel agent is not merely for making reservations, however. A good travel agent booking a flight for a customer will know what general discounts are in effect based on how long your stay will be, how far in advance you are able to make your reservations, whether you are making a simple round trip or adding extra stops, and other factors. He or she will also likely be able to suggest suitable accommodations or packages that offer the kinds of services you want.

In the case of package tours, you want to be sure that the tour operator can deliver the package being offered. Here again, a local travel agent can be helpful. Most major tour operators have established reputations for reliability—the inevitable occasional foul-up notwithstanding. If there is any doubt, there are trade organizations, described below, that can be consulted about specific questions.

Not all travel agents are licensed, but membership in the American Society of Travel Agents (ASTA), the Alliance of Canada Travel Associations (ACTA), or the Association of British Travel Agents (ABTA) is a safeguard. All ABTA tour operators and travel agents are bonded for your protection. In addition, the British government Air Travel Reserve Fund Act of 1975 gives further financial protection to air travelers on charter or part-charter flights if the air-travel operator is unable to meet his or her financial commitments. ASTA polices its membership through a Consumer Relations and Industry Ethics Committee. For further information, write to ASTA, 4400 MacArthur Blvd., Washington, DC 20007; ACTA, 130 Albert St., Ottawa, Ont., Canada K1P 5G4; or ABTA, 50–57 Newman St., London W1P U.K. In addition, a number of larger American tour operators have formed the United States Tour Operators Association, whose members post a bond to reimburse consumers if a tour operator fails to deliver a product or goes bankrupt. For a list of members, write to USTOA at 211 East 51st St., New York, NY 10022.

Package Tours vs. Independent Travel. Time, convenience, individuality, and cost are the factors to consider when it comes to choosing an all-inclusive, fully escorted tour, a loose plan-your-own-itinerary package tour, or totally independent travel.

Package tours are the easiest to arrange and probably the most economical and efficient way for a first-time traveler to the Caribbean to get a taste of several of the islands. Other packages offer stay-put vacations at one resort, with all meals, sporting fees, and other services included. For avid tennis or golf players these tours, or similar packages provided by resorts, will be far more economical than paying on a per-use basis. Either way, the operator arranges for all plans, boat, and other transportation; transfers wherever needed; tour guides, and generally commodious accommodations. Flight-plus-lodging for many such tours often works out to be less expensive than the flight alone would be if booked as a regular economy fare. Thus, even if you prefer arranging for accommodations at a place other than that offered by the tour operator, and even if you have no intention of participating in any group activities, it may still be in your best interest to purchase the entire package.

Traveling independently allows for greater freedom than does tour travel, but as stated, it is also frequently more expensive. Traveling off-season saves anywhere from 20–40% even for nonpackage visitors, as does staying at small inns and guest houses rather than large hotels.

TOURIST INFORMATION SERVICES. The fountainheads of information on the Caribbean are the *Caribbean Tourism Association*, 20 E. 46th St., New York, NY 10017 (212–682–0435) and the *Eastern Caribbean Tourist Association*, 220 E. 42nd St., New York, NY 10017 (212–986–9370). They can supply you with news of the latest developments for places in the Caribbean, particularly for those areas that do not maintain their own tourist offices.

U.S. Addresses. *Anguilla Tourist Information Office*, 25 W. 39th St., New York, NY 10018 (212–840–6655).

Antigua Tourist Board, 610 Fifth Ave., Suite 311, New York, NY 10020 (212–541–4117).

Aruba Tourist Bureau, 1270 Ave. of the Americas, Suite 2212, New York, NY 10020 (212–246–3030); plus offices in Miami, FL (1–800–3ARUBAN).

Barbados Board of Tourism, 800 Second Ave., New York, NY 10017 (212–986–6515); plus offices in Los Angeles, CA, and Winter Park, FL.

Bonaire Information Office, 1466 Broadway, Suite 903, New York, NY 10036 (212–869–2004).

British Virgin Islands Tourist Board, 370 Lexington Ave., New York, NY 10017 (212–696–0400).

Cayman Islands Department of Tourism, 250 Catalonia Ave., Suite 604, Coral Gables, FL 33134 (305–444–6551).

Curaçao Tourist Board, 400 Madison Ave., Suite 311, New York, NY 10017 (212–751–8266); plus offices in Miami, FL.

Dominican Republic Tourist Information Center, 485 Madison Ave., New York, NY 10022 (212–826–0750); plus offices in Miami, FL.

French West Indies Tourist Board, (Guadeloupe, Martinique, St. Barthélemy, St. Martin), 610 Fifth Ave. New York, NY 10020 (212–757–1125). Or contact the French Government Tourist Office in Chicago, IL or Beverly Hills, CA.

Grenada Tourist Office, 141 East 44th St., New York, NY 10017 (212–687–9554).

Haiti Govt. Tourist Bureau, Rockefeller Center, 1270 Ave. of the Americas, New York, NY 10020 (212–757–3517); plus offices in Miami, FL.

Jamaica Tourist Board, 866 Second Ave., New York, NY 10017 (212–688–7650, 800–223–5225); plus offices in Chicago, IL and Los Angeles, CA.

Puerto Rico Tourism Information Office, 1290 Ave. of the Americas, New York, NY 10019 (212–541–6630, 800–223–6530).

St. Lucia Tourist Board, 41 East 42nd St., Suite 315, New York, NY 10017 (212–867–2950).

St. Maarten, Saba and St. Eustatius Tourist Office, 1500 Broadway, Suite 2305, New York, NY 10036 (212–840–6655).

St. Vincent and the Grenadines Tourist Board, 220 E. 42nd St., New York NY 10017 (212–986–9370).

Trinidad & Tobago Tourist Board, 400 Madison Ave., Suite 712–714, New York, NY 10017 (212–838–7750 or 800–521–0250).

Turks and Caicos Islands Tourist Board, P.O. Box 592617, Miami, FL 33159 (305–592–6183).

U.S. Virgin Islands Tourist Information Office, 1270 Ave. of the Americas, New York, NY 10020 (212–582–4520).

Canada Addresses. *Antigua Department of Tourism,* 60 St. Clair Ave., Toronto, Ont. M4T 1L9 (416–961–3085).

Barbados Board of Tourism, 20 Queen St. W., Toronto, Ont. M5H 3R3 (416–979–2137).

Bonaire Tourist Information, 815 A Queen St. E., Toronto, Ont. M4M 1H8 (416–465–2958); plus offices in Montreal, Que.

British Virgin Islands Tourist Board, 801 York Mills Rd., Suite 201, Don Mills, Ont. M3B 1X7 (416–283–2239).

Cayman Islands Department of Tourism, 11 Adelaide St. W., Suite 406 Toronto, Ont. M5H 1L9 (416–362–1550).

Eastern Caribbean Tourist Association (Antigua, Montserrat, Nevis, St. Kitts, St. Lucia, St. Vincent & the Grenadines). Place de Ville, Suite 1701, 112 Kent St., Ottawa, Ont. K1P 5P2 (416–236–8952).

French Government Tourist Office (Guadeloupe, Martinique, St. Barthélemy, St. Martin), 1 Dundas St. West, Toronto, Ont. M5G 1Z3; 1981 Ave. McGill College, Montreal, P.Q. H3A 2W9.

Grenada National Tourist Office, 143 Yonge St., Toronto, Ont. M5C 1W7 (416–368–1332).

Haitian Government Tourist Office, 113 Simonston Blvd., Toronto, Ont. L3X 4L9 (416–886–3398); plus offices in Montreal, Que.

Jamaica Tourist Board, 2221 Yonge St., Suite 507, Toronto, Ont. M4S 2B4 (416–482–7850).

Puerto Rico Tourism Information Office, 10 King St. E., Toronto, Ont. M5C 1C3 (416–367–0190).

St. Lucia Tourist Board, 151 Bloor St. W., Toronto, Ont. M5S 1S4 (416–961–5606).

St. Maarten, Saba and St. Eustatius Information Office, 243 Ellerslie Ave., Willowdale, Toronto, Ont. M2N 1Y5 (416–223–3501).

Trinidad & Tobago Tourist Board, 145 King St. W., Toronto, Ont. M5H 1J8 (416–367–0390).

Turks & Caicos Islands, 111 Queen St. E., Toronto, Ont. M5C 1F2.

U.S. Virgin Islands, c/o R.B. Smith Travel Marketing Consultants, 11 Adelaide St. W., Suite 406, Toronto, Ont. M5H 1L9.

U.K. Addresses. *Antigua Tourist Board,* 15 Thayer St., London W1 (486–7073).

Barbados Board of Tourism, 6 Upper Belgrave St., London SW1 (235–9155).

Cayman Islands Department of Tourism, 17–B Curzon St., London W1Y 7FE (493–5161).

French Government Tourist Office (Guadeloupe, Martinique, St. Barthélmy, St. Martin), 178 Piccadilly, London W1V 0AL (491–7622).

Grenada High Commission, 102–105 Grand Building, Trafalgar Square, London SC2 (01–839–5922).

Jamaica Tourist Board, Jamaica House, 50 St. James St., London SW1 (493–3647).

Trinidad and Tobago Tourist Board, 20 Lower Regent St., London SW1 (839–7155).

U.S. Virgin Islands, 25 Bedford Square, London WC1 (637–8481).

West India Committee (British Virgin Islands, Nevis, St. Kitts, Turks and Caicos), 48 Albermarle St., London W1 (629–6353).

 TIPS FOR BRITISH VISITORS. Passports. See *Practical Information* in each island chapter for specific passport and visa requirements. Some islands require passports; others do not but may require a "British Visitor's" passport, generally available from the post office.

Insurance. We heartily recommend that you insure yourself to cover health and motoring mishaps, with *Europ Assistance,* 252 High St., Croydon CR0 1NF (680–1234). Their excellent service is all the more valuable when you consider the possible costs of health care in the Caribbean. They have a large network of multilingual staff, available 24 hours a day, around the globe, allied to sophisticated medical services in all those countries in which they operate, as well as having air-ambulance facilities permanently available. Their services for stranded motorists are equally extensive. (*Note:* This insurance will not cover Haiti or the Dominican Republic.)

Tour Operators. The price battle that has raged over transatlantic fares has meant that most tour operators now offer excellent budget packages to the Caribbean. Among those you might consider as you plan your trip are—

Bahos, 47 Chippenham Rd., London W9 (286–5281).

Caribbean Connection, Belgrave House, Bath St., Chester CH1 1QL (0244/41131).

Caribtours, 161 Fulham Rd., London SW3 6SN (581–3517).

Club Méditerranée, 62 South Moulton St., London W1 (409–0644).

Dream Islands of the World, G.L. Travel Management Ltd., 37 Victoria Rd., Surbiton, Surrey (390–1166).

Hayes and Jarvis, 6 Harriet St., Knightsbridge, London SW1 (235–3648).

Heritage Travel, 2 Lower Sloane St., London SW1 (730–7098).

Jetsave Travel, Sussex House, London Rd., East Grinstead, West Sussex RH19 1HD (0342/312033).

Kuoni Travel, 33 Maddox St., London W1 (499–8636).

Rankin Kuhn Travel, 13/17 New Burlington Pl., London W1 (439–4121).

Speedbird Holidays, Alta House, 152 King St., Hammersmith, London W6 (741–8041).

Tradewinds Holidays, 66–68 Brewer St., London W1R 3PJ (734–1260).

Air Fares. We suggest that you explore the current scene for budget-flight possibilities. Though standby fares are unfortunately a thing of the past—except for some possible summertime connections—airlines do offer APEX and other fares at a considerable saving over the full price. Quite frankly, only business travelers who don't have to watch the price of their tickets fly full price these days—and find themselves sitting right beside APEX passengers!

Villa- and Apartment-Rental Agencies. Renting an apartment or villa has become a very popular and economical way of vacationing in the Caribbean islands. Below are some agencies based in the U.K. that can arrange such accommodations for you in the Caribbean.

American Express, 19/20 Berners St., London W1 (637–8600).

Bajan Services Ltd. (Barbados), 36 Edbury St., London SW1 (730–8706).

Continental Villas, 38 Sloane St., London SW1, (245–9181).

Jamaica Association of Villas and Apartments, 21 Blandford St., London W1 (486–3560).

Palmer & Parker (Montserrat), 63 Grosvenor St., London W1 (493–5725).

Speedbird Holidays, 152 King St., London W6 (741–8041).

Cruise Lines. *Costa Lines,* Suite 21, Duke St. House, 415–417 Oxford St., London W1 (493–4707).

Fred Olsen Lines, 11 Conduit St., London W1 (491–3760).

Norwegian Caribbean Lines, Clareville House, Oxendon St., London SW1 (839–4214).

Royal Caribbean Cruise Line, 35 Piccadilly, London W1 (434–1991).

P&S Travel, 3 Cathedral Place, London EC4M 7DT (248–6474), has passenger-freighter travel to the Caribbean.

Yacht Charter Agencies. *Camper & Nicholsons (Yacht Agency), Ltd.,* 16 Regency St., London SW1 (821–1641).

Castlemaine International, 48 Abermarle St., London W1 (629–1122).

Crestar Yacht Charters, Colette Ct., 125–126 Sloane St., London SW1 (730–9962/5).

Halsey Marine, Ltd., 22 Boston Place, Dorset Square, London NW1 (724–1303).

Sun Days Charters, Ltd., Weald House, Pluckley, Kent TN27 OSN (023–384/432).

Worldwide Yachting Holidays, c/o Liz Fenner, 35 Fairfax Pl., London NW6 (328–1033, 328–1034).

WHEN TO GO. The Caribbean "season" has traditionally been a winter one, usually extending from December 15 to April 14. The winter months are the most fashionable, the most expensive, and the most popular for cruising or lazing on the beaches, far from the icy North, and most hotels are heavily booked at this time. You have to make your reservations at least two or three months in advance for the very best places. Hotel prices are at their highest during the winter months; the 20–40% drop in rates for "summer" (after April 15) is the chief advantage of "off-season" summer travel. Cruise prices also rise and fall with the seasons.

The flamboyant flowering trees are at their height of glory in summer, and so are most of the flowers and shrubs of the West Indies. The water is clearer for snorkeling, smoother in May, June, and July for sailing in the Virgin Islands and the Grenadines.

The Caribbean climate, air-conditioned by the trade winds, approaches the ideal of perpetual June. Average year-round temperature for the region is 78° to 85°. The extremes of temperature are 65° low, 95° high, but as everyone knows, it isn't the heat, but the humidity that makes you suffer, especially when the two go hand in hand. You can count on downtown shopping areas being hot at midday any time of the year, but air-conditioning provides some respite. Stay near beaches, where water and trade winds can keep you cool, and shop early or late in the day.

High places can be cool, particularly when the Christmas winds hit Caribbean peaks (they come in late November and last through January), but a sweater is sufficient for warmth from the trade winds.

Since most Caribbean islands are mountainous (notable exceptions being the Caymans, Aruba, Bonaire, and Curaçao), the altitude always offers an escape from the latitude. When it's 90° in the sun in Port-au-Prince, Haiti, it's a good

10° cooler on the heights of Kenscoff above the capital. Kingston (Jamaica), Port of Spain (Trinidad), and Fort-de-France (Martinique) are three cities that swelter in summer, but climb 1,000 feet or so and everything is fine.

What about rainy seasons and hurricanes? You don't have to worry about either. Hurricanes can sweep through, but the warning service is now so highly sophisticated that planes can change course in midflight to avoid any disturbances and everything can be battened down ashore in plenty of time to ride out the storm. The rainy season, which usually refers to the fall months, consists mostly of brief showers interspersed with sunshine. You can watch the clouds come over, feel the rain, and remain on your lounge chair for the sun to dry you off. A spell of overcast days is "unusual weather," as everyone will gladly tell you.

Generally speaking, there's more planned entertainment in the winter months. The peak of local excitement on many islands, most notably Trinidad, St. Vincent, and the French West Indies, is Carnival.

PACKING. Given the destination, you should not need an excessive amount of baggage—dress on the islands is light and casual, with a sweater or jacket suggested only for cooler evenings. Major airlines limit you to checking two bags plus one carry-on, which must fit under you seat. There are charges for extra baggage and sporting equipment such as golf clubs. Local airlines still limit baggage allowances by weight. Other hints: Nylon tends to be warmer than dacron-cotton combinations, so the latter among permanent-press materials would be preferable; business meetings call for standard business attire; bareback dresses and décolletage for women are not a good idea in Latin-oriented countries and in the less-touristed islands; nude sunbathing *is* fashionable in the French West Indies, but not elsewhere; be prepared for the sun, which scorches even tried-and-true Caribbeanists. Have a long-sleeved shirt, a hat, and long pants or beach wrap, as well as sun-block lotion—the last best brought in plentiful supply from home, since it will be more expensive to purchase on the islands. It's wise, too, to bring along insect repellant. If you plan to explore more than the coast, be sure to bring comfortable walking shoes with non-slip soles. Film for your camera is also more expensive if purchased in the Caribbean.

WHAT WILL IT COST? Since we are covering more than 35 islands and dozens of off-shore cays, we have studied each area individually and given a projected daily estimate for *two* persons within each island section. This daily rate includes hotel accommodations, three meals, tips, taxes, service charges, and a one-day tour of the island, by either taxi or rental car.

The *most* expensive tropical landfalls are Aruba, Barbados, St. Martin, and Curaçao. The *least* expensive are the smaller retreats, such as Saba, Montserrat, Anguilla, and Bonaire. The recent devaluation of the Jamaican dollar makes prices there quite attractive.

But bear in mind that once the *off-season* begins (from Apr. 15 through Dec. 14), you can save anywhere from 20–40% per day. Also check out the year-round package-charter plans (see *Tour Operators* in this section or in individual chapters, and contact them for week-long holidays at substantial savings).

SEASONAL EVENTS. Special events on each island are covered in "Special Events" in the individual island chapters. In addition, national holidays and celebrations generally take place on New Year's Day, Good Friday, Easter Sunday, Whit Monday (seven weeks after Easter Monday), the Queen's Birthday, Christmas Day, and Boxing Day. Many islands also have special ceremonies to celebrate their own independence day.

MONEY. The value of some island currencies changes with great frequency and very radically; some are subject to inflation, others to devaluation. We urge you to change only what you anticipate spending in each country, since exchange bureaus and banks charge a commission when you buy and again when you exchange any unspent balance back to U.S. dollars or other currency. Banks and government-approved exchange houses give the best rates; hotels will also change currency but generally at lower rates. You can purchase small packets of foreign currencies prior to leaving—enough to have for immediate arrival transportation and tipping needs. Look under the heading "Foreign Money Brokers and Dealers" in the Yellow Pages.

Note: Always be sure you ask, if a price is quoted in dollars, *whose* dollars are meant—theirs or yours. U.S. dollars tend to be worth considerably more than those of the various Caribbean currencies. In each island chapter, we have quoted the exchange rate at press time in the section called "Money." *Because of the recent erratic fluctuations of the dollar and other currencies, we strongly recommend that you recheck rates prior to your departure—and possibly while you are gone, if it is for an extended stay.*

Credit Cards. Major credit cards—American Express, Diners Club, Mastercard and Visa—are generally accepted at larger hotels, restaurants, and stores accustomed to entertaining foreign visitors. If your interests are off the beaten track or you stay in guest houses or go in for out-of-the-way dining or handicrafts, you will probably have to pay with cash or traveler's checks. There may even be some room for bargaining when paying with cash, since locals know that the U.S. dollar in particular is worth more to them than their own currency. When charging, you will be billed at the rate of exchange in force on the date of billing.

Traveler's Checks. Traveler's checks are the best way to safeguard travel funds. They are sold by various banks and companies in American and Canadian dollars and in pounds sterling. Most universally accepted, and useful in most places, are those of *American Express, Bank of America, Citibank, Thomas Cook, Barclays, Lloyds, Midland,* and *National Westminster.*

TRAVELING WITH PETS. When heading to the Caribbean, we recommend leaving your pets with friends at home or boarding them at an appropriate facility. Bringing pets out of and back into the country—whatever your point of origin—can involve quarantine time and considerable hassles; also, resort hotels rarely have facilities for animals.

HOTELS AND OTHER ACCOMMODATIONS. *General hints.* Plan ahead and reserve a room well before you travel to the Caribbean. Otherwise, you may find yourself completely stranded, especially during high season. If you have reservations but expect to arrive later than 5:00 or 6:00 P.M., advise the hotel, inn, or guest house in advance. Some places will not, unless so advised, hold reservations after 6:00 P.M., and they may insist on having an advance deposit or your credit-card number to guarantee the room for the night. Also during high season, reserve well in advance and be sure to find out what the rate quoted includes—European (EP = no meals), American (AP = three meals), or Modified American (MAP = two meals) Plan, use of sporting facilities and equipment, and the like. Be sure to bring your deposit receipt with you in case any questions arise when you arrive at your hotel.

Given the vast differences in standards and accommodations in the various countries and islands covered in this book, it would be impossible (and misleading) to establish uniform categories such as deluxe, first-class, etc. Instead, we have used categories to indicate price rather than quality and have tried to include the most useful information for each hotel, inn, and guest house listed in the country chapters, such as whether they offer such features as pools, beach, sporting equipment, restaurants, air conditioning, and other amenities. Prices are intended as a guideline only. The larger resort hotels with the greater number of facilities are, naturally, going to be more expensive. But the Caribbean is full of smaller places that make up in charm, individuality, and price for what they lack in activities—and the activity is generally available on a pay-per-use basis elsewhere.

TIME SHARING. By this time everyone is acquainted with the time-sharing procedure—find a condominium, apartment, or villa, buy it outright, and pay the mortgage off by renting it out to other visitors. You will be obliged to furnish it completely and have the accommodations in perfect order for visiting guests. They pay the rent; you continue mortgage payments. In most cases the rental firm takes care of bookings; in all cases you are allowed to use your place only for specified weeks of the year.

It can be an investment, or it can be a total failure, unless you spend a great deal of time on the Caribbean island you choose to see the way tourism is going. Bankruptcy is ever-prevalent, so be sure of your firm ahead of time. Many hotels jumped on the bandwagon and continue to do so, leasing their rooms on a time-share basis. Several have given up, but others continue to try to make ends meet by selling off whatever they can.

Before you invest, make sure that the number of tourists visiting a particular island will want special accommodations such as yours. If they are in resort hotels they may, but if they are in do-it-yourself condo complexes they may not. The Cayman Islands, St. Thomas, and St. Martin continue to be the successful places, whereas St. Croix and others have failed. There is a bill before the British Virgin Islands legislature to ban time-sharing, and other islands may follow suit, so choose carefully. That idyllic place in the sun won't be your home away from home for more than the realtor's schedule allows, and even though you have chosen the property as a long-term investment, you may find yourself vacationing somewhere else.

Island by island, see our *Practical Information* section, where time-sharing possibilities are included.

DINING OUT. The cuisine changes from island to island, depending largely on the influences of early settlers and traditions. Increasingly, however, as more of the islands gain their independence, local cooking styles are becoming more defined. As with hotels, the island chapters provide details pertaining to price category, quality of food and service, ambiance, etc. We have also indicated which restaurants do or do not accept credit cards. For those that do, we have used the following abbreviations: AE = American Express; DC = Diners Club; MC = Mastercard; V = Visa.

TIPPING. Some Caribbean hotels have adopted the European custom of automatically adding a service charge to your bill—usually 15% but sometimes as little as 10%. Use your own discretion when tipping over and above that for exceptional services rendered. Where no fee is added, tip is based on services delivered. In restaurants and nightclubs, and for room, beach, or poolside hotel service, 15% is standard. At hotels, maids should be left $1 a night for a stay of three or four days, 5% for a stay of a week. Porters and bellmen are tipped $.50 per bag and something extra for unusually heavy items such as golf clubs. (See *How to Get There by Sea* section in this chapter for information on tipping on a cruise ship.)

TIME ZONE. Most Caribbean nations are in the Eastern Standard time zone. Barbados is in the Atlantic Standard Time zone, which is one hour ahead of Eastern Standard Time.

ELECTRIC CURRENT. 110 to 120 volts A.C. is the general rule throughout the Caribbean and the Bahamas, but there are a number of exceptions. Before you leave, check "Electric Current" in the *Practical Information* section on the island you plan to visit.

SENIOR-CITIZEN AND STUDENT DISCOUNTS. Discounts for older and younger travelers are less common in Caribbean resort areas than in the United States and Europe. Some hotel chains generally offer senior-citizen discounts and will grant them when requested wherever the traveler might be. Thus, it is a good idea to carry some form of senior citizen ID. Similarly, it can't hurt to have a student ID. The one that is recognized worldwide is issued by the *Council on International Educational Exchange,* 205 E. 42nd St., New York, NY 10017, or 312 Sutter St., San Francisco, CA 94108. Canadian students should apply to the *Association of Student Councils,* 44 St. George St., Toronto, Ont. M5S QE4.

HINTS TO HANDICAPPED TRAVELERS. The major airlines can usually accommodate wheelchair passengers when notified in advance. An excellent brief guide to airline travel for people confined to a wheelchair or with other handicaps is available free from *TWA,* 605 Third Ave., New York, NY 10016. Other excellent sources of information:

Consumer Information Center, Pueblo, CO 81109; request publications on handicapped travel.

Society for the Advancement of Travel for the Handicapped, 26 Court St., Brooklyn, NY 11242; this organization maintains a list of tour operators who arrange travel specially for the handicapped.

U.S. Government Printing Office, Washington, DC 20402, publishes a booklet titled *Access Travel* with data on 220 airport facilities worldwide.

George Washington University, Rehabilitation Research and Training Center, Ross Hall, Suite 714, 2300 I St. NW, Washington, DC 20037, publishes a booklet for those with lung problems ($1.25).

Facts on File, 460 Park Ave. S., New York, NY 10016 publishes *Access to the World: A Travel Guide for the Handicapped,* by Louise Weiss. It costs $14.95, plus $2 shipping and handling.

HEALTH. Few real hazards threaten the health of a visitor to the Caribbean. Poisonous snakes are hard to find, and the small lizards that seem to have overrun the islands are harmless. The worst problem may well be a tiny predator, the "no see'um," a small sandfly that tends to appear after a rain, near wet or swampy ground, and around sunset. If you feel particularly vulnerable to insect bites, bring along a good repellent.

Even people who are not normally bothered by strong sun should head into this area with a long-sleeved shirt, a hat, and long pants or a beach wrap. These are essential for a day on a boat, but are also advisable for midday at the beach. Also carry some sun-block lotion for nose, ears, and other sensitive areas such as eyelids, ankles, etc. Be sure to take in enough liquids. Above all, limit your sun time for the first few days until you become used to the heat.

If a serious problem arises, your hotel should be able to help you find a doctor. Help also is available from the *International Association for Medical Assistance to Travelers,* which provides a directory of approved English-speaking doctors. Membership is free, and several Caribbean countries participate. Fees are $20 for an office call, $30 for a visit to a home or hotel, and $35 for a Sunday or holiday visit. For information write in the U.S. to IAMAT, 736 Center St., Lewiston, NY 14092; in Canada, 188 Nicklin Rd., Guelph, Ont. N18 7L5; in Europe, 17 Gotthardstrasse, CH 6300 Zug, Switzerland. A similar service is provided by *Intermedic,* 777 Third Ave., New York, NY 10017, but there is an initial charge of $6 per person, $10 per family.

No special shots are required for most Caribbean travel; where they are, we have made note of it in individual chapters.

Food and Water. Food-preparation and storage facilities have improved greatly in recent years. The only precautions we offer are the ones we'd recommend anywhere: avoid mayonnaise that has been sitting on a buffet in the sun; be sure the fish served is fresh; be wary of unfamiliar berries and herbs. If there is a question about the local water, you will find bottled water in your hotel room and available in the dining rooms. Otherwise, you can assume that the tap water and water in carafes in your room are potable. If you are heading into remote regions, go armed with *Halazone,* a small pill available in most drugstores. It may make the water taste funny, but it renders it potable. Fresh milk is available in the more-developed Caribbean countries, though it is usually expensive. To be on the safe side, travel with powdered or canned milk if you are traveling with small children.

The very attractive, shiny-leaved Manchineel tree, which lines many beaches and can be found on most islands, is highly poisonous. Even the water from its leaves after a rain can make you break out in a rash, its sap can cause blisters and temporary blindness, and a nibble of the crabapple-like fruit can cause throat contractions, which can be fatal. Avoid it—and any other plants—until you've checked with someone knowledgeable. (Oleander, poinsettia, and many other beautiful plants and trees are also highly poisonous.)

AIRPORT DEPARTURE TAXES. Refer to "Taxes and Other Charges" in individual island chapters.

CUSTOMS. If you plan to travel with foreign-made articles, such as cameras, binoculars, and expensive timepieces, it is wise to put with your travel documents the receipt from the retailer or some other evidence that the item was bought in your home country. If you bought the article on a previous trip abroad and have already paid duty on it, carry the receipt. Alternatively, you can register such items with customs prior to departure. Otherwise, on returning home, you may be charged duty (for British residents, Value-added Tax as well).

The islands and countries to which you are going welcome tourists, and customs formalities are simple. Unless otherwise specified under the individual countries, you can bring in anything for your personal use.

U.S. residents may bring home $400 ($800 from the U.S. Virgin Islands) worth of foreign merchandise as gifts or for personal use without having to pay duty, provided they have been out of the country more than 48 hours and provided they have not claimed a similar exemption within the previous 30 days. Every member of a family is entitled to the same exemption, regardless of age, and the exemptions can be pooled. Included for travelers over the age of 21 are one liter of alcohol (one gallon from the Virgin Islands), 100 (non-Cuban) cigars, and 200 cigarettes. Only one bottle of perfume trademarked in the U.S. may be brought in. Beyond the first $400, there is a flat tax of 10% of the fair retail value on the next $1,000 worth of merchandise. After $1,400, duty is at the discretion of the customs agent, depending on the type of goods you wish to bring in. Unlimited amounts of goods from certain designated "developing" countries may be brought in duty free; check with U.S. Customs Service, Washington, DC 20229. Puerto Rico counts as American soil, so a stopover there can invalidate your 48-hour restriction if you're on a weekend jaunt. The Virgin Islands' free-port status exempts them from this restriction.

Gifts valued at less than $50 may be mailed to friends or relatives at home, but not more than one per day (of receipt) to any one addressee. These gifts must not include perfumes costing more than $5, tobacco, or alcohol.

Canadian residents may bring in 50 cigars, 200 cigarettes, 2 lb. of tobacco, and 40 oz. of liquor duty free, provided they are declared in writing to customs on arrival and accompany the traveler in hand or checked-through baggage. These are included in the basic exemption of $150 a year. Personal gifts should be mailed as "Unsolicited Gift—Value under $25." Canadian customs regulations are strictly enforced; you are recommended to check what your allowances are and to make sure you have kept receipts for whatever you have bought abroad. For further details, ask for the Canada Customs brochure "I Declare."

British residents, except those under 17 years of age, may import duty free the following: 200 cigarettes or 100 cigarillos or 50 cigars or 250 grams of tobacco; 1 liter of spirits over 38.8% proof or 2 liters of other spirits or fortified wine, plus 2 liters of still table wine; 50 grams of perfume; 1/4 liter of toilet water; and £28 worth of other normally dutiable goods (this last to include not more than 50 liters of beer).

AN INTRODUCTION TO THE
CARIBBEAN

by
KAY SHOWKER

Kay Showker is the author of Fodor's Egypt *and* Fodor's Jordan and the Holy Land. *Her interest and travel in the Caribbean began when she was an editor at* Travel Weekly, *where she covered the region for more than a decade. She continues to be a freelance writer for leading magazines and newspapers across the country. She was the first recipient of the Caribbean Tourism Association's Award for her contribution to tourism through her journalistic efforts.*

The Caribbean—the word rolls off the tongue with a strange yet pleasant and melodic sound, immediately piercing the mind's eye with flashes of bright sun, blue seas, and brilliant colors. Familiar yet foreign, close yet far, it is a place in Eden we have reserved all for ourselves.

To be sure, the Caribbean is the exotic world of the tropics, voluptuous with the green of the jungle etched by pearl-white beaches and caressed by turquoise waters—the idyllic landscape from which vacation posters and brochures are made, luring you to paradise where you can play out the most sybaritic of your fantasies.

27

Yes, it is all this and much more. The Caribbean Sea stretches across more than one million square miles. Its islands—some smaller than one square mile, others larger than fifteen of our states—possess the geographic features and variety of a continent. These lands, rich in a heritage drawn from the four corners of the globe, comprise as many independent countries as Europe. Little wonder the Caribbean is called the Eighth Continent of the World.

For most visitors, the Caribbean is an escape hatch, the nearby romantic spot to run away from winter, leaving coats and boots at the airline boarding gate. The place to shed clothes and worries and run, carefree, away from the stresses of the workaday world, the grime and crime of the city, the crowds in the subway, and the exhaust fumes on the freeway.

Escape you can. It is an escape to the good life where warm, lazy days are followed by cool, velvet nights, where even the tensest, toughest urban survivor of corporate life can be tranquilized by the gentle sounds of the water quietly lapping at the shore.

To call the Caribbean unique is to reduce it to the prattle of tourist brochures. After all, there are islands throughout the world ringed by white sand beaches and green with swaying palms, where gentle tradewinds cool the air and temper the sun.

Yet nowhere among the world's islands is there another group where the spectacular generosity of nature has been matched by the energy and ingenuity of man to create a culture as rich, diverse, and distinctive as that of the Caribbean. It is a world of many worlds and a world of its own.

Defining the Caribbean

But first let's define the Caribbean. From the coast of Florida to the coast of Venezuela, a crest of islands splits the Atlantic Ocean to cradle the Caribbean Sea. The northern tier, closest to the U.S., is known as the Greater Antilles and is made up of Cuba, (not covered in this guidebook), the Caymans, Jamaica, Haiti, Dominican Republic, and Puerto Rico.

The British colony of the Turks and Caicos, directly west of Florida and north of the Greater Antilles, lies entirely in the Atlantic Ocean, but because of its proximity and similar tropical environment, it is usually counted as being part of the Caribbean.

The islands of the eastern and southern Caribbean—greater in number but smaller in size—make up the Lesser Antilles. The Eastern Caribbean islands start with the Virgin Islands on the north and curve south to Grenada in two groups: the Leewards (United States and British Virgin Islands, Anguilla, St. Maarten, St. Bart, Saba, St. Eustatius, St. Kitts, Nevis, Antigua, Barbuda, Montserrat, and Guadeloupe); and the Windwards (Dominica, Martinique, St. Lucia, Barbados, St. Vincent and the Grenadines, and Grenada).

The islands of the eastern Caribbean vary greatly in terrain, culture, and development. Although some have been developed for tourists, most are quiet, lovely corners of the world only small numbers of tourists have discovered.

The southern Caribbean lies off the coast of Venezuela, also in two groups: three islands of the Netherlands Antilles—Aruba, Bonaire and Curaçao—on the west; and the two-island nation of Trinidad and Tobago on the east.

Nature's Extravagance

Along the 2,000-mile Caribbean chain nature provides an extravaganza of beauty, color, and variety. Thickly carpeted mountains and volcanic peaks drop to sun-bleached shores under a sky azure and turquoise at one moment, red and purple another. Between the towering mountains and the sea, waters cascade into rivers and streams and disappear into swamps and deserts; trees laden with spices and fruit perfume the air.

Across the landscape, fields of flowers and flowering trees brilliant with the scarlet and magenta of their blossoms host a multitude of birds and butterflies that flit about under the warm sun. A quick tropical shower refreshes the air and leaves a rainbow overhead.

At eventide, when the sun melts in a crescendo of red, orange, and pink, a chorus of birds introduces the nighttime show of stars that dance across an indigo sky until the violet break of the early dawn.

And this is only the stage above the ground. Below the sea, exotic fish dart around mountains of coral in a wonderworld often proclaimed the most beautiful in the world. Here, in the coolness of the sea, are ever-shifting rainbows of iridescent fish, some less than two inches long, others measuring two feet. Endlessly they flutter through the crystal waters, circling the purple seafans, burrowing into boulders of coral and sponge, hiding in caves and grottos, and even in the wreckage of sunken ships.

Move in closer to any island and you will find each has its own personality with some unusual aspect—the divi-divi tree of Aruba, the turtles of the Caymans, the rain forests of Dominica, the spices of Grenada, the vervet monkey of St. Kitts, the Pitons of St. Lucia—and the list goes on.

Some islands have as much diversity as a continent a million times their size. The desert in Puerto Rico is only a short drive from the only rain forest in the U.S. Park Service. On tiny Aruba, tranquil waters wash miles of beach along the south shore while waves crash endlessly against the rocky north coast. In the Dominican Republic the mountains rise to 10,000 feet in view of the coast. More than 3,000 species of plants, 600 of which are unique to the island, cover Jamaica. The varieties of fern alone number in the hundreds.

The vibrance of the Caribbean does not stop with the landscape; it is reflected in the people and their cultures, which have evolved from a cornucopia of histories, traditions, music, dance, art, architecture, and religions belonging to people from around the world.

Diversity of People and Cultures

But who are these people and where did they come from? One face shows its forebears came from England, another from China, another from Africa. There are Indians, French, Irish, Dutch, Americans, Swedes, Levantines, and more. Sometimes the blond hair or the black eyes or the costume are clues. But more often the mingling has been so extensive that people do not know their origin or their roots have been long since forgotten.

Before Columbus sighted the New World in 1492, the lands of the Caribbean region were populated by Indian tribes—the peaceful Arawaks or Tainos and the fierce Caribs, from whom the sea takes its name. Within a century after Columbus's voyages, the native population had almost vanished because of war, disease, and enslavement.

Traces of the tribes are few, but new excavations and research, especially in Puerto Rico, Jamaica, and the Dominican Republic, are helping us learn more and gain a better understanding of these early settlers. Today their only survivors are a small group of descendants of the Carib Indians on the island of Dominica.

In the wake of Columbus came waves of explorers, settlers, plunderers, merchant sailors, pirates, traders, and slavers from Portugal, Spain, Italy, England, Ireland, France, Holland, Denmark, and Sweden. More came from Greece, Turkey, and Syria; more from Africa and Asia.

The West Indies, as the region was known, became a pawn in the battle for the New World which raged among the European nations for two centuries. While the Europeans fought, they plundered the region's riches and searched for a route to the East. No one can be proud of this ugly time in history, when in the name of king and country men were little more than tyrants and thieves.

In time, Spain, England, France, Denmark, and Holland carved out spheres of influence, hoisted their flags on various islands, and set about to colonize their newly claimed lands. Seeing the potential for new fortunes in sugar and rum, and, later, cotton and tobacco, they replaced the decimated Indian population with African slaves to work the land.

Early in the nineteenth century, when slavery was abolished in the British colonies (two decades before its abolition in the U.S.), the Africans were replaced by indentured labor from India, China, and other Asian lands. At the turn of the century and afterward, the mass immigration of Mediterraneans to America in search of a better life spilt into the islands. The most recent wave—Americans and Canadians looking for investment, retirement, the good life, or all three—has been gathering strength since the 1950s and shows little signs of subsiding.

Across the centuries, the settlers, the sailors, the slaves, the merchants, the workers, and the visitors brought with them parts of their own native cultures—their church steeples, their temples, their brogue, their high tea, their high mass, their masks, their drums, their colors, their songs, their dances, their high-rises and their hamburgers—and out of this melange has grown a Caribbean culture as rich and varied as the landscape of the islands where it flourishes.

Vitality in the Arts

While it might be difficult to define or describe an Antiguan, a Haitian, or a Jamaican, there is no mistaking the lilt of a Bajan voice or a Trinidadian song. Haitian art is instantly recognizable. The beguine began in Martinique, the merengue in the Dominican Republic. Calypso and steel bands were born in Trinidad, reggae in Jamaica, and salsa in Puerto Rico.

The late reggae king Bob Marley, showman Jeffrey Holder, and dancer/choreographer Rex Nettleford may be the most famous performers from the Caribbean, but throughout the islands there is talent and creativity that throbs with rhythm and pulsates with color.

Audiences around the world have witnessed the quality and skill of the National Dance Theatre of Jamaica. Art galleries in Puerto Rico and Jamaica are robust with works by local artists and sculptors that burst with the joy and cry with the anguish of their creators.

From Jamaica and Haiti to Martinique and Trinidad fabrics cascading with color and jewelry bold in design have found their way into the world arena of high fashion. Oscar de la Renta is a Dominican.

One of the best times to see the creative energies of the Caribbean is during a celebration such as Carnival when half the island is on parade. Carnival, which has often grown up around local events, is celebrated at various times of the year and not only during the traditional pre-Lenten festival.

The grand-daddy of all Caribbean carnivals is Carnival in Trinidad, which rivals Rio's in spectacle and makes Mardi Gras in New Orleans pale by comparison. But Crop-Over in Barbados, which comes from the celebration of the harvest, is held in June or July; Carnival in Antigua, which began as a welcome to the British monarch during her visit, takes place in July or August.

If Caribbean arts are a composite of world cultures, so too the architecture. Warm-weather adaptions of English country churches and Spanish cathedrals stand alongside Dutch farmhouses and Danish manors. Victorian gingerbread mansions are pauses in the tango of brightly painted houses in the towns and villages of Haiti. Minarets and steeples pierce the sky of Trinidad; the oldest synagogue in the Western Hemisphere is a Curacao landmark.

The Potpourri of Caribbean Cuisine

Where better to find the Caribbean's combination of natural wealth and cultural richness than in its cuisine? It evolved over the centuries— and has been revolutionized in the past decade.

When the Spaniards came to the New World, they were introduced to exotic fruits and vegetables such as maize (corn), cassavas, peppers, papayas, chocolate, avocados, and potatoes by the native Indians. The Spaniards and other Europeans adopted the new ingredients and eventually many of them became basic elements in classic Spanish and French cuisines.

As others from around the world arrived in the Carribbean, they added their specialties to the pot with a touch of Dutch, a dash of Danish, a particle of Portuguese, a pinch of English, and a drop of African. In time, the Chinese, Indians, Indonesians, Greeks, Turks, and Arabs contributed as well.

From this potpourri evolved a Creole or West Indian cuisine eaten by the local people, with such standards as black bean soup in Puerto Rico, pepperpot and curried mutton in Jamaica, mutton stew (called *goat water*) in St. Kitts/Nevis, callaloo in Grenada and Trinidad, salted fish, known as *ackee* in the Virgin Islands, and fish cakes called *accra* in Guadeloupe. Outsiders seldom had the opportunity to sample native dishes since only a handful of small hotels and guest houses served them.

After independence a new generation of chefs in hotels and restaurants—some born into the native tradition, others new to the region— began to fashion a new and sophisticated Caribbean cuisine. The new cuisine is based on the region's fresh local products—fish, vegetables, fruit, and herbs—and includes new dishes as well as new versions of the old ones.

Caribbean cooks are being encouraged to be creative by their restaurant and hotel associations, which stage annual competitions judged by international food critics. These events have resulted in such wonderful creations as Breadfruit Souffle and Breadfruit Vichyssoise, Cold Papaya Bisque, Crab and Callaloo Soup, Flying Fish in Crust, Lobster Calypso, Fricasse of Red Snapper, Callaloo Quiche, Chicken Creole with Mango, Soupsop Chiffon Pie, Avocado Ice Cream, and Banana Lime Tart, to name a few.

In Guadeloupe, the annual Fête des Cuisinieres or Cooks' Festival in August is not only a women's cooking competition, in which each contestant strives for the most original and remarkable creation, but a major celebration for the entire island.

Caribbean cuisine is heavily influenced by the market—a cultural medley where Africa meets the Caribbean and mixes with the Orient; where pyramids of mango, melon, banana, papaya, pineapple, and pomegranate and stacks of coconut, cassava, yams, plantain, okra, dasheen, and peppers mingle with the cinnamon, nutmeg, cloves, and coffee along with mountains of clothes and shoes to be haggled over by the townfolk or villagers and, sometimes, by visitors too.

Variety of Ambience and Activity

As with nature, so too with the islands' style and ambience. No two islands are alike; each has its distinctive personality and special charm. Each casts its spell.

Some islands are tiny idyllic hideaways far from the beaten path, with names familiar only to mapmakers and yachtsmen. Some are big in size or big on action; some seem larger than they are because of their strong identity and regional influence.

Some islands are developed; others are developing. Some pulsate with the Caribbean beat; others are so quiet one can hear only the sounds of nature. Some have a glittering nightlife with casinos and cabarets, supper clubs and gourmet restaurants; others are rural and rustic. And some islands have some of it all.

There are islands where the emphasis is on sports; others are noted for a single sport. There are islands that emphasize shopping or dining or gambling. Some islands have activity and entertainment to keep you busy every hour of the day. Others test your ability to enjoy simple pleasures.

Few islands fit neatly into one category only; most have distinguishing features that contrast and overlap. Picking the right one for you is a very personal matter and will depend on the kind of holiday you want. The ideal place for your first honeymoon would probably not be right for a second one. An island good for your children might not be as enjoyable when you are alone.

On most islands you can find a range of accommodations from simple guesthouses, charming little hideaways, housekeeping apartments or villas, and camping sites to sleek hotels, elaborate resorts, and private islands devoted to only one resort. But the majority of accommodations is in small hotels of twenty to fifty rooms operated by individual owners or families, which insures the warm and friendly atmosphere that makes the Caribbean so special. Most hotels are on or near a beach and have their own swimming pool and watersports facilities or can arrange them for you.

Something for Everyone

Needless to say, not all islands appeal to everyone. Yet everyone, whatever their interests—sports, history, culture, music, gambling, shopping, dancing, cuisine, entertainment—can find something, and probably many things, which will appeal to them in the Caribbean.

As an example, consider sports. Few places in the world can match the range of sports and recreational facilities that is easily accessible and readily available in the Caribbean—or the spectacular settings in which they can be enjoyed.

From Turks and Caicos on the north to Aruba on the south, there are more beautiful beaches and better year-round sailing than in any other region in the world. You can also swim in a pool, river, stream, and even under a waterfall or sail in small boats, big boats, bareboat, or crewed.

You can climb mountains, fish in the ocean, and scuba dive any month of the year. There is tennis, golf, horseback riding, polo, surfing, windsurfing, waterskiing, parasailing, rafting, rowing, river fishing, snorkeling, squash, soccer, cricket, baseball, archery, bowling, badminton, ping-pong, hiking, biking, camping, and hunting—and probably others we've overlooked.

If you are less athletic or want simply to enjoy nature and the outdoors, you can stroll along a bougainvillea-laden lane, picnic by a secluded cove or wander along a mountainside overlooking the sea's turquoise waters.

You can jog or stretch out for the day on mile-long, powder-fine sands with no more company than a couple of birds, spend an afternoon gathering shells and butterflies, or watch the pelicans flit and flutter at the water's edge.

Throughout the Caribbean there are national parks, bird sanctuaries, underwater trails, and mountain paths where you can capture magnificent panoramas. Or you can get a close-up look on a safari through a rain forest, a walk into the crater of a volcano, or a hike through deep ravines and rolling meadowland—with a stop to explore some caves along the way.

It's also easy to take up a new sport. You can learn to play polo in the Dominican Republic, study sailing in the Virgin Islands, and bone up on tennis at more than 100 resorts with tennis complexes complete with instructors, clinics, and special tennis packages. Indeed, the Caribbean offers any number of ways to improve your body, stretch your mind, develop a new hobby and pick up a lot of information along the way.

Learning Vacation

A visit to any Caribbean island is a visit to a foreign country—even to those, such as Puerto Rico and the U.S. Virgin Islands, that are under the American flag. You can order lunch in French in Haiti or Martinique, pick up some golf tips in Spanish in Puerto Rico or the Dominican Republic, and have a Dutch treat in St. Maarten.

You can count francs in Guadeloupe, pesos in the Dominican Republic, and gilders in Curaçao, and enrich your stamp collection with mementoes from such off-beat places as Anguilla, Dominica, Saba, Nevis, and the Grenadines.

Yet while you experience a new culture, new cuisine, new sights and sounds and foreign languages, you have the security of knowing that English is used and understood throughout the islands. It's the best of both worlds—the exotic flavor of a foreign land in surroundings as familiar as home.

The Caribbean can be a learning experience in the traditional sense, too. Historic monuments and museums, beautifully restored plantation homes and sugar mills, old forts, harbors, and warehouses, churches and synagogues bring the region's history to life and make sightseeing a painless and entertaining way to brush up on the past.

Amateur archeologists and history buffs can start with the Indian petroglyphs in Aruba and Bonaire, pick up a handful of ancient flintstones on Long Island off the coast of Antigua, walk the ramparts of El Morro in Puerto Rico, and climb to the magnificent Citadel in Haiti or Brimstone Hill in St. Kitts.

In the heart of Santo Domingo, the capital of the Dominican Republic, in the Old City of San Juan in Puerto Rico, or Nelson's Dockyard in Antigua, you can walk through the colonial history of the New World. Here many of the oldest buildings in the Western Hemisphere have been magnificently restored and are alive with art galleries, boutiques, cafes, restaurants, inns, and museums.

You can see Columbus's tomb enshrined in the oldest church in the Western Hemisphere in Santo Domingo; Peter Stuyvesant standing in a park on Curaçao; Alexander Hamilton remembered at his birthplace in Nevis; Napoleon's Josephine gracing the Savannah in her birthplace of Martinique—all reminders of the span and complexity of the Caribbean's history.

Learning about the Caribbean's history is also a way to help understand some of the region's current problems. While you might prefer not to think about these as you prepare for a holiday, we would be remiss not to mention them.

Beyond the Beaches

Most people who visit the islands as tourists see only a part of Caribbean life. But beyond the beaches and tourist enclaves, there is a life that takes in the farmer and the fisherman and the factory worker. It is the teacher in her classroom, the doctor at his hospital, the policeman on the street, the sailor in his boat. It is cricket, a soccer match, a cockfight, a baseball game, afternoon tea. It is ordinary people trying hard to find *their* place in the sun and meeting a number of life's hurdles along the way.

Soon after the Europeans moved into the Caribbean to stay, their governments back on the continent made demands which caused islanders to rebel long before Boston's famous tea party. But only Haiti was successful in making a complete break and, not long after our own revolution, established the first black republic in the Western Hemisphere.

The other islands of the West Indies remained the outposts of European empires—exploited or neglected or both—until the Spanish-American War caused Spain to surrender her holdings and World War II caused Britain, France and the Netherlands to change their relationships with most of their colonies.

One by one the islands have made the choice between keeping their European bonds or going it alone. For most of the new island nations the road to independence has been turbulent. Their resources can be easily summed up: their people and their natural beauty. Even in the best of times it's not easy to meet the needs of growing populations.

But over the past decade the path was made all the rougher by the oil crisis, inflation, and the world-wide recession, which stretched their meager resources to the breaking point.

Out of the experience a new Caribbean personality is being shaped, which is historically bound to Europe, emotionally bound to Africa or Latin America, and economically bound to the United States. Slowly the islands are finding their way—some having changed direction several times—but the problems have not disappeared, as newspaper headlines frequently remind us.

Tourism is one of the few bright spots but it is fragile. The tourist dollar pays for schools, roads, hospitals, and a myriad of the other necessities in the islands. Islanders know it, but it does not mean they like it—particularly those who are not the direct beneficiaries. And, alas, the attitude of some visitors is less than helpful.

Americans tend to judge the Caribbean more harshly than they judge any other place in the world. If it does not measure up to our expectations at all times, we are instantly critical. We arrive in Paradise with our motors still in overdrive and expect—indeed, demand—that everyone get a move on. If hotel service doesn't resemble what we find in a New York coffee shop at noon, we start complaining.

A recent article in the travel section of the *New York Times* described the writer's visit to Barbados. At a bus stop he asked for directions from a Bajan waiting in line and received a short, polite response but no follow-up conversation. This encounter led the writer to conclude the natives were not friendly.

Having traveled from one end of the Caribbean to the other for almost two decades, we can say without hesitation the people of the Caribbean are as warm as their sunshine and as friendly as their music. They have grace, dignity, wit, and enormous talent. Meet them with respect and a genuine smile, and you will reap a harvest as beautiful and bountiful as the landscape.

ANGUILLA

by
CLAIRE DEVENER

A member of Air France's New York public relations team for over fifteen years, Claire Devener is now a free-lance public relations consultant, writer, and tour guide. She is also a contributing editor to two other guidebook series as well as SHOP Magazine.

Long a sleepy little outpost known only to a few visitors, Anguilla (pronounced An-*gwee*-lah) has finally been discovered. Realizing its tourism potential, the island recently took its first steps to reach out and beguile. Last year it was featured in several prominent publications and on U.S. network television. Now there's every sign that Anguilla is well on its way to becoming the most "in" destination for Caribbean cognoscenti. But the present government under chief minister Emile Gumbs (who also happens to be minister of tourism) is determined to protect Anguilla's natural resources and beauty. New hotels will be kept small and select . . . no mass tourism or casinos here, rather an emphasis on quality, unspoiled surroundings, friendly people, and scattered low-rise facilities so visitors can continue to enjoy the feeling that this is their own private paradise.

Past and Present

Christopher Columbus supposedly sighted the island on his second voyage in 1493 and named it for its spindly, eel-like shape. No attempt to colonize it was made, probably because the notoriously fierce Caribs had already set up housekeeping on what they called Malliouhana.

In 1650, English settlers arrived on Anguilla from St. Kitts. A band of "wild Irishmen" were the island's first invaders in 1688, followed—twice—by the French, in 1745 and 1796; but the hardy Brits held out. The islanders' reputation as fierce fighters probably protected them from further marauders, and Anguilla was left in peace. In 1871, Anguilla, with St. Kitts, became a component unit (a British administrative designation) of the Leeward Islands Federation, to which Nevis was added in 1882. Anguilla never cared for this forced union and subordinate status and twice petitioned the Colonial Office (in 1875 and again in 1958) for direct British rule. Both pleas were ignored. In 1967, when the three-island colony was granted self-government as an Associated State, the eel squealed and made a stab at total independence by declaring itself a republic and refusing to return to to the fold. For the next two years Anguilla conducted its own affairs, first through an interim council, then through a group of elected leaders. In 1969 a "Peacekeeping Force" of British paratroopers parachuted from the sky and landed on Anguilla. They were greeted with garlands of flowers, happy smiles, and waving Union Jacks. The troops languished on the beach but also were talked into helping a team of Royal Engineers build roads and schools and to improve the port by the industrious islanders. Finally, in 1971, Britain arranged for a three-year "cooling off" period to allow the Anguillians more time to decide the future course of their island. A British Commissioner worked closely with the 1968 elected council until a new and separate constitution was established in 1976, providing for a ministerial system of government. The island elects a seven-member House of Assembly and its own leader who together handle most of the internal affairs; a British governor is responsible for public service, the police and judiciary and external affairs.

The stable economy is based on fishing, lobster pronging, farming, salt and boat-building. Anguilla's racing boats are sought after by world competitors. The colorful fishing and pleasure craft are part of Anguilla's famous carpentry industry that also produces fine doors, furniture, and carvings. Tourism promises to become an increasingly important part of the island's future.

EXPLORING ANGUILLA

Wall Blake Airport and Blowing Point ferry terminal, on Anguilla's southern shore, are the principal ports of entry for those arriving from St. Maarten. The trip, on one of five rather racy motorboats, will be fast and generally quite comfortable.

As you exit the immigration building at the end of the dock, you'll see a neat line of taxis whose drivers are eager to be your tour guides. There are few sightseeing attractions on Anguilla and in fact a drive around the island won't give you much insight into Anguillan life at all.

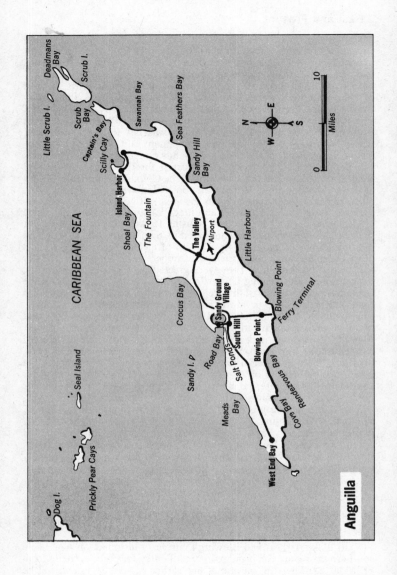

Anguilla

The island's population is spread out with no apparent center or concentration of houses or shops—unless you want to call its one and only stop light, in The Valley, a focal point. Anguilla is unusual in that nothing is as it seems from the outside. Hidden down dirt roads, paths, and byways that crisscross the island's one long road, are some of the most charming small hotels that any island has to offer; good restaurants; incredible powdery white-coral beaches; fine snorkeling and diving; and gracious, spirited people whose verandahed homes have a very special character of their own. You really need to spend a few days here before you get a feeling for this island—then you may decide you never want to leave!

Unless you have some specific destination in mind, your driver will probably head up to the main road from Blowing Point and turn west to Rendezvous Bay and a beautiful, long, half-moon beach flanked by sand dunes, perfect for sunbathing—and a swim.

A few miles north of Blowing Point is one of two salt ponds where the picking, harvesting, and packing of salt for export may be watched —if it happens to be harvest time. And that is up to how much rain Mother Nature has let loose, for salt is formed by the eventual evaporation of the ponds. Nearby Sandy Ground on Road Bay is the most developed of the beaches, with a commercial pier, small restaurants, guesthouses, a hotel, a few interesting boutiques, a charming new hotel and two water-sports centers.

In the northeast is Island Harbor, the center of Anguilla's lobster-fishing industry. Brightly colored fishing boats are lined up on the sand, nets are spread out to dry, and there are two restaurants—including Smitty's, where lots of island action takes place on Saturday nights.

The Fountain is a huge underground cave with an ever-present source of fresh water. There are Arawak artifacts and petroglyphs at the bottom of the strong, steel ladder, but we advise visiting this place with someone knowledgeable, like archaeologist Nik Douglas, who is also secretary of Anguilla's Archaeological and Historical Society. The less adventuresome will probably opt to continue on to Shoal Bay.

This two-mile-long, L-shaped beach is breathtakingly beautiful. More than likely it will be here that you will decide to stay put. Ask your driver to pick you up in time to get the last boat back to St. Martin. Relax and enjoy the crystal clear water, the offshore underwater gardens, a long walk, and several beach bars. If you feel like you've finally found paradise, you're definitely an Anguilla person. As for those 29 other gorgeous beaches, they'll still be there to explore at your leisure when you come back.

PRACTICAL INFORMATION FOR ANGUILLA

FACTS AND FIGURES. Anguilla covers 35 square miles of arid, beach-fringed land located 11 miles north of St. Martin/St. Maarten; 70 miles north of St. Kitts, and 150 miles east of Puerto Rico. The island is 16 miles long and four miles across at its widest point. Crocus Hill is its highest point, just 213 feet above sea level. Scrub Island, Dog Island, Prickly Pear Cays, and Sandy Island are among Anguilla's offshore cays and it also administers Sombrero Island with its vital lighthouse. The population numbers 7,019, predominantly of African ancestry but mixed with Irish, Spanish, and French. Anguilla is one hour ahead of eastern standard time. English is the official language.

WHEN TO GO. The weather is just about always fine. Cooling trade winds are prevalent year-round and keep the relative humidity at about 75%; average temperatures around 80 degrees F. Scattered showers can occur at any time; real rains tend to come between July and October. A fun time to be in Anguilla is during the boat races which take place on New Year's Day; Easter Monday; Anguilla Day (May 30); and during Carnival Week, which begins here the last Friday in July. Some smaller guesthouses keep the same rates year-round; larger properties reduce prices by 30% for the summer season.

 PASSPORTS AND VISAS. U.S. citizens will need proof of identity in the form of a passport (preferably valid, but expired is OK), birth certificate, voter's registration card, or driver's license with photo. Visitor passes are valid for stays of up to three months.

 MONEY. The local currency is the Eastern Caribbean Dollar, now approximately EC $2.68 = U.S. $1. Most places quote in local currency, but U.S. dollars, traveler's checks, credit cards, and even personal checks are widely accepted. Banking hours are 8:00 A.M.–noon Mon–Thur, with an additional two hours added, 3:00 P.M.–5:00 P.M. Fri.

WHAT WILL IT COST

A typical day on Anguilla in season for two persons will run:

	U.S. $
Hotel accommodations on the beach, including taxes	$140
Breakfast, lunch, and dinner at hotel or island restaurant	100
Tips	25
One-day sightseeing by rental car or taxi	35
Total	$300

 HOW TO GET THERE. By air. *Windward Islands Airways* flies from the Juliana Airport on St. Maarten three times a day. *Air BVI* comes in from San Juan via St. Thomas, St. Kitts, or Tortola three times a week; *LIAT* from St. Kitts and Antigua. *Air Anguilla* and *Tyden Air* provide air-taxi service on request from St. Thomas, San Juan, Tortola, St. Maarten, Saba, Statia, and St. Barts.

By sea. Daily water shuttle service to the point of entry at Blowing Point. Five fast motorboats each leave Marigot, on the French side of St. Martin, a minimum of seven times a day from 7:30 A.M. to 4:30 P.M. The trip takes about 20 minutes and the boats can accommodate 30 passengers. The cost is $10 round-trip. Private charters and reduced-rate commuter tickets are also available.

AIRPORT TAX AND OTHER CHARGES. There is an 8% government tax on all accommodations, plus an additional 10% for service. There is an island departure tax of U.S. $5.

 TELEPHONES AND EMERGENCY NUMBERS. You can call Anguilla 24 hours a day by dialing the area code (809) + 497 + the local 4-digit number. Cottage Hospital, located in The Valley, has 24 beds, X-ray facilities, an operating room and lab; tel. 2551. Police headquarters, tel. 2333 are in The Valley.

HOTELS. Tourism is just beginning here, but Anguilla offers some excellent values and an amazingly attractive choice of lodgings that range from small, luxurious resorts to simple, immaculately kept guesthouses. The largest hotel has just 20 rooms and seven villas. We call $260 and up *Super Deluxe;* $150–250 *Deluxe;* $110–149 *Expensive;* $65–109 *Moderate;* and below $60 *Inexpensive* per day for a double during the winter season.

Cap Juluca. *Super Deluxe.* Maundays Bay. Tel. 2779. Named after the Arawak's Rainbow God of good luck, this is Sue and Robin Ricketts' much awaited new endeavor backed by a consortium of U.S. investors. On a lovely 2-mile stretch of sand, the sparkling white oasis is to be totally Moroccan in style with Moorish domes, arches, low walls, and courtyards. Initial plans were to get the main house with restaurant, a Casablanca-style bar called *Rick's Place,* freeform pool, one of three tennis courts and one or two luxurious 2-story, 4-bedroom villas open early in 1986. Accommodations will range from luxury doubles, one-to three-bedroom suites and complete 4-bedroom villas. Eventually this 170-acre property that extends all the way down to Cove Bay will offer a total of 60 rooms and a section of private villas each with its own pool. This new complex had reservations requests before construction even commenced summer of '85.

Malliouhana. *Super Deluxe.* Maids Bay. Tel. 2111. This magnificent property is now managed as well as owned by Annette and Leon Royden. 20 over-size rooms are in the main building, while 7 two-story villas contain three-bedroom suites that can be converted into smaller one- or two-room suites (3 have wheelchair access). Baths are king-size with deep tubs, separate showers, much marble, and mirrors. Larry Peabody is responsible for the fabulous decor and quality is the keynote here from fixtures and furnishings to facilities and services. The 25-acre property set in tropical gardens includes a long powdery white beach as well as a small secluded cove; three cascading fresh water pools, three competition tennis courts, a complete watersports center, and a private yacht available for guest excursions. The gourmet restaurant is under the direction of Jo Rostang of La Bonne Auberge, and a concierge, complete beauty salon, and small but well appointed conference room provide for every need. Splendid as it is, we somehow felt a curious lack of warmth, spontaneity, and congeniality, perhaps best explained right now by the newness of it all.

Cinnamon Reef Beach Club. *Deluxe.* Little Harbour. Tel. 2727. 14 individual cottage suites—nine beachside, five more up on a bluff—are decorated for a truly tropical feeling. The suites are spacious split-level affairs with sitting rooms, sleeping areas with two full-size beds, dressing rooms, and big baths with sunken showers. There is no extra charge for anything, and that goes for the three paddle boats, four 12-foot sailboats, two windsurfers, rowboat, snorkeling equipment, fishing rods, and tennis racquets and balls. The beach is on a well-protected cove with an offshore reef for nearby snorkeling. Two Deco Turf tournament-level tennis courts are perfectly maintained and there's a 40- by 60-foot freshwater pool. Much time and effort have gone into this family-owned property. Special attention to small details—extra-long beds; nightly turndown service; the yellow, red, and orange toucan flag you raise for "beach service"; and their own desalinization plant and generator—assures the comfort of guests.

Coral Bay Resort. *Expensive.* Just outside The Valley. Tel. 2151. This attractive 5-acre seaside hotel offers ten totally refurbished blue and white bungalows with 17 one-bedroom suites, 2 two-bedroom suites, and 2 two-bedroom villas with kitchenette. Not luxurious but comfortable and informal and young American manager Gary Rodrigues really goes out of his way to make his guests happy. There's a beach but the shallow cove is not the best place for swimming. A saltwater pool solves this problem and Anguilla's best beaches are just a short drive. Double hammocks are strung in the trees, the staff is friendly, and the restaurant *Pineapple Annies* offers good food, a pleasant terrace, and frequent entertainment. Horseback riding was planned as well as a complete activity program and poolside bar.

Cul de Sac. *Expensive.* Blowing Point. Tel. 2461. At the end of a dead-end road, this informal yet sophisticated hideaway has six well-appointed, self-contained cottages. Each studio has a large twin bedroom/living area, kitchen, and oceanfront terrace. There's a small saltwater pool and tiny, secluded man-made beach. The elegant bar and lounge has good local entertainment nightly, and excellent West Indian specialties are served in the pretty restaurant at both lunch and dinner. This quiet little hideaway's guests have full use of Malliouhana's luxurious facilities and there's frequent shuttle bus service. Eustace Guishard is your cordial, caring host at this small and special spot.

The Mariners. *Expensive.* Sandy Ground. Tel. 2671/2815. Another new and very pretty place. Nine traditional West Indian gingerbread cottages nestle beneath the cliffs among flowers, palms, and sea-grape trees. The varied accommodations, which can handle a total of 54 guests, include double rooms, studios, suites, two-bedroom apartments, and one air-conditioned three-bedroom apartment. Some have kitchenettes; all have ceiling fans, shutters, shaded verandas, and color schemes to match their pastel-hued exteriors. The setting is idyllic—a nice beach set with turquoise-and-white umbrellas that match sea and sand and an attractive terrace restaurant with a view. The bar and lounge can be lively with visiting yachtsmen; there are barbecues on Thursday, West Indian feasts on Saturday.

Rendezvous Bay Hotel. *Moderate.* Rendezvous Bay. Tel. 2549. The Gumbs family will greet you on your arrival and make you instantly at home. There are 70 acres of beachfront here, and the 20 rooms in two motel-style units got a lot of refurbishing recently, including updated baths. A real family-style atmosphere with meals served on tables on the long terrace, an honor bar, and convivial fellow guests who enjoy the informal way of life. There's a Sunfish available to rent, free snorkeling equipment, and one tennis court.

Inter-Island Hotel. *Inexpensive.* Lower South Hill. Tel. 2259. Neat as a pin, this Anguillian guesthouse is set up on a hill with good views of the Caribbean from its verandas. The 12 immaculate, modestly decorated rooms all have private baths. There are also two spacious, well-equipped apartments with separate entrances on the ground floor. A homey restaurant serves guests hearty breakfasts and excellent West Indian specialties at dinner (both meals included in the price). TV may be watched from comfortable overstuffed chairs in the sitting room and cars can be arranged. Road Bay beach is three miles away.

Lloyd's Guesthouse. *Inexpensive.* The Valley. Tel. 2351. No frills here, just 14 neat and tidy rooms, some with private bath, in a pretty green-and-white shuttered house just a five-minute walk from Crocus Bay Beach. The Lloyds are gracious hosts and give guests good value for their money, with generous breakfasts and homestyle cooking at dinner (both meals included in the price). Two simple but fully equipped beach apartments are also available.

Yellow Banana. *Inexpensive.* Stoney Ground. Tel. 2626. This comfortable 12-room inn is built above a supermarket. The simple, sparkling clean accommodations include just two with private bath; two with W.C. Food is fine, the owners accommodating, and one of the Caribbean's best beaches, Shoal Bay, just a short bike ride or drive away. Breakfast and dinner included in the price.

 HOME AND APARTMENT RENTALS. The local tourist office maintains a complete listing of apartments, cottages, condos and villas that are sprouting up all over Anguilla. Two reliable on-island brokers are Jim and Judy Henderson at Sunshine Villas (Box 142, tel. 2149) and Jillian Carty at PREMS (Box 256, tel. 2596/2777). Both represent about a dozen well-maintained private homes to rent by the week. Ms. Carty also handles homes and land for sale.

Housekeeping accommodations are plentiful and well organized. Highly recommended are:

Carimar Beach Club. *Expensive.* Maids Bay. Tel. 2744. Six-building condo project on the beach next to Malliouhana. 24 two-bedroom units, 2 tennis courts, resident manager. Half scheduled for completion 1985; the rest during 1986.

Shoal Bay Villas. *Expensive.* Shoal Bay. Tel. 4250. Complex of 26 condominiums set on a splendid two-mile sweep of sand. Studios, one and two-bedroom apts., duplexes. 10 units, and *Happy Jack's* beach bar opened late 1984; 12–16 more apts., pool, restaurant, and shop should be ready for '86.

Skiffles. *Expensive.* Lower South Hill. Tel. 2619. Tropical luxury for 20 guests in 5 two-bedroom villas. Built, owned and very attractively decorated by Susan and John Graff, a charming couple from Indiana who discovered Anguilla almost 10 years ago. Fine sea views from floor-to-ceiling windows and 32′ porches; fully-equipped kitchens; cooks available for hire; fresh-water pool. Reserve well in advance, already booked for February '86 at presstime.

Easy Corner Cottages. *Moderate.* South Hill. Tel. 2433. "Mr. Anguilla" Maurice Connor's 17 bright, spacious, and well-equipped one- to three-bedroom apartments. Terraced down a hillside overlooking the salt pond and Road Bay. Popular with families and conveniently located, so reserve well in advance in August as well as the winter season.

Masara Resort. *Moderate.* Katouche Bay. Tel. 2323. Mac Brook's apartments continue to improve and there are now 4 one-bedroom and 2 two-bedroom accommodations. Construction continues and by winter of '86 there should be a restaurant, tennis court, and six more two-bedroom units, set high above the sea.

Merrywing. *Moderate.* Rendezvous Bay. 15 very large apartments (3 one-bedroom; 12 two-bedroom) and two 3-bedroom private villas. Negotiations for the takeover and expansion of this choice 49-acre property were under way at presstime. Check *Villa Vacations* (212–517–3088) on the status of this attractive beachside complex.

Palm Grove. *Moderate.* Sea Feathers Bay. Tel. 4100. Ronald Webster's new 10-room development has spacious, spread out two- and three-bedroom apartments, a fine little beach that's perfect for children, TV, telephone, and lots of island atmosphere. Excellent family accommodations.

Sile Bay Beach Apartments. *Moderate.* Sile Bay. Tel. 2470. Four 1-bedroom apts. and 4 studios face the sea and small pool. Managers Mandy and Roy Bossons also plan to open a larger version of their popular Crocus Bay pub here late in 1985. Excellent snorkeling with equipment, windsurfers, and Sunfish free for guests.

Rainbow Reef. *Moderate.* Sea Feathers Bay. Tel. 2817. Charlotte and David Berglund's four well-equipped two-bedroom bungalows are set on 3 seaside acres. They also have a nice studio and two 2-bedroom apartments at **Sunni Isle** (*Inexpensive*) where there's a pool, a fabulous view of St. Martin, and David's fascinating nutriponic vegetable greenhouses.

Bayview. *Inexpensive.* Sandy Ground. Tel. 2239. Rupert Carty's three beachside apts. are simply furnished and without hot water, but this is a super-relaxed, friendly place with many repeat guests.

Harbor Lights. *Inexpensive.* Island Harbor. Tel. 4435. Four quite attractive and modern studio apartments with kitchenettes; the only accommodations on this picturesque part of the island.

Seahorse. *Inexpensive.* Rendezvous Bay. Tel. 2751. Four large, fully-equipped one-bedroom cottages, two right on the water. Very casual atmosphere where guests usually get together to barbecue in the evening at the seaside grill. Windsurfer, Sailfish free for guests.

Seaview. *Inexpensive.* Sandy Ground. Tel. 2427. Two new and very large 3-bedroom apartments right on the salt pond.

The White House. *Inexpensive.* Sandy Ground. Tel. 2711. Janice and Emile Gumbs' authentic colonial house has one attractive downstairs apartment and a garden cottage on the salt pond that can both accommodate up to 4. If you're adamant about hot water, verify in advance.

 HOW TO GET AROUND. Taxis are readily available and are inexpensive—and many of the drivers double as tour guides for the day. Cars are available to rent at about $24–35 per day. The largest agencies are *Maurice Connors* (tel. 2433); *H & R* (tel. 2656/2606); *Apex* (tel. 2642); *Budget* (tel. 2217); and *Island Car Rental* (tel. 2723). A local driver's license is necessary but most rental agencies can supply this; fee is U.S. $5; validity three months. Contact *Anguilla Rentals* (tel. 2510); *Boos Cycle* (tel. 2323) or *Dyal Cycles* (tel. 2719/2510) for bicycles, mopeds, scooters, and motorbikes. Remember—driving here is on the *left!*

TOURIST INFORMATION SERVICES. On the island, the *Anguilla Tourist Office* is in The Valley, tel. 2759. For sources closer to home, see Tourist Information Services section in the *Facts at Your Fingertips* chapter.

SPECIAL EVENTS. Anguilla Day (May 30) celebrates the island's secession from the Associated State of St. Kitts and Nevis. The end of July and early August are devoted to Carnival and major boat races.

TOURS. Island tour operators include *Bennie's Tours* (tel. 2221); Keith Gumbs' *Mellow Tones Tours* (tel. 2680); and *Nell Taxi and Tours* (tel. 2409). Any taxi driver will also be delighted to show off all there is to see. A tour around Anguilla should run about U.S. \$40. Excursions to Prickly Pear Cays, Sandy Island, or Dog Island for snorkeling, diving, a picnic, or simply sunbathing may be arranged through *Tamariain Water Sports Ltd.* at Malliouhana (tel. 2798/2111); *Island Water Sports* at Road Bay (no tel.) or *Neville Connor* at Blowing Point (tel. 2395).

BEACHES. Beaches and bays abound on Anguilla no matter which side of the island you're on. On the northern strip *Shoal Bay* is a true beauty—L-shaped with beautiful tiny shells and excellent snorkeling. *Captain's Bay* is secluded and romantic; crescent *Road Bay* has the commercial pier and several small restaurants; *Island Harbor's* horseshoe-shaped beach is best for watching the fishermen bring in their lobster and seafood catch; *Barnes, Maids,* and *Long Bay* are three linked beaches whose talcum-powder sand seems to stretch on and on and *Little Bay,* a secluded cove backed by high cliffs, is best reached by boat. The southern shore has *Cove Bay,* with its sheltering coconut palms; *Maunday's* 2-mile-long stretch and *Rendezvous* with dunes and good shelling—and that's only a third, this "beach island" has over 30.

PARTICIPANT SPORTS. Watersports. Water-skiing, windsurfing, sailing, fishing, snorkeling and diving are offered by *Tamariain Water Sports,* at Malliouhana. (Tel. 2798/2111.) Iain Grummitt is a P.A.D.I.-licensed instructor who will give the resort course as well as certification courses. *Island Water Sports* at Road Bay rents jet skis, windsurfers, small sailboats, snorkeling equipment, and rafts, and offers **waterskiing. Fishing** is best arranged through Mariners (tel. 2671) where small boats and windsurfers are also rented. Experienced sailors will enjoy a **day-sail** aboard *Baccarat,* a comfortable 52' racing yawl that can also be chartered for longer sails. Departs daily from Road Bay at 9:30 A.M.; \$50 per person includes an excellent lunch and open bar (tel. 2470). *Ninja,* anchored off Blowing Point (tel. 2592), is a comfortable, new 60' catamaran that is available for day-sails, picnic cruises or longer charters (\$600 per day, maximum 30 passengers).

There are **tennis** courts at Rendezvous Bay Hotel, Malliouhana, Cinnamon Reef, and in The Valley. Horseback riding is now available through Coral Reef Resort (tel. 2151). Four thoroughbred saddle horses may be taken on half-day tours through forest paths or rented by the hour; lessons also arranged.

SPECTATOR SPORTS. Boat racing is the island's national sport and major meets take place on Easter Monday; Anguilla Day (May 30); during Carnival Week, which begins the last Friday in July; and New Years Day. Races are an occasion for the whole island to get together to cheer their favorite and enjoy the barbecues and bands before, during and after the race. **Cricket, soccer** and **softball** matches may be viewed in Webster Park in The Valley; check the local tourist office for dates of scheduled games.

MUSIC, DANCE, AND STAGE. There's a lot of musical talent here that ranges from Bankie BanX, Anguilla's own reggae superstar with four recordings, to the Mayoumba Folkloric Theatre, which presents song-and-dance skits depicting Caribbean and Anguillian culture to the beat of African drums and a string band. Then there's Keith Gumbs and The Mellow Tones, a multifaceted group that has also done recordings; Sprecker, an excellent guitarist; Amelia and Friends, much loved for their quiet ballads and Calypso melodies; talented pianist Frankie Rogers, and popular string and scratch bands such as Sleepy and the All Stars, the Smoky Mountain Boys, and Happy Hits. Steel Vibrations, a relatively new pan band, often entertains at barbecues and West Indian evenings.

 SHOPPING. Shops are few and far between but *The Anguilla Craft Shop* in new quarters next to the library in The Valley has some nice bags, hats, straw and shell work, hardanger, embroidery, macramé, homemade hibiscus wines, pepper sauce, jams, and marmelades made from exotic tropical fruits. This is sponsored and run by the island's National Council of Women, one of several groups encouraging handicraft and cottage industry. Anguilla's carpenters are well known for their beautiful carved doors and furniture and if you are in the market for a racy sea craft, the island boat-builders are some of the Caribbean's best. For fashionable beach and resortwear try *La Romana* at Malliouhana; *Cinnamon Reef's* new boutique; the *Sunshine Shop* in South Hill; The *Riviera Boutique* at Road Bay; and small, locally owned shops such as *The Clothesline, Olive Branch,* or *Blue Waters* in The Valley. *Mariner's Boutique* stocks Naf-Naf, the popular French manufacturer of jumpsuits and other comfortable cotton clothing.

 RESTAURANTS. Lobster is truly king of the sea on Anguilla, but there's lots more on this small island. We call $25 and up per person for a three-course meal *Expensive;* $15–24 *Moderate;* below $15 *Inexpensive.*

Cinnamon Reef. *Expensive.* Little Harbour. Tel. 2850/2727. Dependably fine food prepared by a talented Anguillian chef. Don't miss the wonderful homemade yogurt ambrosia and a dozen other creative luncheon salads; excellent West Indian and Continental specialties with a tropical touch at dinner. Lobster, Black Angus steak, and a fresh catch of the day, prepared simply with lime butter, are always available in addition to the daily changing menu. Some of our favorite dishes here are the Caribbean fish or pumpkin soup, curried conch or goat, and roast duckling in blackberry sauce. The dining room is airy and expansive with well-spaced wooden tables and an array of straight, winged, and lacy fan-backed chairs. Friday night poolside barbecues and nightly entertainment in and off-season. No credit cards.

Cul de Sac. *Expensive.* Blowing Point. Tel. 2461. Candlelit dining indoors or on the small terrace is very popular, so reservations are a must. Somewhat hectic on Thursday evenings before the Mayoumba show, so we suggest just drinks that night and a more leisurely meal another evening. Anguillian chef Gwennie whips up the island's best conch fritters and chowder as well as some tasty seafood preparations at both lunch and dinner. AE, V.

Fish Trap. *Expensive.* Island Harbor. Tel. 4488. Patricia Van Dyck holds forth in the kitchen while husband Thierry takes good care of their guests out on the small terrace. This charming Belgian couple have created one of the island's best restaurants as well as its warmest and friendliest. Patricia's tomato pie, grilled crayfish with garlic butter, and seafood pasta are special treats, but everything here is usually good. Seafood is the freshest, as this is the beach where the fishermen bring in their daily catch. Popular at both lunch and dinner even though it's about half an hour's drive from most hotels. AE.

Malliouhana. *Expensive.* Maids Bay. Tel. 2731. Five young French chefs including Philippe Rostang, two gracious maitres d'hôtel, and the menu are all direct from Antibe's La Bonne Auberge where master-chef Jo Rostang oversees all from afar . . . too far perhaps. The setting is splendid—linens, crystal,

porcelain, and silverware chosen with taste; the Anguillian waiters still somewhat unsure but obviously well trained in the finesse of soigné service; the menu
light and creative, and the food good . . . though far below our expectations.
Unevenness is one flaw, and perhaps the fact that everything here must be
imported is another factor. A rather complicated Bavarois of smoked salmon
could be perfectly prepared, but its sauce was too strongly concentrated; a
simple salade Nicoise was a disaster, while a crunchy green bean salad with
creamy tomato sauce was a delight. With a cellar capacity of 50,000 bottles we
were sorely disappointed at the very limited wine list with nary a great vintage
to be had. Daily specials are always excellent, as are the dessert offerings. We
hope that after a year's experience, the bugs will all get ironed out and perfection
will prevail. No credit cards.

The Mariners. *Expensive.* Sandy Ground. Tel. 2671. We definitely recommend the Thursday-night barbecue and the Saturday-evening West Indian dinner—both excellent values at U.S. $18. Food here has improved dramatically
over the last year, but be prepared to wait, as the 18 pretty terrace tables are
so pleasant that people tend to linger. Dinner is very popular, but so is lunch,
and late-afternoon snacks are served until 5:30 P.M. The bar and lounge can be
lively, especially when there is live entertainment. The comfortable bar and
lounge area are both pleasant for drinks and there is frequent entertainment.
AE, MC, V.

The Barrel Stay. *Expensive to Moderate.* Sandy Ground. Tel. 2831. This
intimate thatched-roof beachside bar and restaurant took off in popularity last
year when dinner reservations were difficult to come by. Good and casual, but
the attractive tables made from real barrel stays are rather uncomfortable. Fresh
grilled lobster, a house bouillabaisse, and other seafood are the specialties at
both lunch and dinner . . . but candlelight evenings are best. AE.

Ferryboat Inn. *Moderate.* Blowing Point. Tel. 2613. John McClain's homemade soups, burgers, and seafood are well prepared and very reasonably priced.
Breezy little terrace where, when dinner is finished, McClain plays bartender
and good conversation and stories take over to amuse local residents and visitors
alike. No credit cards.

Johnno's Fish Pot. *Moderate.* George Hill. Tel. 2728. John Edwards's breezy
hilltop restaurant has a view, small bar, soft music in season, and a good
following. If the weather has been bad, check to see that he has fresh fish, as
his menu is limited when seafood is not available. **Johnno's** on the beach at
Road Bay is *de rigueur* for Sunday barbecue lunch, when there's a band, lots
of St. Martin yachts and motorboats over, and plenty of friendly, barefoot
people. No credit cards.

Lucy's Harbour View. *Moderate.* South Hill. Tel. 2253. Lucy Halley learned
her culinary tricks in St. Martin so her West Indian dishes have a definite French
flair. This is a nice terrace with a view over Road Bay, and Lucy's whole fish
Creole-style, grilled lobster, and crispy chicken legs with sautéed potatoes are
island legends. Open lunch and dinner; be prepared to stay awhile, since all is
cooked to order. No credit cards.

The Palm. *Moderate.* The Valley. Tel. 2668. Owner/chef John Richardson's
pasta dishes and lobster stew prepared with onions, sweet pepper, garlic,
tomatoes, and paprika are special treats, as is his chicken grandmére. Six tables
are covered in cheery red-and-white checks; there's lots of greenery including
a palm tree growing up through the roof in the middle of this very unpretentious
but very good little dining room. No credit cards.

Palm Palm. *Moderate.* Sandy Ground. Tel. 2287. Béatrice and Gérard
Boyer's friendly beachside bistro where croissants are baked fresh for breakfast,
omelettes and burgers are popular at lunch, and some good Creole and French
specialties are served up at dinner. Food here is uncomplicated but well prepared and you get good value for your dollar, especially with the $8.50 daily
special. Pedal boats and Sunfish available for guests. No credit cards.

Pineapple Annies. *Moderate.* Coral Bay Resort. Tel. 2151. The seaside terrace
is perfect if it's not too windy and the long bar is always a stopping-off place
for interesting local residents. The menu changes often at both lunch and dinner
but usually is a good mix of West Indian and Continental. If they're doing the
seafood pizza, shrimp curry Corito, or crayfish you won't go wrong, but every-

thing here is fresh and good, though simply prepared. Entertainment just about every night in season. AE, MC, V.

Rendezvous Bay Hotel. *Moderate.* Rendezvous Bay. Tel. 2549. No menu, as the set lunches and dinners are mainly for guests; but the cook's reputation is such a good one many outsiders join them—but only if they have called in advance. Authentic West Indian chowder, pumpkin soup, pork chops, lobster, and seafood combinations may be among the choices, but everything is always well prepared. Desserts here are usually a treat. The dining terrace is long, as are the tables, where service is informal family style. No credit cards.

Riviera. *Moderate.* Sandy Ground. Tel. 2833. Sylvaine and Didier's special spot for satisfying seafood with both French and West Indian accents. Lunch features salads and omelettes; dinner might include a highly seasoned fish soup—a meal in itself for some—grilled lobster with lime butter, spicy conch, or pepper filet; French bread and tasty desserts. A nice spot on the sea. AE, V.

Amy's Bakery And Snack Bar. *Inexpensive.* Blowing Point. Tel. 2775. Enjoy chicken and chips, pizza, quiche, chops, and scrumptious cakes and pies on the premises or carry them out. No credit cards.

Aquarium. *Inexpensive.* South Hill. Tel. 2720. A good local spot for fish, shellfish, turtle, whelks, and conch prepared the Anguillian way—and that means well seasoned. Only eight tables here, best to call and see what's on the menu so they can start preparing in advance. Little atmosphere, but the home cooking makes up for that. No credit cards.

Pepper Pot. *Inexpensive.* Near the stoplight in The Valley. Tel. 2328. Cora Richardson's bar, restaurant and pasty shop draws roti lovers like a magnet. This spicy West Indian mouthful is made of boneless chicken, tanias, celery, pepper, onion, garlic, and local peas, a full meal in itself at only $5 EC. Cora also does complete dinners—lobster, whelks, and conch with dumplings that visitors in the know as well as local residents can't resist. No credit cards.

Roys. *Inexpensive.* Crocus Bay. Tel. 2470. Roy and Mandy Bossons planned to open a second tropical pub on the property of Sile Bay Beach Apartments in fall 1985. Whether one or both exist you'll still be able to find Roy's fish and chips, West Indian pork fricassee and sinfully rich chocolate rum cake. The original bar and restaurant was very casual and laid-back; the new place should be somewhat different, but still attract the same faithful crowd of "expats". No credit cards.

NIGHT LIFE AND BARS. Anguilla nightlife is pretty quiet during the week but all the hotels do offer good local entertainment until around 11 P.M. nightly during the high season. Bankie BanX, Anguilla's own reggae superstar, has been on an extended European tour, but when he's on the island, do try to catch one of his performances, perhaps at his own club, *Bankies,* in The Farrington. Thursday evening performances of the Mayoumba Folkloric Group at *Cul de Sac* is one show that should not be missed. *Pineapple Annies* at Coral Bay resort can draw a lively crowd on Friday and Saturday. The regular Saturday night bash at *Smitty's* in Island Harbor was somewhat out of favor last year, with just a small crowd gathering early for a beer and barbecued chicken before going on to dance till the wee hours at *Dragon's Disco* in South Hill. Musician Keith Gumbs planned to open his new nightclub *Keg's Palace* in George Hill last summer and should be providing some more musical activity nightly.

POSTAGE. Airmail letters to the U.S. require EC $.60, postcards EC $.25.

ELECTRIC CURRENT. Anguilla uses both 110 A.C. and 220 A.C., so check with your hotel before plugging in appliances.

SECURITY. This is a quiet, peaceful island where crime is almost nonexistent; nonetheless, don't tempt fate by leaving valuables unattended. Even though it is usually marked, learn to identify the Manchineel tree. Its fruit is poisonous, and its sap can badly blister skin.

ANTIGUA

by
DAVID P. SCHULZ

David P. Schulz, a freelance writer living in New York, is the author of sixteen books on leisure activities including sports, travel, and recreation. He also writes for magazines and newspapers on subjects ranging from travel, recreation, and leisure to business, finance, and history.

Antigua is the largest of the British Leeward Islands. Its 108 square miles are the limestone and volcanic remnants that have built beach-fringed, scrub-covered islands throughout the Caribbean. But Antigua is more than that. They say they have 365 beaches, one for every day of the year, and we don't doubt it. Thirty miles north lies its sister island of Barbuda.

Antigua is roughly circular and ringed by jagged coves, silent bays, and small harbors, each with its sun-swept beach. Hotels have been strategically placed around the island shores, which gives the country a resort look if you take only the coastal road. Inland, however, you'll see what the island nation is all about with its rain forest—now rejuvenated after having suffered a prolonged drought—pineapple groves, and banana trees, and tiny villages with open-air fruit and vegetable markets that let you know you really are on a tropical isle.

To add to it all, Antigua has a major attraction in its English Harbour. This is a well-done restoration of the eighteenth-century dockyard that was home for Admiral Lord Nelson and his British navy fleet.

More up-to-date are two gambling casinos that are aglitter until the early hours of the morning.

Past and Present

Discovered by Columbus in 1493, Antigua was named for Santa María la Antigua of Seville. The accepted pronunciation has always been English, however—An-*tee*-ga with a hard g. The island was colonized by English planters from St. Kitts in 1623. After a brief period of French occupation in 1666, it was formally given to England by the Treaty of Breda in 1667, and it has remained British ever since, abandoning its crown-colony government only when the committee system was introduced in 1951. In 1967, in the British government's first move to grant eventual independence to the former colonies, Antigua became an associated state within the British Commonwealth. On November 1, 1981, Antigua achieved full independence.

As an independent country, Antigua/Barbuda is going through the growing pains so typical of newly created nations as it tries to broaden its economic base from one heavily dependent upon tourism to one with diversified agriculture and industry.

EXPLORING ANTIGUA

The two major points of reference are the capital city of St. Johns on the northwest side of the island and English Harbour on the south side. St. Johns, with a population of about 35,000, or nearly half of the island's 75,000 people, is the focal point for business and tourist activity with more than half of the country's hotels just minutes away by car. The new Deepwater Harbour, where as many as forty cruise ships dock each month during the winter season, is about a mile from the center of St. Johns with its shops and restaurants. (There is also shopping available at Deepwater Harbour.) Coolidge Airport, with its spacious and modern new terminal, is just a few miles east of St. Johns.

St. Johns

The town can be seen in one day, especially if you just want to skim the high points, but to see the major attractions, sample the local cooking, and engage in some serious gift-shopping, at least one long day or two separate trips would be in order.

The marketplace in St. Johns is a bustle of activity on Fridays and Saturdays for local residents, but its location at the south end of town (where Market Street forks into Valley Road and All Saints Road) is somewhat off the tourist path. There are a few buys for visitors, but the market is mostly for locals who come to buy and sell. It's fascinating to hear them bargain loudly for the fruits, vegetables, fish, and spices. Many of the old-timers will smile and say "Good morning," expecting you to return the greeting. If you want to take pictures, expect to part with a few coins, and be sure to ask first.

Most of the shops, banks, and restaurants in town are located in the area bounded by Newgate Street on the north, Redcliffe Street on the south, the water on the west, and Independence Avenue on the east.

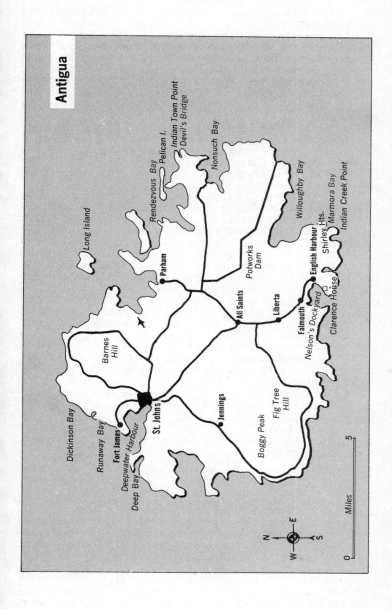

Antigua

Long Island

Rendezvous Bay
Pelican I.
Indian Town Point
Devil's Bridge
Nonsuch Bay
Willoughby Bay
Shirley Hts.
Marmora Bay
Indian Creek Point

Parham

Potworks Dam

All Saints

Liberta

English Harbour

Clarence House

Falmouth

Nelson's Dockyard

Barnes Hill

St. Johns

Jennings

Fig Tree Hill

Boggy Peak

Fort James
Deepwater Harbour
Runaway Bay
Dickinson Bay
Deep Bay

Miles

0   5

N
E
S
W

Just across Independence Avenue are Government House, the Botanical Gardens, and the Recreation Grounds, where some first-rate cricket may be seen. The busiest shopping areas are clustered near the water along Redcliffe, St. Mary's, and High streets, which are intersected by Thames, Market, and Corn Alley. Here, too, are many of the public buildings you may want to visit including the Tourist Bureau (at Long and Thames), the cable office (Corn Alley and High), and the post office on lower Long Street near the water. There is a philatelic window where you can buy the special stamps that make cards sent back home so appealing.

The Old Court House on Market Street between Long and Church now houses the archaeology museum and the Archives, a collection of Antiguan historical records and documents. Also worth a look is Ebenezer Methodist Church (on St. Mary's Street), built in 1839 to replace a smaller building. It is Methodism's mother church in the West Indies.

St. John the Divine Cathedral dominates the town from its hilltop position at Long and Temple streets. Surrounded by the traditional churchyard and graves, this Anglican cathedral was begun in 1845 to replace a stone building started in 1745 that had been destroyed by an earthquake. The first church on the site, however, was a wooden structure built in 1683. The figures of St. John the Baptist and St. John the Divine, erected at the south gate of the present structure, are said to have been taken from one of Napoleon's ships and transported to Antigua in a British man-o'-war.

There are some other points of interest in the St. Johns area. Redcliffe Quay (pronounced "key") consists of a number of restored old buildings housing shops and restaurants at the foot of Redcliffe Street. Police headquarters on Newgate near Market Street is noteworthy because it was formerly the arsenal. Part of the fence is made of firelocks and bayonets. There are two interesting memorials: the Westerby Memorial on lower High Street, erected in 1888 in memory of Moravian Bishop George Westerby; and the Cenotaph on East Street at High Street, built as a memorial to Antiguans who lost their lives in World Wars I and II. Further from the center of town are the Antigua Rum Distillery near Deepwater Harbour and, about a half-mile to the northwest, Fort James, built as a lookout point for the city and harbour of St. Johns. Its ruined ramparts, built in 1703, overlook small islands in the bay, and its cannons still point out to sea.

The Interior

As you head out of town and round the island, the sights are mostly scenic—and, of course, there are the beaches. Antigua's heartland is dotted with churches. They tell the history. Each small village has its church, and some of the more famous include St. Johns in town and St. Barnabas at the village of Liberta. Known in the area as the Chapel of Ease, the church was built more than a hundred years ago of Antiguan green stone. Green Bay was built by the Moravians in 1845 for the emancipated slaves, and the Spring Gardens Church, begun in 1755, was also for the slaves, who, prior to that time, had worshiped under the old sandbox tree.

St. George's, the military church for the island's troops in the last century, has been restored and is used for regular Sunday worship. St. Paul's Church at Falmouth has been rebuilt on the site of the church used for the troops during Nelson's day. The Georgian church at Parham Village, St. Peter's, was built in 1840, following plans of Thomas Weekes, and English architect. It was considerably damaged by an earthquake in 1843, but the octagonal structure is still worth a visit.

English Harbour

Seeing Nelson's Dockyard involves a thirty-mile round trip from St. Johns. Along the way, you'll pass some small villages and mid-island homes that have been spruced up with the island's relatively recent prosperity, and many that have not. The waving fields of sugar cane have diminished in recent years in favor of the more profitable fields of scruffy-looking sea-island cotton and acre upon acre of pineapples. Stone sugar mills still punctuate some of the most magnificent coastal scenery in the Caribbean, while Boggy Peak can be seen in the south-west section. At 1,330 feet, it is the highest point on the island.

Nelson's Dockyard was built in 1784 in "landlocked" English Harbour, so protected from the open sea that approaching yachtsmen rush to their charts, wondering if they've somehow missed the place. Horatio Nelson arrived here in 1784 and became commander-in-chief of the Leeward Islands Squadron. Under his command was the Captain of HMS *Pegasus,* Prince William Henry, Duke of Clarence, who was to ascend the throne of England as William IV, the "sailor king." He was Nelson's close friend and best man at his wedding to young Fannie Nisbet, which took place on the island of Nevis in 1787. A must on your exploring list is Clarence House, the handsome stone residence built for the prince on the heights opposite the dockyard.

The whole of Shirley Heights and English Harbour are fascinating to history buffs. The buildings have been reclaimed by the Dockyard and Shirley Heights restoration groups and the Society of Friends of English Harbour. The Dockyard, whose museum in the Admiral's House has a display of Nelson mementos (porter's lodge, guardhouse, engineer's workshop, sail loft, paymaster's house, capstans, bollards, etc.), is a vivid reminder of history, a living monument to the men and their commanders: Nelson, Rodney, Hood. The historical part need not take you more than an hour at the most, and the area is fun for the lore that comes from today's sailors and others who saunter around the boats tied up at the present active dockyard.

Clarence House is open to visitors when the prime minister is not in residence. From its perch on the hillside overlooking English Harbour, the Duke of Clarence, once Prince William Henry and later King William IV, could look over the dockyard and his *Pegasus* as she rode at anchor in the harbor.

Shirley Heights, a short drive from the sea-level harbor, is a hillside fortification that is being restored. Impressive at sunset. A restaurant at the site provides the opportunity for leisurely investigation. The Admiral's Inn sometimes plans evening entertainments at Shirley Heights.

The West Coast

Instead of cutting across the middle of the island to get from St. Johns to English Harbour, travel the long route along the Caribbean coast. This pleasant ride through gentle hills takes in the seacoast scenery. Several of Antigua's better-known beach hotels are located along the route, as is the archaeological site at Jolly Beach where the earliest settlement on the island has been found, dating to 1775 B.C.

The East End

Ruggedly beautiful and isolated, the eastern third of the island is home to exclusive properties such as the Half Moon Bay Hotel, the Mill Reef Club, and St. James' Club as well as man-made Potworks Dam and Lake, Indian Town, and the natural wonder of Devil's Bridge.

Indian Town, at the northeast point of the island, is one of Antigua's national parks and the site of another archaeological excavation, this one of the more recent Carib Indian occupation. Nearby, breakers roaring in with all the Atlantic's accumulated force have carved Devil's Bridge and created blowholes with fuming surf.

A newer sight is the lake that now monopolizes the east-central section of Antigua, although it has shrunk because of a prolonged dry spell in recent years. The result of the Potworks Dam, the lake was filled in the late 1960s by rainfall and at one time provided most of the island's water supply.

Barbuda

This sparsely inhabited island thirty miles north of Antigua—the whole population of 1,200 lives in Codrington—is sixty-two square miles of wilderness surrounded by wide beaches protected by coral reefs. Hunting, fishing, and diving opportunities are excellent. Martello Tower, the only historic ruin, is believed to have been a lighthouse built by the Spanish before the English occupied the island. LIAT has regularly scheduled daily flights from Antigua. Air and boat charters are also available. Coco Point Lodge has 27 rooms and a few guesthouses, although additional accommodations are planned.

PRACTICAL INFORMATION FOR
ANTIGUA/BARBUDA

FACTS AND FIGURES. Antigua has an area of 108 square miles. Temperature ranges from 71 to 86 degrees in summer, and the island has an average annual rainfall of about 40 inches, though in recent years there has been less. Independent since Nov. 1, 1981, Antigua/Barbuda has a population approaching 75,000, of whom only about 1,200 live on Barbuda, all in Codrington. English is the official language and the majority of the population is descended from African slaves of the British colonial period. Tourism is the major source of foreign exchange and the enlarged Coolidge Airport is an important transfer point for travelers heading further south in the eastern Caribbean.

WHEN TO GO. Antigua/Barbuda has a long winter season stretching from the Independence Day activities at the end of October to Sailing Week early in May, though winter rates are generally in effect from mid-December to mid-April. Off-season room rates are 33%–45% less. The dry season is January through March, but no month averages as much as five inches of rain. Temperatures rarely fall below 70 degrees or rise above 90 F.

PASSPORTS AND VISAS. U.S. and Canadian citizens need only proof of identity. A passport is best, but a birth certificate or voter's registration card will do—a driver's license will not. In addition, all visitors must hold a return or ongoing ticket. British citizens need proof of citizenship plus a return ticket.

MONEY. The Eastern Caribbean dollar (EC) is the local currency, which at press time is figured at EC $2.60 = U.S. $1. Be sure which currency is being used, since most places quote in EC dollars.

WHAT WILL IT COST?

A typical day on Antigua for two persons during the winter season will run:

	U.S. $
Hotel accommodations, including breakfast and dinner	$175
Luncheon in town or at another hotel	20
Tips, service charge, and room tax	30
One-day sightseeing by rental car (self-drive)	35
Total	$260

HOW TO GET THERE. By air. *American, Pan American,* and *BWIA* have direct service from New York; *Pan Am, BWIA* and *Eastern* from Miami. *BWIA* also flies from San Juan and Toronto, *Air Canada* from Toronto, and *British Airways* from London. *Air Florida* provides freight service from Miami. *LIAT* flies out of home base Antigua for down-island destinations. LIAT also has daily flights from Antigua to Barbuda, 15 minutes away, with a round trip costing EC $92. Air and boat charters are available, as are tours to Barbuda—either day trips or overnight stays—through Paradise Tours, High St., St. Johns (tel. 24786) or Wadadli Travel & Tours (tel. 22227/8).

By boat: Antigua is a very popular cruise-ship stop during the winter season, when as many as 40 cruise ships dock at Deepwater Harbour each month.

AIRPORT TAX AND OTHER CHARGES. There is a 6% government tax on hotel accommodations, as well as a 10% service charge. The airport departure tax is EC $10 per person.

TELEPHONES AND EMERGENCY NUMBERS. The area code for Antigua is 809 then dial 46 followed by the local 5-digit number. Emergency services vary from section to section, and your hotel should have the numbers for local help. Holberton Hospital (tel. 20251) in St. Johns is a 210-bed facility with X-ray, intensive care unit, laboratory, surgery, and a 24-hour emergency room. St. Johns' police telephone number is 20045; police headquarters is 20125.

HOTELS. The resort hotels are stretched out all along the island's best beaches. Because so many of them are a distance from the city, most guests take advantage of the MAP plan. Therefore, our categories are based on accommodations for two during the winter season with breakfast and dinner included (unless otherwise noted). Rates are in U.S. dollars. We call $190 and above *Deluxe;* $150–$189 *Expensive;* under $150 *Moderate.* There are less expensive places to stay, including some very nice apartment and cottage accommodations with light housekeeping facilities, called self-catering in Antigua.

Deluxe

Anchorage Hotel. Box 147, St. Johns. Tel. 20267. This gracious and sprawling resort at Dickenson Bay two miles north of St. Johns has 99 rooms with recently refurbished accommodations: deluxe beach rooms with a/c; fan-cooled rondavals with king-sized beds; lush garden rooms with a/c and sea view for most, and a/c cottage rooms. Sandy white beach with complimentary water sports including windsurfers, pedaloes, Sunfish, snorkeling, and waterskiing. Excursion and glass-bottom boats available, plus three tennis courts and pro Mary McLean. Evening entertainment. Cordon Bleu chef creates menu magic.

Curtain Bluff. Box 288, St. Johns. Tel. 3115. This is the most dramatic resort on the island, in that it's on a peninsula on the southwestern coast, on the way toward English Harbor, with the leeward sea on one side and the windward on the other. Fifty beautifully decorated rooms, each with a balcony overlooking the water, add to the charm here. Fine dining and a selection of spots for sipping, such as their indoor round bar or tree-shaded patio. There are three tennis courts, a pro shop, and on the beach, water-skiing, sailing, snorkeling, and scuba diving. No credit cards.

Half Moon Bay. Box 144, St. Johns. Tel. 32101. The surf is directly in front of the 100-room property, and the calm Caribbean waters are just a walk along the sand away. The food is excellent, with a full breakfast on your private terrace a sign of what is to come later on. Delectable tropical fruits, oversized salads, lobster, red snapper, and other specials from the sea are just a few of the choices. Jackets required two evenings a week in season, but it's informal during the summer. Activities include a freshwater swimming pool, tennis courts, a nine-hole golf course, and water sports.

The Inn at English Harbour. Box 187, St. Johns. Tel. 31014. If ever there was a place with quiet charm and centuries-old history, this is it. Just 30 rooms on a hilltop across the bay from and overlooking Nelson's Dockyard. Some of the cottages are available on the bluff, others on the beach at Freeman's Bay below. Breakfast and lunch are served at both locations; dinner is on the terrace at the top. All water sports and tours of the historic dockyard add to the pleasures.

Long Island Resort. Box 243, St. Johns. Tel. 32176. Informal luxury at its best, with 28 rooms split between cottages and a multi-unit facility at one end of Jumby Bay Beach. Quiet and private are watchwords, with miles of trails to cover on the 300-acre private island 4½ miles northeast of Antigua. Choice of beaches. Complimentary water sports, tennis, bicycles. Free ferry to Antigua. Rates include lunch as part of full American plan.

Expensive

Antigua Beach Hotel. Box 63, St. Johns. Tel. 22069. On a hilltop with a beautiful view of Hodges Bay, this 44-room property offers tennis and a large freshwater pool on the premises, with a beach just a short walk down the hill. Casablanca restaurant features international cuisine.

Blue Waters Beach Hotel. Box 256, St. Johns. Tel. 20290. There are 49 beachfront rooms here at Soldier Bay set in a tropical garden at the edge of the sea. Garden suites and studio apartment available. Meal plans can be EP or full American. Dining room features West Indian dishes, elaborate buffets, and barbecues. A full watersports program as well as a freshwater pool, tennis, archery, sailing, and fishing for daytime activities; music in evenings.

The Copper and Lumber Store Hotel at Prince William Carreenage. Box 184, St. Johns. Tel. 31058. At Nelson's Dockyard, English Harbour. With 14 rooms/suites, some furnished in contemporary style, others in 18th century georgian with dormer windows, ceiling timbers, mahagony and brass bathroom fixtures, and slate floors. Rates are EP since all have fully equipped kitchens.

Galley Bay Surf Club. Box 304, St. Johns. Tel. 20302. An ideal getaway in an exclusive spot on the northwest coast. The setting is superb, with the 28 rooms and villas in Gauguin-style thatched-room complexes on the lagoon. The beach is long and quiet; perfect for swimming, shelling, and snorkeling. When the mood suits, there are also tennis to play and horses to ride. Excellent food served on the terrace overlooking the water, and music for dancing later on.

Halcyon Cove Beach Resort and Casino. Box 251, St. Johns. Tel. 20256. 150 rooms spread around freshwater pool courtyard and beach overlooking Dickenson Bay. Expansive beach for sunning, in addition to snorkeling, windsurfing, waterskiing, and sailing. Tennis courts, plus chance to play nearby 18-hole Cedar Valley course. Interior dining room or Warri Pier restaurant over the water. Music, dancing, and, of course, the casino in the evenings.

Hawksbill Beach Hotel. Box 108, St. Johns. Tel. 20301. There are 75 rooms with terraces, almost all with beach view, plus the Great House luxury villa. Freshwater pool, 4 beaches, and 37 acres of grounds makes this place unique on the island. Choice of two dining rooms, plus regular entertainment. Complimentary watersports except slight charge for waterskiing.

Jolly Beach Hotel. Box 744, St. Johns. Tel. 20061. With nearly 500 rooms, this is the largest hotel in eastern Caribbean. White sand beach at Lignumvitae Bay, 15 miles from St. Johns, it offers a full range of free water sports, 8 tennis courts, freshwater pool, shuffleboards, and volleyball. Two open-air restaurants, beach restaurant, coffee shop, ice cream parlor, and 7 bars. Nightlife includes entertainment, disco, slot machines.

Moderate

Admiral's Inn. Box 713, St. Johns. Tel. 31027. Enchanting 14-room hotel in historic building at Nelson's Dockyard, English Harbour. Rooms are simple but charms abound. Superb food in indoor dining room or on the terrace. Beach at Freeman's Bay is a short, complimentary boat ride away. Same people operate the Falmouth Beach Apartments with 25 efficiency units.

The Barrymore. Box 244, St. Johns. Tel. 21055, 24062/3. 32 rooms a/c with private baths, two efficiency units with full kitchens. Close to town, yet with horseback riding, swimming pool, and shuttle service to the beach. Elegant dining at *DuBarry* restaurant on premises.

Barrymore Beach Apartments. Box 244, St. Johns. Tel. 24101/40. Studios, one- and two-bedroom units with kitchens as well as the Great House and other luxury villas. Beautiful white sand beach or freshwater pool. Perfect place to get away from it all. When not cooking in, *Satay Hut* restaurant features local and Asian specialties at reasonable prices.

Blue Heron Beach Hotel. Box 185, St. Johns. Tel. 31421. A new facility designed for surf, sand and sun lovers with 40 neat, efficient rooms at Johnson's Point beach, with its view of Montserrat on the horizon. Water sports available. Meals in the *Rookery* dining room are first rate, with selection from international or West Indian menus, especially at breakfast.

Galleon Beach Club. Box 1003, English Harbour. Tel. 31081. Comfortable cottage-style living here in a lovely colony overlooking Freeman's Bay at the edge of English Harbour. Accommodations are in well-furnished one- and two-bedroom cottages, each with full bath, living room, and full kitchen. Cook for yourself or try *Colombo's Restaurant and Bar* for the best Italian food on the island. This is a popular spot, so even though you're staying at the club, make reservations ahead of time. Beach options for daytime fun include swimming, snorkeling, sailing, and water-skiing. Nelson's Dockyard is just a few minutes away. Ideal for families who want to combine sports and sightseeing.

Long Bay. Box 442, St. Johns. Tel. 32005. 20 rooms, 5 cottages. A favorite with British travelers. Beach features coral reef in water shallow enough to walk to. Water sports equipment for rent, including a 31-ft. trimaran. Bar/restaurants at beach and in main building. Brand new tennis court.

New Antigua Horizons. Box 54, St. Johns. Tel. 21318. Peace and quiet, with 33 rooms, 24 overlooking sea, 9 with garden view, all with private terrace or patio, a/c available at extra charge. Swimming pool, tennis court, and almost all water sports. Fishing trips can be arranged. Kitchen puts emphasis on seafood with local flavor.

Runaway Beach Hotel. Box 874, St. Johns. Tel. 21318. 36 rooms grouped in several buildings stretched along the beach. Many of the units are efficiency apartments with cooking facilities. There is also a freshwater pool and watersports equipment available for rental.

TIME-SHARING CONDOMINIUMS. If you are interested in condominiums, contact the Antigua/Barbuda Tourist Board before your departure for the island.

HOME AND APARTMENT RENTALS. Cottages, apartments, and villas are available on Antigua and Barbuda, generally renting for periods of a week or more. Availability and rates are subject to change according to season and demand. These include Barrymore Beach Apartments (Box 244), Antigua Village (Box 159), Cape Coast Cottages (Box 1044), and Dian Bay Resort (Box 231). Check with the Antigua/Barbuda tourist board when making plans if you are interested in villas or self-catered units.

HOW TO GET AROUND. Taxis are readily available at Coolidge Airport and the Deepwater Harbour when cruise ships dock. Rates are posted at the airport and drivers are supposed to carry a rate card with them. A trip from the airport to St. Johns is U.S. $5.50, for example, while a taxi from St. Johns to Nelson's Dockyard and Clarence House would run $29.40.

If you are planning a trip across or around the island, a rental car may be more economical. There are several reputable local firms and some affiliated with U.S. agencies such as *Avis, Budget, Dollar, Hertz,* and *National.* Rates run about $35 per day. You will need a valid driver's license and a temporary permit for which the fee is U.S. $10. And remember to drive on the *left* no matter whether you rent a left-hand- or right-hand-drive car.

TOURIST INFORMATION SERVICES. In Antigua, the Antigua/Barbuda Department of Tourism is at Thames and Long Sts. (tel. 20480). On-island information supplied here. For sources closer to home, see the Tourist Information Services section in the *Facts at Your Fingertips* chapter.

SPECIAL EVENTS. Major events and celebrations include Independence Day (and the half-marathon and fun run conducted in association with it) on or about November 1; Carnival Week in early August, Sailing Week in late April or early May; and the two tennis weeks, the men's in January and the women's tourney in April.

TOURS. There are half-day and full-day island tours, some on land and others to offshore cays. The major attraction here is *Nelson's Dockyard* at English Harbour on the south coast, but there are also round-the-island excursions, which include visits to *St. Johns,* the *rum distillery,* and famous *Fig Tree Hill.* You can negotiate with one of the taxi drivers or contact one of the sightseeing-tour operators. Among them are: *Alexander Parrish, Ltd.* (tel. 20387), *Antours* (tel. 24788), and *National Tours, Ltd.* (tel. 21239).

PARKS AND GARDENS. Located near the government building on the east end of St. Johns with the entrance opposite the East Bus Station just off Independence Avenue, the *Antigua Botanical Gardens* have a small but lovely collection of flowering shrubs and tropical trees offering some invitingly shady places to relax. There are also a number of wildlife areas, some of which have park status, others of which have less formal protection.

The *Boggy Peak* area on the southwest side of the island is a tropical evergreen rain forest with lianis and epiphytes, silk cotton trees, locust trees, and large ferns.

One of the most mature stands of trees on the island can be found at *Weatherills Hill* on the northern end of the island not far from the Anchorage Hotel.

Here there is a closed canopy of trees up to 30 feet high dominated by wild cedar, turpentine, loblolly, boxwood, willow, and fig trees.

The *Mill Reef* area in the extreme east is now an officially protected area, and the *Marine Park Seaquarium* is a cage built over a coral reef located below Fort Charlotte just outside English Harbour.

 BEACHES. This is an island for beaches—the Antiguans claim to have 365 of them, one for every day of the year. The powdery sands come in white, pink, and shades of tan. There are obviously too many to list and though all are open to the public, some are more popular than others, including *Dickenson Bay,* location of so many resort hotels; *Five Islands,* in the area around Hawksbill Hotel, with four secluded beaches; *Carlisle Bay,* located at Old Road where a large coconut grove adds to the tropical paradise image; *Long Bay,* a sheltered beach on the Atlantic side not far from Devil's Bridge; and *Half Moon Bay,* a pink-shelled crescent with excellent snorkeling opportunities.

 PARTICIPANT SPORTS. Ever since Admiral Lord Nelson came in as commander-in-chief of the British royal navy's Leeward Islands Squadron in 1784, **sailing** these waters has been a feature attraction. Most of the resort hotels have **Sunfish** available for trying your hand across the gentle sea, and a few have **windsurfers** for a fast ride with the breeze. Should you want to make a full week of it, contact *Nicholson Yacht Charters* at English Harbour (tel. 31059) or write ahead to their office at 9 Chauncy St., Cambridge, MA 02138. Other yachts can be chartered through hotels, including Curtain Bluff, Half Moon Bay, Long Bay, and Hawksbill Hotel. There are **deep-sea fishing** charters operating out of Falmouth Harbor, Nelson's Dockyard, and Mamora Bay. In addition, the *Jolly Roger* and the *Pride of Orca* both offer group cruises daily out of Dickenson Bay.

In addition to offering **swimming** (with 365 beaches), the resort hotels either offer directly, or can make arrangements for, **scuba diving** and **snorkeling.** Serious **runners** can participate in the Antigua Half-Marathon held during the several-day celebration of Independence Day (Nov. 1), which attracts an international field, or they can participate in the more leisurely fun run held at the same time.

Tennis is popular enough to draw pros for three week-long tournaments (men in January at several of the hotels, women in April and mixed doubles in November at Half Moon Bay) and there are lesser competitions at the more than half-dozen hotels with courts. **Golf** is not a major island pastime, but there is an 18-hole course at Cedar Valley, three miles north of St. Johns, where visitors can sign up for short-term memberships, and a nine-hole course at the Half Moon Bay Hotel where there are no greens fees for hotel guests.

 SPECTATOR SPORTS. In addition to all the matches during the **tennis** weeks competitions and the racing during the Antigua **Sailing** Regatta, **cricket** is the country's national game with important matches played at the Recreation Grounds at the east end of the city near Independence Avenue during the season, which runs February to July. **Horse racing** has been revived at Cassada Garden Race Track, east of St. Johns on the road to the airport. There are at least ten meetings a year, generally around major holidays such as Valentine's Day, Easter, Independence Day, Christmas, etc., with legalized betting on the events. Also soccer, basketball, and track & field.

 HISTORIC SITES AND HOUSES. *Nelson's Dockyard* at English Harbour wins hands down for the best restoration on the island, if not in the eastern Caribbean. Most of the small buildings are now as they were in the 18th century, with a sail loft, an engineer's workshop, and a paymaster's house among them. The home in which Admiral Nelson lived is now a museum, and one of the Georgian buildings is now an apartment hotel for sailing buffs.

Clarence House, on a bluff overlooking the dockyard, was built for the Duke of Clarence when he served here as a seaman in Nelson's squadron. The duke later became King William IV of England, and the house has been used to entertain visiting royalty ever since. Country residence of the prime minister, Clarence House is open to the public when he is not in residence.

Fort Berkeley, at the western end of English Harbour, was the most important bastion in the 18th century in that it stood guard against invaders coming along the southern shore and into the landlocked harbor. *Fort James,* just outside the city of St. Johns, took care of fortifications for the northwestern part of the island.

 MUSEUMS. The *Admiral Nelson House,* the restored home where Lord Nelson supposedly lived, is now a museum. Whether he actually lived there or not, there is enough memorabilia tracing his life and the history of the British royal navy in the Caribbean during the 19th century to warrant a visit. The *Dow Hill Museum,* near English Harbour, has a small, compact collection of Indian artifacts from centuries-old Arawak villages. Museum hours are usually 8:00 A.M.—4:00 P.M. daily except Sundays and holidays. There is a small museum at Shirley Heights near English Harbour. In St. Johns, the Old Court House (Market St. between Long and Church) now houses the archaeology museum and the state archives.

MUSIC, DANCE, AND STAGE. Other than nightclub performances and special shows at the hotels, most serious performing arts take place at the University of the West Indies campus, located at the east end of St. Johns near the Recreation Grounds.

 SHOPPING. Many shops still operate the traditional hours of 8:00 A.M. to 4:00 P.M. daily except Sunday, closing 12:00–1:00 for lunch and at noon on Thursdays or Saturdays or both. Not all do, however, especially those that are most tourist oriented. Duty-free shops offer bargains in liquor, fragrances, and jewelry, while locally made items include pottery, straw work, Antigua rum, and local scenes and designs printed on fabric, shirts, scarves, bags, etc. Some shops accept credit cards, but many do not, so be sure to check. Prices are posted in either U.S. or EC dollars, sometimes both, and clerks will accept either currency in payment.

Redcliffe Quay at the foot of Redcliffe St. is an interesting maze of shops selling both domestically produced and imported goods. The shops along St. Mary's, High, and Long Sts. sell to both locals and tourists—most of the tourist shops are along St. Mary's St. Artist George Kelsick sells his hand-printed fabrics at *Kel-Print* on St. Mary's St. (at Temple) and several stores specialize in apparel made entirely or partially from West Indian sea-island cotton. Hans Smit, who bills himself at *The Goldsmitty,* plies his trade at 8a Redcliffe Quay, not far from *Serendipity,* featuring goods from the British Isles, and *A Thousand Flowers* with its local batik. *The Scent Shop* on High St. offers the obvious fragrances in addition to watches, jewelry, ceramics, and Waterford crystal while honoring all major credit cards. You can find hand silk-screened originals at *Sugar Mill Boutique* on St. Mary's St., and local crafts and clothes at *Sun Fun,* 71 Newgate St. behind the cathedral.

 RESTAURANTS. The accent here is on fresh-caught fish, but most restaurants offer a variety and you'll have no trouble finding continental, American, or West Indian-style cooking. Lobster is a big local favorite, as is spicy curried conch and local produce, especially the sweet Antigua black pineapple. Most menu prices are quoted in EC dollars, often in both EC and U.S. currency. Be sure to check. Dinner reservations may be needed, especially in season. Same with credit cards. The following categories are in U.S. dollars for a three-course meal without wine or beverage, per person: over $20 is *Expensive;* $13–$19, *Moderate;* under $13, *Inexpensive.* (Note: 10% service charge and 6% government tax may or may not be included in menu prices.)

Expensive

Admiral's Inn. Nelson's Dockyard, English Harbour. Tel. 31027. This is a delightful and historic place to dine, either on the terrace or indoors in a 18th-century setting. Seafood, especially lobster, and steaks are specialties.

DuBarry's. At the Barrymore Hotel. Tel. 21055. The newest elegant spot has a generally French menu sprinkled with Oriental-influenced treats such as a Szechuan-style crispy fish appetizer and sweet-and-sour pork chops. The ambience is a cross between continental sophistication and Caribbean relaxation.

L'Aventure. Dian Bay. Tel. 32003. Tastefully furnished rooms in what was once a private villa. Continental cuisine with a good selection of European and California wines. Croissant sandwiches popular at lunch. Boned rack of lamb with special filling in pastry shell is a dinner specialty. AE, MC, V.

Le Bistro. Hodges Bay. Tel. 23881. Superb French cuisine served in a small and intimate candlelit restaurant. It's run by a French couple who is always on hand to offer friendly personal service. The chef is also from France and prepares steaks, seafood, lobster, and duckling in a variety of delectable ways. They are open only for dinner, and a reservation is required.

Le Gourmet. Fort Road, St. Johns. Tel. 22977. Lobster the specialty, with the only live lobster tank on the island. Rest of menu features other seafood and continental cuisine, including Swiss gschnätzlets (veal in sauce). Reservations suggested but not required. AE, MC, V.

Moderate

Cockleshell Inn. Fort Rd., just outside St. Johns. Tel. 20371. Wonderful seafood, including cockles, and fresh-caught fish specialties make this small tavern a very popular place. Be sure to make a reservation. Open for dinner only, from 6:00 P.M. until midnight. AE, DC, MC, V.

Colombo's. Galleon Beach Club, English Harbour. Tel. 31081. Run by Sardinians who make every effort to please, and they do. Full Italian menu with regional specialties included. Good food, and lots of it.

Country Pond House. Upper Nevis St., St. Johns. Tel. 24508. A cozy spot in a 200-year-old house that once held a combination art gallery/pizzeria. Emphasis is on straightforward preparation of a few offerings that change regularly. Pasta with cockles is a local favorite. AE.

Parrot Cage. Fort Road, St. Johns. Tel. 23861. One of the newest restaurants in town, serving dinner only. Crowd tends to be late and local. Specials include beef kabob and chicken brochette, plus lobster of course. AE.

Pier 5. Crabbs Marina. Tel. 32114. Popular dockside spot for decent sandwiches and fries or more leisurely seafood entrees. Very casual during the day but some yachtspeople will dress for dinner, though it's not required. MC, V.

Satay Hut. On Runaway Bar near Barrymore Beach Apartments. Tel. 24140. A relaxed waterfront beach bar and restaurant with everything from hamburgers, hot dogs, pizza, and sandwiches to grilled fish, steaks, lobster, and the only Indonesian satay available on the island. Other Asian dishes also featured occasionally.

Spanish Main. Independence Ave., St. Johns. Tel. 20660. West Indian and American dishes are special here, with everything from hamburgers and omelets to conch and lobster specialties. The atmosphere is friendly, and the decor interesting—this two-story building was once the governor's mansion.

Victory. 3 Redcliffe Quay, St. Johns. Tel. 24317. Bar moved up front and kitchen to one side, making food service faster and more efficient, and food is still as good as ever with continental cuisine and local foods. Popular with daytime shoppers and with locals in the evenings. AE, MC, V.

Inexpensive

Brother B's. Long St., St. Johns. Tel. 20616. The place to really sample Antiguan dishes and all the stews and vegetables indigenous to the West Indies. Informal, perfect for lunch on the patio when shopping or sightseeing.

Chalet Suisse. Redcliffe Quay, St. Johns. Tel. 24221. Combination coffee house/delicatessen, with wide selection of gourmet meats and cheeses to eat in, take out, or take home. Sandwiches overstuffed by Antiguan standards. Also features a selection of packaged snacks and delicacies from U.S., UK, Europe.

Darcy's. Kensington Ct., St. Johns. Tel. 21323. Grilled lobsters popular with tourists at lunch. Sandwiches and plates available for those with smaller appetites. Garden setting ideal for a mid-afternoon beverage break.

18 Carrot. Church St., St. Johns. "Antiguan-style international" food, with emphasis on health and nutrition in salads and vegetables, although burgers and sandwiches available. Lunch only. A discotheque at night.

Golden Peanut. High St., St. Johns. Tel. 21415. Busy place in heart of shopping and business district with wide range of sandwiches, cold plates, and local favorites like conch curry and lobster prepared several ways.

 **NIGHT LIFE AND BARS.** Most of the resort hotels offer regular entertainment, with calypso singers, steel bands, limbo dancers and folkloric groups featured on different nights. *The Victory* at 3 Redcliffe Quay has entertainment on weekends and Tuesday nights, while *The Big Pineapple* on Market St. (between Redcliffe and St. Mary's) is popular with locals when bands play Thursday, Friday, and Saturday nights. *Solid Gold* at Market and Hawkins Sts. and *18 Carrot* on lower Church St. are popular discos in St. Johns.

 CASINOS. There are two hotel casinos on the island open from early evening until 4:00 P.M. with a "reasonable attire" dress code. Slot machines, blackjack, roulette, and craps tables draw gamblers to the *Halcyon Cove Resort* on Dickenson Bay and the *Flamingo* on a bluff overlooking St. Johns (enter from Queen Elizabeth Ave. on the east end). The *St. James's Club* has a private casino. *Jolly Beach Hotel* has a roomful of slot machines, as does the *Gold Coin* on Corn Alley in St. Johns, which is open from early in the morning until well past midnight.

POSTAGE. Airmail letters to North America cost EC $.60 and postcards are EC $.40. The post office is located at the foot of High Street.

ELECTRICAL CURRENT. Most hotels operate on 110 volts A.C. and usually have a plaque saying so near outlets for plug-in appliances. Most of the rest of the island is supplied with 220 volt A.C. current.

 SECURITY. Few problems at any of the hotels, but casinos attract a gambler crowd. The streets of St. Johns are fairly empty at night and it would be advisable not to walk around alone late at night. It is wise not to leave unattended valuables in your room or on the beach.

ARUBA

by
ANITA GATES

Anita Gates is a New York-based freelance writer and a contributing editor of Frequent Flyer *magazine. She is also the author of three books on careers and the job market. Her first visit to Aruba was in 1972.*

Aruba is not quite beautiful, but visitors seldom realize it when caught by her charms as Americans and Europeans have been for the past two decades.

First, there are the beaches: seven miles long and pure powdery white on the southwestern coast. And there is the equatorial sun, shining down through bright blue skies almost every day of the year. Cooling trade winds rustle through nearby palm trees.

Then there are the divi-divi trees, those odd-looking plants bent completely sideways by the winds, dotting the *cunucu,* Aruba's flat countryside. The air is dry here, more comfortable than in most tropical climates. Season upon season of it have created an odd Caribbean desert of kiwi and sea grapes, rock formations and aloe plants, cacti named for their shapes: bushi, round and red; cadushi, tall and green.

Aruba is the westernmost of the Netherland Antilles Leeward Islands, just fifteen miles from the Venezuelan coast. Both the Dutch and Spanish influences are strong. The spoken language here, for instance, is Papiamento—a blend of Dutch, Spanish, Portuguese, Indian and almost every other tongue that has ever been spoken here. Everyone speaks English too, having studied it since the fifth grade, as well as Dutch—the official language used in newspapers and schoolrooms.

Anyway, what's there to understand? For vacationers, Aruba exists merely as the row of elegant hotels along the beach, their casinos, the sophisticated shopping streets of Oranjestad and the calm turquoise Caribbean beyond.

Past and Present

Aruba's modern history got off to a rather undistinguished start. The Spaniards declared it a useless island and never bothered to record the exact date of discovery. Rather offhandedly, they claimed it in 1499.

The Arawak Indians were there before the Spanish (although 2,000-year-old pottery fragments prove they were far from the first inhabitants), but were shipped off to work in Santo Domingo's copper mines. When the Dutch took control in the 1630s, they brought the Indians back to tend their own livestock, then forbade other European settlements.

In the centuries that followed, Aruba's economy depended first on gold mining, then on aloe plantations. In 1929, Lago Oil opened one of the world's largest refineries here, thanks to the island's proximity to the Venezuelan oil fields. The refinery remained an important employer until its closing last spring. Now tourism stands alone as the leading industry here.

Through it all, the Dutch have remained. The governor of the Netherlands Antilles, based in Curaçao, is a representative of the queen. A lieutenant governor is in charge of Aruba and the *staten* (senate) is the island's legislative council, elected every four years.

Now Aruba wants its independence. At least, enough Arubans do to have forced a constitutional conference agreement on separate status for the island, to be granted in 1986. A target date of 1996 has been set for real independence. Although the transition appears calm enough now, only time will tell.

Meanwhile, the island appears to be almost a model society with little of the real poverty that afflicts some other Caribbean islands. Good housing, food supplies, medical coverage, and a literacy rate near 100 percent mean that the Arubans are, understandably, contented with their lot. And that means a friendly tolerance of the North American, South American, and European visitors who crowd their streets and beaches throughout the year. When Arubans smile and say *bonbini* (welcome), most of them actually mean it.

EXPLORING ARUBA

Aruba, at approximately twenty miles by six, is small enough to explore in one day. When you arrive at the Princess Beatrix Airport in the south central part of the island, you'll probably drive west through Oranjestad to your hotel on the southwest beach. Most of your fun in the sun and socializing will go on in these areas, but other parts of the island have their own appeal.

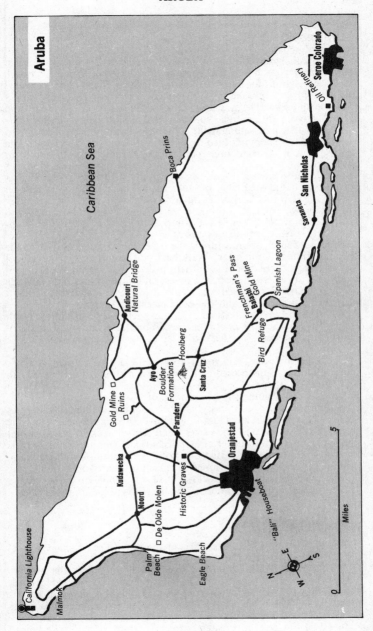

Aruba

Caribbean Sea

California Lighthouse
Malmok
Palm Beach
De Olde Molen
Noord
Eagle Beach
Kudawecha
Historic Graves
"Bali" Houseboat
Oranjestad
Paradera
Gold Mine Ruins
Ayo
Hooiberg
Boulder Formations
Santa Cruz
Bird Refuge
Frenchman's Pass
Balashi Gold Mine
Spanish Lagoon
Andicouri
Natural Bridge
Boca Prins
Savaneta
San Nicholas
Seroe Colorado
Oil Refinery

Miles

N E S W

0 5

Oranjestad

Aruba's charming Dutch capital is best explored on foot. Take a taxi or bus from your hotel, and start at the corner of Lloyd G. Smith Boulevard (named for a former general manager of the Lago Refinery) and Arnold Shuttestraat.

If you should arrive by cruise ship, you'll dock very near here. And if you arrive early enough, you may find a ship from Venezuela or another nearby port selling fruits, vegetables, and other goods right on the dock. After shopping turn right and walk one long block until you see the Bali Restaurant houseboat in the harbor. You've arrived at Shuttestraat.

Oranjestad's main attraction is shopping, so turn left onto Shuttestraat, bear left at the plaza, and take the second right. You're now on Nassaustraat, Aruba's most fashionable shopping street. And wherever you turn now, you'll find things to buy: from jewelry and watches to beautiful embroidered tablecloths and duty-free perfumes. The shopping section ends around Dwarsstraat.

Beautiful Dutch architecture is the other most important reason for spending time in Oranjestad. Walk back to the corner of Olde School Straat and go three blocks south (toward the harbor) to Wilhelminastraat. This is where the capital's oldest and most interesting buildings are found. Oranjestad itself was founded in 1790. Walk west and find old homes, the library, and the old Protestant church.

When you reach Shuttestraat again, turn left and go one block south (toward the harbor) to Zoutmanstraat. You'll find the small archaeological museum here, worth a short visit to see artifacts of Aruba's cave dwellers.

One block to the east and you'll be in front of Fort Zoutman, Aruba's oldest building. Constructed in 1796, it saw action against the British and Curaçao troops. The William III tower, named for the Dutch monarch of that time, was added in 1868.

Walk one block south and you'll be in Queen Wilhelmina Park, a small pocket of palm trees and flowers overlooking the sea. A marble statue of the queen is at the eastern end. Or go back to Nassaustraat and turn north at the corner of Hendrikstraat to see the Saint Francis Roman Catholic Church. Just behind it is the numismatic museum, displaying coins and paper money from more than 400 nations.

Many of Oranjestad's shops close for siesta, from noon to two, giving you an opportunity to try one of the downtown restaurants.

East to San Nicolas

Some of the most historical parts of the island are outside Oranjestad. Drive east toward the old capital, San Nicolas.

Taking L.G. Smith Boulevard east, you'll soon pass the airport. Look to your left for a glimpse of Hooiberg (better known as Haystack Mountain). At 541 feet, it is Aruba's second highest elevation and its most visible natural landmark. There are several hundred steps up its side, but legend has it that no tourist ever cared to try the ascent.

Just past the drive-in theater, a road on your left will take you to Frenchman's Pass. According to local tradition, some French invaders and Indians battled here in the early 1600s for control of Aruba. You'll also find ruins of the Balashi gold smelting works here, one of several reminders of the island's nineteenth-century gold rush.

Back on the main road, you might want to turn right into the area called Spanish Lagoon, where pirates once hid away to repair their ships. The Marina Pirata restaurant here is the perfect stop for seafood.

Driving further, you'll come to Savaneta, Aruba's oldest town. Here is another famous seafood restaurant, Brisas del Mar, ideal for a casual lunch overlooking the water.

When you reach San Nicolas, you'll find that memories of the recently closed refinery still dominate the former capital. If you want to shop, try the pedestrian mall just behind the Astoria Hotel on Crijnssen-straat. For eating out, your choices include the Astoria's Chinese restaurant or Charlie's Bar, a Dutch-style tavern on Main Street.

Most of the beaches just outside San Nicolas are fine for swimming. Few visitors frequent them, but only because there are no resort hotels on this part of the island. Tourists are more than welcome at the Aruba Golf Club, just north of San Nicolas.

The Rugged Northern Coast

On the north and windward side, Aruba still belongs to nature. The Atlantic waters are much too rough for swimming, the terrain is barren and rocky, and the beaches are deserted. This can be a beautiful drive, with some sightseeing of natural phenomena along the way.

Drive northwest from San Nicolas and stop first at two old Indian caves, Guadirikiri and Fontein. Both were used by Aruba's long-ago Indian inhabitants, and Fontein has some still-undeciphered writings on its walls. Guadirikiri Cave is just east of Fontein Cave. Don't let the "ancient Indian drawings" here fool you; they were added by a European movie company that filmed here a few years ago. Note: these are real caves—with real bats inside!

Your next stop is Boca Prins, a small cove for secluded sunbathing. What you've come to see, however, is just beyond. White sand dunes rise suddenly from the rocky landscape. If you're feeling athletic, climb to the top and slide down one; devotees say it's like sledding without benefit of a sled. Or remain standing and enjoy the dramatic ocean view.

If you want to drive to Aruba's highest point, 617-foot Jamanota, now's the time to make the detour inland. Otherwise, keep driving north; the real beauties are ahead.

All beaches are public in Aruba, but some are so secluded you'd never know it. You'll come to Daimari first and pass a coconut plantation on your way to it. The Papiamento sign there is not a warning to trespassers; it means "Coconuts are not sold here."

The next beach is Andicouri, considered Aruba's most magnificent secluded spot and just the place for the most romantic picnic of your vacation. To get there, however, you have to pass through another coconut plantation—private property—and the owners generally ask for a small admission fee before letting you drive through. A new road recently was built to avoid this problem, but many visitors still take the shortcut. They say the beauty here is well worth the price.

Aruba's natural bridge is just north of here, carved and hollowed by eons of wind and sea. After you see it, drive inland to Ayo, a tall and unusual rock formation. The stones have been balanced atop each other precariously for centuries. Scientists who believe Aruba was once part of the South American continent theorize that a volcanic eruption blew the two land masses apart, and this is how the rocks landed. A little further inland is Casi Bari, an even larger formation that seems more like a great rock garden. You can climb part of the way up Ayo and all the way to the top of Casi Bari's largest formation for lovely, if somewhat breezy, island views.

Your final stop is at the Chapel of Alto Vista. This small church is barely thirty years old, but it stands on the site of a chapel built in 1750 where Aruba's first modern religious services were held.

Palm Beach and Environs

It's almost certain that you'll stay in one of the hotels stretched along the white sandy beach that thrice changes name—from Druif to Eagle to Palm—on Aruba's breathtaking southwestern coast. Exploring this area can simply mean hotel-hopping for dinner, dancing, gambling, and late-night entertainment. During the day, it's easy to stroll from your hotel's beach to another and simply drop in for a neighborly poolside lunch or drink, wearing your shorts or swimsuit.

The Caribbean shore here is the center of Aruban tourism, primarily because it offers the best swimming, sailing, snorkeling, fishing, scuba diving, and just about every other water sport devised. The most pleasant way to explore this aspect is to take one of the many tours available, which range from diving expeditions to sunset cruises and glass-bottom boat excursions.

You should also drive or taxi past the hotel strip for at least a quick look at the island's westernmost point. Just beyond the hotels is Malmok, where Aruba's wealthiest families live. Malmok Beach is open to the public, of course. And if you haven't already seen it from a sailing or snorkeling tour, here is the wreck of the German ship *Antilla,* scuttled in 1940. Malmok is considered the finest spot on the island for both shelling and snorkeling.

Almost at the very end of the island is the California Lighthouse, standing above open fields of aloe and cactus. You can drive past the lighthouse to the westernmost tip and stop to enjoy the view.

On your way back, turn inland just before the Americana Hotel to the town of Noord. Here is the Church of Santa Anna with its 115-year-old oak altar.

Sunsets are spectacular anywhere along the beach, so settle in at your favorite poolside hotel bar. Then enjoy dinner at Papiamento, The Mill, or one of Aruba's other elegant restaurants.

PRACTICAL INFORMATION FOR ARUBA

 FACTS AND FIGURES. Aruba lies in the south of the Caribbean, just 12 degrees north of the equator and 15 miles north of the Venezuelan coast. With an area of fewer than 75 square miles (19.6 miles by 6.5 miles at its widest point), it's the middle-sized island of the Leeward Netherlands Antilles—larger than Bonaire and smaller than Curaçao. Almost 68,000 people of 42 distinct nationalities make their home here. Native Arubans (who have a mix of Arawak Indian, Spanish, and Dutch ancestry) are joined by thousands of Dutch, South Americans, North Americans, and Chinese. Their language is Papiamento but everyone also speaks English.

Oranjestad, named for the royal House of Orange, has been Aruba's capital city since 1790. Its busy harbor is on the island's south central coast. San Nicolas, the former capital, is on the island's eastern end. The island's hotels are concentrated along the beaches just west of Oranjestad.

 WHEN TO GO. It's almost always 82° F and sunny in Aruba, winter or summer. Winter is considered high season, however, lasting from November to April. Low season offers similar weather and lower hotel rates. The months of October, November, and December are considered the island's rainy season but, since the annual rainfall is fewer than 20 inches, this is not normally a reason to stay away. Humidity is low throughout the year, and the trade winds never stop blowing.

 PASSPORTS AND VISAS. U.S. and Canadian citizens need only proof of identity, such as a passport, birth certificate, or voter's registration card. A driver's license won't do. British citizens don't need passports either, but must have a British Visitor's Passport, available from any post office. Passports are required of all other visitors. All visitors to Aruba must hold a return or ongoing ticket.

 MONEY. The guilder or florin is the Netherland Antilles' unit of money, subdivided into 100 cents. In English, it's called a guilder; in Dutch, it's the Netherland Antilles florin; thus, the symbol NAfl. It is issued in all denominations, including a square nickel, which makes an unusual souvenir. The official rate of exchange is U.S. $1 = NAfl 1.77.

WHAT WILL IT COST?

A typical day for two during high season will probably run:

Standard double room at one of the beach hotels	$120
Full hotel breakfast	15
Lunch at a moderate downtown restaurant	20
Dinner at one of the island's popular spots	60
Restaurant and hotel tips, taxes, and service charges	40
One day of sightseeing by rental car	30
	$285

 HOW TO GET THERE. By air. *American Airlines* flies nonstop from New York; *Eastern* from Miami. *ALM*, the Dutch Antillean airline, flies in from Miami and San Juan, and also links Aruba with Bonaire, Curaçao, and St. Maarten. There are special excursion fares, and Aruba can be included in a Curaçao or Bonaire round trip if you make plans in advance.

By Sea. Cruise ships out of Miami, Ft. Lauderdale and San Juan call at Aruba year-round.

AIRPORT TAXES AND OTHER CHARGES. The airport departure tax is $7.75 (or NAfl 13.50) per person. All room rates are subject to a 5% government tax. Hotels also normally add a 10–15% service charge.

 TELEPHONES AND EMERGENCY NUMBERS. Country code for Aruba is 599. Medical services are available at Horacio Oduber Hospital, opened in 1976 near Eagle Beach (tel. 24300). Hotels also have physicians on call and can make hospital, doctor, or dental appointments for you. For police, phone 110 or 24000.

 HOTELS. The Arubans don't bother much with street addresses, but no visitor has ever gotten lost trying to find his hotel. All of them are lined up neatly along the powdery white sands of the Caribbean, stretching west from Oranjestad along L.G. Smith Blvd., a street also known as Palm Beach in this part of town. It's all the same neighborhood, so your biggest decision is whether to stay in a high-rise hotel (all except the Playa Linda have casinos) or a low-rise (more informal settings).

Hardly anybody arrives in Aruba without a hotel reservation. A large percentage of visitors come here on vacation packages with hotel included, a money-saving plan highly recommended. Tourism officials report, however, that visitors aren't planning months and months ahead as they used to. A great number now call their travel agents or book a package through an airline mere weeks ahead.

We call $120–$150 EP *Expensive;* $80–$115 *Moderate;* anything below that *Inexpensive.* Prices quoted are in American dollars and are for two people sharing a room in high season. Off-season (April–November) hotel rates can drop by 20–50%, although the weather is just as wonderful. Some hotels raise their winter rates at Christmas and during Carnival week (mid-February).

Expensive

Americana Aruba Hotel & Casino. Box 280. Tel. 24500. This luxurious 200-room high-rise on Palm Beach attracts an American clientele of all ages with its casino, huge pool, and tennis courts. Guest rooms are cheerful with white furniture and small terraces. There's a gallery of seven shops, including a barber and a branch of Kan Jewelers. Dining choices include *Villa Fiorita* for an informal breakfast, lunch, or dinner; *Le Café,* with a French sidewalk cafe decor for sandwiches, omelets, and the like; and *Las Mañanitas Steakhouse* for more elegant and more expensive fare. There's similar dining and live entertainment at the hotel's spacious supper club, the *Stellaris Restaurant and Showroom.* Or enjoy live music and fancy drinks at *Le Club,* with a view of the pool. No TV, but otherwise luxury accommodations. It's the third hotel from the end of Palm Beach, between the Playa Linda and the Aruba Caribbean.

Aruba Beach Club. 53 L.G. Smith Blvd. Tel. 24595. Here is an attractive, Spanish-style low-rise resort with an open-air lobby leading directly to patio, gardens, and pool. The beach is just beyond, and it's populated with a combination of time-share owners and "regular" hotel guests like you—mostly American and mostly young to middle-aged marrieds. The mood can border on elitism, but in a very informal way. All 133 tastefully decorated rooms have TV, a small patio or balcony, and a kitchenette (but there's an extra $15-per-day charge for non-time-sharers to use it). You can really make yourself at home here. The on-premises deli is almost a supermarket, complete with liquor on sale. And when you don't feel like cooking, you can relax in a director's chair at the open-air *Cayena Garden* for breakfast, lunch, and dinner—or drop into romantic *La Taverna.* This stretch of Druif Beach is particularly nice. Tennis, a selection of small shops, and video games for the kids and other fanatics.

Aruba Caribbean Hotel & Casino. 81 L.G. Smith Blvd. Tel. 22250. Built in 1959 as the island's first luxury hotel, the *Aruba Caribbean* was closed down completely last year for renovations by its new Dutch owners (Golden Tulip Hotels). The 200-room hotel should have reopened its doors by this season, and in grand old style. We're assuming they'll still have the pool, tennis courts, water sports, ocean-view rooms, casino (Aruba's first), and most of its half-dozen spots for dining and entertainment.

Aruba Concorde Hotel & Casino. 77 L.G. Smith Blvd. Tel. 24466. Aruba's only true high-rise (18 floors). The main lobby is multi-textured with marble, burl, chrome, light wood, and cranberry formica—and alive with a sophisticated, well-dressed crowd, many of them South American. Guest rooms, almost 500 of them, feature tasteful and colorful furnishings, good-sized terraces with ocean views, unstocked mini-fridges, and color TV. The casino is Aruba's largest, and there are handsome shops on the lower level. Dining choices include *Adriana* for sophisticated Italian cuisine, the huge and elegant *La Serre* for a continental dinner, and its next-door neighbor, *Rendez Vous Gourmet,* perhaps for an intimate late-night supper. *Club Arubesque,* off the main lobby, is a nightclub complete with showgirls. Tennis, water sports, pool.

Divi Divi Beach Hotel. 93 L.G. Smith Blvd. Tel. 23300. Once the mecca for America's swinging singles, the ultra-casual Divi Divi now attracts vacationers of all ages. There is still an air of barefoot playfulness here, however; past guests have scratched their names, graffiti-style, on the cactus. An open-air lobby leads to the pool area, surrounded by eating and drinking places, and the beach. A total of 152 guest rooms includes 40 casitas (garden bungalows with patios) and 20 lanais, which open directly onto the beach. The decor is dark Spanish wood with tile floors and small patios or terraces. The Divi Divi's restaurant is the *Red Parrot,* a large dining room with a continental menu. Tennis courts and shops, but no TV. Located beside the Aruba Beach Club.

Playa Linda Beach Resort. 87 L.G. Smith Blvd. Tel. 25298. There are only suites, 60 of them, at this pyramid of understated elegance. Open since July 1983, Playa Linda is a time-share resort where vacationers can rent unpurchased suites by the day or week, as at any hotel. The mood, however, is more like a club with hotel services. The smaller suites have brown louvered doors dividing the bed and sitting/dining areas; the larger ones have two bedrooms, one small bath and a master bath with its own dressing room. All have kitchenettes, although non-time-share guests get only running water and the refrigerator turned on, and balconies. The Playa Linda also seems the most private of Aruba's hotels, and its clientele is mainly the tanned, well-groomed, somewhat conservative American set. When the whole thing is completed, possibly this year, there will be 185 rooms—but never a casino. TV, drug store, game room. Water sports and tennis can be arranged. All three meals are served at the informal open-air *Palapa Restaurant.*

Moderate

Aruba Palm Beach Hotel & Casino. L.G. Smith Blvd., Palm Beach. Tel. 23900. Formerly the Sheraton, this 200-room blue tower is an excellent choice for vacationers who love water sports and nightlife equally. The DePalm water-sports tours leave from here. Then evenings can be spent gambling at the casino, enjoying the live entertainment in the glitzy blue *Galactica Lounge,* dining in the *Rembrandt Room,* or all three. Another dining choice is the open-air *Steak Pub* on the lower level, overlooking the pool. Guest rooms are pleasant and spacious with tiny balconies, baths with separate dressing areas, and big walk-in closets. No TV. Pool, tennis courts, and shops.

Bushiri Beach Hotel. 35 L.G. Smith Blvd. Tel. 25216. The Bushiri is an eye-catcher, a long, low, and attractive new building and the first beach hotel you encounter driving out of Oranjestad. Service is the attraction here; the entire staff is in training at a hotel school associated with the property. All 50 pleasant guest rooms have TV, carpeting, and the beach (right outside your door). Because of its easy proximity to town, the Bushiri attracts some businesspeople as well as vacationers. Breakfast, lunch, and dinner are served—expertly—at the *Flamboyan* restaurant here. Pool, pool-side bar, cafeteria.

Holiday Inn. Box 408. Tel. 23600. Aruba's own twin towers, connected by a central lobby and a big central pool, stand at the western end of Palm Beach and of hotel row. The guests here are almost all from the U.S., with a heavy emphasis on family. Children under 12 stay free with their parents, and the pool area includes beachside swings and other play equipment. The health club is a big attraction. Guest rooms, almost 400 of them, are spacious and attractive with balconies and TV. Many were refurbished in a contemporary peach and aqua color scheme last year. In addition to the casino, there are several choices for evening entertainment. *The Palm Beach Room* offers dinner and late-night cocktail shows with the closest thing Aruba offers to top-name entertainment. The plush dark green disco, *L'Esprit,* is open for happy hour and late-night dancing. The *Empress of China* restaurant is open for dinner with dark atmosphere and Cantonese specialties, while *Salon International* serves breakfast, lunch, and dinner in a casual setting overlooking palm trees and the beach.

Tennis courts, an extensive water-sports program, and a good selection of lobby shops, including a deli.

Manchebo Beach Resort Hotel (Best Western). Box 564. Tel. 23444. This unassuming small hotel just happens to have the most spectacular and least crowded (most deserted) beach on hotel row. The Manchebo Beach is where middle America and Europe meet. And this is where a certain reclusive 1930s film star hid away in recent years when she wanted to be alone. All 72 guest rooms have patios or balconies facing the beach, carpets, color TV's, and unstocked mini-fridges. There's special theme entertainment, and food virtually every night, or guests can eat at the *Fish Restaurant* or romantic *French Steak House.* Drugstore/gift shop and tour desk. Free transportation to *Talk of the Town,* Manchebo Beach's sister hotel in Oranjestad.

Talk of the Town Restort Hotel (Best Western). Box 564, L.G. Smith Blvd. in Oranjestad. Tel. 23380. What's a nice resort like this doing in downtown Oranjestad? Attracting a mix of American and European visitors, from honeymooners to families with children, as it has since 1965. There's a huge pool in the very pleasant Spanish-style inner courtyard, the beach is right across the street, and free transportation is available to Manchebo Beach, its sister hotel. Talk of the Town's 62 guest rooms overlook the courtyard and feature TV, carpeting and unstocked mini-fridges. Some have kitchenettes. *Talk of the Town* restaurant is one of Aruba's best-known gourmet dining experiences. Guests may also visit the *Pool Bar,* the *Moonlight Grill,* and the *Contempo Disco,* or stroll across the street to *Surfside,* the hotel's beach restaurant under the stars. Jacuzzi, water sports, shops, tour desk.

Tamarijn Beach Hotel. 64 L.G. Smith Blvd. Tel. 24150. The Divi Divi's sister hotel is newer (1977), larger (204 rooms) and even more attractive in its low-key way: Spanish style, white with brown balconies. What the two hotels have in common are open-air lobbies (this one with hanging plants galore), an air of barefoot elegance (the staff likes to say that jackets are reluctantly permitted) and a reputation for a feel-at-home atmosphere. The Tamarijn's cheerful guest rooms all have ocean views with patios or balconies. Guests come in all ages and sizes, but most are American and many are repeat visitors. There's a poolside bar open till 1 A.M., but the real restaurant here is the *Palm Court.* Continental dining in a casual setting attracts Arubans as well as vacationers. Tennis courts, and a small arcade of shops, but no TV.

Inexpensive

Astoria Hotel. 6 Crijnsenstraat, San Nicolas. Tel. 45132. Small commercial hotel in the heart of Aruba's former capital. Ten air-conditioned rooms, cocktail lounge, Chinese restaurant. The town's pedestrian shopping mall is nearby.

Central Hotel. Downtown Oranjestad. Tel. 22260. A 30-room commercial hotel with air conditioning in some rooms. Restaurant and bar. Room rates include continental breakfast.

Hotel Victoria. Downtown Oranjestad. Tel. 23850. Many South American businessmen stay at this 30-room commercial hotel at the end of Nassaustraat. Cocktail lounge, restaurant. All rooms air-conditioned.

 HOME AND APARTMENT RENTALS/TIME SHARING Daily, weekly, and monthly rates are available at many of the rental properties. A complete list of non-hotel accommodations and current rates is available from the Aruba Tourist Bureaus in New York, Miami, and Oranjestad. Some possibilities:

Aruba Beach Club. 53 L.G. Smith Blvd. Tel. 24595. Time-share apartments with kitchenettes in this sophisticated beachside low-rise. See hotel section for description.

Camacuri Apartments. Fergusonstraat 46B, Oranjestad. Tel. 26805. Air-conditioned units with two double beds, kitchenettes, color TV, private porch, and maid service. Five-minute walk from the downtown beach at Surfside and a ten-minute drive to the beach hotels. Inexpensive weekly and monthly rates.

Dutch Village. L.G. Smith Blvd. Tel. 24150. Deluxe studio, one-bedroom, and two-bedroom time-share apartments next door to the Tamarijn Beach

Hotel. The Divi Divi Hotel Corporation owns this resort, so you get access to all their restaurants, pools, bars, tennis courts, and beaches.

Edge's Apartments. 458 L.G. Smith Blvd. Tel. 21072. In the fashionable Malmok area, 11 oceanfront apartments with air conditioning, color TV, kitchenette, private patio, and whirlpool. Inexpensive daily and weekly rates.

Playa Linda Beach Resort. 87 L.G. Smith Blvd. Tel. 25298. A choice of 60 elegant one- and two-bedroom suites at this beautiful time share resort. See hotel section for description.

Talk of the Town Resort Hotel. P.O. Box 564, Oranjestad. Tel. 23380. This downtown hotel now has low-priced guesthouses nearby. Air-conditioned rooms, kitchen facilities, shared bathrooms, maid service, and guest-card access to all Talk of the Town restaurants, bars, and the Surfside beach restaurant. Daily rates.

The Vistalmar. Bucutiweg 28, Oranjestad. Tel. 28579. One-bedroom seaside apartments with fully equipped kitchens, sunporches, TVs, telephones, and maid service. Ten minutes from hotels and beaches. Inexpensive daily and weekly rates.

HOW TO GET AROUND. Taxis are always available at your hotel or in Oranjestad (dispatch office tel. 21604), but the fixed fares (no meters) are generally expensive. The current airport-to-hotel fare is $8 to the low-rises and $10 to the high-rises, which are slightly farther away. A short drive from one hotel to another or from the hotel into Oranjestad will run $3–$5 or so. Rates are $1 higher on Sundays and after midnight. Tipping the driver 15% or so is the thing to do, but not mandatory.

Consider sightseeing by taxi. The drivers speak English, are generally helpful, and can be hired for a flat rate of $20 per hour for a carload of up to five people.

Rental cars are available from a number of local and international firms, including *Avis* (tel. 28787), *Budget* (tel. 28600), *Dollar* (tel. 25651), *Hertz* (tel. 24545), *InterRent* (tel. 21845), *Marco's* (tel. 25889) and *National* (tel. 21967). Rates vary by season, but generally run from $25 to $35 per day. Mileage is sometimes free, but usually not for a one-day rental. You must be at least 21 years old and have a valid driver's license.

Mopeds can be rented at *Rent-A-Chappy* (tel. 25975) for $20–$25 per day.

For inexpensive trips between the beach hotels and Oranjestad, buses run hourly. The fare is $.60 or one guilder, and exact change is preferred.

TOURIST INFORMATION SERVICES. The Aruba Tourist Bureau on the island is at 2 Arnold Schuttestraat in Oranjestad (tel. 23777). For sources closer to home, see the Tourist Information Services section in the *Facts at Your Fingertips* chapter.

SPECIAL EVENTS. *Carnival* is the winter highlight, and Aruba now claims to be the world's third-largest celebrator (after New Orleans and Rio de Janeiro) of this pre-Lenten revel. The biggest day is the Grand Parade, with colorful costumes and floats, on the Sunday before Ash Wednesday. But the elections of various carnival queens, *tumba* (a local music style) contests, and the smaller steel-band parades called *jump-ups* go on for weeks before. The off-season festivals (*Watapana* in Oranjestad and *Sanifesta* in San Nicolas) weren't held in 1985, but might return by popular demand this year or next.

TOURS. DePalm Tours, 142 L.G. Smith Blvd. Oranjestad. Tel. 24400, has a near-monopoly on the Aruban sightseeing business. Reservations can be made through their main office or their hotel branches. Water-sports tours leave from the seaside DePalm office beside the Aruba Palm Beach Hotel. Others begin with pick-up at your hotel or cruise ship. Some of the most popular tours include: *Round the Island* (2½ hours) an ideal orientation tour that includes the oak altar at the Church of Sta. Anna, Casi Bari natural bridge, the ruins of a 19-century gold mill, and Spanish Lagoon. *Trimaran Sailing* (two or three hours) lets you choose a morning, afternoon, or sunset voyage aboard the 42-foot, two-mast *Seaventure.* (The morning cruise includes a one-hour swimming and snorkeling stop, and lasts three hours.) Two complimentary drinks included. *Sunset Cruise and Beach Barbecue* (3½ hours) leaves late afternoon (Thursdays only) on the 65-foot *Dreamboat* for a relaxing cruise down the Caribbean coast to the beach of the Surfside Restaurant where you'll enjoy a barbecue dinner and dancing to steel band music on the beach (dinner and one rum punch included). *Glass-Bottom Boat Cruise* (1½ hours) lets you explore underwater Aruba, from coral formations and tropical fish to shipwrecks, without moving from your seat. One of the newer and livelier tours is the *Fun Cruise* (4 hours), a trip to a private beach including lunch, unlimited rum punch, and a treasure hunt. De Palm's other offerings include 2½- or 3-hour sailing cruises on *Mi Dushi,* a 75-foot ketch built in 1928; *Marlab,* a three-hour scientific tour led by marine biologists; full-day sailing cruises on the *Tranquilo,* including lunch, swimming, and snorkeling; and full-day tours to Curaçao, Bonaire, or Caracas. Scuba diving, snorkeling, deep-sea fishing, horseback riding, and boat rides are also available.

 PARKS AND GARDENS. *Queen Wilhelmina Park* is a small, pleasant oasis of tall palms and tropical flowers overlooking the harbor. Located at the eastern entrance of Oranjestad, the park is always open, always free of charge, and ideal for a short afternoon stroll.

 BEACHES. *Palm Beach* and *Eagle Beach* come together on the island's western shore to form a seven-mile stretch of powdery-white beauty that is Aruba's claim to fame. The Caribbean waters here are turquoise, calm, and perfect for swimming. The sand is never too hot to walk on and the trade winds cool you constantly. But don't let the comfort of this paradise lull you into forgetting suntan lotion; it's easy to burn this close to the equator.

The beaches on Aruba's northern (Atlantic) shore are beautiful for strolling and for solitary picnics, but the waters are much too rough for swimming or snorkeling. All Aruban beaches are public but, in the case of *Andicouri,* a beautiful, secluded beach on the northern shore, you may have to pay an admission fee if you take the shortcut through private property to get there.

You'll find gentler waters at locations near San Nicolas, like *Baby Beach,* but tourists rarely go there.

 PARTICIPANT SPORTS. Water sports. The action here includes sailing, snorkeling, waterskiing, and windsurfing—all available at most beach hotels. Scuba diving among the coral reefs and to sunken wrecks is extremely popular. Visibility can be 90 feet or better under good conditions. *DePalm Watersports* (tel. 24400) rents all necessary equipment and offers instruction. Several deep-sea fishing boats are available for half- and full-day charters. They include the *Mari Indi* (tel. 23375), *Gina* and *El Delfin* (for either, tel. 24400), *Teaser* (tel. 25088), *Sweet Mary* (tel. 27985), *Raivera* (tel. 23600, ext. 281) and *Macabi* (tel. 22756). Both the *Raivera* and *Macabi* have a four-person minimum for charter.

Tennis courts are located at most hotels, some lighted for night play.

Golf is an unusual experience at the Aruba Golf Course, 82 Golfweg, near San Nicolas. The nine-hole course on the southeastern end of the island offers some special challenges: oiled-sand greens, goats that wander over the fairways, and the ever-present trade winds. Daily greens fee, $5; caddy fee, $3; clubs rental, $4. Tel. 93485.

Horseback riding can be arranged through DePalm Tours or directly through Rancho El Paso (tel. 23310). Five trips a day, including a 2-hour beach ride, are scheduled. To find it, turn right between the hospital and the Concorde Hotel, then follow signs.

Physical fitness is the sport at Body Language, Aruba's health and fitness center at the *Eagle Club,* 12 Engelandstraat (tel. 22808). For a $7.50-per-day fee, vacationers can have full use of the sauna, whirlpool and gym, with its Nautilus-style machines and free weights. Massage, waxing, and beauty services are available by appointment. Open till 8 P.M. on weekdays and from 10 to 4 on Saturdays, the gym is casual, generally uncrowded and within walking distance of the low-rise beach hotels.

SPECTATOR SPORTS. There are no professional sports teams but you can see amateur soccer, softball, and baseball played at the side-by-side stadiums on Fergusonstraat, just outside Oranjestad.

HISTORIC SITES AND HOUSES. *Fort Zoutman,* built in 1796 to protect the new capital from invaders, is Aruba's oldest building. Located at the corner of Zoutmanstraat and Oranjestraat, one block north of Queen Wilhelmina Park, it was constructed on what was then the coast. Armed with four cannons, it saw action only twice (in 1799 and 1805). Since then it has served as the police department, a government building, and a prison. The tower that now forms the fort's entrance was built in 1868 and has served as both a lighthouse and a public clock. The initials on the tower, WIII, stand for William III, who was king of the Netherlands when the tower was built. The *Arubana Museum* was opened here in 1984.

The buildings on *Wilhelminastraat* in Oranjestad are among the oldest and most interesting in Aruba, many Dutch style with gables and pastel facades. Look for the old Protestant Church (built in 1846 and the island's second-oldest building) at the corner of Shuttestraat. Diagonally across from it you'll find a government building dating back to 1911 and the handsome Aruba Public Library, originally built as a school in 1888. Down the street are #8 (built in 1923–25) and #7 (built in 1937–38), two very photogenic mansions built as private residences.

Be sure to take a look at 21, 27, and 35 Wilhelminastraat as well. Although they have been modernized, they were built in 1877 and are believed to be Oranjestad's older standing residential buildings.

Alto Vista Chapel. Our Lady of Alto Vista was built in this northwestern corner of Aruba in 1952, but its history stretches back two centuries. Here, in the early 1700s, prayer meetings were held under a tree or in a hut. The first chapel was dedicated on this spot in 1750. The antique Spanish cross used in processions then is now inside the new building and is the oldest work of art in the Netherlands Antilles. When the first chapel was closed and crumbled away in the 1800s, Arubans continued to revere the spot and pray near its foundations. There is now an annual pilgrimage here in October.

Santa Anna Church. Noord. The carved oak altar inside, created by Dutch sculptor Hendrik van der Geld in 1870, is the reason most people visit this church. The stained glass windows are German and represent the four *fiscals* (laymen preachers) of Alto Vista. The 1877 rectory, to the right of the church, is one of Aruba's oldest buildings. To get to Noord, turn inland between the Playa Linda and Americana Hotels.

Frenchman's Pass. Aruba's gold rush began in 1824 on the northern coast and lasted for almost a century. In 1899, Aruba Gold Concessions Ltd. built a smelting works in the center of the island near Frenchman's Pass. Its crumbling walls, kettles, and ovens are still here.

German Shipwreck. On May 10, 1940, a German warship, the *Antilla,* lay at anchor off Malmok Beach. When word came that the Netherlands Antilles had been drawn into the war, the captain scuttled his ship and the wreck has been lying there ever since. It can be seen from the high-rise beach hotels, but the best way to get a close look is to go on one of the sailing, snorkeling, or diving tours that go near it.

Spanish Lagoon. Pirates used to sneak away to this spot on the southeastern coast, just west of Aruba's oldest town, Savaneta. They came to repair their ships. Some say gold pirate treasure is still buried here.

 MUSEUMS AND GALLERIES. *Archaeological Museum,* corner of Zoutmanstraat and A. Shuttestraat. Tel. 28979. Aruba is rich in prehistory and, although little is known about the Indians who lived here one and two thousand years ago, many of their artifacts have been found. This small collection, housed on the second floor of a charming yellow-and-green building, includes burial urns, skeletons from the pre-ceramic period, stone tools, cooking pots, and a number of shell and chalk artifacts. Open Monday–Friday, 8:00 A.M. –12:00 noon and 1:30–4:30 P.M.; weekends by appointment only. Free admission.

Arubana Museum, Fort Zoutman, corner of Zoutmanstraat and Oranjestraat. Everything Aruban is the theme of the island's newest museum. Its three rooms house everything from conch shells and coins to donkey saddles and a wooden "cactusgrab." Open Monday–Friday 9:00 A.M.–4:00 P.M. and until noon Saturdays. Admission is one guilder (about 60 cents).

DeMan Shell Collection, 18 Morgenster. Tel. 24246. This permanent shell collection occupies one room of a private home. By appointment only.

Numismatic Museum, J.E. Irausquinplein 2-A (behind the St. Francis Catholic Church). Tel. 28831. Mario Oder established the Museo Numismatico in 1981 with his private collection of more than 30,000 items from 400 countries. You'll find three air-conditioned rooms full of money—coins and paper, ancient and new, some from countries that no longer exist (like Latvia), some unusual (like the coins used in leper colonies or the Chinese currency with Nixon's picture on it)—and Oder's son Ruben eager to answer your questions. Open Monday–Friday 7:30 A.M.–12:00 noon and 1:00–4:30 P.M., Saturdays till noon and Sundays by appointment only. Admission is free, but you may want to drop a little something into the contribution box. It, and the Parsons table it sits on, are made entirely of Aruban square nickels.

 MUSIC, DANCE, AND STAGE. What there is takes place at the Cas di Cultura in Oranjestad (located at Vondellan and L.G. Smith Blvd.). Depending on when you arrive, you might find a drama festival, a Venezuelan choir, a children's theater performance, or an exhibition of paintings by Caribbean artists. There is no "season"; activities are scheduled year-round. Advance programs may not be available, however, so look for bulletins of events posted at hotels or notices in the English-language newspaper.

 SHOPPING. Duty-free is the magic word here, although the shops can't compare with those on sister island Curaçao. Nassaustraat is Aruba's Fifth Avenue, offering good prices on china, crystal, jewelry and perfume. The *Aruba Holiday* green sheet, distributed free, is a good guide to the shops and their merchandise.

Most stores are open from 8:00 A.M. to noon, close for lunch, then reopen from 2:00 to 6:00 P.M. Some are closed on Tuesday afternoons and all are closed on Sundays, except when cruise ships are arriving on that day. Major credit cards are accepted almost everywhere, and U.S. dollars are accepted almost as often as the local currency.

Don't even think about haggling. The Arubans don't believe in it and, in fact, find it even more offensive than most American merchants would. Bonus: There's no sales tax, so the price you see is the price you pay.

Some stores to explore:

Aquarius, 9 Nassaustraat. The trendiest, most fashionable clothing store in town with lots of chrome, track lighting, and rock music in the background. The names you'll see include Fiorucci, Louis Feraud, and Fendi. Everything chic for women, men, and kids.

Aruba Trading Company, 14 Nassaustraat. Now it's a two-part store and both sides are very fashionable. *Le Gourmet* is small, but has room for Dutch cheeses, Fortnum & Mason teas, French bloc de foie gras, wine, liquor, spices, Swiss chocolate, and other chic food. The department store side offers women's, men's, and children's clothing, a large cosmetics and perfume bar, Delftware, Limoges, and other gift items.

La Bonbonniere, 75-B Nassaustraat. A tiny gourmet shop worth looking into. Chocolates, rum cakes, caviar, Cuban cigars.

Boulevard Shopping Center, L.G. Smith Blvd. If you like the convenience of several shops under one roof, drop in here. You'll find local fashions, souvenirs, T-shirts, leather goods, shoes, handicrafts, and computers at its various shops.

Ecco, Nassaustraat between Emmastraat and Hendrikstraat. Leather goods, including Ferragamo and Bruno Magli shoes. Men's department on second floor. The mini-casinos here—assortments of chips, dice, cards, and roulette wheels in handsome wooden boxes—make perfect gifts.

Fanny's, 7 Nassaustraat. Cosmetics, toiletries, and perfumes up front. Resort wear and the like in back.

Gandelman's, 5 Nassaustraat. Glamorous jewelry and watches, plus all the Gucci accessories from key chains to handbags.

El Globo, Nassaustraat. Electronics, cameras, and souvenirs.

Harms Brothers, 17 L.G. Smith Blvd. This is the duty-free shop, offering free delivery of your purchases to the airport or cruise ship. Liquor, wine, cigarettes, cigars, perfume, T-shirts, Dutch wooden shoes, and a complete delicatessen.

Kan Jewelers, Nassaustraat between Emmastraat and Hendrikstraat. Small, elegant and a long-respected name here. The names you'll see include Rolex, Rado, Concord, Rosenthal, and Les Musts de Cartier. Beautiful jewelry too.

New Amsterdam Store, 10 Nassaustraat. Perhaps Aruba's best department store prices. Men's, women's, and children's clothing, tablecloths and napkins, souvenirs, Delftware. All in an informal atmosphere.

Palais Oriental, corner of Nassaustraat and Emmastraat. Christofle silverware, Lladró procelain, jewelry, crystal, glassware, embroidered tablecloths.

Penha & Sons, 11 Nassaustraat. An old name in Aruba, offering a wide selection of perfumes. Men's clothing too.

Spritzer & Fuhrmann, corner of Nassaustraat and Hendrikstraat. All four corners, that is. The main store sells watches, jewelry, and gifts. The second sells china, crystal, and flatware, with jewelry downstairs. The third specializes in porcelain and crystal, or pick up an elegant snail-serving set as a gift. The fourth Spritzer & Fuhrmann is Optica Moderna, selling sunglasses, binoculars, and magnifying glasses, among other things. Perhaps the best-known shopkeepers in the Caribbean, and a class act.

Airport shopping is good but limited. Your choices are a branch of Kan Jewelers, a small duty-free shop almost completely devoted to liquor (some cigarettes and cigars, too), a food store specializing in cheese and chocolates, and the Van Den Bergh gift shop with a selection of perfumes and souvenirs.

 RESTAURANTS. Aruba is a melting pot of nationalities, and its restaurants reflect them all. Fresh local seafood is the real specialty here, and you should try some typical Aruban foods, if only side dishes like *plantains* (similar to bananas, but cooked) and *pan bati* (beaten bread, thick as a pancake). But you'll probably have time to enjoy several of the cuisines available here— French, Italian, Chinese, Indonesian, and the others. One nice twist about Aruban restaurants is that they aren't all bound to one specialty; some seafood restaurants serve Chinese food, steak places serve seafood, and so on.

Settings range from very casual to romantic and elegant. Even the most formal restaurants, however, simply call for jackets for men and a nice sundress, worn with dress-up sandals, for women. All but the most informal spots accept major credit cards and take dinner reservations.

You'll find that most Aruban menus list prices in both U.S. dollars and Netherlands Antilles guilders. And the service charge is almost always included.

We call $8 or less per entree *Inexpensive;* $9–$15 *Moderate;* $16 and above *Expensive.*

Expensive

La Dolce Vita. 164 Nassaustraat. Tel. 25675. In its first five years, this canopied Italian restaurant in a former private home won its reputation as Aruba's best. New owners have made some changes, but it's still one of the island's most popular spots. Start with antipasto, then go on to a sophisticated veal dish with pasta on the side. Dinner only. AE, MC, V.

The French Steak House. Manchebo Beach Hotel. Tel. 23444. Candlelight dining on gourmet specialties from veal stroganoff and lobster pompadour to steak au poivre or Steak Diane Flambee. Dinner only. AE, V, MC.

The Mill (De Olde Molen). Near Palm Beach. Tel. 22060. This red windmill, built in Holland in 1804 and reconstructed here 20 years ago, has become an island landmark. Inside you'll find elegant continental cuisine, from veal cordon bleu to chateaubriand, with ambiance to match. To get there, turn right (inland) at the Aruba Concorde Hotel. The restaurant can be seen easily from the road. Dinner only. AE, MC, V.

Palm Court. Tamarijn Beach Hotel. Tel. 24150. Continental fare in a tropical setting of rattan chairs and blue-and-white striped awnings. Dress casually and if you're in the mood for lobster, just ask. They're flown in live from Maine. Dinner only. AE, MC, DC, V.

Papiamento. 7 Wilhelminastraat. Tel. 24544. Put this one at the top of your list. New Dutch-Aruban managers, Lenie and Eduardo Ellis, have turned this 1930s mansion into the most sophisticated restaurant on the island. The interiors are cool and spacious with stone walls, pale hardwood floors, multi-level seating, copper chandeliers, and huge bouquets of silk flowers. The menu is international, with veal saddle, rack of lamb, and fish specialties among the favorites. Dinner only. Oyster bar and live music at cocktail hour. AE, MC, V.

Le Petit Bistro. Aruba Caribbean Hotel. Tel. 22250. A formal French restaurant at the hotel's pool level. Chateaubriand and rack of lamb for two are among the specialties. Lunch and dinner. AE, MC, DC, V.

The Red Parrot. Divi Divi Beach Hotel. Tel. 23300. A large and lovely dining room with heavy Spanish wooden chandeliers and touches of stained glass. Continental cuisine. Dinner only. AE, MC, DC, V.

Talk of the Town. Talk of the Town Hotel. Tel. 23380. This low-lit, all-red French restaurant in downtown Oranjestad has been winning culinary awards for years. The veal dishes are excellent, or order the Caribbean's best frog's legs. Dinner only. AE, MC, DC, V.

Moderate

Astoria Hotel. 6 Crijnssenstraat, San Nicolas. Tel. 45132. Devotees say this restaurant offers Aruba's best Chinese food. Lunch and dinner. AE, MC, V.

Bali Floating Restaurant. Oranjestad on the harbor. Tel. 22131. Right across from the bus station and tourist office. Inside, there's rijsttafel, curries, steaks, and Javanese specialties. Casual, festive atmosphere with lots of bamboo and cactus. Lunch and dinner, or drinks overlooking the harbor at the Bamboo Bar. AE, MC, V.

Buccaneer. Noord. This well-known, informal seafood restaurant is worth a visit for the decor alone. Every booth in the right-hand dining room has its own private aquarium so patrons can watch marine life float by. The bar is the prow of a ship with a seashell collection under glass. To get there, turn inland between the Playa Linda and Americana Hotel, make a right at the Airoso Apartments and follow the signs. No reservations are taken here, so come early and expect to wait. Dinner only. AE, MC, DC, V.

The Captain's Table (formerly La Posada Criolla). 4 Wilhelminastraat. Tel. 26772. The Ellises, who also run Papiamento, have turned this old *cunucu* (Aruban countryside) house into a restaurant specializing in unusual fish dishes and regional specialties. Dinner only. AE, MC, V.

Cattle Baron. 228 L.G. Smith Blvd. Tel. 22977. Steaks are the specialty in this Western-style building with wagon wheels leaning against the wooden porch. To find it take the first right past the hospital. Lunch and dinner. AE, MC, DC, V.

Dragon Phoenix. 31 Havenstraat. Tel. 21858. Chinese food in a very authentic Chinese atmosphere. Lunch and dinner. AE, MC, V.

El Gaucho. 80 Wilhelminastraat. Tel. 23677. Aruba's only Argentinian restaurant so far. Enjoy beef grilled over charcoal or one of the seafood specialties, all with gaucho music in the background. Lunch and dinner. AE, MC, V.

Heidelberg. 136 L.G. Smith Blvd. Tel. 33020. Aruba's first German restaurant offers wiener schnitzel, sauerbraten and the like. Dinner only. AE, MC, V.

Kowloon. Corner of Emmastraat and Nassaustraat. Tel. 24950. Oranjestad's best address for all kinds of regional Chinese cuisine—Hunan, Szechuan, Cantonese and more. Lunch and dinner. AE, MC, V.

Marina Pirata. Spanish Lagoon. Tel. 47150. If you want huge portions of seafood in a very casual open-air seaside restaurant, this is the place to come. The ceiling is covered with palm leaves, the bar is built of rum kegs, and the red snapper is bigger than the plate. You can get octopus provençal, poultry or steak too—then sunbathe after eating. To find it, follow L.G. Smith Blvd. east from Oranjestad. Take the second right after the airport (it's across from the drive-in movie) and follow the signs. Lunch and dinner. AE, MC, V.

Ocean. 124 Arendsstraat. Tel. 28207. When you want seafood, your spouse wants Chinese, and the other couple want steak, this is the choice to make. Set on a somewhat industrial street, it offers no view, but does have an interesting Chinese salad bar and good food. Lunch and dinner. AE, MC, V.

La Paloma. Noord 39. Tel. 32770. Choose seafood or local specialties in this country-house setting. Take the first right (inland) between the Americana and Playa Linda, then look for the white house with the orange roof on your left. Dinner only. AE, MC, V.

Papagayo. L.G. Smith Blvd. Ctr. Tel. 24140. Beautiful caged birds, lots of greenery, a romantic harbor view, and an emphasis on service have made Papagayo one of Aruba's most fashionable eating spots. The accent is northern Italian, with offerings like saltimbocca romana and linguine with lobster and seafood. Lunch and dinner. AE, MC, DC, V.

Roma Mia. 156 Nassaustraat. Tel. 28639. Authentic Italian fare in a former private home near La Dolce Vita. Dinner only. AE, MC, DC, V.

La Serre. Aruba Concorde Hotel. Tel. 24466. When you're in the mood for a truly elegant setting, consider this huge hotel dining room, decorated in formal red with shirred white curtains. The continental menu is in French, the entertainment is live but discreet, and this is the place to dress up a little. Dinner only. Two seatings, 7:00 and 9:30 P.M. AE, MC, DC, V.

Surfside's Garden Restaurant. L.G. Smith Blvd. Tel. 23380. On the other hand, if you want to dress very casually and eat at a picnic table on the beach, with only palm trees and the constellations looking down at you, go to Surfside. Steaks, seafood, and all the exotic dishes served on the many special theme nights are catered by the Talk of the Town Restaurant across the street. Dinner only. AE, MC, DC, V.

La Taurina. 149 Nassaustraat. Tel. 26780. This homey restaurant serves Spanish specialties, seafood, and steak. Have paella with sangria or a Spanish wine. Lunch and dinner. AE, MC, V.

Trocadero. 152 Nassaustraat. Tel. 21210. A wide choice of dishes in an informal setting. Seafood choices range from green turtle steaks and baby shark fillets to basic lobster and shrimp. Steaks, Oriental food, and curries are available too. Lunch and dinner. AE, MC, DC, V.

Inexpensive

Beep Beep. 68 Wilhelminastraat. Tel. 24717. Cantonese, Chinese, and Indonesian food in a casual setting. The Road Runner cartoon character is this restaurant's symbol for fast service—thus the name. AE, MC, V.

Brisas del Mar. 222-A Savaneta. Tel. 47718. This friendly, homey ten-table seafood restaurant overlooking the water is something of a local phenomenon, just as popular with residents as with vacationers. Don't go for the decor (a giant stuffed-animal shark hanging over the kitchen's pass-through window). Go for the pan-fried fish Aruban style, breaded conch, scallops, smelts, or squid. To find it, drive east from Oranjestad on L.G. Smith Blvd. to the town of Savaneta, about ten miles away. Lunch and dinner. No credit cards.

The Cellar. 2 Klipstraat. Tel. 24543. It could be a small pub in Amsterdam with its dark wood bar and cozy booths. The Cellar is right in the middle of Oranjestad's shopping district. The food is casual, but the atmosphere is perfect and the international wine and beer lists impressive. Lunch and dinner. No credit cards.

Chefette. Bubali 105-C. Tel. 23270. West Indian soul food is the specialty here. Seafood and steaks too. Dinner only. AE, MC, V.

De Dissel. 1 Hospitalstraat. Tel. 24229. Dutch pea soup, "croquet balls," and other casual but hearty foods in a Dutch tea room with a touch of Old World charm. Breakfast, lunch, and late afternoon snacks. No credit cards.

Mido. 5 Dwarsstraat. Tel. 22134. Informal Chinese restaurant at the eastern end of Oranjestad's main shopping street. Lunch and dinner. AE.

Taco El Toro. 12 Klipstraat. Tel. 25736. Aruba's first Mexican restaurant and a favorite with residents. Lunch and dinner. No credit cards.

 NIGHT LIFE AND BARS. All the glamor and glitter you could wish for is found every night in the high-rise beach hotels—and in a few selected spots around the island. If all you want is an after-hours drink, perhaps with live background music, several Aruban bar/restaurants stay open until 3:00 A.M. or later. You might run into your croupier there, winding down after a long night at the casino. Some late-night possibilities in Oranjestad include *The Cellar* and *Taco El Toro.*

Visitors who want to explore the less-touristed nightspots of San Nicolas may want to drop in at *Chesterfield's Night Club,* 57 Zeppenfeldstraat (tel. 45109). Have a drink and a snack at *Charlie's Bar* at 56 Main Street, authentically Dutch and open until midnight. The truly adventurous may want to stroll and explore the seamen's bars here, across from the refinery, complete with legalized ladies of the evening.

Back at the beach, even the low-rise hotels usually have dancing to live music in a lobby bar or at poolside. For more action or a real show, consider these possibilities:

Club Arubesque, Aruba Concorde Hotel. Tel. 24466. There's a two-drink minimum at the 11:00 P.M. Las Vegas-style show, complete with showgirls. Try to get one of the plush tables for two or four near the small stage, or a cozy banquette in the back.

Contempo, Talk of the Town Hotel. Tel. 23380. This disco is the place to dance the night away after a gourmet dinner at the hotel restaurant.

L'Esprit, Holiday Inn. Tel. 23600. The decor is dark green and plush at this elegant lobby-level disco, open from 10:00 P.M. to 2:00 A.M. Sunday is Calypso night with limbo and calypso dance contests. Big-screen videos every night.

Galactica Lounge, Aruba Palm Beach Hotel. Tel. 23900. Just stroll from the casino into this glitzy blue disco-like club. There are 8:30 and 11:30 P.M. shows with guest performers.

Holiday Inn, Tel. 23600. On Friday nights, poolside is the place to be for the weekly Carnival show. This is your chance to see the colorful costumes and music that highlight Aruba's yearly Carnival celebration. Traditional barbecue and steel-band music.

Indian Rock Garden, Hooiberg. Tel. 29154. This out-of-the-way disco is a favorite with Arubans, and looks from the outside like a stone cave with a door in the shape of a dragon's mouth. To find it, drive east from Oranjestad on Nassaustraat, which will turn into Cumana. Drive toward Haystack and, when the steps up the mountain are on your right, turn left. You can't miss it.

Palm Beach Room, Holiday Inn. Tel. 23600. This lobby-level club offers the glitziest of entertainment, like its recent Rio-style review. The 9:30 dinner show includes a four-course meal. The 11:30 cocktail show includes two drinks.

Scaramouche, L.G. Smith Blvd. Shopping Ctr., upstairs. Tel. 24954. This is Aruba's "in" spot, and you'll see its red lip-print symbol everywhere. The glamorous atmosphere, colored lights, and disco music go on until 5:00 A.M.

Stellaris Restaurant and Showroom, Americana Aruba Hotel, Tel. 24500. Dinner shows featuring continental cuisine and live entertainment at this large supper club.

CASINOS. The liveliest we've seen in the Caribbean. Slot machines ring out constantly and the roulette, baccarat, and blackjack tables seem always to have potential winners waiting in the wings. Each casino has different hours, with some opening certain games in the morning and afternoon. All, however, are open late. No one under 18 is permitted to play.

The Alhambra, across from the Divi-Divi Hotel, is the newest and definitely one of the best. This 8,000-square-foot fantasyland has it all, from baccarat and roulette to nickel slots and an impressive costumed doorman who'll shake your hand for luck.

All others are in the high-rise hotels (the *Holiday Inn, Concorde, Americana Aruba, Aruba Palm Beach* and, when it's reopened, the *Aruba Caribbean*). And they're just as popular, packed with vacationers until the wee hours of the morning.

POSTAGE. At press time, airmail rates from Aruba to the U.S. and Canada were NAfl .60 for postcards and NAfl 1.00 for letters.

ELECTRIC CURRENT. The current here is 110 to 120 volts A.C.

SECURITY. Aruba is one of the safest and most law-abiding islands in the Caribbean, but there's petty crime even in paradise. Pickpockets are considered the closest thing to hardened criminals here, and a purse-snatching is front-page local news. Most Arubans didn't even lock their homes until recent years. Essentially, you and your belongings are safe just about anywhere on Aruba you'd think about going. A midnight walk along the beach is relatively safe and, if you decide to stroll along the highway from one hotel to the other, you're probably in more danger from oncoming traffic than from potential muggers. Downtown Oranjestad is basically safe too, because discos are open late at night. The island's only dangerous neighborhood is The Village, north of San Nicolas, and few tourists have ever found reason to go there. Still, there's no reason to be careless, or to leave valuables lying around. Several hotels offer free safe-deposit boxes built into your guest room closet. A deposit is put on your bill, but you pay only if you fail to return the key at check-out time.

BARBADOS

by
BARBARA A. CURRIE

Barbara A. Currie is a writer, photographer, and publicist who has traveled, lived, and worked in the Caribbean since 1975. She is an avid scuba diver and saltwater angler and specializes in writing about those attractions in the Caribbean. Ms. Currie is a regular contributor to Skin Diver, Diver *and other water-sports magazines.*

Barbados has been a popular tourist destination since the eighteenth century. It was considered by the English to be one of the healthiest places in the Empire, and Europeans claimed that bathing in the surf near Bathsheba cured a variety of illnesses.

This easternmost island in the Windward chain has retained all its natural attractions and added or improved on many others. Today, this independent 166 square mile Caribbean nation prides itself on being almost completely self-sufficient in terms of its basic needs, and the result is a sense of national pride that makes the Barbadians some of the most likeable of all West Indians.

Barbados can easily substantiate its tourism claim that "it has it all," unless casinos are a prerequisite for your holiday. It offers a tradewind-cooled climate, averaging 80 degrees; health and pure-water standards so elevated that the place had a heyday as the sanitarium of the West Indies; an atmosphere that ranges from ultrasophistication, mainly on the western St. James coast, to barefoot hospitality on the Atlantic side;

miles of powdered coral beaches, both pink and white; and thousands of quick-smiling Bajans.

In addition to a network of almost 860 miles of good paved roads and reliable public transportation, Barbados offers visitors a greater variety of tropical scenery and places of historic interest than other Caribbean countries many times its size. The west coast, tranquil and protected in the lee of the northeast trade winds, has the most beautiful beaches and luxurious resorts; the east coast is rugged and dramatic, with pounding surf and jagged, rocky coastline at times suggesting the British Isles. The interior parishes are a patchwork of rolling hills, plains of sugar cane, and lush patches of tropical forests.

Past and Present

The Barrancoids (Amerinds), the Arawaks, and the Carib Indians were three very different groups of early inhabitants of this island, but western civilization credits a Portuguese explorer with the discovery of Barbados in 1536. He named it Los Barbados, presumably for the abundance of ficus trees, whose aerial roots resemble beards. The Portuguese decided not to settle here, and almost a century passed before the British established the first settlement at Holetown, in what is now St. James Parish, in 1627. Since Barbados lies outside the gentle curve of the Caribbean islands, it was spared the clashes and invasions sparked by the eighteenth-century wave of piracy experienced by neighboring islands, and remained a British protectorate until it peacefully chose independence in 1966.

Bajans are the descendants, for the most part, of slaves brought in to work the plantations after the sugar cane was introduced from Brazil in the 1630s. The Barbados planters seem to have had a more enlightened attitude toward their slaves than the French and Danes exhibited on their islands. As a result of relatively humane plantation conditions, Barbados was spared the horrors and brutal recriminations of a slave uprising.

Barbados was under British rule for over 350 years, and during the two decades since Independence many have referred to it as "Little England." Many British traditions are integral parts of life in Barbados: cricket is a national obsession; tennis is still played on grass courts in some clubs; driving is on the left and traditional Commonwealth holidays are observed. Barbados' legal and court systems still follow the British system, and her national language is English.

Today, tourism and sugar form the base of Barbados' economy. This island produces a major share of Britain's sugar supply, as well as some of the finest rum in the world. In addition to sugar, Barbados produces a cornucopia of fruits and vegetables—almost every inch of the island's fertile soil is cultivated.

Since declaring its independence on November 30, 1966, Barbados has had a history of orderly political transition from one administration to the next. Its democratic government consists of a governor general, who is the head of state and represents the queen. Executive authority is vested in the prime minister and cabinet (privy council) who are collectively responsible to the parliament. The prime minister is appointed by the governor general as the member of the house of assembly best able to command the support of the majority of its members. The normal term of office is five years, although the ruling party may call elections at any time to seek a new mandate.

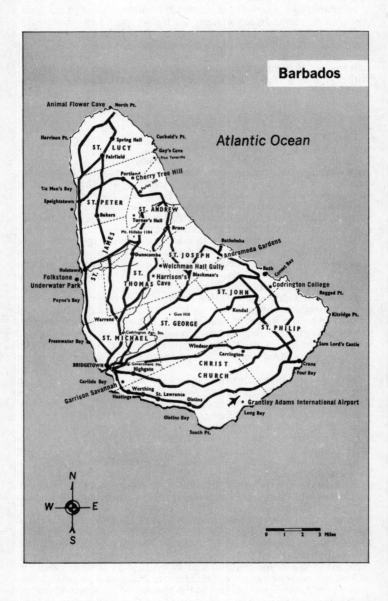

EXPLORING BARBADOS

Many of St. James' coastal hotels provide transportation from the airport, and all can arrange for taxis. However, your tour of Barbados should really begin in the capital, Bridgetown. Depending on where you stay in St. James, Bridgetown is a five- to twenty-minute drive along the main road. When the road forks, bear right and it becomes a modern two-lane highway that deposits you on Bridgetown's western edge, by the Tourist Board on Harbour Road. An excellent suggested walking tour, complete with city map, is available here. Also, you may decide from here to take a taxi into town, as Bridgetown traffic can be confusing on weekdays.

Bridgetown

Bridgetown is the primary duty-free district of Barbados, and Broad Street its main shopping artery. Cruise ships from all major Caribbean lines call here each week, and the capital can be busy on those days when ships are in port.

A minute's walk from the tourist office is Pelican Village, an arts-and-crafts center on Princess Alice Highway near the harbor. Behind this is the Government Handicraft Division of the Industrial Development Corporation, where visitors are welcome to wander and watch basketweaving, pottery making, and other crafts. Temple Yard, on the same highway but a little closer to town, is where the Rastafarians have their craft market, which specializes in leather work. Lord Nelson's Statue, erected in 1813 (twenty-seven years before Nelson's column in London's Trafalgar Square) stands in the center of Bridgetown's Trafalgar Square. On the north side of the Square are the public buildings that house the House of Assembly, notable for its stained glass windows depicting English sovereigns from James I to Queen Victoria. The fountain in the Square was erected in 1865 to commemorate the introduction of a public water system to Bridgetown. Broad Street is in the center of town, about about a ten-minute walk west of the landing dock.

The Careenge, or inner harbor, is located south of the Square and the bridge across it has no name, though it is the structure that gave the city it's name. St. Michael's Cathedral, east of the Square, behind the modern financial building, was originally built in 1665; destroyed by a hurricane in 1780, it was rebuilt only to be badly damaged by another hurricane in 1831. Since then it has escaped further damage. This is where George Washington is said to have worshipped when he visited in 1751. On Upper Bay Street is an eighteenth-century house where Washington and his brother Lawrence stayed for £ 15 a month.

South of Bridgetown is the Barbados Museum, with a fascinating collection of old maps, sailors' valentines, coins, Indian artifacts, domestic arts and crafts, and exhibits of local wildlife. Nearby is Garrison Savannah, a fifty-acre tract of land that was once the parade ground for the British regiment and is now a sports center and park where cricket matches and horseraces are the main activities. The landmark that marks this site is the faded red brick clock tower of St. Ann's Fort, one of the few structures that survived the hurricane of 1831.

Driving south from Bridgetown, on Christ Church Road/Maxwell Coast Road, you'll pass through an area of smaller beach resorts: Hastings, Worthing, and St. Lawrence in Christ Church Parish. On this coastal road is Christ Church, the site of Chase Vault and one of the strangest riddles of psychic phenomena. According to the story, the coffins of a local family rearranged themselves in a sealed vault, which so upset the people of Barbados that in 1820 they were ordered removed and buried in churchyard graves.

The Wild Atlantic Coast

The first part of your drive along the main road from Bridgetown is through flat corridors of sugar cane. Beyond Crane, on the southeast coast, the scenery is beautiful, getting more and more so as you drive southeast along the wildly spectacular Atlantic coast, which, with its cliffs, plunging headlands, and sometimes turbulent surf, reminds many travelers of the coasts of Brittany and Cornwall. One of the showplaces here is Sam Lord's Castle, an early nineteenth-century mansion in the midst of an estate that overlooks the sea. Sam Lord's Castle now stands tall in the center of a Marriott Hotel development, fortunately low profile in the area of the castle.

Sam Lord was a kind of landlubber buccaneer whose chief pastime was luring ships to the reef by hanging lanterns in the palm trees so that mariners, seeing them at night, thought they were the lights of ships anchored in a safe harbor. It was an old trick, practiced successfully in Cornwall and by the Nags Head banders on the treacherous Hatteras reef. When the ships ran aground on the shoals, Sam Lord and slaves took possession of the cargoes, dispatching any sailors who had not drowned.

It must have been a lucrative business. Sam Lord imported Italian artisans to make his castle a thing of beauty; the plaster ceilings are their work. The present owners have kept it up in the style to which Sam Lord was accustomed. The place is furnished with splendid antiques, not the least of which are Sam Lord's mahogany four-poster bed and a wardrobe in whose lavishly carved doors we detect the fine Italian hand of the imported artisan. Visitors are welcome at a nominal fee.

Nearby is Ragged Point, where you can witness the strength of the Atlantic surf and see almost the entire east coast of Barbados to Pico Tenerife. To find it, look for the East Point Lighthouse.

Next stop is Codrington College, which, despite its splendid avenue of towering palms, will remind you of Oxford. The flora may be tropical, but this is an English school in spirit and appearance, the oldest (1716) in the British West Indies. Just to the north is St. John's Church eight hundred feet above the sea and affording a sweeping view of the spectacular windward coast. The church dates from the seventeenth century. Its rosy stone exterior has the patina of age.

Vacationers interested in seeing what life in a West Indian plantation great house might have been like can visit Villa Nova, built from coral limestone in 1834 and reopened in early 1976 for visitors. Furnishings are mostly Barbadian antiques, made from local mahogany. Situated in St. John parish, the great house sits on a hilltop, amid six acres. Prince Philip and Queen Elizabeth have been guests at the great house. It is open Monday through Friday, from 10:00 A.M. to 4:00 P.M.

Heading North

At Bathsheba the Atlantic booms against the cliffs, dashing high on "a stern and rockbound coast," which is obligingly modified here and there to form stretches of beach. Heading north along the east coast road, you'll find Andromeda Garden, a magnificent tropical rock garden on the side of a cliff, whose natural beauty provides a photographer's playground. Many different kinds of tropical flowers, plants, and trees small waterfalls and tiny pools provide one of Barbados' loveliest settings. In the same area is another floral festival, Flower Forest, an attraction with over one hundred species of tropical flowering plants and trees, and the island's newest visitor attraction of this nature.

Overlooking Bathsheba, the views get even more spectacular. Belleplaine looks like a toy village from this height.

Your next stop, about seven miles away will be Cherry Tree Hill and St. Nicholas Abbey. Legend says there was once a magnificent cherry orchard here which was swept away in a landslide. There is a spectacular view of the Scotland District from this site. St. Nicholas Abbey, nearby, is the oldest house in Barbados, probably built before 1660. It's located beyond an avenue of mahogany trees, considered to be the finest display of this species in Barbados.

To the southeast from Cherry Tree Hill is Farley Hill National Park where, in the late 1800s, Thomas Brigg's plantation house was one of the showplaces of the colonies, and a favorite place for visits by royalty. Only the ruins of this plantocracy palace remain, as its grandeur was destroyed by fire in 1887. To the east is Morgan Lewis Mill, donated to the National Trust by its late owner; it is the only sugar mill in Barbados with all its working parts intact.

Farther south and almost in the center of the island is Welchman Hall Gully. It is a valley rimmed by cliffs, inhabited by wild monkeys and planted and preserved as a botanical garden. The bearded fig trees grow here, the island's sole clove tree survives, and there are nutmeg, cocoa, citrus, banana, coffee, and bamboo trees, and other tropical flora. The cliffs are studded with stalactite- and stalagmite-filled caves. Harrison's Cave, near Welchman Hall Gully, is one of the newest attractions in Barbados. This spectacular cave is viewed by train tour on a mile-long underground ride that feels like a prehistoric odyssey through a stone forest of stalactites and stalagmites. In this area you'll also find Chalky Mount, whose potters are busy at work preserving a three hundred-year-old craft of Barbados. Look for family names of Devonish, Cummins, and Harding. They fashion local clay into attractive jugs, jars, and bowls.

You can cut straight west across the island to Speightstown, the second "city" of Barbados, or you can make a loop to North Point at the top of the island and visit the fascinating Animal-Flower Cave. This is actually a series of sea grottoes that can be visited only at low tide. The animal-flowers (local name for sea anemones) live in shallow pools left by the receding tide.

Speightstown, on the leeward coast, is your next destination. If you drive directly from Farley Hill, take the road to Six Men's Bay just north of Speightstown. It passes through the cane fields, dotted with the ruins of sugar mills and old plantation houses. At Six Men's Bay, there are other nostalgic reminders of a different past—old cannons and an anchor lie by the water as if no one has bothered to pick them up for the past hundred years. Here, too, are ruins of a few buildings in which they used to dry whale blubber. At Speightstown, there are more guns pointed out to sea and many old buildings.

The Platinum Coast

When you leave Speightstown you are offically on Barbados' celebrated Platinum Coast. The road follows the coast south from St. Peter into St. James Parish. The contrast between this and the eastern shore could not be greater. If the latter was Brittany, this is the Mediterranean, calm, brilliant, luxurious. Just outside of Speightstown is Heywoods Barbados, the Barbados government's 306-room, $17 million resort complex (actually seven resorts). This resort is special, and worth a stop to see how a well-planned government project can enhance an island's tourism industry.

The center of the Platinum Coast is Holetown, taking its name from the town of Hole on the River Thames. Its church, one of the oldest in the West Indies, is as fashionable as the Abbey. Its font is dated 1684; its bell commands that "God bless King William. 1696." In the town an obelisk marks the spot where Captain Catlin of the *Olive Blossom* is presumed to have landed in 1625, although the monument decrees it, mistakenly, as 1605.

PRACTICAL INFORMATION FOR BARBADOS

HOW TO GET THERE. By air. Barbados' facilities at Grantley Adams Airport have made it the hub of the southern Caribbean, with flights fanning out to Trinidad, St. Vincent, and St. Lucia. Daily nonstop flights come in from New York via *American Airlines* and *BWIA.* BWIA and *Eastern Airlines* fly direct from Miami. *Air Canada* has nonstop and direct flights from Montreal and Toronto; BWIA from Toronto. From Europe, there is frequent *British Airways* and BWIA service from London. The best bets for direct, interisland air connections are LIAT and BWIA, which link Barbados and all the neighboring islands.

By sea. Bridgetown, Barbados is a very popular port of call for ships making the longer down-island cruises from Florida and San Juan.

FACTS AND FIGURES. Easternmost of the Caribbean Islands, Barbados is part of the Windward Islands group, and is the crossroads for visitors traveling to other island members of this region. Barbados actually lies in the Atlantic Ocean, but enjoys the same climate as its Windward neighbors, with an average year-round temperature between 77 and 85 degrees F. Rain falls sporadically between July and November.

Shaped roughly like an avocado, Barbados is 21 miles long, 14 miles at its widest point, and occupies 166 square miles. Its west coast has some of the Windwards' most beautiful golden sand beaches, while its eastern shoreline is rugged and windy, with dramatic surf that suggests the Scottish coast. The interior is plains of sugarcane and lush, rolling hills—but no mountains. Barbados' highest elevation is Mt. Hillaby, at 1,105 ft. A wide variety of tropical trees and flowers grow here.

The country's population of 270,000 is one of the region's most literate, with a national literacy rate of 97%. Almost 80% are of Afro–West Indian descent with the remaining minorities including 3% white and European; 1% East

Indian and 16% of mixed racial origin. The main religion is a mixture of Protestant sects.

Sugar production and tourism are the island's economic mainstays, and it is a popular vacation destination among better-than-average-income travelers from the U.S., Canada, Germany, and the U.K.

Bridgetown, the capital, lies 30 minutes west of the airport on the Caribbean coast, and is an important port of call for major cruise ship lines each week. The island's duty-free shopping district and harbor are located here.

North of Bridgetown is the St. James Parish district, the famous "platinum coast" of Barbados which is the most developed area of the island's tourism industry.

The people, known as Barbadians (Bajan is now used as an adjective, not as a term of ethnic identification), speak English with a lilting local accent. Barbados is not only a fertile island, but also has one of the purest water supplies in the world, as well as its own supply of crude oil.

The national symbol is also the traditional dish of Barbados, the flying fish.

Barbados observes Atlantic standard time, one hour ahead of the eastern U.S.

 WHEN TO GO. Year round, Barbados offers a warm, sunny climate, but the months of July through November are predictably wetter than the others. However, the summer hotel rates, as well as airfares, are reduced dramatically during the summer off-season between April and December 1. Bargains abound on luxury beachfront hotel rooms and rental apartments, and fewer people are enjoying the island's multitude of activities. If you ask Barbadians when the best time to come really is, they'll tell you it's late June through early August, when the month-long Crop Over celebration, a combination of Carnival and independence festivities, is held.

 PASSPORTS AND VISAS. U.S. and Canadian visitors must be in possession of a valid passport or some other document satisfactorily establishing their identity (birth certificate or voter's registration card will do; a driver's license will not) and a return or ongoing ticket. A passport is not required of British citizens if they embark from Great Britain, have a return ticket, and plan to leave within six months. They must have proof of identification. A visa is not necessary.

 MONEY. Barbados has its own currency, the Barbadian dollar, which equals about U.S. $.50. American and Canadian dollars are accepted everywhere, but you'll get a better rate if you stop at a bank and deal in local currency. You'll see almost everything quoted BDS.

WHAT WILL IT COST?

A typical day on Barbados during winter season for two persons will run:

	US$
Hotel accommodations at one of the large beachfront resort hotels	$130
Breakfast at the hotel	16
Lunch at a moderate in-town restaurant	20
Dinner at the hotel or moderate restaurant	50
Tips or service charges at restaurants and hotels	20
One-day sightseeing by tour or rental car	40
Total	$276

AIRPORT TAX AND OTHER CHARGES. There is an 8% government tax on all hotel accommodations, plus a 10% service charge. The airport departure tax is BDS $12 or approximately U.S. $6.

TELEPHONES AND EMERGENCY NUMBERS. The area code for Barbados is 809. Information: 119; Ambulance: 61113; Police: 112; Fire department: 113. With the exception of emergency numbers, all phone numbers here are seven-digit and begin with 42.

HOTELS. There are hotels and inns to suit every pocketbook, and they line every shore. You'll find luxury living along the west coast; comfortable and more reasonable accommodations in the Hastings-Worthing area, southwest to east from Bridgetown; and a few properties along the east coast. Most hotels provide some kind of transportation to town, and taxi service is always available.

We call U.S. $170 and above *Deluxe;* $120–$160 *Expensive;* $80–$119 *Moderate;* and anything below that *Inexpensive.*

Deluxe

Coconut Creek Club. St. James. Tel. 42–02076. Luxury cottage colony at St. James, with 48 housekeeping units set out on beautifully landscaped grounds. Private beach, freshwater pool, dining room, pub, bar pavilion for entertainment and dancing. Breakfast and dinner are included in their rates.

Cobblers Cove Hotel. St. Peter. Tel. 42–22291. A comfortable and unpretentious hotel about 11 mi. up the coast from the capital. 38 luxurious efficiency units with kitchenettes and balconies or patios. They have their own white-sand beach with water sports available; a swimming pool; tropical bar; dining terrace.

Colony Club. St. James. Tel. 42–22335. On the beach at St. James, this seven-acre cottage colony is one of the most attractive of the Bajan "residential clubs." There are 75 luxuriously appointed rooms, all with private patios. Dining room (exchange dining if you like), cocktail terrace, swimming pool, water sports on the beach, and brilliant gardens to stroll.

Coral Reef Club. St. James. Tel. 42–22372. This superb property has 75 rooms, many in cottages scattered around the grounds, with exotic names such as Jasmin, Frangipani, and Bamboo. You'll live the good life here, with luncheon on their terrace and gracious evening wining and dining. Entertainment includes dinner dances and beach barbecues. Freshwater pool; the option for any water sports you select.

Discovery Bay Inn. St. James. Tel. 42–21301. 75 rooms facing the sea on four tropical acres. Small swimming pool, open lounge and dining room, dancing and entertainment during in-season evenings.

Glitter Bay. St. James. Tel. 42–24111. A lovely property on the calm western shore. The accommodations are in 21 units surrounded by tropical gardens at the edge of the sea. The units vary, with six of them in three-bedroom penthouses; twelve in two-bedroom suites; and three in one-bedroom suites. The rooms are plush, large, and airy and all units have fully equipped kitchens. Gourmet dining at the *Piperade Restaurant;* dancing; nightly entertainment. Swimming pool; all water sports; golf nearby.

Sandpiper Inn. St. James. Tel. 42–22251. The 34 rooms here are clustered around the swimming pool. There is a fine beach just steps away from watersports options. Open-air bar and restaurant.

Sandy Lane. St. James. Tel. 42–21311. One of the Caribbean's most famous, this St. James beachfront resort combines 18th-century elegance with 20th-century luxury in 115 contemporary rooms and suites. The building is a lovely example of neo-Palladian architecture, with rooms arranged for a sea view. Everything is airy and plush, with such striking effects as ornate mirrors and crystal chandeliers against a background of coral-stone walls. There are five tennis courts; an 18-hole championship golf course; a free-form swimming pool; and a 1,000-ft. beach where all water sports are readily available. In addition, the two restaurants, two cocktail lounges, and nightly entertainment are guaranteed to keep you busy once the sun sets.

Tamarind Cove. St. James. Tel. 42–21332. Very attractive beachfront resort on the sands along the west coast. The architecture is Spanish; the 43 rooms are in one- and two-bedroom suites. Dining on the terrace; swimming in the pool or in the sea. All water sports available.

Expensive

Barbados Hilton International. Needhams Point. Tel. 42–60200. About five minutes from Bridgetown; 184 rooms and suites, all with balconies. This attractive, five-story building has a New Orleans-style courtyard with all the tropical foliage to charm. Elegant dining room with West Indian and international cuisine. Coffee shop and lounge; tennis courts; swimming pool; 1,000-foot beach where all water sports are available; and shops for browsing and buying.

Carlisle Bay Beach Resort (Holiday Inn). Box 639, Bridgetown. Tel. 42–50886. Lots of action here, with 138 rooms in the seven-story main building and in smaller garden cottages. Most rooms have two double beds with bath, private balcony, and radio. Freshwater pool and patio, busy beach with water sports available. Two restaurants, three bars, entertainment nightly.

Cunard Paradise Beach Hotel. St. James. Tel. 42–29498. Formerly known as the Paradise Beach Resort, this west coast beachfront property has been a popular spot with the younger set from the U.S. and Canada for several years. Convenient to Bridgetown, it has a beach with a regatta of rental boats and a variety of aquatic and nocturnal activities that keep things moving night and day. All the expected amenities: seaside bar, dining rooms, nightly entertainment, plus a well managed diving operation. 180 rooms, very pleasant.

Heywoods Barbados. St. Peter. Tel. (800) 223–9815 (U.S.). This multi-million-dollar resort complex owned by the country's government opened in January 1984. A sprawling 306-room complex combines seven separate resorts, each with its own decor and theme, on a 31-acre site trimmed by almost a mile of prime beach. Offers scuba diving and full water sports center; a nine-hole executive golf course; five tennis courts; three freshwater pools; shuffleboard; two air-conditioned squash courts; conference rooms; and a shopping mall with a variety of boutiques and services. Close to the beach is a marketplace for local crafts with some excellent buys. Nightly entertainment and a variety of restaurants complete this unusual resort. Individual hotel/apartel decor varies. This beautifully landscaped complex is one of the most unusual and attractive properties in the Caribbean, and worth a trip to visit.

Mariott's Sam Lord's Castle. St. Philip. Tel. 42–37350. On the sea at St. Philip, about 14 mi. east of Bridgetown. It isn't really a castle with tower and moat, but an impressive mansion surrounded by 71 acres of beautiful grounds, gardens, and a fine beach. The seven rooms in the main house have canopied beds. Downstairs the furniture is Sheraton, Hepplewhite, and Chippendale, the china is Spode, and some of the paintings are by Reynolds. The rest of the property's 259 rooms are in surrounding cottages. Two swimming pools, a mile-long beach, and tennis courts lighted for night play. *Wanderer Restaurant* for Continental dining. Nightly entertainment, and even a few slot machines.

Sandy Beach Resort. Worthing. Christ Church. Tel. 42–89033. A delightful hotel on the south shore with 139 rooms in 89 suites, all with patios or balconies facing the sea. Large swimming pool; all water sports, including scuba certification and options for deep-sea-fishing trips and harbor cruises. Drinks and entertainment at their *Sand Bar* poolside; excellent food, including a special West Indian buffet weekly at their *Green House* restaurant.

Southern Palms. St. Lawrence, Christ Church. Tel. 42–87171. A luxurious plantation-style hotel on a fine 1,000-ft. stretch of pink sand on Barbados' south coast. Its 95 rooms offer a variety of accommodations, from standard bedrooms to deluxe oceanfront suites with kitchenettes, and one four-bedroom penthouse. Located close to Dover Convention Center, this is a convenient businessman's hotel. Large pool, tennis courts, complete water-sports center on premises. Excellent food at the *Le Petit Flambe* dining room each evening, and the new *Unicorn I* disco is a popular nightspot.

Moderate

Barbados Beach Village. St. James. Tel. 42–03181. 84 nicely furnished units with a choice of twin-bedded rooms, studios, apartments, and duplexes. On a nice stretch of St. James beach, this hostelry has terrace bar, seaside restaurant, swimming pool with pool bar, and a disco nightclub.

Barbados Windsurfing Club Hotel. Maxwell, Christ Church. Tel. 42–89095. This small, 26-room hotel originated as a gathering place for windsurfing enthusiasts at the Windsurfer Beach Pub, and is now a complete school and center for the sport. Rooms are unpretentious but comfortable and spacious, overlooking the fishing village of Oistins on the south coast. Bar and restaurant on the premises, and special jazz band nights each week; all sports can be arranged, but the emphasis here is on learning and perfecting windsurfing skills on top sailboards. Low-key and congenial setting.

Casuarina Beach Club. St. Lawrence Gap, Christ Church. Tel. 42–83600. This luxury 64-room apartment hotel on 900 ft. of pink sand on the island's quiet south coast takes its name from the towering Casuarina pines which surround it. A quiet, lovely setting which offers a dramatic contrast to the platinum coast resorts. Large freshwater pool, tennis, squash courts on the premises, and bar and restaurant on the beach. Other activities, including scuba and golf, can be arranged through the resort. A popular place for those who prefer self-catering holidays in a secluded setting convenient to nightlife and shopping.

Club St. James. Vauxhall, St. James; Box 671C, Bridgetown. Tel. (800) 432–1707 (U.S.). A very special new resort on the west coast, whose "all-inclusive vacation" package is patterned after sister resorts Couples and Hedonism II in Jamaica. Week-long vacations run Mon.–Fri. and everything from airfare to drinks and cigarettes is included in the price. The club also sells day passes for BDS $60 which permit visitors to use the pool, water-sports facilities, and other sports, and include meals and drinks. The resort has 131 attractive rooms, rambling across a lush tropical garden setting, in a variety of accommodations. There are 54 hotel rooms, 55 one-bedroom suites, 14 two-bedroom suites and 8 penthouses. Freshwater pool with swim-up bar; Nautilus fitness center; running program; air-conditioned squash court and sauna on the premises; and all other sports, from scuba to golf and tennis, can be arranged by the resort. So far the club has proved popular with young professionals from the U.S. It's the only resort of its kind in Barbados.

Crane Beach Hotel. St. Philip. Tel. 42–36220. On a cliff overlooking the dramatic Atlantic coast, this remote hilltop property has changed hands hundreds of times but still remains one of Barbados' special places. Accommodations today are in suites or one-bedroom apartments in the main building. Air-conditioned bedrooms are available at the beach club next door. Two swimming pools, a nice restaurant with an extensive wine cellar, and two bars for entertainment.

Sichris Hotel. Worthing. Christ Church. Tel. 42–75930. This "discovery" is not only a comfortable and convenient self-contained resort, but also the ideal place for businessmen whose stay in Barbados requires a quiet place to work as well as accessibility. Just a few minutes from Bridgetown, the 24 air-conditioned one-bedroom suites all have kitchenettes, private balcony or patio, and phones in each unit. Bar, restaurant, and pool on the premises, and a two-minute walk from the beach. It has reasonable rates and an attentive manager.

Southwinds. St. Lawrence, Christ Church. Tel. 42–87181. The first resort venture by the esteemed Divi Hotel group on Barbados, this unusual and attractive complex is actually the expanded and renovated completion of the 36-room beach club on St. Lawrence Beach. The multi-million-dollar facilities include 116 one-bedroom suites with living room, kitchen, and balcony, and a few two-bedroom suites. Sports facilities include tennis, squash, and a variety of water sports, including plans for a complete dive operation (at press time this was not finalized). The new wing is set in a beautifully landscaped tropical garden which enhances the natural beauty of the resort's wooden architecture. Friendly atmosphere, superb service, bar and restaurant, and nightlife nearby make this a popular place for couples.

Sunset Crest Resort. St. James. Tel. 42–74710. A very popular resort with families, particularly Canadians, who find the villas and apartments and nearby shops the ingredients of a very reasonable self-catering holiday. This resort resembles a small village with its collection of one-, two-, and three-bedroom villas spread around a center with supermarket, deli, beauty shop, bank, department store, and recreation area with clubhouse, two large pools, pitch-and-putt golf course, and tennis courts. Across the road is the Beach Club which has two pools, two restaurants, a bar and games room, as well as a fine stretch of beach. The Merrymen play at the weekly beach barbecue.

Inexpensive

Accra Beach Hotel. Rockley Beach. Tel. 42–77866. 21 housekeeping suites nicely furnished; 53 rooms in all. Dining room, cocktail lounge, and beach bar. Water sports.

Atlantis Hotel. Bathsheba. Tel. 43–31526. Warm, pleasant atmosphere here in a nice location on the Bathsheba coast. Just 12 rooms on a bluff overlooking the sea. Their dining room is especially good, particularly for true Bajan dishes for lunch and dinner.

Caribbee Hotel. Hastings, Christ Church. Tel. 42–67888. This 53-room hotel on the southwest coast has been a popular vacation spot for decades for those who want a simple place to stay at a very reasonable rate. Caribee also has 36 one-bedroom apartments for guests who want self-catering facilities. The resort emphasizes inexpensive accommodations with all necessary amenities on the premises and shopping and dining within walking distance.

Island Inn. St. Michael. Tel. 42–60057. If you're looking for an indigenous inn, this is the one; with 22 rooms in a local and informal atmosphere. This property is across the street from the Holiday Inn and down the road from the Hilton International, so you'll be able to enjoy all their action within a few easy paces. Their restaurant serves Barbadian specialties, and their popular nightclub swings until the early hours.

Ocean View. Hastings. Tel. 42–77821. A 40-room oceanfront hotel convenient to town and especially popular with businessmen. Traditional atmosphere and antiques make it a homey place. Its airy seaside restaurant is serene and the staff, very friendly; this is a popular dining spot, known for its fine local seafood and traditional Barbadian cuisine.

 HOME AND APARTMENT RENTALS. Cottages, villas, and apartments have long been a part of the vacation life of Barbados, and now the rental of private homes is running a close second. Many are in the Hastings-Worthing area; some are scattered along the St. James coast, and others are in the Parish of St. Peter.

The Barbados Board of Tourism has a complete listing, with prices on and off season included. (see Tourist Information Services in the *Facts at Your Fingertips* chapter).

Private homes for rent range from servant-staffed four-bedroom, three-bath estates with swimming pools, to comfortable seaside cottages that are fully equipped. Rates can be as low as $700 per week for a seaside cottage that accommodates four people, to $3,000 per week for a well-staffed home that can accommodate eight. Contact: *Caribbean Holidays, Inc.*, 711 Third Ave., New York, N.Y. 10017 (tel. 212–573–8900) for their full-color brochure listing available properties on Barbados.

TIME-SHARING CONDOMINIUMS. *Rockley Resort and Beach Club.* Suite # 512, Rockley Resort, Christ Church, Barbados, W.I. Tel. 42–61325. Just five mi. from Bridgetown, these one- and two-bedroom air-conditioned accommodations with balconies or patios make Rockley a perfect island vacation home. There are six swimming pools on the premises, five tennis courts, squash courts, and volleyball and croquet facilities. There are also a health club, a dining room, a cocktail lounge, and a pool bar. Special playground for children and free shuttle bus to the city complete the package.

HOW TO GET AROUND. It's a long taxi ride from Grantley Adams Airport to the hotels at St. James on the western shore. Taxis are not metered, so discuss the fare in advance and make sure whether the rate quoted is in Barbados dollars (BDS) or U.S. Typical fares from the airport to hotels in the Bridgetown orbit (Hilton, Holiday Inn) run BDS $20; to St. James, BDS $35.

Cars are available for rental through *Avis* (tel. 42–61247); *Hertz* (tel. 42–75094); *National* (tel. 42–60603), and several local firms. You must have a valid driver's license, register it with the police at the airport or the Central Police Station, and pay a driver's-registration fee of BDS $10. Rental cars run U.S. $30–35 per day. Pick-up and delivery of rental cars can be arranged at some hotels.

If you choose the island buses, you'll pay BDS 75¢ for the full route or part thereof—in other words, roundtrip fare from the last scheduled stop to Bridgetown is $1.50.

TOURIST INFORMATION SERVICES. The *Barbados Board of Tourism* has its head office on Harbour Road in Hastings (tel. 42–72623). For sources closer to home, see the Tourist Information Services section in the *Facts at Your Fingertips* chapter.

SPECIAL EVENTS. The biggest yearly event on Barbados is the Crop Over Festival, a month-long celebration that begins with a parade through the streets and continues with folk dancing, calypso, and steel-band concerts. Festival King and Queen contests and fancy-dress balls add to the fun. Everyone on the island participates at one time or another from mid-June to mid-July. It ends on Kadooment Day, the first Monday in July.

The Holetown Festival takes place in February. This is a three-day celebration to commemorate the landing of the first settlers to Barbados in 1627. Included are spectacular cultural events, a massive handicrafts display, a variety of entertainment including concerts, water and land sports, and religious services in St. James on the west coast.

The Oistins Fish Festival takes place in early April. Check with the Barbados Board of Tourism (tel. 42–72623) for the exact dates. This is a festive tribute to the fishermen in the quaint and historic fishing community of Oistins in the parish of Christ Church. Flying-fish-boning competitions, all sorts of entertainment, and an open-air bazaar make it all a delight for townspeople and visitors.

TOURS. Any of the following local tour operators will arrange a tour tailored to your interests, from shopping and sightseeing to day trips to neighbor islands. If you hire a taxi, there are fixed rates: BDS $30 for the first hour or any part of it, and a reduced hourly rate after that. Be sure to establish your rate at the beginning. We recommend Freddie Mapp at *Dear's Garage,* Roebuck St., Bridgetown (tel. 42–63200) for reliable and entertaining island tours built around your sightseeing wishes. Others in Bridgetown and St. Michael Parish include: *Barbados Transport Co-Op Society,* tel. 42–86565; *Johnson Stables and Garage Ltd.,* tel. 42–64205; *Paul Foster Travel,* tel. 42–65166; *United Taxi Owners Association,* tel. 42–61496; *Caribbean Safari Tours Ltd.,* tel. 42–75100.

For organized tours at an exceptional rate, *L.E. Williams Tour Co.* offers 80-mile island tours departing at 10:00 A.M. each day from your hotel. The BDS $75 includes lunch at the Atlantis Hotel in Bathsheba and free drinks on the tour, which will take you to Bridgetown, St. James' beach district, Animal Flower Cave, Farley Hill, Cherry Tree Hill, Morgan Lewis Sugar Mill, the east coast, St. John's Church, Sam Lord's Castle and Oistins fishing village, and St. Michael Parish.

The Barbados National Trust has an excellent program of walking tours of historic areas, as well as an island-wide spring and fall Open House Program. Price for open house tours is BDS $6 per day per home or BDS $18 for an inclusive tour which includes transportation, entrance fee, and drinks. The National Trust program allows access to private homes of historic merit which are not normally open to the public. The walking tours are planned in 14 different locations, all over the island, designed to cover five miles in three hours. These guided tours are a particularly good opportunity for photographers. For information on both programs, check local papers or contact the *National Trust Headquarters* at 42–62421.

 PARKS AND GARDENS. Barbados is a brilliant green island no matter where you travel, but its special spots in this category are:

Andromeda Gardens. This favorite place offers everything that a miniature botanical garden should. There are thousands of tropical plants, trees, and shrubs in blossom throughout the year; a lily pond; and an inspired rock garden that is a treat on its own. The gardens overlook the dramatic Bathsheba coast above Tent Bay on Barbados' eastern shore in St. Joseph Parish. Open daily 9:00 A.M.–4:00 P.M., admission U.S. $1.50.

Barclay's Park is located on the scenic and rugged east coast road, north of Bathsheba in St. Joseph Parish, where the beach is pounded by big breakers rolling in from the Atlantic. This is a lovely picnic area, with a restaurant and other facilities in a seafront wooded area. Open daily, no admission charge.

Farley Hill National Park is located in the central northern section of St. Peter Parish and provides a panoramic view of the rugged Scotland District highlands and a sweeping view of the Atlantic coast. Casuarina, mahogany, and whitewood trees, a beautiful avenue of royal palms, and a tropical fruit orchard are among the natural attractions here. The main sight is the ruins of historic Farley Hill House, once owned by Sir Graham Briggs, who entertained royalty here. The building was later destroyed by fire. Open daily until dark; no admission charge.

The Flower Forest is on East Coast Road north of Bathsheba, St. Andrew. Eventually this park will cover 50 acres, but at present only eight have been developed. The collection of tropical flowers and flowering plants is nevertheless a fabulous photographic opportunity. The forest contains more than 100 species, including delicate orchids, ginger lilies, ferns, puff ball trees, and a variety of fruit and palm trees. Another reward is the stunning view of the east coast and Mt. Hillaby. Open daily 9:00 A.M.–4:00 P.M., admission U.S. $1.50.

Folkstone Park, located on the west coast in St. James Parish, encompasses land and sea. The land area has two tennis courts and a children's playground; a Marine Museum which displays the local marine life in diagrams and exhibits is another feature. The Folkstone Underwater Park is a section offshore that has been declared a marine park in which all forms of marine life are protected and no fishing or collecting is permitted. Visitors can snorkel with equipment rented from a nearby facility or view the sea life from a glass-bottom boat. Open Mon.–to Fri. 10:00 A.M.–5:00 P.M.; Sat. & Sun. 10:00 A.M.–6:00 P.M. Admission fee is BDS $1 for adults and 50¢ for children.

Queen's Park, like Farley Hill National Park, has a historic building as its central attraction. This one is King's House, the residence of the commander of the British troops in the British West Indies until 1909. The Parks and Beaches Commission is now attempting to restore the grounds to their original splendor. On the park grounds is one of the largest trees in Barbados, the "boabab" tree, measuring more than 61 ft. across and estimated to be over 1,000 years old. The old King's House has been restored and converted into a theater with an exhibition room on the lower floor. Located here is the "Steel Shed," which houses the Barn Theatre and a restaurant. Open every day 9:00 A.M.–5:00 P.M. No admission charge to the park, which is open during the same hours. Queen's Park is located slightly east of Bridgetown proper—you'll want to take a taxi here, as it's a long walk from Trafalgar Square.

BEACHES. The best beaches are found along the island's leeward west coast in Christ Church, St. Michael, St. James, St. Peter and St. Lucy. Although public access may not always exist, *beaches are public areas.*

Christ Church, which is actually the south coast, has excellent reef-protected beaches safe for swimming and snorkeling. Highlights are in the *St. Lawrence Gap area,* near Southern Palms and Casuarina Cove.

In St. Michael, the best swimming beaches are *Greaves End,* between the Hilton and the Holiday Inn in Aquatic Gap; *Browne's Beach* near the Bay St. fish market; *Brandon's Beach,* two miles west of Paradise Beach Hotel, and Fresh Water Bay near *Paradise Beach.*

In St. James, *Payne's Bay* marks the beginning of a fine west-coast stretch which runs through Sandy Lane Bay north to the Miramar Hotel in north St. James.

In St. Lucy, north of Speightstown, over a mile of uninterrupted sand lies on the beachfront of *Heywoods Barbados resort complex.*

Barbados' east coast offers stunning scenery and some superb sunning beaches, but swimmers must be extremely careful here. The surf is rough on the Atlantic side, and strong currents do exist. The best areas are *just off East Coast Road near Bathsheba;* small beach areas at *Long Pond* and *Tent Bay; Bath,* in St. John Parish; *Crane Beach,* below the clifftop Crane Beach Hotel; *Sam Lord's Castle resort beach;* and *Four Bay* southwest of the Crane Beach Hotel.

PARTICIPANT SPORTS. Barbados is one of those rare Caribbean islands where there is as much to do on land as there is on sea. Play 18 holes of **golf** at the Sandy Lane Club (tel. 42–21405) or nine holes at the Rockley Resort (tel. 42–75890). There are also **squash** courts at Rockley and at the Barbados Squash Club (tel. 42–77193).

Horseback Riding through the rolling hills of Barbados and along its east coast beaches is an exhilarating experience and can be arranged through *Sharon Hill Riding Stables,* tel. 42–50099; *Sunbury Riding Stables,* tel. 42–36780; and *Country Corral Stables,* tel. 42–22401.

Tennis courts lighted for nighttime play as well as day matches exist at most major resorts, and at the *Paragon Tennis Club,* tel. 42–72054. Most courts expect appropriate tennis dress.

Scuba Diving is another exciting offering, still unknown by most visitors. Two excellent diving operations on Barbados' west coast will furnish all certified divers' needs, and offer basic instruction to interested non-divers. *Willie's Watersports,* whose headquarters is at Cunard Paradise Beach Hotel (tel. 42–51060/42 –62273) and *The Dive Shop Ltd.* (Paki's Watersports), located between the Hilton and the Holiday Inn in Aquatic Gap (tel. 42–69947) are our recommended sources.

Deep-Sea Fishing charters can be arranged on the *Jolly Roger* (tel. 42–60767) and *Captain Patch Cruises* (tel. 42–72525).

Water sports, including sailing, waterskiing, and other activities, can be found at many west coast and south coast beach resorts or arranged through Willie's Watersports and The Dive Shop Ltd.

Windsurfing rental equipment and expert instruction are available at the *Barbados Windsurfing Club Hotel* (tel. 42–89095).

SPECTATOR SPORTS. Barbadians claim, "you name it, we play it," from cricket to polo during the various sporting seasons. **Cricket** is the nation's most popular sport, and the local season runs June through December or early January, but the island's best sportsmen participate in international best matches during the rest of the year. Local papers publicize the sites of current matches, and taxi drivers always seem to know how to get there.

Soccer is almost as popular, and the season runs from January through June. Information on local "football" (as it's known here) schedules is available through the Barbados Football Association (tel. 42–44413).

Rugby fans can contact the Barbados Rugby Association at 43–56455 for current Club schedules at the Garrison Savannah.

Polo matches are played at the Polo Club in St. James on Wednesdays and Saturdays during the Sept.–Mar. season, and visitors are welcome for a BDS $5 admission fee. This is a fascinating experience with lots of action and club T-shirts make fine souvenirs.

Horse racing is a very popular sport in this country which has its own Stud Book Authority to insure quality breeding. There are two racing seasons, Jan.–May and July–Nov., with races held every other Saturday at the Garrison Savannah, between Bridgetown and Hastings (Christ Church). Admission to the grandstand is U.S. $6. Information: Tel. 42–63980. Dress on the Garrison is smart casual!

 HISTORIC SITES AND HOUSES. *Government House:* This wonderful old mansion was rented as a residence for the governor in 1702 and eventually purchased by the Barbados government as a permanent home for the governor general. No tours here, but see the home, which is interesting to see for its architecture and layout from the outside.

Villa Nova. Built in 1834, this grand plantation great house has been perfectly preserved and over the years has housed and hosted British royalty. The antiques within are worth the visit, and the beautifully landscaped gardens surrounding it are an added bonus. Located in St. John Parish. Open Mon.–Fri. 10:00 A.M.–4:00 P.M., U.S. $2 admission charge.

Sam Lord's Castle. Located about 45 minutes from Bridgetown in St. Philip Parish on the southeast coast. This impressive mansion, which the privateer Sam Lord built and furnished with the wares of ships he caused to run aground on the east coast, is the most impressive on the island. Just nine rooms, but each replete with paintings by Reynolds; furniture by Chippendale; and china by Spode. Not only can you take a tour through the manse, but you can stay in one of the rooms. They all have four-poster beds and every antique of the era you can imagine. Guided tours Monday through Saturday; U.S. $3.50 per person.

Codrington College. Located in St. John Parish near Consett Bay, this property is now a theological seminary, but was once the home of Christopher Codrington when he was governor of the Leeward Islands in 1698. *St. John's Church* nearby is not only interesting in itself, but has a historic cemetery. One of the stones in the churchyard reads, "Ferinando Paleologus—from ye Imperial Lyne of ye last Christian Emperors of Greece—1655–1678." No admission charge.

St. Nicholas Abbey, located in St. Peter Parish, dates back to 1650 and is said to be one of the few homes built in authentic Jacobean style. The home is dramatically furnished with antiques and English and Barbadian furniture. Open to the public 10:00 A.M. to 3:30 P.M., Mon.–Fri.; U.S. $2.50 entrance fee.

Chase Vault. Christ Church Parish Church is the location of this famous site where one of psychic phenomena's unsolved riddles has puzzled the population since 1820, when coffins of deceased members of the Elliot family mysteriously rearranged and, in some cases, damaged themselves in this sealed vault. Located in Christ Church about seven miles from Bridgetown.

Chalky Mount. A fascinating old village on the coastal road in St. Andrew Parish on the east coast. Pottery has been crafted here for 300 years, and you can find a variety of items for sale.

 MUSEUMS AND GALLERIES. *The Barbados Museum,* the only museum in the country, is situated at the Garrison in St. Michael, 1½ mi. from Bridgetown. It used to be a military prison but today houses a collection of memorabilia tracing the history of Barbados. The museum is also a center for art shows and cultural activities. Open Mon.–Sat., 9:00 A.M.–6:00 P.M., U.S. $2 admission fee.

Several galleries on the island offer the opportunity to buy or just to admire local works. Among them are the *Pelican Art Gallery,* at Pelican Village in St. Michael, and the *Hilton Gallery,* at the Hilton International Hotel.

MUSIC, DANCE AND STAGE. The culture of Barbados provides some of its liveliest entertainment. Most large resort hotels offer at least one floor show each week during the season, featuring acts such as limbo dancing, fire-eating, calypso dancers, and other local entertainers. In recent years, dance has become a vibrant part of Barbadian life, and in an effort to involve visitors in this aspect of local culture, local dance troupes offer regular performances which are advertised in the daily newspapers and island tourist publication.

Special stage shows portraying the culture and heritage of the island offer an entire evening's entertainment for visitors. "A historical celebration of Barbadian culture" describes "1627 And All That . . . ", now in its sixth year at the *Barbados Museum* every Sunday and Thursday. The price includes a tour of the museum, dinner, and the two-act dance show. Both events average U.S. $30 per person.

"The Plantation Tropical Spectacular" is a 90-minute stage presentation featuring a cast of 30 performers. Dancers accompanied by live bands take the audience on a journey through Barbados history from the original settlers through modern Carnival festivities during the Crop Over Festival. The admission price includes a Bajan buffet and entertainment by a steel band during dinner. Located at the *Plantation Restaurant* in St. Lawrence Gap.

Barbados' best known band, "The Merrymen," plays a combination of calypso and "Caribbean pop" known in many overseas countries. This popular group plays each week at the *Plantation Restaurant, Sunset Crest Resort* in St. James and at other hotels. Locations and other details appear in the local press.

Barbados has several excellent steel bands, including the "Barbados Steel Orchestra," one of the best of its kind in the Caribbean. These talented musicians perform each week at select hotels, and, once again, the *Advocate* is the best source of current information.

For theater buffs, there are several local drama groups, including the "Green Room Theater Club" and the "Barbados National Workshop Theatre," that stage a variety of productions throughout the year at local theaters such as the *Combermere,* the *Queen's Park Theatre,* and the *Queen's Park Steel Shed.* Check the daily paper for details and dates.

SHOPPING. Most Bridgetown shopping is department store style, with *Cave Shepherd Y. DeLima, Da Costa & Musson,* and others on Broad St., the island's Fifth Avenue. Always ask if there is an in-bond department. It may take you longer, but the prices will be better. Among the several reliable jewelry shops are *Y. DeLima* (both the Broad St. shop and the branch in Hastings); *Louis I. Bayley* on Broad St. for Rolex watches; *J. Baldini* on Broad St. for Eterna and Longines watches, Brazilian jewelry, and Danish silver; *Correia's* on Price William Henry St. for diamonds, semiprecious stones, cultured pearls, and other items.

Local tailors can make items on the spot. Your hotel can suggest some names or, if their list is short at the time of your visit, contact the Barbados Board of Tourism at Marine House for names.

Among the items made with the visitor in mind are place mats, rugs, handbags, dresses, dolls, and the usual shell jewelry. At *Pelican Village,* the outlet for the local handicraft and home industry, you can watch some of the items in the making. The Village is on the outskirts of town and, in addition to the cluster of conical shops, there is the *Government Handicraft Center.* The shop on the main floor carries items made from pandanus grass—rugs, place mats, bags, etc. Khus khus place mats are popular too. You can also visit the *West Indies Handicrafts* at Pierhead Lane, famous for one-ft.-square fiber mats made into floor coverings.

The best island-designed fabric that we've seen is that sold at *Caribatik Island Fabrics* at the Crane Beach Hotel, a 10-min. drive east of the airport in the direction of Sam Lord's Castle. The fabric is batik dyed in a studio at Falmouth, Jamaica, under the watchful eye of the Chandlers. Items for sale in the Barbados shop include wall hangings, caftans, halter dresses, neckties (made from left-overs), and fabric by the yard, the cotton selling at about $7 per yard. Designs are interesting and colorful.

The *Beach Market* at Heywoods Barbados offers a variety of nice local crafts, including wall hangings, woven placemats, hats, embroidered items, shellcraft, and jewelry. One stall operated by the Barbados Industrial Development Board is particularly interesting, a kind of local craftsmen's co-op. Saturday is the busiest day here.

Another excellent source of Barbadian crafts is *The Best of Barbados* shops, located at the Sandpiper Hotel, Hilton, Skyway Plaza and Sam Lord's Castle. They offer a variety of souvenirs designed and made in Barbados, depicting many areas of Barbadian life.

The *Barbados Museum Shop* has a good selection of books on a variety of Caribbean topics and a small selection of West Indian articles and souvenirs, including old prints of Barbados.

Mall 34, a new shopping area in Bridgetown's central Broad St. district, has about 20 shops with merchandise ranging from duty-free items to local quality crafts.

Shops are usually open from 8:00 A.M. to 4:00 P.M. Mon.–Fri. and Sat. 8:00 A.M.–noon. Weekday banking hours are 8:30 A.M.–1:00 P.M. Mon.–Thurs.; Fri. 8:30 A.M.–1:00 P.M. and 3:00 P.M.–5:30 P.M.

 RESTAURANTS. For a small island, Barbados offers a lot of variety in dining; from sophisticated, pricey haute cuisine to simple local fare of fish and bammie. We won't discourage you from trying any of the continental establishments while you're on Barbados, but you shouldn't leave without sampling some of the best indigenous West Indian dishes in the Caribbean.

Barbados produces a cornucopia of fruits and vegetables, including such exotic tropical ones as soursop, star apple, papaya, and mango. Fresh fruit is abundant on menus here, especially at breakfast.

Flying fish is a Barbadian specialty, and its delicate flavor and texture make it the most popular local seafood. It is usually served lightly breaded and fried with peas 'n rice, a local staple composed of rice cooked in coconut milk with any one of a number of beans, such as pinto, kidney, or pigeon peas. Other local specialties include lobster (the clawless Caribbean kind), dolphin fish, kingfish (wahoo), and curried goat.

Local soups can be a meal in themselves, thick and spicy and unlike the kind you'd find at home. Callaloo soup is a delicious vegetable soup made from a locally grown spinach-like vegetable, okra, crab meat, and seasonings.

The local hot sauce is made from treacherous Scotch Bonnet peppers and is *very* hot—one drop will be plenty, so be forewarned.

Barbados is one of the region's leading producers of rum and its Mount Gay is known as one of the best in the world. The true planter's punch is made with dark rum, fresh lime juice, and simple syrup, topped with fresh nutmeg. Once you try a local rum punch this way you'll discover how the drink tastes best. Banks is a light, refreshing locally brewed beer.

We call dinner at U.S. $25 per person without drinks *Expensive;* $16 to $24 *Moderate;* and anything under that *Inexpensive.* Lunches on the same scale: U.S. $15 and above, *Expensive;* $9–$14 Moderate; and anything below that, *Inexpensive.*

Note: When you arrive in Barbados, try to get a copy of the *Visitor* and the *Advocate* newspapers. Each will have listings in their dining sections of weekly special events, which are numerous during winter season. Some of the best dining buys on Barbados are the lavish buffets and barbecues held at the larger hotels each week. Average cost per person for all-you-can-eat seafood, Barbadian, or a mixture of entrees ranges from U.S. $12 to U.S. $22. Also listed is a host of inexpensive restaurants, too numerous to mention here.

Expensive

Bagatelle Great House. St. Thomas Parish. Tel. 42–02072. This converted plantation home, hidden in the hills, puts you into the colonial life of Barbados. For added charm, it has castle overtones and offers intimate terrace dining at tiny tables for two, or within its stone walls at King Arthur—variety round-tables. Dining is by candlelight, with Continental and local cuisine featured. Expensive wine list to add to the pleasure of dining elegantly. Reservations are a must. AE, MC, V.

La Cage Aux Folles. Payne Bay, St. James. Tel. 43–21203. A very intimate restaurant with seating for only 22, acclaimed as Barbados' true gourmet French restaurant. Its unusual tropical French decor includes a cage of colorful parrots and macaws—hence the establishment's name. You'll notice lots of fresh flowers decorating the room, and enjoy soft background music during dinner. The menu is simple, but the quality of food and manner of preparation merit the size of the tab. Lobster and beef are exceptional here, and a good wine list is available. Reservations a must. Dinner only. AE, MC, V.

Greensleeves. St. Peter. Tel. 42–22275. The poolside setting and elegant touches of fresh flowers, soft music and fine service under the stars make this a very romantic setting. On one of the most extensive menus Barbados offers, you'll find such entrees as frogs legs, duck a l'orange, Steak Diane and other continental offerings. Or choose from 16 appetizers, 10 soups, 22 main courses and a dozen desserts. Dinner only and reservations are a must. AE, MC, V.

Piperade. St. James. Tel. 42–24111 (Glitter Bay Resort). This elegant terrace restaurant, decorated in shades of pink and green, has an interesting menu and one of the most extensive wine lists on the island, including fine vintages from France, Italy, Spain, Germany, and Portugal. Nightly entertainment comple-ments a menu whose unusual shrimp dishes and house specialty Filet de Boeuf Pecheur (seasoned filet topped with mushrooms and curried shrimp) and highly recommended. Reservations a must. Dinner only. AE, MC, V.

Moderate

Brown Sugar. Bridgetown, just behind the Island Inn. Tel. 42–67684. A special place to sample Bajan foods, all prepared according to tradition. Their daily lunch buffet is a bargain, popular with local businessmen because of the wide variety of local specialties and reasonable price. You won't need dinner later! Pleasant colonial garden setting, with dinner served by candlelight on linen-covered tables. AE, MC, V.

Flamboyant. Worthing, Christ Church. Tel. 42–75588. Barbadians favor this spot for evening dining in a cozy and nicely decorated old Barbadian home. Generous portions of local and European dishes—some with German accents. Casual dining for dinner only. AE, MC, V.

Green House. Sandy Beach Hotel, Worthing. Tel. 42–89033. Delectable dining here in an ideal setting—candlelight, soft music, sea breezes. Specialties always include Bajan bouillabaisse, delicately poached fillet of sole, and a sea-food combo. Friday nights are special here, when they feature Bajan Cohoblo-pot, a marvelous outdoor buffet set up at the edge of the beach. The finest samplings of Barbadian cuisine, along with exotic fruits and vegetables. Make reservations. AE, MC, V.

The Hide-away. St. Thomas Parish. Tel. 42–21902. On the other side of the mini-moat and lily pond from Bagatelle Great House, this restaurant is open-air, informal, and fun. Everything from great fondues to lobster for dinner. Snacks and sandwiches are served much later then the place becomes a nightclub that swings until 3:00 A.M. AE, MC, V.

Da Luciano Ristorante Italiano. Highway 7, Hastings. Tel. 42–75518. Clas-sic Italian fare served in the restored living room of an old Victorian home. Excellent food and lots of it. AE, MC, V.

Luigi's. St. Lawrence Gap, Christ Church. Tel. 42–89218. Superb Italian food and lots of it, plus a variety of seafood dishes, all served in a small Neapolitan setting. Open for dinner only. Call for reservations. AE, MC, V.

Ocean View Hotel. Hastings, Christ Church, Tel: 427–7821. This charming, gracious old hotel dining room overlooks the sea on Barbados' south coast. Airy and tropical, the setting is as pleasant as the service is attentive. For years this unpretentious dining spot has been a favorite with Barbadians and visitors for excellent Barbadian dishes, including "sea eggs" (sea urchins) in season. Open for lunch and dinner, casual dining. AE, MC, V.

Pisces. St. Lawrence Gap, Christ Church. Tel. 42–86558. One of the island's best for seafood dinners. The atmosphere is homey and the fare delectable. Open for dinner only. Reservations required. AE, MC, V.

Plantation Restaurant. St. Lawrence, Christ Church. Tel. 42–85048. Weekly Wednesday Bajan Buffets and Tuesday entertainment by The Merrymen are two outstanding attractions for this restaurant which is a renovated old Barbadian residence surrounded by spacious grounds above the Southwinds Resort. Cuisine here is a combination of French and Barbadian, served inside or on the terrace. Casual dining for dinner only. Reservations suggested. AE, MC, V.

The Virginian. Sea View Hotel, Hastings, Christ Church. Tel. 42–77963. Another spot popular with the local crowd for intimate surroundings and some of the island's best values in food. Seafood, shrimp, and steaks are the specialties, all good and courteously served. Dinner only. AE, MC, V.

Witch Doctor. St. Lawrence Gap (across from Pisces), Christ Church. Tel. 42–87856. An attractive restaurant whose interior is a cascade of tropical plants. Traditional Barbadian dishes and fresh local seafood are the specialties here and done very well. Open for dinner only, casual dining, but reservations are suggested, especially in winter season. AE, MC, V.

Inexpensive

Atlantis Restaurant. On the windward coast at Bathsheba. Tel. 42–31526. This is one of the most delightful luncheon spots on the island. Small, friendly, and informal, with tables set out overlooking the sea. Bathsheba is a fishing village, so all the fish specialties have been plucked from the sea earlier in the day. The menu is limited, but not the food. No credit cards.

 NIGHT LIFE AND BARS. There are entertainment and dancing at most of the resort hotels every evening. Swingers will find several places to enjoy until the early hours of the morning. The *Rendezvous Disco* at the Rockley resorts is one of the most popular on the island. *The Hide-away,* adjacent to the Bagatelle Great House, is another favorite.

There are disco sounds nightly at the Hilton's *Flambeau Bar.* Other nightclubs and discos include:

The Carlisle, Bay St., St. Michael. Tel. 42–79772. An open-air disco open nightly, with the added attraction of a U.S. $12 steak special on Mondays.

Belair Jazz Club, Bay St., Bridgetown. Tel. 42–79772. Go late if you want to see this nightspot at its busiest, with a melting pot of people and live jazz nightly.

Alexandra's, Bishop Court, Bridgetown. Patterned after the original Alexandra's in Stockholm, this is one of the more elegant clubs in Barbados, housed in a 170-year-old plantation house. Live music Mon.–Sat.

Unicorn I, Southern Palms Hotel, St. Lawrence, Christ Church. Tel. 42–87171. One of the island's newest discos; intimate but modern decor; popular with the younger crowd. Open nightly at 9:00 P.M.

Club Milliki, Heywoods Barbados Resort, St. Peter. Tel. 42–24900. The club's name is a West African word meaning "welcome," which is the atmosphere. Smart casual dress; cover charge for non-guests. Good music and a lively crowd. Open nightly from 9:00 P.M.

Within 25 years of Barbados' settlement in 1627, legend says, there were over 100 drinking houses on the island. Today, there are over 1,600 "rum shops," about ten per square mile.

A few popular watering holes where you can enjoy good conversation and reasonably priced drinks are: *The Ship Inn,* St. Lawrence Gap, Christ Church, tel. 42–89605; *The Coach House,* Paynes Bay, St. James, tel. 43–21163; *The Windsor Arms,* Hastings, Christ Church, tel. 42–77831; *The Boat Yard,* Bay St., Bridgetown, tel. 42–94806; *Barbados Windsurfing Club,* Maxwell, Christ Church, tel. 42–89095; *The Abbeville Pub,* Rockley, Christ Church, tel. 42–77524; *The Rosebank Inn,* Rockley, Christ Church, tel. 42–77273; *Ye Olde*

English Pub, St. Lawrence Gap, Christ Church, tel. 42–85777; *Boomers,* St. Lawrence Gap, Christ Church, tel. 42–88439.

POSTAGE. Air mail rates to the U.S. and Canada are BDS 65¢ per ½ oz., 45¢ for aerograms and postcards; to the U.K. 76¢ per ½ oz. for letters and 50¢ for aerograms and postcards. To other parts of the West Indies, 50¢ per ½ oz. for letters and 35¢ for aerograms and postcards.

ELECTRIC CURRENT. The current here is 110 volts/50 cycles.

SECURITY. Barbados enjoys a reputation as a friendly island where visitors can expect to encounter few, if any, unpleasant incidents. As in other destinations, you should take the usual precautions to safeguard your valuables and not leave them lying around your room or unattended on the beach. Every island has its share of petty thieves, and there is no reason to tempt fate.

In previous years, Barbados had earned some negative comments in the foreign press about pesky beachboys, but if that plague persists it must have gone underground, as the great swarms of anxious young men eager to please visiting females seem to be gone now. Of course, as the saying goes, "you can get anything you want if you flaunt it."

BONAIRE

by
BARBARA A. CURRIE

Bonaire is a "desert" island both stark and startling. There isn't another inhabited island in the Antilles whose natural attractions compare with the unique ecosystem and magnificent desolation of this island located only fifty miles north of Venezuela.

Within its arid 112 square miles, Bonaire shelters a curious collection of creatures, protected by government-enforced conservation laws and a rugged wilderness landscape. The northern quarter of Bonaire comprises the 13,500-acre national park, Washington/Slagbaii (pronounced Slag-Bay), a true naturalist's Eden. Created in 1978, the park is a sanctuary for over 150 species of migratory birds, including flamingos; yellow-winged parrots, also known as the Bonairean "lora"; Caribbean parakeets; and yellow orioles. Hidden in the forests of finger cactus and plains of divi-divi trees and aloe plants are large iguanas, wild donkeys, and goats. Along the rocky coast is one of the Caribbean's most breathtaking collections of secluded sandy coves, carved into the limestone shoreline by centuries of surf action.

The landscapes and fascinating geological formations vary—from a moonscape and Mohave Desert to "snow and ice" scenes in the southern section's solar saltworks. In the island's center, civilization, in the form of Bonaire's quaint and impeccably tidy capital of Kralendijk, separates the lowland from the gradually rising "highlands" to the north.

Bonaire is much more than a birdwatchers' and naturalists' haven. Offshore congeries of coral gardens and colorful marine life have earned this island a reputation as one of the world's finest scuba-diving destinations. From its limestone coast, extending three miles out and 200 feet down, is one of the Caribbean's richest collections of marine life. It is protected by law as Bonaire Marine Park.

Despite its discovery by divers and naturalists, this quiet Dutch island remains an uncommercial refuge. It resembles sister islands Aruba and Curaçao—the other two-thirds of the Dutch "ABC" island trio—only in its geological origin, and is not everyone's ideal vacation hideaway.

In addition to its unusual natural attractions, Bonaire also enjoys a reputation as a quiet, friendly, and safe island. The official language is Dutch, but Papiamento—a local dialect that's a fusion of Dutch, Spanish, Portuguese, French, and English—is much more popular. Both English and Spanish are widely spoken, however.

Past and Present

Bonaire was discovered in 1499 by Amerigo Vespucci, but the island had been inhabited for centuries by Arawak Indians. Vespucci named the island after the Arawak word "bo-nah," or "low country."

Between 1527 and 1633, the Spaniards attempted to colonize the island. However, in 1634, the Dutch occupied Curaçao and two years later laid claim to neighbor Bonaire, in order to use the ABC islands as a military base against the Spanish forces.

The Dutch West India company began to develop Bonaire in 1639 and salt production, corn planting, and stock breeding were introduced. For the next 160 years, the Dutch West India company ran this island, importing about 100 slaves from Africa to work the salt ponds. Bonaire's present population of 9,200 is a mixture of Dutch, African, and Indian descent.

The British occupied the island briefly during the early 1800s, but by 1816 the Dutch had regained control and set up a government plantation system based on Brasil wood, aloe vera, and other commercial crops. After slavery was abolished in 1863, government operations proved unprofitable and the island was divided and sold.

A severe economic recession for the next sixty years, forced many Bonaireans to migrate to Aruba and Curaçao to work the oil industry. But in the 1950s Bonaire's economy began to recover. The island's first hotel opened in 1951, and tourism was introduced; the salt pans, modernized to use solar energy, became one of the most successful plants in the world; and an enlarged power plant and 8,100-foot runway at Bonaire's airport assured the island's future development.

Throughout these decades of rapid progress, the people of Bonaire have been constantly concerned about protecting their unique and fragile ecology. Bonaire was the first of the Netherlands Antilles to enact strict environmental legislation, incorporating the surrounding reef system into Bonaire Marine Park and reserving thousands of acres of wilderness as wildlife sanctuary and flamingo preserve.

As one of the ABC islands of the Netherlands Antilles (an autonomous part of the Kingdom of the Netherlands), Bonaire is governed by the mother country, Holland. Each island has its own locally elected legislative council and executive council, called an island council. The twenty-two-member Parliament, or Staten, is made up of representatives from all island councils, and is based in Willemstad, Curaçao. A governor appointed by the Queen of the Netherlands represents the Crown, and Bonaire has a lieutenant governor, who resides in Kralendijk, the island's capital.

Political plans agreed to in the spring of 1983 include Aruba's separation from its sister ABC islands in 1986, and the independence of the entire group in 1996.

EXPLORING BONAIRE

Bonaire's quaint and tidy capital of Kralendijk, located about five minutes north of Flamingo Airport on the island's central west coast, is the logical starting point for a tour of the island, which is twenty-four miles long and three to seven miles wide. The harborfront town is a short walk from the Carib Inn and Flamingo Beach Hotel, which lie to the south along J.A. Abraham Boulevard, the road that leads from the airport into Kralendijk. Bonaire Beach Hotel and Habitat are about half a mile north of Kralendijk along the north coastal road.

The widely distributed Bonaire Holiday Guide published on the island contains a detailed map of the capital, which is a useful reference source for a walking tour. Shopping is limited in Kralendijk, but you will find some interesting local handicrafts at the Fundashon Arts Indistria Bonariano just south of town on J.A. Abraham Boulevard. This road becomes Breedestraat (Broad Street), Kralendijk's main thoroughfare for small department stores, boutiques, restaurants, and a few duty-free and jewelry stores. The Bonaire Tourist Bureau and the post office are also located on Breedestraat, toward the center of town. Crossing Breedestraat, at the intersection opposite Spritzer & Fuhrmann duty-free, is Kerkweg Street, which is the location of several supermarkets, the ALM ticket office, and a handful of snack shops and better restaurants, including Bistro Des Amis and Rendezvous.

Parallel to Breedestraat, beginning immediately after the Flamingo Beach Hotel, is the narrow waterfront avenue of C.F.B. Hellmundweg. It leads to South Pier and North Pier (customs is nearby), and the most picturesque part of Kralendijk. Several old government buildings, banks, and commercial structures along the waterfront have been attentively restored or freshly painted and preserved in the traditional Dutch architectural style. Along this avenue is an old fort, complete with cannons aimed at the harbor, and a square with fragrant mimosa trees sheltering a plaque commemorating the 1944 visit of Eleanor Roosevelt.

The town fish market remotely resembles a miniature Greek temple just north of North Pier. Local fishermen moor their small wooden skiffs on the shoreline here and unload their early-morning hauls before noon each day, offering fresh snapper, dolphin, and wahoo, nearby is a produce market.

From Kralendijk two tours are possible, each requiring from a half day to a full day or more, depending on how seriously you take your photography—and how many hours you want to spend snorkeling or beachcombing along the coast. For the south tour, take J.A. Abraham Boulevard out of Kralendijk, past the Flamingo Beach Hotel.

South Bonaire

Drive south along the South Scenic Route. One of the first sights you'll see on this excursion is the five hundred-foot Trans World Radio antenna, a 500,000-watt Protestant missionary station, established in 1954, that now has a worldwide audience.

A little farther south is the sprawling solar saltworks, whose "snow-drifts" are really the signs of a thriving salt industry operated by the Antilles International Salt Company. These "ponds" are harvested twice a year and serve as both a major source of income for the island and the breeding and roosting ground for the famous flock of wild flamingos.

A word of advice: if you want to witness the colorful exodus of the birds, plan to arrive just before sunset. Visitors are NOT permitted to enter the Pekel Meer breeding sanctuary, part of the solar saltworks area, but if your timing is right you'll see the legendary pink cloud on the wing at sunset over the salt ponds.

Just beyond the salt pans is an area barren in appearance but rich in history. Its local name is Rode Pan. Here you'll find two groups of tiny slave huts, built of stone in 1850 to house slaves imported from Africa to work the pans, and three thirty-foot obelisks built in 1838 to guide to port the ships coming to load salt. The huts have been restored to their nineteenth-century condition, complete with thatched-cane roofs. Note: Islanders will tell you that this area is the best viewing point for the sunset flight of the flamingos departing for Venezuela.

Continuing on, you'll encounter the Willemstoren, the island's first lighthouse, built in 1837. To the north are two of Bonaire's most picturesque spots, Sorobon Beach and Boca Cai at Lac Bay. Offshore you'll find good snorkeling, and along the shore you'll see pink-and-white hills of conch shells bleached by the sun. Cai is actually a fishing village, and it's best to see this settlement on Sunday, when many of the islanders turn out for a beach picnic on this beautiful stretch of sand. There's even a small island "restaurant" that serves strictly local seafood and cold beer.

North Bonaire

Heading north from Kralendijk, you'll follow Breedestraat, which becomes the North Scenic Route on the outskirts of town. Continue along the coast about half a mile past the marina, Bonaire Beach Hotel and Casino, and the Habitat resort. If you're planning a serious expedition into Washington/Slagbaii National Park on the island's northern section, plan on *at least* a full day. The dramatic scenery you'll encounter en route and inside the park limits will demand constant photo stops, and an unhurried tour of the park's three "plantations" takes time as well (Washington, Slagbaii, and the western area of Brasilia).

Touring Tip: Rent a four-wheel-drive vehicle—the park's rocky dirt roads are winding and rough on conventional vehicles.

The park will be your ultimate destination on the North Scenic Route tour, and as you head north, you'll see a very different landscape as the elevation rises along the coast, which offers several excellent panoramas for photographers. About fifteen minutes north of the Bonaire Beach Hotel is a site called "1,000 Steps," marked by a lime-stone staircase carved into the cliff to the left of the road. There are

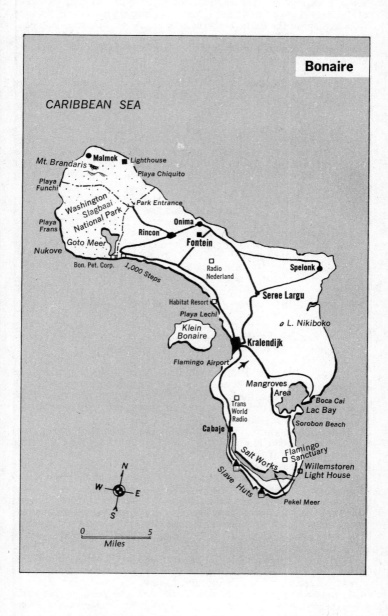

Bonaire

CARIBBEAN SEA

Mt. Brandaris
Malmok
Lighthouse
Playa Chiquito
Playa Funchi
Washington Slagbaai National Park
Park Entrance
Playa Frans
Onima
Rincon
Fontein
Nukove
Goto Meer
Bon. Pet. Corp.
1,000 Steps
Radio Nederland
Spelonk
Seree Largu
Habitat Resort
Playa Lechi
L. Nikiboko
Klein Bonaire
Kralendijk
Flamingo Airport
Mangroves Area
Boca Cai
Lac Bay
Trans World Radio
Sorobon Beach
Cabaje
Flamingo Sanctuary
Salt Works
Willemstoren Light House
Slave Huts
Pekel Meer

N
W E
S

0   5
Miles

actually sixty-seven steps leading down to a small cove with excellent offshore snorkeling and diving. (One-way traffic begins a short distance from here, after the Radio Nederland headquarters building. You cannot come back this way to reach Kralendijk, but must follow the cross-island road to Rincon and the main entrance of Washington/Slagbaii, and return via the main road through the center of Bonaire.)

As you continue along the last mile of the North Scenic Route, you'll see the storage-tank facilities of Bonaire Petroleum Corporation to the north. The road to Rincon and Washington/Slagbaii Park is clearly marked; if you continue north, you'll reach an unpaved road leading around the BPC facilities, which are fenced in, and continuing into the Brasilia section of the national park. The road does not connect with the other two park sections, but leads to two beautiful locations; Nukove, a secluded cove with superb snorkeling just south of Playa Frans; and a large brackish inland lake, which is the occasional roost of a large flock of flamingos. These sites are located just off the road, which ends at Playa Frans. To return to the entrance to the Brasilia section, you must backtrack along the same cactus-lined road.

On your left on the cross-island road you'll see Goto Meer, one of the largest inland brackish lakes, where you'll almost certainly see flamingos feeding in the shallows.

The entrance to Washington/Slagbaii National Park is on the northeastern side of Bonaire, and the park is open from 8:00 A.M. until 5:00 P.M., with a $1.50 per person admission charge. You will receive a map and instructions from the park attendant on touring the area, whose dirt roads are clearly marked with scenic-route directional signposts and location names. The park is sprawling and has over forty miles of sidetrips to coastal coves and inland vantage points, salinas and birdwatching points. We strongly recommend that you study the map carefully and buy a copy of the Netherlands Antilles National Parks Foundation guidebook to the park at the entrance gate.

NOTE: Motorcycles and two-wheeled vehicles of any kind are not permitted in the park. There are no concessions or snack bars beyond the gate, so visitors are advised to bring along a thermos or cooler with drinks. The entire park area is a forest of tall finger cactus and dense bush, with startling rock formations and rugged hills. This is desert and can be very hot at midday.

The highest point on Bonaire, Mount Brandaris, with an elevation of 784 feet, is located in the north-central part of the park. There is no route to the top of this peak.

When you leave the park and head south, you'll reach a fork in the unpaved road. The route to the left will take you along the coast to Boca Onima, where you'll see a small signpost marking the way to a thirty-foot-high limestone ledge. Below, the overhang of the ledge juts out like a partially formed cave entrance; you'll see designs and symbols inscribed in faded red on the limestone that are believed to have been left by the Arawak Indians centuries ago. Other inscriptions can be seen at Fontein on a similar geological structure.

This same fork leads into the paved main road, which will take you south past Seroe Largu, an excellent elevated site for viewing the entire area of Kralendijk and the southwest coast.

If you take the road to the right at the fork south of the park, you'll pass through Rincón—a collection of well-kept pastel-colored cottages and century-old buildings that is Bonaire's oldest village—and on to a well-paved road leading back into Kralendijk. Or, you can follow the mid-town sign to another paved road, which veers to the left and trace the central and southeast coast until it becomes a dirt road leading to Spelonk and the rugged eastern most point of Bonaire. This road curves back into the road leading to Kralendijk.

Klein Bonaire

This 1,500-acre island located a half-mile off of Kralendijk is flat, rocky, uninhabited—and beautiful. Its untouched beach and the coral gardens surrounding it make it a very popular picnic spot. Day trips can be arranged through your hotel.

PRACTICAL INFORMATION FOR BONAIRE

FACTS AND FIGURES. Bonaire is the second largest of the six Netherlands Antilles islands, which include Aruba, Bonaire, Curaçao, St. Maarten, Saba, and St. Eustatius. It is located 50 miles north of Venezuela and 1,720 miles south of New York, away from the hurricane belt of the Caribbean.

Volcanic in origin, Bonaire occupies 112 square miles and is an arid island whose highest elevation is Brandaris Hill, 784 ft. Cactus, scrub brush, and divi trees grow in a terrain very similar to that of desert regions of the southwest U.S. and the Baja peninsula. There are large solar salt ponds on the southern part of the island.

Bonaire's population of 9,200 is of Dutch and West Indian descent and although the official language is Dutch, most islanders speak Papiamento, a difficult dialect for visitors to understand. It combines Spanish, Portuguese, Dutch, English, and French with a profusion of local idioms. English and Spanish are widely spoken on the island, however.

Although Bonaire receives only 22 inches of rainfall per year, drinking water is available at all resorts, which have supplies of distilled and desalinated water for guests. The year-round climate is very tropical, with sunshine and occasionally stiff (16 mph) breezes from the southeast. The average land temperature is 82 degrees F and the water temperature averages 80 degrees.

The capital and main shopping district is Kralendijk, located on the island's central west coast. Directly offshore is the 1,500-acre, flat, rocky, and uninhabited island of Klein Bonaire.

Bonaire operates year-round on Atlantic standard time, one hour ahead of eastern standard time.

WHEN TO GO. Bonaire is blessed with a year-round fine climate. While its arid nature may be a problem for those who live there, it's ideal for visitors, who can be assured of good weather almost any day they arrive. Winter months will be breezier but in general you can plan to go to Bonaire during any month and expect sunshine and clear seas. The average temperature is 80°. As in the other Caribbean destinations, hotel and airline rates are dramatically reduced during summer season, April 15–Dec. 1.

PASSPORTS AND VISAS. U.S. and Canadian citizens need only some proof of identity, such as a passport, birth certificate, or voter's registration card. A passport is not necessary for British citizens; however, they must have a "British Visitor's" passport, available from any post office. Passports are required of all other visitors. In addition, all visitors to the island must hold a return or ongoing ticket.

MONEY. The currency of the Netherlands Antilles is the NA florin, or guilder. The official rate at which banks accept U.S. dollars is NAf 1.77; traveler's checks at NAf 1.79. The rate of exchange at shops and hotels ranges from 1.75 to 1.80. The guilder is divided into 100 cents and there are coins of 1 cent, 2 ½, 5, 10, and 25 cents as well as 1- and 2 ½-guilder coins. Paper money is issued in denominations of 1, 2 ½, 5, 10, 25, 50, 100, 250, and 500 guilders.

WHAT WILL IT COST?

A typical day on Bonaire in season for two persons will run:

	U.S.$
Hotel accommodations	$90
Breakfast and dinner at hotel or in-town restaurant	60
Luncheon at moderate restaurant	15
Tips or service charge at the restaurants; tax and service charge at the hotel	15
One-day sightseeing by taxi or rental car	45
Total	$225

HOW TO GET THERE. By air. *American* and *Eastern* offer daily flights from New York to Curaçao and Aruba, with connecting service to Bonaire via *ALM*. Eastern and ALM also offer daily jet service from Miami to Curaçao and Aruba, with connecting service via ALM. From Miami, ALM offers direct service to Bonaire once a week. ALM also has direct service to Curaçao and Aruba from other Caribbean spots including San Juan, St. Maarten, St. Kitts, and Trinidad.

AIRPORT TAX AND OTHER CHARGES. You'll pay a straight 15% on your hotel bill, which breaks down to a 10% service charge for gratuities, plus a 5% government tax. There is an airport departure tax of U.S. $5.75.

TELEPHONES AND EMERGENCY NUMBERS. To call direct from the U.S., dial 011–599–7 plus the number on Bonaire. Within Bonaire, telephones are located only at hotel front desks or the central office in Kralendijk. In an emergency, dial 0 for the operator.

HOTELS. There are just a handful of hotels on Bonaire, all with an emphasis on the sea. Water-sports centers and dive shops can be found at each property, with choices of everything from boating to snorkeling and scuba diving. We call $70 and up *Expensive* and anything below that *Moderate*.

Bonaire Beach Hotel and Casino. *Expensive.* Kralendijk. Tel. 8448; in U.S. (800) 526–2370 or (201) 566–8866. Formerly the Hotel Bonaire and Casino, the island's largest hotel is now managed by the British and has undergone a refurbishing program. Spread across 12 acres and encompassing a 600-ft. beach called Playa Leche, the property has 145 air-conditioned rooms with private bath, a dining room, cocktail lounge, coffee shop, and nighly entertainment. Outdoor attractions include tennis courts, beach bar, and casino; open from 6 P.M. until 3 A.M. For divers, the Bonaire Scuba Center offers complete scuba and underwater photography center and special packages which include diving and free use of all water-sports equipment. Non-divers can rent sunfish, windsurfers, and snorkeling equipment.

Flamingo Beach Hotel. *Expensive.* Bonaire. Tel. 8285; in U.S. Box 686, Ithaca, NY 14850. Tel. (800) 252–6232 in NY and (800) 847–7198 elsewhere. All that a small resort hotel should be. Right on the beach with accommodations in sea-front rooms or in individual cottages. Now has 110 rooms, freshwater pool, Jacuzzi, beach bar, small boutique, and large area for terrace dining overlooking the sea. The hotel's two restaurants include an informal seaside restaurant and the slightly more formal *Chibi Chibi,* named after the local birds of the same name. KiBoKe Pakus, the hotel's unusual boutique, reflects the impeccable taste of Alice Hughes; her husband Peter operates Dive Bonaire, the best-equipped scuba and underwater photo center on Bonaire and one of the finest in the Caribbean. Last year, the *Flamingo Beach* opened the island's only casino, a small, delightful diversion adjacent to the hotel, and it has been dubbed the "world's only barefoot casino." While the staff may be in black tie, you can dress in shorts and other island garb.

Carib Inn. *Inexpensive.* Box 68, Bonaire. Tel. 8819. This friendly, seven-room seaside resort is run with very personal attention by 10-year residents Bruce and Liz Bowker. Most of the guests are divers, and Bruce operates a small, full-service dive operation at the resort, which offers daily dive trips and scuba lessons on request. All rooms have refrigerator and electric kettle; 3 are complete efficiency apartments. One of Bonaire's best accommodation buys, walking distance to town; pool and small beach at resort. No restaurant; outdoor facilities, in addition to the dive shop, include a small beach. Very reasonable rates, even in season.

Habitat. *Moderate.* Bonaire. Tel. 8290. With only 19 air-conditioned rooms, the Habitat is more like a guesthouse for dedicated divers than a hotel. It is also the domain of a colorful long-time Bonaire resident, Captain Don Stewart. The nine two-bedroom cottages have kitchenettes and patios, and there are a limited number of small single rooms. The "out-island" ambience of this seaside resort is enhanced by hammocks slung between the trees. A complete dive center, Aquaventures, provides divers with everything they need, including photo supplies and services. Habitat is also the home of Dee Scarr's Touch the Sea program, an unusual diving experience. Dee leads reef trips for small groups to see her tamed sea creatures offshore.

HOME AND APARTMENT RENTALS. Bachelor's Beach Apartments. Tel. U.S. (202) 244–5046. Located on the waterfront, on Bonaire's south scenic route, just a mile from the airport. Completely furnished, with full kitchens, fine ocean view and diving right offshore. **Bonaire Beach Bungalows.** Box 155, Bonaire. Tel. 011–599–78585. These 7 two-bedroom, air-conditioned villas are just 15 feet from the ocean and fully furnished with electric kitchen; large patio area; diving arranged through local operators. Five minutes from Kralendijk. **Bonaire Sunset Villas.** Box 115, Bonaire. Tel. 011–599–78291. This operation offers a variety of one- and two-bedroom cottages and two- and four-bedroom houses with waterfront locations, available for daily, weekly, or monthly rentals.

HOW TO GET AROUND. Walk in town and take a taxi elsewhere. You can rent a car for $35–$45 per day there. *Avis* (tel. 8310) has offices at the airport, at the Flamingo Beach Hotel, and at the Hotel Bonaire. Other firms are *Boncar* (Budget) (tel. 8300), which also has offices at these locations, or *Erkar* (N.V.), a local firm (tel. 8536). To get from the capital to the airport by taxi costs about $4.50, and about $10 to the hotels.

TOURIST INFORMATION SERVICES. The *Bonaire Government Tourist Board* has its main office at # 1 Breedestraat in Kralendijk (tel. 8322). For sources closer to home, see the Tourist Information Services section in the *Facts at Your Fingertips* chapter.

SPECIAL EVENTS. The biggest events on Bonaire are its **February** Carnival celebrations, with dancing and parades in the streets, and Annual International Sailing Regatta in **October,** and the Queen's Birthday on **April** 30. In celebration of Her Majesty's day, the lieutenant governor hosts a cocktail reception at his home and everyone is invited (tourists too).

TOURS. The Bonaire Trading Company is the oldest established tour service on the island, operating as *Bonaire Sightseeing Tours.* They offer a complete island tour (which can be spread over two days) for $16, or individual north and south island tours for $10 each per person. Each tour lasts about two hours. (tel. 8300). Other tour services are available through *Avis Flamingo Tours,* with representatives at the airport; Flamingo Beach Hotel; Bonaire Beach Hotel; and *Achie Tours* (tel. 8630).

PARKS AND GARDENS. *Bonaire Marine Park:* Roughly the entire coastline around Bonaire and Klein Bonaire, from the highwater tidemark down to 200 ft. "Marine park" means this entire area is protected, and basic park rules prohibit spearfishing; taking of any shells or coral, alive or dead, from the reefs; damaging the reefs by stepping on or anchoring on coral or littering the area. *Swimming, diving and snorkeling are permitted.* This island's coral reefs are populated by one of the Caribbean's most colorful collections of marine creatures. Visibility, year-round, ranges from 70 to 100 ft., and there are more than 50 easily accessible dive sites and numerous shallow locations perfect for snorkelers.

Washington/Slagbaii National Park. This 13,500-acre game preserve is the first of its kind in the Netherlands Antilles and occupies almost all the northwestern portion of the Island. The park is open seven days a week from 8:00 A.M. to 5:00 P.M. Entrance fee is $1.50 per person, children under 15 no charge. The best bird-watching time is in the morning. No hunting, fishing, or camping allowed. Visitors are requested not to frighten the birds or animals and not to damage or remove anything from the grounds. Two routes are laid out through the park: a 15-mi. "short" route and a 22-mi. "long" route, marked by yellow and green arrows respectively. As befits a wilderness sanctuary the roads are a bit rugged.

BEACHES. Bonaire has beaches ranging from white to pink sand, many of them hideaways you'll find on your own. The uninhabited island of *Klein Bonaire* is a tiny treasure to enjoy and to picnic on. Arrangements for a day away can be made through most hotels and dive operations. Other special beaches are Sorobon Beach at Lac Bay.

There are many beaches along Bonaire's west coast, which is the leeward side of the island and lacks the strong surf and currents of the eastern side. Swimmers will find they prefer this side of the island, and should practice caution when attempting to swim on the windward coast.

PARTICIPANT SPORTS. Deep-sea fishing, snorkeling, scuba diving, sailing, and **windsurfing** can be arranged through *Dive Bonaire* at the Flamingo Beach Hotel (tel. 8285), the *Bonaire Scuba Center* at the Bonaire Beach Hotel (tel. 8448); *Aquaventures* at the Habitat (tel. 8290), and the Carib Inn (tel. 8819).

HISTORIC SITES. Historic island attractions include the *Salt Pans* in the south and the *slave huts* in the same area. Near the oldest village on the island (Rincón), at Boca Onima and Fontein, you'll find the *Indian inscriptions* that are more than 500 years old on overhanging limestone ridges. The *Willemstoren*, built in 1837, is Bonaire's oldest lighthouse.

MUSEUMS AND GALLERIES. For something really different, contact the studio at the *Radio Nederland Wereldomroep* in Kralendijk (tel. 8472) and make arrangements to see their fascinating two-hour sight-and-sound presentation of radio and electronic artifacts from the early 20th century period, when "progress was introduced" to Bonaire.

MUSIC, DANCE, AND STAGE. Folklore dance and music groups perform occasionally on Bonaire, and concerts are held by other organizations. If you're curious about local culture and arts, contact the Cultural Center, tel. 8558.

SHOPPING. Bonaire is not a shopping isle, but for the limited browsing and buying you may be doing, there are small branches of *Spirtzer and Fuhrmann* downtown and at the Bonaire Beach Hotel, with duty-free buys on china, silver, and crystal. The *Ki Bo Ke Pakus* (What do you want?) shop at the Flamingo Beach Hotel has interesting batik, dashikis, and island-made jewelry.

In Kralendijk, you can find quality gold and precious gemstone jewelry and Rolex, Seiko, and Ebel watches at *Littman Jewelers* on Breedestraat, opposite the Tourist Board office. Handicrafted products in wood, leather, and sterling can be found at *Ayulla*, which has a selection of crafts from many Latin American countries as well; *Fundashon Arte Industria Bonairiano*, an arts-and-crafts center on J.A. Abraham Blvd., offers locally made items fashioned of black coral, goat skin, wood, and stained glass. *Heit's*, on Kaya Bonaire on the waterfront, stocks an interesting variety of souvenirs and jewelry, film, and camera supplies. Locally made ceramics can be found at *MOR-ANG Ceramics* on J.A. Abraham Blvd., just north of Flamingo Beach.

RESTAURANTS. Flamingo Beach offers a different menu each night (Indonesian rijsttafel on Tuesday; French fare with wine on Wednesday; an old-fashioned barbecue with a calypso band on Saturday); and the Bonaire Beach Hotel favors Continental and West Indian cuisine with a variety of both on the menu each night.

Do try the Kralendijk restaurants, not only for the food, but for the opportunity to meet Bonarians. We call $22 per person *Expensive;* $15–$22 *Moderate;* and below that *Inexpensive* for dinner.

Beef Eater. *Moderate.* 3 Breedestraat. Tel. 8081. This small, English-run restaurant offers consistently superior quality continental cuisine and excellent, fresh local seafood. Good service, memorable dining. Open Monday through Saturday for dinner only, and reservations are a must. AE.

Bistro Des Amis. *Expensive.* 1 Kerweg. Tel. 8003. The finest you'll find in French cuisine on this Dutch isle, with escargots and coquille St. Jacques among the house specialties. Excellent wine selection, and a nice bar for sipping same as you wait. Open for dinner only, daily except Monday. Reservations necessary. AE, MC, V.

China Garden. *Moderate.* Breedestraat. Tel. 8480. Curried dishes and Chinese specialties we found disappointing and overpriced for quality this year. Lunch and dinner daily except Tuesday. No reservations needed. No credit cards.

Den Laman Aquarium Bar & Restaurant. *Expensive.* Tel. 8955. Seaside restaurant north of town specializing in local seafood. While you wait, you can watch the live entertainment in the 9,000-gal. aquarium, which has a technicolor array of denizens of the deep you may never have seen. Specialties include charbroiled butterfly conch, red snapper Creole, and their homemade cheesecake. Open for dinner only from Wednesday through Saturday. Reservations a must. AE, MC, V.

Mona Lisa Bar & Restaurant. *Moderate.* Downtown. Tel. 8308. Sounds Italian, but it's really as Dutch as can be. Under new management from Holland, this small café offers superb Dutch, local, and Indonesian dishes at some of Bonaire's best prices. Unusual items include Bami Goreng, sate, and Java honden Portie. Open daily except Wed. for breakfast, lunch, and dinner. No credit cards.

Zeezicht Bar & Restaurant. *Expensive.* The name translated means "sea view," and this restaurant on the harbor of the capital city has it all. Tel. 8434. You can dine on the terrace as you watch the sunset, or in the air-conditioned, indoor dining room. Start with their oysters in hot green sauce; try the local freshcaught fish, which make up the bouillabaisse; then their platter, which is a combination of fried filet of fish, oysters, lobster, shrimp, and conch. Open for lunch and dinner daily. No credit cards.

The Rendezvous. *Moderate.* Kerkweg in Kralendijk. Tel. 8454. Next to Maduro & Curiel's Bank, this is a convenient resting place for shoppers right downtown. Open from 9:00 A.M. until 11:00 P.M. for pastries, expresso, and light refreshments—best for people-watching on the shaded terrace. Full lunch and dinner menus offering excellent variety of selections, including steaks and local seafood. Cafe atmosphere and casual dress. Closed Sunday mornings only. AE.

Great China, 14 Breedestraat. Tel. 8886. Don't overlook this tiny restaurant in town; it offers an extensive menu of Chinese and local dishes of superior quality at very reasonable prices. Open daily except Sun. from 11:30 A.M. until 10 P.M. V, MC.

NIGHT LIFE AND BARS. The *E Wowo* (means "the eye" in Papiamento) is the only place on the island to be for dancing after dark. It's a well-designed club on the second floor of one of the oldest Dutch Colonial buildings on the island. There is a small entry fee, which varies according to season, but if you want to swing until dawn this is the place. You should also check with the Flamingo Beach Hotel and Bonaire Beach Hotel, which schedule entertainment several nights a week. The *Dryfellars Divers' Bar,* located on the waterfront on Helmundweg, within walking distance of Flamingo Beach, is a charming bar full of atmosphere, run by a young Dutch couple who welcome visitors like friends. Low-priced drinks, good snacks and sandwiches and a favorite roost of locals. Worth several stops.

CASINOS. Bonaire has two casinos, one at Flamingo Beach Hotel and one at Bonaire Beach Hotel. Both open at 6 P.M.

POSTAGE. Airmail postage rates to the U.S. are NAf. 1.00 for letters and NAf .65 for postcards; to Canada, NAf 1.10 for letters and NAf .70 for postcards; to the U.K., NAf 1.25 for letters and NAf .80 for postcards.

ELECTRIC CURRENT. The current here is 127 volts on 50 cycles. This can cause some appliances to blow out, so you should check with your hotel or apartment manager about the best method for preventing problems. Normally, you can prevent overheating by using small appliances only for short periods of time.

SECURITY. Bonaire is one of the friendliest and least crime-plagued of the Caribbean islands. Visitors should take the normal precautions about securing money, credit cards, jewelry, and other valuables simply to avoid tempting the few petty thieves who inevitably inhabit any place catering to vacationers.

THE BRITISH VIRGIN ISLANDS

by
TONY TEDESCHI

Tony Tedeschi is a New York-based writer and photographer. His credits include Penthouse, Holiday, American Way, *and dozens of other magazines and newspapers around the country.*

The difference in these islands is a matter of positioning, not only in the good fortune of their overall placement in the eastern Caribbean, but in the way the islands lie in relation to each other. Like dice tossed from a gambler's cup, they have managed to arrange themselves, for the most part, in two parallel lines running from northeast to southwest, with a channel in between. On the one side are Tortola, Beef Island, Guana, the Camonoes, and Scrub; on the other, Norman, Peter, Salt, Cooper, Ginger, Fallen Jerusalem, and Virgin Gorda. Between is the Sir Francis Drake Channel. Anegada lies off to the north and Jost Van Dyke is due west of Tortola.

The formation of the principal islands protects the channel from the sea, allowing for some of the most beautiful sailing waters found anywhere on earth—and therein lies the unique personality of "the B.V.I." (British Virgin Islands). With the founding of The Moorings in 1969, yacht chartering became the most popular vacation activity in the B.V.I., and today several hundred yachts ply these waters with a diverse collection of sailors from the serious to the first-timers, who can charter with a captain and crew. At any given time, about half the islands' visitors are aboard the yachts, which limits demand for land-based facilities, keeps development in check, and allows the islands to maintain their natural beauty.

In the B.V.I., the sunrises are yellow, blue, and beautiful; the sunsets are orange, purple, and staggering. The breeze blows through the channel most of the time and the water is all the colors of blue from pale aquamarine to deep royal. There are dozens of white, sandy beaches and secluded anchorages, and the places to stay are among the most pleasant in the Caribbean. These islands are *the* place to leave your frenetic pace behind and let the sky and the sea help you unwind.

Past and Present

The islands were discovered by Columbus at the turn of the fifteenth century, but Spain did little about them. The first appearance of the British was in 1628, but the Dutch from nearby St. Maarten moved in—with little regard to title—and began the lucrative sugar production for which they would become famous throughout the Caribbean. Thus the area became part of the rich rum-sugar-slave triangle between the Caribbean, the colonies to the north, and Africa. For the next hundred years, the area was a watery jousting ground for the British, French, Dutch, Danes, Spaniards, and the privateers who swore allegiance to no crown.

In 1773, the islands were granted a charter by the British crown and they have been a stable part of the British Empire ever since. A planter class, built around slave labor, developed in the eighteenth century and trade with the new American colonies was a mainstay of the economy. With the emancipation of the slaves in 1834, the sugar-based economy fell apart and the area remained somewhat depressed until the 1960s when visitors began flocking to the islands.

Tourism, now recognized as the key to the economic livelihood of the B.V.I., is encouraged and developed with a strict eye toward maintaining the natural beauty of the area. The present chief minister is a former head of the tourist board and his government is committed to the intelligently planned development of the tourism plant.

EXPLORING THE BRITISH VIRGIN ISLANDS

Tortola, the principal island of the British Virgins, is also the only island where you can do any real exploring by land. It is on Tortola that most of the islands' 12,000 people live, most in three small towns: East End, West End, and Road Town, the capital. Taking the day to tour Tortola, however, is worth the trip—if your stomach can stand some precipitous climbs in the mountains that form the center of the island. Since you'll want to sample the beaches as you explore, come equipped with bathing suit, cover-up, the requisite towels and lotions—and don't forget your camera. Do forget to bring lunch; there are some wonderful places to eat along your route.

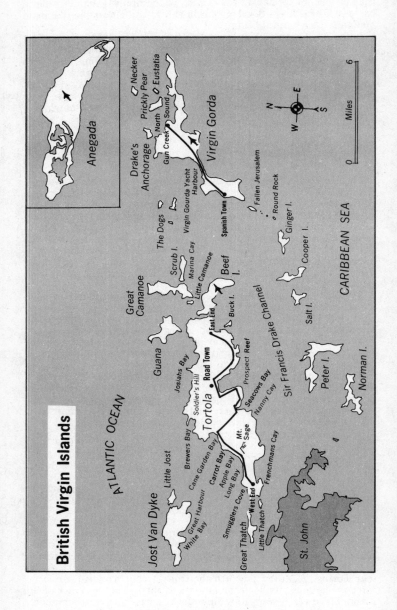

British Virgin Islands

Road Town to West End, Tortola

Head out from Road Town and travel southwest along the shore, where there are some beautiful vistas just beyond Prospect Reef at Sea Cows Bay. Here the road winds right down to the water's edge, from which you'll see Peter and Norman islands in the distance across the channel.

Stop off at Nanny Cay, a newly developed marine center—one of the largest in the Caribbean—and take a look at some of the beautiful yachts that tie up here. It may whet your appetite for some sailing! Nanny Cay is home base for the Tortola Yacht Charters fleet. Check out TYC's C&C 49-footers, some of the sleekest yachts available for charter.

From Nanny Cay the road continues along the water to West End. There is a small community here, with a grocery store (where you might want to sip something cool) and a post office (where you might want to pick up some colorful stamps). This is also one of the busiest ports in the B.V.I. It is here that the water taxis *Bomba Charger* and *Native Son* deposit passengers from their daily runs to and from St. Thomas in the U.S. Virgin Islands.

Continue on around to Soper's Hole, a favored anchorage of charter yachts visiting West End, and consider stopping at Bananas for a snack. There is a beautiful view of the bay, the yachts, and the island of St. John, USVI, in the distance.

The Atlantic Coast to Tortola's Hills

From West End, the road swings round to the north shore of Tortola, which is the side that faces the Atlantic. Here lie the most dramatic beaches on the island. Stop first at Long Bay, which is a classic C-shaped stretch of beach. The small, pyramidal-shaped island just offshore makes a scene reminiscent of Copacabana in Rio, except that the beach at Long Bay is seldom crowded. You might want to stop here for a bite at the open-air beachside restaurant, situated among the ruins of an old fort.

Beyond Long Bay is Apple Bay, and for a special luncheon, continue on to Sugar Mill Estate Hotel.

From Sugar Mill Estate, the road climbs into the hills, where you should be prepared for narrow, very curvy roads, some just single lane. Your only clue that someone may be coming the other way is the honk of a horn, which is a good precaution to take yourself each time you swing a blind curve. By now you should have sighted Mt. Sage, the highest point on the island, and below it Carrot Bay. Almost every curve for the next several miles opens upon lovely, high-vantage-point vistas of the beautiful bays below and the other islands in the distance. In this part of the island, the lush farmland yields sweet potatoes, avocados, bananas, and sugar cane. The terrain is so steep that farmers still use donkeys. When you reach Windy Hill, stop and take a picture; the view is spectacular.

Back to Tortola's Bays and Road Town

You descend now to Cane Garden Bay, a must stop. One of the most beautiful spots in the BVI, Cane Garden Bay is great for swimming, snorkeling, windsurfing, admiring the yachts, and watching the sun travel across the sky. Stop for a hamburger and a cold drink at Stanley's. You may also want to buy one of the T-shirts emblazoned with the famed tire swing—and of course, take a swing on the tire, strung from a gigantic palm tree at beachside.

From here, head further north to Soldier's Hill, where you'll find mango and breadfruit trees and brilliant hibiscus and flamboyant, all overlooking Brewer's Bay. If you're a potential camper, stop here and take a look at the grounds.

Now you're headed back to Road Town, the vest-pocket capital, where you will want to stop at one of the shops for a souvenir T-shirt, some casual tropical fashions, local jewelry, or a bottle of the B.V.I.'s famed Pusser's British Navy Rum. You may also want to browse through the Tropic Isle Shopping Center at Village Cay Marina and, if you do, don't miss the Ample Hamper, a gourmet shop that sells everything from mint toffee and anchovy sauce to rum pepper sauce and BVI native seasoning, both made in Tortola from native recipes.

As for the other islands, their principal attractions are their resorts, natural beauty, and serenity.

PRACTICAL INFORMATION FOR
THE BRITISH VIRGIN ISLANDS

FACTS AND FIGURES. The British Virgin Islands are about 60 miles east of Puerto Rico and about 20 miles east of the U.S. Virgin Islands. There are more than 50 islands in the chain, most tiny. Only about a dozen of the islands are inhabited. The total population is about 12,000, most of whom live on Tortola, with about 1,000 on Virgin Gorda. Principal islands besides Tortola and Virgin Gorda are Anegada, Jost Van Dyke, Peter Island, Cooper Island, Norman Island, Salt Island, and Beef Island (which is attached to Tortola by a small bridge). The key cities are Road Town on Tortola and Spanish Town on Virgin Gorda, although both are quite small by any standards.

The islands are volcanic, surrounded by coral reefs. There are dozens of beautiful white sandy beaches, many palm-fringed. Most of the islands are hilly or even mountainous. The highest peak is Mt. Sage on Tortola. The islands are home port to one of the largest charter boat fleets in the world.

WHEN TO GO. The weather is as close to perfect in the B.V.I. as anywhere on earth. Daytime temperatures range between 75 and 85 degrees year-round. Temperatures are about ten degrees cooler at night. In August, the hottest month, temperatures may climb above 90. Tropical storms, if they occur, usually come during late August through September.

PASSPORTS AND VISAS. U.S. and Canadian citizens are required to produce proof of citizenship—a passport, birth certificate, voter's registration card, or the like. Alien residents must have an alien card or valid passport. All visitors must have a return or onward ticket. British subjects must have valid passports.

MONEY. U.S. currency is used, even though the British Virgin Islands issued its own currency in 1973 in honor of the islands' 200 years of constitutional rule.

WHAT WILL IT COST?

Typical expenses for two people will run approximately:

Room at moderate hotel	$90
Breakfast at hotel, including tip	8
Lunch at inexpensive restaurant, including tip	10
Dinner at moderate restaurant, including tip	35
Sightseeing bus tour (van and driver for two hours)	35
Evening drink	4
Total	$182

HOW TO GET THERE. By air. From the United States, major airlines service San Juan, St. Thomas and St. Croix, where you can make connections to the BVI. There is no direct service. Be sure you know just where you're going in the B.V.I., because there are some direct routes that avoid intermediate stops on other islands. Some routes are combinations of air and sea.

Air BVI and *Crownair* fly from San Juan, Puerto Rico, and St. Thomas, U.S. Virgin Islands, to Beef Island Airport (Beef Island is connected to Tortola by a bridge). Air BVI also has shuttle service to Anegada.

By sea. From St. Thomas, U.S. Virgin Islands, the *Bomba Charger* and *Native Son* water taxis ferry passengers across to West End and Road Town, Tortola, in less than an hour. *Bomba Charger* also serves Virgin Gorda and Jost Van Dyke. *Speedy's Fantasy* serves St. Thomas, Road Town, and Virgin Gorda. For schedule and other information, call: *Bomba Charger,* 495–4545; *Native Son,* 495–4617; *Speedy's Fantasy,* 495–5240. Peter Island, Biras Creek, and other out-of-the-way spots have their own boats to fetch you upon arrival, if you've planned ahead and given them advance notice.

AIRPORT TAXES AND OTHER CHARGES. There is a departure tax of $5 per person for those departing by air, $3 per person by sea. All room rates are subject to a 5% hotel accommodation tax.

TELEPHONES AND EMERGENCY NUMBERS. The area code for the B.V.I. is 809. You need not dial the area code when making calls within the B.V.I., even if your call is from one island to another. To get operator assistance, dial 0; police and fire, 999; hospital, 998.

HOTELS. Prices for accommodations in the B.V.I. are a classic case of supply and demand. There are just not that many rooms available. Add to that the fact that much of what is available is considered luxury resort and it all totals up to some of the most expensive rates in the Caribbean. Since demand for a getaway to the sun is greatest in the winter season—December 16–April 15—expect to pay about twice as much in season, or, if you prefer the optimistic viewpoint, about half as much in the off-season. Since accommodations are limited, plan to book space as far in advance as possible. For the winter season, as much as a year in advance is not out of the ordinary.

Price categories (based on double occupancy) are: *Super Deluxe,* $250 per night and up; *Deluxe,* $150–250; *Expensive,* $100–150; *Moderate,* $70–100, *Inexpensive,* less than $70. Most of the high-end prices come with two or three meals per person, double occupancy. (There is a 5% hotel accommodation tax.)

ANEGADA

The Reefs Hotel. *Expensive.* Anegada. (the only address). Get there by air from Beef Island Airport. Tel. 494–3425. 12 rooms. The only place to stay on

Anegada. It's on the beach, has a beach bar and a restaurant. Sport fishing and scuba diving are main attractions and clientele are young people who favor these kinds of water-oriented activities. Nothing else to do. Rates include all meals.

JOST VAN DYKE

White Bay Sandcastle. *Deluxe.* P.O. Box 7174, St. Thomas, U.S.V.I. 00801 (mailing address only). Get there by air from Beef Island Airport. Tel. 494–2462. Four octagonal cottages are nestled among the palms and bougainvillea to provide an ideal away-from-it-all atmosphere. Informal housekeeping arrangements just perfect for families or self-sufficient couples. Beautiful beach, favored by visiting yachts. Excellent restaurant. You can also be picked up at Red Hook dock on St. Thomas. Rates include three meals.

MARINA CAY

Marina Cay Hotel. *Super Deluxe.* P.O. Box 76, Road Town, Tortola. Get there by launch from Beef Island. Tel. 494–2174. 12 rooms in A-frame buildings on beautiful little island, just off Beef. Informal and an ideal atmosphere for water sports. Special shoreside dining area for yachters who anchor here, but hotel guests have priority at hilltop open-air restaurant. Rates include all meals.

MOSQUITO ISLAND

Drake's Anchorage. *Deluxe.* Box 2510, Virgin Gorda. Tel. 494–2254. Wonderful, secluded getaway on island in middle of Gorda Sound, just a short hop from top Virgin Gorda resorts. All water sports. Lovely beach. Two luxurious villas. Rates include all meals.

PETER ISLAND

Peter Island Hotel and Yacht Harbor. *Super Deluxe.* P.O. Box 211, Road Town, Tortola. Get there by launch from Tortola. Tel. 494–2561. 52 rooms. A special resort that is spread out on the only 775 developed acres of this island. 32 harbor suites, 20 suites in new units along beach. Furnished in Scandinavian modern. Central clubhouse with reception area. Lounge, grill room, bar, game rooms, and salt water swimming pool. Beach facilities at palm-fringed Deadman's Bay, one of the Caribbean's most beautiful bays. Fine dining with variety of dishes served in formal dining room or restaurant on beach. All marine facilities; three tennis courts. Spectacular hilltop villa—The Crow's Nest—rents for about $1,500 per night. Rates are MAP; include all meals at Crow's Nest.

TORTOLA

Prospect Reef Resort. *Expensive.* P.O. Box 104, Road Town, Tortola. Tel. 494–3311. 131 rooms. Luxury units clustered on shore of Sir Francis Drake Channel. Many units include kitchenettes. Villas are two bedrooms with courtyard, living area, and modern colorful appointments. Small harbor and other yachting facilities, including fleet of boats available for rental by the day or longer. Two restaurants, two bars. Swimming pool and dive tank. All water sports, including dive shop run by George Marler, technical advisor for underwater scenes of the movie, *The Deep,* filmed off Salt Island. Clientele is mixed families and singles—resort is favored by Americans and Europeans. Sunrises are very dramatic.

Fort Burt Hotel. *Moderate.* P.O. Box 187, Road Town, Tortola. Tel. 494–2587. Seven Rooms. In old fort on hill overlooking Road Harbour; terrific view. Boat to private beach. Restaurant and bar on main road below and on waterfront—perhaps the most favored watering hole in Road Town. Frequented by charter crews and locals, good spot for local color.

Long Bay Hotel. *Moderate.* P.O. Box 433, Road Town, Tortola. Tel. 495–4252. 37 rooms—some on hillside, others on beach—within sound of the surf. All accommodations have kitchenettes. Excellent cuisine. Breakfast and lunch served at beachside open-air restaurant. Dinner is in hillside dining room. Saltwater pool. Clientele is families and singles; also favored by honeymooners.

The Moorings—Mariner Inn. *Moderate.* P.O. Box 139, Road Town, Tortola. Tel. 494–2332. 40 rooms. Within walking distance of Road Town center. Principally overnight stop for charters, but good buy for non-charterers. Rooms all have balconies and kitchenettes. Very good open-air restaurant. Informal, popular local bar. Freshwater pool, tennis courts. Home base for The Moorings, largest yacht charter fleet in the Caribbean.

Sugar Mill Estate Hotel. *Moderate.* P.O. Box 425, Road Town, Tortola. Tel. 495–4355. 21 rooms. Built in the ruins of old sugar mill. Great location with beach on north shore. Pool on hill above. Great restaurant and night spot. Rooms have kitchenettes. Excellent collection of Haitian paintings, many for sale.

Treasure Isle Hotel. *Moderate.* P.O. Box 68, Road Town, Tortola. Tel. 494–2501. 40 rooms. One of the first hotels on the island. Convenient stopping place in a tropical setting with sea view from private verandas overlooking Road Harbour. Freshwater pool, three tennis courts, squash court. Beach club on lovely, secluded Cooper Island, across channel. Good spot for active people.

Cane Garden Bay Hotel. *Inexpensive.* P.O. Box 570, Road Town, Tortola. Tel. 495–4639. Ten rooms. On one of the most popular bays in the B.V.I. Swimming, snorkeling and the afternoon sun are wonderful here. You can also windsurf or sail a Sunfish. Rooms are modest, but location is priceless.

Smuggler's Cove Hotel. *Inexpensive.* P.O. Box 4, West End, Tortola. Tel. 495–4234. Seven rooms. Four units on beach, three on hillside. Restaurant, beach bar. Selection of water sports. Informal atmosphere and a place to be on your own, if you so choose.

Village Cay Marina. *Inexpensive.* P.O. Box 145, Road Town, Tortola. Tel. 494–2771. 13 rooms. One of the better things to come out of the extensive landfill project at the waterfront. The overnighting here has a nautical emphasis, since facilities are used by charterers. Two restaurants: one informal, dockside; the other elegant, upstairs. Short walk to Road Town center.

VIRGIN GORDA

Biras Creek Hotel. *Super Deluxe.* P.O. Box 54, Virgin Gorda. Guests are met by taxi at Virgin Gorda Airport, taken to jetty for short launch trip to hotel; they can also come by sea via launch or charter boat. Tel. 495–5455. 30 rooms. Spectacular 150-acre location on narrow neck of land, with channel on one side, Caribbean on the other. Two-suite cottages, each with twin bedroom, bath—with outdoor shower—sitting room, patio. Freshwater pool, tennis courts. Guests can bicycle to and from beach at Deep Bay. Marina for 30 boats. All meals included in rates. Superb European-oriented cuisine and extensive wine list, served in hilltop dining room with spectacular view.

Bitter End Yacht Club. *Super Deluxe.* P.O. Box 46, North Sound, Virgin Gorda. Guests are met by taxi at Virgin Gorda Airport or can come by sea via charter boats. Tel. 494–2746. 35 rooms. Popular with yachtsmen and sea-lovers in search of barefoot lifestyle. Wonderful location near reef for excellent snorkeling. Cottages on hillside above beach. Excellent open-air restaurant; lively clubhouse bar. Owners make arrangements for day charters. All meals included.

Little Dix Bay Hotel. *Super Deluxe.* P.O. Box 70, Virgin Gorda. Tel. 495–5555. 84 rooms. Typical Rockresort—i.e., elegant hideaway with very rich atmosphere. Lovely rooms in cottages stretched around 400 lush acres. Sparkling beach front, all water sports, full marina. Five tennis courts, commissary, shopping center. Delightful restaurant in central pavilion. Offers combination plans with sister resort at Caneel Bay Plantation on nearby St. John in U.S.V.I. All meals included.

Tradewinds Resort. *Super Deluxe.* P.O. Box 64, Virgin Gorda. Tel. 494–3151. New sister hotel to Biras Creek. Built in the hills overlooking North Sound. Beautifully elegant restaurant. Complete watersports activities.

Olde Yard Inn. *Deluxe.* Olde Yark Inn. P.O. Box 26, Virgin Gorda. Tel. 495–5544. 11 rooms. Small hideaway with unusual features, including one of the finest private collections of books in Caribbean, housed in breeze-swept gazebo.

French cuisine and extensive wine cellar. Large welcoming bar-dining room area overlooking the sea. Wonderful beaches short drive away. Water sports and horseback riding arranged. Hiking trails up to Gorda Peak. Rates are MAP.

Leverick Bay Hotel. *Expensive.* P.O. Box 63, Virgin Gorda. Tel. 495–5450. 29 rooms. Two three-bedroom houses rented by the week. Freshwater pool, two beaches, marine facilities, all water sports. Restaurant and beach bar.

Fischer's Cove Beach Hotel. *Moderate.* P.O. Box 60, The Valley, Virgin Gorda. Tel. 495–5252. Eight rooms at half to a third of those at more famous resorts—and this hotel has its own beach. Restaurant is known for its seafood, but there is also a commissary for do-it-yourselfers. Small boats for rent, great snorkeling. Horseback riding.

Guavaberry Spring Bay. *Moderate.* P.O. Box 20, Virgin Gorda. Tel. 495–5227. 14 rooms. Built—literally—among and even atop the giant boulders strewn along the channel side of Virgin Gorda. It's just a few mintues' walk to "The Baths," one of the most beautiful beaches in the Caribbean, or the less-frequented Spring Bay. Units are one- or two-bedroom, with living room, kitchen/dining area, bathroom, and sundeck.

Ocean View Hotel. *Inexpensive.* P.O. Box 66, Virgin Gorda. Tel. 495–5230. 12 rooms. A friendly, guesthouse atmosphere, prevails at this hotel. Meals served at the O'Neal family restaurant, noted for its seafood.

 HOME AND APARTMENT RENTALS. There are several homes, apartments, and cottages available for rent on a weekly, monthly, or longer basis. Contact the B.V.I. Tourist Board, 370 Lexington Ave., New York, NY 10017, (212) 696–0400, or at P.O. Box 134, Road Town.

Among the properties to consider are:

Nanny Cay Apartments. P.O. Box 77, Road Town, Tortola. Tel. 494–2422. Small condominium development on Tortola. Between Road Town and West End, the complex overlooks a marina. Two-bedroom apartments have kitchen, two bathrooms, and maid service. Weekly rates are $200–350.

Josiah's Bay Cottages. P.O. Box 89, Road Town, Tortola. Tel. 494–3176. Three cottages. Just off lovely, secluded beach, 12 minutes from airport, but a million miles from earth, it seems. Set on grounds of 18th-century "Great House," cottages include bedroom, living room/dining area, kitchen, bath, and terrace. Definitely away from it all.

 HOW TO GET AROUND. Taxis are readily available on Tortola and the drivers can also arrange for island tours. You can rent a car through *Avis* (494–2154), *Budget* (494–2639), *Hertz* (494–3322), *National* (494–3179), *International* (494–2516) and local *Alphonso* agency (494–3137), all in Road Town. On Virgin Gorda, there is also Virgin Gorda Tours Association, (495–5252). There are no rental counters at the airport, but the rental agencies will deliver a car to your hotel. You'll need a temporary driver's license, available for $5 at police headquarters or from rental firms. Rates begin at about $20 per day. And remember rules of the road are British—drive to the *left*.

 TOURIST INFORMATION SERVICES. The *British Virgin Islands Tourist Board* has an office in Road Town. Tel. 494–3134. It's open from 9:00 A.M. to 5:00 P.M. Monday through Friday. For sources closer to home, see the Tourist Information Services section in the *Facts at Your Fingertips* chapter.

SPECIAL EVENTS. Carnival (the first weekend in August) and the Spring Regatta are the special highlights throughout the B.V.I.

TOURS. Island tours of Tortola are available from any number of van tour companies. Their telephone numbers are in the directory. They can also be contacted through hotels. There are no scheduled tours per se. For $35, one to three people can rent a van and driver for two hours, which is ample time for a complete tour around the island. Each additional person is $8. Time over two hours is prorated. Try *Travel Plan Tours,* Road Town, tel. 494–2347; or *David Winter Sightseeing Tours,* Road Town, Tortola, tel. 494–2214.

BEACHES. On **Tortola** the two most popular beaches are *Cane Garden Bay* and *Long Bay* on the north coast. On **Virgin Gorda,** try *The Baths, Spring Bay, Deep Bay* at Biras Creek, *The Bitter End* and *Little Dix Bay.* On **Peter Island,** *Dead Man's Bay* is a wonderful tree-lined beach. On **Anegada,** try *Loblolly Bay* or *Turtle Bay.* On **Jost Van Dyke,** the beach is *White Bay.*

PARTICIPANT SPORTS. Sailing in the British Virgin Islands is some of the best in the Caribbean. Modern marinas have full supplies and yachts may be chartered from: *The Moorings,* P.O. Box 139, Road Town, tel. 494–2332; *Caribbean Sailing Yachts,* P.O. Box 157, Road Town, tel. 494–2741; *West Indies Yacht Charters,* Maya Cove, Tortola, tel. 495–2363; *Tortola Yacht Charters,* Nanny Cay Marine Centre, Tortola, tel. 494–2221.

Tennis courts are available at Long Bay Hotel, Treasure Isle Hotel, Prospect Reef Resort, and The Moorings Mariner Inn, all on *Tortola.* On *Virgin Gorda* there are courts at Biras Creek Hotel and Little Dix Bay Hotel. The *Peter Island* Hotel and Yacht Harbour also has courts.

Board sailing or windsurfing is very popular in the B.V.I. and is available at literally any of the major hotels and from *Boardsailing BVI* at Long Look, P.O. Box 537, Tortola. Tel. 495–2447.

Scuba diving is excellent in the B.V.I. Some of the top centers are: *Aquatic Centers,* at Prospect Reef Resort, P.O. Box 108, Tortola, tel. 494–2858; *Underwater Safaris,* at The Moorings, P.O. Box 139, Tortola, tel. 494–3235; *Blue Water Divers,* at Nanny Cay Marine Centre, P.O. Box 437, Tortola, tel. 494–2847; *Dive BVI, Ltd.* at Marina Cay, P.O. Box 76, Tortola, tel. 494–2174; *Kilbrides Underwater Tours,* North Sound, Virgin Gorda, tel. 494–2746.

SPECTATOR SPORTS. Spectator sports in the B.V.I. include **softball** from March to July on Saturday and Sunday afternoons; **basketball,** August-November, Friday, Saturday, and Sunday afternoons; **cricket, soccer,** and **rugby** on an unscheduled basis throughout the year. The best matches are played by schools and clubs. Inquire at tourist office for specific schedules.

HISTORIC SITES. Norman Island. *The Caves.* On the channel side of the island, approachable only by boat, "The Caves" are part of the local lore, which hints of pirate treasure. You can enter some of the larger caves by dinghy—if you had treasure to hide, these caves would be as likely a spot as any. Norman is said to be Robert Louis Stevenson's "Treasure Island." It is, however, uninhabited.

Salt Island. *Wreck of the Rhone.* The British mail ship *HMS Rhone* went down off Salt Island in a 19th-century hurricane, and today forms a natural dive spot with zillions of fish and beautiful coral formations counterpointing the remains of the hull and masts. Best explored as a scuba dive, the water is nonetheless clear enough to enable you to see the outlines of the ship from the surface with a snorkel, if you choose to drop anchor nearby. The *Rhone* was the location for the underwater scenes in the movie "The Deep."

Tortola. *Anglican Cathedral.* Old Main St., Road Town. The oldest church in the B.V.I., it was built in the early 1900s.

Callwood Rum Distillery. Cane Garden Bay. No phone. Just off the main road. An example of rum-making the old-fashioned way, i.e., in a moonshiner's-delight contraption, complete with cauldrons, twisting cooper pipes, etc. Finished Arundel Rum is stored in old kegs. Open most of the day.

Virgin Gorda. *Old Copper Mine.* Near southeast corner. Remains of old Spanish mine, circa 16th century. Includes foundations of old fort and chimney of old smelter. You can view the mine's cavernous opening, but do not enter.

 MUSEUMS AND GALLERIES. Tortola. *Folk Museum.* Across from the post office on the Main Square. No telephone. Odd hours. Examples or artifacts, antique island furniture, historical displays.

Roger Barnett's Collections. On Old Main St. 495–2352. Odd hours. Watercolors of island settings.

Joseph Hodge's Gallery. Palm Grove Shopping Center. No telephone. Odd hours. Oil paintings of island scenes.

MUSIC. Music in the B.V.I. is of the Caribbean steel band variety, with a local touch called "fungi." Reggae is also popular here, as is current pop music.

 SHOPPING. Except for Road Town, Tortola, and the Virgin Gorda Yacht Harbour, shops are limited. The luxury hotels have boutiques with a few items but otherwise, forget it. Nonetheless, you may want to pick up some of the B.V.I.'s famous rum or seasonings as gifts.

Tortola. In Road Town, there are several shops that are worth a visit and some carry handicrafts and unusual gifts impossible to find among the Danish-French-Italian imports on the larger islands.

Pusser's Rum Shop, Old Main St., is not to be missed. This B.V.I. spirit, which is known throughout the Caribbean, comes in a handsome decanter-like bottle, which has spawned a whole series of crocks and flagons. Also for sale here are all sorts of gifts and wearing apparel, most with the rum's motto, "Splice the Main Brace" (loose translation: "take five for rum ration").

The *Cockle Shop* has colorful "flags" of the B.V.I., rare West Indian and B.V.I. stamps; lovely local watercolors; replicas of old West Indian coins fashioned into ornaments; Cuban cigars; French perfumes; English Wedgewood; imported jewelry; wines and liquors at below St. Thomas prices. This is one place for you to pick up Florence Lewisohn's *Tales of Tortola.*

At the the Tropic Aisle Shopping Center at Village Cay Marina, you'll find the *Stowaway Boutique* for women's wear; *Crown Jewelers* for gems, and the *Carousel Gift Shop* for imported china and crystal. *Caribbean Handprints* has a broad selection of items fashioned from original silk-screen fabrics. Be sure to stop in at the *Ample Hamper,* a gourmet shop with merchandise ranging from mint toffee and anchovy sauce imported from London's Fortnum and Mason's to rum pepper sauce and B.V.I. native seasoning, both of which are made from native recipes in Tortola.

Virgin Gorda. At the marina, there are two areas: one owned and operated by Little Dix–Rockresorts hierarchy, with a commissary, boutique, Harbor master's office, etc.; the other (which looks similar unless you know the difference) with private shops, wine shop, supermarket (with astronomical prices), pharmacy, the *Spouter* for ice cream, and the *Bath & Turtle,* a pub. There is a wonderful, wide assortment of T-shirts at *Dive BVI.* Stop by *Tropical Handicrafts,* where you get local jewelry and a lesson in lore from Kuanda Leonard.

 RESTAURANTS. In the B.V.I., most favored recipes are seafood, for obvious reasons. Almost everything else has to be imported and thus tends to be more expensive. Most restaurants offer varied fare, including seafood and an array of continental dishes, with a selection of specific European specialties. Higher-priced hotels are noted for their cuisine. Owners of smaller properties often feature favorite recipes. Reservations are generally essential since the chef cooks to the house count. Price categories, based on average three-course dinner for one, excluding beverages, tax, or tip, are as follows: *Deluxe,* over $25; *Expensive,* $20–25; *Moderate,* $10–19; *Inexpensive,* less than $10.

BEEF ISLAND

The Last Resort. *Moderate.* Trellis Bay, Beef Island. Tel. 495–2520. Very informal. Cross the water via launch or dinghy. Among house specialties are home-made pumpkin soup, roast beef and Yorkshire pudding, and roast duckling in brandy sauce. Proprietor Tony Snell entertains after dinner on guitar with very witty original songs. No credit cards.

JOST VAN DYKE

Abe's at Little Harbour. *Inexpensive.* No telephone. The address is the same as the name. Very informal. Open for lunch and dinner. Featured choices are chicken, fresh fish, and lobster. No credit cards.

Rudy's. *Inexpensive.* Tel. 494–3450. No address—you'll find it. Very informal. Try lobster sandwiches and family-style dinners. No credit cards.

PETER ISLAND

Yacht Harbour. *Deluxe.* Peter Island Hotel & Yacht Harbour, Peter Island. Tel. 494–2561. Reservations necessary. For a special evening, make reservations here for dinner and dancing. Elegant dining room with varied menu, featuring seafood and continental cuisine. Veranda out back overlooks channel and twinkling lights of Road Town across the water. Personable general manager, David Benson, and his wife Gae often will join you for an after-dinner cocktail. Jacket for men, dress for women recommended. AE, CB, DC.

TORTOLA

Fort Burt. *Deluxe.* Road Town, Tortola. Tel. 494–2587. Breeze-swept setting at top of hill above harbor, classical music accompanies wonderful cuisine. Try the cauliflower soup, conch fritters, lobster Sir Francis Drake and pina colada cheesecake.

Upstairs. *Expensive.* Village Cay Marina, Tortola. Tel. 494–2771. Reservations necessary. Elegant dining with seafood specialties. Extensive wine list. Jackets suggested. AE, CB, DC.

Carib Casseroles. *Inexpensive.* Road Town, Tortola. Tel. 494–3271. Basically a take-out restaurant but nice for lunch on tiny patio. Try beef and green banana curry, sweet-and-sour pork, chicken in white wine. Great selection of hot and cold soups and rich delectable desserts. No credit cards.

Maria's. *Moderate.* Road Town, Tortola. Tel. 494–2595. Local specialties. Try anything with lobster, conch, or fish. No credit cards.

Peg Leg Landing. *Moderate.* Nanny Cay, Tortola. Tel. 494–2512. On stilts, above the breakers. Excellent seafood. Try the dolphin strips for an appetizer and the snapper entree. AE, CB, DC, MC, V.

Stanley's. *Inexpensive.* Cane Garden Bay, Tortola. Tel. 495–4520. Nothing special to recommend it except the location—on a beautiful bay—and Stanley himself. Setting somehow makes hamburgers taste better and beer seem colder. Famous tire swing at beachside. No credit cards.

Sir Francis Drake Pub. *Inexpensive.* At Fort Burt Hotel, Road Town, Tortola. Tel. 494–2587. Local hangout on water's edge. Hamburgers are tops. Also try chicken or scampi dishes.

Skyworld. *Moderate.* Ridge Road, Tortola. Tel. 494–3567. Incredible view from atop mountain of both U.S. and British Virgin Islands. Good seafood and beef dishes. AE, MC, V.

VIRGIN GORDA

Biras Creek. *Deluxe.* Biras Creek Hotel, Virgin Gorda. Tel. 495–5455. Reservations necessary. Dining room is atop hill, reached via stone walk from marina. Channel is on one side, Caribbean on the other. Food specialties are seafood and European dishes. Excellent cuisine, spectacular view. Generally only one item on menu per dinner, sometimes two, so inquire before making the trip or take your chances—whatever they serve will be excellent. AE, CB, DC.

Little Dix Bay. *Deluxe.* Little Dix Bay Hotel, Virgin Gorda. Tel. 495–5555. Reservations necessary. Elegant dining. As expansive a menu as found anywhere in B.V.I., with seafood and Continental specialties. Jackets required. Dresses suggested for women. AE, CB, DC.

Bitter End Yacht Club. *Expensive.* Bitter End Yacht Club, Virgin Gorda. Tel. 494–2746. Reservations suggested. Favored rendezvous for cruising yachtsmen. They start early with champagne breakfast, offer a buffet and club lunch of antipasto buffet, lobster crepe or club sandwich, hamburger, and dessert. For dinner try lobster, fresh fish, steak entrees. AE, CB, DC.

The Wheelhouse. *Moderate.* Ocean View Hotel, Virgin Gorda. Tel. 495–5230. Informal. Popular with lunchtime crowd from nearby harbor. Try seafood dinners, local island specialties. AE, CB, DC.

The Bath And Turtle. *Inexpensive.* Yacht Harbour Shopping Center, Virgin Gorda. Tel. 495–5239. "Pub Fare" served from noon 'til nine. Food ranges from hamburgers and sandwiches to steak and local lobster. No credit cards.

 NIGHT LIFE AND BARS. Night life is not the reason to vacation in the B.V.I., where the emphasis is decidedly on the sun-packed days. There are no real nightclubs or discos, per se, and even the after-dinner entertainment in hotels and restaurants is at a minimum. Pub-like atmosphere prevails in Road Town. Hotel nightspots are in keeping with the image of the particular hotel: Peter Island is sophisticated, Prospect Reef features "fungi" band one or two nights per week, *Sir Francis Drake Pub* has occasional live pop music. There are no casinos, no music halls, cabarets, or piano bars.

POSTAGE. Airmail rate to the U.S. is $.40 per half ounce.

ELECTRIC CURRENT. The current here is 110 to 120 volts A.C.

 SECURITY. The B.V.I. is one of the safest places in the Caribbean. There is little or no crime involving tourists. The judicial system is very strict with wrongdoers. Tourists can feel safe anywhere in these islands and really do not even need to lock the doors to their hotel rooms, although there is never any reason to tempt fate.

CAYMAN ISLANDS

by
BARBARA A. CURRIE

Less than a decade ago, turquoise sea, turtles, and tremendously friendly people were the trademarks of this obscure British Crown Colony sleeping 480 miles south of Miami and 180 miles northwest of Jamaica.

Although those remain traits of Grand Cayman, Cayman Brac, and Little Cayman, this trio has developed dramatically since 1976 and now enjoys a reputation as both a major offshore financial center and tax haven, and a growing refuge for vacationers whose prerequisites for paradise are as simple as year-round sunshine, sand, and sea.

The Cayman Islands occupy less than one hundred square miles, but their aquatic attractions give them high marks in Caribbean tourism. Not only do these islands rank as one of the top four scuba-diving destinations in the world, but during 1984 they emerged as the hottest new spot for big-game fishing in the Caribbean. Likewise, the 450-plus banks in George Town, the capital, attract thousands of businessmen each year. Fins and finance are the mainstays of the island's economy.

Grand Cayman's Seven Mile Beach is one of the finer beaches in the West Indies, and the abundance of quality condominium beachfront apartments available for self-catering holidays makes this island increasingly popular as a family destination, particularly in summer months.

Cayman Brac, eighty miles east of her "big sister" island, is the real visual jewel of this trio, a tiny, somnolent limestone speck of less than twenty square miles. A majestic bluff rises gradually to 140 feet at the island's eastern tip. Pirate legends and torturous bluff-top caves make this island a "must" for at least a day trip—and much longer for amateur naturalists and divers.

Little Cayman, seven miles north of Cayman Brac, has a "permanent" population of twenty-seven on eighteen square miles of unspoiled West Indian wilderness. This diminutive dollop of tropical flora wears a thick cloak of coconut palms and offers superb bonefishing, flycasting for small tarpon in a landlocked lake and the kind of isolation many travelers discover only after years of globe-roaming.

The official motto of the Cayman Islands has always been "He hath founded it upon the seas," and the green sea turtle, which once populated these coasts by the thousands, remains the national symbol. But beyond the sun, sand, and sea which have lured over 200,000 visitors annually in recent years is another important "s": safety. These islands remain one of the most politically stable and overall crime-free countries in the Caribbean.

Past and Present

Columbus discovered the Cayman Islands (specifically, Cayman Brac and Little Cayman) on his fourth and last voyage to the New World, on May 10, 1503. He named the islands "Las Tortugas" because of the quantity of sea turtles that populated these coasts. He was followed in 1586 by Sir Francis Drake, who renamed them Caymanas, allegedly for crocodiles he encountered in the mangrove swamps (although many naturalists wonder if the reptiles weren't actually large green iguanas).

Regardless of what nature of wildlife originally populated this obscure trio, by the seventeenth and eighteenth centuries they had become a popular refuge for buccaneers, including such rogues as Sir Henry Morgan, Edward "Blackbeard" Teach, and Neal Walker. Legends claim there are still undiscovered caches of treasures in the caves of Cayman Brac.

There are no documents to prove it, but historians of the islands believe the first settlers were deserters from Oliver Cromwell's army who defected to Little Cayman and Cayman Brac around 1668 from the base in Jamaica. But from 1734, when the first recorded settlers arrived, until a century later, the Cayman Islands attracted a mixture of transplanted (some say shipwrecked) Welshmen, Scots, Irishmen, and Englishmen whose customs are still visible in the contemporary Caymanian way of life, as well as in the West Indian brogue which blends a curious combination of Anglo-Caribbean accents.

A famous Cayman curiosity is its tax-exempt status. Legend has it that the tragic "Wreck of the Ten Sails" was responsible. A convoy of Jamaican merchantmen bound for England wrecked off Grand Cayman's East End in 1788, and the Caymanians proved their heroism by rescuing all of the passengers aboard the fleet of ten ships. As a reward, King George III decreed the islands' freedom from taxation.

Cayman was attached to Jamaica until that country achieved independence in 1962, and in the past twenty-three years has consistently resisted pressure to follow suit, chosing to remain a British Crown Colony.

The country's economy is based on the offshore financial industry and tourism, and Caymanians enjoy one of the Caribbean's highest standards of living. Here the intermarriage of Anglos and West Indians, dating back a century, has led to an absence of racial prejudice.

Observers of Caribbean politics attribute Cayman's reputation for political stability to its attachment to Great Britain. The present constitution came into effect in 1972, creating a legislative assembly which is the lawmaking body of the islands. It consists of twelve elected members (MLAs) from six electoral districts and three official members: the chief secretary, financial secretary, and attorney general. As a British Crown Colony under this constitution, the Cayman Islands are governed by a governor who is the appointed representative of the Queen.

Elections are held every four years, and there is no party system yet in the Cayman Islands.

Grand Cayman remains the tourism center of these islands, but during the past few years both Cayman Brac and Little Cayman have begun to develop more facilities to allow visitors to enjoy the special serenity and charm of the sister islands. There is no gambling, nor are there any resorts over five stories anywhere in the islands. To prevent modern plundering of Cayman's magnificent surrounding reefs, the Cayman Islands Watersports Association and the islands' twenty-two dive operations enforce the conservation motto of "take only pictures and leave only bubbles."

EXPLORING THE CAYMANS

The three members of the Cayman Islands trio are as different from each other as the five districts within Grand Cayman. The Cayman Islands have never been known for their topside attractions—they lack the dramatic panoramas of other Caribbean islands, or the lush vegetation of their neighbor Jamaica. Regardless of how many of the islands or districts you choose to tour, you'll miss the real "soul" of the Caymans if you don't take time to meet the Caymanians themselves in your travels. While those in in George Town may be too harried caring for customers, the outlying areas are more relaxed and will give you a much better idea of the real spirit of the Caymanians, which originally lured tourists to these islands.

Grand Cayman

Although Grand Cayman is relatively easy to explore on your own (and the sister islands even easier), the most enjoyable way to wet your feet and whet your curiosity about this country's culture is to begin with an organized island tour by one of the established tour operators, or by private taxi—the older cabbies have a delightful repertoire of local fables to amuse their passengers. You'll hear about duppies and May Cows and things that went thump in the night—and how to cook conch or smoke marlin.

If you do choose to strike out on your own, you'll want to rent a car or moped for at least two days to allow for a relaxing trip around Grand Cayman's seventy-six square miles.

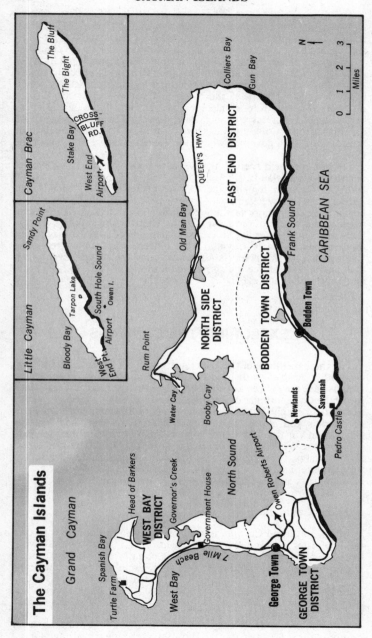

The Cayman Islands

Grand Cayman

Little Cayman

Cayman Brac

WEST BAY DISTRICT

NORTH SIDE DISTRICT

BODDEN TOWN DISTRICT

EAST END DISTRICT

GEORGE TOWN DISTRICT

Turtle Farm
Spanish Bay
Head of Barkers
West Bay
Governor's Creek
Government House
North Sound
7 Mile Beach
Owen Roberts Airport
George Town
Water Cay
Booby Cay
Rum Point
Newlands
Savannah
Pedro Castle
Bodden Town
Frank Sound
Old Man Bay
QUEEN'S HWY.
Colliers Bay
Gun Bay
CARIBBEAN SEA

N
0 1 2 3 Miles

Sandy Point
Bloody Bay
Tarpon Lake
South Hole Sound
West End Airport
Owen I.

The Bluff
The Bight
CROSS-BLUFF RD.
Stake Bay
West End Airport

Before you begin exploring, ask for one of the colorful and well-illustrated maps of the three islands distributed by the Cayman Islands Department of Tourism. Most hotels have them at the front or activities desk.

You may read or hear about the "dozens of beaches" of these islands, but that's more exaggeration than reality. Grand Cayman's west coast, the most developed area of the entire colony, is where you'll find its famous Seven Mile Beach, and it is a beauty. But the best snorkeling locations are off the ironshore (coral ledge area) south of George Town on Grand Cayman's west coast, and in the reef-protected shallows of the island's north and south coasts, where coral and fish life are much more varied and abundant. Other good beaches include East End, at Colliers, by the Tortuga Club; Cayman Kai; Rum Point by the Retreat; and Water Cay, also near Rum Point.

George Town

George Town is the capital and seat of government of the Cayman Islands, as well as a busy harbor that is the entry point for the approximately 120,000 visitors who arrive on twelve to fourteen major cruise ships each year. An average of three ships call each week year-round in this city, which has become one of the top eight cruise-ship destinations in the Caribbean in the past few years.

Shopping, rather than sightseeing, is the main attraction here, although there are several points of interest to note during your stroll around George Town: the old Marine Building on the waterfront; the Clock Monument to King George V; the Legislative Assembly Building on Fort Street; and the Courts Building opposite. Also on the waterfront is the historic Lands and Surveys office building, one of the few remaining examples of traditional gingerbread architecture in George Town. (Just south of George Town, down the almost-hidden drive past the Island Taste snack bar, is an area named Pantonville, where you'll see three more restored examples of gingerbread-style buildings, dating back almost a century.)

Don't be surprised if you can only distinguish a few of the 450-plus banks among this important financial center's many modern buildings. In truth, the majority of these are "B-licensed" institutions engaged strictly in the offshore financial industry—not the full-service banks you deal with overseas.

Competition-class shoppers and serious spenders may find their downfall in George Town. There's abundant bounty in the duty-free category in the form of watches, china, crystal, porcelain, and some perfumes and jewelry. Prices, according to serious Caribbean bargain hunters, rival those in the U.S. Virgin Islands. Interesting local crafts are limited to black coral jewelry and some thatch work. However, in George Town's many boutiques you can find a variety of different—and often pricey—fashions, from sophisticated labels like Fiorucci in Elizabethan Square to the exciting eastern Caribbean batiks manufactured in St. Kitts for Sea Island Cottons on the waterfront.

In 1985, a new museum of marine artifacts from the collection of a Key West treasure hunter, the late Art McKee, opened in Grand Cayman, located on the top floor of Bob Soto's Freeport building.

Although not a true museum, there is one fine showplace you shouldn't miss. Black Coral And, a small, elegant emporium on Fort Street, is as difficult to describe as it is to leave. Although it specializes in black coral jewelry and other creations, this entire store is a dazzling display of the workmanship genius of sculptor Bernard Passman, whose talent in black coral has been recognized by royalty three times. Passman designed the official gifts presented on behalf of the Cayman Islands Government to HRH Prince Charles and Princess Diana for the royal wedding; a gift presented to Queen Elizabeth and HRH the Duke of Edinburgh to commemorate the first royal visit in February 1983; and even Prince William was honored by a Passman creation.

And on Harbour Drive next to Ruth Clarage, there is another must for black coral buffs, Black Coral Jewelry and Other Fine Gems. Owners Richard and Rafaela Barile are true entertainers (former vaudeville folk) whose talent in this craft caught the attention of such VIP visitors as Jimmy and Rosalynn Carter, Muhammad Ali, and Paul Hopkins. Barile and his Caymanian staff produce exquisite work, rich in detail and in our estimation *underpriced* for the quality.

North to Seven Mile Beach and West Bay

Drive along West Bay Road north from the George Town limits, past dozens of small hotels and low-slung condominium apartments, then park your vehicle. The attractions on Grand Cayman are Seven Mile Beach (actually only five and a half miles long) and the variety of water sports the island's west coast beach area offers. Headquarters for this collection of aquatic activities are Bob Soto's Diving Ltd. and the water-sports concession called Aqua Delights, located on the beach of the Holiday Inn Grand Cayman. Between them they can arrange everything from a resort course in scuba to jetskiing and windsurfing.

This area is Grand Cayman's busiest vacation center, and most of the island's accommodations and restaurants, as well as several new shopping centers, are located along this "gold coast" strip.

Just north of Le Club Cayman resort is Government House, the residence of the Governor. It is not open to the public, but you can park outside the entrance and take photographs. The royal poincianas and surrounding gardens are spectacular in June.

West Bay has two well-known attractions, the Cayman Turtle Farm Ltd. and the tiny village of Hell. To get to the Turtle Farm, turn left at the fork just beyond Silver Sands Cafe and continue for about two miles. This is *not* a Marineland-type tourist attraction with performing reptiles, but a research center dedicated to saving several endangered species of sea turtles from extinction. Established in 1968 by private enterprise and now owned by the Cayman government, the farm raises green sea turtles from eggs through young adulthood rather than collecting specimens in the wild. It is the only scientific operation of its kind in the world, and depending on the season, you may be able to watch adult females nesting—or see a new crop of tiny hatchlings. An educational exhibit in the main building relates the historical significance of the green sea turtle in these islands, and the adjacent gift shop has an amusing collection of 'turtlebelia" souvenirs. (Note: U.S. citizens cannot take home any greenturtle products, including jewelry or oil, due to the U.S. Customs regulation banning the import of these products.) The farm is open daily and admission is charged.

A few minutes away is the village of Hell, where you can buy postcards and stamps at the tiny wooden post office and have them postmarked "HELL, Grand Cayman." Just a trident's throw west is the very local roost, The Club Inferno, and to the rear is an eerie acre of limestone outcroppings, a bleak and barren area which gave this village its name a century ago.

George Town South to South Sound and Savannah

Hidden along the coastal road from George Town south are many of the remaining small Caymanian-style cottages. Most are decorated with colorful "sand gardens," sandy plots planted with varieties of tropical plants and flowers.

The Seaview Hotel, the oldest in the Cayman Islands, recently renovated but still charming with its famous "Shipwreck Bar," is minutes south of the capital. A stop here—especially during prime "watering time"—should introduce you to a local cast of characters. If you miss them here, try the Sunset House bar a few minutes south on the seaside.

This part of Grand Cayman's west coast is "ironshore," a coral ledge which meets the sea and provides sharp-edged contrast to Seven Mile Beach. The snorkeling in the shallow water near the shore is very good and at times *superb,* especially directly off the Sunset House and South Cove dive resorts, and in the cusp of Smith's Cove just a minute farther south. The gentle sandy entrance to Smith's Cove, although secluded from the road by a thick cluster of sea grape trees, is a popular spot and easy to locate.

Continue along this coastal road a few miles until, after a sharp bend, you encounter a complete change of terrain. Here lies Grand Cayman's "Piney Forest," a canopy of towering Australian pines with its own special beauty. The Cayman Islands cricket, football (soccer) and rugby pitches can be seen north of the road in South Sound.

Continue east, back to the road which leads to Bodden Town (there's only one). Pedro's Castle, allegedly the eighteenth-century haunt of pirates, is now a ramshackle structure that's a popular local bar and restaurant, with a fine panoramic view of the south coast. Nearby on a back road is Bat Cave—ask for directions from any Caymanian.

Bodden Town

The original capital of the Cayman Islands, Bodden Town is a quaint village. A local entrepreneur has opened part of his property to the public as the Pirate's Caves of Bodden Town, a small underground cave system where eighteenth-century rogues may have sought shelter. From there, you can ask directions to the Slave Wall—and listen to different local versions of its history.

Several miles east is Breakers, whose primary attraction is the Lighthouse Club, appropriately named for its central structure. This is a good place to stop for excellent refreshments, whether native liquid or seafood, before continuing either north to North Side and Cayman Kai or east to Collier's Village and Queen's Highway.

North Side

Some say this area of Grand Cayman reminds them of the outer islands of North Carolina, with stretches of sand protected by the fringing reef several hundred yards beyond. It's also favored by islanders for weekend escapes. Lack of crowds or activity and some of the islands' most beautiful beach areas (Rum Point by the Retreat and, further south, Water Cay) lure residents who arrive by car or boat, especially on Sundays.

During summer months, you'll be able to hear and probably see the indigenous red-headed Cayman parrots in the brush along the roads, and large land crabs often scurry at night across the pavement.

Queen's Highway and East End

A bit east of the "intersection" in Old Man Bay, the road connects with the stretch joining North Side with East End. Eight miles of well-paved road offers panoramas of the "last Grand Cayman frontier" and numerous opportunities for secluded snorkeling and picnics. Queen Elizabeth II cut the ribbon officially opening this road in February 1983 and a plaque at its eastern edge proclaims it "Queen's Highway" in her honor. It links Old Man Bay with Grand Cayman's least-developed district, East End, whose scenes are very West Indian. Offshore, past Collier's Village and the Tortuga Club, you'll see what's left of the wreck of the M.V. *Ridgefield,* a 7,500-ton liberty ship that went aground on the reef under suspicious circumstances during the Bay of Pigs invasion in 1962.

Between the villages of East End and Breakers, the south coast ironshore is perforated by small underwater caves or "blowholes." When there's surf action these resemble mini-geysers, sending spumes of salt spray twenty to thirty feet in the air.

Cayman Airways is the link for day trips or longer excursions to the sister islands, which, eighty miles east, are too distant for the average visitor to reach by local boat.

Cayman Brac

"Miss Elo," Cayman Brac's most famous taxi guide, can meet you at Gerrard Smith International Airport and take you on a tour of this very friendly—and very un-touristy—sister island. It's highlight is its eastern tip, a 140-foot sheer cliff which plummets into the Caribbean. "Brac" is Gaelic for bluff; the Brackers are even more hospitable than their cousins in Grand Cayman, and welcome visitors, whether they choose to climb the bluff and hike the lighthouse trail, search for over 140 species of migratory birds sighted on this island; explore the caves, bonefish, snorkel, or dive its virgin underwater territory. The natural beauty of the island and the natural warmth of the 1,700 Brackers make this a special experience. Don't leave without meeting Eddie and Idalee Scott in Watering Place—Eddie is a master craftsman in a multitude of media, from black coral to native wood.

Cayman Brac is not known for its beaches, but there is a nice sandy patch at Tiara Beach and, farther east, at the Brac Reef Beach resort. Excellent snorkeling can be found immediately offshore of the Buccaneer's Inn on the island's north coast. Don't visit Cayman Brac without stopping at both south coast hotels, the Tiara Beach and Brac Reef Beach. We find these two resorts rank among the finest and friendliest small hotels in the Caribbean.

Little Cayman

Little Cayman could have been the tropical counterpart to Thoreau's Walden Pond, given the solitude and self-reliance it inspires. Three small lodges offer comfortable accommodation and access to excellent fishing (bonefish, tarpon, and gamefish offshore), but Little Cayman's most elusive treasure is the unparalleled beauty of the underwater panoramas off its north coast at Bloody Bay and Jackson Point sites prized by experienced divers. This island has been actor Burgess Meredith's refuge for a decade and its dedicated patrons guard it jealously, hoping progress will never reach its palm-choked coast. Little Cayman's south coast is the "center of civilization" and is where you'll spend most of your time, sunning on Owen Island or bonefishing in South Hole Sound lagoon.

PRACTICAL INFORMATION FOR
THE CAYMAN ISLANDS

 FACTS AND FIGURES. The Cayman Islands are a British Crown Colony consisting of Grand Cayman, Cayman Brac, and Little Cayman. The largest of the trio, Grand Cayman, occupies 76 square miles and has a population of approximately 16,600. Cayman Brac and Little Cayman, 82 miles northeast of Grand Cayman, are much smaller, with 12 and 10 square miles respectively. Cayman Brac's population is approximately 1,700, while Little Cayman has only 27 permanent residents.

The islands are the lowlying tops of submerged mountains and are composed of limestone, rather than volcanic rock. The only island with an elevation over 60 ft. is Cayman Brac, whose backbone is a majestic bluff rising to 140 ft. at the island's eastern tip.

The capital and seat of government is George Town, which is also the main harbor. There are three points of entry with customs and immigration facilities: George Town Harbor for ships and pleasure boats; Owen Roberts International Airport on Grand Cayman, and Gerrard Smith Airport on Cayman Brac.

The official language is English.

The islands are on eastern standard time year-round and *do not* change to daylight savings time in April.

Although the water is generally safe to drink, little fresh water is available and most comes from cisterns or the desalination plant on Grand Cayman. You should inquire about potability at your resort.

 WHEN TO GO. The Cayman Islands enjoy summery temperatures and sunshine almost year-round. The rainy season is officially from June through November. Average temperatures range from 75–85 degrees F year-round, slightly higher during August and September.

Since the prevailing winds shift from southeast to northerly in the winter months, there is always a leeward side to each island, making diving and water sports possible all year. Most divers consider May through September the prime scuba time in these islands, coinciding with the low summer season rates at most hotels and condominiums—which can be as little as half the winter season tariff.

For anglers, gamefishing is also good year-round, but the month of June has proved particularly good for blue marlin and dolphin.

Weatherwise, the best time to go to the Cayman Islands is anytime. To take advantage of the best buys in accommodations (and find fewer other people visiting), late April through late November is the best time to travel.

PASSPORTS AND VISAS. U.S., Canadian, and British visitors must have some proof of identity (passport, voter's registration card, or birth certificate), as well as a return or ongoing airline ticket.

MONEY. The Cayman Islands dollar is based on the U.S. dollar, but not at par. U.S. $1 = about 80¢ Caymanian. This rather lopsided exchange rate often confuses, if not shocks, visitors, so be prepared. The U.S. dollar does not go very far here; Grand Cayman is an expensive island any way you look at it, and you have to scout for value within your budgetary restraints. It's advisable to exchange U.S. dollars at the bank and when you tour or shop be sure, when prices are quoted, which dollar you're discussing.

WHAT WILL IT COST?

A typical day for two persons during the winter season will run:

	U.S.$
A moderate hotel on Seven Mile Beach (MAP), including breakfast and dinner at the hotel	$160
Light luncheon at the hotel or in town	25
Tips or service charges at restaurants, hotel tax and service charges	20
Rental car or island tour	30
Total	$235

HOW TO GET THERE. By air. Miami is the major gateway, with daily flights provided by *Cayman Airways* and *Republic Airlines.* Cayman Airways also flies non-stop between Houston and Grand Cayman, and between Miami and Cayman Brac. *Air Jamaica* has service from Kingston; Interisland service is aboard Cayman Airways.

At press time, Cayman Airways was operating weekly service between Miami and the Turks and Caicos Islands, continuing on the Grand Cayman via Kingston.

Arrival on Grand Cayman is at the new, multi-million-dollar Owen Roberts International Airport. The attractive and spacious modern complex opened in January 1985. On Cayman Brac, the point of entry is Gerrard Smith International Airport.

AIRPORT TAX AND OTHER CHARGES. There is a 6% government tax on hotel rooms, plus a service charge that ranges from 10–15%. The airport departure tax is U.S. $5. Cayman coins are issued in denominations of 1 cent, 5 cents, 10 cents, and 25 cents with indigenous flora and fauna on the obverse of each coin. Bills are issued in different colors: $1 (red), $5 (blue), $10 (green), $25 (brown), and $100 (orange).

Credit cards are *not* widely accepted, particularly at restaurants.

TELEPHONES AND EMERGENCY NUMBERS. The area code for the Cayman Islands is 809. The prefix for all Cayman telephone numbers when dialing long distance is 94 followed by the appropriate 5 digits. Within the Caymans it's only necessary to dial the 5-digit number. A modern automatic telephone system links the islands via submarine coaxial cable, enabling Cayman operators to dial numbers worldwide, with 24-hr. service. For police or any emergency, just dial your hotel operator.

HOTELS. The Holiday Inn Grand Cayman is the only large hotel located on Seven Mile Beach. However, in January 1985, a $6.5-million conference center opened on West Bay Road, part of the Transnational House office complex, which resembles Mount Vernon transplanted to the tropics. In most resorts and dive lodges you'll find comfortable quarters and facilities typical of those in American chain hotels. In general, the most luxurious units are found in the 30-plus condominium apartment complexes that dot Grand Cayman's coastline. Wherever you stay, the emphasis will be on maintaining that relaxing "turtle pace" the Cayman Islands are famous for. We call $160 and above *Deluxe;* $100–159 *Expensive;* $85–99 *Moderate* and below that *Inexpensive.* These rates are in U.S. dollars and based on double occupancy. *Note:* when obtaining rates, be sure to inquire which meal plan is included. Most hotels will quote an EP (no meals) rate, but many offer MAP and occasionally AP rates, which can save you quite a bit in these islands where food prices in restaurants are high.

GRAND CAYMAN

Caribbean Club, *Deluxe.* Box 504, West Bay Rd. Tel. 949–2593. This delightful cluster of 18 pastel-pink villas is nestled on one of the most picturesque sections of Seven Mile Beach. Each two-bedroom villa is distinctively decorated in the owner's taste and all have fully equipped kitchens.The units fan out behind the main buildings, which houses one of the island's finest restaurants (commanding better-than-casual attire from its patrons). The upstairs Green Turtle bar is a popular luncheon spot overlooking the Caribbean Club grounds and nearby sea. Water sports and tennis.

West Indian Club. *Deluxe.* Box 703, West Bay Rd. Tel 949–2494. The nine one- or two-bedroom units available for vacation rental rate are some of the most exquisite to be found on *any* island, as each one's decor reflects a labor of love and imagination of its owner. The club resembles a colonial manor house, with spiral staircase at the entrance confined by clusters of multicolored bougainvillea. The beach beyond is so quiet you might think it was private property. All units have fully equipped kitchens; price includes half-day maid service (full days can be arranged).

Beach Club Colony. *Expensive.* Box 903, West Bay Rd. Tel. 949–2023. "The slow vacation" is the slogan of this small hotel, which was once the prize property of Seven Mile Beach. After complete refurbishing and reorganization of the bar and restaurant, Beach Club's 41 units have been restored to the romantic charm that attracted a loyal following a decade ago. Every kind of water sport can be arranged on the premises. This is a small hotel with lots of personality and a friendly, attentive management and staff who remember how to treat customers as guests. The food in the *Marlin Room* and out on the seaside *Grape Tree Terrace* is excellent. Their weekly West Indian breakfast buffets and seafood buffet lunches are one of the island's best buys.

Holiday Inn Grand Cayman. *Expensive.* Box 904, West Bay Rd. Tel 947–4444. All the expected Holiday Inn accoutrements in 215 rooms on Seven Mile Beach. You'll find more water sports here than you can imagine, along with a freshwater pool and tennis (with resident pro if you need him). The *Chez Jacques* restaurant offers good local seafood and excellent prime rib; the *Terrace Room* has casual coffee-shop style dining all day. The *Wreck of the Ten Sails Lounge* offers entertainment six nights a week by Barefoot Man and Band.

Cayman Kai Resort. *Moderate.* P.O. Box 1112, North Side. Tel. 947–9556. This charming "community" on Cayman north coast claims to be "the Cayman you came here for," capturing and preserving that out-island ambience and serenity. The resort consists of 26 sea lodges with kitchenettes and a main complex with restaurant, two bars, tennis court, dive and water-sports shop, and small "Kai-missary" with groceries and sundries for those who wish to cook for themselves. Rental beach houses and very attractive Island Houses (apartments) complete the vacation options here. Water Cay beach and marina.

Ron Kipp's Cayman Diving Lodge. *Inexpensive.* Tel. 1–800–327–8223. A comfortable 17-unit dive lodge that offers access to some of the island's finest dive sites, 30 minutes east of George Town. Excellent vacation packages available.

Also part of the Cayman Kai development is the new luxury condominium resort complex, **The Retreat,** located where the old Rum Point Club lured island isolationists. This development sells its facilities as "the private world of the privileged few," and the view and beach alone might convince you. Health and recreational facilities are an exclusive "plus" here. (Tel. 948–0952/50.)

Sunset House. *Moderate.* P.O. Box 479, South Church St. Tel. 949–5966. "Low-key or laid back" might describe the 42 comfortable rooms on the ironshore south of George Town. A well-run dive operation, congenial staff, and one of the most amusing and popular local bars on the island make this resort a favorite with divers. Excellent shore diving and snorkeling and a good restaurant and other attractions. The ongoing cast of local characters—especially the local fishing fraternity—that gathers at "My Bar" (a thatched-roof seafront structure) makes this a great place to "meet the people."

Spanish Cove. *Inexpensive.* Box 1014, West Bay Tel. 809–949–3765. These 96 nicely appointed units, pool, restaurant, bar, and complete dive shop make this a popular selection with discriminating divers. Lovely lush landscaping and quiet setting, worth finding on Cayman's north coast.

Cayman Islander. *Inexpensive.* P.O. Box 509, West Bay Beach. Tel. 949–5533. A pleasant property with 69 air-conditioned rooms around the pool. Seven Mile Beach is just across the road. What's unique and fun here is that you exchange your money for doubloons and pay for all extras in buried-treasure replicas. They have a restaurant and offer an informal and friendly setting, impeccably furnished and clean rooms with satellite TV, and free admission to the new Cayman Islander Nightclub.

Seaview Hotel. *Inexpensive.* P.O. Box 260, S. Church St., Grand Cayman. Tel. 949–4990. This recently renovated 16-room hotel has been the favorite roost of long-time visitors and businessmen for over 30 years. Located just south of George Town on the ironshore it's quiet, clean, comfortable units and friendly Caymanian staff. Freshwater pool, *Shipwreck Bar,* ample parking seaside behind the hotel.

CAYMAN BRAC

Brac Reef Beach Resort. *Moderate.* Cayman Brac. Te. 948–7323. The latest source of Brac pride is this new 40-room resort on the island's breeze-cooled south coast. Designed, built, and owned by Bracker Linton Tibbets, the resort lures divers and those vacationers who come to savor the special ambience of this tiny island while enjoying quality accommodations, pool, beach, snorkeling, and a good local restaurant.

Buccaneer's Inn. *Moderate.* P.O. Box 68, Cayman Brac, Tel. 948–7257. This 34-room property is simple, almost rustic, but still very friendly. Located opposite Brac Reef, but on the West End's north shore, with the airport runway separating the two at this tip-of-the-island point. Swimming pool; restaurant; bar on the beach featuring entertainment at the edge of the sea. All three meals included in the daily rate.

Tiara Beach Hotel. *Moderate.* Cayman Brac. 948–7313. The esteemed Divi Hotel Corp. took over this 33-room property, formerly the Brac Reef I, and improved the facilities, including the beach area, upgrading them to the organization's standards. Nice beach, saltwater pool, tennis court, and diving. Bonefishing can be arranged with local guide. Restaurant and bar on premises.

Scuba diving is a big attraction of the Brac, and all hotels offer packages through Brac Aquatics, Ltd.

LITTLE CAYMAN

Dillon Cottages. *Moderate.* c/o Capt. Dillon Kirkconnell, Cayman Brac. Tel. 949–4321. Located near the grass airstrip, these two cottages offer simple surroundings on this secluded isle. A great way to "rough it" without camping out, and enjoy the special serenity Little Cayman offers.

Kingston Bight Lodge. *Moderate.* Little Cayman. Tel. 948–3244. This small, 12-unit fishing lodge became so popular with bonefishermen and tarpon enthusiasts that the resort was often full—and overfull at times—in years past. All the facilities and potential are still there, but the resort was sold in 1984 and had not reopened at press time. Check with the Dept. of Tourism before making plans.

Southern Cross Club. *Moderate.* Little Cayman. U.S. tel. (318) 222–0517. These nine rooms set in an idyllic palm-fringed beach setting on Little Cayman's south coast, have all the ingredients for an unforgettable "castaway holiday" in a simple but very spirited out-island resort. Although it claims to be a private club, it will accommodate you if space permits. Call for information—the resort closes during certain periods. Diving and fishing are excellent here, and bird-watching has been called some of the Caribbean's finest at the nearby sanctuary.

Sammy McCoy's Guest House. *Moderate.* Tel. (809) 948–8326. This small, cozy diving and fishing resort opened in 1985 on Little Cayman's north coast. Very reasonable rates and Sammy's infectious good nature make this locally run resort a promising vacation prospect for the future. Five rooms, superb diving and snorkeling right offshore. Meals included in rates.

CONDOMINIUMS. At least a dozen condominium complexes, most of them beachfront and all at least "on the water," fall into the Expensive price category. They offer self-catering holiday options in some of the finest units of this nature you'll find on any Caribbean island. Studios, one-, two-, and three-bedroom units are available. Assume each will have a full electric kitchen and simple, but ample, utensils supplied for dining in. A few favorites (all on Grand Cayman), both for quality of facilities and friendliness of management and staff:

Harbour Heights. Box 482, West Bay Rd. Tel. 949–6364. The 19 two-bedroom, two-bath units of this complex remain some of the nicest on the beach, and the personality of this 13-year-old property comes from the TLC invested by owners and management working together. Freshwater pool, lovely beach, and a feeling of seclusion. No tennis.

Lacovia. *Deluxe.* Box 887, West Bay Rd. Tel. 949–6364. Completed just over a year ago, this 34-unit apartment complex has already won repeat clientele who appreciate the high quality of layout, design, and decor Lacovia has brought to Seven Mile Beach. One-, two-, and three-bedroom suites, each with full electric kitchen and private patio or balcony overlooking a large swimming pool, Jacuzzi, and exotic tropical gardens of oleander, bougainvillea, and crotons. Saunas, tennis courts, beach, recreation center/clubhouse with 150-person capacity. Small shopping center and a variety of dining within walking distance.

London House. Box 1356, West Bay Rd. Tel. 947–4060. One of the friendliest condominium properties on the northern end of Seven Mile Beach, this 20-unit complex is managed and staffed by Caymanians. Freshwater pool, patio barbecue area, and a half-dozen hammocks under casuarinas on the beach. A lovely, relaxing location.

Moon Bay. North Side, Box 38. Tel. 947–2057. A newcomer on the Cayman condominium listing, this 26-unit property overlooks the fringing reef off Pease Bay on the island's south-central coast. A half-hour ride from Seven Mile Beach, Moon Bay's lure is its serene seaside location "miles from anywhere" but with every possible amenity and superbly landscaped garden setting. Freshwater pool, large patio area, excellent snorkeling and windsurfing in the reef-protected shallows offshore, and new tennis courts.

Pan Cayman House. Box 440, West Bay Rd. Tel. 809–947–4002. A long-established favorite refuge of many of Cayman's most loyal patrons. The ten two- and three-bedroom beachfront apartments offer no extracurricular activities, just a beautiful secluded setting and a feeling of comfort the staff works hard to preserve. Located in the center of Seven Mile Beach.

Spanish Bay Villas. Box 2067, Spanish Bay. Tel. 949–3272. These 12 one- and two-bedroom apartments are located on the north coast, right next door to Spanish Cove resort. The excellent facilities of their neighbor property, combined with the quality of the seaside units, make this an exceptional self-catering vacation opportunity for divers. The famous north wall is just one-quarter mile offshore. The villas are in West Bay, nine miles north of George Town.

Tarquynn Manor. Box 1362, West Bay Rd. Tel 947–4038. Tarquynn's 20 two-bedroom units and three-bedroom penthouse suites have a substantial list of repeat customers, attracted by the beautiful setting and attentiveness of the manager and Caymanian staff. Newcomers will find a warm welcome—if they're fortunate enough to find space.

Victoria House. Box 636, West Bay Rd. Tel. 947–4233. Built by Canadians with exquisite taste, this 25-room resort on the beach remains one of the island's finest. Tennis and extremely friendly management and staff are lagniappe; the units themselves are lovely.

Villas of the Galleon. Box 952, West Bay Beach. Tel 949–6485. This very popular property is nestled on the beach between the Holiday Inn and Le Club Cayman—the two "hot spots" of Seven Mile Beach. The 48 units preserve a feeling of privacy amidst all the activity, however. Courteous and capable management and staff.

Villas Pappagallo. Box 952, Barkers, West Bay, Tel. 949–3568. One of the most distinctive condominium properties on Grand Cayman, with 42 one-, two-, and three-bedroom apartments unusual for their Mediterranean design and decor. On the most distant developed waterfront location on Grand Cayman's northwest coast. Excellent snorkeling right offshore, freshwater pool, and a very quiet, secluded location, racquetball courts and a hydrotherapy spa. Spanish Cove welcomes Pappagallo guests for scuba diving. New epicurean restaurant opened on property in 1985.

The Cayman Islands Department of Tourism can provide you with a complete list of condominium and small rental apartments available in the *Moderate to Inexpensive* price range—and there are lots of them, including beachfront units on Seven Mile Beach. During summer season, many of the properties listed above as "Expensive" become "Moderate to Inexpensive." Check before you book. Hospitality World, Ltd., can help you rent a condominium to suit your needs. Contact Suite 205, 7220 N.W. 36th St., Miami, FL 33166. Tel. (800) 232–1034.

 HOME AND APARTMENT RENTALS. Apartments, cottages, and guest houses vie with all the villas and hotels available on Grand Cayman. They range from two to three bedrooms, are mostly oceanfront, and many also have swimming pools. Prices during the winter season range anywhere from $40–170 per day.

Cayman Rent a Villa can assist you in locating a rental house or cottage. Contact Box 681, Grand Cayman. Tel. 947–4144.

 HOW TO GET AROUND. A fleet of taxis meets all planes arriving at Grand Cayman's Owen Roberts Airport. Your fare to town will be about $5 and to most hotels along Seven Mile Beach between $8 and $10. From the airport to the Tortuga, way out at the northern point, runs about $30, but they will meet you if you let them know your arrival time in advance.

Cars are available for rental but not at the airport. Best bet is to phone as soon as you reach your hotel. However, cars can be left at the airport on your departure. The rental companies will issue you a driving permit (U.S. $3) as long as you have a valid driver's license. Among the firms are: *Hertz* (tel. 92280); *Budget Cayman Rent-a-Car Ltd.* (tel. 95605); and *National Car Rentals* (tel. 94790); but our favorite firm is *CICO/AVIS*—the cars are better maintained than most and the staff courteous and helpful. Plus toll-free U.S. reservations: 1–800–331–1212. Local: 92468. Driving is on the left.

You can also rent bicycles, mopeds, and motorbikes on Grand Cayman from *Caribbean Motors* (tel. 94051) or *Cayman Cycle* (tel. 95721).

Taxis are stationed at all the major hotels, and island buses zip back and forth into George Town all day. If you haven't rented a car or taken an island tour, this will be the most inexpensive way to travel. Buses out to the East End operate on a less frequent schedule, so check with your hotel for times. And remember, always check to see whether you'll be paying in Cayamian or U.S. dollars.

On Cayman Brac, cars are available through *S & H Rentals* (tel. 87347), and mopeds through *Brac Reef Beach Hotel.*

TOURIST INFORMATION SERVICES. The Department of Tourism operates information booths at the Tourist Landing Dock on the waterfront in George Town, and at Owen Roberts International Airport. Its main office is on the second floor of the Government Administration Bldg. ("Glass House") in George Town. Tel. 94844, Ext. 175. For sources closer to home, see Tourist Information Services section in the *Facts at Your Fingertips* chapter.

SPECIAL EVENTS. The highlight, and the most outstanding event here, is Pirate's Week in October. Colorful costumes and parades along with treasure hunts, elaborate buffets, dancing, and sports tournaments, but the highlight is when Caymanians dress up as rogues and wenches, board a replica of a galleon, invade the harbor, and capture the governor. There's a mock battle, but it surely looks authentic, as if the swords were drawn by the buccaneers who commanded the sea lanes more than 200 years ago. Batabano, a local costume parade and carnival sponsored by Rotary, is a fun even worth attending during April.

June is Million Dollar Month in the Cayman Islands, a month-long series of saltwater fishing tournaments offering huge cash prizes including $1 million to the first angler to break the existing IGFA all-tackle record for Atlantic blue marlin in Cayman waters.

TOURS. There are a variety of island tours, but the most impressive are those you take underwater. Coral reefs, sunken wrecks, and marine gardens are spectacles to be seen and can be easily arranged through a number of aquatic operators (see *Participant Sports*). On land, island tours by taxi should really be limited to a half day, since there really isn't enough to see to warrant a full day. Two Caymanian-owned and -operated tour services offer a wide and interesting variety of island tours, from shopping tours of George Town to round-the-island lunch trips with snorkeling stops. Congenial young Caymanian guides make this a very worthwhile and enjoyable investment. Contact *Tropicana Tours,* tel. 95499 or *Greenlight Tours,* tel. 79560.

The *Kon Tiki* is a new party "raft" offering day and night cruises, with live band and copious rum punch off Seven Mile Beach. Tel. 96062 for times and tickets.

North Sound beach/picnic/snorkeling cruises and a variety of outings at sea can be arranged through Crosby and Gleason Ebanks at *C&G Watersports* on West Bay Road. Tel. 93954, 93372, or 93240.

For glass-bottom-boat rides and snorkeling tours, *Bob Soto's Diving Ltd.* (tel. 92022/92483) and *Surfside Watersports Ltd.* (tel. 92724) can accommodate you.

BEACHES. Grand Cayman's west-coast stretch of *Seven Mile Beach* is the showpiece of fine, powdery sand and the island's primary topside vacation attraction. Grand Cayman has several small beaches which might better be called coves, including *Smith's Cove* off South Church St., south of the Grand Old House—a popular bathing spot on weekends for residents.

A small but pretty beach is right off the Ports of Call restaurant north of George Town, and is officially called *Pageant Beach.*

Small beach areas on the south coast offer excellent snorkeling within the sheltered area inside the fringing reef. You can find them *behind the Crow's Nest restaurant* near Sand Cay in South Sound, at *Beach Bay Condominiums* in Spotts, and at *Moon Bay* in Pease Bay.

At East End, the *Tortuga Club Beach* can be lovely if it's kept clean of seaweed tossed ashore by the tradewinds. Other tiny coves can be discovered by exploring the shore along Queen's Highway on the way to North Side.

Seldom discovered by visitors unless they're staying out there are the beautiful beach areas of *Cayman Kai, Rum Point* and, even more isolated and unspoiled, *Water Cay.* These are favored hideaways for residents and popular Sunday picnic spots.

On **Cayman Brac,** both *Tiara Beach* and *Brac Reef Beach* resorts have fine small beaches, better for sunning than snorkeling.

Little Cayman's *Sandy Point,* on the eastern tip, and *Owen Cay* beaches are exquisite isolated patches of powder worth every effort to reach by boat.

PARTICIPANT SPORTS. Scuba diving is still king of sports in the Cayman Islands, with deep-sea fishing running close behind. Twenty-three dive operations and numerous related services such as underwater photography centers serve an estimated 40,000 divers annually. You can learn to dive here, through short resort or full certification courses; other divers must have "c-cards" to prove they are certified. Two-tank dives average $30–35; full certification courses $300. Recommended operations (although all are very competent) are *Sunset House Divers; Bob Soto's Diving Ltd.; Quabbin Dives Ltd., Don Foster's Dive Grand Cayman Ltd.,* and *Spanish Cove* for learning to dive. Literature on all operations can be obtained through the Grand Cayman office of the Dept. of Tourism. On Cayman Brac, *Brac Aquatics, Ltd.* offers scuba and snorkeling.

Deep-sea fishing here is a bonanza, with the waters teeming with blue marlin, wahoo, bonita, and barracuda. Contact Charterboat Headquarters (tel. 74340), the clearinghouse for booking charters, or *Quabbin Dives Ltd.* (tel. 95597), to make arrangements. Prices run about $300 for a half day; $500 for a full eight hours. On Cayman Brac and Little Cayman, deep-sea fishing and bonefishing can be arranged through hotels.

One of the major events of world sportfishing is Million Dollar Month, a month-long series of salt water fishing tournaments in June. Huge cash prizes—including $1 million to the first angler to break the existing IFGA all-tackle record for Atlantic blue marlin in Cayman waters—lure hundreds of serious anglers for the entire month. Information can be obtained from the Million Dollar Month Committee, P.O. Box 878, Grand Cayman.

Many hotels and apartments have **tennis** courts, many of them lighted for night play. Some are for resident guests only; others, such as the Caribbean Club, and the Holiday Inn, welcome visitors and charge a small fee.

Water skiing, wind surfing, or simply **swimming** the calm waters are other pleasures offered at or through the major resort hotels. New to Grand Cayman and unique in the Caribbean is the Britannia Golf Course, where Jack Nicklaus has added a new concept of the sport—a course designed for the "Cayman short ball." Future plans include a 246-room Hyatt. Information on this unusual course is available from Box 1698, Grand Cayman. Tel. 949–7440.

SPECTATOR SPORTS. Cricket, rugby, and **soccer** matches are held throughout the year, with teams coming in to compete from other islands. Contact the Department of Tourism (tel. 94844) for times and places. Usual venue is the playing fields located just off South Sound R., about five minutes from George Town.

HISTORIC SITES AND HOUSES. Many of the old homes have gone but there are still a few that show off the distinctive Caymanian architecture. Almost gingerbread in appearance, they are single- and double-story structures with ornate hand-carved trim and zinc roofs. Some have been restored in George Town, with the finest examples on South Church St. just past the harbor. They are in an area called *Pantonville,* since all three homes were built, and are still owned, by the Panton family. Another two-story historic structure is the *Thompson House* just out of town on the airport road. None of the "historic homes" are open for public viewing, as they are now either private homes or offices where visitors would be an intrusion.

The rocks and tiny village called *Hell:* The limestone formations and crags give visitors a different look at Grand Cayman away from the resort area, but the main attraction here is the *Hell Post Office,* where tourists get a kick out of sending postcards to friends which are postmarked "Hell."

The Old Court House. This is the last of the old government buildings to be preserved and is another classic Caymanian building on the harbor front in George Town. The Lands and Survey Department has its offices here now, but you're welcome to visit.

 MUSEUMS. *The Cayman Brac Museum,* in the Old Government Administration Bldg. at Stake Bay. contains a carefully assembled collection of tools and artifacts that depicts life in the early part of this century. An admirable effort by the islanders to preserve the past and well worth seeing. Open Mon.–Fri. 9:00 A.M.–noon and 1:00 P.M.– 4:00 P.M.; Sat. 9:00 A.M.–noon. Free. On Grand Cayman, visit the marine artifact collection of the late treasure hunter Art McKee, located in in Soto's Freeport building in George Town.

 MUSIC, DANCE, STAGE. *The F.J. Harquil Cultural Center,* located behind the Cinema I & II on West Bay Rd. is the most exciting nightlife development on Grand Cayman during the last decade. Live drama, musical comedy, variety shows, and cabarets are offered for those who crave culture rather than action during their visit. The island's Inn Theatre Company season runs Oct.–June, featuring fine performances by local company members. Concerts and theatre performances by international artists are scheduled at other times. Call the box office at 95477 for current program offerings.

The various publications that appear each week on Grand Cayman will give you complete listings of all special events, dances, and concerts. Make a point of picking up at least one of the three newspapers *(Caymanian Compass, Sun* and *The Pilot)* published weekly.

 SHOPPING. Grand Cayman offers the finest selection of quality black coral craftsmanship in the Caribbean, and connoisseurs of this form of jewelry and art will be tempted to overspend here. You'll find George Town an unexpected treasure, with china, crystal, watches and jewelry at excellent duty-free prices from 25–40% less than in the U.S. Shops are along the harbor front or just a block or two away. The main shopping thoroughfares are Harbour Dr., along the waterfront; and Fort St. and Cardinal Ave., both perpendicular to Harbour Dr. Other emporiums include Elizabethan Square, off Sheddan Rd., and Anchorage Square, off N. Church St. Both plazas offer an exclusive collection of quality shops featuring clothing and other items.

Soto's Freeport Building on Harbour Dr. houses a branch of *Soto's Freeport Ltd.* duty-free collection and two boutiques, *Temptation Ltd.* for sophisticated U.S. and European ladies' fashions, and *The West Indian Sea Island Cotton Shop,* for colorful, casual cotton Batik clothing and embroidered items from St. Kitts/Nevis in the eastern Caribbean.

Other harborfront shops worth exploring are *Arden, English Shoppe, Cayman Camera,* and *Artifacts Ltd.,* side-by-side facing the tourist dock and cruise-ship landing.

Ruth Clarage for hand-printed original designs that make stunning Caribbean sportswear—everything from scarves to short or long dresses.

Kirk Freeport Plaza, on Cardinal Ave., is large and filled with a wonderland of watches; a wide selection of crystal by Lalique and Baccarat; and Hummel and Lladro figurines. There are dozens more choices, but make sure you check your hometown prices in advance so you'll know exactly how much you're really saving.

Treasure Cove, also on Cardinal Ave., hugs the waterfront and looks just like an English Tudor cottage. The china, such as Rosenthal, Royal Doulton, and Wedgwood, is attractively displayed, as is the crystal.

The *Grand Cayman Craft Market* on Cardinal Ave. is a tongue-in-cheek title for a tiny hole-in-the-wall packed floor to ceiling with souvenirs associated with "the islands," from thatch baskets and Panama hats to Haitian carvings and an assortment of hammocks. The real attraction is the personality who owns and operates this Caribbean curiosity shop, John Gunter, a transplanted Jamaican whose size and enthusiasm make him one of the island's memorable characters.

For black coral creations, be certain to visit *Black Coral And* on Fort St., next to the Cayman Airways Ltd. office, and *Black Coral and Other Fine Gems,* next to Ruth Clarage on the waterfront.

Shopping on Cayman Brac is limited, with small shops at the *Brac Reef Beach, Tiara Beach,* and *Buccaneer Hotels,* but the highlight here is a visit to *Ida-Lee's* jewelry shop for beautiful items carved from black coral.

RESTAURANTS. An unfortunate discovery for many visitors is the high cost of eating out on Grand Cayman, and a little known fact is that the best value for dollar exists in the small native nooks specializing in West Indian fare (there is no indigenous "Cayman cuisine," only adaptations of island-style dishes).

Local specialties include conch (pronounced konk), the meat of a large pink mollusk served stewed in coconut milk, as conch fritters, chowder, or tenderized and pan-fried as cracked conch. Fish, including snapper, grouper, wahoo, tuna, dolphin, and marlin can be served simply or spiced with peppers, onions, and tomatoes. Curried goat and chicken are other favorites.

Caribbean (spiny) lobster is available here, but it is usually very expensive, as the shellfish is in short supply in local waters. And, unfortunately, the only traditional dish of the Cayman Islands, turtle, is often difficult to find on the island. The government forbids the killing of wild sea turtles, and the scaling down of the activities of the Cayman Turtle Farm in recent years has resulted in a shortage of meat. If you go the Cayman Islands expecting to savor turtle stew or turtle steak, you'll have to phone around to find out which restaurant has it on the menu that day.

Dining on Grand Cayman can be very expensive. Prices are usually quoted *in Cayman Dollars* with 15% gratuity added automatically in the better restaurants. An important note: very few places accept any credit cards! We call $16 CI ($20.50 US) and up per person for entree only for dinner, *Expensive;* $9–$15 CI *Moderate,* and anything below that *Inexpensive.*

The following restaurants are all on Grand Cayman:

Expensive

Caribbean Club. West Bay Rd. Tel 92593. Reservations are a must here. The food is superb, as is the setting. Quiet, intimate, and unhurried service. The menu is extensive, as is the wine list. All credit cards.

Chez Jacques. Holiday Inn Grand Cayman. Tel. 74444. Imaginative continental menu featuring seafood specialties and famous for its prime rib portions. Quiet, relaxed atmosphere, with free admission to the Wreck of the Ten Sails nightclub included in the price of dinner. All credit cards.

Grand Old House, Petra Plantation. South Church St. Tel. 92020. The home was built in 1900, and the Victorian look hasn't changed. Dining by candlelight on the veranda overlooking the sea or in an airy greenhouse setting in the gazebo. The most ambitious menu on the island features exotic lobster dishes, rijsttafel rack of lamb, and a variety of French and West Indian specialties. Originally called the Petra Plantation, the great-house atmosphere remains. Reservations are a must. No credit cards.

Lobster Pot. North Church St. Tel. 92736. Right on the water on an open terrace, and usually crowded because of its fine food. Its menu comes in the form of a mid-19th century newspaper. Among the many choices are conch chowder, turtle soup, seafood curry, fresh fish, and Key lime pie. Reservations required. No credit cards.

Galleon Beach Restaurant (at Le Club Hotel). Tel. 92692. This dining establishment on Seven Mile Beach offers a romantic seaside (and ocean-view) setting with candlelight dining on seafood and prime beef. Inside dinners only. AE, MC, V.

Periwinkle. West Bay Road. Tel. 92927. The new Periwinkle is delightful; epicurean Italian cuisine supervised by chef who was with the Caribbean Club for many years. Excellent and imaginative menu and wine list. AE, MC, V.

Reefcomber Island Grille. West Bay Road. Tel. 95575. A new establishment offering excellent, unusual Texas-style cuisine (fajitas, enchiladas), prime rib, steaks, seafood, and interesting menu of extras. Good lunches, attentive service, and comfortable atmosphere. AE, MC, V.

Seaview Restaurant. Seaview Hotel, S. Church St. Tel. 94990. Dine by candlelight on a tropical veranda made more enjoyable by courteous service. Seafood is the specialty but it's pricey for the quality. AE, V, MC.

Moderate

Almond Tree. North Church St. Tel 92893. This is the island's only thatchroof restaurant. Creative and potent tropical drinks to sip while you wait for one of their seafood specialties. The emphasis is usually on the catch of the day, soup and salad included. All credit cards.

The Cracked Conch. Selkirk Plaza, West Bay Rd. Tel. 95717. Generous portions and well prepared seafood make this one of the most popular lunch and dinner spots on Grand Cayman. Try their conch creations before you leave. Local fish and lobster are excellent here too. AE, MC, V.

The Lighthouse Club. Breakers. Tel. 72047. Attractive oceanfront setting and breeze-cooled location complement the menu here which emphasizes West Indian seafood dishes. AE, MC, V.

The Marlin Room. Beach Club Colony Hotel, West Bay Rd. Tel. 92023. Quiet, candlelit atmosphere with a menu that combines both excellent West Indian–style dishes and a variety of continental entrees. Seafood is the specialty here, dinner only. Reservations are suggested. AE, MC, V.

Pagoda. West Bay Rd. Tel. 95475. This Chinese restaurant is the only one on the island and serves excellent food to eat in or take out. Nice lounge while you wait for either one. AE, MC, V.

Inexpensive

Capt. Bryan's Seafood. N. Church St. (on the waterfront). A new lunch and dinner spot with a nautical theme and attractive seaside patio offers fresh local seafood and West Indian specialties including fried lobster and stewed conch at very reasonable prices. A short walk north from George Town on the sea side. No credit cards.

Cayman Arms. Harbour Dr. Tel. 92661. Small English pub overlooking the waterfront. A friendly and informal place, it is a favorite for its thick strawberry daiquiris. No credit cards.

Crow's Nest. South Sound Rd. Tel. 96216. Open daily for lunch and dinner. House specialties in this modest little restaurant include shrimp, cracked conch, conch fritters, and other local seafood. Customers can use the sandy beach and snorkeling area out back for daytime recreation. No credit cards.

Island House Restaurant. Church St., West Bay. Tel. 93017. Reservations, please! Excellent Cayman-style cooking—coconut grouper, conch, turtle, and lobster in an informal, warm atmosphere. Owner Kenrick Welds runs one of West Bay's best small eateries. Open daily for lunch and dinner. No credit cards.

Island Taste. S. Church St., George Town. Tel. 94945. Famous for their meat patties (spicy pastries filled with highly seasoned beef) and West Indian dishes. Very informal and very reasonable, a popular quick lunch and take-out stop for George Town's business folk. Lunch only. No credit cards.

Ribbs Unlimited. Off West Bay Road, adjacent Cayman Islander nightclub complex. One of the best buys on Grand Cayman, patterned after the Tony Roma's rib chain in the U.S. Huge portions, superb ribs and chicken, onion loaves, etc. A must for anyone homesick for that kind of fare, or for those seeking value for dollar. AE, MC, V.

Sheila's Restaurant. Goring Ave., George Town. Tel. 95237. Breakfast, lunch, and dinner (winter season only) weekdays, with daily lunch specials for under $7 in portions that will fill you. West Indian specialties, conchburgers, steaks, and salads. Excellent soups, too. No credit cards.

NIGHT LIFE AND BARS. Grand Cayman has expanded significantly in the last year in this area, with the addition of the new *Cayman Islander Nightclub* complex off West Bay Road. Live music and huge interior with dance floor, open 6 nights a week. Admission is CI $5—but free to Cayman Islander Hotel guests. Their island floor show, "Caribbean Cabaret," is excellent, using talented young artists (Tel. 95533).

At the Holiday Inn, the *Wreck of the Ten Sails* is still popular with the local crowd and the dance floor is a great gawking place for islanders and visitors. Entertainer "Barefoot Man" (and Band) are a decade-old tradition on Grand Cayman and always worth a visit. Admission is free to hotel guests, $5 for others.

Le Club Cayman, formerly Galleon Beach, offers nightly entertainment (except Sunday) in the beachfront lounge. Local and international artists change weekly or monthly, depending on season.

The Windjammer Lounge in the Falls Center on West Bay Rd. is Cayman's most sophisticated nightclub, offering everything from jazz to quiet piano music —check local newspapers for current performers.

The Tradewinds, one of the Caribbean's most popular calypso bands, tours Grand Cayman from October through May or June, appearing at the *Ports of Call* patio on N. Church St. near George Town and a variety of other spots. Their performances are well-publicized and should be a must on your nocturnal activities agenda. Wherever they play, expect a lively crowd of locals; admission is usually $5–8.

Weekend dancing under the stars is a big attraction at the *Royal Palms Hotel.* Poolside barbecue and entertainment every Saturday for a fixed price of under $20.

POSTAGE. The Cayman Islands Philatelic Bureau, located in the main post office in George Town, offers one of the most colorful collections of postage stamps in the Caribbean on souvenir first day covers for collectors. The stamps of these islands make an excellent, inexpensive souvenir and can be purchased Mon.–Sat. from that office.

At press time, air mail postage to the U.S. and Canada is C.I. 20 cents per half oz. for letters and C.I. 10 cents for postcards; C.I. 40 cents to the U.K. for letters and C.I. 15 cents for postcards. A rate increase is under consideration for 1985, but your hotel front desk can advise you on current rates.

ELECTRIC CURRENT. The current here is 110 to 120 volts A.C.

SECURITY. "The islands time forgot" have remained the islands crime forgot by comparison with more developed destinations, but visitors are always urged to use *common sense* in securing valuables including wallets, jewelry, expensive cameras, and dive gear. Even paradise has occasional snakes and thievery does occur. Leaving valuables in view and doors unlocked offers more temptation than some characters can resist. This applies to night spots as well: Don't leave purses unattended while on the dance floor.

CURAÇAO

by
NANCY B. CLARKE AND ADRIENNE HENZEL

Nancy B. Clarke was a contributing editor to the Best of the Caribbean *guide book. In Venezuela, she worked with the* Caracas Daily Journal, *and later wrote a monthly economic newsletter for the Republic of Colombia. Adrienne Henzel has studied and worked in Madrid, where she reviewed restaurants for U.S. publications. She has traveled extensively in Europe and Latin America. She and Ms. Clarke are compiling a cookbook on traditional Spanish foods.*

Although Curaçao lies less than forty miles north of South America, the influence is strictly Dutch colonial. The homes are scrubbed and gleaming and, painted as they are in a variety of pastel colors, give the island a sparkling storybook look. The largest of six islands that form the Netherlands Antilles, Curaçao covers 173 square miles and is home for 165,000 people.

While Curaçao has its share of beaches, they can't compare in length and breadth with those of its sister islands, Aruba and Bonaire. The emphasis on this island is on smaller, cove-style beaches, shopping, fine dining, and the enchanting capital city of Willemstad. The official language is Dutch, but the dialect of the people is a mixture of Dutch, English, Spanish, Portuguese, Indian, and African. It's called *Papiamento.* Sounds difficult, but you'll be surprised at how much of it you can understand, especially if you know a little Spanish. You don't have to know Papiamento to get along. As one Curaçao businessman put it: "We are Dutch, so we all speak English."

Past and Present

Curaçao was discovered, not by Columbus, but by Alonzo de Ojeda —or Amerigo Vespucci, depending whose history book you read—in 1499, and was first occupied by the Spaniards in 1527. In 1634, the Dutch arrived under the auspices of the Netherlands West India Company, banished the Spanish governor and four hundred assorted Spaniards and Indians to Venezuela, and set up a colony. Peter Stuyvesant became its governor in 1642 and held the post for three years before heading north to New York. Over the years the British and the French made stabs at capturing the island until the Dutch claim was firmly sealed by the Treaty of Paris in 1815. In 1954 Curaçao became an autonomous part of the Kingdom of the Netherlands, with an elected parliament and island council, and a governor who is appointed by the queen to represent the Crown.

Curaçao is politically stable and has a well-earned reputation for religious and racial tolerance. On two occasions, Curaçao gave asylum to Simón Bolivar, the liberator of South America. Today, some forty nationalities comprise the island's population.

EXPLORING CURAÇAO

Thirty-eight miles long and shaped like an elongated bow tie, Curaçao stretches northwest, pointing to its sister islands, Aruba, to the north and Bonaire, to the south. The better hotels are scattered along the southern, leeward side of the island. For water people, this shore also has the better beaches and coves. Piscadera Bay (with the Concorde and Las Palmas Hotels) is a five-minute cab ride to the principal city and capital, Willemstad. Curaçao International Airport is near the center of the island. Regular cabs are readily available and moderately priced. The public bus system is dependable and inexpensive, but make sure you carry small change in florins for boarding.

Once you've settled in your hotel and tested the Caribbean water and sun, you'll want to visit Curaçao's charming capital city, Willemstad.

Willemstad

The Santa Anna Bay cuts right through Willemstad like an Amsterdam canal. A pontoon bridge connects the eastern area, the Punda, with the Otrabanda, literally, the "other side."

Willemstad is a pleasure to explore. Allow plenty of time and set a leisurely pace for shopping, sightseeing, and picture-taking. You'll be impressed with the cleanliness of Curaçao's capital.

Stores are open Monday through Saturday but, when cruise ships are in port, may open on Sunday for a few hours. Everything is centrally located within about a six-block radius in the Punda section, so Willemstad is best explored on foot. Comfortable, flat shoes are in order, as there are some cobblestone streets left.

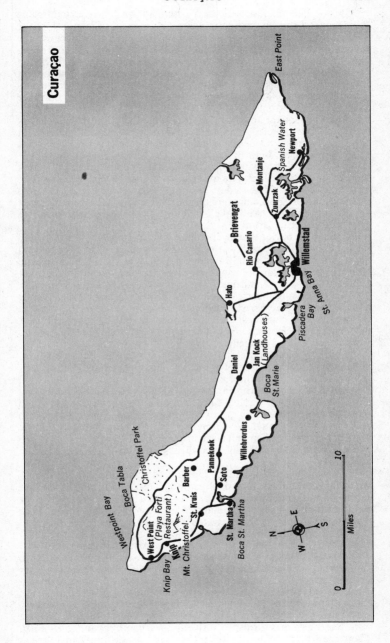

A good place to start is at the Waterfort, just two blocks from the Punda side of the Queen Emma pontoon bridge and the mouth of the Santa Anna Bay. This bastion dates from 1634, and its walls form the foundation of the towering Curaçao Plaza Hotel. When you see the big ships pass so close to it, you'll know why the hotel is the only one in the world that carries marine collision insurance. Cannons still point toward the ocean and iron links still remain from an age when visitors weren't so friendly and residents had to close off the harbor entrance from invaders and pirates.

Cross Piar Square and you'll see the beautifully restored Fort Amsterdam. Once the city's major fort, it is now the seat of government and the governor's residence. Within the fort's walls is Curaçao oldest Protestant church, built in 1742.

Now head north toward the Queen Emma pontoon bridge. Watch it swing open to let ships pass into and out of the harbor, which it does an average of thirty times a day. Watch people scrambling to get across this seven hundred-foot floating bridge to avoid the fifteen-minute wait for the trip by ferry. And take a ride on the ferry yourself, for a free taste of Caribbean salt air.

The pontoon bridge that sways under your feet was built in 1888, and used to be a toll bridge. Turn right at the taxi stand on Breedestraat and you'll pass Spritzer and Fuhrmann, the Tiffany's of the Caribbean; then stop by the colorful New Amsterdam store and a handful of other tempting shops in handsomely restored Dutch Colonial buildings. Turn left at Columbustraat and visit the very special Mikve Israel Synagogue. It is the oldest synagogue in continual use in the Western Hemisphere. Its congregation was founded in 1651 by Sephardic Jews who came from Holland. Note the magnificent brass chandeliers and carved mahogany ornaments.

Leaving the museum, go left. At the end of the street, on Madurostraat, two blocks away, is the bustling floating market. (Have your camera ready.) Each morning, dozens of schooners come from Venezuela, laden with tropical produce. They tie up on the small canal and display their wares. You'll hear good-natured bartering and you'll see rows of fresh mangoes, papayas, and exotic vegetables, next to fish and fabrics—all for sale or to photograph. As this nautical produce mart is a morning affair, plan on stopping by while the action is still lively—and the day still cool. Activities start at 6:30 A.M. and wind up at 3:30 P.M.

Walk west now to the end of Caprileskade, and turn left on Heerenstraat for more browsing and bargaining. Turn back toward the water one block to Handelskade and the Café Italia, a friendly sidewalk cafe right across from the ferry landing. Stop here for an icy lemonade or a steaming cappuccino, and watch the passing parade of ships and humans. Free shuttle buses pick up hotel guests immediately to the left of the bridge's Otrabanda side. There is a taxi stand there, too.

On the Otrabanda side of the pontoon bridge see the statue of Pedro Luis Brión, which dominates the square called Brionplein. Another point of interest on the Otrabanda, but farther out on Leeuwenhoekstraat, is the Curaçao Museum, a former military hospital that was carefully restored as a fine example of Dutch architecture. Its gardens, containing specimens of all the island's plants and trees, are worth a visit. The museum is furnished with antiques, paintings and *objets d'art*. There are art exhibitions, as well as relics of the primitive Indian tribes that once lived on these islands.

At Chobolobo you'll find the Senior Liqueur Factory, distillers of the original Curaçao liqueur, made from oranges grown locally. Close by, in the Gaito residential district, is the Centro Pro Arte, where concerts, ballets, and plays are presented. Exhibits of paintings, sculpture, and other arts are held on a regular basis.

North of the Scharloo residential section is Fort Nassau, an impressive bastion built in 1792 on a 220-foot-high hill overlooking the city. It once housed the military. Today, it welcomes visitors who come to explore and then to dine at its fine restaurant or to dance in its intimate discoteque/nightclub, Infinity. The Fort Nassau Restaurant's terrace bar is the perfect place to watch the Caribbean sun set.

West Point

To explore the northwest part of the island, follow the main road toward the village of Soto. You'll find the landscape arid and cactus spiked. Some cacti rise more than twenty feet, and the divi-divi trees bend to the will of the trade winds. Flaming flamboyant trees punctuate the dry countryside from time to time, and you'll see a few picturesque thatched native huts that have not yet succumbed to the new and modern. It is in this countryside, or *cunucu,* that you may hear the happy rhythm of the *tumba,* Curaçao's "national" dance, with its traces of everything from the Latin American rumba to an Irish jig. Throughout the *cunucu* you'll see families weaving straw, women pounding cornmeal, and native fishermen casting their nets, occupations that are as old as time. Stop at the Jan Kock House, built in the mid-seventeenth century. Rumored to be haunted, it is one of Curaçao's oldest buildings. Hours are irregular so be sure to call before planning a visit.

Drive past tiny pastel cottages, twenty-foot-tall cacti and scattered windmills, which supplement private water and electrical supply. Goats ("chici bestia" in Papiamento) wear triangular wooden collars to prevent them from escaping through fences.

Stop for a swim or to enjoy the view at Knip Bay. (No changing facilities.) This protected cove, backed by sheer cliffs, is usually fun on Sundays, when there is sometimes impromptu music and dancing.

Drive on toward West Point and you can't miss Mt. Christoffel, looming 1250 feet to your right. The very special cove at West Point resembles Spain's Costa Brava. A wonderful place for a swim. High above the beach is the Playa Forti Restaurant, a casual place with what is definitely one of the best views of the ocean on the entire island. The Playa Forti offers delicious local dishes and super fresh seafood.

Leaving Playa Forti, stop at the lookout point over Santa Marta Bay. The landscape here is similar to that of Southern California. You'll also come to two historic homes. Ascensión Plantation is a meticulously restored plantation house used as an "R & R" home by the Dutch navy. If you can arrange a visit for the first Sunday of the month, they host a weekly open house. Doors are open to all from 10:00 A.M. until noon and Dutch hospitality prevails. Landhuis Santa Marta, just off the main road to West Point, and about forty minutes outside of Willemstad, is worth a stop. It is situated on a hill overlooking acres of land amassed by its former owners. You'll get a real feel for how the good life was lived in Curaçao in the early 1700s.

If time permits, make a stop at nearby Boca Tabla, where the sea has carved a grotto. You can sit safely in the back of it and see and hear the waves roll in. If you plan to explore here, bring sturdy shoes.

From your stop at Boca Tabla, head back toward Christoffel Park. This 4,000-acre preserve requires at least two to three hours to explore. There are unusual geological formations, strangely shaped divi-divi trees, and the petite Curaçao deer. The park is open from 8:00 A.M. to 3:00 P.M. but visitors are not admitted after 2:00 P.M. At the entrance to the park you'll notice the impressive Landhuis Savonet. The landmark is not open to the public, but feel free to admire it from a distance.

Eastern End of the Island

Landhuis Brievengat is just a ten-minute drive northeast of Willemstad, near the Centro Deportivo sports stadium. It contains the original kitchen with eighteen-inch-thick walls, fine antiques, and watchtowers, later used for lovers' trysts.

East of Willemstad on Spanish Water Bay, you'll pass private yacht clubs which draw fishermen from far and wide for special fishing tournaments. A swing along the eastern part of Curaçao can be done in an hour or so. It should include a stop at Santa Barbara Beach (called "Boca"). It's busy, bustling, and the place to be on Sundays. It has changing facilities, a snack bar, and lots of activity.

PRACTICAL INFORMATION FOR CURAÇAO

FACTS AND FIGURES. The largest of the Netherland Antilles islands, Curaçao is 42 miles east of Aruba and 30 miles west of Bonaire. It is 38 miles long and 7 miles wide, at its widest, with a population of 165,000.

Curaçaoans are an ethnic blend of Spanish, Dutch, African, and Portuguese. Although Dutch is the official language, Papiamento is the spoken language of the people. It's a musical mix of Spanish, Portuguese, and African. Most everyone is fluent, to different degrees, in English and Spanish. The island's highest point is at its northwestern tip, Mt. Christoffel, at 1,250 feet.

Curaçao's coastline has 38 beaches and coves. Its southeastern shore is sheltered from the constant tradewinds and offers the best swimming, boating, and snorkeling.

WHEN TO GO. The winter months, December 15 to April 15, are the most popular time to visit Curaçao. Hotel prices usually run 15 percent higher then.

Curaçao's climate is delightfully tropical all year round, with an average temperature of 80 degrees. Steady tradewinds provide cooling breezes and evening temperatures rarely dip below 75. Curaçao has no rainy season. The average rainfall of only 20 inches allows for few showers, and these are of short duration.

The island is not in the hurricane belt and there are no sharks in its waters.

PASSPORTS AND VISAS. U.S. and Canadian citizens need some proof of identity. A passport is best, but a birth certificate and voter's registration card will do—a driver's license will not. In addition, all visitors to the island must hold a return or ongoing ticket. British citizens need not have a passport if they carry a "British Visitor's" passport, available from any post office; a visa is not required if stay does not exceed three months.

 MONEY. The guilder or florin (both names are used interchangeably, although prices are marked with *fl.*) is the Netherlands Antilles' unit of money, which is subdivided into 100 cents. The official rate of exchange is U.S. $1 = 1.77 NAfl.

It's not necessary to change U.S. dollars into florins. Dollars are accepted universally. However, you'll want to change $10 or so into local currency for using pay phones, cigarette vending machines, and for bus fares.

WHAT WILL IT COST?

A typical day on Curaçao in season for two persons will run:

	U.S. $
Hotel accommodations	$ 90
Full breakfast at the hotel	12
Lunch at a moderate restaurant	20
Dinner at one of Curaçao's finest restaurants	50
Tip or service charge at the restaurants; tax and service charge at hotels	20
One-day sightseeing by rental car	30
Total	$222

 HOW TO GET THERE. *American Airlines* flies nonstop from New York; *Eastern Airlines* nonstop from Miami. *ALM,* the Dutch Antillean Airline, flies in from Miami and San Juan and also links Curaçao with Aruba, Bonaire, and St. Martin. There are special tour packages and excursion fares, and Curaçao is included in an Aruba or Bonaire round trip if you make your plans in advance. Remember to reconfirm your return flight 48 hours in advance. Many cruise ships make Curaçao port of call.

AIRPORT TAX AND OTHER CHARGES. There is a 5% government tax on all room rates. Hotels also add a 10% service charge to your bill. The airport departure tax is $5.75 per person.

 TELEPHONE AND EMERGENCY NUMBERS. Phone service in Curacao is reliable and waiting time to call the U.S. is usually about 15 minutes.

Curacao's area code is 599–9. Hotel operators are helpful in placing calls and most hotels do not add extra charges for this service.

Police, fire: 44444; ambulance: 625822; St. Elisabeth's hospital: 624900 or 625100; telegram: 613500; taxi central dispatch number: 84574; U.S. Consulate: 613066.

 HOTELS. Strangely enough, on an island that is thirty-eight miles long, there are just seven large hotels, all in or within ten minutes of Willemstad, with the exception of one out on Santa Marta Bay near the island's northern tip. For a double room without meals in winter, we call $90 and above *Expensive;* $70–89 *Moderate;* below that *Inexpensive.* Peak season is mid-December to April 15, when rates are about 15% higher.

Expensive

Concorde Hotel. Piscadera Bay. Tel. 625000. Formerly the Curaçao Hilton. Built on the site of old Fort Piscadera. 200 rooms face the bay or the sea. Water sports are especially popular here, with dive boats, Boston Whalers, deep-sea-fishing excursions, and waterscooters all available at their dock. Freshwater pool with poolside eating and drinking area; two bars; the elegant *Willemstad Room* for continental dining; lively casino and entertainment and dancing in their *Tambu Bar.* Planned children's activities and babysitters available.

Holiday Beach Hotel and Casino. Coconut Beach. Tel. 625400. Each of the 200 two-double-bed rooms here has a private balcony. Swimmers and sunbathers have a choice of the beach or the large freshwater pool just a short walk away. All water sports and tennis courts available. Beach buffets and nice dining indoors, with the *Casino Royale* to enjoy afterward. Plenty of other activities available, from beach exercise classes to movies.

Las Palmas Hotel and Beach Resort. Piscadera Bay. Tel. 625200. A well-run and nicely landscaped property offering relaxed, friendly ambience. Hotel has 98 air conditioned rooms in addition to 94 fully equipped villas. There's a mini-market for those who choose to cook in the villas. For those who don't, there's a pleasant garden coffee shop and the *Chevere Pub and Restaurant,* with music nightly, including lively folklore and Caribbean shows. Lounge around an Olympic-sized freshwater pool or take a five-minute walk to small private beach also frequented by Dutch residents. Tennis courts are lighted for free day or night play. Also available are a variety of water sports. Hotel is 1½ miles from Willemstad and has free shuttle-bus service to the capital. Packages available.

Moderate

Coral Cliff Resort and Beach Club. Santa Marta Bay. Tel. 641610. A perfect getaway in a secluded area about a half hour's drive from the city. 35 rooms in cottages, all with air conditioning and kitchenettes. Patio restaurant for dining overlooking the sea; tennis courts; marina; and private beach. Options for sailing, snorkeling, and windsurfing. An ideal spot for families.

Curaçao Plaza Hotel. Plaza Piar, Williamsted. Tel. 612500. Curaçao's first high-rise hotel, now newly refurbished. Built into the massive walls of a 17th-century fort at the entrance to Willemstad's harbor. The ramparts rising from the sea have been left intact and now serve as a promenade for guests. 254 rooms, some in the tower, which have balconies overlooking the water. No beach here (beach privileges at major hotels however) but a swimming pool, two restaurants, a nightclub, and a discotheque. Special nights for a folkloric show, poolside barbecue, and elaborate Sunday buffet. For added entertainment the casino is open until the early hours.

Princess Beach Hotel and Casino. M.L. King Blvd., Willemstad. Tel. 614944. 140 rooms with ocean view, on a small beach that is one of the best in the Willemstad area. Olympic-size saltwater pool and pool deck for casual dining; glass-bottom-boat trip to underwater park. By 1986 the new main building, replacing one destroyed by fire, will be ready with a new casino, health spa, and self-service restaurant.

Inexpensive

Avila Beach Hotel. Willemstad. Tel. 614377. On the sea in Willemstad's residential section. 45 air-conditioned rooms spread out from the 200-year-old former governor's mansion. Romantic, open-air *Belle Terrace* restaurant prides itself on Danish specialties, a Viking pot, weekly smorgasbord, and well-prepared local dishes. Cocktail lounge and bar. Allow a minimum of 15 minutes to walk to town. A good value here with plain but clean rooms and a friendly and comfortable atmosphere.

 HOME AND APARTMENT RENTALS. There are very few rentals available on the island. Your best bet is to contact the *Curaçao Tourist Bureau* (see Tourist Information Services in the *Facts at Your Fingertips* chapter) or write to *Caribbean Home Rentals,* Box 710, Palm Beach, Fla. 33480.

HOW TO GET AROUND. There are public buses at minimal charge for trips to the airport, to the suburbs, or out into the country. But on arrival, you'll probably prefer to take a taxi. The drivers have an official tariff chart, with fares running from $11 to Willemstad to $9 to Picadera Bay, depending upon your hotel location. Taxis at other times are moderately priced, but confirm the fare with the driver before departure. There is an additional 25% surcharge after 11:00 P.M., so if you're out at night, be prepared. Taxis are usually readily available at the hotels; in other cases, call Central Dispatch at 84574 and they will provide one for you.

Most hotels have complimentary bus service to and from Willemstad, so check with them for times and pickup points. Free ferry service is provided across St. Anna Bay for pedestrians when the pontoon walking bridge is closed to traffic.

You can rent a car for $25–30 per day (gasoline and mileage charges are extra) at the airport or in town. Among the firms are *Avis* (tel. 611255); *Budget* (tel. 83466); or *National Car Rental* (tel. 613924). Note: Car speedometers and road signs are in kilometers.

TOURIST INFORMATION SERVICES. The *Curaçao Tourist Bureau* has an office at Plaza Piar in Willemstad (tel. 613397). Its main office is at Schouwburgweg z/n, Willemstad (tel. 77122). For sources closer to home, see Tourist Information Services in the *Facts at Your Fingertips* chapter.

SPECIAL EVENTS. Carnival is king here and is a fierce competition to select the official tumba theme song, election of a new king and queen, and partying in the streets. Momentum builds to Shrove Tuesday, with an endless carnival parade and more tumba. This giant party ends at midnight with the burning of an effigy of King Momo (Judas). Hotel accommodations are scarce, so book well in advance if Carnival is your thing. In addition, on this international island, there are added celebrations.

TOURS. Your hotel tour desk can make arrangements with a reputable tour operator. Among those tours offered are: *City and Country Tour* (2½ hours), $10.00, NAfl. 17.50, which includes visits to the Curaçao Liqueur Factory, the Botanical Garden, the Brievengat Church, and old Fort Nassau, situated on a hilltop overlooking the city and the harbor. *Island Tour* (5½ hours), $20, NAfl. 36. You'll drive through the countryside and along the coast to Westpoint at Curaçao's northern tip. This tour includes luncheon at the Playa Forti Restaurant, swimming, and a stop at Boca Tabla, a coral grotto carved by the sea. *Island Country Drive* (3½ hours), $14, NAfl. 25. This tour is pretty much the same as the Island Tour but doesn't include luncheon or swimming. For sightseeing by sea, glass-bottom-boat trips and harbor tours are also available. There are also night tours, including dinner and show, a visit to the club or casino from $22, NAfl. 40. Reserve through your hotel or directly with *Taber Tours* (tel. 76637 and 76713), or *ABC Tours* (tel. 625200 and 675105). Day trips to Aruba and Bonaire by private plane cost $115, NAfl. 200 per person.

You can hire a taxi for sightseeing for about $15 per hour.

PARKS AND GARDENS. *St. Christoffel Park.* A beautifully laid-out wildlife preserve covering 4,000 acres at the western end of the island. At 1,250 ft., this is the highest spot on the island, but you'll have to reach the peak on foot. Down below is a 35-mi. network of roads around and up the hills, showing off wildlife roaming free and several species of birds. Allow at least two hours to explore. The park is open from 8:00 A.M. to 3:00 P.M. but no one is admitted after 2:00 P.M. Admission is $1 (NAfl. 2).

Seaquarium. Striking, free-as-the-breeze architecture makes this a "must" visit. See the majesty of life underwater—coral that glows, sponges that don't, and 300 varieties of tropical fish. Stroll along a shark canal, dolphin and turtle ponds. Snacks and bar. Open Sun.–Thurs. 10 A.M. to 10 P.M.; Fri. & Sat. 10 A.M. to midnight. Admission: adults, $5.50 (NAfl. 9); children, $2.75 (NAfl. 4.50). Tel. 616670.

BEACHES. Curaçao can't boast the long powdery sands of its sister islands of Aruba and Bonaire, but it does have a variety. The *Avila Hotel* and *Coral Cliff Resort* have private beaches; the *Concorde, Holiday Beach, Las Palmas,* and *Princess Beach Hotels* have both beaches and pools.

There are public beaches at *Westpoint* in the north and *Daaibooi* on the south side of the island. There are also nice private beaches where you will pay a small entrance fee and have shower and changing facilities. Both *Jan Thiel* and *Santa Barbara* are on the eastern end and, in addition to swimming, attract snorkelers and scuba divers. Santa Barbara is currently the most popular. It has changing facilities and a snack bar. The entrance fee for both beaches is $3.35 (NAfl. 6) per car.

PARTICIPANT SPORTS. All sports are available here, both on land and on water. **Sailing, waterskiing, wind surfing, snorkeling, scuba diving,** and **cruising** on a Boston Whaler or a waterscooter provide all the action you'll need on the sea. Rental equipment and instructions for all are available through Piscaders Watersports, which has its headquarters at the *Concorde* (tel. 25000). They can also arrange **deep-sea-fishing** excursions for a half or full day.

On land, you can play **golf** at the Golf and Squash Club near the Shell refinery. Powerful tradewinds and sand greens offer a different challenge. Greens fees for nine holes are $10; caddies are $2 for nine holes; clubs can be rented for $3 a day. Make arrangements in advance by calling the Golf Club Bar (tel. 92664). There are **tennis** courts at most of the hotels, some lighted for night play. For **horseback riding,** contact Rancho Alegre (tel. 79160) for rides by the hour or longer excursions by reservations

SPECTATOR SPORTS. The graceful windsurfers, bobbing sailboats, and commercial ships passing by make the water on ongoing spectacle in Curaçao. The modern and comfortable Centro Deportivo stadium, with a seating capacity of 12,000, is ten minutes from town. It is the scene of professional and amateur **soccer** matches. The soccer season runs March through October. Admission starts at $7 for international games and escalates according to the quality of teams playing.

Good amateur **baseball** is also played from March to October. Check with your hotel to learn who's playing when.

HISTORIC HOMES AND SITES. There are several historic homes on Curaçao, but the most famous, and the most delightful to see, are the small Dutch-gabled houses, painted in pastel colors, all along St. Anna Bay in Willemstad. Just once glance and you'll feel as if you're in Holland. Visiting hours for most historic houses are 10:00 A.M.–noon, 2:00–4:00 P.M. daily. Most are closed on the last Sunday of the month.

There are several old plantation homes ("Landhuis") to visit outside the city, such as *Landhuis Santa Marta* on the Western side of the island. *Jan Kock Landhuis,* which was built in 1650 northwest of Willemstad, is open to the public but has irregular hours (tel. 88088). The *Ascension Plantation,* up on the northeast coast, is where the Dutch navy holds open house every Sunday from 10:00 A.M. until noon. *Landhuis Brievengat,* 4 Rheastraat, is just a ten-minute ride from the center of town, near the sports stadium (tel. 78344). You'll get a good feeling for how the upper crust lived in the early 1700s. Hours: 10:00

A.M.–noon and 2:00 P.M.–4:00 P.M. Admission $1, NAfl. 2. Closed last Sunday of the month. *Landhuis Savonet,* at the entrance of St. Christoffel National Park, is lovely to see, but not open to the public. The *Roosevelt House,* located in the Scharloo residential area of Willemstad, is the U.S. consul general's residence and is so called because the house was a tribute from Holland to the U.S. in thanks for American assistance during World War II.

Few Caribbean islands are without their old fortresses, and Curaçao is no exception. *Fort Amsterdam,* near Piar Square in Willemstad, is a formidable bastion that was built as one of eight forts to protect the island from invaders. Today it houses the governor's residence and the Dutch Reformed Church. Look for the English cannonball embedded in its southwest wall to get an idea of one of the battles decades ago. No admission fee.

Fort Nassau, high on the Ceru Sablica, a hill overlooking the harbor, was built in 1792 and is the most impressive today because within its ramparts there is delightful restaurant and terrace bar.

Other historic sites to see in town include the *Mikve Israel-Emanuel Synagogue* 29 Kerkstraat (tel. 611067), built in 1732 and the oldest in the New World. It is open to visitors Mon.–Fri. 9:00–11:45 A.M.; 2:30–5:00 P.M. The Jewish Museum is in the synagogue's courtyard. See also the ultramodern *Brievengat Church,* with its unique baptismal pool; and the 18th-century Protestant church behind the governor's palace.

MUSEUMS AND GALLERIES. *The Curaçao Museum* (tel. 623777), across from the Holiday Beach Hotel, off Eeuwensweg, is housed in a century-old former plantation house. This small jewel is filled with artifacts, paintings, and antique furnishings and affords the opportunity to trace the island's history. Open from 8:00 A.M. to noon and 2:00 to 5:00 P.M. daily. Closed Mondays and last Sunday of the month. Admission $1.50, NAfl. 2.

The Octagon House, Penstraat St. (tel. 6254524). Within walking distance of the Avila Beach Hotel is well worth a visit. It is unusual in appearance and rich in history. Now a museum, it was once the home of patriot Simón Bolívar's family. Open 8:00 A.M. to noon and 2:00 to 6:00 P.M., Monday through Saturday. No admission fee.

MUSIC, DANCE AND STAGE. Local musicians specialize in the tumba and Latin American rhythms. Even if you don't favor the salsa, you'll be caught up with Curaçao's infectious music and in awe of the lovely dancing. The annual Carnival celebration, winding up on the eve of Ash Wednesday, is a giant block party.

Local folklore groups demonstrate the African, European, and Caribbean influences in traditional Curaçao dances. Seeing one of their performances is a must. The folklore group Nos Antiyas is especially good. They sing and dance Curaçao's folk music with great gusto. Check with your front desk to learn at which hotel they are appearing. Show usually includes a buffet dinner featuring specialties of Curaçao.

SHOPPING. Curaçao is a haven for shoppers, not only because it is a free port, but because the cosmopolitan character of the city is reflected in a staggering array of merchandise displayed in a wide variety of shops. Most of the shops are concentrated in the Punda, the oldest quarter of Willemstad, a section that seems to have been invented for happy tourist browsing. Stores are open Mon.–Sat., 8:00 A.M. to noon, 2:00 P.M. to 6:00 P.M. When cruise ships are in port, shops may be open for a few hours on Sunday.

The chief shopping streets are Heerenstraat, Breedestraat, and Madurostraat. Heerenstraat is a pedestrian mall, as is Gomezplain. Both are closed to traffic, and their roadbeds have been raised to sidewalk level and covered with pink inlaid tiles.

The range of bargains here extends alphabetically from antiques to Zulu sculpture and includes Swiss watches, French perfume, gems, silver, crystal, cameras, hand-embroidered linen tablecloths, ivories, china, Indian brass, Dutch tiles, and Delftware. If you don't see it, keep looking. But remember that although the Netherlands Antilles are a GSP area, this type of exemption from U.S. customs duties applies only to some local products. Pick up a copy of the *Curaçao Holiday* yellow sheet for a full listing of shops and specifics on current good buys. The degree of savings you make will depend on the part of the country you're from or the city in which you live. Among the best shops in Willemstad are:

Boolchand's, Heerenstraat 4B, behind a facade of red-and-white-checked tiles. French perfumes, British cashmere sweaters, Italian silk ties, Dutch dolls, Swiss watches, and Japanese cameras.

El Continental, Heerenstraat 24–26. Fine gold jewelry mounted with precious and semiprecious stones, Swiss watches, Hummel figurines, British woolens, and cashmere sweaters.

Gandelman Jewelers, Breedenstraat 35. This fine shop at 35 Breedenstraat offers a sparkling selection of diamonds, gold, and gemstones. Gucci accessories —wallets, keychains, and belts make nice gifts.

Julius L. Penha & Sons. On the corner of Breedestraat and Heerenstraat, in front of the pontoon bridge. For French perfumes, Hummel figurines, linens from Madeira, Delftware, and handbags from Argentina, Italy, and Spain.

Kan Jewelers, Breedenstraat 46. Swiss watches, semiprecious stones, and Rosenthal china, crystal, and flatware.

New Amsterdam Store, Gomezplain or Breedenstraat 29. Three different shops to choose from, all so busy, that they don't even close for the noon *siesta.* Designer fashions, gold and silver jewelry, watches, imported lines, and Delft pottery are among the many items they sell.

Spritzer & Fuhrmann, Heerenstraat 2. They are the leading jewelers in the Netherlands Antilles. Danish silver, Delftware, Limoges, diamonds, emeralds, china, Lladro figurines—you name it, they have it. Service here is especially attentive.

The Yellow House. La Casa Amarilla has a complete line of French perfumes and cosmetics. Also leather goods, imported fashions, and Hummel figurines.

Black Koral. A tiny shop at the Princess Beach Hotel, east of Willemstad (tel. 614944). Owner and expert diver Bert Knubben polishes rare black coral and fashions it into elegant jewelry and pendants. Prices start at $15 for a small pendant. In the orient the material was used as a talisman to ward off evil, sorcery, and disease. Shop open daily 10:00 A.M. to 5:00 P.M.

 RESTAURANTS. The basic cuisine of Curaçao is Dutch, with Latin American, Indonesian, and Chinese complements. Favorite seasonings include curry powder, soy sauce, nutmeg, cumin, and ginger.

Perhaps the most famous Indonesian dish set before the tourists here is *Rijsttafel,* or rice table. A mountainous portion of rice is accompanied by a choice of at least twenty side dishes. *Erwtensoep* is a famous Dutch pea soup thickened with fat pork and sausage. Don't plan to eat anything else with it—it's two meals in itself. Then there's *keshi yena,* cheese, usually of the Edam variety, stuffed with meat or fish and gently baked.

The cosmopolitan character of Curaçao is reflected in its food. You can find French, Italian, Argentinian, Swiss, Chinese, Indonesian, and typical American meals. Seafood is always good, with wahoo, dolphin, and red snapper most in demand.

As for drink, there are imported wines, beer from Holland and the U.S., and locally brewed *Amstel,* the only beer in the world that is distilled from sea water; the Holland Gin, or *Jenever,* which the Dutch down neat like schnapps; and there's *Curaçao,* the liqueur that is made from island-grown bitter oranges.

We call $8 and under *Inexpensive;* $9–$15 *Moderate;* $16 and above *Expensive.*

Expensive

Bistro le Clochard. In the Rif Fort at the entrance to the harbor. Tel. 625666. This is a romantic and intimate restaurant. The inobtrusive background music doesn't always quell the rumbling—it's the Caribbean surf pounding against the old fort's walls. Swiss and French dishes specially prepared to order including chateaubriand and broiled barracuda. Reservations required.

De Taveerne. On Eridanusweg, near the Promenade shopping center. Tel. 70669. Fine dining in the whitewashed wine cellar of a magnificent converted country estate, once called Landhuis Groot Davelaar. Innovative young Dutch chef serves a cold fish appetizer that's smoked on the premises, savory grilled lobster, tenderly prepared veal, and other continental offerings. Blessedly soft background music and cosy nooks make for a special evening. Popular with locals and visitors. Reservations suggested. Open Mon.–Sat., 12:00 noon–3:00 P.M. and 7:00–11:00 P.M. Dress is casual during the week, dressier on Saturday. AE, DC, MC, V.

La Bistroelle. Behind the Promenade Shopping Center. Tel. 76929. You'll have to take a taxi to find it, but it's worth it for the Victorian atmosphere, which includes chandeliers and red-backed velvet chairs. Marvelous French fare, most of served *Flambé* at your table: escargots, bouillabaisse, poached salmon steak in champagne, to name just a few. Reservations required. AE, DC, MC, V.

Moderate

Belle Terrace. Avila Beach Hotel, Penstraat 130–134. Tel 614377. Delightful seaside restaurant in a 200-year-old mansion. Different specialties every night, such as the popular Curaçao dishes *keshi yena* (stuffed Edam cheese) and *sopito* (fish-and-coconut soup). Find a beef barbecue another night or a fondue bourguignon on another. Creative salad bar adds to it all. AE, DC, MC, V.

Bellevue Bar/Restaurant. At Parera just outside the Punda. Tel. 54291. You'll find the true spirit of Curaçao here, with waitresses in folkloric costumes and Dutch music playing in the background. They specialize in seafood and Creole dishes. For something really different, try their *sopi juana* (iguana soup).

Fort Nassau Restaurant. On a hilltop overlooking Willemstad. Tel. 613086. Perfect for the view from this old battlement, which was built in 1792. Have drinks on the terrace and meals inside the fort. Extensive menu, with the emphasis on French and international dishes. Their lobster and red-snapper specialties are delicious, as are those which are traditionally Dutch. Vegetables include sauteed green squash and curried papaya. AE, DC, MC, V.

Rijsttafel Restaurant Indonesia. 13 Mercuriusstraat, Cerrito. Tel. 612606. Just outside of town, but the best bet is take a taxi—it's not easy to find. This top restaurant used to be on the waterfront and is as popular today in its new location as it was then. *The* place for authentic *rijsttafel*, a feast that seems never ending but ever appealing. AE, DC, MC, V.

Playa Forti. Westpoint, on the northern tip of the island. Tel. 640273. This memorable spot is only open from 10:00 A.M. to 6:00 P.M. It's on a cliff above the beach to offer terrific views, but the food is even better. They specialize in authentic local dishes, such as *sopi di playa,* a Curaçaoan thick fish stew. Don't miss it!

Golden Star. Socratestraat 2. Tel. 54795. This small, unpretentious restaurant serves out some the best in local food. Owner Marie Burke has been overseeing her immaculate kitchen for 13 years. She transforms only the freshest produce into dishes such as "bestia chiki" (goat stew), shrimp creole, and delicately seasoned grilled conch, all served with heaps of fried plantains, rice, and avocado. There's also steaks and chops, all beautifully prepared. Attracts local and European businesspeople. Open 11:00 A.M. to 1:00 A.M. Well worth the five-minute cab ride for a lunch break from downtown shopping. Dress is informal. AE, DC, MC, V.

NIGHT LIFE AND BARS. The action really centers on the casinos here, but there's lots more. Folkloric shows (from $15, with wine), at the hotels; entertainment, musical reviews, and music for dancing at *Tambu Lounge* and at the Curaçao Plaza's *La Cave de Neptune,* both of which swing until well after midnight. Don't miss the *Discoconut* (tel. 54291) at the Bellevue Restaurant just outside the Punda. Its action begins once the dinner hour is over.

Dancing starts seriously after 11:00 P.M. There is a good choice of lively clubs and discos. But the "in" place now is *Infinity.* Just downstairs from the restaurant at Fort Nassau, its special features are a waterfall wall, very intimate atmosphere, and lulling mood music. Drinks are $3. A sure stop after dining upstairs. Casual attire during week, dressier on weekends. No cover.

The Tunnel, near Las Palmas Hotel, Piscadera Bay area, on Goeroeboeroeweg. Tel. 624608. This is a cozy, romantic club with live Latin, local, and disco music. Entrance fee varies according to group appearing. Casual attire. Mixed drinks are $3 each.

La Fontaine, on Cascoraweg, near the Zoo, is a 15-minute drive from town. This nightclub seats 300 and is as popular with locals as tourists. No entrance charge on weekdays; $6 on weekends.

Studio Club, on Ontarioweg, Salinja, is open daily from 9:00 P.M. and offers live entertainment on weekends (tel. 612272).

CASINOS. There are casinos at the *Concorde,* the *Curaçao Plaza,* the *Holiday Beach* and the *Princess Beach Hotels.* The atmosphere is lively and comfortable, and complimentary drinks are served by all. The Concorde's hours are 9:00 P.M. to 4:00 A.M. All other casinos open at 1:00 P.M. and close at 4:00 A.M. When cruise ships are in port the Curaçao Plaza, in downtown Willemstad, opens its doors at 11:00 A.M. Minimum age for entering casinos is 18 years. Casual dress permitted; jackets required at the Concorde. Women not admitted in shorts after 9:00 P.M.

POSTAGE. Rates for sending an airmail letter to the U.S. and Canada are: U.S. $.55 or 1 NAfl.; a postcard, U.S. $.30 or NAfl. .60.

ELECTRIC CURRENT. The current here is 110 to 130 volts A.C. American razors and hairdryers function on this current.

SECURITY. Curaçao has a low crime rate, but visitors are wise to place passports and valuables in their hotel safe. Cab drivers are courteous and dependable. Emergency or late-night cabs may be obtained by calling the central dispatch number, 84574/6.

DOMINICA

by
DAVID P. SCHULZ

The island of Dominica (pronounced Dom-in-*ee*-ka,) is twenty-nine miles long, and fifteen miles wide. It is situated in the eastern Caribbean between the French islands of Guadeloupe to the north and Martinique to the south.

Most of the population lives in settlements in the low-lying coastal areas with perhaps 20,000 in the capital city of Roseau in the south and another 5,000 in Portsmouth, the second-largest city, in the north. The island is also home to the last remnants of the Carib Indians.

Abundant rainfall in the interior makes for lush vegetation as well as cash crops. Water is exported by the tankerful to more arid neighbors. Among the unique forms of wildlife are the Sisserou, or Imperial, parrot and the rednecked, or Jacquot, parrot, both found only in Dominica.

English is the official language of the country, but a French patois is widely spoken. Maps list both English and Creole place names.

Past and Present

Dominica, or Sunday Island, was named by Christopher Columbus on Sunday, November 3, 1493, on his second voyage to the New World. European efforts to subdue the fierce Carib Indians were so unsuccessful that in 1749 Britain and France agreed to let the Indians have the island. Nonetheless, the fertile soil and plentiful rainfall soon attracted French and English planters. The fighting between them became so fierce and frequent that even the warlike Caribs took to calling the island "waitukubuli" ("land of many battles"). The French burned Roseau in 1795 and left Dominica only after extracting a ransom of 12,000 pounds from the British. Dominica remained a British colony until 1967 when it gained some self-government; it became fully independent on November 3, 1978, exactly 465 years to the day after its discovery. Today it is a sovereign democratic republic headed by a president and seven ministers, including a prime minister.

EXPLORING DOMINICA

The Caribbean, or western, side of the island is where the major cities, most of the population, and all of the hotels are located. Major point of entry is Canefield Airport on the west, or Caribbean, side of the island about three miles from the capital city of Roseau. A project is under way to lengthen the runway and add lights for night landings. The older Melville Hall Airport on the northeast coast is well maintained and used by private aircraft and for day-hops from neighboring islands. Portsmouth, with the best harbor in its protected northwest coast location, is the major port of entry for yachts.

Given the small size of this almond-shaped island, virtually any destination is within reach on an easy day trip. Distances in Dominica are measured in time rather than miles, especially when moving east-west across the island's mountains. The highways ringing the island's perimeter have been, or are now being, upgraded, so that hiring a self-drive car is not the adventure it once was. Many roads in the mountains, however, are still rutted and pocked by potholes. In some areas roads are reduced to mere tracks best negotiated by four-wheel-drive vehicles. For some of these remote destinations, a hired driver and car or a tour with Wilderness Adventure Tours or Dominica Tours, formerly Anchorage Tours, may prove more rewarding.

Roseau

The capital city lies on the flat delta of the Roseau (or Queen's) River in the southwest part of the island. It was never an impressive city, and hurricanes have taken their toll on colonial-era and other historical buildings, most of which are grouped along Bay Front and High Street. The city is small and street marking so irregular that addresses, where they exist, are seldom used. A meandering walk through town (less than ten minutes in any direction) will take you past most of the landmarks, churches, shops, and other sights. The real attractions in Dominica lie outside of the city. Roseau's harbor area is functional—agricultural products are here loaded on small boats which transfer them to freighters farther out in the deep water, and water is piped to tankers some distance from shore. The Anglican, Roman Catholic, and Methodist churches can be found easily by looking up for the steeples. Other buildings of note include the post office on Bay Front and, behind it, the Old Market where craft-selling has replaced food-trading.

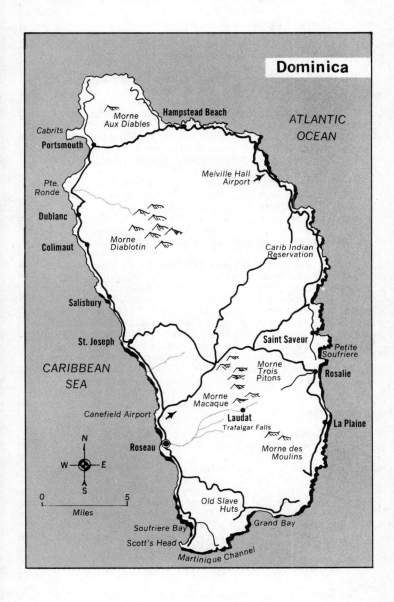

Dominica

ATLANTIC OCEAN

Morne Aux Diables

Hampstead Beach

Cabrits

Portsmouth

Pte. Ronde

Melville Hall Airport

Dublanc

Colimaut

Morne Diablotin

Carib Indian Reservation

Salisbury

St. Joseph

Saint Saveur

Petite Soufriere

CARIBBEAN SEA

Morne Trois Pitons

Rosalie

Canefield Airport

Morne Macaque

Laudat

Trafalgar Falls

La Plaine

N
W E
S

Roseau

Morne des Moulins

0   5
Miles

Old Slave Huts

Soufriere Bay

Grand Bay

Scott's Head

Martinique Channel

On the southern edge of the city are the botanical gardens and, rising behind the city, the peak of Morne Bruce. From it you can get an excellent view of the city and harbor.

Morne Trois Pitons National Park

The road up the Roseau Valley branches not far from Roseau, with the right leg leading to Trafalgar, the other to Laudat and the national park. The temperatures become noticeably cooler very quickly.

Just beyond the village of Trafalgar is Papillote Garden, the Papillote Hotel, and the path to Trafalgar's twin waterfalls. After exploring the garden or orchids, begonias, and other exotic plants, follow the trail to Trafalgar Falls as it winds through light forest and past small rivulets to an observation platform where there is a fine view of the main fall and the top of the other falls.

The Valley of Desolation is an active fumarole area (a fumarole is a crack through which gases escape from the molten lava below) with a harsh sulphuric environment at the foot of the hills that form the basin of Boiling Lake. The lake is believed to be a flooded fumarole rather than a volcanic crater and is approximately seventy yards wide with an unknown depth. Water temperatures measure 180 to 197 degrees F at the edges.

The village of Laudat is a departure point for many of the attractions in Morne Trois Pitons National Park, including a challenging trail to the Valley of Desolation and Boiling Lake, the second largest such lake in the world. The park itself covers more than 5,000 acres and much of it is wild and pristine. If you stay on the trails you won't really need a guide, but sensible shoes and clothing are necessary. There are trails leading to Freshwater and Boeri lakes, vast stretches of rain forest, Middleham Falls, and many of the island's noted mountain peaks.

The Emerald Pool is the most accessible point in the park, located about three and a half miles from Pont Casse on the transinsular road that leads to the town of Castle Bruce.

The East Coast

The Atlantic coast offers a rugged landscape of dramatic cliffs, jagged points, and waterfalls down to the ocean, but a current road map is a must in order to chart a course, avoid roads too rough for your vehicle, and orient yourself. After the trip, on improved roads, across the island to Castle Bruce, the north road leads to the Carib reserve, the south to a river estuary where dugout canoes in the making can be seen. Further south, and back toward the interior, is the Emerald Guest House, a convenient meal stop. The area around the nearby community of Saint Sauver has small holdings of bananas, bay oil, spices, and coconuts. At the edge of the village is the Bay Oil Distillery, complete with water supplied by bamboo pipes. Explore the quaint church and old estate house. A path behind the church leads to a stony beach where local fishermen land their boats. The beach also provides sheltered bathing.

The road ends a few miles south of Point Soufriere. Hikers can continue to Rosalie where there are an old aqueduct and water wheel, excellent river bathing (recommended over ocean bathing because of potentially dangerous undertows), and an expanse of black-sand beach.

To reach Rosalie by car means retracing the route to Pont Casse but taking the southerly road which forks off about halfway back, before you reach Pont Casse.

Carib Reservation

The reservation encompasses an area of 3,700 acres set aside in 1905 and communally owned by the last descendants of the Carib Indians living in the islands. The people have adopted a Creole lifestyle but have maintained the traditional skills of basket-weaving, canoe-building, and carving. Thatched huts with traditional roofing and plaited walls serve as craft shops, best known for baskets made from reeds dyed various colors that are waterproofed by weaving wild banana leaves between reed layers. Farming and fishing are the main occupations. Attractions on the reservation include the Roman Catholic church at Salibia, whose altar was fashioned from a canoe, and the L'escalier Tete Chien (Snake Staircase) at Sineku, a hardened lava flow that juts into the ocean and is the subject of several Carib legends.

Northeast Coast

Red cliffs and gold sand distinguish the secluded beaches in the area on the Atlantic coast north of the Carib Reserve. It can be reached by following the road to Melville Hall Airport from the central crossroads point of Pont Casse. Here rivers twist through mangrove forests and coconut fields and fishing villages dot the shore. Londonderry Beach, not far from Melville Hall Airport, is noted for its roaring breakers and quiet river. Reefs provide interesting snorkeling and diving at Woodford Hill and Hampstead Beach. There are also inviting beaches at La Taille Bay, Anse Noir, Anse-du-Mai, and Hodges. Calibishie is a charming fishing village where experienced amateurs can try their hand fishing in the Guadeloupe Channel. (Fees vary and arrangements should be made at least a day in advance.) Hiking trails lead to the northern tip of the island at Penville and La Haut.

Portsmouth and Cabrits

Prince Rupert Bay, on the northwest (Caribbean) coast, is the best and most beautiful harbor on the island with more than two miles of sandy beach shaded by coconut trees. The quiet town of Portsmouth features a memorial to Lord Cathcart at Burroughs Square, a handicraft shop at Banjamin Park and the Indian River Inn—a popular bar and starting point for an Indian River Adjoupa Boat Ride. North of town is the Cabrits, a spectacularly beautiful peninsula dominated by two steep hills separated by a narrow valley with one of the few surviving woodland forests in the Caribbean. The eighteenth-century Fort Shirley, being restored by local historian Lennox Honychurch, is definitely worth a trip. The footpath up the hill is smooth and gently graded.

West Coast and Layou Valley

The west coast between Roseau and Portsmouth lies in the "rain shadow" of the interior and thus is usually dry and dusty. Here are several small coves and black-sand beaches, some accessible only from the sea. The Layou Valley is luxuriant and green with virtually every type of tropical crop growing along the river banks. The fields of Hillsborough Estate grow tobacco for local cigars and cigarettes. The Layou River, Dominica's largest and longest, is dotted with pools and riverside beaches ideal for picnics. A full day's activity is a swim and hike down the river from Belles Village. The Layou sweeps through dramatic gorges with steep-sided pools alternating with waterfalls and rapids. You'll end up at the main road near Clarke Hall Estate (not open to visitors) where your transportation can meet you.

Southwest Coast

The road south from Roseau passes through the village of Pointe Michel, settled by refugees from Martinique when Mount Pelee erupted decades ago. Approaching the village of Soufriere, there is a panoramic view of Sourfiere Bay with Scotts Head rising on the other side. Pleasant beaches and snorkeling locations are plentiful. Turning east at Soufriere will lead to Sulphur Spring, where steaming fumaroles are visible. The village church contains dramatic murals depicting village life. The road leads to Scotts Head, with its views of the Caribbean, the Atlantic, and the island of Martinique off in the distance.

PRACTICAL INFORMATION FOR DOMINICA

 FACTS AND FIGURES. Dominica is 29 miles long, 16 miles wide, and covers an area of 290 square miles. It is centrally located in the thousand-mile-long Caribbean archipelago, between the French islands of Martinique and Guadeloupe. The population of 76,000 is concentrated along the coastal areas. The interior is the most mountainous of the Caribbean islands and is largely covered with lush rain forest. An agricultural country, whose manufacturing and tourism sectors are still developing, Dominica exports bananas, coconut, grapefruit, limes, cocoa, essential oils, spices, and flowers. English is the official language, though Creole patois is widely spoken. The two airports are Canefield, near Roseau, and the larger Melville Hall on the northeast (Atlantic) coast. Dominica is on Atlantic Standard Time, one hour ahead of Eastern Standard Time. The roads form, essentially, a circle around the island's perimeter with an "X" through the middle and a few spurs going up into the mountains from the coast. In many areas, especially in the mountains and the interior, the roads are reduced to tracks passable only in a four-wheel-drive vehicle, and even then not without some difficulty.

 WHEN TO GO. Daytime temperatures range from 75 to 90 degrees F, with the coolest months December through March. Temperatures, especially at night, are cooler in the mountains. Weather is generally dry along the coast, especially the west coast, with storms infrequent. Dry season is January to June, with rainfall averaging 40 inches a year on the coasts, and four to five times that in the mountainous rain forest.

PASSPORTS AND VISAS. No passports or visas are required from U.S. or Canadian citizens, but proof of citizenship is required (birth certificate, voter's registration card, etc.).

MONEY. The Eastern Caribbean dollar (EC) is the official currency, Figure U.S. $1 = EC $2.60. Local prices, especially in shops frequented by tourists, are often quoted in both currencies, so be sure to ask.

WHAT IT WILL COST?

A typical day in Dominica for two persons during the winter season will run:

	U.S. $
Hotel accommodations, including breakfast and dinner	$ 90
Lunch at a restaurant	25
Tips, hotel taxes, and services	20
Car rental (self-drive)	35
Total	$170

HOW TO GET THERE. By air. By connecting flights with international airlines through Antigua, St. Lucia, Guadeloupe, Martinique, Barbados, Trinidad, and Puerto Rico. *LIAT* flies south from Antigua and Guadeloupe, north from Trinidad, Barbados, and Martinique. *Air Caribe* flies direct from San Juan; *Winlink* from St. Lucia; *Air Martinique* from Fort de France, and *Air Guadeloupe* from Pointe-a-Pitre.

AIRPORT TAX AND OTHER CHARGES. There is a 10% government tax and a 10% service charge in lieu of tipping included in hotel bills. The airport departure tax is U.S. $3 or EC $8.

TELEPHONE AND EMERGENCY NUMBERS. The area code to dial Dominica is 809 and the local access code 445. Direct telephone, telegraph, teletype, and telex services via Cable & Wireless (West Indies) Ltd. Emergency telephone numbers are available through the hotel, since most guest rooms do not have telephones.

HOTELS. There's a surprising variety, though their number is limited and there are fewer than 350 rooms on the whole island. As there is only one road, none uses a street address although hotels do list a P.O. box in Roseau. Each hotel has something different to offer. Informality is the rule, and there is a variety of options in meal plans. Major credit cards are generally accepted. Official season is December–April, with some facilities offering the same rates year-round and others lowering rates 10–20% May–November. Most offer discounts for stays of a month or more and all impose the 10% government tax and 10% service surcharge.

Staying on Dominica costs less than on most islands. For double occupancy in season with two meals (MAP), $60–$100 is *Moderate;* under $60, *Inexpensive.* Reservations can be made through the tourist board. Telex: 8649 Tourist Do.

Anchorage. *Moderate.* Box 34, Roseau. Tel. 2638, 2369. The 36 rooms at this waterfront (no beach) hotel a half-mile south of Roseau are in two buildings, one three-storied with sea-view balconies, the other motel-style, along the water. With restaurant, bar, swimming pool, and yacht mooring, it caters to both tourists and businessmen. Headquarters for a variety of water sports and safari tours of the island. EP. Service charge not included in bill.

Castaways. *Moderate.* Box 5, Roseau. Tel. 6245. Dominica's first resort hotel with 27 rooms in quiet isolation 11 miles north of Roseau. Founded by Bill Harris and now run by daughter Linda. Meals served in large dining area with spacious lounge and cocktail bar overlooking sea. Tennis court recently added. Offers photo-safari and garden tours in association with Wilderness Adventure Tours. Lower rates in off-season. MAP.

Layou River Hotel. *Moderate.* Box 8, Roseau. Tel. 6281/5. A 44-room family resort on Dominica's largest river offering air-conditioned rooms, conference center, and baby-sitting services. Swimming pool. EP. No credit cards.

Layou Valley Inn. *Moderate.* Box 196, Roseau. Tel. 6203. New facility in the foothills of Morne Trois Pitons. Ideal for hikes to Freshwater Lake or Boiling Lake. Five rooms with spacious private baths. EP, MAP, FAP.

Reigate Hall. Renovating this has been a labor of love for Gordon Harris. Scheduled to open for 1985–86 season with 15 a/c rooms, swimming pool, tennis court, an extensive game and activities room. Free shuttle to town, a mile away. French-oriented continental menu planned.

Sisserou. *Moderate.* P.O. Box 134, Roseau. Tel. 3111. A 20-room facility on the water half-a-mile south of Roseau with bar, restaurant, and pool. Frequent entertainment. Single, double, and triple rates available. MAP.

Springfield Plantation. *Moderate.* Box 41, Roseau. Tel. 1401, 1224. A former plantation, in a secluded mountain setting with 25 units: some hotel rooms and some apartments. Freshwater swimming in nearby streams and pools; trail maps available for nature hikers. MAP.

Coconut Beach. *Inexpensive.* Picard Estate, Portsmouth. Tel. 5393. A new beachfront development just south of Portsmouth; six of its 11 units opened in 1984. Some units are air conditioned and some include light housekeeping facilities. Snack bar and restaurant specialize in barbecued fish and steaks.

Emerald Safari Hotel. *Inexpensive.* P.O. Box 20, Roseau. Tel. 8631. Popular with Europeans and located in the interior near the famed Emerald Pool, this place serves as headquarters for hikers, birders, and adventurers. Restaurant on premises. Bungalows and cabins available. EP.

Papillote. *Inexpensive.* P.O. Box 67, Roseau. Tel. 2287. A nature retreat in the mountain rain forest near spectacular Trafalgar Falls. Rooms are neat and family suites are available. Hosts Cuthbert and Anne Jean-Baptiste have exotic birds, gardens, hot mineral pools and waterfalls, river bathing, a craft center, and restaurant featuring local specialties. Safaris and walks arranged. MAP.

Portsmouth Beach. *Inexpensive.* Box 34, Roseau. Tel. 5142, 5130. Companion to the Anchorage near Roseau, so combination north-south stays can be arranged. Many of the 100 rooms are used by medical school students. Restaurant, bar, and swimming pool, as well as a beach and water sports. EP.

 GUESTHOUSES. Dominica has several guesthouses, whose accommodations range from rudely efficient to clean and comfortable. Most are in the Roseau area.

Castle Comfort (tel. 2188) is on the water on the outskirts of town between the Anchorage and Sisserou hotels with 6 rooms plus 10 in new unit slated for September 1985 opening. Rates U.S. $5 and up. MAP.

Continental. 37 Queen Mary St., Roseau. Tel. 2215/6. Ten rooms, most a/c, half with private bath, toilet. Doubles from U.S. $48 EP to U.S. $89 MAP.

The Kent-Anthony (tel. 2730) at 3 Great Marlborough St. in Roseau offers 21 rooms in the middle of town, not all with private toilet and shower, but a good bargain at U.S. $20–$28 for doubles, EP.

San Souci Manor. (tel. 2306). Box 373, Roseau. Upscale luxury in hills overlooking Roseau and harbor. Three spacious units with kitchens, meal preparation available at extra cost. Color TV, swimming pool, free chauffered ride to town in morning. Double: U.S. $70 with continental breakfast.

Upright House (tel. 4005) at 48 Goodwill Rd., Roseau, has rooms are named after signs of the zodiac. Ten rooms, some with private shower and toilet, with doubles ranging from U.S. $28–39 depending upon meal plan.

 HOW TO GET AROUND. There are taxis at the airports, with rates to Roseau and the hotels fixed by the government and posted on cards drivers are supposed to carry with them. From Canefield to Roseau is U.S. $10 and from Melville Hall U.S. $40. Two reliable car rental agencies are *Wide Range Car Rentals,* 81 Bath Rd., Roseau, tel. 2198, and *Valley Rent-a-Car,* Goodwill Rd., Roseau, tel. 3233. Daily rates are U.S. $25–$35; weekly $160–

220. Deposit and a visitor's driving permit for EC $20 are required. Car and driver may be hired at rates starting at U.S. $15. Tips extra.

 **TOURIST INFORMATION SERVICES.** The *Dominica Tourist Board* operates out of offices on Cork St. in Roseau, tel. 2351 or 2186; or write to Box 73, Roseau, Dominica, W.I. For sources closer to home, see the Tourist Information Services section in the *Facts at Your Fingertips* chapter.

 SPECIAL EVENTS. Major celebrations and traditional religious holidays include Carnival, in the spring during the days preceding Ash Wednesday, and the fall festivities that begin with Creole Day in late October (when native dress is worn and native patois is spoken exclusively) and culminate in National, or Independence, Day ceremonies on November 3.

 TOURS. Both package tours and custom-designed excursions can be arranged through *Wilderness Adventure Tours* (81 Bath Rd., Roseau, tel. 2198) and *Dominica Tours* (Anchorage Hotel, Roseau, tel. 2638). Arrangements can also be made through your hotel. Prices vary greatly depending upon number of persons, length of tour, and type of vehicle required, with prices per person ranging from U.S. $20–45 per person for day tours. Tours of the rum distilleries, coconut processing plant, plantations, and other factories are not regularly scheduled, but sometimes can be arranged through your hotel.

 PARKS AND GARDENS. *Morne Trois Piton National Park* was the first national park established among English-speaking Caribbean islands. Most visitors enter the park via the village of Laudat (about seven miles from Roseau) and then travel three more miles to the first of the major attractions inside the park, Freshwater Lake. The *Botanical Gardens* off High St. in the southern end of Roseau were established in the 19th century, but are only now recovering from hurricane devastation in the early 1980s.

 BEACHES. There are no private beaches on the island and the Castaways is the only true beachfront hotel. Most of the beaches are black sand, betraying the island's volcanic origins. The best beaches, which remain sandy well out into the sea, are in the northwest area around *Portsmouth.*

PARTICIPANT SPORTS. Walking, hiking and **mountain climbing** are Dominica's chief sports. The island is a favorite for birdwatchers and botanists since portions of the interior are relatively untouched by human development. Among the destinations that lure hikers and adventurers are the Carib Reserve, Boiling Lake, the freshwater lakes, Beori Crater lakes, Emerald Pool, and Trafalgar Falls. The trek up Morne Diablotin (4,747 ft.) should be undertaken only with a guide since many of the trails are overgrown and subject to washouts after heavy rains. There are two reliable tour operators who provide guides: *Wilderness Adventure Tours* (tel. 2198), under the direction of Albert Astaphan, which offers some real exploring packages and some, described as "arduous," that take you in four-wheel-drive vehicles to starting points before leading you further into the rugged interior. Prices range from U.S. $20 to $30 and can include lunch or not. *Dominica Tours* (tel. 2638) features water-sports tours as well as trips to some of the more popular attractions in the interior. Packages range from U.S. $12 for a motorboat trip to $44.

Hunting, and **fishing,** especially for local crayfish and frogs, is allowed during a strictly controlled season, roughly September to February.

The **swimming** here is generally in resort pools, on black-sand beaches or in the freshwater rivers, pools, and mountain lakes. **Snorkeling** and **windsurfing** are available at many hotels. **Scuba** gear is not as common and *Dive Dominica,* located at Castle Comfort in Roseau, is the only professional dive shop on the island. Derek Perryman and his staff are qualified instructors offering everything from novice instruction to challenging, day-long dive trips.

SPECTATOR SPORTS. For spectators, **cricket, soccer,** and **basketball** are played at the amateur level in season, with schedules posted in public places in Roseau and at hotels.

HISTORIC SITES AND HOMES. The few ruins and historic buildings have not really been restored and are rather ramshackle and nondescript.

 SHOPPING. Natural splendor is still the major attraction of Dominica, not shopping, but there are several shops and boutiques selling straw baskets, shell carving, and other handicrafts produced by Dominicans and Carib Indians. *Caribana Handicrafts* at 31 Cork St. (tel. 2761) in Roseau features hats, baskets, and wall plaques made both in the store and in the villages, and has a large selection of wood, coconut carvings, and other items crafted by Caribs. *Tropicrafts,* on Turkey Lane (tel. 2747) is where *vertivert* is fashioned into floor mats with geometric, flower, and fish motifs. Hats, baskets, and wall plaques are also made on site for sale (or shipping directly to the States via prepaid order). Also available are shell-encrusted picture frames and bamboo furniture. Locally produced rums (there are two distilleries on the island), cigars, pepper sauces, bottled water, syrups, guava cheese, and coconut-oil soaps are available in stores and supermarkets.

RESTAURANTS. The emphasis is on freshness. Cooks use local vegetables as well as such island delicacies as "mountain chicken," which is really a local frog called *crapaud;* crayfish or "river shrimp," and land crabs served stuffed or in a stew. Many garden vegetables are locally grown, as are green and sweet bananas, wild figs, kush-kush yams, and a root substituted for potatoes called "dasheen." Most hotel and guesthouse dining rooms serve à la carte menus if you want to eat out or are touring the island. And you have the option of having your hotel pack a picnic lunch for you. Dining hours are posted, with lunch generally from 12:00 P.M. to 3:00 P.M., and dinner 7:00 P.M. to as late as 11:00 P.M., usually earlier at the hotels. Given the scarcity of restaurants, there are really only two price ranges: more expensive and less expensive, but for purposes of classification, a three-course meal per person in EC dollars is *Expensive* if over $35; *Moderate,* $25–$35; *Inexpensive,* under $25.

La Robe Creole. *Expensive.* 3 Victoria St., Roseau. Tel. 2896. Reason enough to visit Dominica, as Erica Burnett-Biscombe brings out the best in local crapaud, crayfish, crabs, *lambi* (conch), *bouke* (lake prawns), and lobster, as well as root vegetables like cush-cush yam and dasheen. Many dishes available only during the legal hunting season, September–April. Callaloo and crab soup made with dasheen leaf and coconut milk is a must. Fish and meats are grilled over local charcoal. Open 9 A.M. to midnight. Shorts, swimsuits discouraged. AE, MC, V.

Coconut Beach Grill Bar. *Moderate.* Picard Estate, Portsmouth. Tel. 5393. Open-air beachfront location perfect for relaxing over cooling drinks while waiting for your charcoal-broiled fish or steaks. Cold platters and sandwiches available, too, including hamburgers for the homesick. Mountain chicken delicious when available during the season. AE.

The Orchard. *Moderate.* Queen Mary St. and Fields Lane, Roseau. Tel. 3051. Joan Cools-Lartigue puts her considerable talents to work on a menu that features creole favorites like black pudding, roti, crabbacks, conch, and lobster. Relaxed, shady garden setting. Open for lunch and dinner. No credit cards.

Guiyave. *Inexpensive.* 15 Cork St., Roseau. Tel. 2930. Features a light snack and sandwich menu in a walk-up setting. No credit cards.

The Mouse Hole. *Inexpensive.* 3 Victoria St., Roseau. Tel. 2396. Downstairs from, and affiliated with, La Robe Creole, this shop features a selection of salads, sandwiches, and snacks for takeout only. No credit cards.

 NIGHT LIFE AND BARS. After-dark activity is not the lure of Dominica, but *La Robe Creole* has light jazz on weekends, while hotels such as the *Castaways* and *Sisserou* feature local entertainment on an irregular basis. *The Warehouse Disco* and *Nite Box (Venue) Disco* in Roseau are open on weekends but attract more locals than tourists.

POSTAGE. First class (airmail) letters to the U.S. and Canada cost EC $.60 and postcards EC $.30.

ELECTRIC CURRENT. 220–240 volts, 50 cycles; transformer required for American appliances.

 SECURITY. A small, relatively homogenous population with an agricultural heritage contributes to an early-to-bed, early-to-rise ethos that discourages illicit behavior and crime. Of course, when you are a tourist in any foreign country, you should exercise reasonable caution in carrying money and valuables, but here there is nothing special to be afraid of.

DOMINICAN REPUBLIC

by
TONY TEDESCHI

It may be a matter of some dispute whether the bones and ashes in the big black box opposite the altar in the Cathedral of Santa María la Menor in the Dominican Republic really are the remains of Christopher Columbus, but if his spirit is restless, there can be no question that the Dominican Republic is where it roams. Santo Domingo is a treasure trove of structures, furnishings, and artifacts dating back to when Columbus founded the city and called there during his further explorations of the Caribbean. But the capital, and the rest of this island country, is also very much a place of today, with luxury hotels, vibrant nightlife, wonderful beaches, and all kinds of activity—all of it, however, respectful of a tradition that is the oldest in the New World.

Past and Present

The Dominican Republic comprises the eastern two-thirds of Hispaniola, the island it shares with Haiti to the west. The name is a derivation of La Isla Española ("the Spanish island"), which Columbus called it when he first sighted the island on December 5, 1492. The island enjoyed a period of flourishing growth during the first half of the sixteenth century, when the Spanish colonial period was at its peak. In 1509, Columbus' son, Diego Colón, came to the island as viceroy with his wife, Maria de Toledo, the niece of King Ferdinand. During this period, the city of Santo Domingo was built and became the hub of Spanish commerce and culture in the New World.

Gold and silver finds on the newly discovered continents turned interest to Mexico and Peru, and Hispaniola declined politically and economically. In 1586, the British explorer Francis Drake attacked the capital city and put it to the torch, while he waited for a ransom the city could not seem to muster. After less than a century, the proudest Spanish city of America had become little more than a ghost of its former self.

Thus began nearly four centuries of misfortune for the island. French buccaneers seized the western third of Hispaniola, a land grab that was legalized by the Treaty of Ryswick in 1697. The French then extended their sway over the whole island, renaming it Saint Domingue, and became rich on sugar and the slave trade. The whole brilliant but ill-conceived structure toppled in the wake of the fires of the slave revolt that established the first black republic in Haiti in 1804.

Five years later, the Dominicans, with British help, revolted and reestablished Spanish rule on their two-thirds of the island; in 1821, they proclaimed their independence from Spain. However, the Haitians invaded the new country a year later and reoccupied it for another twenty years, until Juan Pablo Duarte led the movement that drove out the Haitians and established Dominican independence in 1844.

For more than a century after the end of the Haitian occupation, the Dominican Republic endured a succession of "men on horseback," who were for the most part military dictators ruling with iron fists. Twice the U.S. Marines occupied the country (1916–24 and in 1965) and once the U.S. almost accepted an offer to annex the country. Beginning in 1930 and for a period of thirty-one years, the Dominican Republic was in the control of Rafael Trujillo, a dictator of unmatched cruelty. In 1961, Trujillo was assassinated by a group of more than a dozen men who had finally had enough.

The past dozen years have been a period of political stability; elections and transitions of government have caused only a few nervous moments. The country has prospered of late and has a very healthy tourism industry, with ambitious plans for expansion of the tourism plant, particularly on the north coast at Puerto Plata. A large foreign debt, however, has depressed the Dominican peso against foreign currencies, and while that means a U.S. dollar goes a long way in the Dominican Republic, it also suggests the destabilizing effects this negative exchange situation may have on the domestic economy. The next few years will be important ones for the Dominican Republic and may indicate whether once again the country will assume a leadership role in the region.

EXPLORING THE DOMINICAN REPUBLIC

As the eastern two-thirds of the island of Hispaniola, the Dominican Republic is bounded by Haiti to the west, the Atlantic Ocean to the north and the Caribbean Sea to the South. To the east, across a channel, lie Puerto Rico and the Virgin Islands. The country's principal attractions are the capital city of Santo Domingo on the south coast, where the Ozama River empties into the Caribbean; La Romana, also on the

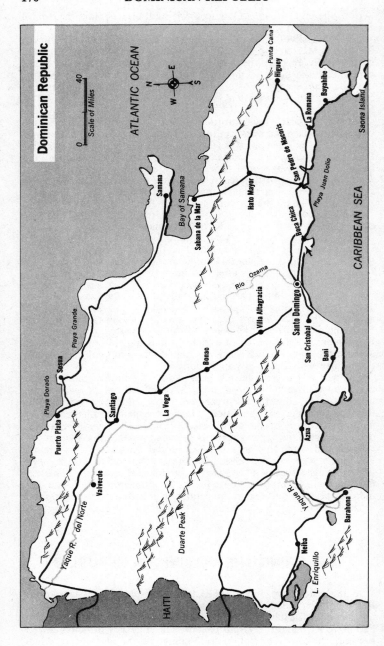

Dominican Republic

south coast, about two hours by car east of Santo Domingo; and Puerto Plata, a new tourist resort area on the north coast.

Santo Domingo

Any exploration of the Dominican Republic should begin where western civilization in this part of the world began—at the old city of Santo Domingo. Here, at the junction of the Rio Ozama and the Caribbean, in an area of about a dozen city blocks, the structures of the nearly 500-year-old city of Columbus have been preserved, restored, rehabilitated, and refurnished in the style of the period. Beginning at La Atarazana, there is the colonial commercial district, with its shops, restaurants, and galleries. Across the plaza is the Alcázar, the castle of Diego Colón, Columbus' son, who was the island's viceroy. Built in 1514, the castle was restored in 1957, with a painstaking reassembling of authentic relics from the museums of Spain. It is a marvel of sensitive reconstruction. Furnished with beautiful paintings, statues, and tapestries of the period, the castle is equipped as it was when the viceroy held court here, right down to the dishes, the salt cellars, and the viceregal shaving mug. Much of the art and furnishings was donated by the University of Madrid. Coral limestone walls, forty inches thick, were patched and strengthened with blocks from the original quarry, and the twenty-two rooms are cooled by breezes wafting through unglassed windows and open patios.

Across Calle Emiliano Tejera, opposite the post office on Calle Isabel la Católica, is the House of Cord, where Diego Colón lived while the Alcázar was being constructed. Built in 1502, this is the Western Hemisphere's oldest standing house, miraculously spared by hurricanes and the ravages of Francis Drake. The latter, who burned Santo Domingo block by block finally desisted when he received his ransom in this very house.

Traveling south on Calle Las Damas, you will come to the Museum of the Royal Houses, containing wonderful artifacts of the period; the Chapel of Our Lady of Remedies, where the early colonists worshipped; the National Pantheon, an eighteenth-century Jesuit convent that now serves as a mausoleum for prominent Dominicans—the Hostal Nicolás de Ovando, once the home of a prominent colonial and now a working hotel. Two blocks further south is the old Fort Ozama, with its impressive Tower of Homage, dating back to 1503.

A right on Padre Billini will take you by the Convent of St. Clare, built for the Clarisa Sisters in 1522; and the Museum of the Dominican Family, containing furnishings of the nineteenth century housed in the home of Francisco Tostado, an actuary of the sixteenth century. At Arzobispo Merino, make another right for a short, one-block side trip to an astonishing place, the Cathedral of Santa María la Menor, the oldest cathedral in the New World. The cathedral, with its splendid Renaissance facade and vaulted Gothic interior, was begun in 1514 and took two decades to complete. In the nave guarded by four baroque columns, carved to resemble royal palms, the remains of Christopher Columbus are said to lie in a black box and marble sarcophagus.

Back traveling west on Padre Billini, you pass the Convent of Santo Domingo, where early sixteenth-century lectures in theology so impressed Pope Paul III that he granted it the title of university, making it the oldest institution of higher learning in the New World. Next are the eighteenth-century Chapel of the Third Order and the sixteenth-century Church of Regina Angelorum. When you reach Palo Hincado, head one block south to see the Gate of Mercy, where Duarte declared the Dominican Republic free of Haitian annexation in 1844. About a mile north is the Fortress of Concepción, which was the northwestern defense post of the old city.

East to La Romana

Heading east on the Las Américas highway, you travel along the beautifully landscaped Caleta Park, which rims the sea. About a twenty-minute drive from the city is Boca Chica Beach. It is the most popular beach, since it is closest to the capital, and a good place to mix with the warm and friendly Dominicans. About an hour out of the capital is the city of San Pedro de Macoris, one of the best spots in the country to catch a baseball game. Baseball is the national sport of the Dominican Republic, and it is played in San Pedro at Tetelo Vargas Stadium, which is visible just off the highway on your left. On the eastern edge of the city is the Brugal Rum distillery and beyond that the cane fields begin, staying with you most the way to La Romana.

The two biggest attractions at La Romana are Casa de Campo and Altos de Chavón. Casa de Campo is a sprawling 7,000-acre resort, where you can golf on either of two courses, play tennis, polo, trap shoot, ride horses, indulge in every water sport under the sun—you name it; they've got it.

Just three miles beyond Casa de Campo is Altos de Chavón, to which you can drive or take one of the free shuttle buses from the resort. A re-creation of a medieval village, Altos de Chavón has been designed to show the lifestyle that Columbus brought to the New World. It is spread out on the cliffs overlooking the Río Chavón. You'll feel centuries slip away as you walk the cobblestoned streets, admire the buildings with their wrought-iron Spanish balconies, then rest in the shade of one of the courtyards, ablaze with bougainvillea. The focal point of the village is St. Stanislaus, the church named after Poland's patron saint in honor of Pope John Paul II, who visited the Dominican Republic in 1979 and left some of the ashes of St. Stanislaus behind. Art galleries, shops, a regional museum of archaeology, a quaint ten-room inn, and five restaurants fan out from the church's plaza. There are also a very popular discotheque and a Grecian-style amphitheatre.

North to Puerto Plata

The drive from the southern coast to the north will take you about four hours, plus or minus a half-hour, depending on traffic. It is a trip through lush green areas of palm and banana, orange groves and rice paddies, truck farms and cattle ranches. Be careful of the occasional ominous-looking brahma bull along the side of the road or the slow-footed farm horse taking its sweet time to cross in front of your car. Along the way you will pass through small, picturesque towns like Villa Altagracia and Bonao, where Falconbridge is mining nickel. You'll go by dozens of colorful roadside eateries that offer chicharrones (fried pork rinds), chicken, ripe pineapples, juicy mangos, and avocados,—any of which you can buy for a few centavos.

About two-thirds of the way up the highway you will come to Santiago, a business city and the capital of the state of Cibao. Here you

Photo by Barbara A. Currie

The Caribbean is known for its beaches, bays, and gentle trade winds. Pigeon Point Beach, Tobago, is idyllic for swimming. In the crystal clear waters of Bonaire, Netherlands Antilles, a diver gets a closeup view of a pufferfish.

Photo by Chris McLaughlin

Photo by Barbara A. Currie

The noble Georgian-style Government Square is in Jamaica's
Spanish Town, only 12 miles from Kingston. The historic
community was the island's capital during the Spanish
occupation in the 16th century. Meanwhile, Saturday is
market day for most local people in the Caribbean.

Getting to know the people—such as these two Cayman Island charmers in their school uniforms—is always an enticement to stay longer. Many visitors choose apartment living, even in historic spots such as restored Nelson's Dockyard in Antigua. *Courtesy of Antigua Dept. of Tourism and Trade*

Photo by V. Puzo

Contrasting islands, contrasting harbors: St. Croix, where hobiecats, sailboats and windsurfers ply the waterfront, and St. Thomas, where dozens of cruise ships anchor.

Courtesy of Caribbean Tourism Association

can stay at a guesthouse, eat in the local restaurants for just a few pesos, or, again, enjoy a baseball game in this city where baseball is king.

You reach the Atlantic near Puerto Plata on the Amber Coast. You are now 150 miles north of Santo Domingo. It was here that Columbus made his landing on December 5, 1492, and where his brother founded the settlement he called Puerto Plata Villa. If you have time, you can search around for amber, a fossilized pine resin formed fifty million years ago. The Dominican Republic is the world's prime source of this beautiful stone and you can pick up a treasure of amber in any of a hundred small shops throughout the country for a fraction of what it costs elsewhere.

In Puerto Plata you will find the Fortress of San Felipe, which guarded the island from the British pirates and the fierce Caribe Indians. It has been carefully restored to the way it looked in 1540 and stands at the entrance to the harbor, now host to frequent cruise ships. East of the city is the Playa Dorada, "golden beach," and it is here that the Dominican Republic is building its principal beach resort area. Already in place are brand-new hotels with a total of more than 1,000 rooms, and at least that many more are planned for the next few years. It's a great place to golf, ride horses, swim, sun, or try your skill at water sports.

Samana

East of Puerto Plata is Samana, where the *Turtle Dove,* a sailing vessel bearing several hundred escaped American slaves from the Freeman Sisters' underground railway, was blown ashore in a gale in 1824. The escapees settled and prospered and today their decendants number several thousand. They speak the English of the United States south of 150 years ago, worship in Protestant churches, and call their villages Bathesda, Northeast, and Philadelphia.

There is a beautiful beach and a beautiful bay at Samana, but the real attraction here is the sport fishing, considered to be some of the best in the world. You can rent a sport-fishing boat for a day or two and try for the trophies that run the waters of the Dominican Republic, or rest your weary bones along the beach in this beautiful—and out-of-the-way—spot.

PRACTICAL INFORMATION FOR
THE DOMINICAN REPUBLIC

FACTS AND FIGURES. The Dominican Republic is a country of 19,000 square miles, located on the eastern two-thirds of the island of Hispaniola, which it shares with Haiti. It is home to four million inhabitants. The capital and largest city is Santo Domingo, with 800,000 residents. The principal resort areas are at La Romana on the south coast, Puerto Plata to the north, and Samana to the northeast. A country of dramatic terrain, the Dominican Republic has major mountain ranges—including the highest mountain in the Caribbean, Duarte Peak—as well as miles of cane fields and fruit groves and beautiful palm-fringed beaches. The language is Spanish and the predominant racial group is mestizo (or mixed blood). About 95% of the population is Roman Catholic. With a predominantly agricultural economy, the Dominican

Republic is a major exporter of sugar, not to mention tobacco, cacao, coffee, fruits, and vegetables. It has extensive amber deposits and the largest operating gold mine in the Caribbean.

 WHEN TO GO. Climate in the Dominican Republic is typically Caribbean. Year-round temperatures average 77 degrees, with the hottest stretches between June and September; the coolest, December through April, which is *the* season. The rainiest time of the year is mid-August through the end of September, which is the tropical storm season in the Caribbean. January and February are perhaps the best time to go, when the days are warm and the evenings pleasantly cool.

 PASSPORTS AND VISAS. U.S. citizens need proof of citizenship. A passport is best but an original birth certificate with a raised seal is also acceptable. A driver's license is not acceptable. British and Canadian citizens need a valid passport, but no visa if staying less than 90 days. All visitors must buy a tourist card (U.S. $5), which should be obtained beforehand through a participating airline, but can also be purchased upon arrival at the airport in the Dominican Republic.

 MONEY. The Dominican peso is divided into 100 centavos. The rate of exchange against the U.S. dollar fluctuates. At press time, U.S. $1 brought between R.D. $2.50 and $3.20.

WHAT WILL IT COST?

A typical day for two persons in season will run:

	$U.S.
Hotel accommodations in Santo Domingo	$ 70
Breakfast at the hotel	8
Luncheon at a moderate restaurant	15
Dinner in town or at the hotel	25
Taxes, tips, and service charges	15
Car rental for one day	20
Total	$153

 HOW TO GET THERE. By air. *American Airlines* and *Dominicana Airlines* fly nonstop from New York to Santo Domingo. Both also fly nonstop from New York to Puerto Plata. From Miami, *American, Dominicana* and *Eastern* fly to Santo Domingo. Both *Prinair* and *Dominicana* have nonstop service to Santo Domingo from San Juan.

By sea. Santo Domingo is served by *Home Lines, Norwegian American, Paquet,* and *Royal Viking Cruise Lines. Royal Viking* and *Paquet* call at Puerto Plata.

By land. You can travel by land to the Dominican Republic from Haiti, but it's best to check on the border situation since traffic is often restricted between the two countries.

AIRPORT TAXES AND OTHER CHARGES. Airport departure tax is U.S. $20. There is a 5% government tax on hotel rooms, plus a 10% service charge.

TELEPHONE AND EMERGENCY NUMBERS. The area code in the Dominican Republic is 809. Police 682–3000; fire department: 682–2000; ambulance service: 689–4288.

HOTELS. The Dominican Republic was the site of the first hotel in the New World and it seems the country has been building them ever since. There is a very ambitious development plan underway, especially at Puerto Plata on the north coast, where a resort community has literally been built in less than five years. Prices are reasonable everywhere, especially if you take advantage of package plans. We will call prices over U.S. $150 a night for a double room *Deluxe;* $100–150 *Expensive;* $75–100 *Moderate;* and under $75 *Inexpensive* (all based on high-season rates). A 5% room tax is levied on all hotel bills, plus a 10% service charge on rooms, nightclubs, and restaurants.

SANTO DOMINGO

El Embajador. *Expensive.* Ave. Sarasota. Tel. 533–2131. A special hotel, with 310 large and luxuriously furnished rooms. It has everything: fine dining at *Jardín de Jade Chinese* restaurant; dancing and entertainment at *La Fiesta Lounge;* a swinging discotheque called the *Embassy,* which draws residents and visitors from other hotels. There is a lively casino as well. For the activities-minded, there is a large swimming pool, tennis courts, and free transportation to nearby beaches.

Hotel Santo Domingo & Hispaniola. *Expensive.* Ave. Independencia. Tel. 532–1511. Actually two hotels (385 rooms) on one 24-acre site in the midst of downtown, just off the main boulevard along the sea. Recently sold by Gulf + Western to private investors. Interiors were designed by Oscar de la Renta, the Dominican fashion designer, and they're beautiful—marble and tile, tapestries, lots of color, slatted blinds, ceiling fans. Hand-crafted Dominican furniture is everywhere, including the guest rooms. The *Alcazar Restaurant* serves international cuisine in an intimate setting; *El Vivero* features Italian specialties. There are also open-air bars, lounges with entertainment, and the *Neon 2002* discotheque, one of the liveliest in the city. Two Olympic-size swimming pools and three all-weather, lighted tennis courts.

Sheraton Santo Domingo. *Expensive.* Ave. George Washington. Tel. 685–5151. This 11-story, ultramodern hotel has 260 rooms, most with a view of the sea and the main boulevard. All have color TV and a service bar. *Antoine's* restaurant serves French and continental specialities and is one of the best in the city. In addition, there are the *El Yarey* piano bar and lounge and the *Omni Disco.* Also a very popular casino. Swimming pool with poolside bar, night-lighted tennis courts and a full health club.

Dominican Concorde. *Moderate.* Ave. Anacaona. Tel. 532–2531. Originally the Loew's Dominicana, this eight-story, 316-room edifice features modern decor. There is a rooftop restaurant and lounge with dramatic views, and ground-floor restaurant, lobby piano bar, and casino. Pool area is large and shaped in various geometric forms. Largest convention facilities in the city. Located in residential area, away from downtown, near Los Indios Park.

Hotel Lina. *Moderate.* Ave. Maximo Gomez. Tel. 689–5185. First achieved fame for its restaurant, operated by ex-dictator Trujillo's chef. Formerly a 64-room property completely refurbished and reopened in 1984 with 221 rooms and suites. Now includes restaurant, cafe, piano bar, night club/discotheque, and casino. Also two pools, health club, and tennis courts.

Hostal Nicolás de Ovando. *Inexpensive.* Las Damas. Tel. 687–7181. Called the oldest hotel in the New World, this 60-room property is in the old colonial sector of the city, within a short walk of most of the important monuments. The old Spanish decor runs throughout the hotel, with beamed ceilings and carved mahogany doors, combined with native Dominican tiles and artwork. The restaurant features Dominican specialities. There is also a swimming pool.

San Geronimo. *Inexpensive.* Ave. Independencia. Tel. 533–8181. 72 nicely decorated rooms. Swimming pool on second-floor terrace. Cafeteria with wide selection of dishes at reasonable prices. *El Castillo Nightclub and Cocktail Lounge* for dancing. Casino.

HIGUEY

Club Mediterranee Punta Cana. *Moderate.* Cabo Engaño. Tel. 567–5228. Situated 145 miles east of Santo Domingo, this is one of Club Med's newest properties in the Caribbean. 600-bed village stretches across 70 acres that curve around a long white-sand beach. All the club accoutrements for dining, dancing, discoing until dawn. Ten tennis courts. Large freshwater pool. All water sports and everything from archery to volleyball for landlubbers. The buffets are elaborate and the wine flows free and freely. All-inclusive rate covers everything but hard liquor.

PUERTO PLATA

Dorado Naco. *Expensive.* Box 162. Tel. 586–2019. Lovely 150-room property on the beach. One- or two-bedroom apartments or spacious penthouses. All have fully equipped kitchens and there is a well-stocked commissary on the premises. If you choose not to cook, you can enjoy excellent dining room and poolside buffets. Freshwater pool with deck and bar, golf, horseback riding, bicycles, and motorbikes. All water sports. Very creative management designs spate of activities to keep patrons occupied, i.e., fashion shows, pool games, donkey races on beach, etc.

Jack Tar Village. *Expensive.* Playa Dorada. Tel. 586–3800. Self-contained community of 200 rooms in cottages along beach in tropical setting. One fee includes all meals, drinks, water sports, greens fees, transportation to town—everything. 18-hole Robert Trent Jones golf course curves around property. There are also tennis courts, clinics, and horseback riding. The all-inclusive fee keeps you on the premises, but you really won't mind.

Playa Dorada Hotel. *Expensive.* Playa Dorada. Tel. 586–3988. A Holiday Inn beach resort property. 253 air-conditioned rooms on a long stretch of beach. Each room has balcony and terrace. Surroundings are impeccably landscaped. Swimming pool, just a few steps from the beach with swim-up bar. Excellent dining room. Disco here is swinging-est night spot on the beach. Tennis courts, horseback riding, biking, golf, water sports.

Villas Doradas. *Expensive.* Playa Dorada. Tel. 586–2770. Brand-new aparta-hotel with 100 one- to four-bedroom fully air-conditioned units with kitchenettes. *Las Garzas* restaurant serves continental cuisine. Swimming pool. On beach, with all water sports. Horseback riding. Across from golf course.

Costambar. *Inexpensive.* Box 186. Tel. 586–3828. One-, two-, and three-bedroom apartments on wonderful breeze-swept beach. Swimming pool, basketball, volleyball, and tennis courts. Horseback riding. Dining in club restaurant overlooking pool and beach.

Hotel Montemar. *Inexpensive.* Box 382. Tel. 586–2800. Very pleasant 45-room hotel just outside town of Puerto Plata. Also six beachside cottages, across the highway. Large swimming pool and lovely open-air dining room. Nine-hole golf course. Hotel also serves as school for young Dominicans interested in careers in the industry, so you may have more than the normal complement of service personnel tending to your every need.

LA ROMANA

Casa de Campo. *Deluxe.* Box 140. Tel. 682–9656. A class act, built by Gulf + Western and sold recently. Plush resort, set on 7,000 acres of beachfront land on the southeast coast, has all luxuries, plus a variety of activities not available anywhere else on the island. There are 350 casitas, casita suites, and one-, two- and three-bedroom golf-and-tennis villas, plus 150 condominium apartments available for rental. You have a choice of four restaurants, which offer everything from quick snacks to French fare served flambé. There are seven bars for casual sipping by day or dancing by night. For golfers, there are *two* Pete Dye championship courses—one around the shoreline, the other in the hills. La Terraza is the resort's tennis village, with accommodations in villas and 17 tennis courts, eight lighted for night play. Other sportsmen can enjoy polo at the only club of its kind in the Caribbean. Facilities include polo equipment, lessons, two polo fields, and the option to schedule matches. There are seven swimming pools—one with a swim-up bar—and a wide variety of water sports, including canoeing, beach parties, and yacht cruises. There is also a complete health club with exercise equipment, racquetball, squash, sauna, jacuzzi and massage.

La Posada Inn. *Inexpensive.* Box 140. Tel. 682–9656. Just five minutes from Casa de Campo and part of the Altos de Chavón medieval village, this delightful ten-room inn was also built by Gulf + Western. Opened just a few years ago, La Posada will make you feel as if you've lost a few centuries somewhere. All rooms are air-conditioned and have private patio and balcony on cliff overlooking the Rio Chavón. Choice of five restaurants in surrounding courtyards. *Genesis* disco swings until wee hours. Open-air, Grecian-style amphitheater features top entertainment.

SAMANA

Bahia Beach Resort. *Moderate.* Samana Bay. Tel. 538–2142. 105 rooms on cliff above the beach in one of the best game-fishing areas of the Caribbean. Excursions to Cayo Levantado Island—it's 30 minutes away by boat, but deserted beaches are the reward. Intimate dining rooms, pool, all water sports.

 HOW TO GET AROUND. Taxis are readily available at the airport and major hotels and can also be hailed in the streets. (All prices quoted in pesos.) The minimum charge in town is $1.50; the hourly rate, $5. The airport is quite a distance from the city, and taxis run approximately $20. There is also express-bus service from the airport to Independence Plaza in the center of town for $2.50 per person. The buses leave five times a day on weekdays, twice a day on weekends. In town there are also *públicos,* small blue-and-white or red-and-blue cars, which run regular routes, stopping to let passengers on and off. The fare is less than $1. The bus fare from Santo Domingo to Puerto Plata is $7.50. Cars are available for rental at the airport or in Santo Domingo. There are several firms, with rates that vary from $20–$60 per day depending upon the make and size of the car. Among those to contact are: *Avis* (tel. 532–2969); *Budget* (tel. 565–5678); *Hertz* (tel. 688–2277), and *National* (tel. 566–2747).

 TOURIST INFORMATION SERVICES. In the Dominican Republic, contact the Office of Tourism on Calle César Nicolás Pensón (tel. 688–5537) or the Tourist Information Center at Calle Arzobispo Merino 156 (tel. 687–8038), both in Santo Domingo. In Puerto Plata, visit the Tourist Office on Gregoria Luperón (tel. 586–2216). For sources closer to home, see the Tourist Information Services section in the *Facts at Your Fingertips* chapter.

 SPECIAL EVENTS. The Merengue Festival, which takes place in July, has really caught on and rivals carnival celebrations elsewhere in the Caribbean. It's a ten-day party, with outdoor bands and orchestras on the Malecón in Santo Domingo. Festivities include a fish fair, folkloric performances, an artisans fair, and a gastronomic festival in which all the hotel chefs present their specialties.

 TOURS. There are half-day sightseeing tours of Santo Domingo and full-day tours throughout the country. Contact *Amber Tours,* 39 Ave. Sarasota (tel. 532–3080); *Prieto Tours* (Gray Line of Santo Domingo), 201 Arzobispo Merino (tel. 682–8426); and *Turinter,* 4 Ave. Navarro (tel. 685–4020) for a specific list of options and prices. Also, if you'd like to ad-lib your own tour with the assistance of a knowledgeable bilingual guide, try the *Association*

of Tourism Guides (Asociación de Guía de Turismo), Ave. Benito Monción (tel. 682–7066).

 PARKS AND GARDENS. The following are all in Santo Domingo. *Parque Independencia,* or Independence Square, where the colonial section ends and modern Santo Domingo begins, is a popular gathering place, especially on Sundays. *Paseo de los Indios* is a five-mile-long park which runs south of Ave. Anacaona in the western sector of the city. It commemorates the native Indians and is a lovely place to spend time enjoying the fountains, lakes, and profusion of flowers along the footpaths. There are also train rides through the park. *La Caleta Park,* along Ave. Las Americas toward the airport, is a pleasant spot on the rim of the sea. It is dotted with ponds, paths, and picnic areas. There are also exhibitions and a small cafeteria. *National Botanical Gardens,* at Arroyo Hondo in the northern section of the city, are among the largest such gardens in the Caribbean, with examples of virtually all the flora of the Dominican Republic beautifully displayed. There are train rides with guides. Also a Japanese garden, various lakes for small boat rides, and a cafeteria.

 BEACHES. The closest, most pleasant beach near Santo Domingo is *Boca Chica,* about a 20-minute ride east of the city. It is the most popular with the local people. Farther east are *Embassy* and *Juan Dolio.* About two hours east of Santo Domingo, near La Romana, are *Las Minitas* and *Bayahibe,* the latter reached by a short launch ride. Club Med has a long and beautiful beach at its location near Punta Cana. At Puerto Plata on the north coast, there are some 70 miles of beaches, the most popular of which are at *Playa Dorada,* where the new resort hotels are opening (see "Hotels"). Also wonderful beaches at *Playa Grande* and *Sosua,* near Puerto Plata.

 PARTICIPANT SPORTS. Tennis is very popular in the Dominican Republic and played throughout the country. Many hotels have courts—there are 17 at Casa de Campo and 10 at Club Med. Tennis clinics are part of the program at most of the hotels offering tennis.

Golf is available in Santo Domingo at the Santo Domingo Country Club. Most hotels can arrange guest privileges. There are two Pete Dye championship courses at Casa de Campo and a Robert Trent Jones championship course at Playa Dorada. Hotel Montemar in Puerto Plata has a nine-hole course.

Water sports are an integral part of the activities at all the beach resorts. You can snorkel, windsurf, sail, and, in some places, scuba dive. Scuba-diving trips to offshore reefs also can be arranged through *Mundo Submarino,* 99 Gustavo Mejía Ricart in Santo Domingo (tel. 566–0344).

Horseback riding is also available at most seaside resorts. Casa de Campo, for example, has a dude ranch with 2,000 horses.

Game fishing can be arranged through most hotel tour desks. Particularly good at Samana.

Polo. Casa de Campo has two polo fields and gives lessons.

 SPECTATOR SPORTS. Baseball is a national passion here. The country has sent top stars to the major leagues, including Juan Marichal, who was recently inducted into the Hall of Fame. Season here is off-season in the U.S.: October–February. Best games at Quisqueya Stadium in Santo Domingo, Cibao Stadium in Santiago, and Tetelo Vargas Stadium in San Pedro de Macoris.

Polo. There are matches at Sierra Prieta in Santo Domingo and Casa de Campo in La Romana.

HISTORIC SITES AND HOUSES. In Santo Domingo the old colonial sector along the Rio Ozama is a living historic site. You cannot walk a block without coming to some centuries-old building or church, the remains of a fortress or a section of the city wall, all reminders of the original Spanish presence in the New World. Some of the most significant include:

Cathedral of Santa María la Menor, Arzobispo Merino at the foot of Arzobispo Nouel. Finished in 1523, this is the oldest cathedral in the New World. A fine example of ecclesiastical design, it contains what Dominicans claim are the remains of Christopher Columbus. Open 9:00 A.M.–6:00 P.M., Mon.–Sat. Sunday masses begin at 6:00 A.M. Free admission.

The Alcazar, just off Emiliano Tejera at the foot of Las Damas. Built in 1514, this was the palatial home of Diego Colón and his wife, María de Toledo, when Columbus' son served as viceroy. Completely restored with furnishings, artwork, and artifacts, many donated by leading museums in Spain. Open 9:00 A.M. –6:00 P.M. Small admission charge (about U.S. $.50)

The Atarazana, on La Atarazana just off Emiliano Tejera, across from the Alcazar. A restored commercial area of the period whose cobbled streets now contain shops, galleries, and restaurants. Various hours.

The Pantheon, on Las Damas, near the corner of Mercedes. Once a Jesuit monastery, this is now the final resting place of prominent Dominicans. Wonderful architecture. Open 9:00 A.M.–6:00 P.M., Tues.–Sun. Small admission.

Casa del Cordón, at the corner of Emiliano Tejera and Isabel la Católica. Built in 1503, it is the oldest stone dwelling in the New World. It was the home of Diego Colón while he awaited the completion of the Alcazar. Also called the House of Cord. Open 9:00 A.M.–6:00 P.M., Tues.-Sun. Admission is free.

Tower of Homage, on Paseo Presidente Billini, overlooking the Rio Ozama. Built in 1503, the tower is the most dramatic part of the old Ozama Fortress, designed to protect the city from attack. Open 9:00 A.M.–6:00 P.M., Tues.–Sun. Admission is free.

Bastidas House, on Las Damas, just off El Conde. Excellent example of a civil dwelling dating to the 16th century. Open 9:00 A.M.–6:00 P.M., Tues.–Sun.

Concepción Fortress, on Palo Hincado at Isidro Duarte. The northwestern defense post of the wall around the old city. Examples of watchtowers and cannon positions. Open 9:00 A.M.–6:00 P.M., Tues.–Sun.

Fathers of the Land Mausoleum, at the foot of El Conde off Palo Hincado. Modern mausoleum built in 1976 to honor the heroes of the modern republic—Duarte, Sanchez, and Mella. Open 9:00 A.M.–6:00 P.M., Tues.–Sun.

Gateway of Mercy, on Palo Hincado at Arzobispo Portes. The southwestern entry point of the old wall around the city. It was here that Duarte proclaimed the country's independence from Haiti in 1844, after 22 years of annexation.

Hostal Nicolás de Ovando, on Las Damas, just south of Mercedes. Once the home of a wealthy city dweller of the early 16th century, this is now an operating hotel in a building that has seen four centuries.

Our Lady of Remedies Chapel, on Las Damas at the foot of Mercedes. Small chapel for the first citizens of the colony. Open 9:00 A.M.–6:00 P.M., Mon.–Sat.; Sunday masses begin at 6:00 A.M.

Our Lady of Mercy Convent, on General Luperon and the corner of Jose Reyes. Built in 1555 and sacked by Sir Francis Drake, it contains the only remaining cloister from the period. Open 9:00 A.M.–6:00 P.M., Tues.–Sun.

Santa Barbara Church, on Ave. Mella between Isabel la Católilca and Arzobispo Merino. Build in 1562 to honor the patron saint of the artillery, it is the only example of a combination church and fortress. Open 9:00 A.M.–6:00 P.M., Mon.–Sat.; Sunday masses begin at 6:00 A.M.

Santo Domingo Convent, at the corner of Padre Billini and Duarte. The building was constructed 1510, and theology lectures began here in 1532. It was granted the title of university in 1538, and is the oldest such institution in the New World. Open 9:00 A.M.–6:00 P.M., Tues.–Sun.

San Nicolás Bari Hospital on Hosto, between General Luperón and Mercedes. The first hospital in the New World, opened in 1503, it functioned for several centuries. Open 9:00 A.M.–6:00 P.M., Tues.–Sun.

In **Puerto Plata,** note the centuries-old architecture of the buildings in the town, then visit the *Fort of San Felipe,* on the shore road, just east of the harbor.

It's an excellent example of a Spanish harbor fortification. Today it overlooks the docking place of giant cruise ships. Small admission fee. Ride the cable car to the top of *Isabel de Torres Peak* (2,565 ft.), on Autopista Duarte, for a spectacular view of the town and surrounding area. A huge statue of Christ the Redeemer commands the summit. Price is R.D. $2.

 MUSEUMS AND GALLERIES. You can get a wonderful taste of Dominican culture and the history of Hispaniola at a host of museums around the city of **Santo Domingo.** A good place to begin is *Museum of the Casas Reales* (Royal Houses). Once the headquarters of the colonial government, today it features an incredible collection of furnishings and artifacts from Dominican history, including great treasure troves of silver, gold, china, and crystal recovered from sunken vessels. On Las Damas, near the corner of Mercedes. Open 9:00 A.M.–6:00 P.M., Tues.–Sun. Small admission fee.

Museum of the Dominican Family provides a good look at how Dominicans lived in the 19th century. The building is the old colonial house of Francisco Tostado, built in 1516. On Padre Billini, near Arzobispo Merino. Open 9:00 A.M. –6:00 P.M. Small admission fee.

Duarte Museum, once the mansion of the father of the modern republic, Juan Pable Duarte, now contains furnishings and memorabilia of the 19th century. 138 Isabel la Católica. Small admission fee.

In the large and beautiful Cultural Plaza in the center of downtown Santo Domingo, there are three museums clustered around a quadrangle. The *Museum of Dominican Man* traces the country's history from pre-Columbian times to the present. The *Museum of Natural History* provides insights into flora and fauna of the area. And the *Gallery of Modern Art* has excellent examples of the work of Dominican and foreign artists. Small admission fee for each.

In addition to the Gallery of Modern Art, there are fine galleries for browsing or buying, scattered throughout the city. Many have good selections of works by local painters and sculptors. Worth a look are the *Nader Gallery* on La Atarazana, *El Greco Gallery* on Ave. Tirandentes, and *Carias Art Gallery* on Ave. Mexico. Business hours are 9:00 A.M.–6:00 P.M., Mon.–Sat.

In **La Romana,** you will want to visit the *Regional Museum of Archaeology* at Altos de Chavón for exhibits of both the pre- and post-Taino Indian periods. Open 9:00 A.M.–9:00 P.M. every day. Free admission. There are also two art galleries at Altos de Chavón, which feature rotating exhibitions of local painters, sculptors, and photographers. Open 9:00 A.M.–9:00 P.M. Sun.–Thurs., 10:00 A.M. –10:00 P.M. Fri. & Sat.

In **Puerto Plata,** along what is known as "The Amber Coast," visit the *Museum of Dominican Amber,* which features an extensive collection of amber pieces, some with wonderful fossils trapped more than 50 million years ago. Corner of Duarte and E. Prudhomme. Open 9:00 A.M.–5:00 P.M. Mon.–Sat. Admission is free.

 MUSIC, DANCE AND STAGE. The merengue is the national dance of the Dominican Republic and you'll hear and see it everywhere, performed by everyone from the smallest troupes to the largest folkloric groups. There are three principal theaters in Santo Domingo. *The National Theatre* in the ultramodern Cultural Plaza features performers, orchestras, and theater companies from all over the world. Ave. Máximo Gómez (tel. 682–7255). *Palace of Fine Arts* features dance festivals and theater presentations. Ave. Independencia (tel. 682–6384). *Casa de Teatro* features folkloric shows. On Arzobispo Merino (tel. 689–3430).

 SHOPPING. If you bring back nothing else from the Dominican Republic, you should consider some amber jewelry. The Dominican Republic has the largest deposits of the semi-precious stone and the prices are the best anywhere. You might also consider a piece made from larimar, a recently discovered stone thus far found only in the Dominican Republic.

In **Santo Domingo,** there are a number of wonderful shops around the Alcazar, most of them featuring jewelry, paintings, other crafts, and some straw works. Among the best are *Ambar Tres* at 3 La Atarazana, *Méndez* on Ave. 27 de Febrero, and *Artesanías Dominicanas* with two shops, one at 24 Tienda and the other on Ave. 27 Febrero. At *Plaza Criolla* you will find a whole collection of shops and boutiques selling everything from perfume to jewelry, fashions, and crafts. At the corner of Ave. 27 Febrero and Anacaona. Other local buys are carved mahogany figurines and bowls, embroidery, and straw items at *Mercado Model,* a spotless model market, which also features displays of fruits and vegetables, baskets, hats, sandals, and other island souvenirs. You should bargain here to get the price down. At the *Centro de los Héroes* shopping area, you will find Swiss watches, French perfumes, liquor, and other imports at duty-free prices. Mella St. is the principal shopping street, El Conde a close second.

In **Puerto Plata,** visit the *Tourist Bazaar* with its seven showrooms featuring excellent selection of amber and larimar. There are also paintings, sculpture, seashell and coral jewelry, island fashions, straw goods, and macrame. 61 Duarte. At the *Factory Gift Shop,* before choosing among the wonderful selections of amber and larimar, you can watch the jewelry being crafted by jeweller Ramón Ortiz and his craftsmen. They will also make custom pieces. 23 Duarte.

In **La Romana,** there are some beautiful shops at the Altos de Chavón re-created medieval village. A sampling includes: *L'Atelier,* for local amber, larimar, and coral jewelry; *Everett Designs,* a workshop as well as store, specializing in gold and silver designs; *Flamboyan,* furniture and decorating articles—fabrics, bedspreads, etc.; *Bouganvilia,* Dominican crafts, including ceramics, leather, silkscreen, and embroidery, some made by artisans of the village; *Qu'iavon,* featuring embroidered shirts for men and women and a wide assortment of casual sportswear; *Macramé Chavón,* with a wide assortment of bags, belts, placemats, etc.; *Oscar de la Renta/Freya,* designer clothes by de la Renta, featuring his tropical line.

 RESTAURANTS. Dining out in Santo Domingo is a real treat, especially in the old colonial section and along the waterfront, where the gracious atmosphere adds to the enjoyment of the fine food. Many restaurants specialize in continental Spanish, Italian, and French cuisine, as well as Dominican favorites. Seafood is featured on just about every menu and it is excellent here. Some local country snacks you might want to try include *chicharrón* (fried pork rind) and *calletas* (flat biscuit crackers). Also you might want to sample some Latin dishes such as *arroz con pollo* (chicken with rice) and *tortilla de jamón* (spicy ham omelet). Presidente and Bohemia are the local beers. Bermúdez and Brugal are the local rums. Food and beverages are usually inexpensive in the Dominican Republic, due largely to the favorable exchange rate. Wines tend to be expensive, however, because they are expensive to import. There is a 10% service charge added to the check.

We will call R.D. $20 and up for dinner *Expensive;* $10–19 *Moderate;* below that *Inexpensive.*

SANTO DOMINGO

Continental

Alcazar. *Expensive.* Hotel Santo Domingo. Tel. 532–1511. This superb restaurant, designed by Oscar de la Renta, has an elegant Moorish setting. Excellent international fare. Sea bass filet with crab meat au gratin is one of the specialties. AE, DC, MC, V.

Antoine's. *Expensive.* Hotel Sheraton. Tel. 685–5151. Delicious cuisine served in intimate setting on a par with that of fine restaurants of other world capitals. Try imperial stew, made with lobster, shrimp, and scallops. Extensive menu features no less than 20 desserts. AE, DC, MC, V.

Lina. *Expensive.* Hotel Lina. Tel. 689–5185. This restaurant has been an institution for more than a quarter-century, made famous by the proprietor, ex-personal chef to Trujillo. Although it serves a varied fare, its accent is Spanish—the paella is a must. AE, DC, MC, V.

Mesón de la Cava. *Expensive.* Ave. Mirador del Sur. Tel. 533–2818. A great experience, which begins when you descend more than 50 feet into a natural cave. Choice of seafood excellent, also wonderful beef dishes. Try the prime filet with dijon flambé or the tournedos Roquefort. AE, DC, MC, V.

Fonda de la Atarazana. *Moderate.* 5 La Atarazana. Te. 689–2900. Continental, plus some wonderful Dominican touches. Try the sea bass, the kingfish dominicana, or the shrimp brochette. AE, MC, V.

Dominican

La Bahia. *Inexpensive.* 1 Ave. George Washington. Tel. 682–4022. Again, seafood is tops. Informal, a place where you'll want to linger because everything looks—and is—so good. Try the *sopa paludica* (a thick fish soup made with fish, shrimp, and lobster and served with tangy garlic bread), and the *espaguettis a la canona* (spaghetti covered with seafood). MC, V.

El Castillo del Mar. *Inexpensive.* 2 Ave. George Washington. Tel. 688–4047. Wonderful, open-air setting by the sea along the main thoroughfare. Seafood here is special—try the sea bass castillo (smothered in onions, tomatoes, peas, and seasoned with basil) or the lobster thermidor. The fish soup for starters is well worth the few pesos you will pay for it. MC, V.

Chinese

Jardin de Jade. *Moderate.* El Embajador Hotel. Tel. 533–2131. Chinese food at its best and lots of it. Peking duck (of course) is a specialty, but there are dozens of other choices. AE, DC, MC, V.

French

Chez Francois. *Expensive.* 53 Padre Billini. Tel. 688–7549. Small and special restaurant in the colonial section serves memorable French dishes and has a fine selection of imported wines. AE, DC, MC, V.

Italian

Il Buco. *Expensive.* 152-A Arzobispo Merino. Tel. 685–0884. Informal decor and a lot of camaraderie in this restaurant, which has won gastronomical awards. Full menu includes dishes from all over Italy. The green lasagna alla garisenda is one of the award-winners and deservedly so. AE, DC, MC, V.

Vesuvio. *Expensive.* 521 Ave. George Washington. Tel. 682–2766. One of the best Italian restaurants anywhere. Everything from the meat and seafood, pasta and cheeses, to the desserts is freshly made, caught, grown, or killed. Endless menu with specialties like *calamares al vino blanco* (squid in white wine sauce), *scaloppina al tarragón* (veal with taragon), and on and on. DC, MC, V.

Da Ciro. *Moderate.* 38 Ave. Independencia. Tel. 689–6046. A happy place to be, with wandering musicians serenading as you dine and patrons joining in the singing. Antipastos and pasta dishes are oversized and delicious, but the menu doesn't stop there; it includes seafood, chicken, and beef dishes prepared in more than a dozen different ways. DC, MC, V.

Vesuvio II. *Moderate.* 17 Ave. Tiradentes. Tel. 567–7330. An offshoot of, and less formal than, the original Vesuvio, but with a menu that is equally as ambitious. More than two dozen seafood dishes alone, along with all the antipastos and homemade pasta specialties. DC, MC, V.

Spanish

El Caserío. *Expensive.* Ave. George Washington. Tel. 689–7779. Extensive menu with specialties like paella valenciana, seafood zarzuela, blue fish with anchovies, leg of lamb segovia. Also wonderful desserts like chocolate cake caserío. AE, DC, MC, V.

LA ROMANA

The re-created medieval village of Altos de Chavón has six wonderful restaurants, offering a varied mix of cuisine. They are:

Tropicana. *Expensive.* Casa de Campo. Tel. 682–9656. Elegant setting, with glass windows that are removed to let in the cooling breezes. Beef and seafood dishes are specialties. Don't miss the sea bass. AE, DC, MC, V.

Café del Sol. Moderate. Tel. 682–9656, ext. 2346. Outdoor cafe with view of village and distant mountain range. Serves pizza and assorted light dishes. AE, DC, MC, V.

La Casa del Río. *Moderate.* Tel. 682–9656, ext. 2345. Continental specialties in dining room perched on a cliff above the Rio Chavón. AE, DC, MC, V.

Los Chinos. *Moderate.* Tel. 682–9656, ext 2353. Chinese specialties, from egg rolls to sweet-and-sour dishes. AE, DC, MC, V.

La Fonda. *Moderate.* Tel. 682–9656, ext. 2350. Thoroughly Dominican—specialties include sea bass in coconut sauce and goat stew. AE, DC, MC, V.

La Piazetta. *Moderate.* Tel. 682–9656, ext. 2339. Italian restaurant designed in medieval style with strolling minstrels to add to the mood. Wonderful menu featuring fresh cheeses and pastas. Try any of the veal dishes. AE, DC, MC, V.

PUERTO PLATA

Dorado Naco. *Expensive.* Tel. 586–2019. Varied fare, with seafood specialties. Excellent cuisine presented nicely in indoor restaurant or on deck above pool area. Chefs here won lion's share of culinary awards at recent country-wide competition. AE, DC, MC, V.

Playa Dorada Holiday Inn. *Expensive.* Playa Dorada. Tel. 586–3988. Continental cuisine in spanking-new restaurant. Again it's seafood, particularly the lobster. AE, DC, MC, V.

Los Pinos. *Moderate.* Hermanas Mirabal. Tel. 586–3222. Continental menu, plus Dominican specialties. Also try the omelets. AE, MC, V.

Roma II. *Inexpensive.* Corner E. Prudhomme & Beller. Tel. 586–3904. In center of Puerto Plata. Not much more than open-side structure under metal roof, but turns out some of the best pizza you'll ever have. Pizza dough and pasta made fresh daily. Pizzas cooked in wood-burning oven. Other specialties include *spaghetti con pulpo* (octopus), *filete chito* (steak with garlic), and a whole complement of pastas and special sauces. No credit cards.

San Pedro de Macoris. *Inexpensive.* Ave. Independencia. Tel. 529–2877. Piano Restaurant and Dugout Bar. A great spot, especially if you're a baseball fan. San Pedro is home to some of the best players in the world and here you're apt to spot Joaquin Andujar of the Cardinals, Juan Samuel of the Phillies, Raphael Ramirez of the Braves, or others. Owner Freddie Natera hosts a radio show after local games (Oct.–Jan.). Try shrimp or lobster dishes for dinner; chicken sandwiches for lunch. AE, MC, V.

 NIGHT LIFE AND BARS. The Dominican Republic is where the merengue was born, so Dominicans have a definite feel for, and love of, music and dancing. There is an excellent selection of nightclubs/discotheques around Santo Domingo, some with entertainment as well as music for dancing. The following is a selection:

Santo Domingo. *Alexander's Club,* 23 Calle Pasteur. No telephone. A hot spot where the young go to dance to disco and a good blend of rock 'n' roll. *Bella Blu,* 519 Ave. George Washington. Tel. 689–2911. Caters to the over-25 crowd, Wide variety of musical programs, which change every night. *José,* 555 Ave. George Washington. Tel. 688–8242. Dancing until 4:00 A.M. Two shows nightly. *Las Palmas,* Hotel Santo Domingo. Tel. 532–1511. Trés chic. *Neon 2002,* Hotel Hispaniola. Tel. 533–7111. Lots of flash, great lighting, hot music. *Omni,* Hotel Sheraton. Tel. 685–5151. Elegant, exciting. Great continuous slide show of Dominican scenes.

La Romana. *Genesis,* Alto de Chavón. Tel. 682–9656, ext. 2340. Where else can you disco to the latest sounds in a medieval setting, in a re-created medieval village, high on a cliff above a tropical river? If that doesn't sound tempting, why bother to go dancing? A little rock, some new wave, rhythm and blues, mixed with salsa and, of course, the merengue.

CASINOS. There are a number of casinos at the major hotels in Santo Domingo, each offering a full complement of table games, including blackjack, craps, and roulette. Hours for Dominican casinos are 3:00 P.M.–4:00 A.M. every day. Jackets are required. You must be over 18 to enter. The most popular casinos are: *Dominican Concorde,* Ave. Anacaona. Tel. 532–2531. *El Embajador,* Ave. Sarasota. Tel. 533–2131. *Hotel Lina,* Ave. Máximo Gómez. Tel. 689–5185. *Naco Hotel,* an Nicolásdentes. Tel. 566–3131. *San Gerónimo,* Ave. Independencia. Tel. 533–8181. *Sheraton Santo Domingo,* Ave. George Washington. Tel. 685–5151.

POSTAGE. Airmail postage to the U.S. is about U.S. $.39.

ELECTRIC CURRENT. The current here is 110 to 120 volts A.C.

SECURITY. The Dominican Republic is home to a congenial people who are known for their friendly attitude toward visitors. Traveling about the cities or the countryside, either by day or night, presents no unusual problems of security beyond the normal degree of discretion and caution one must exercise anywhere.

GRENADA

by
SALLY CUMMINGS

Sally Cummings is a freelance writer who has been traveling and writing about it since 1975. She has been published in various newspapers, including the Christian Science Monitor, *the* Dallas Times Herald *and the* Miami News, *as well as in nearly all the leading U.S. travel industry trade publications. Since 1981 she has been writing and producing* The Plaza Newsletter, *a popular quarterly published and distributed by the Plaza Hotel in New York. She lives in Manhattan.*

The aroma of nutmeg, cinnamon, and cocoa fills the air on Grenada, also known as "The Spice Island of the Caribbean." Plantations within its 120 square miles grow much of what is in your spice cabinet—fresh bay leaves, allspice, cinnamon, saffron, cloves, and at least half-a-dozen others, in addition to the nutmeg introduced on the island in 1843. The crop flourished and is now Grenada's biggest export, although unfortunately it is not a tremendous profit-maker. Nutmeg from Africa and the Far East, although far milder, is a big competitor. You'll grow used to the pungent aroma and spicy flavor of nutmeg after just a few days of eating and drinking in Grenada—particularly if you indulge in the rum punches. Grenadian rum punches are not the frothy, fruity concoctions you'll find elsewhere in the islands; here they are simply rum, a bit of syrup, lime juice, a dash of bitters, and a generous dusting of nutmeg—and delicious.

Grenada is the most southerly of the Windward Islands and its terrain includes lofty mountains, deep valleys, cascading waterfalls, white-sand beaches, and picturesque harbors. It is covered with lush rainforest, the essence of "tropical." Less than half an hour by air from Barbados to the northeast, and only ninety miles from Trinidad, its neighbor to the south, this island is easily accessible by land or by sea.

Past and Present

Grenada's recent history put it on front pages everywhere in the autumn of 1983. But its colonial history is typically Caribbean—a tug-of-war between two European powers.

Columbus noticed the island on his third voyage in 1498; he bypassed it, but not before naming it Concepción. No Europeans tried to colonize it, however, until 1609, when the British arrived and were quickly sent packing by the ferocious Carib Indians. The French were more determined in 1650 and succeeded, after a series of bloody skirmishes, in literally pushing the Caribs off the island. (The Indians jumped from Le Morne des Sauteurs, or Leapers' Hill, on the north coast, rather than subject themselves to capture.)

In 1762 the British moved in on the French, beginning the seesaw of power that became a familiar tale on many of the Windward Islands. The French regained control in 1779 but ceded it again to the British under the Treaty of Versailles in 1783. Slave uprisings and trouble fomented by the remaining French on the island plagued the government until slavery was abolished in 1834.

In 1967 Grenada became an associated state of the British Commonwealth. It was given complete internal autonomy while Britain remained responsible for defense and external affairs. Total independence was granted in 1974 under Grenada's first prime minister, Sir Eric Gairy, who had won popular support in the early 1950s by organizing trade unions among farmworkers.

Gairy's administration, despite his early support of workers, was not the triumph of democracy some might have hoped. It was constantly at odds with a youthful political party, the New Jewel Movement, that had been formed in 1973 under Maurice Bishop.

In March 1979, while Gairy was out of the country, Bishop and other members of the NJM seized power. As the island's second prime minister, Bishop tried to develop it according to Marxist doctrine and established ties with Cuba, the Soviet Union, and other Communist governments. However, divisions developed within his own party, and in October 1983 he was imprisoned. The government was taken over by Deputy Prime Minister Bernard Coard and Army Commander Hudson Austin. Bishop and several supporters were murdered.

At that point the United States was encouraged to intervene. Troops invaded the island on October 25 and airlifted out the American students there who were attending St. George's University Medical School. Coard and Austin were arrested and resistance to the American invasion was quickly put down.

If the U.S. invasion—which Grenadians always refer to as "the rescue"—was controversial elsewhere, it was greeted with almost unanimous support—even jubilation—throughout the Caribbean (Cuba excepted, of course). American visitors to Grenada will find themselves treated as if they had personally sent the Rangers in and put down the coup, delivering the people from a Marxist regime most of them dreaded.

In December 1984, Herbert A. Blaize was elected Prime Minister of Grenada. With $57.2 million in U.S. aid, his government is beginning to rebuild Grenada's economy, focusing on agriculture, light manufacturing and tourism. Rebuilding roads and installing a new telephone system (to replace an outdated hodgepodge) are priorities.

Since October 1983 Grenada has been extremely stable and peaceful. U.S. and Caribbean military troops have largely been withdrawn, now that they have trained a Grenadian police force. Visitors to the country before and after the invasion have noticed a definite change in the atmosphere—there's now a palpable sense of hope, relief, and relaxation. Grenadians are earnest about building tourism to supplement agriculture in their economy. Tourists are warmly welcomed and extremely safe.

EXPLORING GRENADA

The northern and central regions of Grenada are very fertile and are given over to agriculture—not only to spices but to all kinds of fruits and vegetables (a bounty deliciously reflected in Grenadian cuisine). The southern tip of the island, just below St. George's, is the heart of the resort area, site of virtually all of Grenada's most important hotels and of Grand Anse Beach, one of the Caribbean's most beautiful.

The new airport at Point Salines, which opened in late 1984, is located at the southwest tip of the island, within a fifteen- to twenty-minute drive of most of the hotels. (The old airport, Pearls, is high up on the east coast, an hour's drive from St. George's.)

St. George's

Grenada's capital city and major port is one of the most picturesque and truly West Indian towns in the Caribbean. Pastel-painted warehouses cling to the curving shore along the horseshoe-shaped Carenage; rainbow-colored houses rise above it and disappear into the green hills.

St. George's can be toured on foot in a couple of hours. Start on the Carenage; the pier where ocean liners dock is at one end, the homey Turtleback restaurant with its open-air tables is at the other. In between are the post office, the library, a number of small shops (don't miss Spice Island Perfumes for locally-made suntan lotions, beauty creams, and gifts), the Grenada Tourist Board, and two more good restaurants, Rudolf's and the Nutmeg. The Nutmeg is on the second floor above a bookshop, and its huge open window provides a great view of the harbor.

From the west end of the Carenage (you can pick up a map of the city at the tourist office) take Young Street to the Grenada National Museum, where there's a small but interesting collection of ancient and colonial artifacts and recent political memorabilia.

Take any of the streets off to the left to the Esplanade, the ocean side of town. Here you'll find Grencraft, the National Handicrafts Center, where local goods are sold. Nearby is the Yellow Poui Art Gallery, which exhibits and sells Caribbean art, antique engravings, and other fine arts. Across the street is a row of tiny shops selling similar goods,

Grenada

CARIBBEAN SEA

Green I.
Levera I.
Levera Pond
Levera Bathway
Grenada Bay
Sauteurs
Duquesne Bay
ST. PATRICK
Victoria
ST. MARK
St. Mark's Mts.
Mt. St. Catherine
Great River Bay
Pearl's Airport
Pearl's Bay
Gouyave
Belvidere
Dougaldston House
ST. JOHN
Grenville
Marquis I.
ST. ANDREW
St. Andrew's Bay
Grand Rey
Concord Falls
Grand Etang L.
Gt. Bacolet Bay
Willis
Annandale Falls
ST. GEORGE
ST. DAVID
Grand Mal Bay
St. Paul's
St. George's
Morne Jaloux
St. David Point
Grande Anse Bay
Grand Anse
Westerhall Pt.
Pt. Salines
Lance-aux-Epines
Prickly Bay

N
W   E
S

0   1   2   3
Miles

as well as treats like guava jelly (a soft candy) and coconut fudge. From there Granby Street will take you past Market Square, which comes alive with vendors selling fresh produce early Saturday mornings.

St. George's Anglican Church (built 1828), St. Andrew's Presbyterian Church (built 1830), and St. George's Methodist Church (built 1820) are all nearby on their respective hills. The Anglican church, at the head of Gore Street, is lined with plaques representing Grenada in the eighteenth and nineteenth centuries.

Rising above the point that separates the harbor from the ocean is Fort George, built by the French in 1708 and now open to tourists.

The fastest way from the Carenage to the Esplanade is through the Sendall Tunnel. Take it if you're too tired to tackle the hill.

To explore the rest of the island, rent a car, hire a taxi, or sign up for a guided tour. If you're planning to do any hiking into the interior, bring long pants and a long-sleeved shirt as protection against mosquitoes, sharp-edged leaves, and branches. And don't forget a bathing suit!

The West Coast

The coast road north from St. George's winds past soaring mountains and valleys covered with banana and breadfruit trees, palms, bamboo, and tropical flowers. At Concord Falls, about eight miles north of St. George's, you can hike for two miles up into the hills and take a refreshing dip. About fifteen minutes farther north is the town of Gouyave (pronounced like the first syllable of guava), center of the nutmeg industry. At Dougaldston Estate, near the entrance of the town, you can see cloves, cinnamon, mace, nutmeg, allspice, and cocoa in their natural state and laid out on giant trays in the sun for drying. (Old women slowly walk barefoot through the spices, shuffling them so they dry evenly.)

Not far away is Levera Beach, a long expanse of sand lined with sea grapes and palms where the Caribbean meets the Atlantic. The islands in the distance are the southernmost Grenadines.

If it's lunchtime and if you've made reservations, head south for the short drive to Betty Mascoll's seventy-seven-year-old plantation house, Morne Fendue. The big two-story house was built by Mrs. Mascoll's father of hand-chiseled, colored stones mortared with lime and molasses. Outside, poinsettias grow in riotous profusion; inside, amid Victorian antiques and lace curtains, Mrs. Mascoll serves superb West Indian cuisine and arguably the best rum punch on the island.

The East Coast

From St. George's, a tour of the east coast should start at Westerhall, the Beverly Hills of Grenada, known for its beautiful villas, gardens, and views. From there a dirt road leads to Bacolet Bay, a ragged peninsula in the Atlantic where the surf pounds against uninhabited beaches for miles. About fifteen or twenty miles north is Grenville, the island's second city, a good place to stop for seafood. As in St. George's, Saturday is market day here, and the town fills with local people doing their shopping for the week. Grenville also has a spice-processing factory open to the public.

If you take the interior route back to St. George's, you'll see how lush and mountainous the island really is. You'll wind upward through the rain forest until you're surrounded by mist, then back down into the sun. Stop to gaze at Grand Etang Lake, a thirteen-acre, glasslike expanse of cobalt water in the crater of an extinct volcano. The area is a bird sanctuary and forest reserve, and fishing and swimming are permitted.

Another place to stop is Annandale Falls, where a mountain stream cascades fifty feet into a pool surrounded by liana vines, elephant ears, and other tropical flora—a good swimming and picnic spot.

Grand Anse and the South End

Grenada claims to have forty-five accessible white-sand beaches, but despite the charms of secluded little coves, none is lovelier than Grand Anse Beach. About a fifteen-minute taxi ride south of St. George's, it is a gleaming two-mile curve of sand and clear, gentle surf. To the south it ends in a jutting palm-covered point; to the north you can see the narrow mouth of St. George's harbor and the pastel houses climbing the hillsides above it. The sunset is particularly beautiful at Grand Anse; enjoy it over cocktails at Spice Island Inn, whose open-air tables are practically on the beach.

Most of the island's hotels are in Grand Anse or the adjacent community, Lance aux Epines (pronounced "lance-au-peen"), so most of the island's night life is concentrated here. The Sugar Mill swings until late, provided one of the Caribbean's occasional power outages doesn't shut down the stereo.

Spice Island Yacht Charters in Lance aux Epines rents everything from Sunfish and windsurfers to fifty-foot yachts, with or without crew.

The Grand Anse shopping center has a supermarket/liquor store, a clothing store, a shoe store, a record shop, and a gift shop with luxury items (English china, Swedish crystal) at prices competitive with duty-free prices elsewhere in the Caribbean.

Grenada's Grenadines

Grenada also holds claim to three small islands of the Grenadines to the north—Carriacou, Petit Martinique and Isle de Ronde—as well as a handful of uninhabited specks where most of the action is the lowering of sails by charter yachts that anchor in the harbors. Carriacou's colonial history paralleled Grenada's, although its minute size (thirteen square miles) and distance from Grenada (sixteen miles) make it of much less significance. A chain of hills runs through the center of Carriacou, from Gun Point in the north to the favorite, protected harbor of Tyrrel Bay in the south. Inter-Island Air Transport makes daily flights to and from Grenada and a scheduled schooner makes regular, if not daily, runs. Hillsborough is the main town, and the main social season is August, when the annual Carriacou Regatta brings sailors and yachts from throughout the Caribbean. Tour operators in Grenada offer chartered day-cruises to the island.

Five miles northeast of Carriacou, Petit Martinique's 486 acres hold about six-hundred year round inhabitants, most of whom are employed, like most of Carriacou, in boat-building and seamanship. Like Carriacou and Grenada, Petit Martinique was settled by the French.

PRACTICAL INFORMATION FOR GRENADA

FACTS AND FIGURES. Located in the eastern Caribbean, Grenada is the southernmost of the Windward Islands, 12 degrees north of the equator. Trinidad lies 90 miles to the southeast, Barbados 125 miles to the northeast. Grenada is 21 miles long and 12 miles wide at its widest point, with an area of 120 square miles. Volcanic in origin, the island is mountainous in the interior and extremely fertile. It is called The Isle of Spice because of the variety of spices it produces for export, nutmeg chief among them. Most of its 110,000 inhabitants live in and around St. George's, the capital, a port city on the west coast, and in Grenville, on the east coast. The nation also includes three much smaller islands, Carriacou, Isle de Ronde, and Petit Martinique, which are part of the Grenadines. English is the official language.

WHEN TO GO. The temperature in Grenada stays at about 83 degrees F 12 months a year. September through December is considered the rainy season; daily showers lasting from a few minutes to half an hour or so can be expected. On the other hand, perfectly sunny weather for days at a stretch is equally common during rainy season. As far as hotel rates are concerned, the "high" season lasts from December 15 to April 15. Prices fall by 20% to 40% the rest of the year.

PASSPORTS AND VISAS. For U.S., Canadian, and British citizens, proof of citizenship and a return air ticket are required for entry into Grenada. A passport, even an expired one, is the best proof of citizenship; a birth certificate or voter-registration card will also suffice.

MONEY. Grenada uses the Eastern Caribbean dollar; $2.65 E.C. = $1 U.S. All prices referred to herein are in U.S. dollars unless otherwise noted, but be sure to ask which dollars are referred to when you make purchases and business transactions in Grenada. They usually take E.C., except in places that cater especially to U.S. tourists. Be prepared to pay for nearly everything—accommodations, food, and sundries—in travelers' checks or cash; credit cards are not yet widely accepted. Money can be exchanged at any bank or at hotels.

WHAT WILL IT COST

A typical day on Grenada for two people during the season will run:

	$U.S.
Better-than-moderate hotel accommodations, including breakfast and dinner	$150
Lunch at a moderate restaurant	12
Tips, hotel taxes, services	30
Car rental or sightseeing	45
Total	$237

HOW TO GET THERE. By air. *BWIA* serves Grenada from New York and Miami. Another way to go is on *LIAT* out of Barbados (via St. Vincent) or Trinidad. *Inter-Island Air Service* has scheduled service between Grenada and Carriacou.

By sea. At least half a dozen major cruise lines, including Cunard, Norwegian American Cruises, Paquet Cruises, and Sun Line Cruises, include St. George's on some of their Caribbean cruises. Inter-island schooners offer shuttle service between Grenada and the neighboring islands of Carriacou, Petit Martinique and Isle de Ronde.

TAXES AND OTHER CHARGES. There is a 7½% government tax on hotel rooms plus a 10% service charge. There is an airport departure tax of E.C. $15, about $5.66 U.S. currency.

TELEPHONES AND EMERGENCY NUMBERS. To dial Grenada long distance, you must go through the operator. St. George's Hospital (tel. 2051, 2052, 2053) offers all facilities. Your hotel operator will have the number for the nearest police and fire stations. The telephone system in Grenada, never very efficient, is now being redesigned. Until it is complete, contact the hotel operator to put through any long-distance calls you want to make or, in St. George's, use the cable and overseas telephone office on the Carenage at Hughes St. Until coin telephones are installed, place your local calls from hotels.

HOTELS. In January 1985 Grenada had only about 400 first-class hotel rooms, 200 of which were occupied by U.S. troops and diplomats. New construction is now underway and at least one new hotel will open in 1986; check with the tourist office or your travel agent.

Accommodations range from simply furnished kitchenette suites to stylish, Caribbean-style elegance, but most fall somewhere in between. There are no pretentiously posh hotels—Grenada is a simple place and its hotels have been furnished accordingly. Most of the hotels are owned and run by Grenadians; those that aren't are run largely by British or American expatriates who love the simplicity of Grenadian life. Because the hotels tend to be small—10 to 20 rooms in many cases—they have an intimate feel, and the manager might well become a friend.

Also because of their small size, Grenada's hotels generally do not have their own golf courses, marinas, or tour services. All the hotels will arrange fishing and boating expeditions, golf, island tours, and other activities if you just ask.

The following hotels are in St. George's or in the resort area south of it. For double accommodations, including two meals during the winter season (December 15–April 15), we call U.S. $150 and up *Deluxe;* $100–149 *Expensive;* $85–99 *Moderate;* and anything below that, *Inexpensive.*

Unless otherwise noted, winter rates are strictly MAP—that is, breakfast and dinner included. In the summer season (April 16–December 14) most of the hotels offer EP rates (no meals) and CP rates (breakfast only). The price difference between EP and MAP is usually $20–40, depending on the category of the hotel.

During the summer season prices fall by 20–40%. A 10% service charge in lieu of tipping and 7½% government tax are added onto each bill. *Credit cards are generally not accepted.*

It's best to book your hotel through a travel agent. Alternatively, some hotels have U.S. representatives through which you can make bookings; these are indicated below. Until more hotels open, early booking is a good idea. However, Grenada has a hotel association which has up-to-date information on which hotels have vacancies, and they can often book rooms on short notice. (Grenada Hotel Association, P.O. Box 440, St. George's, Grenada, W.I. Tel. 4475; Telex 3425GA; Cable GREHOTA.)

Note that most hotels and restaurants in Grenada outside St. George's don't have street addresses; there are few enough of them that everyone—and certainly cab drivers—know them well.

Grenadian cuisine is excellent, and the food served in hotel restaurants is no exception. When one is outstanding, we've mentioned it; but all are very good.

The Calabash. *Deluxe.* Prickly Bay, Lance aux Epines. Mailing address; P.O. Box 382, St. George's. Tel. 4234, 4334. The 22 kitchenette suites here are set on a wide green lawn that ends on a pretty, curved beach. There's a yacht and charter-boat anchorage on the other end of the cove. The clientele is mostly couples of all ages and families; many of them, like the owner, English. Tennis and windsurfing are offered. The most deluxe suite has its own private, semi-indoor pool. The open-air restaurant is friendly and comfortable.

Secret Harbour Hotel. *Deluxe.* Lance aux Epines. Mailing address: P.O. Box 11, St. George's. Tel. 4439, 4548, 4549. The island's most luxurious resort consists of 20 roomy, Mediterranean-style units set on a ridge overlooking Mt. Hartman Bay. Each unit has two antique four-poster beds, a balcony with a gorgeous view of the bay, and a giant bathroom with a window in the shower that overlooks the sea. There's a pool, a tennis court, and a small private beach. The restaurant and lounge are popular at night; owner/manager Barbara Stevens is a charming hostess. The clientele is mostly couples of all ages and celebrities. Represented in the U.S. by David B. Mitchell and Co., 200 Madison Ave., New York, NY 10016; (212) 696–1323.

Spice Island Inn. *Deluxe.* Grand Anse Beach. Mailing address: P.O. Box 6, St. George's. Tel. 4258, 2818. Spice Island has the distinction of being right on the beach. Twenty of its suites face the water; the other ten are surrounded by walls that enclose small, private swimming pools. The atmosphere here is lively; the bar and restaurant open onto the sand. The restaurant is very popular. Families and couples of all ages make up the clientele.

Cinnamon Hill and Beach Club. *Expensive.* Grand Anse. Mailing address: P.O. Box 292, St. George's. Tel. 4301, 4302. There are 20 one- and two-bedroom suites, eight of them on Grand Anse beach and the rest scattered among the bougainvillea on the hillside above it. The kitchens are fully equipped; the rate does not include meals, but you can have breakfast cooked and served in your suite for about U.S. $7. There are tennis courts, squash courts, a pool, and a putting green, and two suites with their own private pools. Couples of all ages and families stay here; the atmosphere is lively. MAP, CP, and EP plans year round. Represented by International Travel and Resorts, INC., 25 West 39th Street, New York, NY 10018; (212) 840–6636; (800) 223–9815.

Grenada Beach Hotel. *Expensive.* Grand Anse. Mailing address: P.O. Box 441, St. George's. Tel. 4371. This hotel, the largest in Grand Anse, was used to billet U.S. troops through the first quarter of 1985. Plans call for it to reopen 150 rooms in December 1985, with more to be added in 1986. It has a pool and tennis courts and is situated on Grand Anse Beach next door to the Spice Island Inn. Much of the winter season night life in Grand Anse centers around this hotel because of its nightly entertainment: steel, reggae, or pop bands who play for dancing and listening by the pool. Each room has two double beds; some face the beach, others overlook the pool. Sailing and windsurfing are also available. The Grenada Beach offers both MAP and EP rates year-round. Couples and families make up the clientele.

Horse Shoe Bay Hotel. *Expensive.* Lance aux Epines. Mailing address: P.O. Box 174, St. George's. Tel. 4410. Six secluded, Spanish-style villas perch on a hillside overlooking a small private beach. Each villa has one or two units consisting of two bedrooms and a kitchen, laundry room, and patio. The double beds are giant mahogany four-posters, fit for royalty, and each villa has a back-porch utility sink so guests can clean the fish they catch. The hotel will arrange fishing expeditions; tennis, sailing, scuba diving, and snorkeling are also offered, and there's a freshwater pool. The clientele is mostly couples. The handsome restaurant overlooks the sea.

Ross' Point Inn. *Moderate.* St. George's. Mailing address: P.O. Box 137, St. George's. Tel. 4551. This inn is set on three-and-a-half acres on a point two miles south of St. George's harbor and half-a-mile north of Grand Anse Beach. Owned by the same family since 1928, Ross' Point has 12 simply furnished rooms sleeping two or three. The snorkeling off the point is said to be the best on the island, and a car shuttles guests to and from Grand Anse Beach if they perfer to swim there. Ross' Point is a quiet place; its owner, Curtis Hopkin, is an elder statesman in Grenadian and Caribbean tourism. The kitchen is renowned for its superb West Indian cuisine. (Note: After the 1983 invasion, the U.S. took over Ross' Point as its embassy. This was to be a temporary arrangement, but at press time the embassy still had not relocated to permanent quarters. Check with your travel agent or with the hotel association.)

Twelve Degrees North. *Moderate.* Lance aux Epines. Mailing address: P.O. Box 241, St. George's. Tel. 4580. Joe Gaylord built and opened this secluded, modern cottage hotel in 1968. It has six one-bedroom and two two-bedroom apartments. Modern and spare, they have Spanish tile floors, cream-colored walls, and lots of light. They sit atop a hill that slopes down to a swimming pool and, beyond that, a small beach that's good for snorkeling (bring your own gear). Rates are EP; each apartment has a kitchen, which the hotel stocks with staple food items before you arrive; the food is billed to you at cost. (Anything you don't want can be returned and you won't be billed for it.) You supplement the store with your own purchases; the hotel will run you down to the supermarket. Your own maid comes in every morning to prepare breakfast, tidy up, do the laundry, and fix lunch. The hotel has no restaurant, but the hotels and restaurants of Grand Anse and Lance aux Epines are nearby, within walking or cabbing distance. There's a Sunfish and a sailing dinghy for rent and a free tennis court. The clientele is definitely adult; children under 12 are not allowed. During the winter season there's a minimum stay of one week.

Blue Horizons Cottage Hotel. *Moderate.* Grand Anse. Mailing address: P.O. Box 41, St. George's. Tel. 4316. This comfortable, family-oriented hotel has 16 kitchenette suites sleeping two, three, or four, some with living rooms and all with terraces. The individual units are set among the palms around a large, sunny lawn and swimming pool. Grand Anse Beach is a five-minute walk down the hill. Rates are without meals, but the hotel has an excellent, reasonably priced restaurant, *La Belle Creole.* Royston's Rental Cars is based here.

The St. James Hotel. *Inexpensive.* Grand Etang Road, St. George's. Mailing address: P.O. Box 131, St. George's. Tel. 2041, 2042. This 100-year-old former private home has been a hotel since 1950. It is located in the west end of St. George's, set on a hill between the Carenage and the Esplanade, and is a gracious retreat amidst the bustle of town. There are 16 simple rooms, both singles and doubles, with nice views. Most have a private bath; some share a bath with the room next door. Rate plans include one, two, or three meals or none at all. In the dining room, superb West Indian cuisine is served. A shuttle bus takes guests to and from Grand Anse Beach; you can order a picnic lunch to take with you. The clientele includes businesspeople from other islands and abroad, students on a budget, and a variety of others, mostly adults.

 HOME AND APARTMENT RENTALS. Your travel agent or the Grenada Hotel Association can book space at these establishments, all of which are convenient to Grand Anse Shopping Center.

The Flamboyant. Grand Anse. Mailing address: P.O. Box 214, St. George's. Tel. 4247. Sprinkled on a hill above the south end of Grand Anse Beach, these simple cottages have one or two bedrooms each for a total of 22 bedrooms. The view of the beach and of St. George's in the distance is wonderful. Many of the guests are students or teachers at St. George's University School of Medicine, which is based nearby. Maids and cooks are available.

Maffiken Apartments. Grand Anse. Mailing address: P.O. Box 124, Grand Anse, St. George's. Tel. 4255, 4522. Four modern stucco units on a terraced hill; each contains a fully furnished apartment for up to four people. Maid service is provided and cooks are available. Grand Anse Beach is five minutes away.

South Winds Holiday Cottages and Apartments. Grand Anse. Mailing addresses: P.O. Box 118, St. George's. Tel. 2351, 2399. Five two-bedroom and six one-bedroom apartments are fully furnished; maid service and cooks are available. Some units are individual, others are in a two-story, motel-style building and all have patios. Grand Anse Beach is 500 yards away.

HOW TO GET AROUND. Local buses, actually mini-vans (a recent innovation), ply the road between St. George's and Grand Anse. Hail one anywhere along the way, pay E.C. $1, and settle in for one of the most hair-raising rides of your life. (The more runs per day, the more the drivers earn—so they drive fast!) Taxis are plentiful and metered, and rates are posted at the hotels and at the pier on the Carenage in town. The trip from downtown to Grand Anse is about U.S. $6. From the airport to Grand Anse is about U.S. $12. Cabs are plentiful at all hotels and on the Carenage, at the pier, and next to the tourist office.

Rental cars cost about U.S. $40 a day or $220 a week with unlimited mileage. Gas costs about U.S. $2.50 per gallon. Your hotel will arrange the rental for you, or try the following places in St. George's: *David's,* Church St., tel. 2351; *Huggins,* Young St., tel. 3316; and *MacIntyre Brothers,* Young St., tel. 3316, 2514, or (after hours) 3428. In Grand Anse: *Royston's,* Blue Horizons Hotel, tel. 4316. You will need to present a valid driver's license, and remember to drive on the left!

TOURIST INFORMATION SERVICES. The Grenada Tourist Board in the center of the Carenage (P.O. Box 293, St. George's, tel. 2001, 2279), has maps, brochures, and information on accommodations, tours, and other services. For sources closer to home, see the Tourist Information Services section in the *Facts at Your Fingertips* chapter.

SPECIAL EVENTS. In January, the New Year Fiesta and yacht race leads right into the "Around Grenada" yacht race, attracting international participants. The annual Game-Fishing Tournament in mid-January brings anglers from all over to compete for record catches of dolphin, sailfish, marlin, yellowfin, tuna, and others.

The Grenada Easter Regatta in April includes a week of inter-island and local races, culminating on Easter Sunday with various events and celebrations.

In August the annual Carriacou Regatta is the big event on this island, 16 miles north of Grenada. Usually held the first week of the month, it's a weekend of boat races, music, dancing, and cultural performances. Around the 14th is Carnival Weekend, with steel-band and calypso music and "jump-up" folkloric dancing.

TOURS. Grenada Tours and Travel (Young St., St. George's, tel. 3316, 2514, 2031) offers a selection of tours. *Around the Island* is a 6½-hour tour up the west coast to the spice plantation at Gouyave; then on to Sauteurs; then to the Mascoll plantation house, Morne Fendue, for lunch. The homeward route is through the east-coast town of Grenville and across scenic St. David's Parish. The tour costs U.S. $28 per person. *The Day Sail* includes a stop for swimming, snorkeling, and beachcombing in a deserted cove, plus lunch and rum punches, for U.S. $25. *Deep-Sea Game Fishing* expeditions cost about U.S. $20 per person per hour for a minimum of three hours. The *Carriacou Day Tour* includes air transportation to and from the island, an island tour, a barbecue lunch, and snorkeling for U.S. $118 per person.

A number of car-rental agencies and tour operators in St. George's offer standard tours such as the Royal Drive, which includes the town of St. George's, scenic Westerhall Pt. across the island on the Atlantic coast, a small fishing village, a sugar-processing factory, and Grand Anse Beach. Island tours are also available. In St. George's stop by the tourist office for information or try *Otways Tours* on the Carenage (tel. 2558), *Huggins Travel Service* on Young St. (tel. 3316, 2414), *McIntyre Brothers* on Lagoon Rd. (tel. 2044, 2901) or *Grenada Tours and Travel.* In Grand Anse try *Carin's,* just south of the shopping center (tel. 4363, 4364). Your hotel will also arrange a tour. Driving tours can be arranged immediately; air and sea tours will take a day or two.

If you like, you can hire a cab to give you an island tour for about U.S. $35 per hour, or you can sign up for a group tour. Your hotel and the tourist board will make suggestions.

 BEACHES. Two-mile-long *Grand Anse Beach,* a few miles south of St. George's, is one of the Caribbean's loveliest. It has powdery white sand, gentle surf, and shady palms. All beaches in Grenada are open to the public, so you don't have to be a guest at one of the nearby hotels to use them. *Levera Beach* is at the northern tip of the island where the Caribbean meets the Atlantic. The first of the Grenadines is visible in the distance. Grenada has 45 accessible white-sand beaches; rent a car or boat and seek them out.

 PARTICIPANT SPORTS. Fishing. Deep-sea fishing for marlin, tuna, yellowfin, dolphin, and others is excellent. Self-skippered boats are available for about U.S. $30 an hour; crewed charters start at about $40 per hour. The annual Game-Fishing Tournament is held in mid-January. Tour operators or your hotel can arrange fishing trips, or contact *Grenada Yacht Services,* P.O. Box 183, St. George's, tel. 2508.

Golf. *The Grenada Golf and Country Club* in Grand Anse (tel. 4244) has a nine-hole course with very low rates. Your hotel will make arrangements.

Sailing, diving, snorkeling. *Spice Island Yacht Charters,* Prickly Bay, Lance aux Epines (mailing address: P.O. Box 449, St. Georges, tel. 4342, 4458), offers a range of 40- and 50-foot sailboats for charter, with and without crews. *Grenada Yacht Services* in St. George's (see "Fishing," above) offers organized snorkeling and dive trips to nearby wrecks and coral reefs. A 30-foot sailboat with skipper costs about U.S. $160 a day to charter for sailing and snorkeling; lunch is included and six people can be accommodated. There are very few certified diving instructors in Grenada as yet, so don't count on learning while you're there. Your hotel will arrange trips, as will any of the island's tour operators.

Swimming. Take your pick of beaches around the island, but don't miss Grand Anse.

Tennis. Calabash, Cinnamon Hill, The Grenada Beach, Secret Harbour and Twelve Degrees North are the hotels that have courts, and none charge for their use. If there are no courts where you're staying, ask the desk clerk to call one of the private clubs on the island.

Windsurfing. *Spice Island Charters* on Prickly Bay (see "Sailing, diving, snorkeling," above) rents windsurfers for about U.S. $20 per day or $100 per week.

 SPECTATOR SPORTS. Cricket, one of the most popular sports on the island, is played on Saturday mornings at 10:00 A.M. from January to May. The field is just outside St. George's, near the south side of town.

 HISTORIC SITES AND HOUSES. With the exception of Dougaldston Estate, the spice-processing center at Gouyave, any attractions in this category are in St. George's. Grenada's historic buildings are all currently in use; they are not museums, so visits there are unstructured.

Government House. Located in the hills above town near the top of Woolwich Road. Built in the late 18th century, it is a fine example of early Georgian architecture. Now the residence of Governor General Sir Paul Scoon, who represents Queen Elizabeth II. It was closed to the public after the invasion; check with the tourist board for current status. York House, now the Supreme Court building, and the Registry next door were built around 1800. Located on Church Street, they are open Mon.–Fri. 9:00 A.M. to 3:45 P.M. Since they're public buildings, there is no admission charge.

Marryshow House. Tyrrel St. near Bain Alley (tel. 2451). Built in 1917 and combines both Victorian and West Indian architecture. Open weekdays 10:00 A.M. to 4:00 P.M. No admission charge.

Dougaldston House. An hour's drive north of St. George's near the entrance to the town of Gouyave. It is the center of the west-coast spice-processing industry. Women here sort cinnamon, cloves, cocoa, nutmeg, mace, and other spices and dry them in the sun. Open weekdays 10:00 A.M. to 4:00 P.M. No admission charge.

MUSEUMS AND GALLERIES. *The Grenada National Museum.* Young St. in St. George's. Small but interesting; it houses finds from archeological digs, an exhibit tracing Grenada's Indian cultures, and for some reason, a marble bathtub used by Josephine in Haiti before her marriage to Napoleon. The building itself was built by the French around 1704 and served as a prison until 1880. Open Mon.–Fri. 10:00 A.M. to 4:00 P.M. Admission is $.50 for adults, $.10 for children.

Yellow Poui Art Gallery. On the Esplanade in St. George's near the Sendall Tunnel (tel. 3001, 2121). Exhibits and sells Caribbean paintings and sculpture, antique maps, prints, photographs, and other fine artworks.

MUSIC, DANCE AND STAGE. The *Marryshow Folk Theater,* on Tyrrel St. in St. George's (tel. 2451) is Grenada's first cultural center. Plays, West Indian dance and music, and poetry readings are featured on occasion. More informally, steel, reggae, and pop bands play at many of the hotels in the evenings during the winter season.

SHOPPING. The special souvenir to bring home from Grenada is a little basket of spices cinnamon, nutmeg, mace, bay leaf, vanilla, ginger, and others. You can buy them at the open-air market (Saturday mornings in Georgetown and Grenville), at the various spice factories on the island (most island tours include one, such as *Dougaldston House* in Gouyave), in the gift shops on the Esplanade in St. George's, and in the Grand Anse Shopping Center. Vendors who stroll the beach in Grand Anse each have a specialty: spice baskets; fabric dolls; "Rescue 1983" T-shirts (complete with the Stars and Stripes and the Grenadian flag on the front); hats, fans, and visors woven from green palm; and jewelry of black coral.

Shops are generally open Mon. through Sat. from 9:00 A.M. until 3:45 P.M.; some close for lunch from 11:45 until 1:00. Credit cards are not widely accepted. There is no sales tax. Prices are generally marked in E.C. dollars (U.S. $1 = E.C. $2.65). All the following stores are in downtown St. George's unless otherwise noted.

Grencraft, the National Handicrafts Center (Melville St. at the Esplanade, tel. 2655) is a must. They sell locally made furniture; black and brown coral and tortoise-shell jewelry; and crafts of wood, wicker, straw, and fabric. Also T-shirts, postcards and locally made juices, preserves, candy, and sauces.

Spice Island Perfumes on the Carenage (tel. 2006) is a treasure trove of locally made perfumes, body oils, natural extracts of spices and herbs, shampoos, suntan oils and lotions, teas, and spices. Also other gifts.

Sea Change on the Carenage (tel. 2056) is open from 8:30 A.M. to 5:00 P.M. and carries books, magazines, postcards, stamps, film, paintings, prints, and gift items.

Gittens Pharmacy on Halifax St. (tel. 2165) carries cosmetics and toiletries and fills prescriptions.

Charles of Grenada on the corner of Bruce and Cross streets near the Esplanade (tel. 2306) sells luxury items like imported china, crystal, and cashmere sweaters at prices comparable to or lower than those at many Caribbean duty-free shops.

The Esplanade is lined with clothing and gift shops as well as tiny shops selling baskets, woven hats, and homemade candies. The streets between the Carenage and Market Sq. are full of banks, pharmacies, and other useful shops.

The Grand Anse Shopping Center in Grand Anse includes *The Gift Shop,* another outlet for luxury goods such as watches, leather goods, fine jewelry, imported crystal and china, and framed prints at competitive prices: *His & Hers,* which sells clothing for adults and children—bathing suits, sportswear, novelty T-shirts, batiks, and some English wool sweaters; a record shop; and a shoe store. (American Express cards accepted; closed Sun. and Mon.) *The Grand Anse Food Fair* supermarket is open daily except Sun. and sells liquor and wine as well as food.

RESTAURANTS. Grenada is a cook's—and a food lover's—paradise. Unlike so many islands that have a scarcity of fresh produce, Grenada has everything from cabbage and tomatoes to bananas, mangoes, papaya (called paw-paw), plaintains, melon, callaloo (similar to spinach), breadfruit, oranges, tangerines, limes, christophine (similar to potatoes), avocado—the list is endless. Fresh fish of all kinds, including lobster and oysters, is also plentiful. Conch, known here as lambi, is very popular. Be sure to try one of the exotic ice creams—avocado or nutmeg, for example. Almost all Grenadian restaurants stick to local cuisine, which is varied enough to be continually interesting. International favorites like broiled lobster, omelettes, hamburgers, and fish and chips are widely offered as well.

Rum punches are standard everywhere—but no two places make them exactly alike. Taking a survey to see who makes the best one is a delightful pursuit. The local beer, Carib, is also very popular.

Very few restaurants take credit cards. There's no tax on food. A 10% service charge is sometimes included on the bill; a tip of about five percent above that is customary.

By U.S. standards, dining in Grenada is a bargain. The restaurants in the hotels are generally more expensive than others; a three-course dinner for one, without drinks or tip, will cost from $20–40 in a hotel, $8–20 in most individual restaurants. (All prices are given in U.S. dollars.) Therefore, we've listed most of the hotel restaurants under *Expensive* ($20–40) and others under *Moderate* ($8–20).

Regarding dress codes: Grenada is informal; a man can leave all his neckties at home and still be well-dressed. A white or pastel dress shirt and sport jacket are fine for the hotel restaurants and more than adequate for the others. Women should wear skirts or dresses, rather than slacks, in the evening. Hotel restaurants are open daily; some others close on Sundays. Call to check.

With one exception (see "Special Mention," below) Grenada's noteworthy restaurants are all in St. George's, Grand Anse, or Lance aux Epines, all within walking or cabbing distance from any hotel.

Finally, we haven't listed all the hotel restaurants here; just the most outstanding ones. However, the rule that applies to many U.S. hotel restaurants— that they're never as good as a city's other eateries—does not apply in Grenada. It's almost impossible to get a bad meal here.

Expensive

The Calabash. Lance aux Epines. Tel. 4234, 4334. The open-air restaurant here is small and pretty, surrounded by palms and tropical flowers. Try the callaloo soup. Call for reservations. No credit cards.

Ross' Point Inn. St. George's. Tel. 4551. The West Indian cuisine here is legendary, the ambience at dinner casual but elegant. Call for reservations. (Note: The U.S. Embassy took over the inn in Oct. 1983; check with your hotel to see if it is back in operation.) No credit cards.

Spice Island Inn. Grand Anse. Tel. 4258, 4244. The dining room here is open on three sides and just a few steps from the beach. Reservations are needed for dinner in season only (late Dec. to mid-Apr.). The Friday-night buffet is very popular and a wonderful way to sample all the various types of seafood and salads that are such a large part of Grenadian cuisine. No credit cards.

Secret Harbour Hotel. Lance aux Epines. Tel. 4439, 4548. Secret Harbour is the island's most elegant hotel, though it, too, is casual—the Spanish-tile and red-brick restaurant is open to the breezes of Mt. Hartman Bay. The restaurant generally has a fixed menu for dinner; call before you go. Leave time to have a nightcap in the exceptionally inviting lounge. AE, V.

Moderate

La Belle Creole. Blue Horizons Hotel, Grand Anse. Tel. 4316. This pretty, open-air restaurant looks expensive but isn't. West Indian specialties that are a touch more *haute cuisine* than usual—seafood *en croute*, for example. Make reservations. No credit cards.

The Bird's Nest. Grand Anse (next to the shopping center). Tel. 4264. This very informal place is the exception to the rule: it serves Chinese food. Reservations not necessary.

Ristorante Italia. The Carenage, St. George's. Tel. 3986. Delicious pizza, pasta, and other Italian dishes. Located above Spice Island Perfumes, with broad windows overlooking the harbor. Open for lunch (12 to 2:30) and dinner (6 to 11) Mon.–Sat., closed Sunday. Reservations unnecessary. No credit cards.

Mamma's Bar. Lagoon Road, St. Georges. Tel. 2299. To begin with, Mamma's is very informal—the interior decor might be described as West Indian diner—and completely charming. No menus here; one of Mamma's daughters will set before you whatever West Indian specialties Mamma happened to cook that night—probably some roast turtle, fried chicken, lobster salad, christophine salad, cabbage salad, fried plantain . . . whatever. You will not leave hungry. Not to be missed, but reservations are critical! No credit cards.

The Nutmeg. The Carenage, St. George's. Tel. 2539. On the second floor overlooking the harbor, this simple place has a great view. All kinds of seafood prepared in many ways, including grilled turtle steaks and broiled lobster, as well as fish or chicken and chips, salads, and other fare. Reservations not necessary. No credit cards.

The Red Crab. Lance aux Epines. Tel. 4424. This busy pub serves everything from burgers and fries ($3) to lobster thermidor ($17) in an informal setting— big wooden booths, a dart board, and outdoor tables on a lantern-lit patio. Popular with medical students, soldiers, tourists, locals—a mixed bag that makes a lively and convivial atmosphere. Reservations are not necessary. Open for dinner only, 4:00 P.M. to 11:00 P.M. No credit cards.

Rudolf's. The Carenage, St. George's. Tel. 2241. This informal, pub-like place offers both West Indian cuisine (crab back and lobster salad are specialties) and a few Oriental dishes like Tung Po: breaded pork chops with honey, peaches, and rice. Try the cold tomato and orange soup. Closed Sun. No credit cards.

The St. James Hotel. Lagoon Rd., St. George's. Tel. 2041, 2042. This genteel old hotel, a private home 100 years ago, serves wonderful Grenadian cuisine on white linen tablecloths set with antique Sheffield silver. The chutney, made on the premises, could only have been concocted on the Isle of Spice; it alone is worth a visit. Make reservations. No credit cards.

The Turtleback Tavern. The Carenage, St. George's. Tel. 2241. This very informal place sits right at the end of the Carenage overlooking the water. The menu includes turtle toes (ground lambi, lobster, and other fish rolled into balls and deep-fried) and turtle tart (a delicious raisin-and-coconut pie). On Fridays there's a famous but hard-to-get Grenadian dish called oil down—breadfruit and salted pork steamed in coconut milk and covered with callaloo leaves. Reservations aren't necessary. No credit cards.

Special mention: **Betty Mascoll's Great House** up in St. Patrick's Parish (tel. 9330) near Sauteurs is worth the one-hour drive from St. George's. Mrs. Mascoll serves lunch only, and what a lunch it is. Her buffet usually includes—among other delights—the legendary pepper pot, a stew of pork, ox tail and other meats. Excellent rum punches, too. Reservations are absolutely necessary. No credit cards.

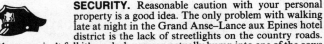

NIGHT LIFE AND BARS. *The Sugar Mill Disco* in Grand Anse (tel. 4401) is the place to go for dancing to reggae, disco, rock-and-roll and oldies. No cover or minimum; no dress code. *The Red Crab,* just down the road from the Sugar Mill in Lance aux Epines (tel. 4424) is a lively pub; closing time is 11:00 P.M. The *Love Boat,* at the inner harbor in St. George's (no telephone), is a sailor's eatery by day, a lively disco on Friday nights. The *Spice Island Hotel,* the *Calabash,* and the *Grenada Beach Hotel* have live music for dancing at least two nights a week. The lounge at the *Secret Harbour Hotel* in Grand Anse (tel. 4439) is popular for late-night drinks.

POSTAGE. Airmail rates for letters are $.22 for half-ounce letter and $.11 for a postcard.

ELECTRIC CURRENT. The current here is 220 volts A.C., 50 cycles.

SECURITY. Reasonable caution with your personal property is a good idea. The only problem with walking late at night in the Grand Anse–Lance aux Epines hotel district is the lack of streetlights on the country roads. When the moon isn't full it's so dark you can actually bump into one of the cows that graze silently by the roadside. St. George's is equally safe.

GUADELOUPE

by
CLAIRE DEVENER

Two islands in one, this butterfly-shaped beauty has some of the Caribbean's most spectacular scenery. The Caribs called it Karukera, or Island of Beautiful Waters, because of its cascades, hot springs, and clear blue-green sea. It's also known as the Emerald Island for its abundance of lush tropical vegetation, forests, fields of cane, and plantations of cocoa, banana, and coffee. But there's much more to captivate the visitor—fascinating folklore, music, song, and dance, colorful madras and foulard, Carnival, the Festival of Cooks, the beguine—all legacies of a heritage that blends the races and cultures of Europe, Africa, and India. And, since it's above all French, Guadeloupe is synonymous with fine food and *joie de vivre*. A smile and two words, *bonjour* and *merci,* are the keys to enjoyment on this tropical paradise.

Past and Present

It was on November 4, 1493, that Columbus discovered Guadeloupe. He went ashore at Ste. Marie, a point near Capesterre on Basse-Terre, now marked with a monument and a sign in Latin. In giving this name to a tropical island, Columbus kept a promise made to the monks of the monastery of Santa María de Guadalupe in Estremadura, Spain. He proclaimed it and the whole archipelago to be the property of their Catholic Majesties, Ferdinand and Isabella.

Thus began the attention from the Spanish conquistadors. Ponce de León and other Spanish soldiers of fortune could not subdue the pugnacious Caribs and never succeeded in colonizing the island. The Spaniards abandoned it in 1604. The French moved in in 1635. Cane was planted, sugar production began around 1644, and thousands of slaves were brought in to work the fields. In 1759, after several skirmishes, the British took control the Guadeloupe for a four-year period ending in the transfer of the French West Indies to the French in exchange for their rights in Canada. One short period of British occupation in 1794 was the only other time that the island did not fly the French tricolor. The Treaty of Paris in 1815 permanently restored Guadeloupe to France. Slavery was abolished and universal suffrage established in 1848. It has been a full-fledged *département* of France since 1946, and in 1974 was given the loftier status of *région.*

Guadeloupe is administered by a prefect who is appointed from Paris by the Minister of the Interior. He is assisted by two general secretaries and two *sous-prefects,* one for Pointe-à-Pitre, the second for the dependencies of St. Martin and St. Barthélemy. There are also two locally elected legislative bodies, the General and Regional Councils, and a consulting body called the Economic and Social Committee. Two senators, three deputies, and two members of the Economic Council represent Guadeloupe in French parliament in Paris.

France's recent efforts to "regionalize" overseas territories by giving them more voice in decisions that affect them continues under Mitterand's government. But "la Métropole" now has increased worries of her own, including a high unemployment rate. This directly affects overseas territory residents, who in the past could find work in the mother country when there was none at home.

In Guadeloupe, the sugar-based economy is shaky. Sugar-producing facilities need modernization, competition from beet sugar is strong, and Guadeloupe is suffering the worst drought in the last sixty years. Bananas, the second most important crop, have been victimized by devastating storm damage and the effects of the drought as well. The net result has been that growing numbers of people are finding themselves without work. Taking advantage of both local unemployment in Guadeloupe and France's preoccupation with her own internal problems, small factions have been nurturing seeds of independence. Their extremist activities have increased to include the occasional placement of bombs in government property such as the Prefecture, as well as in private installations they deem symbols of colonialism. In 1984, the culmination of their efforts was the explosion of fifteen small bombs on the anniversary of the final abolition of slavery in French territories. Although damage was sustained, there were no injuries. Taking credit for these and other isolated incidents in French Guiana, Martinique, and Paris was a Guadeloupe-based, pro-independence group called the Caribbean Revolutionary Alliance. The French government has now banned this organization, making any involvement with them illegal and punishable by incarceration. Factions like these have the sympathies of only 4% of the population. The majority of the island residents are proud to be French and of the fact that they have one of the highest standards of living in the Caribbean.

To produce more jobs, elected local officials are studying measures for the modernization and diversification of the sugar industry. Tourism has flourished since the 1970s and now is the third most important contributor to the island's economy. The number of hotel rooms has nearly tripled in fifteen years and jobs indirectly related to the industry

number nearly 9000. This island is a good place to live, and with the
dollar at an all-time high, a great bargain to visit!

EXPLORING GUADELOUPE

Grande-Terre is a mass of green and silver sugar cane, plantations,
dotted by low rolling hills, windmills, and small villages. The roads are
good, the beaches wonderful. Driving east from Pointe-à-Pitre, a jaunt
of a few miles, will take you to the Fort Fleur d'Epée. Only some of
the walls and a small chapel are left above ground; the real fascination
is the circle of dungeons and passageways below. The view from the
fort overlooking the sea is spectacular.

Gosier is the town that has become the heart of Guadeloupe's vacation life. Bistros, discothèques, and small hotels are hidden down side
streets. Big hotels rise on or near the beach. Ten miles east on the same
road is Ste.-Anne, a little sugar town, neat and prosperous, with a
stretch of magnificent beach that is enjoyed by visitors and fishermen
alike. The Club Mèditerranée's luxury resort, the former Caravelle
Hotel, is at one end of this strand. The route continues, shaded by
flowering pepper trees, to St.-François, where the Les Marines condominiums and the Mèridien and Hamak hotels hold forth and on to
the Pointe des Châteaux at the extreme eastern point of the island.
Lonely and unspoiled, here is a place to remember. The sea flings itself
against huge rocks and the jagged cliffs suggest the majestic headlands
of Brittany. On one of them stands an impressive cross, dominating this
spectacular scene; it is the only sign of man's handiwork here. Not far
away, down a side road, is Pointe Tarare, one of the island's three
naturist beaches.

Le Moule, a short drive from the Pointe heading northwest along the
coast, has a beautiful horseshoe-shaped beach, one of the island's best.
Carib warriors and French and English soldiers once fought here, and
an old cemetery nearby commemorates their ancient conflict with petrified skulls, unearthed by the final victor, the sea.

Basse-Terre

Allow a full day for the eighty-six-mile journey from Pointe-à-Pitre
to Basse-Terre and La Soufrière. This is the "compulsory excursion"
of Guadeloupe, featuring some of the Caribbean's most spectacular
scenery. The terrain of Basse-Terre is far more interesting than that of
Grande-Terre. There's a spectacularly engineered road cutting across
the spine of Basse-Terre called La Traversé. It winds through the
island's newest tourist attraction, the 74,100-acre Natural Park. Walking and hiking paths lead to beautiful sites, impressive waterfalls, picnic
areas, lakes, and rivers. The tourist office in Pointe-à-Pitre can supply
you with a complimentary map.

If you take the east-coast road and head south, you'll pass through
Petit Bourg after crossing the drawbridge over Rivière Salée, the only
river connecting the Caribbean and the Atlantic. Look back to the view
of Pointe-à-Pitre with its prominent "skycrapers" standing as monuments to the French island's prosperity.

The road surface is good around Ste.-Marie, where Columbus landed
and met a flurry of Carib arrows. The East Indians who live in this

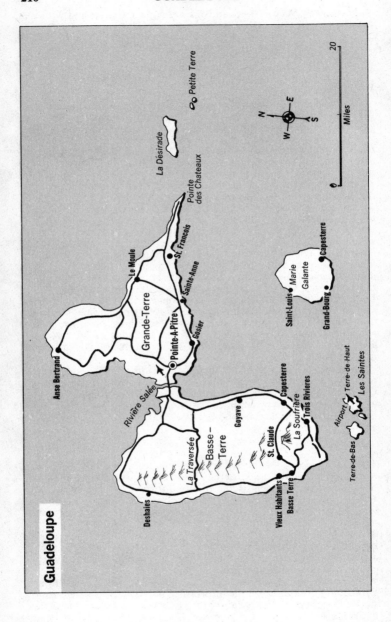

Guadeloupe

vicinity are the descendants of the laborers who were brought in to work the sugar plantations, replacing the freed black slaves.

Past Capesterre, the fishing village of Bananier's small houses slope down to the sea. Trois Rivières is the jumping-off place for a fascinating excursion to the Iles des Saintes. Nearby you can visit the Parc Archéologique des Roches Gravées, where sculptured rocks, heavily incised with Carib engravings, are among the few relics left by the Indians who once dominated the Caribbean.

After Trois Rivières, the road cuts inland, past Dolé-les-Bains with its well-known thermal baths. Shortly after you pass through Dolé, you'll see the village of Gourbeyre and, beyond, the silhouette of Fort Saint-Charles guarding the approaches to Basse-Terre. Basse-Terre is a postcard capital, with beautiful parks, handsome administrative buildings, and a seventeenth-century cathedral, all tucked into a niche between towering Mt. Soufrière and the sea. The steep and narrow road inland leads to St. Claude, a suburb four miles up from Basse-Terre. Here, amid the lushest of tropical trees and gardens, live the wealthy owners of the banana plantations and, more modestly, the higher echelon of the civil servants of France. At St.-Claude, you are already on your way up the slopes of the majestic volcano La Soufrière.

From La Soufrière, you can drive past Rivière Noire and Rivière Rouge to Matouba, in East Indian village where ancient rites, including the sacrifice of animals, are still practiced by survivors of this transplanted people. The black sands of the western shore of Basse-Terre are speckled with fishing villages. Off-shore at Pigeon Island, Jacques Cousteau found some of his most interesting Caribbean specimens.

Iles Des Saintes

Les Saintes are a cluster of eight islands off the southern coast of Guadeloupe, accessible by boats that depart twice a day from Trois Rivières, four times a week from Basse-Terre. If you're planning to go, allow at least an hour for the drive from Pointe-à-Pitre to Trois Rivières. The boat trip, apt to be rough, takes about 45 minutes each way. There is also scheduled small-plane service by Air Guadeloupe and charter service by Caraïbes Air Tourisme and Safari Tours. Not only has Jacques Cousteau spent time in the waters around these remote islands, but naturists have claimed a beach for their third nudist retreat. The eight islands by name are Terre-de-Haut, Terre-de-Bas, Ilet Cabrit, Grand Ilet, La Coche, Les Augustins, Le Pâté, and La Redonde. Terr-de-Haut, the most interesting to visit, has about 1500 inhabitants, descendants of Breton and Norman sailors. They look like a group of Vikings, with apple cheecks, blue eyes, and blond hair. Les Saintois, as they are called, and the Sabans from the Dutch island to the north, are said to be the best seamen in the West Indies. Certainly they are the most picturesque; they still wear unique wide-brimmed, flat straw hats that are often likened to inverted saucers.

The chief settlement of Terre-de-Haut is Bourg, a single paved street following the curve of the fishing harbor. White houses are painted with blue and red trim and occasionally sport a carved balcony or some other touch of Victorian gingerbread. Bourg has several bistros and cafés, a few shops, and timeless primitive charm. Donkeys are the local beasts of burden; fishnets are drying all over the island, strung from poles; children play on the beaches and everywhere else.

The well-preserved barracks, prison cells, and musuem at Fort Napoléon, a reminder of the eighteenth-century battles between Admirals Rodney and De Grasse, may be visited, as may a new botanical garden with an exotic variety of succulents. Terre-de-Haut was made for swimming, sunbathing on splendid beaches and exploring by foot, by bike, or by one of four *taxis de l'ile,* minibuses that run from the airstrip to town and double as tour buses.

Far from the toot of most cruise-ship whistles, Terre-de-Haut does have electricity, running water, a small airstrip, a radio station, and a couple of jeeps and cars. It has also recently become a port of call for some of the windjammers that cruise this part of the Caribbean.

For real exploring get a fisherman to take you over to Ilet à Cabri, whose main inhabitants are a large colony of cats. Walk around the remains of Fort Josephine, built in 1780, and climb up the hill to the island's only structures, six abandoned bungalows, built in the 1960s as part of a vacation complex which was never completed.

On Terre-de-Haut, Le Bois Joli Hotel in the western part of the island overlooks a nice beach, has twenty-one rooms and a pleasant dining room. It's relaxing, quiet, and very informal.

Other overnight possibilities include the ten-room Jeanne d'Arc on the beach at Fond de Curé; or the Kanaoa, a large waterfront villa with excellent food, fourteen rooms and twenty-two new bungalow units. None of these places offers any gala night life, but that's not why you came here.

Marie-Galante

Twenty-seven miles and two hours by the ferry that leaves every day from La Darse in Pointe-à-Pitre; or a fifteen-minute flight by Air Guadeloupe. This flat island, named after Columbus' flagship, the *Maria Galanda,* produces cotton, sugar, and rum, and is the largest of Guadeloupe's dependencies. The women still dress in their colorful madras turbans and long dresses on Sundays, although there is an increase these days in the Parisian style attire that fills the streets of Pointe-à-Pitre.

The capital is Grand Bourg, with a population of about 8000 and a protected beach. Along the shore, there is a handful of spots where you can get an inexpensive meal, usually freshly caught seafood in Creole sauce. If you want to stay overnight, Le Salut (fifteen rooms) and Solédad (eighteen rooms) are the only places, unless the 200-year-old Château Murat finally opens its doors as a hotel. This has been rumored for some time, but as of this writing, the Château remains an impressive, unoccupied building. A new entertainment complex opened recently in Grand Bourg. El Rancho has a 400-seat movie theater, restaurant, terrace grill, snack bar, discothèque, and a few double rooms.

Desirade

A former penal and leper colony, this "longed-for land" was discovered by Columbus during his second voyage. Daily ferries make the trip from the Marina in St. Francois in forty-five minutes. Air Guadeloupe flies in twice a day from Le Raizet Airport. Fishing is the prime activity of the roughly 1600 inhabitants, some descendants of European exiles. The main village of Grande Anse has a pretty church as well as a tiny, very basic hotel, La Guitoune, where excellent fresh seafood is available. Two good beaches on this island, virtually untouched by tourism, are near Souffleur, the boatbuilding village, and Baie Mahault.

PRACTICAL INFORMATION FOR GUADELOUPE

FACTS AND FIGURES. Guadeloupe is actually a 659-square-mile archipelago made up of the two islands of Basse-Terre and Grande-Terre, plus the dependencies of Marie-Galante, Désirade, Les Saintes, St. Martin, and St. Barthélemy. Basse-Terre and Grande-Terre are separated by a narrow four-mile-long seawater channel called Rivière Salée (Salt River). Grande-Terre has 218 square miles and is largely covered with sugar cane, bordered by white-sand beaches, and studded with windmills, low round hills (*mornes*), as well as the majority of resort hotels and fine restuarants. Located here is Pointe-à-Pitre, Guadeloupe's commercial center, whose population is now over 100,000.

Across a drawbridge is the other island, called Basse-Terre (low land) despite the fact that mountains run its length and it is crowned by the highest peak in the lesser Antilles—4,812-foot Mt. Soufrière, an active volcano. This island is larger (312 square miles), less developed, and includes a natural park, tropical rain forests, and cascading mountain torrents that feed a half a dozen rivers. The "low land" appelation refers not to the height of the land, but to the location of the two "wings" in relation to the trade winds. Grande-Terre faces the highest winds; Basse-Terre, with its mountains, is the lee where the winds are "lower." Guadeloupe's capital and administrative center is the town of Basse-Terre, on the southwestern coast at the foot of Mt. Soufrière. Its population is just over 15,000. French and Creole are the official languages, but English is becoming more and more common, especially in larger hotels, restaurants, and other tourist facilities. Guadeloupe is one hour ahead of eastern standard time.

WHEN TO GO. The climate is tropical but tempered by year-round trade winds (*les alizés*) that keep humidity at generally comfortable levels. Temperatures on the coast average 72 to 86 degrees F; in the mountains, 66 to 81 degrees. November through the end of May is the dry season. From July through October, there are short, frequent rain showers; these are heavier and longer in the mountainous areas. During the "Season of Sweet Savings"—mid-April to mid-December—prices are 30-50% lower than those of high season. During this time special packages such as the "Fête Française" tours offer additional savings with a car-rental discount, a free shopping tour, a free dinner with ½ bottle of champagne, and other extras. Carnival, celebrated the two days before Ash Wednesday, is always a lively time to be here; and one of the most colorful island events is the annual Fête des Cuisinières, which takes place on the Saturday nearest to August 11.

PASSPORTS AND VISAS. For visits of three months or less, U.S. and Canadian visitors need a valid passport, or at least one that expired no more than five years before the date of entry *or* proof of citizenship such as a birth certificate with a raised seal or voter's registration. *Either* must be *accompanied* by a government-authorized identification with photo. Check your airline to know exactly what is acceptable. Citizens of the United Kingdom need passports, but no visas. All visitors must have a return or ongoing ticket.

MONEY. The French franc is legal tender here. Figure approximately 10 francs to $1 U.S. The best exchange rate is given at the banks; a hotel's rate may be slightly less. U.S. dollars are accepted in some places, but you will fare much better if you use local currency. Credit cards are widely accepted in resort areas, less so in the countryside and in smaller hotels and restaurants. Banking hours are 8:00 A.M.–noon; 2:30–4:00 P.M. Mon.-Fri.

WHAT WILL IT COST?

A typical day for two persons during the winter season will run:

	U.S.$
Accommodations at a resort hotel on the beach, including breakfast and service charge (average)	$100
Lunch at a moderate restaurant	20
Dinner at hotel or in-town restaurant	50
Tips	8
Car rental for one day	30
Total	$208

HOW TO GET THERE. By Air. *American Airlines* has direct service from New York; *Pan Am* comes in both non-stop from New York and via St. Thomas, and direct from Miami. *Eastern* flights from several U.S. gateways make connections via Miami. *Air Canada* connects Montreal and Toronto to Pointe-à-Pitre. *Air France* has nonstop service from Paris and Fort de France; direct service from Miami, San Juan and Port-au-Prince.

Inter-island carriers include *LIAT* and *Air Guadeloupe*. There is a small airport at St. François, near the Méridien and Hamak hotels, and another at Baillif on Basse-Terre.

By Sea. Pointe-à-Pitre is a port of call for all the major cruise-ship lines.

TAXES AND OTHER CHARGES. Most hotels and restaurants include a 10-15% service charge in their prices. If not it will be added to your final bill. A *tax du séjour* varies from hotel to hotel but the maximum is $1 U.S. per day, per person.

TELEPHONES AND EMERGENCY NUMBERS. To phone Guadeloupe directly from the U.S., dial 011 (01 for person-to-person) + 596 + local number. To call the U.S. from Guadeloupe, dial 19 + 1 + area code + local number. Local information is 12. General hospital, SOS ambulance service (24 hours a day): 82–89–33. Police 82–00–05.

HOTELS. Guadeloupe's hotels have a decidedly French accent and range from 10-room inns to a 270-room resort hotel. We consider $150 and up *Deluxe;* $80–$140 *Expensive;* $50–$75 *Moderate;* under $45 *Inexpensive.* Note: Although hotel personnel, especially front desk personnel, do speak some English, many of the maids, bell- and busboys do not. But no matter, since they are willing, pleasant and smiling.

Hamak Hotel. *Deluxe.* St.-François, Tel. 84–41–80. A secluded property in a lovely garden setting within walking distance of the airstrip, golf course, marina, and casino. 56 one-bedroom suites are located in 28 villas, the best of which are closest to the beach. Each has a private rear patio with outdoor shower, sitting room, spacious bath, and front terrace with hammock. Rooms are attractively decorated and now have telephones and even video/TVs on request. The beach is white sand, water sports are gratis for guests, there's tennis, and both the terrace restaurant and romantic bar are pleasant places to while away an evening.

Auberge de la Vieille Tour. *Expensive.* Gosier. Tel. 84–12–04. Under the management of Frantel, this popular hotel is built around an 18th-century sugarmill. The 82 rooms have been completely refurbished and offer telephone, radio/TV, and pleasant sea views. The 15-acre estate includes gardens, tennis courts, lively *Rum Keg* bar, excellent restaurant in the main building, the *Ajoupa Club,* a thatched-roof outdoor bar and restaurant for lunch and dinnertime barbecues, a large pool, and small white-sand beach.

Méridien. *Expensive.* St.-François. Tel. 84–41–00. A 270-room resort complex that covers 150 acres fronting on a long stretch of white sand. Excellent facilities include formal and informal dining rooms, a new beach bar, large freshwater pool, all water sports, 5 tennis courts lighted for night play, golf across the road, an excellent entertainment program, and a *very* French discothéque. The shopping arcade is a good place to browse *and* buy; rum punch will be served as you check in and the staff is proficient in English.

Village Viva. *Expensive.* Bas-du-Fort. Tel. 83–04–68/06–66. Spectacular new leisure complex that offers 32 spacious rooms in 8 pretty Creole-style houses set in a tropical garden around an enormous swimming pool. Seventh heaven for sports and fitness buffs, with ten artifical grass tennis courts, 2 squash courts, 6 lane bowling alley, exercise programs, and a complete gym. Perfect for families too, with a supervised mini-club to occupy youngsters from 4 to 10 with pottery, painting, and language lessons. Two good restaurants, entertainment, and special rates and services for businessmen complete the well-rounded picture.

PLM Arawak. *Moderate to Expensive.* Gosier. Tel. 84–12–74. On the beach in the resort area outside of Gosier village. There are 150 rooms (some of which could definitely use a thorough sprucing-up) and 8 suites built in 2 wings around the freshwater pool. All have patios or terraces except those in the newer garden wing. The bar is pleasant at sunset when a pianist plays; the new *West Indies Club,* an intimate lounge with soft music, stays open late; and the casino is right on the property. Tennis and water sports available.

Club Méditerranée Caravelle. *Moderate.* Ste.-Anne. Tel. 88–21–00. Located on a spectacular stretch of beach, the 275 rooms are divided among the main building, one three-story and one six-story wing. All are twin-bedded, air conditioned, and have private bath; some have balconies. Those in the main building have elaborate baths. It's typical Club Med style—never a dull moment unless you want one—with six floodlit tennis courts, a pool, sailing, windsurfing, snorkeling, Atari computer workshop, calisthenics, and excellent excursions. This is one of the nicest Club Meds for Americans.

Club Méditerrannée Fort Royal. *Moderate.* Deshaies. Tel. 28–41–10. Small and compact with just 150 rooms in a large main building and white cone-roofed cottages terraced up the hillside. Its "Mini Club" especially designed for children from 5 to 12 years old, makes it ideal for families. Counselors offer the youngsters a full program of activities from 9:00 A.M. until 6:00 P.M., so parents have plenty of time on their own. Spectacular scuba diving at nearby Pigeon Point, rated one of the ten best diving sites in the world by Jacques Cousteau.

La Creole Beach Hotel. *Moderate.* Gosier. Tel. 84–15–00. An affiliate of the Holiday Inn chain, this 156-room beachfront hotel was completely refurbished last year. Attractive, extra-large accommodations feature two double beds, direct telephone, radio and color cable TV. The 17-acre facility offers three restaurants, 2 beaches, large freshwater pool, tennis, scuba center, and all kinds of water sports. English-speaking personnel sport U.S.-flag lapel pins and there's a mini-club to occupy 4–12-year-olds. 100 new condominium bungalows should be completed for the '86 season. This well-managed resort caters to American needs and tastes while still keeping its tropical island charm.

Fleur d'Epée Novotel. *Moderate.* Bas du Fort. Tel. 83–49–49. 190 modern rooms with balconies or patios built in a Y-shaped complex that occupies most of a peninsula. Open and airy lobby with a garden, shops, two restaurants, bar, entertainment, two tennis courts, a fine beach and water sports facilities.

Frantel. *Moderate.* Bas du Fort. Tel. 83–64–44. Nestled among gardens overlooking the bay are 200 large, well-decorated rooms in two- and three-story buildings and bungalows. There's a large freshwater pool, tennis, all water sports (including a scuba center), two restaurants, terrace bar, and *Le Fou Fou*, a popular discothèque.

PLM Callinago Beach Hotel and Village. *Moderate.* Gosier. Tel. 84–12–93. This two story, 41-room hotel is part of a lovely complex on the beach. Rooms are compact but nicely decorated with dressing area, full bath, telephone, and balconies with sea view. French and Creole cuisine are served in the open-sided dining room or on the pool terrace. The Village consists of 96 studios and 22 duplex apartments stretched across the hilltop above the hotel's pool. They are spacious and very attractively decorated. Each has a full kitchen with counter bar set up for meals, as well as patio or balcony,

PLM Sun Village. *Moderate.* Bas du Fort Marina. Tel. 82–14–00 or 83–05–76. Pleasant apartment-style hotel on a hill overlooking the marina and the bay. The 100 studios and duplex suites all have kitchenettes, patios, or balconies. For light, air, and view those highest up facing the large, freshwater pool are best. Excellent French and Creole specialties served at *Le Boucanier;* there's a mini-market with good take-out dishes and a shuttle to the beach at sister property The Arawak. Fine for families and singles who want to do their own cooking once in a while. A car will be useful here in the evening.

Relais du Moulin. *Moderate.* Chateaubrun. Tel. 88–23–96. A country setting between Ste.-Anne and St. François, with 20 bungalows in tropical gardens built around an old sugar mill. There's a lovely pool and an open-sided dining room. A small beach has been added as well as free water sports equipment, and horses may be hired for beach rides on excursions through the hills. Recommended for those who want to be out of the resort scene, yet still close enough to stop by.

La Toubana. *Moderate.* Ste.-Anne. Tel. 88–25–78. Set up on a hill just outside the village of Ste.-Anne in a pretty residential area. 25 bungalows with kitchenettes and terraces, mostly overlooking the sea and spectacular white-sand beach of Club Med La Caravelle. There's a mini-pool, tennis court lighted for night play, French-Creole restaurant whose walls are aquariums, and a breezy bar. Fishing and other excursions may be arranged; video cassettes may also be rented. Casual and relaxed; out of the mainstream but close to everything.

Trois Mats. *Moderate.* St.-François. Tel. 84–41–80. Situated right in the heart of the marina, this apartment hotel offers 24 studios with kitchenettes on the terrace or patio and 12 duplexes with the same layout but an additional bedroom upstairs. Excellent for families. Under the same ownership as The Hamak, so guests have use of their water-sports facilities, tennis court, and beach.

Auberge de la Distillerie. *Inexpensive.* Petit-Bourg. Tel. 94–25–91. A charming 8-room country hideaway just 8 miles outside of Pointe-a-Pitre. The colonial-style main house has a good terrace restaurant and grill room and there's often entertainment around the pleasant pool. Tennis and riding nearby as well as Basse-Terre's fascinating Natural Park.

Auberge du Grand Large. *Inexpensive.* Ste.-Anne. Tel. 88–20–06. Up a side street and right on beautiful Ste.-Anne beach, this casual little inn has ten rooms. Five bungalows are either on the beach or set back in lovely gardens. Mme. Georges Damico is your cordial hostell along with her daughter Micheline, who speaks excellent English. Tranquil, friendly, family-style hotel.

Bougainvillea. *Inexpensive.* 9 rue Frébault, Pointe-à-Pitre. Tel. 82–07–56. In the heart of town, this 36-room hotel caters primarily to businessmen and visitors who need to be in the city. All rooms are air conditioned and have balconies, but not all have full bath. Good rooftop restaurant.

Cap Sud Caraïbe. *Inexpensive.* Chemin de la Plage, Petit Havre. Tel. 88–96–02. This new little "Relais Hotel" is one of the best in the inexpensive category. Attractive setting on a country road between Gosiert and Ste.-Anne, and just a five-minute walk from a quiet beach. Each of the 12 double-bedded rooms is unique. All are air conditioned, nicely decorated, have balconies, and enormous baths. Five face the green fields; seven overlook the sea. Sam Sitbon is the genial host of this friendly, easygoing place; English is limited but a grand effort is made to make everyone feel at home. Guests may use the big kitchen and there's a small bar, TV, and game room. A pool was planned.

Cou Cou des Bois. *Inexpensive.* Montebello, Petit-Bourg. Tel. 95–42–25. Rustic spot in the countryside with 10 simple but spotless rooms overlooking verdant hills. Peaceful setting fine for families on a budget and nature lovers who will enjoy hiking and jogging here. The beach is 10 minutes by car. Owner Léa Béracou, is an absolute Creole charmer as well as a superb cook.

Ecotel. *Inexpensive.* Gosier. Tel. 84–15–66. Part of a hotel school whose staff learns while you vacation. 44 air-conditioned rooms are set in a garden; there's a small bar, swimming pool, and snack bar; free bus to beach. Highlight here is an excellent restaurant where well-known French chefs are invited to prepare gastronomic dinners twice a month, in season.

Les Flamboyants. *Inexpensive.* Gosier. Tel. 84–14–11. An offbeat, friendly, 12-room hotel built around a pretty colonial-style house above the sea. Owners have some interesting plans for '86—24 new apartments, renovation of existing rooms, a pool; but check well in advance, as this bargain is usually booked solid in season.

Relais de la Grande Soufrière. *Inexpensive.* St.-Claude. Tel. 81–41–27. (Closed for renovation at press time so telephone first.) Guadeloupe's original hotel school, with 20 air-conditioned, unusually decorated rooms. Cool mountain setting on the road up to La Soufrière volcano; with students trying hard to please.

Rotabas. *Inexpensive.* Ste.-Anne. Tel. 88–25–60. Another new little gem on a small beach right next door to Club Med. 16 more comfortable rooms were added this year for a total of 44, in bungalows of two each that are named after various shellfish. The gardens are nicely landscaped, there's a pleasant beachside snack bar, good water-sports center and windsurfing school, small boutique, rustic bar, and excellent restaurant serving unusual Creole seafood. Mme. Amélie Kacy and her staff couldn't be more cordial or caring.

HOME AND APARTMENT RENTALS. There are several properties that rent to visitors when owners are absent; we especially recommend the following three:

Le Madrepore. Tel. 83–51–46. 30 studio apartments grouped around a small pool in ten buildings. Located just across the street from the Frantel in Bas-du-Fort, this time-sharing property is well maintained, has a snack bar and a nice view down on the lagoon and marina.

Les Marines de St. Francois. Tel. 84–45–15. 260 studios, apartments, and duplexes of varying size set on ten acres with three swimming pools, two tennis courts, restaurant, and shops. The beach is a five-minute walk, as is a large shopping center, supermarket, golf, the Hamak and Meridien hotels. An excellent facility, convenient to everything and well managed.

Residences Karukera. Tel. 84–44–03. 127 bungalows that include studio's and one- and two-bedroom accommodations. Each has been set up by its owners with furnishings, equipment, etc., so accommodations differ. All are very nicely decorated, have large fully equipped kitchens with big fridge, full stove, and oven; outdoor showers; and gardens or patios. Maids may be hired; there's a private beach down the hill and a good-size swimming pool, tennis, restaurant and snack bar, even a couple of shops. Located on the Pointe des Châteaux road, a five-minute drive from all the activities of St.-François.

HOW TO GET AROUND. Taxis are readily available at the airport, the major hotels and in Pointe-à-Pitre. Fares are government regulated, and are reasonable enough in daytime, but will be 40% higher from 9:00 P.M.–7:00 A.M. Radio taxis may be ordered by calling 92–15–09 or 83–64–27 or 83–09–55. The bus transportation is modern, efficient, and inexpensive. Signs are marked *arret-bus,* but you can flag the driver from anywhere along the road. Buses run 6:00 A.M.–6:00 P.M. Car rentals are available at Raizet Airport, Basse-Terre, Pointe-à-Pitre, and through hotels. They run 140–270 F per day with unlimited mileage. A 14% TVA tax will be added. *Avis, Budget, Hertz* and *National* (Europcar) are all here, along with local firms. Camping cars are available through *Caraïbes Loisirs,* tel. 84–16–41 and *DLC,* tel. 20–55–65. Fully equipped Toyotas sleeping from two to four rent for 2295 F a week for two persons including transfers to and from the airport, unlimited mileage, taxes, and insurance Dec. 1–May 15 and July 1–Oct. 1; 1995 F the rest of the year. A 2000 F deposit will be required.

Bicycles may be rented through *Loca Moto,* tel. 83–21–18; in the St. François Marina; motorbikes from *Erick,* 9 rue de la Republique, Pointe-à-Pitre, tel. 82–05–68; *Le Flamboyant,* Place du March, St.-François, tel. 84–45–51; and *Cyclo Tours,* blvd. du General de Gaulle, Gosier, tel. 84–11–34.

Air Guadeloupe's small planes serve all these islands with frequent flights from Le Raizet Airport.

Désirade: Ferrys leave the St.-François Marina twice daily. Fares are 100 F for adults; 50 F for children; 20 F for infants under two years of age, round trip. The crossing takes 45 minutes. Tel. 84–45–48 or 83–32–67 for schedule changes.

Les Saintes. A ferry departs twice a day from Trois Rivières Mon.-Sat. at 8:30 A.M. and 4:00 P.M.; 8:30 A.M. on Sun. From the capital of Basse-Terre, departures are at 12:30 P.M. Mon., Wed., Thur., and Sat. Both trips take 45 minutes. Tickets 50 F round trip.

Marie Galante. A daily ferry leaves from La Darse near the Tourist Office in Pointe-à-Pitre. This crossing takes two hours and costs 120 F round trip. Schedules are listed in the newspaper *France Antilles,* or call 83–12–45.

Ferry crossings to the offshore islands are apt to be rough and fellow passengers will often include chickens and perhaps a goat or two.

 TOURIST INFORMATION SERVICES. For on-island information, visit *L'Office du Tourisme,* 5 square de la Banque, 97181 Pointe-à-Pitre, tel. 82–09–30. Hours 8:00 A.M.–4:00 P.M. daily, except Wed. and Sat., 8:00 A.M. –noon. Closed Sun. For information closer to home, see the "Tourist Information Services" section of the *Facts at Your Fingertips* chapter.

 SPECIAL EVENTS. The highlights of Guadeloupe's year is its pre-Lenten Carnival, a colorful frenzy of celebrations that last for weeks. Masked revelers and costumed dancers parade in the streets, there are parties and dancing all over the island, all of it coming to a close on Ash Wednesday with a torch-light parade and the burning of "King Carnival."

Another special time is early August when the Fête des Cuisinières, or Cooks' Festival, heralds another parade and celebration. On the Saturday nearest to Aug. 11, in honor of St. Laurent, the patron saint of cooks, Guadeloupe's women chefs parade to the cathedral in Pointe-à-Pitre. They dress in madras and foulard bedecked with traditional gold jewelry, and carry enormous baskets laden with island specialties and trimmed with kitchen utensils. Following a high mass, they all join together for a five-hour feast, complete with singing and dancing. Visitors are welcome but only a limited number of free tickets are available in advance from the Tourist Office.

 TOURS. Island tours may be organized with taxi drivers who have set rates for specific excurions. Samples of excursions and prices may be found in the brochure called *Guadeloupe Bonjour,* available in English at the Tourist Office or from your hotel. Guided bus tours are run by *Georges-Marie Gabrielle* (tel. 82–05–38) and *Petreluzzi Travel* (tel. 82–43–41), both long-established operators with modern buses and English-speaking guides.

 PARKS AND GARDENS. *Natural Park.* Guadeloupe has set aside 74,100 acres of tropical forest, about one-fifth of its entire terrain, as a Natural Park. The prime attraction is Mt. Soufrière, a 4,813-foot volcano, active and well monitored. Highlights include the spectacular three-tiered Carbet Falls near Capesterre, reached by a moderately difficult hike that starts at the end of Habituée Road; Grand Etang (Great Pond), surrounded by luxuriant vegetation; Cascade aux Ecrevisses, a waterfall and pond; picnic areas; well-marked hiking trails through primeval rain forests; and small exhibition buildings devoted to the volcano, coffee, the sea, the forest, and woodworking. There are no dangerous animals or poisonous snakes and the racoon is the park's official mascot. The Tourist Office in Pointe-à-Pitre has an excellent publication detailing fauna, flora, and attractions.

Park Archéologique des Roches Gravées. Near Trois Rivières. Heavily inscibed boulders show Carib drawings and writings. Interesting specimens of island plant life abound along the easy walking paths.

BEACHES. Guadeloupe is ringed by beautiful beaches —white sand along the south coast of Grand-Terre; golden or gray-black sand in the north and south of Basse-Terre. Among the best are: *Ste.-Anne, Raisins Clairs* in St.-François, *Pointe des Chateaux, Le Moule, Anse Bertrand,* and *Port Lousi* on Grande-Terre; the *Deshaies* area, *Clugny, Grande-Anse, Malendure, Vieux Habitants, Trois Rivières,* and *Gourbeyre* on Basse-Terre. There are three naturist (nudist) beaches which are open to all and conformity is encouraged— *Pointe Tarare* near Pointe des Châteaux; the *Ilet de Gosier,* an offshore island opposite the town of Gosier (but only Mon.-Fri.); and *Anse Crawen,* behind the Bois Joli Hotel on Terre de Haut in Les Saintes. Public beaches are usually free but have few or no facilities. Hotel beaches are open to nonguests but a fee will be charged for lounges and changing facilities. Topless sunbathing is prevalent at all hotel beaches; it is not encouraged at public beaches.

PARTICIPANT SPORTS. There is an 18-hole Robert Trent Jones **golf** course adjacent to the Hamak and Méridien hotels in St.-François. An English-speaking pro, clubhouse, pro shop, electric carts (150 F per day) and lessons (85 F per half hour) are available. Greens fees are 150 F per day; 850 F per week in high season; 500 F in low season.

There is a total of 39 **tennis** courts on the island, at least one at every major hotel. Games may also be arranged through the St.-François Tennis Club, tel. 84–40–01.

The underwater natural park surrounding Pigeon Island off the west coast of Basse-Terre has been called one of the world's ten best **diving** sites. Club Med Fort Royal has a fine diving school here for its guests and there are three other excellent operations on Guadeloupe based at Gosier resort hotels. These include the *Karukera Scuba Club* at the PLM Callinago, *G.A.M.A. Scuba School* at the Hotel Frantel, and *Aquafari* at La Creole Beach Hotel. Also *Nautilius Club,* Malendure Beach, tel. 86–70–34, and *Les Heures Saines,* Bas-du-Fort, tel. 87–77 –5. All offer similar arrangements at comparable rates—120 F–300 F for a one-tank dive, depending on operations and diving-site distance. Excursions are also offered to Les Saintes.

Snorkeling is good on the reef just off St.-François and off Ilet de Gosier across from the village of Gosier on Grande-Terre. Two glass-bottom boats, the *Aquarium* and *Nautilius,* make snorkeling trips every day 10:00 A.M.–4:00 P.M. from Basse-Terre's Malendure Beach to Pigeon Island. Price is 70 F for adults; 35 F for children.

Waterskiing, Sunfish sailing, and **pedal boats** are available at all resort hotels, as is snorkeling equipment.

Windsurfing is really the rage here, and Guadeloupe is frequently the location of international competitions. Lessons and rentals at all beachfront hotels.

Sailing is very popular,and both bareboat and crewed boats are available. The Bas du Fort Port de Plaisance Marina has 27 acres of facilities and 700 berths for pleasure craft up to 120 feet long. The *capitainerie* (harbormaster's office) is open Mon.-Fri. 8:00 A.M.–1:00 P.M. and 3:00 P.M.–5:00 P.M. Sat. 8:00 A.M. to 11:30 A.M. Tel. 82–54–85; a second marina is available at St.-François that can accommodate 140 boats. Tel. 84–47–28. Office hours here are 8:00 A.M.–noon; 2:00 P.M.–5:00 P.M. Mon.-Sat. on Basse-Terre is the Marina de Rivière-Sens with 160 berths, tel. 81–77–61. Hours: Mon.-Fri. 8:00 A.M.–12:30 P.M.; 2:00 P.M.–5:00 P.M.; Sat. 8:00 A.M.–noon. Reliable charter companies inlcude *Locaraïbes,* tel. 91–07–80 and *Soleil et Voile,* tel. 82–26–81, both located in Port de Plaisance Marina; *Basse Terre Yachting,* Rivière-Sens Marina, tel. 81–11–45, and *Guadeloupe Chartaire,* Carenage, Pointe-à-Pitre, tel. 82–34–47. Complete sailing courses from one day to two weeks are available from *Evasion Marine,* St.-François Marina, tel. 84–46–67.

Deep-sea fishing for bonito, dolphin, captainfish, barracuda, kingfish, and tuna may be arranged by contacting the *Thalassa,* tel. 82–74–94 in Bas du Fort or the *Flying Lobster* at the Meridien Hotel in St.-François, tel. 84–41–00. The *Fishing Club Antilles* in Bouillante on Basse-Terre runs overnight excursions, tel. 86–73–77.

The Parc Naturel in Basse-Terre offers excellent **hiking** with well-marked trails of varying difficulty and plenty of interesting sights. A helpful brochure outlining hikes is available from the Tourist Office in Pointe-à-Pitre; guided excursions may be arranged through the *O.G.M.C.* in Basse-Terre, tel. 81–45–79 or 85–20–04.

Horseback riding is offered at *Le Relais de Moulin* at Choâteaubrun between Ste.-Anne and St.-François, tel. 88–23–96 and *Le Criolo* at St.-Félix, tel. 84–04–86. Lessons, beach riding, and picnics are all a part of their programs and prices run approximately 300 F for a half-day ride.

The *Papyrus,* a **glass-bottomed catamaran,** does daytime trips to the Ilet de Gosier beach with entertainment and lunch aboard on moonlight sails with a barbecue dinner and dancing. Price for both 230 F. Call 82–87–16 for details.

SPECTATOR SPORTS. The season for **cockfighting** is Nov.–Apr. when frequent matches are scheduled around the island. **Horse racing** takes place periodically at Bellecourt, Baie-Mahault, and the St. Jacques Hippodrome at Anse Bertrand. Check the Tourist Office for exact schedules.

MUSIC, DANCE, AND STAGE. The Folklore Ballet of Guadeloupe performs occasionally at major hotels; again check the Tourist Office for details. The 1800-seat Centre des Arts et de la Culture in Pointe-à-Pitre stages frequent concerts of classical music, jazz, plays, and ballets with both local artists and performers from Europe and the U.S.

SHOPPING Pointe-à-Pitre has small stores along rues Frébault, Nozières, and Schoelcher, the main shopping streets, that offer an excellent selection of French perfumes, cosmetics, men's and women's clothing, crystal, porcelain, leather goods, local souvenirs, and fine wines and liquers. Keep in mind when purchasing luxury goods that many stores offer a 20% discount for payment in traveler's checks and, in some cases, with credit cards.

You'll save as much as 50% on perfumes purchased here—prices are even lower than those in Paris. *Champs Elysées* and *Phoenicia* at the foot of rue Frébault have the best selection of brands, as well as cosmetics, atomizers, ties, scarves, and other small accessories. Phoenicia also has a second, larger branch at 93 rue Nozières.

In the same area, *Seven Sins'* shelves are stocked with all kinds of brandies, liquors, liquors, and fine wines. *Vendôme* has an exclusive on Orlane, Stendhal, and Germaine Monteil cosmetics and also offers a small but always interesting collection of imported fashions.

On the other side of lower rue Frébault are *Rosebleu* and *A La Pensée,* large shops with a good assortment of crystal, porcelains, silver items, and other luxury gifts. Continue up the street to the Place de Marché (Market Square), a fascinating melange of colors, smells, and sounds. Fruit, vegetables, spices, and flowers are sold by madras-dressed, Creole-speaking market women who know how to drive a hard bargain.

Rue de Nozières could be called Fashion Avenue, with tiny boutiques lined up one after the other for five blocks. Each has its own very personal taste and style in clothing for both men and women. Paris is well represented, as is the Côte d'Azur, whose up-beat fashions always set trends. Don't expect much English to be spoken here, so it's a good idea to at least acquaint yourself with your European size equivalents and learn a few basic phrases like *trop petit* (too small), *trop grand* (too big), *une autre couleur* (another color), and, of course, *trop cher* (too expensive).

The French have always done delightful children's clothing and several shops here carry a nice variety. Try *Tom Pounce, Katia, Love, Kickers, Charly,* or *Natalys* on rue de Nozières or *Nanouche* on rue Lamartine.

Designer shoes will seem almost a bargain if you compare their prices in the States. For the best selections of these and other well-known names, head for *Valerie* or *Lady's* on rue André Boisneuf; *Citronnelle* on rue Henri IV; *Chloe, La Cothurne,* and *Ingrid* on rue Lamartine. For stylish sandals and other more reasonably priced models there's *Bata* and *100,000 Chaussures* on rue Frébault.

Antique lovers should not miss *En Temps Longtemps,* 28 rue Sadi Carnot, a pretty two-level store in an interesting old house that carries high-quality local and imported furniture, silver, crystal, and attractive objets d'art at quite reasonable prices. A visit to *Tim Tim* will be a real trip into Guadeloupe's past. Here you can poke through stacks of books, engravings, maps, jewelry, laces, and antique clothes as well as sone massive Creole furniture, all assembled by novelist André Schwartz-Bart and his wife Simone in their lovely colonial mansion at 15 rue Henri IV.

Rue Schoelcher is one of our favorite shopping streets with its balconied old houses and prettily painted, very chic boutiques such as *Falbala,* a tiny shop overflowing with lacy lingerie; *Tipopette* for toys; *l'Artisan Parfumeur,* with its exotic fruit- and flower-based scents; *Selection* for Baccarat, Lalique, and Porcelaine de Paris; *Hibiscus D'Or* for costume jewelry and unusual gifts; and *Floral Antilles* for the most exotic tropical blooms. Located here are also five of Guadeloupe's most fashionable ladies boutiques; *Paul et Virginie, Pok, Jazelle, La Pagerie,* and *Bleu Marine.* Prices are at least 20% less than what you can expect to pay in the U.S. for comparable clothing.

For souvenirs and locally made handicrafts—*doudou* dolls dressed in madras; straw goods; madras table linens, aprons, and cards with colorful collages; and baskets of spices, shells, and wooden carvings—there's *Au Caraïbe,* 4 rue Frèbault; *Eliane Sarkis; King Creole* and *Macabou* on rue Nozières. Records are available at *Debs* on rue Frèbault; *R. Celini* on rue de Nozières.

Hours in town are generally 8:00 or 8:30 A.M.–noon and 2:30 P.M.–6:00 P.M. Mon.-Friday and 8:00 AM.M–noon Sat. Pointe-à-Pitre gets very hot, so try to schedule your shopping early in the morning or after 3:00 P.M.

Bas du Fort has two large commercial areas which remain open until 7:00 P.M. and on Saturday afternoons. The focal point of the *Mammouth Shopping Center,* just off the main highway heading east, is the huge supermarket of the same name. This is a good place to pick up patés, cheese, heat-and-serve dishes, canned delicacies, kitchen gadgets, and some surprisingly attractive and very inexpensive beachwear. *La Boite à Malice* offers absurd and practical knickknacks; *LI-D* carries all the latest high records and photographic materials; and *Orchidée* has put together a tasteful collection of jewelry and gifts.

In the marina area is another shopping plaza with over 20 stores and a half a dozen restaurants. Located here are *Anémone,* which offers very special jewelry; *Dans Un Jardin* for flower-based fragrances, essential oils, soaps, and cosmetics; *A la Recherche du Passé,* with a small but interesting selection of old maps, postcards, and engravings; *Voile 2,000* which specializes in tennis and other sports equipment and clothes; a new *Seven Sins* liquor store; *Atelier des Artistes* for original artwork, jewelry, and gifts; and *Chabada, Sun and Sea, Safari,* and *Eglantine* for men's and women's resortwear.

If you continue along the lagoonside road through a new residential area you'll come to Place Creole and a lovely pink-and-white shop called *La Verandah.* The owner, Bernadette, is an interior decorator and her small gifts and items for the home are most attractively displayed and quite out of the ordinary. Also located here are *La Maison du Rhum,* where a good variety of Guadeloupe's finest rums may be tasted as well as purchased; and *La Maison de l'Artisinat,* a cooperative of 40 local artists who display and sell their work.

The village of Gosier's Main Street has a couple of interesting places and in St.-François there's a small flower-bedecked shopping center located in the marina. Of interest here are *Alamanda* for up-to-the-minute costume jewelry from Paris; *La Goëlane* with elegant resort wear for ladies and men; *Plein Soleil* for tropical-style decorative items for the home; *Le Bambou's* gifts and small souvenirs; *Olivier de St. Mande* with a small selection of handicrafts and plenty of reading matter; a shoe store called *Isabella; St. Gilles Coiffeur; La Boutique de Bee Shirt,* whose hand-screened T-shirts with local scenes are made in Paris; and *Tropi 'Cuir* for leather goods.

Just outside St.-François, at their popular restaurant *Les Oiseaux,* Claudette and Arthur Rollé are concocting some not-to-be missed herbal remedies, spice packets, and wonderful fruit punches, as well as other unusual local artistry all prettily packaged in colorful madras sacks.

Nearby is *The Gourmet Shop,* another good-sized, well-stocked supermarket. In the Les Marines de St. François apartment complex, several new shops have opened including *Blue Wave* and *l'Atelier de Ste.-Anne,* whose hand-painted clothing is especially attractive. For some of the most fashionable resort wear, don't miss *La Créoline* just outside of town on the Usine Ste.-Marthe road. Here talented Geneviève Beiger has her studio and takes orders for her much in demand hand-painted and-screened pareos, beach towels, chemises, and T-shirts. Her beautiful designs are colorful, elegant, and unusual, and are worn by the most fashionable visitors from Paris.

Finally, for last-minute purchases, a group of new shops has opened outside the airport terminal that sell records, gadgets, gifts, accessories, beauty products, T-shirts and other resort wear, shoes, Haitian art, Caribbean crafts, and cut flowers cleared for entry into the States and boxed for travel. The anthuriums, birds of paradise, and heliconia all make a nice long-lasting souvenirs.

RESTAURANTS. Guadeloupe may have the best restaurants in the Caribbean. There's a choice of over 100 dining places that offer classic French and nouvelle French, Creole, Italian, African, Indian, South American, and Vietnamese food. Some are elegant, with service on fine linens and china; others are on the front or back porch of the owner's home. The sea supplies wonderful raw material—lobster, conch, snapper, kingfish, turtle, shark, clams, and sea urchins (known here as *oursin*), as does the land—crab, goat, rabbit, game, unusual tropical fruit, vegetables, and subtle spices. To complement the cuisine are marvelous French wines, champagne, liqueurs, and excellent local rum. Start your meal with a "ti-punch," a tiny but potent mixture of rum, lime juice, and sugarcane syrup that puts a real edge on appetites. Dining is a long and leisurely affair here, and there's no better way to end your evening than relaxing over a strong, aromatic cup of locally grown coffee and a fine old rum or cognac.

The big hotels tend to rely on imported meats and other items, which are sometimes well prepared, sometimes not. The secret here is to get out and try the small local restaurants that are spread out all over the island; that's where you'll experience dining that you'll never forget.

In classifying our restaurant choices we call over $20 *Expensive;* $12–20 *Moderate;* under $10 *Inexpensive* for a three-course meal for one person.

Auberge Landaise. *Expensive.* 2 Chemins, Pliane, St.-Félix. Tel. 84–06–53. One of the island's best dining spots, with an unusual menu that features game—venison, hare, dove, wild boar—from December through spring. Owner-chef Yvette Chantegreil's specialties are mainly from the Landes area, which suggests foie gras, smoked trout, preserved (*confit*) duck and pork, truffles, and wild mushrooms. But she is just as adept at Creole crayfish or conch *tourte* and Basque-style fish soup. The decor is rustic, service on pretty porcelain, and the wine list outstanding. Just 50 diners can be accommodated, so reservations are a must on weekends. Closed Mon. AE, V.

Auberge de la Vieille Tour. *Expensive.* Gosier. Tel. 84–12–04. Chef Jean Le Bihan trained with such master chefs as Vergé and Rostang, but has developed his own forte in the integration of local tropical produce into classic recipes. Some of his more unusual dishes have included conch raviolis with lobster-flavored butter; red snapper supreme with creamy sea urchin sauce; foie-gras-stuffed quail with a cocoanut crust and roast lamb with juniper berries and old rum. The large, pleasant dining room is air-conditioned and has no view, but the menu is varied, wine list superb (though expensive), and service by staff of madras-garbed young ladies is smooth and unhurried. Dinner only. AE, D, MC, V.

Le Balata. *Expensive.* Route de Labrousse, opposite the Mammouth Commercial Center, Gosier. Tel. 82–85–29. Panoramic as well as gastronomic, with a view out over Fort Fleur d'Epée. Service is gracious; the presentation attractive; and the atmosphere relaxed both on the eight-table rounded terrace or in the rustic indoor dining room. Marie and Pierre Cecillon are well-established restaurateurs, and their new hilltop inn is definitely one of Guadeloupe's best dining spots. Pierre is from Lyon, so his menu could include classic fish mousse with lobster sauce; warm chicken-liver salad with croutons and lardons; grilled pigs' feet; a thrush paté or chicken fricassee with cream and wild mushrooms. Creole goat curry; shark steak with chèvre, and his very special way of preparing grilled crayfish are also highly recommended. A special businessmen's lunch is available at 90 F including wine. Open lunch and dinner. Closed Sun. evening, all day Mon. AE, D, V.

Le Bistrot. *Expensive.* Petit Havre (between Gosier and Ste.-Anne). Tel. 88–91–82. New owners Annie and Danny Rossard have kept the same menu that has long made this restaurant a favorite choice of both locals and visitors. Situated on a hill with a splendid view at both lunch and dinner. Start your meal with one of the 15 different fruit-based rum punches, then try Danny's special shark steak with fresh pasta, perfectly grilled fish, or *cassolette du pecheur*, a mini-bouillabaisse. Everything is good. Do be tempted by dessert—tarte Tatin, walnut pie à mode, and homemade rum raisin ice cream with hot chocolate sauce are all very special treats. Dinner reservations necessary. Closed Sun., Mon., and the months of Aug. and Sept. No credit cards.

La Canne à Sucre. *Expensive.* 17 rue Henri IV, Pointe-à-Pitre. Tel. 82–10–19 or 83–58–48. Don't miss Marie-Claude and Gérard Virginius' elegant little restaurant in the center of the city. Gerard's refined and unusual Creole cuisine is unequalled with such original recipes as chicken breast stuffed with conch; *lambi fin gourmet* (ground conch with eggplant, chives, and mushrooms, served in its own impressive shell); a finely textured loaf of seafood (tiny, tender octopus, sea snails, and conch); and passion fruit ice cream soufflé. But expect even more marvels from this popular chef, who recently spent some time at Paris' prestigious Taillevent, internationally acclaimed for creative cuisine. AE, V.

La Cannelle. *Expensive.* Village Viva, Bas-du-Fort. Tel. 83–06–66. New and very elegant, this small restaurant's tables are set with the finest linens, china, crystal, and silverware. The perfect spot for a romantic candlelit gourmet dinner that might feature fresh foie gras, an interesting puff pastry filled with snapper and land crab, and delightfully rich homemade pastries. AE, D, V.

La Louisiane. *Expensive.* Quartier Ste.-Marthe, just outside St.-François. Tel. 84–44–34. A dozen tables in a pretty old colonial house in the countryside. New owner-chef Daniel Hugon is from Cannes and his menu features classic offerings, as well as a Creole dish or two. One nice combination of the two cuisines is his thinly sliced duck breast (*auguillettes de canard*) prepared with dried currants and rum. Closed Sun. evening and Mon. lunch. V.

La Mandarine. *Expensive.* Blvd. de la Plage, Gosier Village. Tel. 84–30–28. Another new and very attractive restaurant where partners (Danielle in the dining room; Harry in the kitchen) work beautifully together to create fine dining in a pleasant atmosphere. Small and cozy, with four tables on a curtained porch, nine more inside. The house hallmark is a touch of orange used in this special kir (made with champagne, cassis, and Cointreau) and in dinner sauces, garnishes, and desserts. Ingredients are top quality, the menu well thought out, the service siogné. Open lunch Tues.–Fri.; dinner every day but Mon. AE, D.

La Plantation. *Expensive.* Marina Commercial Center, Bas du Fort. Tel. 82–39–63 or 83–17–81. A must for gourmets, where Bordeaux-born François Delage offers some of the best fare in Guadeloupe, perhaps even in the Caribbean. Specialties with a tropical touch are added each season but such delights as conch cocktail with grapefruit, scallops with passion fruit, smoked goose breast with roquefort, and duckling with cassis are just a few of the choices among two dozen or so fascinating dishes. The decor is appealing, service careful though not overbearing, and the wine list a small treasure. Open lunch and dinner. Closed Sun. AE, D, MC, V.

Le Baoulé. *Moderate to Expensive.* Blvd. Amédé Clara, on the water side of the lower road in the village of Gosier. Tel. 84–39–50. Albert Descoteaux, the St. Claude Hotel School-trained local chef, still holds forth in the kitchen; but ownership of this popular terraced restaurant is now in the capable hands of former French swimming champion Alain Sumeire and his partner Jacques Marois. Soft music plays in the background; the view out over the Ilet de Gosier is idyllic, and the menu is a good mixture of Creole and French. Coconut soup; "sunset salad" with avocado, rice, walnuts, and lobster; pasta with roquefort; filet of red snapper on a bed of bananas; as well as some delectable dessert creations are among the wide choices. The eight terrace tables are much in demand at both lunch and dinner, so reserve in advance. No credit cards.

Le Flibustier. *Moderate to Expensive.* La Colline, Fonds Thézan (between Ste.-Anne and St.-Félix). Tel. 88–23–36. Fish, lobster, and beef grilled over a wood fire are the specialties of this rustic hilltop farmhouse. A complete dinner that includes a petit punch, mixed salad, grilled lobster, coconut ice cream, and half a pitcher of wine is available at 140 F. Portions are copious and the ambience is fun and lively, as this is a favorite of Club Med staff members from the Caravelle next door. No credit cards.

Le Galion. *Moderate to Expensive.* Ecotel, Montauban Gosier. Tel. 84–15–66. Guadeloupe's second hotel school, where visiting chefs from metropolitan French teach the students to cook and waiters and waitresses learn the proper way to serve by practicing on guests. The menu changes when teachers and students do; but classic choices will always be a good bet here. *Soirées Gastronomiques* (gastronomic evenings) are scheduled twice a month from January through April, when big-name chefs from France are invited to Guadeloupe to prepare gourmet galas (average price 220 F per person) for a limited number of diners. Similar Antillais evenings were also planned for the coming winter season. Call for exact schedule. AE, D, MC, V.

Le Jardin des Gourmets. *Moderate to Expensive.* Montauban, Gosier. Tel. 84–00–55 or 84–34–40. Elisabeth, a former actress and Paco Rabanne mannequin in Paris, is your lovely owner/hostess. Lunch in her pretty, rather sophisticated little dining room stresses grills—fish, beef, lamb, even *pavé de cheval* (horsemeat), the latter a special Gallic preference. Dinner features unique treats such as turkey with pineapple and old rum; crab-stuffed chritophine; a goat- and chicken-liver terrine; shark *colombo* with green tomatoes. Desserts are always a delight as is high tea (which includes herbal and flower-flavored concoctions) served on the front garden terrace. AE, MC.

Les Oiseaux. *Moderate to Expensive.* Anse des Rochers, 3 km. outside St.-François. Tel. 84–48–64. A very special favorite of ours for its tranquil setting and the country-style cooking of congenial owners Caludette and Arthur Rollé. Fish and shellfish fanciers should try *cigale de mer* (sea cricket). This most unattractive, hard-to-find member of the shrimp family has a memorable taste that's somewhere between that of lobster, crayfish, and shrimp—hard to describe but definitely delicious. Sunday lunch, a long relaxed afternoon of fine dining, is extremely popular. You might, however, prefer a less busy day when the Rollés have more time to chat and their refreshing little house pool might just be yours alone. Closed Thurs. No credit cards.

Le Tap Tap. *Moderate to Expensive.* Relais du Moulin, Châteaubrun (between Ste.-Anne and St.-François). Tel. 88–23–96. This attractive 16-table restaurant is set among green pastures and vibrantly hued bougainvillea, alamanda, and hibiscus. Two brothers from Nice do the cooking and there's a 90F lunch menu that changes daily. In the evening and on Sunday, choose from a big menu that features such unusual treats as kingfish marinated in lime with eggplant caviar, veal with crayfish, frog's legs ragout, scallop timbales with ginger and mint, and some scrumptious tropical desserts. AE, D, MC, V.

La Toubana. *Moderate to Expensive.* Ste.-Anne. Tel. 88–25–78/57. Perched on a hilltop in a quiet residential area just outside the village, this restaurant is part of a new bungalow hotel. Brother-and-sister team, Christine and Patrick Vial Collet, has decorated the dining room with giant aquariums along two walls. The effect is a constantly moving and changing scene that includes every imaginable kind of marine life. The small menu offers typical Creole and French dishes, surroundings are pleasant and the poolside terrace a fine place for a sunset drink. D, V.

Auberge de la Distillerie. *Moderate.* Petit-Bourg. Tel. 94–25–91/27–68. Lovely little country hideaway with a poolside terrace and indoor grill room with a rustic bar where rum tasting may be enjoyed. Cuisine is Creole with some especially nice sea urchin dishes, unusual salads, rabbit local style, citronella chicken, guinea hen with bananas, and Caribbean choucroute with pawpaw among the menu choices. AE, V.

Chez Bach Lien. *Moderate.* Blvd. Amédé Clara, Gosier Village. Tel. 84–10–91. Small and elegant. Before-dinner drinks are served in a sitting room furnished with antiques. You will wait, even with reservations, as this Vietnamese restaurant is very popular. Bach Lien herself is now tending her new place in St. Martin, but her kitchen is in the capable hands of a trusted friend who continues her high standards. We never tire of the *nems,* ginger chicken, and carmelized pork but there are three dozen other dishes to choose from. Dinner only. Closed Wed. V only.

Le Bananier. *Moderate.* Gosier. Tel. 84–34–85. Two former employees of the Vieille Tour, Cornelia, the capable maitre d' and Albert, the friendly bartender, recently struck out on their own to create this attractive new spot. Nouvelle cuisine Creole is highlighted, and though we have not yet tried this place, reports received were laudatory. D.

Barbazar. *Moderate.* Marina Bas-du-Fort. Tel. 91–36–19. Now in a far more attractive location, Mme. Barfleur offers her fine Creole dishes in a sophisticated setting. Her different ragouts, curried shark, conch gratin, *burgau* (sea snails), and wonderfully spicy *boudin* and tiny clams are praised by local gourmets and visitors who are accustomed to well-seasoned food. Little English is spoken here, but the ambiance is warm and service always smiling. No credit cards.

Le Boucanier. *Moderate.* PLM Sun Village Hotel, Bas du Fort Marina. Tel. 83–05–76. Not for the tourist looking for local food; but for those who appreciate refined French fare such as stuffed brown trout; veal chops with sherry, wild cepe mushrooms, tomato, and shallots; unusually good smoked kingfish and bonito; lobster coquille and the house brochette, which features kidney; beef *merguez,* lamb, and mushrooms. Félix Teisseire is a transplanted Niçois who has been in the Caribbean 16 years and his food is consistent and dependable; his recipes are varied as they are good. AE, D, MC, V.

Le Carilou. *Moderate.* Village Viva, Bas-du-Fort. Tel. 83–06–66. The very attractive outdoor restaurant of this new complete leisure center. The menu is extensive, ice cream homemade, and the luncheon buffets some of the island's most elaborate. Tropical pizzas, grills, and diverse salads are just a small part of the menu at lunch and dinner. AE, D, V.

L'Enfer Vert. *Moderate.* 2nd floor Galeries Nozières, rue de Nozières, Pointe-à-Pitre. Tel. 91–53–82. A pleasant green-and-white oasis in the center of the city where light, modern Creole food is prepared by a young Guadeloupean graduate of the Ecotel Hotel School. This is a combination restaurant, bar, and lounge where guests get up and play the piano on weeknights; jazz, Brazilian, and other combos take over on Friday and Saturday evenings. There are chess tables, Scrabble boards (in French, of course), and billiards; the crowd is young and international. Closed Sat. lunch and all day Sun. No credit cards.

La Grande Pizzeria. *Moderate.* Bas-du-Fort. Tel. 82–52–64. Rosell Aurières and her chef, Enrico, have pooled their talents to create another popular seaside dining spot. Pizza, pasta, good salads, plus Milanese, Bolognese, and Italian seafood specialties are all on the menu of this animated, open-late terrace. Expansion next door to Rosell's former Albatros restaurant was being considered as a bar with good music for listening or dancing. No credit cards.

Marlen's Restaurant. *Moderate.* 23 rue Gosset. Pointe-à-Pitre. Tel. 83–20–43. In this pretty private home on a side street you'll find the island's most unique and exotic menu. Marlen has spent over 20 years in Africa and is a collector of interesting *objets d'art* as well as recipes. Her nephew Pierre learned Malagasy cooking while attending hotel school in Paris. Together they turn out some very unusual dishes—some fiery, some sweet and mild, all delectable. Open lunch and dinner. V.

La Mouette. *Moderate.* Pointe des Chateaux. Tel. 84–40–57. By far the best of a string of small restaurants along this road. Jacques Nainan has 16 tables on his large terrace and eight more out in the front yard under conical roofed pavilions, ideal for lunching in your bathing suit. Of special interest here is *poisson coffré,* local trunkfish that is prepared stuffed or roasted, as well as all the classic Creole *colombos, ragouts,* and *blaffs.* The hot peppers are served on the side, so it's up to each diner to spice or not to spice. A small combo was planned for Saturday-night dancing and eventually a swimming pool was to be constructed. Closed Sun. No credit cards.

Relais de la Grand Soufrière. *Moderate.* St. Claude, Basse-Terre. Tel. 81–41–27. This hotel-school restaurant has been closed for renovation for some time, so be sure to call first. The terrace and colonial-style dining room were both popular luncheon places with local businessmen, government officials, and visitors touring La Soufrière volcano and the other attractions of Guadeloupe's fascinating Natural Park. No credit cards.

Rosini. *Moderate.* Bas du Fort, across from Frantel. Tel. 83–07–81. Fine, 100% Italian operation. Luciano Rosini and his sister-in-law cook; his wife is responsible for the decor; their six children serve. The menu, in three languages, is extensive, and everything from the fresh pasta to desserts is homemade. This is a lively, friendly place. A new minibus service, available by reservation will pick up two or more guests at their hotel. AE, D, V.

Le Zagaya. *Moderate.* rue de la République, St.-François. Tel. 84–40–94. A small six-table terrace on the beach where lobster, fish, and meat are prepared on the outdoor grill. Try one of the Creole starters and finish up with one of Jean-Marie's fantasy desserts. Very informal and relaxed with classical background music. Open for lunch and dinner. Closed Tues. No credit cards.

Le Cercle. *Moderate to Inexpensive.* Lieu dit "Castel" Lamentin, Basse-Terre. Tel. 25–68–66. Reputedly one of the best for giant crayfish and a good variety of seafood and shellfish. Dinner only; a discothèque operates on Friday and Saturday nights. French is a must here. No credit cards.

Le Chaubette *Moderate to Inexpensive.* Route de la Riviera, Gosier. Tel. 84–14–29. Highly respected chef Gitane Chavalin has a faithful local clientele at both lunch and dinner so reserve in advance. Serves some of the island's best Creole cuisine. No credit cards.

Chez Clara *Moderate to Inexpensive.* Ste.-Rose, Basse-Terre. Tel. 28–72–99. A pretty and popular terraced restaurant where Clara Leseur and her mother turn out some fine family recipes—curried pan-fried skate (*raie*) with green papaya; tiny clams (*palourdes*) in a spicy broth; conch stew, and other Creole delights. Clara is a delight herself, a pretty, chic Guadeloupéanne who left a jazz-dancing career in Paris to run her family's restaurant by the sea. She has abundant charm that pleases her customers as well as the local fisherman who save her their most special catches. Reservations advised. MC.

Chez Rosette. *Moerate to Inexpensive.* Route de Gosier, Gosier Village. Tel. 84–11–32. Suzette Limol has taken over this old established restaurant to continue in her mother's footsteps providing authentic Creole cooking from *boudin* to roast suckling pig. No credit cards.

Chez Violette-La Creole. *Moderate to Inexpensive.* On the eastern outskirts of Gosier Village. Tel. 84–10–34. Multihonored, 6-foot-tall Violetta Chaville the head of Guadeloupe's cuisinières' (lady chefs') association, presides in her well-respected restaurant. Very popular with American visitors for its varied selection of typical Creole dishes; friendly atmosphere, and traditional service by waitresses in madras and foulard. Open lunch and dinner. No credit cards.

Le Karacoli. *Moderate to Inexpensive.* North of Deshaies, Basse-Terre. Tel. 28–41–17. Well-established Lucienne Salcède speaks English and delights visitors to her beachside terrace with what we found to be some of the island's best *accras* as well as turtle *ragout,* coquilles Karacoli, and a good selection of other well-spiced Creole specialties. We like the tables spread out on the sand, with the sea just a few steps away for a convenient dip. There are daily 60-F and 90-F menus at both lunch and dinner. No credit cards.

Le Matété. *Moderate to Inexpensive.* Rotabas Hotel, Ste.-Anne. Tel. 88–25–60. A pretty thatched-roof pavilion in a garden seiting with 14 tables, an attractive brick bar, and some hard-to-find local dishes such as *boudin en papillotte; sea snail (burgot) blaff;* cream of pumpkin soup; crayfish soup; stuffed sea urchin (*oursin*); fricasseed tiny octopus; and grilled crayfish. Open dinner daily and Sunday all day. AE, D, MC, V.

La Nouvelle Table Creole. *Moderate to Inexpensive.* Village Caraibe Hotel, St.-Félix. Tel. 84–04–86. The owner, Jeanne Carmelite, is another of Guadeloupe's best Creole cooks. This, her second restaurant, is a spacious 2-level affair that is often lively at night with local bands entertaining large local dinner parties. Food is fine and ambiance *tres gai*, with hotel guests joining in the festivities. No credit cards.

Ravine Chaude. *Moderate to Inexpensive.* Baie Mahault, Lamentin, Basse-Terre. Tel. 25–60–53. A hot-spring station with an excellent restaurant especially known for its crayfish specialties and other good typical island dishes. Extremely popular weekends when Guadeloupéans gather to enjoy Mme. Mormont's fine fare and partake of the healthy mineral waters. No credit cards.

Au Vieux Port. *Moderate to Inexpensive.* St.-François. 84–46–60. In the village by the fishermen's landing spot, this rustic 12-table seaside terrace offers a simple menu of grilled steak and fish served with excellent local vegetable purees; green salad, and crisp *pommes frites* (French fries). The young owners speak good English and the crowd is usually lively and friendly. Open late at lunch and dinner. No credit cards.

L'Accra. *Inexpensive.* Motel Ste.-Anne, Durivage Ste.-Anne. Tel. 88–22–40. Juditha Dardet is the charming owner of this rustic little restaurant. Typical Creole specialties à la carte and a daily 90F menu with very generous servings are both offered. V.

L'Amour en Fleurs. *Inexpensive* Ste.-Anne. Tel. 88–23–72. Don't be deceived by the basic, unpretentious looks of this little roadhouse across from the St.-Anne cemetery. Jovial Mme. Trésor Amanthe has won a variety of culinary awards and her typical Creole specialties are carefully prepared, well spiced, and authentic. You'll taste the real thing here at rock-bottom prices. Lunch and dinner. No credit cards.

Le Barbaroc. *Inexpensive.* Petit Canal. Tel. 22–62–71. Félicité Doloir was named one of 1983's outstanding cooks by H.J. Heinz and Company. Her rustic 12-table restaurant features old, almost-forgotten Creole recipes and she also conducts Sunday tours that combine culinary and historic highlights of her area. Try *moabie,* a healthy nonalcoholic drink made from tree bark; her incredible "punch de maison," a secret mixture of local fruits and rum; crab paté; mixed seafood coquille; breadfruit or other local vegetable soufflés; or any one of three dozen delicious dishes on her menu. Reservations are a must on weekends, when people come from all over the island to feast. No credit cards.

Chez Dollin-Le Crépuscule. *Inexpensive.* On the road to Carbet Falls, Habituée village, Basse-Terre. Tel. 86–34–56. A good lunch place when visiting the spectacular falls. Stop by on your way up to order crayfish, goat curry, Creole chicken, or maybe one of the copious four-course menus, as you're sure to build up quite a thirst and appetite on your hike. No credit cards.

Chez Honoré-Aux Fruits de Mer. *Inexpensive.* 5 Place du Marché, St.-François. Tel. 84–40–61. A good value 125F menu that includes *crab farci, accras,* fish coquille, *boudin,* grilled lobster, and dessert. Honoré is called the lobster king—he catches his own and will have the prized crustacean when no one else does. Honoré now has a second spot called *La Langouste* at Anse à la Gourde on the Pointe des Châteaux road. Same menu, same prices may now be enjoyed at lunch by the sea. No credit cards.

Chez Jacqueline-Aux Arcades. *Inexpensive.* St.-Félix. Tel. 84–17–36. One of the prettiest of the "Chez" restaurants with an attractive bar. Charcoal-grilled chicken with spicy Creole sauce; cod, vegetable, and lobster accras and stuffed christophine are a few of the specialties. Everything is cooked to order so choose this restaurant when you're not in a rush. No credit cards.

Chez Lydie. *Inexpensive.* St.-Félix. Tel. 84–13–63. Best for dinner or a late lunch, as this simple, very uncommercial restaurant gets crowded and hot at the height of the day. Madras is everywhere—on the walls, tables, and waitresses, who, unless they are from Dominica, won't speak or comprehend much, if any, English. But the satisfying full-course meal you'll have here could include a *ragout de cheval;* tender turtle steak; seafood brochette, or tasty country chicken spiced to perfection if you like it hot. No credit cards.

Folie Plage. *Inexpensive.* Anse Laborde, north of Anse Bertrand. Tel. 22–11–17. Prudence Marcelin is a jolly chef who's thought of everything in her popular restaurant—a shallow pool for the children; a boutique with clothing, souvenirs, and postcards with her own picture; even a discothèque on weekends. This is another reliably good Creole spot where local residents come for Sunday outings. Her *boudin* we found to be one of the island's best. No credit cards.

Le Houelmont. *Inexpensive.* 34 rue de la République, Basse Terre city. Upstairs restaurant facing the Conseil Cénéral in town. Two rustic dining rooms, one with a view, offer a wide selection of good Creole dishes plus couscous and paella. Open lunch and dinner except Sundays. AE, V.

Les Mouillages-Mme. Racine. *Inexpensive.* Deshaies. Tel. 28–41–12. Going on its 18th year, this little spot hidden behind the general store on the sea is well-known to yachtsmen who radio in advance for Mme. Racine's lobster. There's an enormous 5-course menu, popular at both lunch and dinner, so do reserve. No credit cards. Lobster should be ordered in advance and may be enjoyed as part of an enormous five-course menu. Popular at both lunch and dinner, so reserve. No credit cards.

La Pecherie. *Inexpensive.* rue de la République, St.-François. Tel. 84–48–41/ 94. Rustic eight-table porch hung out over the sea where seafood reigns. Dinner is served late; lunch on weekends only. No credit cards.

Pizzeria Napoli. *Inexpensive.* Gosier. Tel: 84–30–53. For fresh pasta, 10 different pizzas, salads and Italian-style meat and fish. Be prepared to wait in this popular spot. Lively, friendly and open until 1:00 A.M. No credit cards.

Poisson d'Or. *Inexpensive.* rue Sadi Carnot, Port Louis. Tel. 84–90–22. Also known as chez Nonore, this harborside restaurant offers a nice view over to Basse-Terre and fine fresh fish. An excellent lunch stop when visiting the pleasant, uncrowded Port Louis beach. No credit cards.

La Reserve-Chez Jeanne. *Inexpensive.* St.-Félix. Tel. 84–11–27. Another simple, unpretentious restaurant for dependable and dependably good home cooking Creole style by Jeanne Carmelite, who does a terrific goat curry as well as other traditional specialties. No credit cards.

 NIGHT LIFE AND BARS. Guadeloupeans love to dance and their joie de vivre is infectious, so you'll probably soon find yourself beginning the beguine with the best of them.

What's considered to be the most "in" disco changes overnight, but those that have survived several seasons are the Frantel's *Fou Fou; Le Caraïbe* in the Hotel Salako; *Newland* in Gosier; *La Chaine* in St.-Fèlix; *Acapulco* and *Neptune* in St.-François. The newest, and by now probably *the* place, is Gerard Dantevieux' multifaceted dining complex and elegant disco, *Mandingo,* on the beach in Gosier. Action starts late, around 11:00 P.M. on weekends, and ends early—in the morning, that is. Weekdays are somewhat more restrained but you'll find plenty of company even at 2:00 A.M.

For quieter moments there's always the *Rum Keg Bar* in the Hotel Vieille Tour in Gosier and the *West Indies Bar* in the PLM Arawak. The latter is a softly lit lounge with music to match. A friendly, English-speaking bartender named James makes Americans feel right at home. *Le Jardin Bréselien* in the Bas du Fort Marina has live Brazilian music and features some lavish ice-cream concoctions and tall drinks that make your head spin as much by their variety of ingredients as the punch they pack. Because of its proximity to a residential area the music here shuts down somewhere around 11:00 P.M.

 CASINOS. Guadeloupe has two, the original in the Marina at St.-François and a second on the grounds of the PLM Arawak in the Gosier hotel area. They're both European style, with no slot machines but plenty of baccarat, blackjack, roulette, and craps tables where the stakes can get surprisingly high. Hours are 9:00 P.M.–3:00 A.M. every evening except Sunday; entrance fee 60 F. A proof of identity with photo is required; tie and jacket is not, but proper dress code (no shorts, etc.) must be adhered to.

SECURITY. Pointe-à-Pitre streets tend to be rather deserted in the downtown area in the evening, so there is no reason to wander around alone here after dark. Guadeloupeans don't do it, why should you? The hotel areas in Gosier, Bas du Fort, and St.-François are quite well frequented but stay on well-lighted pathways. Beware of passing motorcyclists riding double, who have been known to snatch purses and speed off into the night. Valuables should be kept in your hotel's safety-deposit box and not left around on the beach, in unlocked cars, or other public places.

POSTAGE. Postcards to the U.S. require 60 F; letters up to 20 grams take 3.60 F. For Canada, postcards 2 F; letters 2.70 F.

ELECTRIC CURRENT. Voltage is 220 A.C., 50 cycles. American appliances will need French plugs, converters, or transformers. The best is to travel with your own or use dual-voltage equipment.

HAITI

by
TONY TEDESCHI

Most travelers to Haiti are surprised by what they find, for Haiti is a place like no other in the Western Hemisphere. Haiti is a country where the strange rituals of voodoo have been combined with the sedate culture of France. It is a country where men like Toussaint l'Ouverture, Henri Christophe, Jean Jacques Dessalines, and Alexandre Pétion were fighting to free their land from the French less than twenty years after the Americans to the north had freed themselves from the British. It is a country of teeming cities and quiet beaches, lively night life and colorful art, towering monuments and exotic cuisine. But above all, Haiti is a country of warm and friendly people whose welcome to visitors is written all over their smiling faces.

Past and Present

Haiti occupies the western third of the island Columbus called La Isla Española when he landed there in 1492. (Today it shares the island, now called Hispaniola, with the Dominican Republic to the east.) The natives Columbus found living there were called Arawaks or Tainos, "the good people," and they called their land "Hay-ti" (the mountainous country). The Arawaks made the mistake of greeting the Spaniards with gifts of gold, which set off the frenzy for the glittering metal that would cost countless lives among the natives of the New World. Within

Haiti, the population of Arawaks was reduced from a million to just a few hundred in less than fifty years, and that led to the importation of African slaves, which changed the history of Haiti forever. From Africa they came in the holds of slave ships, the *Quimas*, the *Bambaras*, the *Mandinques*, the *Ibos*, and with them came the beat of voodoo drums.

The French moved into Haiti in the late seventeenth century and set up a plantation society with key cities at Cap-Haitien on the Atlantic coast, Port-au-Prince and Gonaïves on the Gulf of Gonâve, Jacmel on the Caribbean. In 1791, however, the black slaves, inflamed by the libertarian ideals of the French and American revolutions, rose up against the cruelty of their masters.

Displeased with the loss of control, Napoleon sent seventy warships and 45,000 men under the command of his brother-in-law, General Leclerc, to seize the ringleader, Toussaint L'Ouverture, bring him and his leading generals, Christophe and Dessalines, to Paris, then reenslave the blacks. A fierce battle ensued. When Toussaint l'Ouverture went to French headquarters to discuss armistice, he was seized, bound, thrown into the hold of a ship, and sent to France to die of starvation and exposure less than a year later.

With the disclosure of this treachery and of Napoleon's intent to restore slavery, Generals Christophe, Dessalines, and Pétion resumed the war, now a war for independence. The French, decimated by the yellow fever that killed Leclerc and others, capitulated in November 1803. France had lost her richest colony and a crucial staging area for Napoleon's designs on North America.

On January 1, 1804, the second declaration of independence in the New World was proclaimed. The country was officially named Haiti. The first black republic was born.

Dessalines was crowned emperor of Haiti as Jacques I, but was assassinated in 1806 and Haiti became a republic with Pétion, a quiet, cultured statesman, ruling in the south; Christophe in the north.

Christophe proclaimed himself king, surrounded himself with a self-appointed nobility and embarked upon a building career in which he constructed eight chateaux and nine royal palaces in fourteen years. More than 200,000 men performed the labors of Hercules in erecting the Sans Souci Palace and the spectacular Citadelle Laferrière. King Henri I committed suicide in 1820 and was buried in the Citadelle.

Haitian history from 1820 to 1957 was a succession of seizures of power by elected officials seeking to extend their terms beyond the law, military assassinations, bloody disputes with the Dominican Republic to the east and a nineteen-year occupation by the U.S. Marines (from 1915–1934). In 1957, François Duvalier was elected president. Duvalier, known as "Papa Doc" because he was a physician before entering politics, altered the constitution to allow himself to become president-for-life, a title he passed to his son, Jean Claude, when he died in 1971. Jean Claude has ruled the country ever since.

The political situation in Haiti, though repugnant to believers in democratic elections, has nonetheless brought a high degree of stability to the country for some twenty-five years. How long the stable situation will last is anyone's guess, since Haiti is one of the poorest countries in the world and there are persistent rumors that Jean Claude is not in good health.

Voodoo

To begin to understand Haiti, you must have some knowledge of the voodoo cult that is a part of so many Haitian beliefs and an inspiration to the country's art and music. Transplanted by the slaves, voodooism today exists side by side with Catholicism, the official religion. The *veve,* a geometric design traced on the ground in corn flour, is the emblem of the diety being summoned. The veve is also believed to be the original inspiration for Haitian painting.

The voodoo ceremony is conducted by a *hougan* (priest) or a *mambo* (priestess) in a charm-trimmed *hounfor,* or neighborhood voodoo temple, decorated with primitive symbols representing various voodoo gods or *loa,* plus a pole, like a painted maypole, in the center, and the *rada,* or sacred drums.

The ceremony builds with the beat of the drums, the singing of the initiated, and the whirling dancers. Participants in the ceremony dance with an abandon that often reaches its climax with the dancer going into a trance. According to voodoo belief, this means the dancer is possessed by the loa; the god has entered the body and soul.

The version of voodoo you will see at the tourist spots is no less exhausting to the first-time viewer than the real thing is to the experienced practitioner. Voodoo, at once cult and diversion, is the most vivid evidence of the survival of the African past in Haiti.

Haitian Painting and Folk Art

The celebrated renaissance in Haitian painting began in 1944, when an American artist and teacher, DeWitt Peters, opened Le Centre d'Art in Port-au-Prince. Three years later, Haitian painting caused a sensation at the UNESCO international exhibition in Paris. In 1948–49, Haitian "primitives" were shown and bought in New York and all over the U.S. The same year, the American poet and art critic Selden Rodman launched the mural movement in Haitian painting. Thirteen tempera murals were painted by native Haitian artists in the Episcopal Cathedral of the Holy Trinity. Soon, the walls of hotels and airport and exposition buildings began to glow with the rich colors of these self-taught primitive artists. Many of the painters are now widely known wherever pictures are exhibited and bought: the late Hector Hyppolite, who was a voodoo priest; Wilson Bigaud, the first Haitian to exhibit at the Carnegie International; Philomé Obîn and Enguerrand Gourgue, whose paintings are part of the permanent collection of New York's Museum of Modern Art.

EXPLORING HAITI

The shape of Haiti resembles the open jaws of a crocodile, with the Golfe de la Gonâve between them. On the northern peninsula is the colonial city of Cap-Haitien with its history of revolution. On the southern peninsula is the coffee-plantation town of Jacmel. At the hinge where the two join is Port-au-Prince, the capital city.

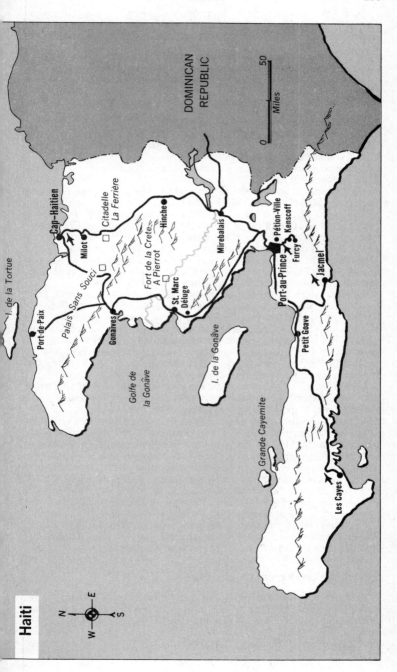

[Note: When traveling in Haiti, don't be afraid to use your horn, especially when crossing intersections and passing other vehicles or pedestrians. It is common practice and makes others aware of your intentions. Bring your passport and tourist card. You *must stop* at police checkpoints, where you will be asked your name and destination, then sent on your way.]

Port-au-Prince

Port-au-Prince is a teeming city of 800,000. It is a place of contrasts, with beggars lining the streets in front of expensive hotels. Exploring the city is an adventure in itself. Its streets are crowded with pedestrians as well as vehicles and beasts of burden.

A logical place to begin your exploration is the Place des Heros de l'Independence in the city center on rue Jean Marie Guilloux between rue des Casernés and rue St. Honore. Here you will see the National Palace; the Mausoleum, containing the bodies of Dessalines and Pétion; the National Pantheon Museum, containing samples of artifacts from each period of Haitian history, including the anchor from Columbus' flagship the Santa María. A few blocks away, off rue Capois, is the Museum of Haitian Art, containing the works of such artists as Hector Hyppolite, the voodoo priest, and Philomé Obin and Enguerrand Gourgue, whose works are now part of the permanent collections of leading museums and art connoisseurs all over the world.

Heading north on rue Capois, make a left on rue des Casernés, then a right on boulevard J.J. Dessalines and travel north about a half-dozen blocks until you get to rue des Fronts Fort. To your left for the next two blocks is Haiti's Iron Market. Housed beneath the roofs of two iron warehouses, the market is a crush of humanity, with vendors selling everything from food to perfume, spices to carvings and paintings. If crowds bother you, you won't like it here. If you enjoy haggling for bargains, there are bargains to be had. Your choice.

One of the many sharp contrasts so characteristic of Port-au-Prince is provided about a hundred yards west of this native bazaar by the International Exposition Grounds, centuries removed from the Iron Market in both atmosphere and architecture. The Exposition Grounds are on the waterfront, just off Harry Truman Boulevard, a wide thoroughfare built in the best spirit of western city planning. The buildings of Haiti's Bicentennial International Exposition are now used as shops and government buildings. The charming illuminated fountain provides a focal point for the area, and there are a number of sidewalk cafes and restaurants in the immediate vicinity. At night, with the fountain illuminated and people strolling through the landscaped plaza, the place still has the atmosphere of a world's fair.

Traveling north on Harry Truman, make a right on rue Pavee. About a half-dozen blocks further on the left is the Cathedral St. Trinité, with its famed murals in the Haitian primitive style.

Pétion-Ville, Kenscoff, and Furcy

Continue out rue Pavee until it joins avenue John Brown on the right, then out of Port-au-Prince, until the street becomes avenue Pan Americaine. You are headed now to Pétion-Ville, the cool and pleasant suburb of Port-au-Prince, in the mountains about two thousand feet above the capital. The road winds through forests and trees supporting vines of crimson blossoms, past modern villas, vintage Victorian mansions, and humble thatched peasant huts. Along the way, you pass the seemingly endless line of strong, graceful women making their way to market with their headbaskets full of the fruits and vegetables of their gardens. In Pétion-Ville, there are lovely hotels, inns, and restaurants that were once the playground of the Creole elite.

Beyond Pétion-Ville, the road continues to wind up the mountain another four thousand feet to Kenscoff, where the farmers and native women display their colorful wares on the slopes, bartering and haggling to make sales. This is the Châlet des Fleurs, with its acres and acres of sweet peas and other flowers grown for air shipment to the U.S. market. It is a spectacular green mountain setting. Tuesdays and Fridays are the principal market days in Kenscoff.

The road, narrow now and twisting and full of switchbacks beyond Kenscoff, ends at Furcy, about seven thousand feet above sea level. From here you can see La Selle (the saddle), Haiti's highest peak, soaring almost nine thousand feet and robed in a mantle of dark green pine. This unique pine forest, in whose dense growth escaping slaves once took refuge, can be reached by a long trek from Port-au-Prince, but it's only for the truly adventurous who can handle the terrible road, a very difficult climb, and an occassional crocodile.

South to Jacmel

A round trip south to Jacmel will take the better part of a day. Jacmel is an unspoiled little town overlooking the bay of the same name. This town, about a two-hour drive from Port-au-Prince, has a strong colonial flavor and some excellent examples of nineteenth-century architecture reminiscent of New Orleans. Its Iron Market was built about seventy years ago in an effort to outdo the one in the capital, but it falls short. Incidentally, that strong, aromatic coffee you've been enjoying since you got to Haiti comes from this area.

If you've got some time head west at Dufort and make a short side trip to the Taino Beach Hotel near Grand Goâve. Here there is a lovely tree-lined white-sand beach where you can enjoy lunch under a palm or a cool drink at the beach bar and refresh yourself with a dip in the sea. Beyond Taino Beach is Le Relais de l'Empereur, the most expensive resort in Haiti, near Petit Goâve.

North to Cap-Haitien

Unless you are prepared to get up very early, drive for almost five hours, spend another five hours exploring, then allot five hours more for the return trip, Cap-Haiten is at least a two-day jaunt.

You drive north out of Port-au-Prince on the highway to Cap-Haitien. Almost twenty miles out of town, near Duvalierville, you will find Ibo Beach, the closest to the city, a lovely white-sand area that is perfect for a dip and some snorkeling. Beginning just beyond the village of Arcahaie, about thirty miles from Port-au-Prince, you enter Haiti's Plage or beach area, so-named because for the next twenty miles you will pass Kyona, Kaliko, Ouanga, Jolly, and Xaragua beaches, plus the Club Med at Montrouis. These are lovely beaches, each with a hotel, and are just right for a stop—if you're so inclined—for a swim in the crystal-clear waters of the Golfe de la Gonâve.

It was at Montrouis, by the way, that Hector Hyppolite's paintings on the door of a roadside bar were discovered by American connoisseur DeWitt Peters, a discovery that launched the Haitian art movement.

Next up is the port city of Saint Marc, whence eight hundred Haitians sailed north to fight in the American Revolution and learned the military lessons that would help them win their own freedom twenty years later. For the next fifteen miles, between Saint Marc and Estere, you will pass lush green rice patties, where workers and oxen labor in the water-logged fields. Then abruptly the land turns arid, with giant cacti reminiscent of the American desert.

Now you enter Gonaïves where, in 1804, Haitian General Dessalines declared independence from France. For the next two hours, you climb and descend three successive mountains, passing peasants along the road, some hawking their fresh produce. Then you'll pass through the old yellow gates into Cap-Haitien.

Cap-Haitien is a colonial town of stone buildings with shuttered windows painted in every color of the rainbow. You may want to stop at the gallery of famed artist Philomé Obin on "L" Street near First, or the Cathedral on "F" Street between Sixteenth and Eighteenth. But the principal reason you have driven all this way is to see the palace of Sans Souci and the Citadelle La Ferrière. To get to both, you take the main highway south out of Cap-Haitien for about ten miles to where the road dead-ends at the village of Milot. Straight ahead, you will see the remains of Sans Souci, wrecked by an earthquake in 1842. Once the palatial home of King Henri Christophe, Sans Souci still evokes a sense of grandeur. At Sans Souci, you can wander through the ruins of the palace. You will also want to step inside the domed chapel. The guides will be happy to show you the very room where King Christophe committed suicide with a silver pistol and golden bullet. (Tip them whatever you feel is appropriate).

From Sans Souci, drive another five miles along dirt road to a second parking lot. Here you begin a two-mile hike to the Citadelle, or you can rent a horse. Either way it is slow going and takes about thirty minutes. When you reach the Citadelle, you will see why it was said a garrison of five thousand soldiers could hold off the siege of an entire army for a year or more. It is an incredible edifice of twelve-foot-thick walls, rising from the sheer cliff face. Two hundred cannons stand guard. You'll wonder how it was ever built and it will not surprise you to learn it took thirteen years and a toll of 20,000 lives.

If you are in the mood for a swim at this point, there are two lovely beaches west of Cap-Haitien, Cormier and La Badie, but each take some time to get to. They are worth the effort if you are spending a day or two at Cap-Haitien.

PRACTICAL INFORMATION FOR HAITI

FACTS AND FIGURES. Haiti is a country of about 10,000 square miles, occupying the western third of the island of Hispaniola, which it shares with the Dominican Republic. It is a very mountainous country (that's what Haiti means in Arawak). Haiti has a population of more than five million, about 80% of which lives in rural areas. Its capital and largest city is Port-au-Prince, with a population of more than 800,000. Other key cities are Cap-Haitien on the north coast, Gonaives on the west, and Jacmel and Les Cayes on the south. French is the country's official language, but the most widely spoken dialect is Creole, a combination of African languages, indigenous Indian, the Norman French of the buccaneers, and the dialects of the French colonists. About 120,000 people visit the country each year, half from the U.S., most of the rest from Canada and Europe. Haiti is one of the poorest countries on earth with the lowest per-capita income in the Western Hemisphere.

WHEN TO GO. Haiti has a very pleasant Caribbean climate. In the coastal areas, temperatures range from 70 to 90 degrees F year-round, with temperatures on the high end during July and August and on the cool end from December through March. Temperatures in the mountains are quite a bit cooler ranging from 50 to 75 degrees. The driest months are December through March. Tropical storms, when they occur, generally come from mid-August through the end of September.

PASSPORTS AND VISAS. All U.S. and Canadian visitors are required to have proof of citizenship. A passport is best, but a birth certificate or voter's registration card will do. A driver's license will not. In addition, you must have an ongoing or return ticket. British citizens must have a passport, but no visas are required.

MONEY. The unit of Haitian currency is the gourde, which equals U.S. $.20. The gourde is divided into 100 centimes, and there are 5-, 10-, 20-, and 50-centime coins. American money and traveler's checks are accepted throughout Haiti at even exchange value.

WHAT WILL IT COST?

A typical day in Haiti for two persons during the winter season will run:

	U.S. $
Hotel accommodations at a moderate hotel, including breakfast and dinner	$85
Luncheon at an in-town restaurant	15
Tip or service charge at restaurant; hotel tax and service charge	15
Rental car for one day or island tour	30
Total	$145

HOW TO GET THERE. By air. All flights into Haiti land in Port-au-Prince. *American Airlines* flies nonstop from New York. *Eastern Airlines* and *Air France* have flights from Miami; *Air France* also flies from San Juan. *Air Canada* makes nonstop flights from Montreal.

By sea. More than 100 major passenger ships call at Port-au-Prince or Cap-Haitien. The principal cruise lines are: *Norwegian Caribbean, Norwegian American, Holland American, Sitmar, Royal Caribbean* and *Paquet Cruise Lines.*

By land. You can travel by land to Haiti from the Dominican Republic, but it's best to keep abreast of the border situation. Traffic is often restricted between the two countries.

AIRPORT TAXES AND OTHER CHARGES. Government tax on accommodations is 5%, plus a 10% service charge. The departure tax is U.S. $10.

TELEPHONES AND EMERGENCY NUMBERS.
Country code for Haiti is 509. The Haitian Telephone
Company provides service via link-ups to all parts of the
world. Charge for three minutes to the U.S. is $4.50; to
Canada $9. For overseas operator dial 09. Information is 110.

Emergencies. Each hotel has a designated doctor, while English-speaking
doctors and dentists are available in Port-au-Prince and provincial capitals. Ask
at your hotel. U.S. Embassy number is 2–0200, Canada's is 2–4231.

HOTELS. There are more plans for accommodations on
the beaches, but so far they are limited in number. Port-
au-Prince has the widest variety, with small inns and
guesthouses vying with retreats that wind up to Pétion-
Ville. Cap-Haitien, Haiti's second city, offers lots to see but only a few places
to stay. The beaches are north of Port-au-Prince on the road to St. Marc, west
toward Petit Goave or south to Jacmel.

In Haiti, we call $200 and up per day for a double room *Super Deluxe;*
$150–199 *Deluxe;* $100–149 *Expensive;* $75–99 *Moderate;* anything below $75
Inexpensive.

PORT-AU-PRINCE AND PÉTION-VILLE

Dunes El Rancho Hotel & Casino. *Deluxe.* Box 71, Pétion-Ville. Tel. 7–2080.
Cool and comfortable, with 115 lavishly appointed rooms. All air-conditioned,
but with mountain breezes, chances are you won't need it. Once a private home,
to which more and more additions have been made, the latest being the island's
newest casino. Two swimming pools, two tennis courts, a fine restaurant, nightly
entertainment.

Royal Haitian Hotel & Casino. *Expensive.* Box 2075, Martissant, Port-au-
Prince. Tel. 4–0258. Lively and attractive property with 82 rooms on 15 acres
overlooking Port-au-Prince harbor. Each room has a terrace with a view.
French and Creole specialties are highlights of cuisine here. Pool-deck restaurant offers breakfast and lunch. Two freshwater swimming pools; two championship tennis courts. By night, music and action in the casino. MAP.

Grand Hotel Oloffson. *Moderate.* 60 ave. Christophe, Port-au-Prince. Tel.
2–0139. Adds new meaning to the word "grand." It looks the way a Caribbean
hotel is supposed to look. Haiti's liveliest and most fascinating place to stay, it
keeps drawing celebrities and returnees who love the atmosphere. Just 24 rooms,
in all shapes, sizes and decors. Rooms are named for those who've slept there—
John Gielgud Suite, Chambre Mick Jagger, etc. French and American fare in
dining room; lively conversation at bar and in sitting rooms; spring-fed swimming pool. Breakfast included.

Ibo Lele Hotel. *Moderate.* P.O. Box 1237, Pétion-Ville, Tel. 7–0845. High in
the hills overlooking the city, this 70-room resort is a perfect cool hideaway just
15 minutes from town. Swimming pool and patio for sunny hours; fine French
restaurant and vibrating *Club Shango* from sunset until the wee smalls. For
added enjoyment, the Ibo Lele has private beach club on Cacique Island, a
20-minute drive and 5-minute boat ride away, for a full day of sunning or
swimming on almost uninhabited stretch of sand. Breakfast included.

Hotel Splendid. *Moderate.* P.O. Box 1214, Port-au-Prince. Tel. 5–0116. And
"splendid" it is, at a very reasonable price. It was a Haitian mansion that has
been completely restored. Today it is an interesting combination of colonial,
Victorian, and Mediterranean styles, surrounded by tropical gardens. Cuisine
is traditionally European, but the pool and relaxation that surround are strictly
Caribbean.

Villa Creole. *Moderate.* P.O. Box 126, Pétion-Ville. Tel. 7–1570. Another
hillside retreat with dramatically furnished rooms. Atmosphere is French-
Creole and delightful. The spacious swimming pool is perfect setting for patio
barbecues and Creole buffets. *Villa Belle Restaurant* is more intimate and more
Parisian. Haitian troubadours play every night. Additional local entertainment
during the winter. Tennis courts on premises for day or night play. Options for
snorkeling and scuba trips to nearby beaches. Breakfast included.

Castel Haiti. *Inexpensive.* P.O. Box 446, Port-au-Prince. Tel. 2–0624. This 100-room property is the only one in the country that soars to heights generally associated with big city hotels. All rooms have balconies that provide bird's-eye views of the city. Good food with elaborate French-Creole buffets the highlight. Nightclub featuring local entertainment, the large swimming pool and wide deck, just minutes from city center. Hotel is a popular spot for tour groups and also caters to meetings and conventions.

CAP-HAITIEN

Cormier Plage Hotel. *Moderate.* P.O. Box 70, Cap-Haitien. Tel. 2–1000. This 35-room property is tucked onto 15 acres of lush tropical beachfront. About half-hour by dirt road west of Cap-Haitien. All sorts of water sports; tennis courts. Creole, European, and seafood specialties on the menu. MAP

Mont Joli Hotel. *Moderate.* P.O. Box 12, Cap-Haitien. Tel. 2–0300. A fine hilltop hotel with 45 air-conditioned rooms, all with spectacular views of the ocean and the city below. Dining room specializes in Creole cuisine; two bars and lounge featuring nightly entertainment by local bands. Swimming and water sports at nearby Rival Beach. MAP

Roi Christophe Hotel. *Moderate.* P.O. Box 34, Cap-Haitien. Tel. 2–0414. This small, 18-room property was originally built in 1724 as a little palace for the French governor. Although it's been refurbished, it hasn't lost its colonial look. French fare featured in the dining room; camaraderie in the busy cocktail lounge. The swimming pool and mini-casino provide modern touches. MPA.

ALONG THE BEACHES

Le Relais de l'Empereur. *Super Deluxe.* Petit Goâve. Tel. 503 (in Port-au-Prince tel. 5–0810). Beachfront property for the rich and chic. Just ten rooms, but decor is lavish. Pool, private beach, all kinds of water sports and activities. Built by former owner of famed Habitation Leclerc, which has closed. All meals included.

Le Xaragua Hotel. *Expensive.* P.O 1734, Déluge. Tel. 2–5000. On Golfe de la Gonâve in small village of Déluge, about 50 miles from Port-au-Prince. 51 air-conditioned rooms on oceanfront are graceful combination of Caribbean tradition and modern construction. Nice beach, freshwater pool, tennis courts. Small restaurant and bar. MAP.

Ibo Beach Club. *Moderate.* P.O. Box 1237, Route Nationale No. 1, Cacique Island. Tel. 7–1200. This is the opportunity to find your own private island and live the barefoot life. All 72 rooms are fully equipped cabanas. Great restaurant serving daily catch, fresh from the sea. Lighted tennis courts. Swimming pool, lovely beach, water sports. Breakfast included.

La Jacmelienne sur Plage. *Moderate.* rue St. Anne, Jacmel. Tel. 2–4899. Lovely beach resort. 40 modern rooms tastefully furnished in Haitian decor, all with terraces overlooking the sea. Large freshwater pool with pool bar and open-air terrace bar above. *L'Ambassador Dorin Restaurant* serves Haitian cuisine, with emphasis on seafood. Horseback riding and excursions to nearby attractions arranged. MAP.

Jolly Beach Club. *Moderate.* P.O. Box 15418, Carries Route du Nord. Tel. 2–9653. On La Gonâve Bay, south of Montrouis. Wonderful new 22-room property. Spectacular view of bay on the one side, Chaines des Matheux mountains on the other. Excellent cuisine featuring seafood and Haitian specialties. Swimming pool, beach with water sports. Tennis courts. MAP.

Kyona Beach Hotel. *Moderate.* Route Nationale No. 1, Montrouis. Tel. 2–6788. Wonderful outdoor-living, fresh air-oriented resort. 18 rooms in bungalows on 600 acres of beachfront property. Terrific lobster specialties in restaurant. Local folkloric shows on Fridays.

Club Mediterranee. *Inexpensive.* Village des Vacances, Commune de Montrouis. Tel. 2–4400. When this club opened in 1980, they called it "Magic Haiti," and it is that. In the small town of Montrouis on the shore, about a 1 ½-hour drive north of the capital. Accommodations for 700 in two- and three-story clusters of bungalows set on 120 acres along deserted white-sand beach. Three

HAITI

separate dining areas. Large freshwater pool and poolside bar. 14 tennis courts. All water sports. Lavish buffets with wine flowing freely during lunch and dinner. Inexpensive when you consider weekly rate is all-inclusive.

 HOW TO GET AROUND. Taxis are not metered, but fares to the hotels from the airport are fixed and the rates are per car, not per person. Current prices are $11 to hotels in Port-au-Prince; $12 to Pétion-Ville; $42 to Taino Beach. Check in advance for all other resorts. In addition to taxis in town, there are also inexpensive ways of getting around. *Publiques* are public cars that can be hailed within the city limits, and *camionettes* (station wagons) make the run up and down the hill from Port-au-Prince to Pétionville. In both cases fares are about $.25 per person.

Rental cars are readily available at the airport and in Port-au-Prince. Rates run $22–30 per day, with unlimited mileage. Among the firms to contact are: *Budget Rent-a-Car* (tel. 6–2324); *Caribbean Enterprises, Inc. (Avis)* (tel. 6–2333); or *Continental Travel Service (National)* (tel. 2–0611). A U.S. or Canadian driver's license is acceptable.

 TOURIST INFORMATION SERVICES. The main office on the island is the *Office National du Tourisme,* on Ave. Marie Jeanne in Port-au-Prince (tel. 2–1720). For sources closer to home, see the Tourist Information Services section in the *Facts at Your Fingertips* chapter.

 SPECIAL EVENTS. The highlights of the year in Haiti are the combination Independence Day–New Year's Day celebrations and the pre-Lenten Carnival, complete with parades, floats and parties.

 TOURS. Haiti is a vast country, and there's plenty to see, from one end to the other—beaches, cities, historic attractions. *Chatelain Tours and Travel Service* (The Gray Line of Haiti) makes it easy. In Port-au-Prince, contact them on rue Geffrard (tel. 2–4468), or in Pétion-Ville call 7–0275. Among the tours they offer are:

Colonial Jacmel. A charming and quiet little city, built in 1698, that has maintained its colonial charm. Enroute you'll drive through native markets, sugar-cane fields, and mountain villages. Full-day tour, $40 per person, which includes lunch.

La Gonâve Island Cruise. Sail on a cabin cruiser to La Gonâve, the mysterious island in the bay of Port-au-Prince. Its curious setting will amaze you—golden-sand beaches, crystal-clear water, and friendly native fishermen. A beach barbecue will be prepared for lunch; masks and fins provided for snorkeling. This tour is approximately eight hrs.; $48 per person, lunch included.

Cap-Haitien and the Citadelle. On this tour, you'll fly from Port-au-Prince to the north coast. From Cap-Haitien, you'll visit the ruins of Sans Souci Palace built by King Henry Christophe in 1804, then ride horseback to the top of the Citadelle, the "eighth wonder of the world," at 3,000 ft. above sea level. Luncheon will be at an in-town restaurant, and there will be a city tour before boarding the return flight to Port-au-Prince. Approximately ten hrs.; $100 per person, including round-trip air fare, luncheon, horses, and guides.

Kenscoff Mountain Tour. This tour heads for the hills and the village of Kenscoff, 5,000 ft. above sea level. It includes a spectacular 15-mi. drive through the mountains, a stop and sampling at the Jane Barbancourt Rum Castle, and at Boutilliers, for a sweeping, 3,000-ft. view. This excursion is three hrs., with morning and afternoon departures; $12 per person.

Association of Guided Drivers. If you want to hire a car and construct your own itinerary with the help of a knowledgeable driver, contact the Association des Chauffeurs Guide d'Haiti (ACGH), Harry Truman Blvd., City of the Exposition. Tel. 2–0330. Drivers are fluent in English, French, Spanish, and of course

Creole. Rates are $10 per hour or $50 per day for up to four people. Group rates are available on minibuses for up to 14 people.

PARKS AND GARDENS. Many hotels have beautifully landscaped gardens of their own that show off Haiti's flora in a profusion of blooms and colors, and the forest trails into the mountains can certainly be called gardens. However, only one place combines the two and adds a healthy dose of Haitian history to boot. This is *Champs de Mars,* or *Place des Heros de l'Independence,* right in the center of Port-au-Prince. The park, laid out in front of the National Palace, is beautifully landscaped and the perfect setting for a stroll, with stops at the giant statues of Haiti's heros. The park is about a half-dozen square city blocks, bounded by rue des Casernes on the north, rue St. Honore on the South, rue de la Reunion on the west and rue Capois on the east. Like all of Haiti, the park is safe for visitors. However, discretion is always advised when wandering anywhere late at night. Incidentally, don't be alarmed by the Haitians who will literally run up to you and begin talking and sometime even tug at your shirtsleeves. Everyone in Haiti is a potential guide for a few coins. Be advised, however, that if you accept and do pay for the guided tour, your footsteps will soon be dogged by more people trying to get in on the act.

BEACHES. Haiti's beaches come in a wide variety. There isn't one that's typical of the country, and that is what makes each special. The most popular are within an hour's drive of Port-au-Prince in the Plage area north of the city, although despite their proximity to the city, these beaches are seldom crowded. These are white sandy beaches on the Gulf of Gonave. Most are accessible by car, others via a short boat ride. They begin at Duvalierville and extend north to Deluge and include *Ibo Beach, Kaliko, Kyona, Jolly Beach,* and *Xaragua. Taino Beach* and *Jacmel Beach* are along the southern peninsula. On the north coast are *Rival Beach, Cormier Plage* and *La Badie,* a short drive from Cap-Haitien. *Cacique* and *Cocoyer beaches* are short boat-rides from the mainland. All Haitian beaches are excellent for swimming and snorkeling. There are also dozens of coves to discover all along the shore. The best bet is to rent snorkeling equipment in advance so you are prepared for any new discovery while exploring the coastline.

PARTICIPANT SPORTS. Tennis. Courts are available at just about all major resorts and many are lighted for night play. Obviously, if tennis is your thing, inquire in advance about facilities.

Golf. There is only one golf course in Haiti, a small nine-holer at the *Pétion-Ville Club,* above Port-au-Prince.

Water sports. Snorkeling, sailing, waterskiing, windsurfing, and scuba diving are available at the beach resorts or can be arranged through in-town hotels. Two special options on the water are those arranged through *Chatelain Tours and Travel* service in Port-au-Prince (tel. 2–4468) or in Pétion-Ville (tel. 7–0275). They are the Yellow Bird Catamaran Cruise, which sails out to the Grand Banc coral reefs (approximately four hrs., $17 per person); and the Tropical Sea Garden Cruise, when non-swimmers can enjoy all that's along the ocean floor, from a glass-bottom boat (approximately three hrs., $18 per person).

SPECTATOR SPORTS. Soccer. Soccer is played almost everywhere in Haiti, but the best matches take place at the *Stade Sylvio Cator* on rue Oswald Durand, almost every night beginning at about 6:30. Haiti has very good teams which are respected throughout Latin America, where this sport is king. Contact the tourist office in Port-au-Prince for specific times and additional sites (tel. 2–1720).

Cockfights. If you have the stomach for it, the real spectator sport in Haiti is cockfighting, which takes place on Saturday and Sunday afternoons.

Cockfighting is a gambler's sport and you'll see a lot of furious negotiating taking place before each duel to the death. Understandably, the loser's handler is often reluctant to call it quits, even when the outcome appears obvious, so you'll often see the handler blowing his hot breath on the back of the fatigued bird's neck to rush a fresh supply of blood to its head. Crowds are largely Haitian, plus visiting tour groups and a handful of individual visitors. Some of the best fights are in Pétion-Ville at Gaguere de Freres on rue de Freres, beginning about 1:00 P.M. Or you can join a 2 ½ hr. Chatelain Tour for $12 per person, which includes admission.

HISTORIC SITES AND HOUSES. Cap-Haitien. The most historic and overwhelming site in Haiti, if not in all the Caribbean, is the *Citadelle La Ferriere* near this northern port city. It was built by Henri Christophe, the self-proclaimed king of Haiti, to protect the island from invaders. The fortress covers 100,000 square feet of solid rock, at an altitude of 3,000 feet. It took 13 years and 200,000 men to build, 20,000 of whom paid the ultimate price. The Citadelle has 12-foot-thick walls, 200 cannons, and accommodations for members of the royal family—which occupy 40 rooms alone. There are accommodations for 4,000 soldiers, who, it is said, could have held off an invading army for a year. To reach the Citadelle, drive to the village of Milot, then up a dirt road to a parking lot. From there hike the last two miles or rent a horse (about U.S. $2.50). Admission is U.S. $1.25, which also includes the Sans Souci Palace.

Companion piece to the Citadelle is Christophe's *San Souci Palace* at the base of La Ferriere mountain. Sans Souci was the showplace of its day. Complete with tapestries, Italian marbles, running water, cooling aqueducts, all the trappings of royalty, it was home to the king and his self-appointed court. Though the palace was wrecked by an earthquake in 1842, its ruins still have a certain grandeur. Both monuments are open 7:00 A.M.-5 P.M.

Port-au-Prince. *The Episcopal Cathedral of St. Trinité,* on rue Pavee at rue Courte, is a showplace of Haitian mural art, with breathtakingly colorful paintings of religious scenes filling its walls. "The Last Supper," showing all the apostles in detail, is perhaps the most impressive and an interesting contrast to DaVinci's interpretation of the same scene.

The Roman Catholic Cathedral on rue Bonne Foi and rue Dr. Aubry has a brilliant rose window and the Old Church on the same grounds dates back to 1720, during the French colonial era. Churches and cathedrals are open all day and are free of charge.

Place des Heros de l'Independence is the cultural centerpiece of Port-au-Prince on rue Jean Marie Guilloux between rue des Casernés and rue St. Honore. Here you will find the *National Palace,* the *Mausoleum* containing the bodies of Dessalines and Pétion, and the new *National Pantheon Museum,* containing artifacts from each period of Haitian history.

The Iron Market takes up two full city blocks on blvd. J.J. Dessalines between rue des Fronts Fort and rue des Cesars. Here for the past century, beneath the roofs of two old iron warehouses, Haitian merchants have sold everything from spices to artwork.

MUSEUMS AND GALLERIES. The primitive art of Haiti was "discovered" in the mid-1940s and began to emerge as a recognized force in the art world in the 1950s. It added a vibrant and colorful element to contemporary art and launched a new wave of painting by local Haitian artists.

Port-au-Prince. *The Museum of Haitian Art* displays about 200 works of the most famous Haitian artists and examples from the latest crop of newcomers. The museum is on rue Capois off rue Oswald Durand. It is open Mon.–Fri., 9:00 A.M.-1 P.M.; Mon. Wed. and Fri. 4:00–6:00 P.M.; Sat. 9:00 A.M.-12:00 noon. Admission is free.

Le Centre d'Art at rue 22 September 1957 has a wonderful collection of the works of many famous Haitian artists. It is open 9:00 A.M.-5:00 P.M. Mon.–Fri. and 9:00 A.M.-12:00 noon Sat. and Sun. Admission is free.

The National Pantheon Museum at Place des Heros de l'Independence is an impressive subterranean structure that opened in 1983. It contains a wide range of relics and works of art, from the anchor of Columbus's Santa María to a sculpture of the feet of famed dancer Katherine Dunham, who lives in Haiti. There are artifacts of Haiti's history from the Arawaks to the Duvaliers. The Pantheon is open Mon.–Sat. 10:00 A.M.-5:00 P.M. Admission is U.S. $3.

There are dozens of galleries all over Port-au-Prince, with paintings in all varieties and price ranges. Among them are *Galerie Nader*, 92 place Geffard, (tel 2–0033), which exhibits works of such masters as Obin, Nemours, La Tortue, and others. Open Mon.–Fri. 8:00 A.M.-5:00 P.M., Sat. 8:00 A.M.-1:00 P.M. *Musé Gallery*, Corner rue Geffard (tel 2–3193) includes all Haitian styles. Open Mon.–Fri. 8:00 A.M.-5:00 P.M.; Sat. 8:00 A.M.-1:00 P.M. *Olivier Studio Gallery*, 124 ave. Christophe (tel. 2–6982) is owned and managed by the painter Raymond Olivier and features his "new face of Haitian painting," a stark modern flavor to the tradition Haitian naive style. Also works of dozens of other artists. Open Mon.–Sat. 8:30 A.M.-6:00 P.M.; Sun. 8:30 A.M.-12:00 noon.

 MUSIC, DANCE, AND STAGE. The unique music and theater of Haiti is a folkloric blend of African, Caribbean, and European influences with, of course, the mystical rhythms of voodoo. Folkloric troupes perform at the various hotels on a rotating nightly basis, generally in conjunction with an outdoor barbecue dinner. Just ask at your hotel about when the troupe will be there, or where it is on any given night. In addition, folkloric music is a principal part of local festivals held throughout Haiti during specific periods to honor local patron saints or to recognize historic events. For example, on May 1 there is a Labor Day and patron saints' celebration in Jacmel on the southern coast; June 15–July 15 is dance schools performance time in Port-au-Prince, featuring performances of classic ballet and modern dance along with traditional folkloric festivities; platron saints' celebrations take place in Cap-Haitien on the north coast July 25 and 26 and August 15. The month of December is concert season in Port-au-Prince, featuring international and Haitian classical music, as well as popular and experimental works performed by local and international ensembles. Inquire at your hotel or at the tourist office for information about times, dates, places, specific types of music, and theater and admission prices.

 SHOPPING. Port-au-Prince. Haiti's most famous, most crowded, and most diverse shopping center is the *Iron Market* on blvd. J.J. Dessalines between rue des Fronts Fort and rue des Cesars, near the waterfront. Here frenetic transactions take place throughout the day. Bargaining is a must, and if you offer half the quoted price, chances are you'll get it. Carved wooden items, masks, and Haitian paintings are for sale all over the market. Go there early in the morning to beat the heat and the heaviest crowds.

Larger shopping marts and boutiques are conveniently situated on the Exposition Grounds on Harry Truman Blvd., near the waterfront, but you'll also find good shops and boutiques scattered all around the city from the sea wall to the residential section and up to the surrounding mountain spots in Pétion-Ville and beyond at Kenscoff. Don't forget, Tuesdays and Fridays are market days at Kenscoff.

The best buys are paintings done by the local artists. Haitian primitives have become world famous, so prices are not what they used to be. But browse through the galleries and you're bound to find something to please your eye and your pocketbook. (See "Museums and Galleries" for some specific suggestions.)

 RESTAURANTS. You'll remember Haiti for its food. The French cuisine is authentic; the Creole specialties, combining French, West Indian, and African elements are exotic and delicious; the seafood is as good as you'll find anywhere. Some special dishes to try are *diri et djondjon* (rice and black mushrooms); *grillot* (fried island pork); *riz et pois* (rice and kidney beans); and guinea hen with sour orange sauce. Langouste flambé is flaming local lobster; *piment oiseau* is a very spicy hot sauce that should be used sparingly; and *grillot et banane pese* (pork chops and bananas) are an island favorite.

The haute cuisine francaise offers every specialty you can name, much of it served flambé. You'll find French wines and champagnes in the better restaurants, but the island drink is rum. The best is Jane Barbancourt, made by a branch of Haiti's oldest family of rum and brandy distillers. Barbancourt rum is rated on a star system, like fine brandies, with five stars being the top of the line. It is often drunk straight up from a snifter.

Food at the hotels is usually good and sometimes excellent, but there are a handful of special restaurants in Port-au-Prince and its suburbs where the atmosphere is almost as fine as the food. To be safe, be sure to make reservations, although in most cases they are not necessary. Dress for all is casual, although shorts are not appropriate for dinner. Hotel restaurants are the best places to eat when you are outside the Port-au-Prince area.

As for dining, we call U.S. $20 and above per person *Expensive;* $15–19 *Moderate;* below $15 *Inexpensive*. A 10% service charge is added at all restaurants. An additional tip may be left, but generally only for extraordinary service.

Chez Gerard. *Expensive.* 11 rue Pinchinat, Pétion-Ville. Tel. 7–1949. Elegant place with tables in a garden setting around a restored mansion. Crepes or escargots make a delectable beginning, followed by a choice of chicken, seafood or beef entrees, all nicely prepared and beautifully served. AE, DC, MC, V.

La Lanterne. *Expensive.* 41 rue Borno, Pétion-Ville. Tel. 7–0479. Deluxe dining in a lovely, restored family home, with dozens of different dishes, served by candlelight around the swimming pool. Try the lobster coquille for an hors d'oeuvre; tournedos bordelaise or langouste Creole is an excellent choice of entree; and bananas flambé make a delightful finale. The menu is extensive and the wine list perhaps the most diverse in Haiti. AE, DC, MC, V.

Le Belvedere. *Expensive.* Morne Calvaire, above the city. Tel. 7–1115. Dining indoors or on the terrace offers spectacular view of the city. Try the foie gras du Perigord as a starter, then inquire about the special veal or lobster dishes. At the end of the meal the cafe irlandais (Irish coffee) adds and international touch. AE, DC, MC, V.

La Belle Epoque. *Moderate.* 23 rue Gregoire, Pétion-Ville. Tel. 7–0984. Pleasant dining in another of Haiti's restored homes. The boeuf bourguignon and curried shrimp entrees are superb. There is also a wonderful selection of Creole dishes. AE, MC, V.

La Recif. *Moderate.* 50 rue Delmas, Delmas. Tel. 6–2605. Wonderful Creole cuisine, especially wide variety of seafood dishes, from king crab to conch, shrimp to lobster. Duck also a specialty. AE, DC, MC, V.

Le Ronde Point. *Inexpensive.* ave. Marie-Jeanne, Cité de l'Exposition. Tel. 2–0621. On the Exposition Grounds, this is an old favorite for Haitian cooking. Fresh seafood specialties are featured, such as lobster marinated in rum and served flambé. Especially pleasant for an in-town lunch. AE, DC, MC.

Place Vendome. *Inexpensive.* Cité de l'Exposition. Tel. 2–3906. French and Creole specialties, nicely served in 18th-century surroundings. Salads are especially good. AE, DC, MC, V.

Rival Beach Club. *Inexpensive.* Rival Beach, just west of Cap-Haitien. No telephone. No credit cards. Just a nice change of pace on a breezy beach. Good lunch spot for a ham or chicken-and-cheese sandwich or a fish brochette.

 NIGHT LIFE AND BARS. There is much to do in Haiti at night, most of it centering around the hotels and restaurants. The nightclubs at the hotels feature live entertainment, either in the native or Caribbean styles or in the pop genre. Many restaurants also feature live entertainment. There is a wandering folkloric troupe that rotates nightly among the different hotels around Port-au-Prince and it is best to inquire at your hotel when the troupe will be there or where you can catch it on any given evening.

The most popular hotel nightclubs are at the *Dunes El Rancho, Royal Haitian, Villa Creole,* and *Castel Haiti* in the Port-au-Prince area; and *Mont Joli* and *Roi Christophe* in Cap-Haitien.

For voodoo ceremonies, there are re-creations at the hotels or *Chatelain Tours* (tel. 2–4468) can make arrangements for you to see an excellent facsimile out in the countryside—a three-hr. tour for $14 per person.

Haiti also has a complement of local bars, discotheques, and nightclubs, but although most are safe to visit, they do tend to represent the seamier side of Haitian life and are only for the more adventurous among us.

 CASINOS. Although there are slot machines at hotels throughout Haiti, there are just two casinos that include a complement of Las Vegas–style games: craps, blackjack, roulette, etc. In both, casual dress is acceptable, although guests generally tend to dress up more for the casinos. You must be at least 18 years old to enter, unless accompanied by a parent.

El Rancho Casino, rue José de San Martin, Pétion-Ville. Tel. 7–2080. At the posh Dunes El Rancho Hotel. Exciting casino in beautiful mountain setting above Port-au-Prince. Open 8:00 P.M.-4:00 A.M. every day.

Royal Haitian Casino. Martissant, Port-au-Prince. Tel. 4–0258. At the Royal Haitian Hotel above Port-au-Prince harbor. Open 9:00 P.M.-3:00 A.M. every day.

POSTAGE. Air mail rates to the U.S. and Canada are U.S. $.25 per ½ oz. for a letter; $.20 for a postcard.

ELECTRIC CURRENT. The current here is 110 to 120 volts A.C.

 SECURITY. International reports have named Haiti one of the safest places in the world for visitors. Almost every hotelier will tell you a favorite story about money being returned by taxi drivers or valuables left behind in hotel rooms being returned by chambermaids. Since Haiti is a very poor country, however, there are countless beggars wherever you turn, most wanting to earn a few pennies by showing you around. Groups of beggars, from young children to old men, will follow you for blocks and it is often difficult to shake them. If you do give money, they will hound you further. It can be disarming and disconcerting. Although there are few horror stories about thieves, muggers and the like roaming the streets at night, judgment should be exercised.

JAMAICA

by
BARBARA A. CURRIE

Jamaica is an experience as difficult to define as it is to forget. Of all the English-speaking Caribbean countries, Jamaica evokes the most emotional response from visitors: It is impossible to feel indifferent about this incredibly beautiful island, or to escape the rhythm of its vibrant cultural pulse.

Sensuous, enticing, enchanting—all describe Jamaica. The visually stunning natural attractions of its north coast resort areas are only a fraction of Jamaica's offerings: lush gardens, waterfalls, an artist's sprawling canvas of exotic flora trimming magnificent sand and seascapes. This is only the backdrop for one of the most fascinating cultures in the West Indies. Jamaica is music, art, legend, and an undefeatable spirit.

Jamaicans themselves provide the most vivid memories; only through knowing them can you begin to understand the soul of this complex country whose people remain proud despite continuing economic strain.

With 4,243 square miles, Jamaica is the third-largest of the Caribbean islands. The island floats in the tropics, directly on the trade routes from Europe to the Panama Canal at the crossroads for air and sea traffic between North and South America. With the two largest Caribbean islands, Cuba and Hispaniola, it forms the Greater Antilles.

While most tourists frequent the north coast at resorts such as Montego Bay, Ocho Rios, and Port Antonio, Kingston is the island's sprawling capital and center for political, intellectual, and artistic life, as well as the home of some of its best entertainment. It is also home for about half of Jamaica's population.

More than forty square miles of Jamaica lie about 5,000 feet, and more than half of the country is over one thousand feet in elevation. But its mountains, while spectacular in their veil of bluish mist, are only part of the scenic wealth. The island has two hundred miles of white, sandy beaches, 120 rivers and streams, and a lush vegetation. All of this is combined in a country only 146 miles from east to west and between 51 and 22 miles from north to south. Visitors sometimes feel as if they're experiencing the grandeur of a continent.

There *are* continental variations in the climate. On the sun-drenched, palm-shaded beaches, you are most definitely in the tropics. But climb two thousand feet or so to one of the typical hill communities like Mandeville, and you'll find the evenings breezy and cool. Another thousand feet, and you'll be reaching for a sweater or sitting happily by a fire. While daytime, sea-level temperatures, even in the dead of winter, will be balmy and sunny, the evenings can be cool enough for sweaters or jackets, particularly now that air-conditioning has invaded the hotels.

Of Jamaica's 2.5 million people, about ninety-five percent are of African or Afro-European descent. In the minority are groups whose ancestors came from Britain, the Middle East, India, China, Portugal, Germany, South America, and other islands of the West Indies. But there has been free intermarriage over countless years, so the faces of Jamaicans are many shades—from black to tan to white. Jamaicans, whatever their racial descent, regard themselves as Jamaicans.

Jamaicans also are proud of their motto: "Out of many, one people."

Past and Present

The first arrival to Jamaica can be traced back to about a thousand years after the death of Christ. A cinnamon-colored Amerindian people paddled their tree-trunk canoes onto its shores from the Orinoco region of South America. These Arawaks may have replaced an earlier, more primitive people, the Ciboneys, who had arrived from Florida and settled on the larger Caribbean islands. The Arawaks had a gentle, idyllic culture based on hunting, fishing, light farming, festivals, and games, but this was when Christopher Columbus landed in 1494.

That was Columbus' second voyage of discovery to the New World. He sailed into what is now called Discovery Bay on the island's north coast. The frightened Arawaks made ugly faces and rude noises but quickly capitulated at the sight of a few sailors armed with crossbars and a fierce dog.

Unlike Columbus' other discoveries, Jamaica did not fall under the Spanish crown but became the personal property of the Columbus family. The first Spanish settlement was established in 1509 at Sevilla Nueva (near what now is is St. Ann's Bay on the north coast), but the settlers soon moved their capital to the other side of the island and founded Villa de la Vega (now known as Spanish Town). The Spaniards were disappointed that the island contained no precious metals and the colony remained small and poverty-stricken.

After 161 years of Spanish domination, the island changed hands. In 1655, an English fleet sailed into Kingston harbor. The Spanish small colony surrendered before the 5,000 British soldiers and sailors.

Under British rule, Jamaica became a base for pirate fleets roving the Caribbean. Leader of the pirates was that famous British buccaneer, Henry Morgan. One of his good friends was the governor of Jamaica, and he and his freebooters operated under the official protection of His Majesty's government made their headquarters a town called Port Royal, on a spit of land across from present-day Kingston. In its heyday, the port was a bizarre bazaar where British merchants could buy pirate booty at big bargains. The waterfront was like a giant flea market teeming with rogues and rascals and their wealthy customers. These Buccaneers won and lost enormous fortunes gambling. That perhaps is why Jamaica to this day does not have, nor want, the casinos that other Caribbean islands use to woo tourists. In the buccaneer days rum flowed freely in Port Royal and prostitution flourished. It was known, in fact, as "the wickedest city in Christendom."

When Morgan was less than thirty years old, he was knighted and appointed lieutenant governor of Jamaica. After Sir Henry died in bed in 1688, Port Royal had a state funeral for him. On June 7, 1692, an earthquake tilted two-thirds of the city into the sea. A tidal wave then came along and finished what the earthquake had started, burying pirate treasure worth a million pounds sterling. Some twentieth-century divers with perseverance have searched the murky waters of the harbor area and found some of it. There wasn't much, but the idea that there may be more is not lost on the thousands who pursue the water sports of snorkeling, scuba diving, and sailing off Kingston's reefs.

Jamaica's eighteenth century was one of prosperity—sugar cane fields flourished, plantation great houses were built for sugar barons, and the export business proved a tropical gold mine. The situation was not so bright, however, for the nearly one million blacks who passed through the slave markets during this period. The slave trade was finally abolished in 1807; slavery itself in 1838.

On August 6, 1962, Jamaica became an independent nation with loose ties to the Commonwealth. It enjoys a democratic form of government with the sixty members of its House of Representatives chosen every five years in general elections. The government is headed by the prime minister, who is assisted by a cabinet of fellow-ministers. The twenty-one senate members are nominated by the government and the opposition party and appointed by a governor-general, who technically represents the queen but whose duties are purely ceremonial.

With the election of Michael Manley in 1976, Jamaica entered a state of economic crisis. He visited Moscow and Havana, flirted with left-leaning countries of the Third World for financial support, and brought about an erosion of confidence among Jamaica's traditional western allies. Middle- and upper-class Jamaicans began leaving the country. Fifty percent of the island's hotel rooms were empty. Nearly half of the island's 24,000 small businesses boarded up their doors. There were power failures, work stoppages, and food shortages.

When Prime Minister Edward P.G. Seaga came to power in 1980, he was quick to re-establish ties with western allies, pay a visit to U.S. president Ronald Reagan, and expel officials of the Cuban Embassy.

Although inflation and unemployment continue to plague the country, tourism is taking root again, and Jamaicans have hopes for the future.

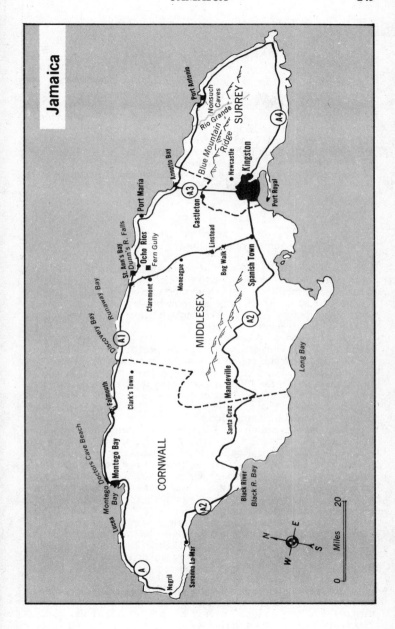

Jamaica

EXPLORING JAMAICA

Most maps of Jamaica show highway names—like A1, A2, and A3—but very few roads have anything remotely resembling a marker. Highways apparently had signs at one time, but these have been knocked or blown down by storms and never replaced. Most Jamaicans along the roadside are happy to give directions. However, when they tell you to "go straight" and the road branches either left or right, they mean "follow the main highway." In most instances, they'll nod their heads in the direction they mean. Roads are narrow and winding, but generally good. Still, some have potholes deep enough to damage a tire, so be careful. And remember to drive on the left!

Kingston

This capital city is often bypassed by visitors other than businessmen, but it does have a number of interesting attractions, particularly cultural ones.

Some of the island's finest hotels are located in Kingston, and those multi-storied towers are filled with rooftop restaurants, English pubs, jazz clubs, glitzy discos, and other entertainment facilities. The New Kingston area, formerly a racetrack, now bustles with hotels mixed in with contemporary office towers, high-rise apartments, restaurants, boutiques, and theaters.

One of the first stops on any visitor's Kingston itinerary should be the stately Devon House, through the iron gates at 26 Hope Road. Built in 1881, the mansion is regarded as one of the country's best-preserved examples of classical architecture. The government brought and restored the house in the 1960s and continues to add period furnishings and other improvements. Former stables surrounding the building have been converted into some of the best craft shops in the entire country, operated by Things Jamaican, Ltd. Also on the grounds are a popular bar and restaurant. The tree in the center of the patio is a mahogany, one of the few surviving specimens around Kingston.

Farther down Hope Road is Kings House, the residence of the governor-general, and nearby, on Montrose Road, is Vale Royal, the residence of the prime minister. Originally an old plantation house from the eighteenth century, it is one of the few remaining structures in Kingston that has a lookout tower on the roof from which shipping movements in the harbor could be seen.

If you schedule your sightseeing just right, you may get a peek at Tuff Gong International, the recording studio built by reggae star Bob Marley before he died of cancer at the height of his career. Close friends of Marley—among them "official" tour guide Marcia Sterling—take tourists through the studio. The house at 56 Hope Road is easily recognized by its exterior colored red, yellow, and green—the colors of the Rastafarian religion. It also flies the Ethiopian flag as a reminder that those of Marley's faith consider the Ethiopian emperor to be divine, the Messiah, a descendant of King Solomon and the Queen of Sheba, and a champion of the black race. Included in the tour is a look at the Ever Brown mural entitled "The Journey of Superstar Bob Marley." It is a fascinating depiction of the musician's life, the beginning of which is shown with Marley in a womb shaped like a coconut. The heart in the center represents the heart of the Jamaican people, who loved him so much.

Don't fail to visit the Institute of Jamaica near the waterfront. In this museum/library, the island story is unfolded in a series of graphic exhibits ranging from Arawak Indian carvings to living examples of Jamaican fauna. There are some fascinating old charts and almanacs here; some stranger-than-fiction documents like the Shark Papers, damaging evidence tossed overboard by a guilty captain and found years later in the belly of a shark; a number of paintings and prints; and an outstanding library.

The University of the West Indies is in a rustic setting almost completely surrounded by mountains. This institution, organized by the various West Indian governments after World War II, is a symbolic achievement of the West Indies Federation. It is the cradle for much of the new thinking that marks the independent countries of the Caribbean. The university also has a bar and disco in the student union that is open to both students and visitors, including tourists. Operated by a guild of undergraduates who pay dues to keep the joint jumping, it is decorated with posters supporting Third World causes and slogans like "Jobs, Not War." But the message over the bar seems to sum up the students' current thinking: "Democracy is based upon the conviction that there are extraordinary possibilities in ordinary people."

To gain insight into another cultural side of Jamaicans, you should pay a call to the National Gallery, which has been relocated from Devon House to 12 Ocean Boulevard in the Kingston Mall near the revitalized waterfront. On display are paintings and sculptures that trace the development of Jamaican art from the 1920s to the 1980s, including works by John Dunkley, David Miller Sr., and David Miller Jr., the "intuitive masters" (so-called because their art was created through a "gut feel" and not according to academic principles). Edna Manley, wife of the second prime minister and a co-founder of the Jamaica School of Arts, also has works on display. And so does Mallica Reynolds, better known as "Kapo," whose sculptures and paintings are among Jamaica's finest. Of special fascination to many visitors will be the controversial statue of Bob Marley by Christopher Conzalez.

For those with a fascination for flowering species, the place in Kingston is the famous Royal Botanical Gardens at Hope. Given to Jamaica by the Hope family after slavery was abolished, the gardens are part of an agricultural center and have about two hundred acres of beautifully landscaped tropical trees, plants, and flowers. They are all clearly identified. Qualified guides are on hand to escort visitors through the grounds and there are free concerts here on the first Sunday of the month. The Coconut Park and Zoo will delight the children.

Before leaving Kingston, be sure to visit the Jamaican Crafts Market near the waterfront. Here more than at any other market on the island, you will be hassled on the outside by "entrepreneurs" who want you to change money at bargain rates (don't, it's against the law); to buy "ganja" (marijuana), cocaine, and other illegal drugs or dubious "gold" jewelry. But once you make it inside, you'll find a pleasant array of arts and crafts that are for sale nowhere else on the island.

Port Royal

While you're in the Kingston vicinity, you should make every effort to make a brief call on Port Royal, the little town that was the haven for swashbuckler Henry Morgan and other villains. One of the famous landmarks is St. Peter's Church, built in 1725 to replace Christ Church, which slid into the sea in the earthquake of 1692. St. Peter's proudest possession? The silver communion plate that the notorious Morgan gave to the church. There are many monuments to distinguished early citizens of Jamaica, not the least of whom was Lewis Galdy, a French emigré who was responsible for the rebuilding of St. Peter's. According to his tombstone, he was flung into the sea during the earthquake, kept himself alive by swimming, and was rescued and returned to the devastated city by boat.

There also is a small Maritime Museum at Fort Charles, which recalls Port Royal's "second life" as headquarters of the British navy in the Caribbean. The fort's foundations were laid in 1655, the year the English captured Jamaica, and it was continually expanded thereafter. With a full complement of 104 guns, it was the strongest in the Caribbean and was never once attacked.

Spanish Town

Also in the Kingston vicinity is the historic community of Spanish Town, the island's capital during the period of Spanish occupation in the sixteenth century, and ruled by the British until 1872. Located only twelve miles west of Kingston, Spanish Town boasts the noblest Georgian square and the oldest cathedral in the Western Hemisphere—Government Square and St. James Cathedral, respectively. It was originally known as Santiago de la Vega, which was corrupted by the English to St. Jago de la Vega, or St. James of the Plains.

Port Antonio

About sixty miles north of Kingston via a winding road is Port Antonio, the cradle of Jamaican tourism. Here, near the turn of the century, the United Fruit Company came in, built a hotel, and started the migration to the beaches of the north coast. Port Antonio was the holiday capital of Jamaica before Montego Bay and Ocho Rios were generally heard of. Clara Bow, Bette Davis, Ginger Rogers, Errol Flynn, Rudyard Kipling, William Randolph Hearst, J.P. Morgan, and others of fame and fortune regularly made the Port Antonio scene. It still holds its own with celebrities. Robin Moore, the novelist, wrote *The French Connection* under a mango tree in his year, and Tommy Tune, the Broadway producer-director-actor, got some of his inspiration for the musical *Nine* while a guest at the elegant Trident Hotel and Villas.

The "must" activity in Port Antonio is not star-gazing but rafting on Jamaica's Rio Grande. The river is a swift Jamaican waterway fed by the torrents and cascades pouring down from the John Crow Mountains, and becomes navigable only as it approaches the sea. Your trip, for about U.S. $45 per raft, starts at a base near Berrydale. It takes about three hours to travel eight miles downstream to the port of Burlington, where the river flows into the Caribbean at St. Margaret's

Bay. The rafts, made of bamboo, accommodate two passengers and a skilled raftsman, who stands near the bow to guide the craft with a long pole. One of some one hundred raftsmen who make one trip each day is Nathaniel Bell—"Call me captain," he says—who has been at the helm for some twenty-nine years and can recite the history of the popular tourist activity.

It's a pleasant journey through tropical scenery, occasionally accelerated by mini-rapids. The pleasures of rafting can be varied by fishing from the raft, photographing Lover's Lane (a rock archway), or swimming when the captain pauses near some tranquil pool. You also can take along a picnic lunch and eat it on the raft or river bank. No need to take along cumbersome drinks, however. Vendors of Red Stripe beer and Coca-Cola appear miraculously around many a bend in the river. At Rafters Rest, the end of your journey, there's another watering hole (a cocktail bar) as well as a restaurant and souvenir shop.

Slightly west of Rafters Rest is Somerset Falls. Somerset is only four hundred feet, and the climb to the top of the falls is largely via a concrete staircase. If you don't have three hours to spend on the Rio Grande, there's a bamboo raft ride part way up to carry you to the main falls. The attraction is open from 8:00 A.M. to sunset seven days a week. Plans call for developing three ponds on the site to let tourists fish for perch and shrimp. Admission is charged.

Port Antonio is especially noted as a Caribbean center for deep-sea fishing. Some say it's the best fishing in the West Indies. The area, in fact, is called "the place where the big ones don't get away," and visitors have been known to pull in twice their weight in dolphins (the local fish, not the mammal) in the course of an hour, a feat that should satisfy any fisherman. It's also the home of the Blue Marlin Fishing Tournament each October. A variety of festivities enlivens the week-long event which attracts international anglers. Marlin, tuna, kingfish, wahoo, yellowtail, and bonefish also swim these waters.

Port Antonio also has what many folks say is the best "jerk pork" in Jamaica—and the place to get it is near Boston Beach. This type of barbecue, delicious wherever you buy it, was developed by runaway slaves, the Maroons, and enabled them to survive by eating wild hog during their many years of guerrilla warfare against English settlers and soldiers. Nowadays, the jerk pork is likely to be of domestic pig, but the "jerking" is still done using green saplings as firewood and special spices, one of which is pimento, as seasoning.

Worth a look—if for no other reason than its beauty—is the Blue Hole, more romantically called the Blue Lagoon. It's a favorite spot for swimmers, skiers, and divers near San San Beach within walking distance from the Jamaica Hill Hotel grounds. Romantics say it's bottomless; spoilsports say it's about 180 feet deep. Some of the island's most elegant villas, including Blue Marlin and Tiamo, are in the vicinity.

Ocho Rios

This center is another of Jamaica's resort areas. Its name doesn't mean what you probably think it does. It's not Spanish for "eight rivers"; it's a corruption of "chorreras," a word meaning spout or waterfall that was applied to the whole stretch of coastline where a series of rivers flowing from the mountains suddenly gushes out of limestone rocks to form beautiful cascades.

Most tourists coming from Kingston take the "main highway"—it's called A1, but so few road signs exist in Jamaica that it's impossible to use them as a navigational aid—through Spanish Town, through the spectacular gorge of Bog Walk, over Mount Diablo, turning right at Moneague, and proceeding by way of Fern Gully, a beautiful gorge shaded by giant tropical ferns.

The "must" in the Ocho Rios vicinity—and indeed, one of Jamaica's most famous spots—is Dunn's River Falls and beach. The clear waters of a mountain stream, rushing down through a wooded gorge, suddenly widen and fall in a transparent film over a natural stone stairway before meeting the warm Caribbean. The cascades and pools of Dunn's River can be explored from a trail that flanks the stream, but the best thing by far is to put on trunks or a bikini and get into the swim. It's a challenging six hundred-foot climb to the top, up wedding-cake tiers of stone in chilly, if not icy, water, It's not a trek for the feeble, the faint of heart or the handicapped. If you go, your best bet is to hire an experienced guide and hold his and others' hands as you climb. A guide will not only lead your way but also warn you about slippery stones. Trust him with your camera and have him take pictures as you tumble and tread your way along. Every Thursday at 7:30 P.M., there is the Dunn's River Feast where a sumptuous buffet is served on the beach near the falls. That's followed by a nighttime climb of the falls, a Jamaican folklore performance, a fashion show and dancing to reggae music.

Another special outdoor event is a night on the White River, featuring a torchlight canoe ride to a clearing along the bank for dinner and a local show.

At least part of your exploring of the Ocho Rios area should be done underwater or with benefit of a glass-bottom boat.

Lovers of flora should visit the Upton Country Club Botanical Gardens and the Shaw Park Gardens, both with fine collections. Shaw Park also has charming waterfalls. Beneath Shaw Park is The Ruins, a former disco that recently was transformed into a delightful bar and restaurant with cascading waterfalls, little streams, and a lush tropical garden.

Fans of Ian Fleming's spy novels also should visit the nearby village of Oracabessa. It's the location of Golden Eye, the villa used by the author as a winter escape from 1946 until his death in 1964. Owned later by reggae superstar Bob Marley the retreat contains 007 memorabilia, including posters from *Goldfinger, Live and Let Die,* and other movies. Situated on spacious grounds that obviously inspired some of the settings for Fleming's fiction, it has its own private beach and occasionally can be rented through Island Records.

Noel Coward's vacation residence, Firefly, is nearby, about 20 miles east in Port Maria. It belongs to the National Trust of Jamaica and is open to the public. Coward's piano is still where it was when he sang "If I Have a Talent to Amuse" for friends who knew he was dying. The composer is buried in a simple grave behind the home.

Montego Bay

Usually called Mo' Bay by anyone who's been in Jamaica more than a day, Montego Bay is, to put it conservatively, the greatest and most, in terms of both clutter and action. The Cage, an eighteenth-century jail for slaves, runaway seamen, and other vagrants, stands in the city's center.

Located between two other popular resorts (Negril and Ocho Rios), Montego Bay has grown from a rustic Indian village into the second-largest city in Jamaica. The Montego Bay area streches twenty miles from Rose Hall around the curve of the bay west to Round Hill and Tryall Golf and Beach Club. It has its own airport, Donald Sangster International, and there are innumerable gilded beachcombers of the international set who have never set foot in any other part of Jamaica.

It all began back at the turn of the century. People didn't swim in those days; they bathed. And only a few hardy souls did that. Bathing was said by some "advanced thinkers" to have a certain therapeutic value, providing of course it wasn't overdone. One of these innovators was Dr. McCatty, a Jamaican physician who indulged in bathing with other daring medical types at a beach he happened to own in Montego Bay. It was a shining, white, unpopulated strand entered through a cave. Residents who saw these physicians carrying on in this "odd" way called the beach Doctor's Cave. In 1906, Dr. McCatty donated the beach to a club he formed and the Doctor's Cave Bathing Club was established. The rest is resort history—and blaring radios, bouncing beachballs, and souvenir shops. The cauldron of humanity that boils and bakes on small Doctor's Cave Beach is a far cry from the elite of those early days. *Everyone* goes to Doctor's Cave Beach these days. Less crowded is Cornwall Beach, next door. There also is a new public beach, the Walter Fletcher, west of Doctor's Cave.

One of the most popular sightseeing attractions in the area is the restored Rose Hall Great House—and "great house" it was indeed perhaps the grandest eighteenth-century plantation house in all the West Indies. The second mistress of Rose Hall was Annie Palmer, reputed to be a sort of female Bluebeard. She is credited by local historians with murdering her three husbands and a plantation overseer who was her lover. She was done in by an unknown assailant. Her amours have been recorded in two novels, *The White Witch of Rose Hall,* and *Jamaica White.* You can take a guided tour of the property and there's a small restaurant and pub on the premises, near the torture chamber.

Another great Great House is Greenwood, built by the Barrett family, from which the English poet Elizabeth Barrett Browning was descended. It is one of several houses in the immediate area which belong to the Barrett family, who once owned all the land from Rose Hall to Falmouth. The poetess' father, Edward Moulton Barrett ("The Tryant of Wimpole Street"), was born at Cinnamon Hill, a private residence located on the hill above Rose Hall. Also born there was his sister Sarah, who became celebrated for her portrait (called "Pinkie") which still is much reproduced on chocolate boxes. The house has a number of oil paintings of the Barrett family, china made by Wedgwood for them, a library with rare books dating from 1697, a fine collection of antique furniture and a collection of extremely rare musical instruments (polyphone, wind organ, and barrel organ) in working order.

For rafting in the area, it's the Martha Brae River, named after an Arawak Indian girl who was credited with supernatural powers. During the Spanish occupation, she was the only villager who knew the whereabouts of a gold mine, so the story goes. The Spaniards tortured her to make her reveal the secret. One day she promised to take them there, but on reaching the river, she called on her powers and changed its course. She and the greedy Spaniards were drowned and her spirit (or "duppy," as they call ghosts in Jamaica) guards the entrance to the mine to this day. A rafting tour—similar to the one on the Rio Grande, but not as long—is available on this gentle river.

If you'd like to see the hills and inland countryside from Montego Bay, the Governor's Coach Tour is a special way. A diesel rail car, the "Governor's Coach," takes you through small Jamaican villages, past banana and coconut plantations, through coffee groves, and as far south as the Appleton Rum). A picnic lunch by the river, rum punch, and breathtaking scenery makes for a most enjoyable day.

Cockpit Country

The Cockpit Country, with its strange pitfalls and potholes carved into limestone by some ancient geological force, is one of the most primitive sections of the whole West Indies. It was there that fugitive slaves of the Spanish took refuge from the conquering English in 1665. From hideouts in these impregnable hills, they waged such relentless guerrilla warfare against the new invaders that the English called for a cease-fire in 1735, on the ex-slaves' terms. The descendants of these unsubdued slaves, the Maroons, live to this day in the Cockpit, free of taxation and other government interference in their affairs, their rights guaranteed by treaty. Only in the event of a capital crime can they be called to account by the government (and we've been told there hasn't been one in two hundred years). Just fifteen miles from Montego Bay, this is the historical "Land of Look Behind," where pairs of British colonials rode back-to-back on a single horse to avoid being ambushed by these fierce fighters for freedom. The Maroons—there are about five thousand of them—are ruled by one of their number known as the colonel, and you should send word ahead before entering their country. The country can be explored on horseback (or gazed upon from a helicopter), and some adventurous tourists have been known to enter from Good Hope. Ask the Jamaica Tourist Board about minibus tours from Montego Bay to Accompong.

Negril

Situated on the western tip of the island, this area grew so slowly that for years it was "Jamaica's best-kept secret." But now that it has become a haven for water sports and the very casual, sybaritic life, it has come into its own. Its accommodations are similar to those the Club Meds offer, with activities planned around the clock. Negril is the place to lead an unfettered beachside life on a seven-mile stretch of glorious sands.

Natural foods and a naturist beach are all part of the scheme of things at Negril today. Scuba diving, snorkeling, sailing, windsurfing, parasailing, and swimming are the daytime activities, and the sorts who like this side of the island keep on playing outdoors even when an occasional storm blows in. A caftan or shirt over your bikini is the proper attire for dining and dancing after sundown.

Mandeville

As you approach Mandeville, you may be reminded of the rolling hills and valleys of Devonshire. The illusion is quickly spiked by the sharp, fanlike outlines of palm fronds and, if the season is right, the red flame of poinciana blossoms and the oranges and grapefruits in the citrus groves. Mandeville has its village green, its Georgian courthouse, its neat cottages and gardens, and above all, its parish church, whose tall steeple would be perfectly at home in the Midlands. The climate is crisper here.

This could be the garden capital of Jamaica. There are private gardens, and each summer there is an exhibit by the Jamaica Horticultural Society. This is the center of the island's citrus industry; in season, the colorful market in the busy town square overflows with the fruits and flowers of this tropic soil.

Less "touristed" and therefore much less expensive than the better-known Jamaican resorts, Mandeville has hill-country isolation and back-country village charm. Horseback riding, cycling, croquet, hiking, tennis, and golf are the diversions here, and you feel more like engaging in them in the cool temperatures. If you want something more active, descend to the coast for deep-sea fishing. Headquarters is the Blue Water Fishing Club at Whitehouse. Prize catches of marlin, tarpon, kingfish, and wahoo have been made in these waters, which rival those off Port Antonio for game fish.

Center for once-popular crocodile hunting (now prohibited) is Black River, the town at the mouth of its namesake stream, the largest navigable river in Jamaica. It has excellent freshwater fishing. The marshy banks of Black River are home for what the people and even the tourist office call alligators, but their snouts are longer and narrower than an alligator's, and their lower teeth clamp shut into marginal notches as do those of a crocodile (not into pits as alligators' do).

PRACTICAL INFORMATION FOR JAMAICA

FACTS AND FIGURES. Jamaica is the third-largest of the Caribbean islands and the largest of the English-speaking ones. While English is the official language, a local dialect, Creole, is also widely spoken. It is basically English in vocabulary and grammar but contains features derived from a variety of African languages, Spanish, and French. With 4,243 square miles, Jamaica measures 146 miles from east to west and between 51 and 22 miles from north to south. Its population presently is estimated at 2.5 million, with half of it in the capital city of Kingston and the surrounding metropolitan area. The country's motto, "Out of Many, One People," refers to a population that is predominantly African and Afro-European in origin, with minority elements coming from the United Kingdom, Indian, China, Syria, Portugal, and Germany.

Temperatures generally range from about 80–95 degrees in the lowlands to about 40 in the mountains. Average rainfall can be above 80 inches.

Agriculture is a major industry, particularly sugar cane and its byproducts of rum and molasses. Other major farm products include bananas, pimento, and coffee. Bauxite mining provides much employment, but the island's mountain ranges are also rich in limestone, marble, pophyry, alabaster, shale, and sandstone. Tourism, on the other hand, is rapidly becoming the main contributor to the national income.

WHEN TO GO. Anytime. But rates are highest in winter (mid-December to mid-April) and cheapest in summer (mid-April to mid-December). Although it is hot all year, the climate is very pleasant and healthy, with extremes tempered by the breezes from the northeast trade winds. Jamaica doesn't have seasons like spring, summer, autumn, winter; temperatures are fairly consistent year-round. The average annual temperature is 80 degrees F, with November and April being the coolest months (but still in the pleasant 70s and 80s). The official hurricane season begins June 1 and continues into October. Throughout this period, you must be prepared for the possibility of a hurricane. Rainy seasons are May/June and October.

 PASSPORTS AND VISAS. Passports are not required for U.S. and Canadian citizens; however, every visitor must have some proof of citizenship (birth certificate or voter's registration card will do—a driver's license will *not*). British visitors must have a passport, but visas are not required. You must have sufficient funds to maintain yourself on the island, as well as a return or ongoing ticket.

To facilitate the visitor's arrival in Jamaica, declaration forms are distributed in flight and customs formalities are kept to a minimum. Virtually everyone is searched upon arrival. In addition to looking for illegal drugs, officers check to see that you don't bring in such restricted items as fresh fruits, flowers, or meat. Canned fruits and vegetables are okay.

Jamaican law also prohibits bringing arms or ammunition onto the island. Visitors carrying a weapon must declare it upon arrival and surrender it to customs authorities. Firearms are returned on departure from the island.

Caveat: Jamaica is very strict about drugs. Possession of "ganja" (marijuana) may get you a jail cell, and you'll most certainly be deported. Above all, don't try to smuggle it out of the country. The authorities are onto all the tricks, including packing it inside pumpkins and sending it home by mail. Coast guard patrols have been strengthened and sniffer dogs that can detect the smell of "ganja" have been introduced at Montego Bay and Kingston airports.

 MONEY. Jamaican dollars are used here, so when prices are quoted in dollars, double-check to see if they mean U.S. or Jamaican. The Jamaican dollar at press time was worth about 20 cents, or JDS $5.00 = U.S. $1.00. Open-market exchange rates fluctuate, and visitors are advised to check the newspapers for the buying rates of foreign currency.

New regulations stipulate that Jamaican currency must be used when paying for anything. Currency can be exchanged at airport bank counters, currently exchange bureaus, or any commercial banks. Be sure you get a receipt. Banks generally are open between 9:00 A.M. and 2:00 P.M. Mon.—Thur. and 9:00 A.M. -noon and 2:30 P.M.-5:00 P.M. Fri.

A receipt will be issued for the exchange transaction, and must be retained to enable you to reconvert Jamaican currency not spent on the island. Only airport bank counters are authorized to reconvert. It is against the law to take Jamaican currency into or out of the country.

WHAT WILL IT COST?

A typical day on Jamaica for two persons during the winter season will run:

	US$
Hotel accommodations at one of the resort areas	$105
Breakfasts at the hotel	15
Lunches at a moderate restaurant	20
Dinners at the hotel or in town	50
Taxes, tips, and service charges	10
Car rental or all-day sightseeing for one day	45
Total	$245

HOW TO GET THERE. By air. Visitors staying in Ocho Rios and Runaway Bay–area hotels, in addition to those at Montego Bay or in the Round Hill–Tryall area or even Negril, will find Montego Bay's Donald Sangster International Airport the most convenient. Visitors to Port Antonio and Kingston will find Kingston's Norman Manley Airport the most convenient. When you arrive at either airport, you can take the shuttle service of *Trans Jamaican Airlines.*

From New York, *American Airlines,* and *Air Jamaica* fly nonstop. *Air Jamaica* and *Eastern* come in from Miami; *BWIA* from San Juan, and *Aeroflot* from Havana. Air Jamaica, the country's national carrier, provides the most frequent services between U.S. cities and the island. They also fly from Toronto. *Air Canada* flies in from Montreal and Toronto. *British Airways* and Air Jamaica come across the Atlantic from London.

By sea. More than 200 cruise-ship calls are made yearly in Jamaica, mostly by ships leaving Miami, Tampa, or Port Everglades on a weekly basis. Cruise ships come in to Montego Bay, Ocho Rios, and Port Antonio. Many of the cruise lines offer land packages before and after the voyage, and a variety of excellent tours ashore are offered in each port. One of the newer cruises goes around the island, stopping at Morant Bay, Lucea, Savannah-la-Mar, and other cities not normally called on.

AIRPORT TAX AND OTHER CHARGES. The airport departure tax is JM $10. An accommodation tax is now in force. This tax is charged for each day you occupy a hotel room. It can range from $4–6, depending on the hotel's category. The smallest charge generally applies to facilities that have fewer than 50 rooms. Some hotels add a 10–15% service charge; others leave it up to your good judgment.

 TELEPHONES AND EMERGENCY NUMBERS. The area code for Jamaica is 809. Police and Air-Sea Rescue, 119; Fire department and ambulance, 110. The numbers are valid for the entire island.

 **HOTELS.** No matter what you desire in accommodations, Jamaica has it all—no fewer than 10,000 rooms in hotels, inns, and guesthouses. If you wish to visit between mid-December and mid-January, book reservations well in advance—at least six to eight weeks. After mid-January there's usually a lull and you can find accommodations on relatively short notice. The plush resort hotels generally are on the north shore in the Montego Bay, Ocho Rios, and Port Antonio area. Negril, on the westernmost point of the north shore, and Mandeville, in the hills, offer the best deals for those on a budget. Kingston, the capital city, offers splendid accommodations for the business traveler and conventioneer, but next to nothing for the tourist in search of a barefoot-by-the-sea holiday.

During the past year, the number of Club Med-style "all-inclusive" vacation resorts has doubled in Jamaica. These offer some of the best holiday bargains anywhere in the Caribbean, operating according to a prepaid plan which includes everything from accommodations and all meals to drinks, cigarettes, and activities.

One of Jamaica's lesser-known bargains is a relatively new program called "INNside Jamaica." Similar to the "Inns of Jamaica" program of the 1970s, it is a seven-day package that gives tourists a chance to choose two or three hotels in different resort areas of Jamaica. If you desire you can sleep in as many as seven different places during the week. It costs U.S. $245 per person, double occupancy, for eight days and seven nights. If you want a car, that can be arranged for an extra U.S. $180 and a refundable deposit of $400. You pay for your own gas and insurance. "INNside Jamaica" doesn't include air fare, room taxes, service charges, or departure tax, but it does include as many as five sightseeing excursions and entertainment in accordance with the offerings of the inns you stay at. Meals (breakfasts and dinners) are U.S. $28 per person daily. Some 25 small hotels—most of them with less than 50 rooms—participate in the program, among them the *Charela Inn* in Negril, the *Mayfair* and *Four Seasons* in Kingston, the *Silver Seas* and *Pineapple Penthouse* in Ocho Rios, the *Silver Spray Club* and *Caribbean Isle* in Runaway Bay, and the *Cariblue* and *Royal Court* in Montego Bay. For information, contact the Jamaica Tourist Board.

Following are some hotel accommodations by area. For double occupancy during the peak winter season, we call $200 and above *Deluxe;* $150–99 *Expensive;* $90–149 *Moderate;* and anything below that *Inexpensive.*

FALMOUTH

Trelawny Beach Hotel. *Moderate.* Box 54, Falmouth. Tel. 954–2450. This 350-room self-contained resort soars up seven stories over four miles of white-sand beach. All rooms are air conditioned and have either an ocean or a mountain view. Two dining rooms, tennis courts, swimming pool, complimentary use of water-sports equipment. This resort now operates under the all-inclusive vacation package format.

KINGSTON

Wyndham New Kingston. *Expensive.* Box 83, Kingston 5. Tel. 926–5430. Formerly the New Kingston, this property has been taken over by the Wyndham Hotel Co and now offers 400 rooms divided between the main 17-story high rise and 7 cabana buildings surrounding the olympic-size pool and gardens. Conference facilities for up to 800, meeting rooms, tennis courts, health club. Three restaurants, including Emperor's Orchid (oriental) and Ristorante de Amore (Italian). Two bars and disco in Jonkanoo Lounge.

Jamaica Pegasus. *Expensive.* Box 333, Kingston 5. Tel. 926–3690. 324 rooms, all air-conditioned, in a 17-story complex near downtown. The plan was to make it a special convention center for Kingston, and today it offers meeting rooms that can accommodate 1,000 people. Facilities include audio-visual services, a variety of restaurants, cocktail lounges, shops, a swimming pool, jogging track, health club and tennis courts. A special tour desk is available to make arrangements for golf, and sightseeing. English-style pub with inexpensive food and frequently outstanding jazz;

Hotel Oceana. *Moderate.* Box 986, Kingston. Tel. 922–0920. This is another high-rise commercial property in the capital. 150 beautifully furnished rooms with excellent views of new waterfront area. Near the National Gallery, government offices, ferry to Port Royal. Caters to conventions; eight meeting and banquet rooms for groups of up to 1,200; cocktail lounge, shopping arcade, swimming pool. Meals not included.

Mayfair Hotel. *Inexpensive.* Box 163, Kingston. Tel. 926–1210. 28 rooms—some with air conditioning, some with private bath—on West King's House Close, near historic Devon House. A quiet, informal guesthouse that is a former great house set in lovely tropical gardens. Meals not included.

Terra Nova Hotel. *Inexpensive.* 17 Waterloo Rd., Kingston. Tel. 926–9334. 34 air-conditioned rooms on beautiful grounds. The main part of the hotel once was a private home. Swimming pool; restaurant, which is especially popular at lunchtime; nightclub. Meals not included.

MANDEVILLE

Mandeville Hotel. *Inexpensive.* Box 78, Mandeville. Tel. 962–2420. This 60-room resort is delightful: shades of Victorian England set down amid spacious tropical gardens. The restaurant and cocktail lounge follow the theme. Perfect for a getaway to the past while enjoying the cool mountain air. Golf privileges at the nearby Manchester Club. Meals not included.

MONTEGO BAY

Half Moon Club. *Deluxe.* Box 80, Montego Bay. Tel. 953–2211. Celebrating its 30th anniversary in 1985, this exquisite 400-acre property is a destination in itself. Owner Heinz Simonitsch lavishes attention to detail on his resort, which recently underwent a $6-million refurbishing and renovation program. 197 rooms in suites and apartments on a lovely expanse of white sand 7 miles east of Montego Bay. Its 18-hole championship golf course is outstanding, and there's a special clubhouse at which you can dine by reservation in the evenings. Squash courts; more than a dozen tennis courts; health spa; water-sports center; freshwater pool. Buffet lunches are served on the terrace; dinner in a more intimate atmosphere; and bonfire barbecues on the beach. Includes some meals.

Round Hill Hotel. *Deluxe.* Box 64, Montego Bay. Tel. 952–5150. Under new management (Omni International Hotels), this is a beauty of a resort on a 98-acre peninsula that juts out into the Caribbean eight miles west of Montego Bay. 101 units, with a choice of a hotel suite or a villa on the hill with a private pool. Landscaped tropical gardens surround them all. Dining by candlelight; entertainment in the evening; tennis; horseback riding; water sports—everything for the good life.

Tryall Golf and Beach Club. *Deluxe.* Sandy Bay, Hanover. Tel. 952–5110. Another world of elegance and atmosphere 12 miles west of town. Accommodations are in the hilltop great house of a former plantation estate or in 50 private villas that make up part of the hotel. Excellent commissary for those in villas, plus regular food-shopping excursions weekly. Magnificent 18-hole championship golf course which slopes down and around the sea. The club is on its own bay, but doesn't have much beach. That will change when the $84,000 beach improvement project is finished. Large pool with swim-up bar and bouillon at 11:00 A.M. each day; tea at 4:00 P.M.; terrace restaurant for some of the finest dining in Jamaica. Includes some meals.

Casa Montego. *Expensive.* Box 16, Montego Bay. Tel. 952–4150. Opposite famous Cornwall Beach. 129 rooms in a building that rises nine stories. They all have terraces and a Mediterranean flair. Open-air bar; dining room; large saltwater pool; disco; shopping arcade. Meals not included.

Rose Hall Beach & Country Club. *Expensive.* Box 999, Montego Bay. Tel. 953–2650. Another of Montego Bay's self-contained resorts. There are 500 air-conditioned rooms here in a seven-story double hotel complex, each with private bath and balcony. Right on the beach, with all water sports; six tennis courts; large swimming pool; 18-hole championship golf course; gourmet dining room; coffee shop; nightclub; disco. Some meals included. This resort underwent a $3-million refurbishing program in recent months, including renovation of the Grand Cornwall Ballroom to include new audio-visual and teleconferencing equipment, and improvements on the golf course.

Royal Caribbean. *Expensive.* Box 167, Montego Bay. Tel. 953–2231. A very attractive setup, with 165 rooms in 12 buildings on the Caribbean at Mahoe Bay. The architecture is Jamaican colonial, and the buildings are neatly arranged in a semicircle around the gardens. Free-form pool; private beach; tennis; putting green; fine dining in their *Patio Restaurant* or on the *Parisienne Terrace* under the stars. A $6.5-million renovation program made a big difference in this resort, including the addition of Discotheque Le Club, open 6 nights until 2:00 A.M., and the Crown Room, a games room.

Carlyle Beach Hotel. *Moderate.* Box 412, Montego Bay. Tel. 952–4140. A pleasant setting; 52 rooms with balconies facing the sea. Beach privileges at the small beach opposite; swimming pool; popular restaurant and pub, with entertainment during the winter season. Meals not included.

Doctor's Cave Beach Hotel. *Moderate.* Box 94, Montego Bay. Tel. 952–4355. Convenient location with 79 air-conditioned rooms opposite the beach. Freshwater pool; restaurant with good food and service; entertainment; options for water sports. Some meals included.

Jack Tar Village. *Moderate.* Box 144, Montego Bay. Tel. 952–4340. This 128-room hotel, high above the water on the outskirts of town, is a typical Jack Tar property, in that the village operates on an all-inclusive, seven-day stay. All water sports; terrace restaurant; beachside bar; snackery; entertainment; casual living within. Weekly rates are $875 for a single, $700 per person for a double. All meals and extras included.

Sandals Resort Club Beach. *Moderate.* Box 100, Montego Bay. Tel. 952–5510. This hotel with 173 air-conditioned rooms overlooking magnificent expanse of private white beach also operates on an all-inclusive, seven-day stay. Price of $1,000 a week per couple includes airport transfers, government taxes, unlimited use of all sports equipment; Jacuzzi and sauna; aerobics classes; oversized swimming pool; self-serve juice bar; entertainment; masquerade, beach, and other theme parties. All meals and extras included.

Montego Bay Club Resort. *Inexpensive.* White Sands, Montego Bay. Tel. 952–4310. 79 air-conditioned studio rooms and suites; rooftop swimming pool, beach rights, restaurant near promenade of specialty shops, tour desk. No meals included.

Upper Deck. *Inexpensive.* Box 16, Montego Bay. Tel. 952-5120. Unique setting high above bay. 109 rooms on three floors, all with full kitchens or kitchenettes. A powder house used by Admiral Nelson in 1782 serves as the commissary. Grill and bar face the bay and offer splendid sunsets with meals and drinks. Swimming pool to keep you cool; beach privileges below. No meals included.

Verney House. *Inexpensive.* Box 18, Montego Bay. Tel 952–1677. Informal and friendly atmosphere here, with 29 balconied rooms overlooking the bay. Spacious gardens around the hillside; nice dining room; swimming pool with bar. No meals included.

NEGRIL

Coconut Cove Hotel. *Expensive.* Box 12, Negril. Tel. 957–4216. These 32 apartment-like units at Rutland Point are on the famous seven-mile strip of beach. Near highway, but hidden away in acres of attractive grounds with tropical flowers and coconut palms. You have a choice of one- or two-bedroom units, many split level with kitchen facilities. In the process of major refurbishing; may provide cooks as well as maids for guests. New restaurant being installed. Beach bar; freshwater swimming pool; complimentary lounge chairs, snorkeling, Sunfish sailing, tennis. Great place for breakfast on the beach. Casual attire; caftan over bikini is considered "dressed." Next door to Hedonism II. Can be *Moderate* if you share one of the larger units, which easily accommodate four. Some meals included.

Hedonism II. *Expensive.* Box 25, Negril. Tel. 957–4200. A 280-room resort where informality and action are foremost. At Rutland Point on the west end of Jamaica. The rooms are in two-story building stretched around the sea. The premise is total hedonism and the concept Club Med–style—every activity and every form of entertainment you can think of. Virtually everything but phone calls and personal laundry are included in weekly package—and that even includes unlimited drinks and cigarettes. Six lighted tennis courts; swimming pool with whirlpool; parasailing; water skiing; Nautilus equipment; library; daily activities; nightly entertainment; one of the best discos in all of Jamaica. No tipping and no guests under 16 years of age.

Charela Inn. *Moderate.* Box 33, Westmoreland. Tel. 957–4277. Intimate, quiet inn with ten air-conditioned rooms with either balcony or covered patio. Near highway, but can hardly be seen. Small, charming, reasonably priced restaurant that combines Jamaican and French cuisine; excellent selection of French wines to complement five-course dinners; enticing crepes, imaginative quiches, and great tarts. Includes some meals.

Sundowner. *Moderate.* Box 5, Negril. Tel. 457–4225. Not luxurious, but perfect if you're a water person. Just 26 rooms on a seven-mile arc at Long Bay Beach, with a pleasant restaurant and every opportunity for a quiet getaway. This traditional favorite emphasizes water sports and will encourage you to do so. Scuba diving is the highlight.

OCHO RIOS

Couples. *Deluxe.* Tower Isle, St. Mary. Tel. 974–4271. A complete, self-contained property on private, palm-lined beach. All-inclusive package (no fewer than seven days permitted) offers everything you could imagine or want. All 152 rooms, including eight "villas," have private bath, balcony, or patio with a view of mountains or the sea. But it's for couples only; no singles, no children. No TV either, but lots of daily and nightly activities, including American vs. Canadian volleyball competitions, staff and guest talent shows, reggae and disco dancing. All water sports; swimming pool; special island for nude sunning; tennis courts; fully equipped Nautilus gymnasium; even deep-sea fishing included in the price. Weight-watcher's nightmare: bountiful breakfast buffets, large lunches, filling dinners, midnight snacks, and all the booze you can drink. Cigarettes are free, too. Gracious staff. Highest occupancy rate of any resort on the island; many repeaters. Figure $1,820 per couple per week during the winter; slightly less off season and during certain winter weeks.
  Plantation Inn. *Deluxe.* Box 2, Ocho Rios. Tel. 974–2501. Delightful resort estate that looks like something out of "Gone With the Wind." Plantation house is at street level; the beach a steep climb below—but you get a dramatic perspective of the seas from your balcony. 82 beautifully appointed rooms; dining and dancing by candlelight on the veranda; fine shops; tennis courts. A memorable place to stay! Some meals included.
  San Souci Hotel. *Deluxe.* Reserve through First Resort Corp., 200 Madison Ave., N.Y., N.Y. 10014. Tel. 212–689–3048 or toll free outside New York 800–235–3505. Extensive refurbishing of 80 rooms and suites of one, two, and three bedrooms, each with private balcony or patio overlooking the sea; kitchenettes in some units. Newly refurbished in elegant, tropical decor throughout. Unusual bar and restaurant; two swimming pools—one fed by mineral springs, the other freshwater—private beach; full scuba and watersports facilities; 12 all-weather tennis courts. No meals included.
  Americana Ocho Rios. *Expensive.* Box 100, Ocho Rios. Tel. 974–2125. A towering 325-room hotel that soars 11 stories over a white-sand beach. It's a bit of an extravaganza, with five restaurants, two swimming pools, tennis courts, a variety of water sports. No meals included.
  Eden II. *Moderate.* Mammee Bay, Box 51, Ocho Rios. Tel. 972–2300. Jamaica's newest all-inclusive resort, formerly the Jamaica Hilton, is for adult couples only. Reasonable ($995 per person, 7 nights), includes all meals, drinks, wine, activities, tips, and taxes. Located on a fine stretch of beach, the resort also offers all water sports including scuba, 5 tennis courts, fitness center, sightseeing tours, greens fees and transfers to golf course nearby, horseback riding. 265 rooms with private balconies.
  Ocho Rios Sheraton. *Moderate.* Box 245. Tel. 974–2201. The largest resort in Ocho Rios, with 370 rooms, on the beach, with all expected mass-market amenities and activities for unadventurous travelers. No meals.
  Shaw Park Beach Hotel. *Moderate.* Box 17. Tel. 974–2552. 118 rooms, smaller full service, all-activity beachfront resort popular with the U.S. market seeking sand and sea. Bar, restaurant, disco, tennis.

PORT ANTONIO

Marbella Club at Dragon Bay. *Deluxe.* Box 176, Port Antonio. Tel. 993–3281. Formerly the Dragon Bay Hotel, this 99-room condo/villa colony is set on 45 acres facing the bay. Prince Alfonso Hohenloe, whose original club put Marbella on the map, has introduced his style to Port Antonio. 33 tastefully furnished villas, all with three bedrooms, three baths, living room, kitchen, and roomy terrace (they can be subdivided to fit your needs); housekeeper daily; you can have meals in your villa, in the courtyard near the greenhouses, or at the beach restaurant. Lots of steps, so elderly may have difficulty. International clientele. Refined cuisine; health programs that combine special menus and exercises; day and night sports and entertainment; beach barbecues; hilltop disco free to club guests and those of other resorts in vicinity, but locals pay.

Plans to be first resort in Port Antonio to install televisions; U.S. programming and five video movies a day. Some meals included.

Trident Villas and Hotel. *Deluxe.* Box 119, Port Antonio. Tel. 962–3265. Among the most elegant accommodations in Jamaica. 12 one-bedroom villas, 14 junior suites, and two others fit for royalty and celebrities, both of which patronize the resort. Exquisite grounds. Spacious, some suites with sitting rooms, porches, balconies, and giant bathrooms. A bit stiff with all the white gloves and silver tureens, but food in the dining room rates with the best in the Caribbean. No choices for dinner. Completely refurbished since Hurricane Allen hit in 1980—and done to perfection. Hideaway for celebrities. Mrs. Errol Flynn has a small boutique on the premises. Jacket and tie a must after 7:00 P.M. You may even feel like dressing to traipse to the pool! Some meals included.

Jamaica Hill Resort. *Expensive.* Box 26, Port Antonio. Tel. 993–3286. This is a luxurious, cottage-style hotel with 44 one-bedroom suites and two-bedroom villas (some split level) spread across flowering and colorful tropical gardens (with plants and trees identified). Air-conditioning; ceiling fans; wicker and rattan furnishings. Most units have kitchens, but resort discourages use because of the mess it can create and the resort's own excellent eating facilities. Casual environment makes nearly every guest feel comfortable. Unique dining in open-air, split-level restaurant built around 100-year-old fig tree; pleasant, open-air breakfast room in blues and whites. Small pool, but beautiful San San Beach is nearby, as is Blue Lagoon for good fishing. Some meals included.

Frenchman's Cove Hotel. *Moderate.* Box 101, Port Antonio. Tel. 993–3224. 24 air conditioned rooms on 44 acres of lush tropical vegetation. Once the "in" place for celebrities. Still represents a good bargain in attractive unspoiled setting. Excellent swimming in sea and river; housekeeper to cook and do laundry; special VIP plan available. Breakfast and dinner included.

Bonnie View Hotel. *Inexpensive.* Box 82, Port Antonio. Tel. 993–2752. 30 rooms, not particularly well furnished, but a few with private verandas overlooking spectacular scenery. Restaurant on top of 600-foot hill has one of Port Antonio's best views of the twin harbors and environs. Meals are moderately priced and delicious, but don't expect anything fancy. Popular with the budget-minded. Large pool and sundeck; local calypso entertainment and video movies some evenings. Meals not included.

PORT ROYAL

Morgan's Harbour Hotel, Beach Club and Yacht Marina. *Moderate.* Port Royal. Tel. 924–8464. Brand-new resort with 24 rooms, each a different color, with air conditioning and ceiling fans, on 22 acres of beachfront at entrance to old pirate's town. Full-service marina; pier bar; restaurant; access to Lime Key Island; plans to expand to 140 or more rooms and add variety of water sports. Nice, casual environment. Meals not included.

RUNAWAY BAY

Jack Tar Village. *Moderate.* Box 112, Runaway Bay. Tel. 973–3404. Jamaica's second, and newest, all-inclusive resort of that chain, formerly the Eaton Hall Great House. Charming 56 rooms which retain some Old World atmosphere. Tennis, all watersports, beach; week-long packages under $900 single.

Jamaica, Jamaica. *Moderate.* Box 58, Runaway Bay. Tel. 973–2436. Formerly the Runaway Bay Hotel and Golf Club, this 152-room resort was taken over by Village Resorts Ltd., the group behind Couples and Hedonism II [extensively renovated]. Minimum 1-week stay includes everything in the price: meals, wine, all water sports equipment, tennis, horseback riding, sightseeing tours, disco, and more. Adults only, over 16 years.

HOME AND APARTMENT RENTALS. They have romantic and playful names like Bluebird, Culu Culu, Cirrhosis on the Sea, Heaven Can Wait, Kiki, and Windrush. They're the villas of Jamaica, and they've been attracting the famous for years. Many villas are available to ordinary tourists at weekly rates. Prices can run anywhere from $400 a week for a two-bedroom cottage to $6,000 per week for a six-bedroom mansion. The best contacts are *Villas and Apartments Abroad,* 19 E. 49th St., New York, NY 10017 (tel. 212–759–1025) and *Jamaica Association of Villas and Apartments (JAVA),* 200 Park Ave., New York, NY 10017 (tel. 800–327–5767).

HOW TO GET AROUND. By taxi. Taxis are best for short hops, tours, or seat-in-car travel for the longer trips around Jamaica. Some taxis are metered, but not all. Establish the price with the driver ahead of time. All licensed taxis display red PPV plates (Public Passenger Vehicle) as well as regular license plates. A cab can be summoned by telephone or by flagging one down. When you travel from your hotel, check with the desk about prices and make arrangements for your driver to wait or to come back at a specified hour to pick you up; it's not always easy to hail a taxi, primarily if you're in some out-of-the-way spot. Trips taken between midnight and 5:00 A.M. have a 25% surcharge on the metered rate. Taxi rates are figured per car, not per passenger.

By bus. Local bus service is good in Kingston and Montego Bay. Throughout the island, and particularly in rural areas, you'll see many mini-buses, white with blue stripes. Like taxis, licensed mini-buses bear red PPV plates. The little vans, which are rapidly replacing larger, old-fashioned buses, are a fast and inexpensive way to get around anywhere, but they usually are very crowded.

By cycles. Bicycles, mopeds, and motorcycles can be rented at the front desks of most major hotels. Rates start from about U.S. $16 for a moped and U.S. $25 for a Honda 125, with deposits of about U.S. $80 and $100, respectively.

By train. A diesel train service runs between Kingston and Montego Bay. Some old routes (to Port Antonio, for example) ended after a hurricane damaged many miles of tracks. The Kingston–Montego Bay run is a trip of nearly five hours, providing a kaleidoscope of life and scenery in Jamaica's interior.

By car. Dozens of car-rental firms are located throughout the island, but it is imperative that you reserve a car in advance—before leaving home. Cars are very difficult to rent once you're on the island. Contact *Avis* (800–331–2112); *Dollar* (800–421–6868); *Hertz* (800–654–3131); or *National* (800–328–4567). To rent a car you must be at least 21 years old with a valid driver's license from any country. An international license is not required. You may be required to put up a security of several hundred dollars before taking possession of your car. Be prepared to pay high gasoline prices. Service stations are closed on Sunday, so plan ahead. In a pinch, however, some entrepreneurs operate a black market. You'll pay enormous prices, but you'll be on your way. In Montego Bay, the operation is located near the Texaco station "by the clock." In Kingston, it near Half-Way Tree on Constant Springs Rd.

By air. *Trans Jamaica Airlines,* the island's domestic airline, operates daily shuttle flights between each of the main resorts—Kingston, Montego Bay, Port Antonio, Mandeville, Ocho Rios, and Negril. During the winter season, these resort areas are linked to one another by two or six roundtrip flights daily, fewer during the off season. Be sure to book well in advance for flights during the winter season. For schedule information, call 923–8680 in Kingston; 952–5401 in Montego Bay. There are also offices you can call in Port Antonio, Mandeville, Ocho Rios, and Negril.

TOURIST INFORMATION SERVICES. The board's main offices in the island's capital city are at Block 11, 3rd Fl., Government Conference Center, Duke St., Kingston. For sources closer to home, see Tourist Information Services section in the *Facts at Your Fingertips* chapter.

266   JAMAICA

SPECIAL EVENTS. The highlight of Jamaica's yearly celebrations occurs on the first Monday in August. This is Independence Day, and the entire population of the island turns out to participate.

TOURS. Several tour operators offer half-day tours in all resort areas on the island. Among the selections are *Great Houses:* Rose Hall, Greenwood, and Devon House. *Plantation Tours:* Brimmer Hall, Prospect, Governor's Coach to rum distillery. *River Feasts:* Dunn's River, Great River, or White River; as well as *city tours* of Kingston, Montego Bay, and Ocho Rios. Contact **Martin's Tours** (tel. 327–5767), **Tropical Tours** (tel. 952–1110), **Greenlight Tours** (tel. 926–2014), or **Estate Tours Services** (tel. 947–2058) for details. For the *Hilton High Day Tour* —dubbed "Up, Up, and Buffet"— featuring a ride in a hot-air balloon, call 952–3343.

PARKS AND GARDENS. Jamaica is a garden in itself, lush and green everywhere year-round. Of its 3,000 flowering species, 800 are found nowhere else on earth. If you're in Jamaica the last Saturday and Sunday in April, don't miss the Jamaica Horticultural Society's annual flower show at the National Arena in Kingston. Other really fantastic flowers shows abound all over the island at different times. Some of the most noteworthy gardens are:

Castleton Gardens, 19 miles from Kingston. Native flora and imported plants and flowers flourish here in the cool of the hill at 2,000 feet above the village.

Royal Botanical Gardens. At Hope near Kingston. 200 acres of beautifully landscaped gardens, with flowering plants, flowers, and trees, all identified.

Upton Country Club Botanical Gardens. Ocho Rios. Small and special, and as "in bloom" as Jamaica is all year.

Shaw Park Gardens. A special favorite for visitors to Ocho Rios. In addition to flowering gardens, Shaw has a series of cascading waterfalls to add to the enjoyment.

BEACHES. Jamaica has 200 miles of glorious beaches. With the exception of the celebrated *Doctor's Cave Beach* at Montego Bay, which is extremely popular with Jamaicans and tourists alike, most of the island's sandy spots are quiet and uncrowded. Some, however, have won acclaim for the best swimming, snorkeling, diving, etc. Swimmers seem to favor *Walter Fletcher Beach* in Montego Bay; eaters seem to go for the *Cornwall Beach* in the heart of town (it has a cafeteria with authentic Jamaican food and the beautiful Almond Tree Bar). Other popular beaches include the seven-mile strip in *Negril, Puerto Seco* at Discovery Bay, *Mallards Beach* in Ocho Rios, *Frenchman's Cove, San San* and *Boston Beach* (also great for "jerk pork") in Port Antonio, *Lyssons* in Morant Bay, and *Bluefields* near Savannah-la-Mar. The most popular public beach in the Kingston areas is *St. Catherine's.* But some of the most delightful— and secluded—beaches in the metropolitan vicinity are along the south side of the road to Port Royal. The offshore island of *Lime Cay,* also near Port Royal, is a favorite spot for local swimmers, skin divers and yachtsmen. Nude sunning and swimming is available on the private beaches of Hedonism II, Couples, Sandals, and Runaway Bay.

Water-skiers give high marks to the famous seven miles of sand in Negril, but then, it gets good grades for virtually all types of water sports. Some Hedonism II guests even windsurf in the warm rain. The Blue Hole (Lagoon) in Port Antonio and the waters off the American Ocho Rios Beach also are good for water-skiing. Most of the major hotel beaches on the north coast have excellent areas for windsurfing, snorkeling, and scuba diving.

PARTICIPANT SPORTS. On the water and on the land, Jamaica offers something for everyone. All the major hotels from Negril to Port Antonio have a full array of **water sports** including **scuba diving** operations at Negril, Montego Bay, Runaway Bay, and Ocho Rios. Divers must be able to show a C-card and should plan to bring their own equipment. Although fish life is often scarce, Jamaica's north coast offers some dramatic underwater scenery, including drop-offs, large sponges, hard corals, and other marine life—enough to provide some interesting dives even for seasoned divers. It's one of the attractions often overlooked by visitors to this country. Divers can make arrangements through almost any resort. Many of the resort hotels have designed winding and interesting **jogging** trails and are adding **tennis** courts for night play as well. Devoted tennis players will want to investigate the Montego Bay Racquet Club, which is a hotel as well as a club for local tennis buffs.

Golf is especially popular in Jamaica. There are eight 18-hole championship courses and one nine-hole to play. Most of the courses are set around terrain that offer more beauty as you accept the challenge of each hole. Fairways wind in and around lush forest, beneath mountains, at the edge of the sea, along gentle streams, and near cascading waterfalls. In *Kingston:* Caymanas and Constant Spring. *Mandeville:* Manchester Club (nine holes). *Montego Bay:* Eden Golf and Country Club, Half Moon—Rose Hall; Tyrall. *Ocho Rios:* Runaway Bay and Upton.

Fishing is especially good in Port Antonio. Licenses are not required. Deep-sea fishing for sailfish, yellowfin tuna, blue marlin, white marlin, wahoo, dolphin (dorado, not porpoise), and bonita can be arranged through your hotel.

Parasailing is one of the highlights at Negril; you can soar into the sky for 25 minutes at $15 for the flight. **Waterfall climbing**—most notably at Dunn's River Falls—is a sport unique to Jamaica.

Horseback riding is especially fine in Montego Bay, where you can gallop along the shore. In other areas, you'll trot through the banana and sugar plantations, then wind your way up into the hills.

SPECTATOR SPORTS. Cricket is the national game. International matches, called "tests," are played at Sabina Park, Kingston, between the West Indies team and those from England, Australia, Pakistan, India, and New Zealand. Football—not the American variety, but **soccer**—is the second most popular national sport. **Polo** matches are held in Kingston and Runaway Bay, **horseracing** at Caymanas Park in Kingston throughout the year.

HISTORIC SITES AND HOUSES. You don't have to be in Jamaica long before you've heard about the island's four top attractions:

Devon House, 26 Hope Rd., Kingston. Situated on the waterfront and built in 1881, this historic mansion features late 19th-century furnishings.

St. Peter's Church. Port Royal. Built in 1725. This historic church has an interesting past—including ties to famous pirate Henry Morgan. The tombstones and monuments are fascinating.

Fort Charles. Port Royal. Built by the British in 1656 to guard Kingston Harbor, this fortress was never once attacked.

Rose Hall. Montego Bay. One of the best-preserved great houses, once owned by the notorious Annie Palmer, who was reputed to have murdered her three husbands—among others. Open from 9:00 A.M. to 6:00 P.M. daily. Admission charged. Guided Tours.

Greenwood. Montego Bay. Built by the Barrett family. Antique furniture and a collection of rare instruments. Open 10:00 A.M. to 6:00 P.M. daily.

Most historic sites and museums are open from 10:00 A.M. to 5:00 P.M. Sat.–Thur.; Fri. 10:00 A.M.–4:00 P.M.

The island also has lots of lesser-known places that might be worth investigating on an extended stay. Some of them are:

Alley Church. In the southern city of Alley, this structure was built in the 17th century to serve the old parish of Vere. The charming brick building contains some early tombstones.

Bustamante House. In Blenheim, the house where Sir Alexander Bustamante, Jamaica's first prime minister, was born has been reconstructed on its site as a national monument.

Fort Augusta. A massive fortification built in the middle of the 18th century to defend the approaches to Kingston Harbor.

Halse Hall. This much-restored great house in the Rio Minho valley was built in the 17th century.

Lacovia Tombstone. The inland city of Lacovia possesses two roadside tombstones said to contain the remains of two men who fought a duel in the 18th century. The coat of arms on one is that of Spencer of Althorp, the family of the Princess of Wales.

Folly. Ruins of a mansion near Port Antonio.

If you'd like to track down these and other sites that most tourists don't see, contact the Jamaican Historical Society, 12–16 "E" St., Kingston. It organizes field trips to places of historical interest throughout the island.

MUSEUMS AND GALLERIES. Kingston is *the* place! *The National Art Gallery of Jamaica* is *the* exhibition hall. Open 10:00 A.M.-5:00 P.M. Mon. through Sat., it houses the island's most comprehensive collection of Jamaican art and is located at 12 Ocean Blvd. in the Kingston Mall near the waterfront.

Others worth exploring include:

Arawak Museum. Whitemarl, Central Village. Exhibits artifacts and the history of the island's earliest inhabitants. Open 10:00 A.M.-5:00 P.M. Mon.–Thur., 10:00 A.M.-4:00 P.M. Fri–Sun.

Fort Charles Maritime Museum. Fort Charles, Port Royal. Exhibits artifacts concerning the maritime history of Jamaica. Open 10:00 A.M.-5:00 P.M. Sat.–Thur., 10:00 A.M.-4:00 P.M. Fri.

The Coin Museum. Bank of Jamaica Building, Kingston. Exhibits Jamaican coins from long ago to present. Open 10:00 A.M.-4:00 P.M. Mon–Fri.

MUSIC, DANCE, AND STAGE. If you think all Caribbean music sounds the same, you've probably not paid much attention to the raw, real rhythm of reggae. It's nothing like calypso, with its steel bands and Harry Belafonte tones, although Jamaicans still play "Yellow Bird" to make the tourists happy. Reggae was born in Jamaica. The mento is the traditional and oldest Jamaican beat, but ska, rock-steady, and reggae have taken over. Reggae is to Jamaica what jazz is to New Orleans. Hey, mom, this is the land of Jimmy Cliff, who made a name for himself in the U.S. with the music from the midnight cult film *The Harder They Come,* and the late Bob Marley, whose ghetto beat has overcome racial, political, religious, and language barriers.

If you're fortunate enough to be in Montego Bay during *Sunplash '86*—this year's edition will be the ninth—you'll hear the finest reggae the island has to offer. Traditionally taking place in August, the event will probably be moved up to June. This four-night concert at the Bob Marley Performing Center attended by some 150,000 people begins about 8:00 P.M. each night and lasts until well past dawn the next day. It has featured performances by Rick James, Skeeter Davis, Gladys Knight and the Pips, Aretha Franklin, the Beach Boys, the B-52s, Rita Marley, Jimmy Cliff, Stacy Lattisaw, you name 'em!

If you can't make this big bash, you can find the reggae sound, mixed with other contemporary dance music, in the island's many nightclubs and discos. (see "Night Life and Bars" section).

Jamaican theater and dance also is lively—and varied. If you visit Kingston between December and March, see the annual national pantomime musical at the Ward Theatre. Drama has really flourished in Kingston over the past 15 years. You'll have a choice of several productions on most nights of the year—comedies, tragedies, musicals, revues, opera, and dance. Check the listings for such theaters as the *Little Theater, Way Out Theater* (in the Pegasus Hotel), *Stage One* and the Creative Arts Center (at the University of the West Indies). In Montego Bay, check the listings for the *Fairfield.*

In March–April, the *Jamaica Folk Singers* stage a major presentation at the Little Theater. In December, the *National Dance Theatre Company* presents a "mini" season of dance at the Ward Theatre.

 SHOPPING. Shopping in Jamaica goes two ways: things Jamaican and things imported. The former are made with style and skill; the latter are duty-free bargains. Jamaican crafts take the form of resortwear, hand-loomed fabrics, embroidery, silk screening, wood carvings, oil paintings and fine arts in other media, and rum. The fashion scene is organized under the Jamaica Fashion Guild banner, and its member companies have current fashion ideas, but others who are not members also offer independent and attractive designs. For sophisticated designs, look in at *Ruth Clarage, Ltd.* in Montego Bay. Lively and popular patterns are available at *Pineapple Palace* with stores in Ocho Rios, at several hotels, and at the City Centre in Montego Bay.

At Highgate, a mountain village on the junction road about an hour from Ocho Rios, near the Brimmer Hall Plantation, the Quakers run a workshop specializing in wicker and wood furniture, floor mats, and other tropical furnishing. They welcome custom orders.

The *Jamaican Crafts Market* near the waterfront in Kingston has a great array of arts and crafts for sale. Open from 8:00 A.M.-5:00 P.M. Mon.–Fri., 8:00 A.M.-6:00 P.M. Sat.

Wood carvings, mostly of lignum vitae (a blond hardwood) and mahogany, are seen on the road—every road! For some time during the slow periods in the sugar fields, workers in the area would try their hand at wood carvings and sell their work from roadside stands. In response to complaints from tourists who'd bought the carvings and found the pieces falling apart or in poor condition, the Jamaica Tourist Board set up wood-carving workshops in conjunction with the Jamaica School of Art. Carving instructors voluntarily give the local craftsmen advice on curing the wood properly and advanced the art.

Jamaican rum is a great take-home gift. Tia Maria, too. That's Jamaica's world-famous coffee liqueur. Rumona liqueur is the world's only rum liqueur and is hard to find outside the island.

In-bond shopping used to mean you selected an item in the store and it was delivered to your flight or boat at a much lower price than if you'd taken it with you. Problems resulted, and visitors now can take purchases directly from in-bond stores—provided they can prove they're visitors. (Liquor and cigarettes still must be picked up at your point of embarkation.) Some bargains—sometimes at as much as 40% off U.S. prices—include Swiss watches, British woolens, Irish crystal, figurines, jewelry, cameras, china, and recording equipment. The top-selling French perfumes also are available alongside Jamaica's own fragrances—Royall Lyme, Royall Spyce, and Royall Bay after-shave for men, and Khus Khus toilet water for women. (Secret of the latter's scent lies in the roots of the Khus Khus grass.)

 RESTAURANTS. Jamaican cuisine is distinctive and delicious. The national dish is ackee and saltfish, which is made of codfish and the cooked fruit of the ackee, an exotic vegetable that grows on one of the trees that was brought here by the infamous Capt. Bligh. It tastes a bit like scrambled eggs and fish. Another typical Jamaican dish is rice and peas, a tasty concoction that really has no peas at all. They use kidney beans, white rice, coconut milk, scallions, and coconut oil. The end result is delicious. Curries are hot and good; curried goat is an island favorite.

Pepperpot soup, another island specialty, is made of salt port, salt beef, okra, and callaloo, and it's greener than the sea and a hundred times as thick.

Patties are what they call Jamaica's staple snack. They can be found everywhere—and vary according to filling and price. You'll find some of the best ones at *Sugar and Spice,* 131 Old Hope Rd., Kingston. This pastry shop, which has two other Kingston outlets at Manor Park Plaza and on Red Hills, also features such tasty take-out treats as cheesecake, pizza, bear claws, Swiss rolls, pineapple and cherry turnovers, cream puffs, and fruit pockets. Patties (basically pastries filled with ground beef and breadcrumbs) are about U.S. $1.25; the other goodies, much less.

A word about ice cream. Jamaica has some delicious tropical fruit flavors— banana, mango, guava, pistachio, etc. When in doubt, go for rum raisin! Our favorite flavors were found at the *Dairy Castle*, which has outlets throughout Kingston. Second choice was *I Scream* in the shopping arcade behind Devon House. For the best in Port Antonio, try *Cool Runnins* at 20 West St.

Jamaica fruits are exotic and delicious, especially the mango. But also try the passion fruit and rose apples, custard apples, pineapple, and of course, bananas. If you come across "Matrimony" on a menu, try it! It's a marriage of slices of orange and star apples in a unique fruit salad.

Jamaica also holds its own as far as "quenchers" are concerned. Drinks made with Appleton or Myers rum are among the best in the Caribbean. Tia Maria, the coffee liqueur, also is of Jamaican origin—as is Rumona, a rum cordial. Soursop also is delicious—sort of like a milkshake.

"Need something for your head?" That's a question someone may ask you in Negril. They're not talking about a hat. They're inviting you to try mushroom tea. Say "no thanks." It's a dangerous brew. It is made from psylicybin mushrooms that grow wild, especially after the rain. Smoked, brewed in tea, and eaten raw, these "magic mushrooms" produce hallucinations that are akin to those produced by mescaline or LSD. Avoid them!

Jamaica's resort areas and capital have too many restaurants to list completely. The following are a few worth trying, but there are many others.

Kingston has the widest range of excellent ethnic restaurants in Jamaica— Cantonese, German, East Indian, Korean, and Continental. You'll be surprised at the choices available. There also are many fine restaurants in Montego Bay and Ocho Rios. Here are a few that may tempt your palate. We call $25 a person for dinner, excluding drinks, *Expensive;* $15–24 *Moderate;* anything below that *Inexpensive.*

KINGSTON

Blue Mountain Inn. *Expensive.* Gordon Town. Tel. 927–7400. On the banks of the Hope River, 1,000 feet high in the mountains, this elegant and memorable restaurant is a 30-minute, JM $40 taxi ride from Kingston, but it operates an inexpensive limousine service (JM $12, less than U.S. $5) from the Pegasus, Oceana, Courtleigh, and Terra Nova hotels. A former great house on a coffee plantation, the inn has maintained the elegance it began with in 1754. The food is continental, with each dish specially prepared. The wine cellar is extensive— some say the best on the island. Candlelight and formal (jackets and ties are required of the gentlemen and a wrap of some sort for the ladies because it's cool in the evening in the mountains). Reservations are a must! Its new German chef has come up with delicious fare. Recommended are the ackee quiche; the scallops of lobster sauteed with shallots; peppers and paprika; and the pork done with cognac and sour cream. Open only from 7:30 to 9:30 P.M. Mon. through Sat. Accepts all major credit cards.

Restaurant Korea. *Moderate.* 73 Kuntsford Blvd. Tel. 926–1428. A rare find—Korea in Kingston. While it may seem paradoxical that the capital of Jamaica has a Korean restaurant in the Bank of Montreal Building, don't try to figure it out. Just go and enjoy Bul Ko-Ki. (Bul means "fire," and Ko-Ki means "meat.") This marinated charcoal specialty can be done with beef, chicken, or pork—and comes with vegetables and rice. The house specialty, Han Jung Sik, is a seven-course dinner for about U.S. $9. It includes everything from wonton soup to lichee nuts, with shrimp tempura and sweet-sour chicken in between. Up handsomely carpeted stairs is a spacious room that seats 80. Gentle Korean music creates the atmosphere, along with clever "windows" made of rice-paper panels and scrolls of calligraphy. The restaurant also has a selection of Japanese and Chinese cuisine. It's open from noon to 9:00 P.M. Mon. through Fri.; 5:00 P.M. to 9:00 P.M. Sat. accepts all major credit cards.

The Hot Pot. *Inexpensive.* 2 Altamont Terr. Tel. 929–3906. Where the locals eat between 7:00 A.M. and 7:00 P.M. Two can easily have lunch for about U.S. $4 each—and that would include some of the best chicken south of Kentucky and perhaps a glass of carrot juice or soursop. Not a single entree is priced more than U.S. $3.30. It's not far from the New Kingston hotel district, but it's kind of hard to find; take a taxi. No credit cards.

St. Andrew Guest House. *Inexpensive.* 13 W. Kings House Rd. Tel. 926–6049. In business at the same location for 16 years, this establishment serves up what may be the best Jamaican food on the island—at a price that nearly every tourist can afford. The "atmosphere" is eclectic, at best. Calendars hang in every conceivable place. The dishes don't match. But that doesn't bother the Jamaican professionals who pay about JM $6 for a taxi ride from their New Kingston skyscrapers to have lunch here. It also has a take-out service. Allow 20–30 minutes after calling in your order. It's open from 8:00 A.M. to 10:30 P.M. daily. No credit cards.

The Surrey Tavern. *Inexpensive.* 81 Knutsford Blvd. Tel. 926–3690. Off the lobby of the Jamaica Pegasus Hotel, this English pub offers a tasty buffet from 12:00 noon to 3:00 P.M. Mon. through Fri. and open-face sandwiches and steak and kidney pie from 7:30 P.M. to 9:30 P.M. Fri and Sat. Even the prices for Red Stripe beer and Monterey wine are reasonable! And jazz groups pop in to jam from time to time. On Sundays, it's open from noon to midnight. No credit cards.

MONTEGO BAY

Diplomat Restaurant. *Expensive.* Queen's Dr. Tel. 952–3353. Old-world elegance and fine dining in an old colonial mansion. Popular with well-heeled Jamaicans and affluent tourists. International cuisine and seafood specialties are featured. Accepts major credit cards.

The Calabash Restaurant. *Moderate.* Queen's Dr. Tel. 952–3891. This 80-seat restaurant is casual—but that doesn't mean shorts or bare feet—and has a variety of seafood specialties. The "house special" is a combination of baked shrimp, lobster, crabmeat, and other Caribbean seafoods in a cheese-and-brandy sauce. Its "house drink" is an exotic combination of Jamaican rum blended with Galliano, Creme de Banana, honey, and fruit juices. It's open from 6:00–9:00 P.M. Accepts major credit cards.

Marguerite's by the Sea. *Moderate.* Gloucester Ave. Tel. 952–4777. A perfect setting overlooking the sea and the Donald Sangster International Airport. At night, you can listen to the waves and watch the lights of the planes landing. The food in this casual, 120-seat restaurant with a "garden" (translated "terrace") is excellent. Try the baked Jamaican lobster with garlic butter or the "daily Caribbean catch" steamed in coconut milk. Marguerite's Banana Split, topped with Creme de Banana liqueur, or Coupe Jamaican, topped with Tia Maria, is a good way to finish off dinner. It's open from 10:00 A.M. to 10:00 P.M., but will let you linger longer. Just get your order in by closing time. 50% discount for children. Accepts major credit cards.

RUNAWAY BAY

Country Life. *Moderate.* Box 184, Brown's Town. Tel. 975–2317. This out-of-the-way mountaintop restaurant—in the midst of a homemade bird sanctuary—is the creation of Joycelyn Melton. Its thatched-roof, open-air dining room is crudely designed and overlooks a coop of chickens, parrots, a banana quit, and a doctor's bird (Jamaica's national bird). Nevertheless, the food is superb—generous portions of boiled lobster, red snapper, curried goat, ackee and salt fish, cabbage and carrots, "Johnny Cakes (a corruption of "Journey Cakes" and like dumplings), and green boiled bananas with "Rundown Sauce" (so called "because it runs down your chin when you eat it"). The price is U.S. $20-$25 if Melton has to arrange transportation to her offbeat (and off-the-beaten-track) eaterie. It's for courageous eaters, but you won't have any problems. Accepts major credit cards.

OCHO RIOS

Moxon's of Boscobel, *Expensive.* Boscobel. Tel. 974–3234. One of *the* top restaurants in the area. It's eight miles east of the main tourist areas along the main coastal road, but worth the trip to dine on continental-style veal, shellfish or chicken in a candlelight setting overlooking the sea. You might like its motto: "Nothing's worth the wear of winning, save laughter and the love of friends." Accepts major credit cards.

The Ruins. *Expensive.* DaCosta Dr. Tel. 974–2442. Somebody else said it, but it bears repeating because it rings true. This outdoor restaurant, which seats 350 in good weather, serves three-star food in a five-star setting. Within walking distance of the Sheraton and Americana hotels, it features 21 entrees. The 11 Chinese ones are best, probably because the three owners, chef, and general manager are Chinese. You'll be struck by the 40-foot waterfall that dominates the environment. The restaurant has an attractive bar adjacent to a tree-shaded wooden deck, and you enter the main dining patios by a footbridge. Local food critics say the Lotus Lily Lobster—lobster tail marinated in sherry-and-oyster sauce with a touch of ginger and onion—is mouthwatering. It's about U.S. $21. Dress is casually elegant. It's open from noon to 2:30 P.M. for lunch and 6:00–10:00 P.M. for dinner, daily except Sun. Accepts major credit cards.

Almond Tree. *Moderate.* Main St. Tel. 974–2813. One of the most popular tourist restaurants in the resort. In the Hibiscus Lodge behind big white walls that hide it from Main St., it has some beautiful views of the Caribbean from the main, open-air dining room. Among its 20 specialties are fondue bourguionne, steak Diane, and red snapper topped with jumbo shrimp and served in a herb sauce. We recommend, however, the crabmeat milanese and seafood soup. The bar is fun; you sit in swings! Reservations are must in season. Accepts major credit cards.

Parkway Restaurant & Lounge. *Inexpensive.* Main St. Tel. 974–2667. Near the roundabout and clock tower, this is where the locals eat. Its fare is predominantly Jamaican, and its prices don't break the bank. However, they do have fine lobster and choice U.S. steak. Very casual. No credit cards.

Little Pub Restaurant. *Inexpensive.* Main St. Tel. 974–2324. In the very center of town and known as "the home of lobsters"—lobster thermidor, lobster curried, lobster grilled, and lobster Creole. No credit cards.

NEGRIL

Charela Inn. *Moderate.* Negril Beach. Tel. 957–4277. Famous for its superb five-course dinners in an elegant indoor or patio setting. It combines French and Jamaican cuisine. Specialties include French onion soup, delicious vol-au-vents, and stuffed baked crab. Dress is "informal, but elegant." In other words, no shorts or bikinis! It's open from 8:00 A.M. "onwards." Accepts major credit cards.

Rick's Cafe. *Moderate.* Negril. This legendary gathering spot on the west end road is famous for its fresh fruit daiquiris, piña coladas, giant lobsters, and bagels. Open at 9:30 A.M. daily, it's a great place for brunch—vegetable omelets, eggs Benedict or coffee, toast, and plantain. It closes at 11:00 P.M. Accepts major credit cards.

 NIGHT LIFE AND BARS. Like on most Caribbean islands, the night life is at its best in many of the resort and hotel bars and discos. The action usually gets going around 10:00 P.M. and continues long into the wee small hours.

The *Negril Tree House* and *Club Kokua* in Negril often have reggae concerts. The nameless *disco at Hedonism II* is one of the hottest nightspots on the island. So is *Epiphany* in the Spanish Court Plaza of New Kingston. Here you'll find not only syncopated reggae but also American "soul." Like their crowds themselves, discos come and go. The trick to finding the action is finding which place has a Thursday-, Friday- or Sunday-night special, like "Ladies Night"

(when women are admitted free) or "Happy Hour" (when drinks are discounted). Most discos pop on Saturdays. Some with a lot of poppin' going on in Kingston these days are *Mingles* at The Courtleigh, *Bohemia* in Half Way Tree, and *Rock and Turntable* on Red Hills Road. In Port Antonio, a good choice is the *Marbella Club* disco. In Ocho Rios, *Footprints* in the Coconut Grove Shopping Center and *Silks* at the Shaw Park Beach Hotel.

Often the best nightlife is right in your own hotel. The *Surrey Tavern* in the Jamaica Pegasus looks peaceful enough when it's serving jumbo sandwiches and shepherd's pie at modest prices (about U.S. $3) in the early hours of the evening, but the place goes berserk about 8:30 P.M. on the weeknights that jazz musicians pop in to jam. Kingstonians, who seem to have a knack for tracking down "the scene," arrive by the dozens.

POSTAGE. At press time, air mail postage from Jamaica to the U.S. or Canada was JM $.45 per half ounce and $.35 for postcards. To the British Isles and Europe, it was $.60 per half ounce. To Asia, Africa, Australia, and the Middle East, $.75 per half ounce.

ELECTRIC CURRENT. The current here is 110 volts A.C. Some of the larger hotels use 220 volts only. Most hotels can supply you with a transformer.

SECURITY. Jamaica is a disarming place—hypnotically beautiful and romantic. But don't let the exotic tropical aura defuse you of common sense. Don't invite trouble by allowing strangers on the street—no matter how friendly they seem—to "show" you around off-the-beaten-track roads in main urban areas such as Kingston. Be on guard—it may sound harsh, but crime does exist in Jamaica. Don't be an innocent abroad or you're fair game.

As in most other places in the world these days, don't leave money or valuables in your hotel room. Be sure always to lock your door—even when you're inside. For valuables, use the safe-deposit boxes offered by hotels; they're usually free.

Carry most of your funds in traveler's checks—you'll get a better currency-exchange rate, for one thing—and be sure to record the numbers in a separate, secure place. Never leave your rental car unlocked or valuables in plain sight in the car, even if it's locked.

MARTINIQUE

by
CLAIRE DEVENER

When Columbus landed at Carbet on the western shore of Martinique, he was sufficiently impressed by the island to note, "My eyes would never tire of contemplating such vegetation." The Caribs' name for their island was Madinina, "Island of Flowers," and it still applies today. Martinique is a bower of bougainvillea, alamanda, hibiscus, frangipani, anthurium, wild orchids, and other colorful blooms.

But Martinique is also a land of unexpected contrasts, a mélange of black, white, and café-au-lait people with African, European, and Indian bloodlines. Landscapes and seascapes that range from luxuriant rain forests, cascades, and black sand in the volcanic north to cactus, salt marshes, a stone desert, and fine white sand in the arid south. Small creeks and sheltered coves indent the craggy Atlantic coast while verdant cane fields and plantations cover the interior.

Martinique is peace and quiet in the countryside, *joie de vivre* in the lively capital and its resort center across the bay. It has large hotels and small inns; peppery Creole plates, subtle Oriental spices, delicate French cuisine, smooth vintage wines, and heady rum concoctions. Multifaceted Martinique draws an eclectic mix of visitors, too. You'll hear both Parisian French and Canadian French, as well as Italian, German, Spanish, Swedish, and more and more English every season. Variety is the spice of life on this tropical island.

Past and Present

Columbus didn't stay after landing in Martinique on his fourth voyage in 1502. Evidently no other colonizers could cope with the Carib Indians either, as the island remained in their hands until 1635, when Pierre Belain d'Esnambuc, a Norman nobleman and adventurer, landed with a group of one hundred settlers at the mouth of the Roxelane River. They immediately set about planting crops and constructing a fort. Less than a year later, a war party of over 1,000 Caribs recruited from all over the Caribbean attacked the settlers. But the fort stood strong and the Caribs were soundly defeated. Belain d'Esnambuc designated his nephew, Jacques DuParquet, as governor of Martinique in 1637. An excellent administrator and diplomat, he managed to keep peace with the Caribs, add to the island's population, set up plots of farm land and introduce sugar cane to the economy. Less than ten years after his appointment, Martinique was already developing a reputation as the "Pearl of the Antilles."

France and Britain fought over the colony, desirable for its important production of sugar, until the nineteenth century. Finally in 1815 Martinique was restored to France once and for all. The island became an overseas department of France in 1946 and was elevated to regional status in 1974.

A prefect, appointed by the French Minister of the Interior, governs the island, and three deputies and two senators represent the island in the French Parliament. Thirty-six representatives form the Conseil Generale, the legislative body, and forty-one the Conseil Regional. Each town also has its own mayor. Martinique has all the benefits of France's social and economic system: free schools and medical care, an excellent network of roads, and one of the highest standards of living in the Caribbean. While a small group of leftists advocates independence, the vast majority of people are very proud of being French and can see no advantage whatsoever in changing that status.

The stable economy is agriculturally based with bananas, pineapple, sugar and rum, coffee, cocoa, and spices the main crops. Tourism has become an important factor over the last decade in bringing the island the hard currency needed for its expansion.

EXPLORING MARTINIQUE

Allow at least a full day to explore Martinique at your own pace, although two or three days would be preferable. There are 175 miles of well-surfaced roads, but don't expect to get around in a hurry on this mountainous island. Local drivers zig and zag in their motorized version of a fast beguine; you may be happier leaving the driving to one of them. If you drive yourself, take it slowly and cautiously, stick to your own side of the road, and equip yourself with a copy of the excellent *Carte Routière et Touristique* (at any bookstore) which shows every nook, cranny and knoll.

If your French is rusty—or nonexistent—take along a phrase book and be prepared to use it, especially in the countryside. Just remember to start all conversations with a *bonjour* and a big smile, don't be shy about gesticulating, and you'll get along fine. And don't forget your bathing suit and camera. There are inviting beaches and coves in every direction and Martinique is scenic.

Fort-de-France

The capital city reminds many Americans of the French Quarter in New Orleans—narrow streets lined with pastel-colored houses and lacy wrought-iron balconies. The fine curving bay is a popular port of call for cruise ships and yachts. If you're staying in the Pointe du Bout resort area, it's best to take the twenty-minute ferry ride across the bay to Fort-de-France, as parking is next to impossible and traffic gets clogged in the narrow streets, especially at rush hours (and there are four since most people go home for lunch!)

Start your city tour with a stop at the Tourist Office, right on the seafront Boulevard Alfassa, and pick up one of their excellent touring maps. *Choubouloute,* a weekly guide, and the Tourist Office's helpful general information brochure, *Une Histoire d'amour entre ciel & mer,* are both filled with everything you need to know about the island, and available here.

The shops in Fort-de-France are filled with French perfume (at the best prices in the Caribbean); chic Parisian and Riviera fashions, crystal, jewelry, and other luxury items as well as local handicrafts, with plenty of good buys. The main shopping areas are along rue Victor Hugo, rue Schoelcher, and the small streets in a six-block area bounded by rue de la Liberté and rue de la République.

Non-shoppers may prefer to take a table at one of the many open-sided cafes that overlook the streets and watch the life of the city. There are over 100,000 people living in Fort-de-France, many of whom seem to have inspired author Lafcadio Hearn to write of a people "straight as palms, supple and tall, colored women and men (who) impress one powerfully by their dignified carriage and easy elegance of movement." Some of the women may be wearing bright-colored dresses, foulards, and intricately tied madras headdresses, but most will be elegantly decked out in the latest from Paris. Another good people-watching spot is La Savane, the main square and park right across the street from the ferry landing. The square serves as both a promenade and playground for the capital. It's also where spontaneous athletes pick up a quick game of soccer. Snack trucks line one side and seem to have an endless stream of patrons. Be sure to see Vital Dubray's white marble statue of Napoleon's Empress Josephine in the center of La Savane. Flanked by royal palms, she is depicted in the flowing high-waisted dress of the First Empire, and faces Trois Ilets across the bay, where she was born Marie-Josèphe Tascher de la Pagerie.

The national hero of Martinique is Victor Schoelcher, the leading French abolitionist whose efforts were instrumental in freeing the slaves of the French West Indies in 1848. On the northwest corner of La Savane, the Schoelcher Library honors his memory. There's no more elaborate facade anywhere in the West Indies. It was constructed for the International Exhibition of Paris in 1889, and its red-and-blue Romanesque portal, Egyptian lotus-petal columns and ochre-and-turquoise tiles were transported in pieces to Fort-de-France and reconstructed amidst royal palms and tamarind trees. Students and scholars hover around the library steps all day, every day, making it an ideal spot to practice your French and meet some of the local people.

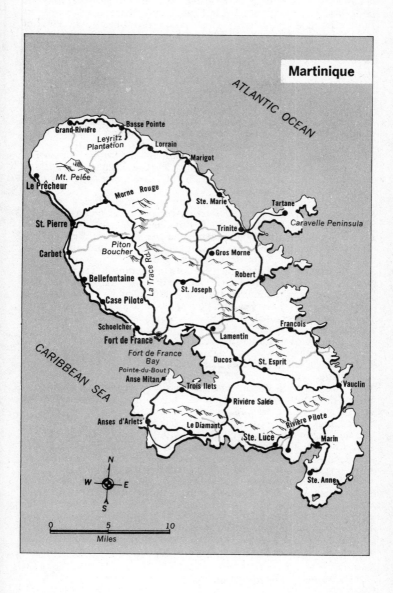

Martinique

ATLANTIC OCEAN

Grand-Rivière
Basse Pointe
Leyritz Plantation
Lorrain
Marigot
Mt. Pelée
Morne Rouge
Ste. Marie
Le Prêcheur
Tartane
Caravelle Peninsula
St. Pierre
Trinité
Piton Boucher
Carbet
Gros Morne
Bellefontaine
Robert
La Trace Rd.
St. Joseph
Case Pilote
Schoelcher
Francois
Fort de France
Lamentin
Fort de France Bay
Ducos
St. Esprit
Pointe-du-Bout
Anse Mitan
Vauclin
Trois Ilets
CARIBBEAN SEA
Rivière Salée
Anses d'Arlets
Le Diamant
Rivière Pilote
Ste. Luce
Marin
Ste. Anne

N
W E
S

0   5   10
Miles

Opposite La Savane on rue de la Liberté is the Musée Départemental de la Martinique containing some interesting Carib and Arawak artifacts as well as old documents and antique furniture. In the center of the city, at the corner of rue Schoelcher and rue Blénac, stands St. Louis Cathedral. The curious metallic spire of this Romanesque-Byzantine-style church is visible from afar.

The North, Caribbean Coast

The coastal drive from Fort-de-France up to St. Pierre (just over twenty miles) is Martinique's classic tourist promenade. The entire circuit can be made in three hours, but it's far more pleasant to enjoy a leisurely lunch along the seaside in St. Pierre then return through Morne Rouge, in the shadow of Mt. Pelée, and the tropical rain forest.

Just past the first northern suburb of Fort-de-France is the fishing village of Fond Lahaye. On its beach you'll see a rare *cocotier à deux têtes,* a two-headed coconut palm.

Leaving Fond Lahaye, the road climbs steeply, offering sweeping views of the Caribbean, and then descends to the picture-postcard villages of Case-Pilote and Belle-Fontaine. Colorful fishing boats carved from gum trees (gommiers) line the shore. Farther north is Carbet, where Columbus landed. Gauguin also lived and painted nearby in 1887. The small museum honoring the artist is worth a visit.

Exploring the ruins of St. Pierre is both fascinating and sobering. The prosperous and cultivated city, once called the "Paris of the West Indies," was buried under an avalanche of fiery cinders and ash in just three minutes after Mt. Pelée erupted at 8:00 A.M. on May 8, 1902. Over 30,000 people perished in the flames and noxious fumes. The only survivor was a prisoner being held in an underground jail cell. Today you can see broken statues toppled from villa gardens and boulevards that eerily vanish beneath a tangle of tropical growth. It is now a sleepy little town of 6,000 residents and little activity. Visit the Musée Volcanologique on its main street. The museum, founded by an American, Dr. Franck Perret, documents the disaster with pictures of the city before the eruption and many relics dug from the debris, including several contorted clocks and watches stopped at 8:00 A.M.

You might want to continue north just a couple of miles to the road's end and Prêcheur, the pretty, historic village where Mme. de Maintenon, Louis XIV's second wife, spent her childhood. There's also an eighteenth-century church and monument honoring Jacques DuParquet, one of the island's most important colonizers.

Return to St. Pierre and head inland for two miles to Morne Rouge, in the shadow of Mt. Pelée. It is possible to climb this continually monitored volcano, but you'll need a guide and it will take you the better part of a day. La Trace, the winding mountain road that goes through the middle of Martinique's lush rain forest, begins at Morne Rouge and ends at Balata Church, a remarkable replica of Paris' Sacre Coeur with a panoramic view down over Fort-de-France.

The North, Atlantic Coast

Take a full day for the one-hundred-mile tour of the northernmost point of the island. Leave Fort-de-France on the new superhighway, pass the cane fields of the plain of Lamentin and the airport, then take the turnoff to Robert. This pretty little fishing village is the birthplace of Aimée Dubuc de Rivery, Josephine Tascher's cousin, who after her abduction by Barbary pirates was taken to Turkey and became the mother of the Emperor Mahmoud II. It's a good place for a swim or an excursion by fishing boat to one of the nine offshore islets.

Five miles up the coast is Trinité, the gateway to the Presqu'ile de la Caravelle (Caravelle Peninsula), a nature preserve and part of Martinique's Natural Park. An entire day could be spent exploring the byways of this hilly, eight-mile-long appendage that juts out into the Atlantic. There are calm coves for swimming on the southern shore; a lighthouse and the ruins of Chateau Dubuc at the western tip; and the fishing village of Tartane in the east, whose palm-shaded beach, small hotel and several "feet in the water" restaurants are especially popular on weekends.

From here you can return to Fort-de-France via Gros Morne, a pineapple center with excellent vistas up and down the coast; and St. Joseph whose forests, rivers, and flowers make an ideal area for hiking.

Should you choose to continue north along the coast, you'll pass the villages of: Ste. Marie, an important agricultural center and the location of the St. James rum distillery and museum; Marigot, "the flower town" with Arawak ruins and fine views; Lorrain, called "the Kingdom of Bananas"; and Basse Pointe, with more pineapple and banana plantations and an excellent view of Mt. Pelée's eastern slope. Nearby is the Plantation Leyritz, a charming country inn where you can take a dip in the pool and have a leisurely Creole lunch.

Return to Fort-de-France via Ajoupa Bouillon and Morne Route, both with anthurium plantations, and the road called La Trace, which zig-zags through a lovely rain forest.

The South

The first stop on this tour is the peninsula of Trois Ilets, a twenty-minute ferry ride across the bay from Fort-de-France (or a 30- to 40-minute drive around the bay through Lamentin and Rivière Salée). The main activity of this area is tourism, centering around the large resort center of Pointe du Bout and the smaller communities of Anse Mitan and Anse-à-l'Ane that cluster along the white-sand beaches facing the Caribbean. The village of Trois Ilets is known for its pottery, straw and wood work, and as the birthplace of Napoleon's Empress Josephine. A small museum in the family estate's former kitchen displays interesting personal papers, period furniture, even a love letter from Napoleon. Two large African tulip trees shade the peaceful grounds and there is also a small botanical garden called the Parc de Floralies.

You'll pass the Empress Josephine Golf Course enroute to Anse-à-l'Ane, where there is a tiny museum with artwork entirely made of seashells, and Anses d'Arlets, where you'll see the beach hung with fishermen's nets set out to dry. Next is Le Diamant and the Rocher du Diamant, known to the English as *HMS Diamond Rock*. This rock was actually commissioned as a sloop of war in the British Navy, who manned it with a garrison of 120 in 1804, and held it for eighteen months in the face of devastating bombardment by French coastal artillery. *HMS Diamond Rock* seemed to be as impregnable as it was unsinkable until the French floated out barrels of rum which were promptly rolled "aboard ship" by the thirsty defenders. History does not record how many British were sober when the French finally took over the rock a short time later.

The village of Diamant has a two-mile-long beach, a major resort hotel, some small guesthouses and restaurants.

Continue heading south to Ste. Luce, another important fishing center whose beaches are popular with campers. It's also possible to hike up in the Forest Montravail, where the view down onto the St. Lucia Canal is superb and there are plenty of good picnic spots. Next you'll pass through Rivière-Pilote, an agricultural area in the mountains and Marin, with its splendid protected bay. This village has a pretty main square and an interesting eighteenth-century church whose richly ornamented interior and multicolored marble altar were retreived from a wrecked galleon headed for Peru. At the southernmost point of the island is Ste. Anne, one of Martinique's most charming villages. It is well equipped with hotels, restaurants, and good beaches. Club Med's Buccaneer's Creek Village is located nearby at Pte. Marin. Several interesting excursions may be made from Ste. Anne, including a visit to a petrified savanna forest and Les Salines, probably the island's most beautiful beach, bordered by coconut palms and generally deserted except on weekends.

Head back the way you came to Marin and Vauclin, another fishing village from which hiking excursions may be made to Mt. Vauclin, the south's highest peak. The next town, François, is known for its Clement rum distillery, restaurants, and reefs. This is the location of many "fonds blancs," shallow, white-sand-bottomed basins between the reefs that are perfect for snorkeling and swimming, including one called Baignoire de Josephine (Josephine's Bath). Excursions may also be made to some of the small offshore islands by making arrangements with local fishermen. Return to Fort-de-France by Lamentin.

PRACTICAL INFORMATION FOR MARTINIQUE

 FACTS AND FIGURES. Martinique is the largest and northernmost of the Windward Islands. It is 50 miles long, 22 wide and has a population of approximately 360,000 of which over 100,000 reside in the capital city of Fort-de-France. The people speak French and Creole with English more and more common, especially in the larger hotels and tourist facilities. Martinique is one hour ahead of eastern standard time.

 WHEN TO GO. A lush land of year-round summer, this island's average temperature varies between 57 and 80 degrees F at sea level; much cooler in the mountains. Weather is warmest and sometimes rainy from September to November. During the "Season of Sweet Savings"—mid-April to mid-December—prices are 30–50% lower than in high season. Special packages such as the "Fête Française Tours" offer additional discounts, excursions, and gifts in their all-inclusive prices. Some are real bargains—as low as $160 per person, double occupancy, for a seven-night stay.

 PASSPORTS AND VISAS. For visits of three months or less, U.S. and Canadian visitors need a valid passport, or one that expired no more than five years before the date of entry *or* proof of citizenship such as a birth certificate with a raised seal or a voter's registration card, *either accompanied*

by a government-authorized identification with photo. Check your airline to know exactly what is acceptable. Citizens of the United Kingdom need passports, but no visas. All visitors must have a return or ongoing ticket.

 MONEY. The French franc is legal tender here. The best exchange rate is given at the banks. U.S. dollars are accepted in some places, but you will fare much better using local currency for meals and incidental expenses. Credit cards are widely accepted in resort areas, less so in the countryside, small hotels and restaurants. Bank hours: Mon.–Fri. 8:00 A.M.–noon; 2:30 P.M.–4:00 P.M.

WHAT WILL IT COST

A typical day in Martinique for two persons in the winter season will run:

	$US
Hotel accommodations at a large on-the-beach resort (including breakfast and service charge)	$102
Luncheon at a moderate restaurant	20
Dinner at the hotel or "in-town" restaurant	50
Tips and taxes	8
Car rental for one day	35
Total	$215

 HOW TO GET THERE. By air. Martinique's Lamentin Airport is 4½ miles from Fort-de-France, connecting the city with flights from the U.S., Canada, Europe, and several Caribbean islands. *American Airlines* flies direct from New York, *Pam Am* from New York and Miami. *Eastern* comes in from Miami, *Air Canada* from Montreal and Toronto. *Air France* serves Miami, San Juan, Haiti, Guadeloupe, Paris, Cayenne, Bogota, and Caracas. *LIAT* serves all islands between St. Thomas in the north and Trinidad in the south. *Air Martinique* flies from Antigua, Barbados, Dominica, Grenada, Mustique, St. Lucia, St. Martin, St. Vincent, Trinidad, and Union, and will also do charters in 9-seat Islander aircraft.

By sea. Fort-de-France is a port of call for all the major cruise-ship lines.

AIRPORT TAXES AND OTHER CHARGES. Most hotels include the service charge in their prices; if not, 10% will be added to the bill. A new "tax de séjour" was implemented last year that differs from hotel to hotel; the maximum is $1 per day per person.

 TELEPHONES AND EMERGENCY NUMBERS. To phone Martinique directly from the U.S., dial 011 (01 for person-to-person) + 596 + local 6-digit number. To call the U.S. from Martinique, dial 191 + area code + local number. For collect or credit-card calls dial 19–590–222. Local information number is 12. The Hôpital de la Ménard, a new, modern medical facility, is on the outskirts of Fort-de-France in Châteauboeuf, Tel. 50–15–5. Ambulance service: 71–59–48. SOS doctor: 70–42–42. Police emergency: 17.

 HOTELS. Martinique has a large variety of hotels ranging from five-room guesthouses to 15-room country inns to a 303-room resort property. Most are clustered at Pointe du Bout and Anse Mitan on the peninsula of Trois Ilets across the bay from Fort-de-France. We call in-season accommodations for two with breakfast *Expensive* if they're $100 and up; *Moderate,* $50–100; *Inexpensive,* below $40.

Bakoua. *Expensive.* Pointe du Bout. Tel. 66–02–02. A well-run, well-equipped hotel that takes its name from the pointed straw hats of the local fishermen. Two suites and 100 air-conditioned rooms are spread out in two hillside buildings and a third at the water's edge. All have been recently redecorated with island-made, rustic wooden furniture; have radio, direct-access telephone, balconies or patios. There's a bar, two restaurants serving Creole and French cuisine, nightly dinner dancing, and a floor show on Friday nights. A pool overlooking the sea, small white-sand beach, two tennis courts and a wide variety of water sports complete the picture.

Casino Hotel La Batelière. *Expensive.* Batelière, northern outskirts of Fort-de-France. Tel. 71–90–41. 218 large, modern rooms on a promontory overlooking the sea with big terraces, radio, and direct-access (though often out-of-commission) telephones. Front desk personnel could definitely be more congenial but a pleasant English-speaking hostess is on duty full time in the lobby. The poolside pizzeria/grill and *Boucaniers* terrace restaurant both have interesting menus, but indifferent service and inconsistent food too often detract from otherwise very attractive settings. Six tennis courts, roomy freshwater pool, small beach, and water sports galore keep guests busy in the daytime; a lively bar with cocktail hour music, casino, and Club 21 discothèque all draw a good crowd of local residents as well as visitors in the evening.

Méridien. *Expensive.* Pointe du Bout. Tel. 66–00–00. This 303-room hotel on its own beach is Martinique's largest. Accommodations are good size and well appointed, all with balconies. There are excellent water-sports facilities, a large fresh-water pool, and two tennis courts. Three restaurants, a lively terrace bar with cocktail-hour music, nightly entertainment, the casino and *Von Von* discothèque provide plenty of diversion for the international clientele.

Leyritz Plantation. *Moderate to Expensive.* Basse Pointe. Tel. 75–53–92. The pride of Martinique, this 18th-century plantation now offers 40 accommodations in assorted, carefully restored structures that range from an elegant manor house to rustic slave cottages to 16 new rooms constructed on the old stone foundation of the former bachelors' dormitory. Don't expect luxury, but rather comfortable country inn style rooms with antique furnishings and lots of character. There's a good restaurant, weekly dinner dancing and folkloric show, tennis court, small spring-fed pool (nearest beach is a 30-minute drive) and best of all, plenty of peace and quiet. All-inclusive 1-week and 3-day spa programs are now offered in association with upstate New York's New Age Health Farm. Fasting, personalized nutrition and beauty programs, even a 2-week medically supervised rejuvenation treatment similar to those given in Rumania are available. The new spa facilities—solarium, Jacuzzi, video lounge, yoga, and figure improvement classes; open-sided beauty salon and massage rooms with splendid views of the surrounding greenery—are also open to regular hotel guests when space permits and appointments are available.

Calalou. *Moderate.* Anse-à-l'Ane. Tel. 76–31–67/78. A 36-room inn built in a tropical garden fronting a quiet white-sand beach. There's a comfortable terrace bar, open-air dining room serving fine Creole and French specialities. Snorkeling, water-skiing, fishing, and sailing are ideal in the calm water and the staff is very friendly and makes a real effort to converse in English.

Club Méditerranée Buccaneer's Creek. *Moderate.* Ste. Anne. Tel. 76–72–72 (8:00 A.M.-9:00 P.M. only). This 300-room hotel is built on 48 acres on a point 27 miles from the airport. The Creole-style village has plazas, avenues, cafés, restaurants, boutiques, and a small marina. Pastel-colored cottages are designed for double occupancy with twin beds, air conditioning, and private bath with shower. The property borders the sea and all water sports are available. There are also six tennis courts, four lighted for night play. As with all Club Meds, a complete week-long holiday is offered for one price—no extras, no tips, aside from personal purchases and drinks at the bar. A special feature here is a complete fitness center.

Diamant Novotel. *Moderate.* Diamant. Tel. 76–42–42. This 180-room self-contained resort is set on 5 acres just 20 minutes south of the airport on the new superhighway. Excellent for families with complete water sports facilities, a large pool, several beaches, two lighted tennis courts, two restaurants, nightclub, video room, and boutiques. The staff's English is good, thanks to a training program initiated last year, and menus offer many U.S. specialties. There's a daily bus service to Fort-de-France, shopping excursions are organized twice a week, and horseback riding is nearby.

Frantel. *Moderate.* Pointe du Bout. Tel. 66–04–04. Not fancy, but very pleasant, 200 rooms arranged around a garden and the large swimming pool. 12 rooms have been upgraded to "superior" which means total refurbishing, sea views, a refrigerator, coffee maker, and TV/video. There are two tennis courts, water sports, a small beach, three restaurants, two bars, nightly dinner dancing, and a popular discothèque called *Le Vesou* that has a fabulous nighttime view of Fort-de-France from its terrace. The staff is especially helpful and friendly.

Manoir de Beauregard. *Moderate.* Ste. Anne. Tel. 76–73–40. A manor house turned inn, with 27 air-conditioned rooms furnished with antiques in both the main house and adjacent garden units. There's a small freshwater pool and sundeck, but the beautiful beach at Les Salines is just a five-minute drive, as is a smaller village beach. A large restaurant serves good French and Creole food, and is popular lunch spot for cruise-ship passengers.

PLM La Pagerie. *Moderate.* Pointe du Bout. Tel. 66–05–30. Located in the heart of the marina and within walking distance of many good restaurants and all the activities of the big resort hotels. The 100 studios are small but cheerful and some have kitchenettes. A large pool is set in the rear garden and has plenty of privacy for sunning.

St. Aubin. *Moderate.* Trinité. Tel. 58–34–77. A gray-and-white gingerbread-frilled colonial house located in the countryside above the Atlantic coast. Ideal for those seeking peace and quiet. The 15 air-conditioned rooms are decorated in modern style. There's a new pool and the beaches of the Caravelle Peninsula are less than 15 minutes away. The French and Creole cuisine of chef/owner Guy Foret is reserved for hotel guests.

Alamanda. *Inexpensive.* Anse Mitan. Tel. 66–03–19. Perfect for families. 24 spacious studios have kitchenettes on their large terraces and can accommodate two to five guests. Set up on a hill but a short walk from the beach and its sister hotel, the Caraïbe Auberge, which has a popular bar and restaurant.

Auberge de l'Anse Mitan. *Inexpensive.* Anse Mitan. Tel. 66–01–12. A very French, 20-room inn with simply furnished air-conditioned rooms, some with balconies overlooking the sea. There's also a comfortable little one-bedroom bungalow down on the sand. Meals are served on the terrace for guests and barefoot informality is the keynote.

Bambou. *Inexpensive.* Anse Mitan. Tel. 66–01–39. A casual beach hotel that's hard to beat at around $27 for two. The 68 rooms are spread out in 34 shingled chalets set back in the garden. Although rustic, they are comfortable, have air conditioning and double or twin beds. Terrace restaurant on the sea draws a good crowd, especially on Sundays when many Fort-de-France families come over for a day at the beach. Frequent barbecues, local bands, and a folkloric show provide entertainment in season.

Caraïbe Auberge. *Inexpensive.* Anse Mitan. Tel. 66–03–19. Another small, informal beach hotel where you'll probably be happier if you speak French. The 19 bargain-priced rooms are simple, immaculate, and air conditioned. Just across from the beach, with an excellent Creole and seafood restaurant, *Le Vivier* in the front garden. Hotel and restaurant are well managed and both are good buys.

Copacabana-Eden Beach. *Inexpensive.* Anse Mitan. Tel. 66–01–19. 8 basically furnished rooms on the sea and 6 bungalows set in a rear garden. Small terrace restaurant and *La Samba* disco on the premises. French is a must here.

Diamant les Bains. *Inexpensive.* Diamant. Tel. 76–40–14. The Andrieu's try very hard to please their guests and make them feel right at home in their friendly 15-room hotel. Some rooms are in the main building, others in bungalows in the garden; all are just two steps from the 2½-mile-long beach that overlooks Diamond Rock. Ambiance is *sympa* and the food is good. Excellent for families but best if you speak some French.

La Dunette. *Inexpensive.* Ste. Anne. Tel. 76–73–90. 18 comfortable but basic rooms, some with sea views from their terraces. An excellent value in a good location in the center of one of the island's prettiest villages and a five-minute walk from the public beach. The attractive, popular terrace restaurant features French and Creole dishes as well as seafood.

Impératrice. *Inexpensive.* Place de la Savane, Fort-de-France. Tel. 70–06–82. 24 air-conditioned rooms in a funky 1950s five-story building (with elevator). There's a garden terrace lounge on the fourth floor and a second-floor restaurant serving a breakfast buffet and French and Creole food throughout the day. Rooms in the front might be noisy, but they overlook all of the activity of the city's center and that makes them the best in the house.

Lafayette. *Inexpensive.* 5 rue de la Liberté, Fort-de-France. Tel. 73–80–50. 24 modern rooms popular with business travelers and visitors who need the convenience of being in the middle of town. The rooms are all individually air conditioned and have private bath. The hotel's restaurant is especially popular at lunchtime and specializes in both French and Creole cuisine. Guests have free use of the Bakoua Hotel's beach facilities in Pointe du Bout.

Madras. *Inexpensive.* Trinité. Tel. 58–21–44. 16 simply furnished, spotless seaside rooms ideal for sports-oriented, French-speaking visitors on a budget. 30 minutes from Fort-de-France at the entrance to the Presqu'Ile de la Caravelle Nature Preserve. Hiking, biking, tennis, and water sports are available at nearby Anse Spoutourne sports center, and excursions with fishermen are easy to arrange. The open-air bar and restaurant are popular with local residents on weekends.

Matador. *Inexpensive.* Anse Mitan. Tel. 66–05–36. 8 large, nicely but simply decorated rooms are built around the ground floor garden of this popular Creole restaurant. Anse Mitan beach is just down the road and the Pointe du Bout resorts within walking distance. Again, you'll be happier if you speak some French, but Raymonde Crico always makes a good effort to make all her guests feel at home.

Rivage Hotel. *Inexpensive.* Anse Mitan. Tel. 66–00–53. Maryelle and Jean Claude Riveti took over this ten-room hotel across from the beach and immediately started redecorating. Plans were to add another six units and possibly a pool. A couple can stay here for around $32 a night with breakfast. Breakfast, sandwiches, and snacks are served in the friendly, informal *Latanier* Bar. The Rivetis are conversant in English and Spanish as well as French.

Victoria. *Inexpensive.* Rond Point de Didier, Fort-de-France. Tel. 71–56–78. Country living five minutes from the city. This is a very attractive 30-room hotel located in a pretty residential area. Good food, cordial service. The pool is pleasant and breezy and the view superb.

HOME AND APARTMENT RENTALS. While the rental situation is not as extensive here as on other Caribbean islands, there are many rustic private homes that are rented to off-island visitors. The Tourist Office is your best source for information.

HOW TO GET AROUND. You'll find taxis at the airport, at the hotels, and in downtown Fort-de-France. Fares are government regulated and will be about 40% higher at night. *Taxis Collectifs* are much less expensive and run bus-like routes to points all over the island, but they are crowded and you may have a long wait. Between Pointe du Bout, L'Anse Mitan, and Fort-de-France, there are frequent (at least every hour) ferries; you pay 7 francs one way; 12 francs round-trip for the 20-minute trip.

Cars are available for rental at the airport, in Fort-de-France, and at some of the hotels. They average about $35 per day. *Avis, Budget, Hertz,* and *National (Europcar)* are here, in addition to local firms. Vespas can be rented at through *Vespa Martinique,* at 3 rue Jules Monnerot in Fort-de-France, tel. 71–60–03.

TOURIST INFORMATION SERVICES. For on-island information, visit *L'Office du Tourisme,* on Blvd. Alfassa, along the waterfront in the center of Fort-de-France. Tel. 71–79–60. Hours: 7:30 A.M.–12:30 P.M.; 2:30 P.M. –5:30 P.M. Mon.–Fri.; Sat. 8:00 A.M.–noon. For sources closer to home, see "Tourist Information Services" section in the *Facts at Your Fingertips* chapter.

SPECIAL EVENTS. The event of the year in Martinique is Carnival, the pre-Lenten celebration that includes parades, masquerades, and dancing and singing in the streets. It goes on every weekend for six weeks and ends on Ash Wednesday with the building of a funeral pyre that will "consume" King Carnival. Another special event is *Fête Nautique de Robert,* a festival of the sea that takes place in the village of Robert on the Atlantic coast in September. It's held in the evening and is dramatic as boats with lights appear in parade form.

 TOURS. May be arranged with taxi drivers who have set rates for specific excursions. The Tourist Office on the waterfront Blvd. Alfassa in Fort-de-France or your hotel tour desk will have the most up-to-date information on motorcoach, boat, or inter-island air excursions.

 PARKS AND GARDENS. *Regional Natural Park* covers about 232 sq. miles. It encompasses the northern tropical volcanic mountains, the southern highlands down to Les Salines beach, and, on the Atlantic side, the Caravelle Peninsula at Trinité. There is a great variety of landscape and vegetation ranging from flowering tropical rain forests and gorges to desolate areas and mangroves. Within its boundaries are campgrounds, hiking and bridal paths, and rural lodging facilities. The Botanical Garden of l'Estripault at Morne Rouge in the north and the new Floralies Park on the grounds of La Pagerie Museum in Trois Îlets are two more of its special attractions.

La Savane in Fort-de-France is a centrally located park serving as a promenade and playground for the capital. Newly landscaped with flowers and fountains and plenty of benches to let you contemplate the sights.

Parc Floral et Culturel, Place José Marti, Fort-de-France. Tel. 71–33-96. Cultural and floral park, aquarium, and geological gallery. Open Tues.–Sat., 9:00 A.M.–noon; 3:00 P.M.–6:00 P.M.

 BEACHES. The southern, white-sand beaches are the best. *Les Salines* near Ste. Anne, and *Diamant* with the offshore landmark of Diamond Rock are the two most outstanding. Pointe du Bout resort hotels have small, sometimes man-made beaches with plenty of room for sunning and water sports in the calm offshore waters. There are nice long stretches of sand at *Anse Mitan, Anse-à-l'Ane* and *Anses d'Arlets.* The Atlantic coast is dangerous except at *Cap Chevalier* and the Caravelle Peninsula nature preserve. In the north are the black-sand beaches of *Carbet, St. Pierre,* and *Prêcheur.* There is no official nudist beach, but topless sunbathing is prevalent at the large resort hotels.

 PARTICIPANT SPORTS. Camping is permitted in the mountains, forests, and on many beaches. Areas with facilities include Diamant, Marin, Ste.-Anne, St. Luce, and Vauclin in the south; Grand-Rivière in the northeast, and Anse-à-l'Ane on the Trois Ilets peninsula. Camping cars may be rented from *WIND* in Troil Ilets. Tel. 66–02–22.

Fishing is best arranged through your hotel desk, with tuna, barracuda, dolphin, and kingfish popular catches. **Surfcasting** is good at Cap Macré, Cap Ferré, and Cap Chevalier in the south.

Hiking and mountain climbing are also very popular with many well-marked trails throughout the Natural Park. Those interested in climbing Mt. Pelée should hire a guide at Morne Rouge. The ascent involves a two-hour hike that is often tricky because tropical growth has hidden deep crevices and other hazards. Other interesting areas include the Caravelle Peninsula Nature Preserve, Gorges de la Falaise, and the thick coastal rainforest between Grand Rivière and Le Prêcheur in the north. The Tourist Office on the waterfront in Fort-de-France has a hiking folder available.

Horseback riding may be arranged through *Ranch Jack Galochat* at Anse d'Arlets. Yel. 76–43–97; *La Cavalle,* Diamant, tel. 76–20–23 (at noon or in the evening) and *Ranch J.R.,* just outside Ste.-Anne, tel. 76–76–88.

Golfers will enjoy the 18-hole, par-71 "Golf de l'Impératrice" at Trois Ilets. The 140-acre championship Robert Trent Jones course is 14 miles long. Electric carts and golf clubs may be rented, and there's an English-speaking pro and a new restaurant. Greens fee is 125F single, 230F couple. Take a bus or taxi from Pointe du Bout hotels.

Scuba divers will find five diving schools around the island—Latitude in the north; Club Med and Diamant-Novotel in the south; Casino Hotel La Batelière just outside Fort-de-France; and Bathy's Club, which serves the Pointe du Bout hotels from the Méridien. All have licensed instructors and well-equipped dive shops. Among the island's more interesting dive sites are the wrecks of St. Pierre, Le Prêcheur, and Ilet la Perle in the north; Cap Salomon and Anse d'Arlets on the Southwest coast; and Ste. Anne and Diamond Rock in the south. **Swimming and snorkeling** are best from the beaches on Trois Ilets peninsula in the south and off the Caravelle Peninsula on the Atlantic coast. The Méridien's *Nautilius* and Casino Hotel La Batelière's *Aquarium,* two glass-bottomed boats, make frequent snorkeling excursions.

There are six **tennis** courts at the Casino Hotel La Batelière and at Club Med; two each at Frantel, Méridien, Bakoua, and Diamant-Novotel. Plantation Leyritz has one court. Most of these facilities have floodlights for night play. Temporary membership at several of Fort-de-France's private tennis clubs may also be arranged—check with your hotel or the Tourist Office for further information. The Tennis Club at the Empress Josephine Golf Course in Trois Ilets has 3 lighted competition courts open to the public for a fee. Reservations must be made in advance, tel. 76–32–81/36–87.

Sailing is very popular and full- or half-day excursions may be easily arranged through hotel activities desks. Bareboat charters are available through *Sodedro,* Pointe du Bout Marina, tel. 66–05–35; crewed charters from the above or *Soleil et Voile,* Pointe du Bout Marina, tel. 66–00–72 or *Ship Shop,* 6 rue Joseph-Compère, Fort-de-France, tel. 71–43–40. The French are fanatical windsurfers so boards are available for rent at all beachside hotels.

"Aquascopes" are docked at the pier in Ste.-Anne and at the Pointe du Bout Marina; they make one-hour underwater excursions several times a day at 80F per person.

 SPECTATOR SPORTS. If a "yole" or "gommier" regatta is scheduled during your stay, don't miss it. These square-sail fishing boats, some constructed especially for racing, and their daredevil crews are a colorful and exciting spectacle. The Tourist Office will be able to fill you in.

Cockfighting is a tradition in Martinique. During the season, January–July, these "combats" take place almost every day. Not for the squeemish, but the spectactors put on a show that far surpasses the rather bloody battle. Sometimes mongoose and serpent fights are also organized, but neither of these events is something that will appeal to the average visitor.

 MUSEUMS AND GALLERIES. *Musée Départemental de Martinique.* 7 rue de la Liberté, Fort-de-France. Tel. 71–57–05. Recently redone, this museum displays relics from the Arawak and Carib civilizations such as pottery, beads and a partial skeleton unearthed in excavations in 1972. Clothing, documents, furniture, and handicrafts from Martinique's colonization are also included. Hours: Mon.–Fri. 8:00 A.M.–noon; 3:00 P.M.–6:00 P.M.; Sat. 8:00 A.M. –noon. Admission 5F.

Musée de la Pagerie. Trois Ilets. Tel. 76–31–07. A charming stone building that was once the estate's kitchen houses mementos of Marie-Josèphe Rose Tascher de la Pagerie, otherwise known as Napoleon's Empress Josephine. Family portraits, a childhood bed and other furniture, even a love letter from Napoleon are displayed. A few yards away is a newer building, the private home of Dr. Robert Rose-Rosette, an expert on Josephine, who put together, owns, and maintains the museum. There's usually a guide, whose English may be hesitant but quite understandable, to show visitors around. A new botanical park has recently been opened on the grounds. Hours: 9:00 A.M.–5:30 P.M. daily except Mon. Admission 8F.

Musée de Coquillages. Anse-a-l'Ane near Trois Ilets. Tel. 76–31–97. Dolls and pictures entirely composed of shells depict the crowning of Napoleon, a local scene, and a folk festival. Hours: 10:00 A.M.–noon; 3:30 P.M.–5:00 P.M., every day but Tues. Admission 6F.

Musée Volcanologique. St. Pierre. Tel. 72–15–16. Founded in 1932 by American volcanologist Franck Perret. The collection includes photos of St. Pierre before and after Mt. Pelée's eruption in 1902, melted glass, twisted musical instruments, and contorted clocks, stopped at 8:00 A.M., the hour of the disaster. Hours: 9:00 A.M.–noon; 3:00 P.M.–5:30 P.M. daily. Admission 5F.

Musée Gauguin. Anse Turin in Carbet. Tel. 77–22–66. Near the beach where Columbus landed in 1502 and Gauguin lived in 1887. Reproductions of some of the artist's Martinique works, documents, letters, and books are displayed. Hours: 9:30 A.M.–5:30 P.M. daily. Admission 5F.

Musée de Poupées Végétales. Plantation Leyritz, Basse Pointe. Tel. 75–53–08. Local artisan and hotel employee Will Fenton has created a collection of dolls, made entirely of natural leaves and flowers, that represent famous women throughout French history. Hours: 7:00 A.M.–6:00 P.M. daily. Admission 10F.

Musée du Rhum. St. James Distillery, Ste. Marie. Tel. 75–30–02. In a pretty old Creole house once occupied by the proprietor of the St. James rum distillery. There's an interesting collection of old "tools of the trade" both indoors and on the grounds—cultivators, a huge copper distilling column, steam engine, even a locomotive. A slide show may be viewed and rums tasted as well as purchased. Hours: Mon.–Fri. 9:00 A.M.–noon; 2:00 P.M.–4:30 P.M.; Sat. 9 A.M.–1:00 P.M.; Sun. 9:00 A.M.–noon.

MUSIC, DANCE, AND STAGE. Don't miss seeing *Les Grands Ballets de la Martinique* during your stay. It's one of the best folkloric troupes in the Caribbean. Thirty young (mostly teenage) dancers, singers, and musicians perform. The beguiling beguine, graceful mazurka, dreamy Creole waltz, and a sensuous calenda are usually presented in a colorful tableau whose inspiration comes from the customs and country legends of the island. The show ends with the melancoly "Adieu, Foulard, Adieu Madras," the story of a Creole girl's hopeless love for a French naval officer whose orders compel him to sail with the tide—the traditional song of farewell in the French West Indies. Presented at the Bakoua, Méridien, Frantel, Casino Hotel La Batelière, and Novotel Diamant on alternating nights.

A new 300-seat Fortin Theater, tel: 66–00–00 ext. 621 has been constructed within the walls of the old fort at the end of the Pointe du Bout peninsula. Each evening at 6:15 P.M. and 8:15 P.M., a multivision presentation traces Martinique's history from the Arawaks to the present. 30 slide projectors, a Cinemascope film projector, quadrophonic speakers and huge screen combine to produce a 55-minute audiovisual spectacle entitled "Martinique, Ile aux Fleurs," by well-known French film director Marcel Carne. French and English soundtracks play at alternating times each evening. Admission is 30F.

On the stage of the new 200-seat Lotus Des Trois Ilets restaurant (tel: 66–00–00 ext. 621) on the other side of the fort, a show follows a gastronomic dinner, both of whose themes will change every three months. The all inclusive price is 230F for dinner at 8:00 P.M., the show at 9:00 P.M.

SHOPPING. Fort-de-France is a good place to buy French luxury imports as most stores give visitors a 20% discount on these goods when purchased with traveler's checks and major credit cards. Shop hours vary slightly but are generally 9 A.M.–1 P.M. and 3 P.M.–6 P.M. weekdays; closed Sat. afternoons. Shops in commercial centers remain open somewhat later.

Roger Albert, probably the Caribbean's most famous perfume emporium, is located at 7 rue Victor Hugo. Prices here are lower than in Paris, and the shop carries all the top names as well as lesser-known marques. Good buys will also be found on leather goods, Cartier and Dupont lighters, cosmetics, crystal, designer scarves and ties, and other gift items. This shop is usually impossibly crowded on days when cruise shops are in port, so we suggest coming back another day or, better yet, heading for their much quieter, but just as well stocked, branch in the Cluny Commercial Center.

On the opposite side of rue Victor Hugo is *Beaufrand*, a similar shop but on a much smaller scale. Other places worth noting on this main shopping street are *R. Montaclair, Venutolo,* and *Grain d'Or* for gold jewelry, both modern and traditional such as hoop earrings and those heavy gold bead necklaces (*collier choux*) that are always worn with "madras and foulard."

In addition to rue Victor Hugo's many fashionable shops, small boutiques carrying the latest French resortwear may be found on rues Lamartine, Perrinon, Moreau de Jonnes, Schoelcher, and Antoine Siger, as well as the Patio de Cluny and Pointe du Bout Marina shopping centers.

Shoes are also a good buy. The best selection will be found at *Siniamin* (Charles Jourdan, Cardin, Xavier Danaud, and Bally) at 7 rue Antoine Siger. For children's wear *Ti Mammelle* and *Jacqueline* on rue Lamartine; *Bebibil* on rue Antoine Siger have things for tots to teens that are both chic and *cher,* but not nearly so expensive as they would be at home.

Local antiques are scarce, but *La Malle des Indes* in the patio de Cluny shopping center often turns up some interesting finds.

Crystal, silver, and china choices are excellent at *Cadet Daniel* on rue Antoine Siger, which carries such names as Christofle, Limoges, Daum, Baccarat, Lalique, and Sevres at big savings.

The distinctive, locally designed handicrafts at the *Caribbean Art Center* (Centre des Métiers d'Art), opposite the Tourist Office on Blvd. Alfassa, should not be missed. This cool, well-arranged showroom stocks hard-to-find recordings, dolls, bamboo, shell, wicker, and straw items and those ingenious and indigenous cloth-collage tapestries. Worked in sections from different colors, patterns, and textures of cloth, these wall hangings start at about $50 and go up into the hundreds, depending on size and artist.

Martinique's rum is some of the world's finest. *La Case à Rhum,* on rue de la Liberté or *Roy du Rum,* on rue Victor Hugo, carry a good selection.

Last-minute shoppers will find *Beaufrand* at the airport for perfumes and as well as the *French Farm,* whose cases contain caviar, cheeses, tinned patés, champagnes, fine wines and rum. There's also a counter that sells anthuriums and other local flowers (all OK'd by U.S. Customs to bring in the U.S.) that make one of the nicest remembrances to carry home.

 RESTAURANTS. Most Caribbean islands have more hotels than restaurants; in Martinique the situation is reversed. You'll find spicy Creole dishes, Chinese, Indian, and Spanish cuisine and, of course, classic French fare. Among the local specialties are *colombo* (curry), *accras* (cod or vegetable fritters), *crabes farcis* (stuffed land crab), *ecrévisses* (fresh water crayfish), *boudin* (Creole blood sausage), *lambi* (conch), *langouste* (clawless Caribbean lobster), and *oursin* (sea urchin). There's also a great variety of fresh fish, tropical vegetables, and exotic fruit. The local cellars are filled with excellent French wines, but the island favorite in the drink department is "le 'ti punch" (little punch), a concoction of white rum, sugar syrup, lime and ice.

You'll get excellent value for your money here. Quality is high and now that the dollar is strong, it's possible to eat a fine three-course meal with wine for around $20—provided, of course, you don't get carried away with foie gras, salmon, caviar, and lobster. We call $20 and up *Expensive;* $12–19 *Moderate;* and below $12 *Inexpensive* for one person for a three-course meal.

Expensive

L'Alizè. Morne Tartenson, Fort-de-France. Tel. 71–30–18. In a cool, green residential area, this is a good place to escape the midday heat of Fort-de-France. Formerly called Le Gargantua, and still popular with local businessmen. The large, awninged terrace has comfortable rattan furniture and a marvelous view down over the capital and the harbor. Chef Pineau's menu features French and Creole specialties at both lunch and candlelit dinner. Closed Sun. V.

La Belle Epoque. Didier. Tel. 70–36–22. Yves Coyac is a talented Martiniquais chef whose forté is light, creative cuisine. His imaginative menus include such unusual treats as poached eggs with chicken livers in Armagnac, seafood in puff pastry with fresh mint, lobster in vermouth with leek greens, Sacher torte with green chartreuse, or a hot apple tart with passion fruit compote. Food, presentation, and service here are excellent and the 9 tables on the spacious terrace of this pretty turn-of-the-century house are much in demand. Lunch and dinner Tues.–Sat. AE, V.

La Biguine. Corner rue Capitaine Manuel and route de la Folie, Fort-de-France. Tel. 70–40–07. Not difficult to get to, but this popular restaurant in an old Creole house is somewhat off the beaten tourist track. Gérard Padra's second floor dining room and downstairs grill room are both attractively decorated and his diversified dishes are always top quality. Some specialties include *Pâté en pot* (Martinique-style mutton soup), tiny soudons (local, sweet clams) on the half shell, conch coquille, excellent steaks, coq au vin, and sliced breast of duck with pineapple. Open lunch and dinner, closed Sun. MC, V.

Le Chateaubriand. Hotel Bakoua, Pointe du Bout. Tel. 66–02–02. This award-winning restaurant has one of the island's most varied menus. For gastronomes: blinis and caviar, fresh foie gras from Strasbourg, and truffled filet mignon in a brioche. Those seeking local specialties will find turtle steak, shark Creole, and chicken curry with coconut. Nouvelle cuisine fans will appreciate Chef Sailhac's duckling in a pink peppercorn sauce or kingfish with a tomato-flavor Bearnaise sauce. Unusual desserts include banana or hibiscus honey mousse. There's dinner dancing nightly, and weekend floorshows on the terrace with a good view across the bay. Open daily for dinner. AE, D, MC, V.

Le d'Esnambuc. 1 rue de la Liberté, Fort-de-France. Tel. 71–46–51. This stylish upstairs restaurant was once the famous Le Foyal. The large menu includes classic French as well as Creole selections. Your phrase book and a sweater will be useful in this air-conditioned spot. One of the few restaurants in town open Sunday evening; but closed Saturday and Sunday lunch. AE, D, MC, V.

La Grand'Voile. Pointe Simon, Fort-de-France. Tel. 70–29–29. The Lyonnais and Creole cooking of owner/chef Raymond Benoit has long been a favorite of both visitors and local residents. The rich fare includes *quenelles de brochet* (pike dumplings with a crayfish sauce), homemade terrines and typical Lyonnaise sausages, tripe, the house artichoke prepared with wild morel mushrooms, good seafood, and a tempting pastry cart. Try to get a terrace or window table for a close-up view of the harbor. Open lunch and dinner. Closed Sun. Reservations imperative at dinner. AE, D.

La Mouïna. Pays Mélé-Voie #1, Lamentin. Tel. 50–26–83. Very hard to find, but another absolute must, for this may well be Martinique's finest restaurant. Magdeleine and Guy Karchesz, the popular former proprietors of Le Foulard, are now happily ensconced in the countryside in a lovely colonial home set amidst colorful tropical blooms. A sublime setting with 12 well-spaced terrace tables and a cozy bar with antique furnishings. Guy's 35 years of culinary experience shines in his small, sophisticated menu which features over a dozen expertly prepared and perfectly presented choices plus four or five daily specialties. Reservations are imperative. Complete directions: On the autoroute to or from the Airport, take the turnoff road marked Robert Trinité, then follow the signs for Jeanne d'Arc, St. Joseph, and Gros Morne. Lunch daily, Friday night dinner twice a month. D, V.

Le Gourmet des Isles. 9 rue Redoute du Matouba, Fort-de-France. Tel. 73–53–45. A cozy, intimate dining room favored by local residents at dinner, businessmen at lunch. Creative Creole fare prepared and served with a special flair. Soft piano music every evening. D, MC, V.

Le Tiffany. Ancienne Route de Schoelcher, near Croix de Bellevue. Tel. 71–33–82. This restored gingerbread mansion is difficult to find the first time but its food, setting, and ambience make it a must—preferably at dinner. The evening meal takes place on one of two candlelit terraces or in the cozy, antique-filled main room. Claude Pradine's talented hand combines classic and modern recipes using fresh ingredients that arrive regularly by air direct from Paris' Rungis market; local products are incorporated into Creole dishes. The menu changes, but special treats include foie gras marinated in sauterne and smoked salmon blinis. You'll find that everything here, including the desserts, will be topnotch. On the small 8-table front porch, a 180F prix fixe menu including aperitif and a pitcher of wine is available from 7:30–10:30 P.M., as well as a marvelous 200F shellfish platter that could feature crab, whelks, oysters, and clams of several varieties. This is the kind of place where you'll linger over conversation, coffee served with delectable home-made chocolate truffles, and a good cognac. Closed Sat. noon and all day Sun. D, MC, V.

Moderate

Calalou. Hotel Calalou, Anse-àl'Ane. Tel. 76–31–67/78. Lunch and dinner are served on two large dining terraces, featuring chef André-Charles Donatien's well-balanced menus. Local produce is used whenever possible, so have some unusual tropical touches. Among the choices are conch with mushrooms, eggplant, and chives; tournedos with green pepper, ginger, mushrooms, and orange-juice sauce; entrecote with chicken livers, rum, and mushrooms; chicken breast stuffed with conch; rabbit in old rum, fine smoked kingfish; even prime ribs accompanied by gratinéed yellow banana, igname, papaya, breadfruit, and christophine. Wednesday evenings feature a Creole dinner and folklore show; Saturdays, there's a barbecue with orchestra for dancing. AE, V.

Le Cantonnais. Pointe de Bout Marina. Tel. 66–03–53. For a change of pace, try M. Guy's large selection of Cantonese specialties. This elegant, antique-furnished Oriental oasis is located in the shopping center just behind the marina. Closed Tues. AE, D, MC, V.

Chez Sidonie. Marina Pointe du Bout. Tel. 66–00–54. Sidonie Pamphile is called Martinique's "Queen of Creole Cuisine." Her popular restaurant is busy day and night. Her large menu features all the typical local specialties with a few classic French dishes added to keep everyone happy. The upstairs tables have a better view, but below you are right in the center of all the colorful portside activity. Closed Mon. No credit cards.

Le Colibri. Morne-des-Esses. Tel. 75–32–19. This is a family operation with owner Clotilde Palladino in her kitchen and her children serving. English is limited, but the Creole food is so good and the atmosphere so pleasant you won't notice. Reserve one of the seven back terrace tables, relax, enjoy the view and a 'ti punch while your meal is prepared to order. Among the excellent starters are *calalou aux crabes,* fish soup, conch or sea urchin tourte, and the house *pièce de résistance, buisson d'écrevisses* —literally a thicket of crayfish, but in this case, six giant fresh-water crayfish arranged around the top of a glass goblet. A tangy tomato sauce flavored with tiny bits of the succulent crustacean, scallions, and thyme is served on the side. Main courses range from cocoanut chicken to quail or suckling pig. Portions are very generous, but be sure to leave room for coconut flan for dessert. Lunch and dinner, closed Sun. evening and Mon. Reservations imperative. AE, D, MC, V.

Le Coq Hardi. 0.6 km rue Martin Luther King, Fort-de-France. Tel. 71–59–64. The best grilled meats in town cooked to perfection over a wood fire. This hillside bistro is located in a pretty old Creole house on one of the main streets that descend into the city from the residential plateau. Closed Sat. lunch all day Wed. AE, D, MC, V.

El Raco. 23 rue Lazare-Carnot, Fort-de-France. Tel. 73–29–16. A nice variety of regional Spanish dishes served in a typically Spanish decor with music to match at dinner. Closed Sat. Sun. and Mon. lunch. AE, V.

L'Escalier. 19 rue de la République, Fort-de-France. Tel. 70–25–22. A young Martiniquais deftly prepares authentic Creole and seafood dishes in this small restaurant with a rustic, country atmosphere. One flight up in a typical balconied building in the center of town. Closed Sun. MC, V.

Aux Filets Bleus. Sainte Anne. Tel. 76–73–42. Set on a palm-fringed beach in a pretty village. Choose your lobster from the glass-topped "vivier" set in the floor, stake out a good table, then go for a swim. The Anglios' excellent cuisine —turtle steak served with gratinéed christophine, fish soup, *crabe farci,* sea urchin, raw clams on the half-shell, fricasseed conch—is in itself worth the trip to this part of the island. Popular with nearby Club Med guests so reserve both lunch and dinner. Closed Sun. evening and Mon. No credit cards.

Le Jardin de Jade. Schoelcher. Tel. 70–05–50. The large, elegant dining room of the former Lido Hotel has a fine view and comfortable, widely spaced tables. Service is efficient and the elaborate menu features excellent Chinese specialties, some Cantonese, some spicy hot, and lots of interesting seafood preparations. Closed Sun. evening and Mon. No credit cards.

Le Mareyeur. Route Principale, Pointe des Nègres. Tel. 71–32–92/72–69–87. A very attractive restaurant not far from the Casino Hotel La Batelière. Shark is one of the menu's highlights as are stingray sautéed in butter, sea urchin, crayfish fricassee, a large fisherman's platter with a variety of ingredients that depends on what's freshest in the market; clam and mangrove oyster tastings. Music on Wednesday and Saturday evenings. Open lunch and dinner. Closed Sun. evenings. AE, MC, V.

Le Matador. Anse Mitan. Tel. 66–05–36. Raymonde Crico holds forth in her 30-table dining room; her husband Francois' domaine is the kitchen. Together they run one of the island's most dependably good Creole restaurants. Popular specialties here are court bouillon, fish, pork, lamb, or chicken colombo, and a tasty roast leg of mutton with a spicy Creole sauce that serves four and must be ordered in advance. Open lunch and dinner, reservations requested. AE, D, MC, V.

Montauberg. Rouge d'Aileron, Morne Rouge. Tel 77–34–11. Situated in the verdant hills facing Mt. Pelée. Spectacular view from the terrace. French and Creole luncheon fare served in this unique setting merits a stop if you are in the area. There are eight rooms in the inn should you be inspired to stay over. Closed Mon. AE, D, V.

Au Regal de la Mer. Anse Mitan. Tel. 66–04–00. Very pleasant garden across from the sea where the former chef of the Frantel, Alain Bourgogne, and his partner Gerard Bobeau offer an excellent assortment of fish and shellfish. Service is friendly, the guests generally lively, and food dependably good as well as attractively presented. The seafood platter is enormous and could easily satisfy two. Dinner only, except Sunday lunch. AE, V.

Typic Bellevue. Blvd. de la Marne. Tel. 71–68–87. If you're looking for out-of-the-ordinary Creole cooking, this is *the* place to head for. Bruno Raphael-Amanrich uses the freshest local products prepared in unusual ways: breadfruit croquettes, sea urchin tourte, crayfish brochette, fricassee of goat, roast suckling pig Boucanier, and baby shark marinated in lime, laurel and herbs, then steamed to perfection and served in a tangy tomato sauce. Open lunch and dinner. Closed Sat. lunch and Sun. AE, D.

La Villa Creole. Anse Mitan. Tel. 66–05–53. The setting is romantic—the oil-lamp-lit back garden of an old wooden house with owner Guy Dawson playing soft guitar at dinner. The food, exotic and traditional, is reliably good: a local salmon terrine served with a light tomato coulis, coconut chicken, a mixed curry of chicken, pork, and mutton, turtle fricassee, grilled kingfish with a basil sauce, lobster flambé in cognac and grilled sirloin with shallots. Closed Sun. Dinner only in high season. AE, D, V.

Inexpensive

Bambou. Anse Mitan. Tel. 66–01–39. Casual, open-air seaside terrace with an extensive menu. Local bands entertain in season and there is a barbecue three times a week. Open lunch and dinner daily. AE, D, MC, V.

Les Brisants. Dostaly, Le François. Tel. 54–32–57. A small Creole inn where the Atlantic surf breaks just outside the door. Excellent seafood and they will also prepare a picnic for you to enjoy on one of the nearby offshore islands. Closed Tues. AE, D.

La Carafe. 11 rue Lamartine. Tel. 73–93–84. The menu of this small upstairs restaurant changes daily but always features some interesting French and Guyanaise specialties. Especially recommended are the eggplant beignets, grilled fish, rabbit in red wine, and everything Guyanaise but particularly the smoked poulet Boucané. Open lunch and dinner. No credit cards.

Chez Gaston. 10 rue Felix Eboue. Tel. 71–45–48. Tony Ardes offers a varied Creole menu in his upstairs restaurant, snacks downstairs all day long. There's a small dance floor and music for dinner dancing and the kitchen is open late.

Brochettes are excellent and unusual here, the room cozy and very popular with local residents. French will be helpful. No credit cards.

Club Nautique-Les Pieds Dans l'Eau. François. Tel. 54–31–00. A simple thatched-roof terrace right on the quai. No decor to speak of, but lunch here means seafood fresh from local fishermen who will also be happy to take you out to the offshore reefs or islands for some snorkeling. The menu depends on the catch of the day; lunch only with a copious 150F three-course lobster menu a favorite. AE, D, MC, V.

Le Crew. 42 rue Ernest Deproge, Fort-de-France. Tel. 73–04–14. A few Creole dishes and plenty of typical French bistro fare: fish soup, salade Nicoise, snails, country paté, frogs' legs, tripe, grilled chicken, and steak eight different ways. All served family style in rustic dining rooms, and there's a daily 60–70F three-course tourist menu. Good generous portions. No credit cards.

Diamant Les Bains. Diamant. Tel. 76–40–14. Another good address for lunch if you are in the southern part of the island. Hubert Andrieu's menu features a nice choice of salads including six different mixtures of hard-to-find avocado; omelettes such as lobster, shrimp, and sea urchin; all the usual Creole specialties; and grilled meat and fish. His terrace is large and airy and the 2½-mile beach overlooking Diamond Rock just steps away. D, MC.

Diamant Plage. Facing the post office in the village of Diamant. Tel. 76–40–48. Lovely 3-level terrace serving such Creole specialties as turtle or shark stew, stuffed shrimp or conch, and superb grilled fish. The sound of the waves is soothing and Octavia Gabrielle's experienced hand provides

La Dunette. Ste.-Anne village. Tel. 76–74–31. Pretty blue-awninged terrace with abundant greenery. The menu is extensive with a large list of salads, well-prepared French and Crelole dishes and nice desserts. If sea urchin is on the menu, don't miss this treat. No credit cards.

La Dunette. Ste.-Anne village. Tel. 76–74–31. Pretty blue-awinged terrace with abundant greenery. The menu is extensive with a large list of salads, well-prepared French and Creole dishes and nice desserts. If sea urchin is on the menu, don't miss this treat. No credit cards

La Factorerie. Quartier Fort, St. Pierre. Tel. 77–12–53. Set in a pretty hillside garden next to the ruins of the Eglise du Fort. This very pleasant al fresco restaurant belongs to an agricultural training school whose three-part program teaches students to serve, sew, and raise crops. Two daily 75F three-course menus are always appealing and the à la carte choices include a wide variety of local specialties. Closed Sat. and Sun. evenings. No credit cards.

Les Mahoganys. Rte. de Caritan, Ste.-Anne. Tel. 76–73–94. Twenty tables on a hillside terrace with bright madras and orange accents. No view, but Lucienne and Gregoire Trime offer large, well-presented portions of lobster, sea urchin, conch, and other seafood. A bit off the tourist track but a nice spot to wile away your day with a long, leisurely lunch. No credit cards.

Restaurant Mally. Route de la Côte Atlantique, Basse-Point. Tel. 75–51–18. This unpretentious little restaurant in Mally Edjam's home has just four tables on her awninged side porch (the best) and a few more inside. It's a long drive and open only for lunch, but you'll need a reservation and your dictionary. If you arrange in advance Mally will do wonderful things to order—papaya soufflé, sea urchin, and crayfish creations; but her fresh local vegetables, soups, curries, stews, and jams are always on the menu. Jams? Oh yes, these guava, pineapple, cornichon, and other exotic *confitures* are meant to be savored at the end of your feast along with a yoghurt or light coconut cake. No credit cards.

Tong Yen. Robert. Tel. 65–17–89. The size and variety of Germaine Bringtown's menu is overwhelming; bring along several friends for maximum tasting of dozens of Oriental/French/Creole/tropical combinations you never imagined existed. The setting on a breezy country hilltop overlooks green fields, flowers, the fishing village of Robert, and the offshore islands in the distance. Tables are especially in demand on weekends, so be sure to reserve. Closed Sun. evening and all day Mon. No credit cards.

Le Vivier. Caraibe Auberge, Anse Mitan. Tel. 66–03–19. In Louis Yang Ting's newly remodeled restaurant, the tables are arranged around a large pool containing an interesting collection of sea creatures—some to be eaten, others just observed. The emphasis is naturally on seafood and it's some of the island's most dependably good. AE, D, MC, V.

NIGHT LIFE AND BARS. With all the *joie de vivre* of Martinique, it is essential to ask locally for suggestions as to current "in" spots. They change frequently but the Tourist Office or your hotel should be up to date.

In and around Fort-de-France are six disco favorites: *Sweety,* 6 rue Captain Pierre Rose; *Hippo Club,* 26 Blvd. Allègre; *Club 21* at the Casino Hotel La Batelière; *Club Bitaco* in Ravine Vilaine; *Club des Iles* on Rte. de Ste.-Thérèse; and *Le Manoir,* Rte. des Réligieuses. *Alibi,* a private club on the premises of the Gargantua, welcomes U.S. visitors as long as management is notified beforehand (Tel. 71–30–18). Piano bars were sprouting up all over town last winter. Among the most popular are the one in the restaurant *Gourmet des Iles,* 9 rue de Redoute Matouba; *New Brummells,* corner rue Ernest Déproge and rue Schoelcher; and *Le Pelican,* 0.5 km Rte. de Châteauboeuf, which also offers jazz, a disco, and video room. *La Carafe,* 11 rue Lamartine, offers good live jazz on Tuesdays, Fridays and Saturdays and *Le Jardin Brésilien,* Rond Pointe de Didier, has live Brazilian music until 11:30 each evening then continues to closing with recorded sounds. This pretty and popular place up in the hills above town also schedules special shows every two weeks. *Le New Cabaret–Chez Gaston* has shows once a week and a live orchestra on Thursday as well as the weekend. Music will usually be alternating beguine, reggae, rock, and slow.

The Meridien's *Von Von;* Frantel's *Le Vesou* in Pointe du Bout and *Le Samba* at the Copacabana-Eden Beach hotel in Anse Mitan all draw local residents as well as visitors and can jump until the wee hours, especially on weekends.

 CASINOS. Martinique has two, one at the Méridien in Pointe du Bout, the second at the Casino Hotel La Batelière on the northern outskirts of Fort-de-France. There are no slot machines but baccarat, blackjack, American roulette, and craps are played. Hours are 9:00 P.M.–3:00 A.M. nightly except Sunday and proof of identity is required (valid passport or driver's license with photo). Entrance fee is 60F at the Meridien, 50F at the Bataliere with the latter open only from November to April. Tie and jacket are not needed but proper attire is required.

POSTAGE. Postcards to the U.S., 2.20F; letters up to 20 g., 3.70F.

ELECTRIC CURRENT. Voltage is 220 A.C. 50 cycles, so American appliances need French plugs, converters, and transformers. Even better, travel with dual-voltage hair dryers, shavers, irons, etc.

 SECURITY. Fort-de-France is a big city so follow the same rules you would at home and those that local residents practice: always lock your car, don't leave valuables in obvious view, and don't flash around your cash in public places. The Pointe du Bout area has a large number of people coming and going, so the same rules on locking cars and valuables hold true here. Use your hotel's safety deposit box if you are traveling with a lot of cash (never advisable, anywhere) or jewelry and don't leave watches or cameras unattended on the beach.

MONTSERRAT

by
BARBARA A. CURRIE

Most first-time visitors aren't prepared for their arrival in this British Crown Colony known as the "little Ireland" of the Caribbean. This tiny, volcanic island of less than forty square miles is not Gaelic but actually very West Indian, and the strongest Irish influence today is found in seventeenth-century records of the island's original settlers, and the surnames of many of today's inhabitants.

Brochures produced by the Montserrat Tourist Bureau in Plymouth, the country's capital, portray the island as the uncrowded, unhurried, and quiet Caribbean of yesterday—and this is not simply propaganda. With one exception—the exhilarating experience of your small aircraft touching down just in time on the tarmac of Blackburne Airport—Montserrat just might be the gentlest of the Leeward Islands. And wherever you travel along the 150 miles of road crisscrossing this island, the people you meet make visitors feel immediately welcome.

The rugged and dramatic nature of Montserrat's terrain is a sharp contrast to the spirit of its people. The label of "emerald isle" is an accurate description of the appearance of this avocado-shaped island with its lush, rolling scenery and volcanic backbone.

With only a small selection of hotels, guesthouses, and rental apartments available, Montserrat has remained distant from the mainstream of eastern Caribbean tourism, despite its location twenty-seven miles (a fifteen-minute flight) southwest of Antigua. The island's 12,500 people, and the few thousand annual visitors don't seem interested in manmade tourism. The natural attractions and the tranquility itself are enough to keep all available rooms filled during the winter season.

Relaxing and hiking may be Montserrat's primary attractions outdoors, but you can also enjoy golf at the Montserrat Golf Club, windsurfing, sailing, tennis, horseback riding, and swimming or sunbathing at Carr's Bay, a golden-sand beach on the north coast. Or explore the black volcanic sand beaches and coves that dot the coastline.

Past and Present

Montserrat, the "saw-toothed mountain," is believed to have been named Santa María de Montserrat for the famous monastery near Barcelona, Spain, by Christopher Columbus, who discovered this speck in the Leeward chain in 1493.

Nobody is certain what brought the first group of settlers to this island in 1632, but evidence suggests that the original Irish settlers may have fled St. Kitts (the first English settlement in the New World, sixty miles northeast of Montserrat) to escape oppressive British policies and find a place to practice their Catholic religion in peace.

Not much was recorded of the island's nineteenth-century development. Sugar was the main crop, but production diminished after slavery was abolished in 1834. According to local historians, sugar was replaced by limes and by the mid-nineteenth century, England had turned to Montserrat as its primary supplier of lime juice—the "fruit" of efforts by transplanted Gloucestershire Quaker Joseph Sturge who developed the crop on the island.

Although plantations are a thing of the past in modern Montserrat, the island has become the cornucopia of the Caribbean. Hundreds of acres of this fertile island are cultivated and produce some of the finest fruits and vegetables in the region.

Montserrat, unlike many of its eastern Caribbean neighbors, has chosen to remain a British Crown Colony. It has belonged to the British for over two hundred years, since the 1783 Treaty of Versailles settled the Anglo-French wars. It was made a part of the Territory of the Leeward Islands in 1956, along with Antigua, St. Kitts-Nevis, and Anguilla, and incorporated into the Federation of the West Indies in 1958. In 1967, Montserrat reaffirmed its desire to remain a crown colony rather than becoming one of the West Indies Associated States.

Under the present constitution, the country is governed by a governor appointed by the Crown. The executive council consists of the governor and five other members. The legislative council includes two official members, seven elected, and two nominated members, presided over by a speaker from outside the council.

EXPLORING MONTSERRAT

For one day at least, put yourself in the hands of one of the taxi drivers. They are not only friendly and informative, but give an excellent and thorough island tour at a reasonable price.

On the road from the airport across to the west coast and Plymouth, the capital city, you'll pass through Harris's Village. The Anglican church there, built in 1900, was blown asunder by the hurricane of 1928

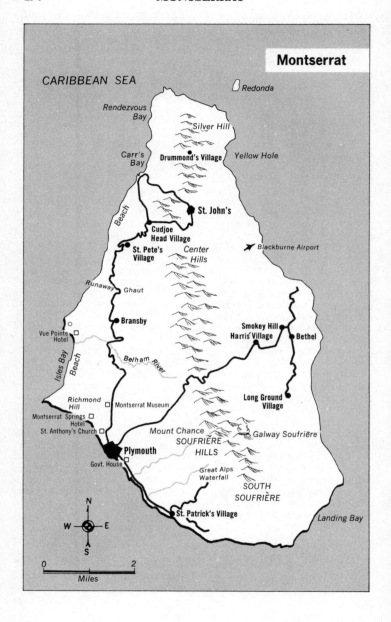

Montserrat

CARIBBEAN SEA

Redonda

Rendezvous Bay

Silver Hill

Carr's Bay

Drummond's Village

Yellow Hole

St. John's

Beach

Cudjoe Head Village

St. Pete's Village

Center Hills

✈ *Blackburne Airport*

Runaway Ghaut

Bransby

Smokey Hill
Harris Village **Bethel**

Vue Pointe Hotel □

Isles Bay *Beach*

Belham River

Long Ground Village

Richmond Hill

□ *Montserrat Museum*

Montserrat Springs Hotel □
St. Anthony's Church □

Mount Chance *Galway Soufrière*

SOUFRIÈRE HILLS

Plymouth

Govt. House

Great Alps Waterfall

SOUTH SOUFRIÈRE

N
W E
S

St. Patrick's Village

Landing Bay

0   2
Miles

and shaken to its foundations by an earthquake in the 1930s. Today it stands rebuilt and impressive. You'll travel through lush, mountainous scenes and see mangoes, papayas, coconut palms, banana plants, and other signs of the fruit and vegetable wealth of Montserrat.

Other sights include the capital city itself, with its population of 12,500 people. Wander around at your own pace, visiting at least four of the churches. And don't miss Plymouth's Saturday market, when produce comes in from all over the island. On market day, this is a West Indian town at its most attractive. One "must see" is Tapestries of Montserrat, upstairs at the John Bull Shop on Old Fort Road. Hand-tufted rugs, wall hangings, and tote bags in exquisite designs are on display—one of the island's best craft buys and most interesting artistic displays.

Plymouth's main street, fringed with Georgian houses built from ballast rock from Dorset, is a beehive, alive with hawkers of tropical produce and handmade items. Boats tie up at the waterfront across from the marketplace, their owners come to trade their goods and their gossip. Other sights include Government House, the residence of the Governor of Montserrat, and its surrounding gardens.

Heading north, you'll come to St. Anthony's Church, on the outskirts of Plymouth, which has been built and rebuilt. The first consecration was sometime between 1623 and 1666, and the rebuilding, after one of the several French-English skirmishes, was in 1730. Freed slaves donated the two silver chalices after emancipation in the 1880s. Beyond Plymouth, on Richmond Hill, is the Montserrat Museum, established by the Montserrat National Trust, a partially restored Sugar Mill, which houses a fascinating variety of artifacts and items on the sociohistory of the island.

Slightly northwest off the Grove Road, which leads to Fox's Bay Road, is Fox's Bay Bird Sanctuary, established in 1979. This 15-acre bog area is a haven for birdwatchers and those wishing a glimpse of Montserrat's wildlife. Trails leading to its interior are marked.

In the hills to the north beyond Belham River is Air Studios, at Waterworks, one of the world's most sophisticated recording studios, owned by Englishman George Martin. Top international stars in the rock industry have recorded albums here. Tours by appointment only (tel. 5678)

Carr's Bay, a thirty-five-minute drive along the north coast, is the place to go for swimming and sunbathing. It is the most popular bathing beach on the island, one of the few that is "regular sand."

South of Plymouth are some of Montserrat's most famous sites. The Great Alps Waterfall is an excursion for the hardy. Although the drive is only fifteen minutes south along the coastal road from Plymouth, the hour-or-more climb requires sturdy shoes and constitution—and a guide, since the growth covers the infrequently trodden path. The rewards are water cascading seventy feet in a pool.

East of Plymouth is Galway Soufrière, a natural phenomenon which will fascinate anyone who has never seen an active volcano. The road here is rugged and the climb up to view the sulfur vents takes about twenty minutes, but you'll get to see an almost prehistoric setting: rumbling volcanic rock, boiling water, and bubbling (and strong-smelling) sulfur pockets.

From this adventure, you may want to continue to Galways Plantation, which is alleged to have been the only Irish plantation in the West Indies during the eighteenth century. This site contains the most valuable remnants of a Montserrat sugar plantation, now being studied through a project sponsored by the Montserrat National Trust.

Northeast of Plymouth there are other places to see such as Runaway Ghaut (or Gut), a precipitous valley where the English and French squabbled two centuries ago, and the agricultural station, not far from the airport. The water sprinkling over the experimental station is a sign of Montserrat's many underground springs. You can also hike up Mt. Chance to Chance's Peak, at three thousand feet the highest point on the island.

PRACTICAL INFORMATION FOR MONTSERRAT

FACTS AND FIGURES. Montserrat is located 29 miles southwest of Antigua in the Leeward Islands. Within its 39.5 square miles is lush, mountainous terrain with many streams and waterfalls, and dense tropical rain forest vegetation. The highest peak is Mt. Chance at 3,000 ft.

The year-round climate is tropical with little variation in temperature (83 degrees F) and abundant rainfall, particularly from September through November.

The population is approximately 12,500, and English (spoken with a lilting West Indian "brogue" reflecting the 17th-century Irish settlers' influence) is the official language.

Montserrat operates on Atlantic time, one hour ahead of the eastern standard time of the coastal U.S.

WHEN TO GO. The winter season (Dec. 15–Apr. 15) is Montserrat's busiest time, and the most difficult time to find both airline space and hotel rooms on the island. In addition to being less "crowded," the summer season, between May and November, offers much lower rates on rooms—at least 25–40% discount. The rainiest months are September through November, so you might want to plan your visit accordingly.

PASSPORTS AND VISAS. U.S. and Canadian citizens need only proof of identity, such as a passport, birth certificate, or voter's registration card (a driver's license won't do). British citizens must have a passport; visas are not required. In addition, all visitors must hold a return or ongoing ticket.

MONEY. The Eastern Caribbean dollar (EC) is the local currency. It is figured at EC $2.70=U.S. $1. Be sure which currency is being quoted; most places quote in EC dollars.

WHAT WILL IT COST?

A typical day on Montserrat for two persons during the winter season will run:

	U.S.$
Hotel accommodations, including breakfast and dinner	$120
Lunch at the hotel or in town	20
Tips, service charges, taxes	20
Car rental or sightseeing by taxi	30
Total	$190

HOW TO GET THERE. By air. Antigua is the gateway. *American Airlines, BWIA,* and *Pan Am* fly there from New York; *Eastern, BWIA* and *Pan Am* from Miami; *Air Canada* and *BWIA* from Toronto; and *British Airways* from London. *LIAT* and *Montserrat Air* provide connections from Coolidge International Airport (Antigua) if arriving jet flights are on time. Charter service by twin-engine aircraft is available through *Executive Air Services* and *Carib Air* in Antigua for the 15-minute flight.

AIRPORT TAX AND OTHER CHARGES. There is a 7% government room tax, in addition to a 10% service charge at the hotels. The airport departure tax is U.S. $5.

TELEPHONE AND EMERGENCY NUMBERS. The area code for Montserrat is 809. The prefix for dialing long distance is 491 followed by the appropriate 4-digit number. The prefix 13 is not necessary when dialing within the island. Montserrat has a 67-bed hospital and five government-employed doctors. Contact your hotel operator for their phone numbers and any other services you might need.

HOTELS. Because Montserrat and its accommodations are so small, breakfast and dinner are very often MAP—included in the daily hotel rate. We call $150 and up *Deluxe;* $120–149 *Expensive;* $80–119 *Moderate;* and anything below that *Inexpensive.*

Vue Pointe. *Deluxe.* Box 65. Tel. 2481. This property is the largest on the island as well as the island's showplace, with 12 rooms and the 28 octagonal cottages, exquisitely appointed, with a large bedroom, a bath, a great view, and privacy. They spill to the black-sand beach below, where there is a beach bar. Swimming pool, main dining room, and lounge areas at the top of the hill. You'll feel at home here because the Osbornes, who own Vue Pointe, will make sure of it. Their Wednesday-night West Indian buffet is a popular event with residents as well as visitors in season. Down the hill is the shoreside bar area and two lighted tennis courts. The hotel also has a small putting green and the Belham River Valley Golf Course is nearby. At press time, the resort was completing a major expansion program, including a 100-seat conference center, beauty salon and delicatessen, new kitchen, and expanded boutique.

Montserrat Springs Hotel and Villas. *Expensive.* Box 259. Tel. 2481. A jewel of a spot, with 29 attractively furnished rooms and superbly appointed 1- and 2-bedroom efficiency suites overlooking the beach at Richmond Hill. West Indian food nicely served on the dining terrace. Olympic-size freshwater pool; health spa with a large hot-water mineral bath and cold-water Jacuzzi. Some evening entertainment during the winter season.

Coconut Hill Hotel. *Moderate.* Box 337. Tel. 2144. This is a renovated plantation house with ten rooms, each with private bath. The atmosphere is casual, pleasant, and very informal. Delicious West Indian specialties served in the dining room. In town but a distance from the usual tourist activities.

Belham Valley Hotel. *Inexpensive.* Box 420. Tel. 5553. An excellent accommodation value during high or low season, this "hotel" is actually several cottages on a hillside overlooking Belham Valley and the river. Montserrat golf course is right below and Uve Point a short walk away. Restaurant on property, but cottages are fully equipped with kitchens.

Flora Fountain Hotel, *Inexpensive.* Box 373. Tel. 2289/2290. Montserrat's newest hotel, catering to businessmen needing comfort and convenience in Plymouth, has 18 air-conditioned rooms and a dining room specializing in Chinese and Indian dishes. Circular construction around a fountain and courtyard.

Wade Inn Hotel. *Inexpensive.* Plymouth. Tel. 2881. A small, ten-room inn/guesthouse. Informal but has a dining room that turns out Caribbean fare that's second to none.

CONDOMINIUMS. *Shamrock Villas.* Contact Doug Kennedy, Montserrat Condominiums, Ltd., Box 180, Plymouth. This is a beautiful property, with 45 one- and two-bedroom apartments and townhouse condominiums. The units are built on a hillside overlooking the sea. Rentals by the week for a one-bedroom villa in season run $350; $1,350 by the month.

HOME AND APARTMENT RENTALS. Villa holidays in Montserrat are luxurious. Most holiday homes have their own swimming pools, terraces, and magnificent views of the Caribbean. Villa rentals normally include the services of a domestic helper and gardener. For information contact *Neville Bradshaw Agencies Ltd.,* Box 270, Plymouth Montserrat (tel. 5270); *D.R.V. Edwards,* Box 58, Plymouth, Montserrat (tel. 2431); *Shamrock Villas,* Box 180, Plymouth, Montserrat (tel. 2974), or consult the *Montserrat Tourist Board,* Box 7, Plymouth, Montserrat.

HOW TO GET AROUND. There is more than 150 miles of good road on Montserrat, and it's worth renting a car to explore. Rental cars can be arranged through your local hotel at U.S. $25–28 per day. A Montserrat driver's license is mandatory and can be obtained at the airport or at the local police station. Your valid license and a fee of EC $7.50 is all that's required. *Remember to drive on the left!*

Taxis are readily available, and your hotel can contact one at any time. The airport is a distance away from the hotels, and taxi rates can range from EC $23–35 for the one-way journey. Be sure to check the approximate fare in advance and be sure you're paying in Eastern Caribbean dollars rather than U.S., which would double the fare.

TOURIST INFORMATION. On the island, contact the *Montserrat Tourist Board* in Plymouth (tel. 2230). For sources closer to home see Tourist Information Services section in the *Facts at Your Fingertips* chapter. Overseas, write the *Montserrat Tourist Board,* Box 7, Plymouth, Montserrat. Tel. (809) 491–2230.

SPECIAL EVENTS. The most important celebrations of the year are festivals held on St. Patrick's Day (March 17), Easter weekend, and Christmas, which is a 9-day celebration beginning on Christmas Eve and ending on January 1, with events organized by a festival committee. All celebrations emphasize the local folklore, music, dance and food of Montserrat.

The main public holidays are New Year's Day, Good Friday, Easter Monday, Labor Day (First Monday in May) Whitmonday (Seventh Monday after Easter Monday), the First Monday in August, Discovery Day (Nov. 11), Christmas Day and Boxing Day (Dec. 26), and recently added St. Patrick's Day, March 17.

TOURS. Tours can be arranged through the hotels and through the *Montserrat Tourist Board* (tel. 2230), with rates running about EC $30 per hour or EC $120 per day. The trip to Galway Soufrière is the highlight, and the nature-trail walk to the Great Alps Waterfall runs a close second. There is also a *Garden Tour,* which is organized by the Rotary Club, during February and March. An all-day island tour is the best bet—you'll tour the mountainous regions, do some bird-watching at the Foxes Bay sanctuary, hikd up to the waterfall, and explore the steaming sulphurous center of the volcano.

The Vue Pointe Hotel (tel. 2481) can arrange cruises of Rendezvous Bay by yacht from Old Road Bay, or interisland yacht cruises, such as an excursion to Redonda for a full day, including luncheon, exploring, swimming, and snorkeling.

PARKS AND GARDENS. The gardens surrounding Government House in Plymouth are beautifully kept and have been so for two centuries. Dozens of other gardens, all private, are lush and colorful and can be part of an island garden tour sponsored by Montserrat's Rotary Club.

 BEACHES. The sands here are a surprise and a delight for visitors. Black-sand beaches to the south; long beige and white strips of sand to the north, provide excellent swimming and sunbathing. *Carr's Bay* and other northcoast coves, including *Little Bay* and *Rendezvous Bay,* on the island's leeward side, are the best swimming and sunbathing beaches, with golden, rather than black volcanic, sand.

 PARTICIPANT SPORTS. All water sports can be arranged through your hotel. There are small boats available for **fishing** and larger craft for half-day or all-day **deep-sea fishing. Horseback riding** along the beaches can be arranged through your hotel. In addition to the quiet and the beaches, many visitors come just to play the 11-hole Belham River Valley **Golf** Course at the Montserrat Golf Club. The fairways run from the beach up the mountainside and are so well kept and challenging that most duffers go around twice. Greens fees run about U.S. $10. Clubs and cart rentals or caddies are available at moderate rates. Excellent **tennis** courts are available at the *Vue Point* and Montserrat Springs Hotels.

SPECTATOR SPORTS. **Cricket** is the island sport, and matches are held from February through June. Check with the Tourist Board (tel. 2230) for places and times.

 HISTORIC SITES AND HOUSES. Admission is free to all sites. *Government House.* Plymouth. This imposing Victorian structure was built in the 18th century and is still an island treasure. Its public rooms may be visited only from 10:00 A.M. until noon on Wednesdays, but its surrounding gardens are open to the public Monday through Friday from 10:00 A.M. until noon.

Fort St. George offers a fine view of Plymouth. Built in the late 18th century, the site is now overgrown, but easily reached and worth the trip for its view.

St. Anthony's Church. Plymouth. On the outskirts of town, this church was originally constructed in 1623 and rebuilt after a French-English battle in 1730. Of special interest are the two silver chalices that were donated by freed slaves in the 1880s.

 MUSEUMS AND GALLERIES. The Montserrat Museum. The museum is housed in an old, restored sugar mill, adding to the history and enjoyment. Admission is free, but donations are appreciated as the museum is staffed by volunteers and is funded entirely by private donations. You'll see photographs of early 20th-century life on the island, Arawak artifacts, maps of historical significance to the island—and a 150-year-old donkey saddle.

 SHOPPING. *Gallery Montserrat* in Plymouth offers handwoven sea-island cotton items and pottery; *Wild Thing Knitwear* nearby sells hand-knitted garments from locally grown cotton. *Perks Punch,* the local liquer, has a rum base, is indigenous to the island, and makes a perfect souvenir. At *The John Bull Shop* and *The EtCetera Shop,* located in Wapping across the bridge in Plymouth, you'll find duty-free crystal, watches, and jewelry, as well as clothing. Some of the finest quality textiles and related products are produced in Montserrat, and you should plan to see the products available from the

Montserrat Sea Island Cotton Company on the corner of George and Strand St. in Plymouth, as well as the beautiful hand-tufted tapestries at *Tapestries of Montserrat,* located in the John Bull Shop on Old Fort Road. *The Government Crafts Shop* near the pier at Queen's Warehouse is a good source of local handicrafts including woven goods, pottery, and even locally made jams. And Vue Point's boutique, *Carol's Corner,* offers more quality local crafts, including leather jewelry and some sea-island cotton items. All stores close at 12:30 on Wednesday and normal shopping hours are 8:30 to 4 weekdays.

 RESTAURANTS. Montserrat's famous "mountain chicken" is actually frogs' legs—the indigenous amphibians are so large their legs could be substituted for ordinary poultry dishes, but the flavor is more delicate and the texture very different. How they are prepared depends on the chef in charge, but fried they are not as delectable as prepared other ways. Goat water, another popular local dish, is goat meat simmered in a thick brown stew with local vegetables including yams, breadfruit, cassava, and pumpkins, seasoned with onions and peppers. Goat, for those who are unfamiliar with it, tastes something like mutton. In addition to dining in Monserrat's elegant hotels, you should plan to try several of the local restaurants, including *The Attic,* on Marine Drive, *The Oasis* in Wapping, and those listed below.

The Belham Valley. *Moderate to Expensive.* Old Towne. Tel. 5553. A variety of native Montserrat and North American dishes. Romantic setting overlooks the valley and river. Recommended specialties are breadfruit vichyssoise, Creole crab and callaloo soup, and mountain chicken. Homemade ice cream in special flavors like soursop. Dinner only. No credit cards.

The Iguana. *Moderate.* Old Fort Road, Plymouth. Garden setting, specialty drinks, and unusual menu catering to the business crowd rather than those in search of island fare. Salads, quiches—and icy lime soup a specialty. Nice resting place for lunch after shopping. No credit cards.

Cynthie's Restaurant. *Inexpensive.* Harney St., Plymouth, Tel. 3285. Open for all three meals and Cynthie prides himself on his local seafood. Lunch averages EC $12 and dinner EC $50 for five-course spread of lobster, less for fresh fish. Weekends, local dishes of goat water and mountain chicken. No credit cards.

Lett's. *Inexpensive.* Marine Drive. Tel. 2396. Specializes in a varied menu from continental fare to Chinese. Outside dining on guesthouse patio, with a different local special each day, and only fresh local vegetables used. Lunch open but dinner by reservation only. No credit cards.

Teacher Jim's. *Inexpensive.* Hideaway Hotel, Rocklands. Tel. 5252. Dinner by reservation only. Beautiful view of the mountains from this old manor house built in 1836. Excellent local food, complete four-course dinner included in the price. No credit cards.

Wade Inn, *Inexpensive.* Parliament St. Plymouth. Tel. 2881. A popular dining spot for fine local fare on an attractively decorated, secluded terrace. "Ask and you shall receive" is the only menu of local dishes available, with seafood the house specialty. No credit cards.

 NIGHT LIFE AND BARS. As on most West Indian islands, there is local—sometimes spontaneous—live music, and special events according to the local social calendar, but no "tourist-type" nightclubs and dances. Hotels organize entertainment on special occasions and can tell you where to go for local music, service club meetings, and other events. For the most part the hotel bars, particularly *Vue Point,* serve as congenial gathering spots where the art of conversation is still the primary form of entertainment. A number of small local night spots welcome visitors in Plymouth, including *La Cave* on Evergreen Drive and the *747 Disco* on Harney Street.

POSTAGE. Montserrat is one of many Caribbean islands whose postage stamps are both interesting and colorful enough to make them popular collectors' items. They can be purchased at the main post office in Plymouth. Overseas airmail postage for letters to the U.S. and Canada is EC $.55; EC $.35 for postcards. To the UK: $EC .70 for letters and EC $.45 for postcards.

ELECTRIC CURRENT. The current here is 220 volts, 60 cycles, and must be converted to 110 for U.S. and Canadian appliances.

SECURITY. This tiny island enjoys a very low crime rate, but visitors are always encouraged to take some precautions in Montserrat as they would in any other destination concerning valuables such as cash, passports, jewelry, and camera equipment. Leaving any items openly displayed in hotel rooms or unattended while sightseeing or swimming is discouraged.

More out of courtesy than as a security precaution, photographers should ask permission before firing away at subjects they may find interesting. Residents can be reluctant, and they appreciate this basic courtesy.

NEVIS

by
BARBARA A. CURRIE

Nevis is one of the most visually stunning and instantly relaxing islands in the Caribbean. The ambience of this 36-square-mile lush green volcanic gumdrop combines fascinating history, a climate known for centuries as a natural spa, cheerful and friendly Nevisians, and striking West Indian scenes. Even without visiting the six historic mineral spa baths at Cades Bay, you'll find a stay on this island revives you. Those baths lured fashionable Europeans in the early 19th century, who came to experience their "curative powers," and earned Nevis the reputation as "the Spa of the Caribbean."

Nevis lies two miles south of St. Kitts. Its slopes rise almost straight up from the sea to Nevis Peak, the island's center, which soars 3,500 feet into the sky. This mountain is joined by a saddle to two lesser peaks, Hurricane Hill in the north and Saddle Hill in the south.

Long beaches, with white and with black sand, and off-shore coral reefs surround the island. Some are edged with rocky promontories, others with long rows of towering palms. Inland, estate houses and plantations prove that Nevis flouished during its heyday centuries ago. But all is quiet today, so quiet in fact that a dozen tourists on the beach will seem like a crowd.

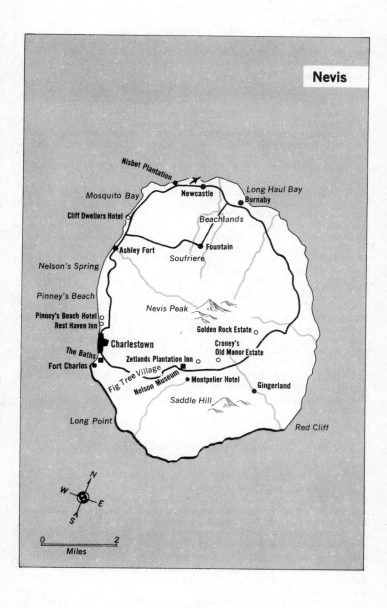

Nevis

Nisbet Plantation

Mosquito Bay

Newcastle

Long Haul Bay

Burnaby

Cliff Dwellers Hotel

Beachlands

Ashley Fort

Fountain

Soufriere

Nelson's Spring

Pinney's Beach

Nevis Peak

Pinney's Beach Hotel

Rest Haven Inn

Golden Rock Estate

Charlestown

Croney's
Old Manor Estate

The Baths

Zetlands Plantation Inn

Fort Charles

Fig Tree Village

Nelson Museum

Montpelier Hotel

Gingerland

Saddle Hill

Long Point

Red Cliff

N
W E
S

0   2
Miles

Past and Present

When Columbus came in 1493, he focused on the mammoth clouds over the island's tallest peak and was reminded of a snow-covered range in the Pyrenees. He christened the island *Nieves,* which in Spanish means "snows." The name held, although the spelling changed over the years.

The next seafarers to arrive were Captain John Smith and his English crew in 1607. They were en route to Virginia to settle the Jamestown colony, but stayed in Nevis long enough for the captain to note, "here we found a great poole, wherein bathing ourselves we found much ease." Permanent colonization took place in 1628 when English Captain Anthony Hilton arrived with eighty planters on board his ship. And so a small colony began, one that would expand with vast sugar plantations and elegant estate houses.

Alexander Hamilton was born here in 1755, and that estate can still be seen in Charlestown, the island's capital. Admiral Lord Nelson, Captain of His Majesty's Ship *Boreas,* was headquartered in Antigua but discovered Nevis as a freshwater stop and returned often enough to court and eventually marry Frances Nisbet, who lived on a sixty-four-acre plantation on the north shore. Their best man was the Duke of Clarence, who was later to become King William IV of England. Their wedding took place at Montpelier Estate, now the site of a sixteen-room hotel. The marriage is recorded at historic St. John's Church in Fig Tree Village.

The "great poole" that Captain John Smith recorded was to become famous for its hot springs and curative waters. The Bath Hotel, an imposing place on a hilltop, was built during the eighteenth century. The word spread, and it eventually became the most important health spa in the British West Indies. It is in ruins today, high above Charlestown, but work has begun on a complete restoration.

Nevis is part of the nation of St. Kitts-Nevis, which became the newest independent country in the Caribbean in 1983, led by Prime Minister Kennedy A. Simmonds.

EXPLORING NEVIS

With its beaches, great houses for fine accommodations, and historic sites, Nevis has more than enough to offer the visitor on tour. The city of Charlestown, once a hub of activity, is quiet today. Most of the excitement occurs when the ferry arrives from St. Kitts, bringing visitors and new supplies of necessary produce.

A few blocks away is the estate where Alexander Hamilton was born. A small museum next door makes history come alive. Charlestown is an easy and interesting self-guided tour through shops and narrow side streets. Maps showing points of interest are available from the Nevis tourist board office off Main St. The best introduction to Nevis is by guided taxi tour. Nevisian cabbies are charming and willing raconteurs who will make your visit more enjoyable by their narrations and asides on the history and folklore of the island.

Among the sites to see are St. John's Church in Fig Tree Village, just a few miles from town. A charming Anglo-Gallic church, it looks as though it had been transported from a Cornish village. Beneath its memorial plaque you'll find the tattered register and an entry that reads: "Horatio Nelson, Esquire, to Frances Nisbet, Widow, on March 11, 1787." A walk through the small graveyard around the church adds to one's sense of history.

It's tricky, but you can drive inland and up toward Nevis Peak. You'll wind and weave your way, and with each bend in the road will find another spectacular view of the island, its beaches and coves.

Although you can make a circular tour of the island, including stops at historic sites, in about four hours, allow a full day. Have the hotel prepare a picnic lunch, or pack your own from the tiny grocery stores on Main Street in Charlestown. Start early so that you'll be able to enjoy the beaches when the sun is at its height. There are no changing facilities, so wear a bathing suit with a cover-up and bring a towel.

Just south of Charlestown are the newly restored, 6 historic mineral baths, now open to visitors, providing an idea of what lured European gentry here a century and a half ago.

Return to the coastal road and head north. Small farms that are sectioned off, and with the surf rolling in, are reminiscent of Scotland. As you round the top of the island you'll pass through Newcastle, once second in importance to Charlestown, now a quiet village and the location of the Newcastle Pottery works, a century-old Nevisian craft where craftsmen fashion clay items and fire them in an open fire of coconut shells.

A few miles southwest on the main road you'll pass Cliff Dwellers Hotel, perched on a 17-acre site 170 ft. high, overlooking St. Kitts. Stop here for a rum punch and experience one of the most spectacular views in the entire Caribbean.

Head south and stop at the white-sand beach on the way to Charlestown. This is one of the island's most beautiful beaches, not only on its shore side, but opposite, where there is a lagoon that looks like a setting from "South Pacific." Take it all in, collect a few shells, and then retreat to the terrace at Pinney's Beach Hotel at the edge of town for a cool drink and to watch the sunset darken St. Kitts across the way.

PRACTICAL INFORMATION FOR NEVIS

 FACTS AND FIGURES. Nevis is in the northern part of the Leeward Island group of the Lesser Antilles in the eastern Caribbean, legally and politically linked to the island of St. Kitts two miles away. The tip of the island's dominant central peak, usually encircled by snow-like clouds, rises into what appears to be an almost perfectly formed cone of 3,232 ft.

The capital city (and only town) is Charlestown, with a population of about 1,200.

The terrain of Nevis encompasses numerous fertile hillsides and seemingly endless stretches of golden-sand beaches formed from coral reef.

The majority of its 9,300 inhabitants, who call themselves "Nevisians," are farmers. They grow mostly vegetables and coconuts.

As on neighboring St. Kitts, the climate can be hot, but its extremes are tempered by breezes from the northeast tradewinds. There is no rainy season. Average annual rainfall is 55 inches. Humidity is low. Average duration of sunshine per day is 8.3 hours. And tropical diseases are virtually nonexistent.

WHEN TO GO. Rates are highest in winter (mid-December to mid-April) and cheapest in summer (mid-April to mid-December). Although it is hot year-round, the climate is pleasant and healthy, with extremes tempered by the breezes from the northeast trade winds. It's never hotter than 92 degrees F, nor colder than 62 degrees. There is no rainy season.

PASSPORTS AND VISAS. U.S. and Canadian citizens need only proof of identity, such as a passport, birth certificate, or voter's registration card (a driver's license won't do!). British visitors must have passports; visas are not required. In addition, all visitors must hold a return or ongoing ticket.

MONEY. The East Caribbean dollar (EC) is the local currency, which, as we go to press, is figured at EC $2.65–2.70 = U.S. $1. Exchange facilities are available at banks. Inns, restaurants, and many shops also accept payment in foreign currency, particularly the U.S. dollar. Major international credit cards are accepted by shops, but not generally by small inns. Many of these, however, accept personal checks.

WHAT WILL IT COST

A typical day on Nevis in season for two persons will run:

	U.S.$
Accommodations at one of the plantation houses, including breakfast and dinner	$150
Lunch at the hotel or a small in-town restaurant	15
Tips/service charges/taxes and other hotel charges	26
One-day sightseeing by taxi or rental car	38
Total	$229

HOW TO GET THERE. By air. Nonstop service from New York to St. Kitts (some days with a connection in Miami) on *Pan Am;* on-again, off-again service and charters from U.S. and Canada to St. Kitts by *BWIA;* from various other Caribbean islands by *LIAT, Windward Islands Airways International* (Winair) and *Puerto Rico International Airlines* (Prinair). Many hotels on Nevis make special arrangements with *Carib Aviation* for hassle-free transfers between Antigua or St. Kitts and Nevis. You can either book through your hotel or contact: Carib Aviation, Box 318, St. John's, Antigua. Tel. (809) 462–3147.

By sea. At least one, sometimes two, round trips (U.S. $7) are offered daily between sister island St. Kitts by the government-owned *M.V. Caribe Queen* ferry, but never on Thursdays (that's maintenance day) or Sundays. (Confirm schedule with tourist board and arrive in plenty of time; it only has 150 seats.) The crossing takes 45 minutes.

AIRPORT TAX AND OTHER CHARGES. Hotels add a 10% service charge and a 7% government tax to your bill. There is an airport departure tax of EC $13 or US $5.

TELEPHONE AND EMERGENCY NUMBERS. The area code in Nevis is 809. For police and fire, dial 99. Dial the hotel operator for other services.

HOTELS. The small inns of Nevis rank among the most exquisite in the Caribbean, offering not only unusual settings and informal atmosphere, but also impeccable standards of service and consistently superior food. Invariably well located and pleasantly furnished, many such "inns" are converted great houses and sugar mills. Many of these hotels offer meals in their daily rate, and we have noted this in the price range for two persons during the winter season. We call $200 and up *Deluxe;* $150–199 *Expensive;* $90–149 *Moderate;* and $89 and below *Inexpensive.*

Golden Rock Estate. *Deluxe.* Box 3, Gingerland. Tel. 5346 or 800–223–5581. One of the most beautiful tropical gardens to be found on any island surrounds this 200-year-old estate. Five individual cottages with fine views and the restored Sugar Mill provide accommodations with modern amenities. The Long House has bar, dining room, library, and recreation room. Other attractions at this elegant inn are superb tennis court and spring-fed freshwater pool. Beach transportation provided daily for guests.

Nisbet Plantation Inn. *Deluxe.* Newcastle. Tel. 5325. This is another lovely island restoration with 35 rooms, most in cottages but some in the plantation house itself. It is situated on the foundations of an 18th-century plantation whose grounds are graced by a tall avenue of cocoanut palms leading to a beautiful beach on the windward coast. Dining room decorated with English antique furniture is exquisite. Tennis, fishing, horseback riding, sailing can be arranged.

Cliffdwellers. *Expensive.* Tamarind Bay. Tel. 617–262–3654. One of our favorite resorts, where a relaxing guesthouse atmosphere, management-inspired camaraderie, superior accommodations, and excellent food are the substance. A trek up the 150-ft. cliff or a ride on the resort tram to view St. Kitts and the Caribbean offers one of the finest views in the islands. 14 guest cottages dot the hill, and there's an ocean-view dining room and terrace bar. The 17-acre site includes large swimming pool, tennis court, 2,000 ft. of ocean frontage and beach, with horseback riding and small golf course nearby. Bostonian owner David Myer is a charming host when he's in residence.

Croney's Old Manor Estate. *Expensive.* Box 70, Gingerland. Tel. 5445. This restored 17th century sugar plantation on the slopes of Mt. Nevis is another gem among island inns, not only because of its stone-cut buildings and luxurious modern bedrooms and suites, but also for the personality of owner Vicky Knorr. 10 spacious, airy rooms with king-sized canopied double beds, fresh water pool, and garden setting. You might come here for the food at the Cooperage Dining Room alone—superb. West Indian and continental fare. Beach transportation provided for guests.

Montpelier Plantation Inn. *Moderate.* Box 474, Nevis. Tel. 5462. At 650 feet, this property includes a grand West Indian great house for drinking and loafing, 16 rooms in well appointed cottages, a big beautiful pool, and a tennis court landscaped carefully into a tropical garden. It also has its own windsurfer and speedboat, a 17-foot Boston Whaler, for waterskiing, snorkeling, and fishing. Beach transportation to Pinney's Beach provided daily for all guests.

Zetland Plantation. *Moderate.* Box 12, Gingerland. Tel. 203–327–3965 or 5454. Restored Sugar Mill is the showpiece of this 300-acre plantation inn resort, whose 22 rooms are housed in 7 double cottages, 4 separate deluxe suites with plunge pools, and the Sugar Mill. Set on the slope of Mt. Nevis with fine view. Tennis court, swimming pool, pavillion bar and terrace, full restaurant facilities and inside dining room in main house. Resort has beach bar/changing room at Pinney's Beach with free transportation for guests.

Hermitage Plantation. St. John-Fig Tree Parish. Tel. 5477. Set in the cradle of Nevis Peak, this small inn is the partially restored plantation of the Pemberton family from Wales, who built the great house in 1740. Accommodations in cottages with individual rooms featuring kitchenettes, canopied beds, and balconies or patios overlooking sea. Plantation grounds of several acres of gardens.

Pinney's Beach Hotel. *Inexpensive,* Box 61, Charleston. Tel. 5207. A comfortable pleasant beachfront property, just a few minutes from Charlestown. 54 rooms in cottages here; high-domed restaurant indoors, terraced outdoors. Some entertainment by local bands in the evening. Swimming on Pinney's long beach is a highlight, and the lagoon adjacent makes it all look like a scene from South Pacific.

Rest Haven Inn. *Inexpensive.* Box 209. Tel. 5208. Just next door to Pinney's Beach, this is the only place on Nevis that has a modern motel look. 30 rooms, most with views of the sea, and many with efficiency units. Restaurant, lounge, small freshwater swimming pool, and just a short walk from town.

HOW TO GET AROUND. It's just a short ride from the airport to Charlestown, but since most of the hotels are further on, the rates vary. There are usually at least a half-dozen taxis at the airport to meet the flights. But before you hire one, ask if your hotel has sent someone to meet you. The drivers are friendly and also good tour guides, but establish the fare in advance. Find out whether the rate quoted is in EC or U.S. dollars, or you may find yourself actually paying double fare. *T.D.C.* on Main St. in Charlestown or *Howell's Multi-Line Services,* tel. 5389 or 5464, are the car-rental agency with rates between $26–38 per day. You must obtain a local driver's license at the Traffic Department in Charlestown at a cost of EC $20. Remember to drive on the left!

TOURIST INFORMATION SERVICES. The St. Kitts–Nevis Tourist Board has offices near the harbor in *Charlestown* (tel. 5494). The St. Kitts–Nevis Hotel Association has offices in *Basseterre, St. Kitts* (tel. 2380). For sources closer to home, see Tourist Information Services section in the *Facts at Your Fingertips* chapter.

SPECIAL EVENTS. Since 1974, Nevis has celebrated Culturama from the last Thursday in July to the first Monday in August. It was organized by the Nevis Dramatic and Cultural Society to preserve traditional customs and local folk art as well as raise funds for a cultural center and theatrical productions. It ends on "August Monday," which marks the abolition of slavery in the West Indies.

The highlight of December—in fact, the entire year—is Carnival Week, which begins Dec. 26 and continues until Jan 2.

TOURS. Both half- and full-day tours are available, some for the historical attractions, others for water sports. Contact *Jans Travel Agency* in the Arcade in Charlestown (tel. 5426). Prices vary depending upon your choice. Don't miss the tour of the Nelson Museum; Alexander Hamilton's birthplace; the Bath sulphur springs; the Jewish cemetery; and the ring of the island's beaches.

BEACHES. A white-sand beach on the west coast is pebbly but well worth a swim; *Pinney's Beach* is long and special. Others along the east and south are small but adequate. On the northern coast the stretch of sand next to the *Nisbet Plantation* is a special spot.

PARTICIPANT SPORTS. To date, **swimming** and **sunbathing** is what is on Nevis and all **water-sports** activities can be arranged through your hotel or through Jans Travel Agency in Charlestown (tel. 5426). The Oualie Beach Pub on Mosquito Bay has **snorkeling, water skiing, windsurfing** (tel. 5329). Most of the hotels have **tennis** courts, and **horseback riding** can be arranged through Spencer Howell, Cane Gardens (tel. 5464).

SPECTATOR SPORTS. Grove Park is the place to go to watch **cricket** (Jan.–July) and **soccer** (July–Dec.). Check with your hotel for dates and times.

HISTORIC SITES AND HOUSES. Nevis is a small quiet island today, but that wasn't always so. Some 200 years ago it was called "the Queen of the Caribees" in that its plantations and health spa drew visitors from all over Europe. In those days it was fashionable to spend time at *The Bath Hotel* for its curative waters. High on a hill overlooking Charlestown, much of it is in ruins but is being restored and there is enough to show how the gentry spent their time during the 18th century. Nearby is *Ft. Charles,* where Nelson kept a lookout for approaching ships.

Montpelier House on Saddleback Hill was the site of the marriage of Admiral Lord Nelson to the young widow Fanny Nisbet. Its sugar mill, signs of plantation resplendence, remain, and it will be restored. *Croney's Old Manor* in Gingerland has its hotel, but also a sugar mill and a good idea of history as plantation life was back when. *Fig Tree Church* contains the register where the original marriage certificate of Lord Nelson is on display.

Golden Rock and *Zetland Plantation* still show signs of those times. They both have hotels on the premises and all the history right next door.

MUSEUMS AND GALLERIES. The *Nelson Museum* in Charlestown has all the memorabilia of Admiral Lord Nelson, who married here. It's open from 9 A.M.–1 P.M. and from 4–5 P.M. daily. Robert Abrahams is the owner and a perfect host. No admission fee. Alexander Hamilton's birthplace and museum on Main St., Charlestown, recently renovated, is another interesting site worth visiting, open weekdays, 9 A.M.–4 P.M.

SHOPPING. *Caribee Clothes* in Charlestown is a must. The prices are high, but the hand-embroidered designs unique. Out in Newcastle, on the north coast, *Newcastle Pottery* makes and sells hand-crafted pots and other ceramics. Just ask anyone nearby and they will be pleased to direct you. And, in town, at the local market, don't miss the local hot pepper sauce. The *Nevis Philatelic Bureau,* on Happy Hill Alley, has a fascinating assortment of recent stamps issues and collectors' items which make excellent and inexpensive souvenirs of the island.

RESTAURANTS. Each inn and resort on Nevis is worth a visit for lunch or dinner, as the cuisine varies according to property, but all offer superior quality at moderate to expensive prices. Reservations for dinner are required for non-guests. In Charlestown, the local watering hole on Main St., the *Longstone Bar and Restaurant,* open 10 A.M.–10 P.M. daily except Sunday, is a good place for drinks, lunch, and dinner. Owner/host Don Williams is a former Yorkshire resident, now 21 years in the West Indies, a real personality and congenial host. Lowest drink prices in Nevis.

NIGHT LIFE AND BARS. What little action there is at night is in the hotels with local entertainment. Each inn or hotel seems to have cultural shows, steel and brass bands, calypso music, folk dances, and other types of programs one night a week. Nevisians and tourists hop around from hotel to hotel. Good local music can be heard at *Dick's Bar* and *Debbie's Disco.*

POSTAGE. Airmail postage from Nevis to the U.S. or Canada was EC \$.35 for postcards and EC \$.55 per half ounce for letters. On the average, airmail letters from the island to the U.S. take eight or ten days. Nevis and its sister island St. Kitts have separate stamp-issuing policies, although both honor the other's stamps. Stamps are beautiful, and you may be more interested in collecting them than in sending them home on letters. The Nevis Philatelic Bureau is on Happy Hill Alley, near the Charlestown harbor.

ELECTRIC CURRENT. The current here is 230 volts A.C. However, electricity supply at some hotels is 110 volts. A transformer is needed for appliances from the U.S. and Canada.

SECURITY. Everybody knows everybody in Nevis, so crime is virtually nonexistent. As in most other places in the world these days, don't leave money and valuables in your hotel room. Carry your funds in traveler's checks—and be sure to record and keep their numbers in a separate and safe place. Never leave you rental car unlocked or valuables in plain sight, even if the vehicle is locked.

PUERTO RICO

by
J. P. MacBEAN

J. P. MacBean is a member of the Society of American Travel Writers and a vice-president of the New York Convention and Visitors Bureau. He has worked for Holiday *magazine, Radio Free Europe Fund, and the Colonial Williamsburg Foundation. A theater specialist, he is also a trustee of the Playhouse Repertory Company. His articles have appeared in* Travel & Leisure, Modern Bride, Horizon, Odyssey, Discovery, Meetings & Conventions, New York Daily News, *and other periodicals.*

Puerto Rico is so complex in its history and culture—so rich in the variety of its activities and attractions—that it would be a great mistake to think of this lovely island as simply another resort area. It is of course a wonderful playground—its beaches are sandy and properly palm fringed; its casinos, discos, and nightclubs quicken pulses; its hotels and *paradores* cater to both the jaded jet setter and the incurable romantic; and its restaurants pay homage to the cuisines of the world.

The decision that faces all visitors to Puerto Rico is what *type* of visit to have. The choices are numerous: a beach vacation in San Juan's fashionable Condado area; a stay in Old San Juan, whose narrow colonial streets and historic sites are easily explored on foot; a drive-around-the-island adventure, stopping in other Puerto Rican cities like Ponce and Mayagüez; a visit to a self-contained resort like Dorado Beach or Palmas del Mar; or a drive to a *parador* like Gripiñas, a former 19th-century coffee plantation in the hills above Ponce. Those who want to get away from it all can even hop a plane to one of Puerto Rico's offshore islands—Culebra or Vieques, for example.

First-time visitors will probably elect to stay in San Juan—in either the old or beachfront sections—and take day trips to various attractions like Luquillo Beach, El Yunque rain forest, Ponce ("The Pearl of the South"), Mayagüez on the western coast, and Arecibo Observatory in the northwestern section of the island.

Because of Puerto Rico's benevolent climate, the island is a popular vacation spot throughout the year. Nevertheless, the crowds tend to come during the late fall to early spring period, escaping the winter weather up north. Puerto Rico attracts a wide variety of visitors: vacationers and honeymooners on package plans, cruise passengers docking at San Juan's handsome old port, sun-seeking Canadians and vacationing college students, the rich and famous checking into luxury resorts like Dorado and Cerromar Beach, and sports lovers flying (or sailing) in for the golf, tennis, fishing, swimming, surfing, scuba diving, and horse racing. Although the sun, the sea, and the casinos are perhaps the biggest initial draws, most visitors leave with rave reviews for the warm and friendly people, the relaxed atmosphere throughout the island, the compelling history and culture, and the fascinating shops, galleries, and restaurants.

For centuries, Puerto Rico had developed artists, musicians, and writers whose work had transcended coastlines and brought them international acclaim. The work of painter Francisco Oller hangs in the Louvre. Puerto Rican writers offer a continuing enrichment to Spanish-language literature. Followers of fine music will recognize the names of pianist Jesús María Sanromá and basso Justino Díaz. The faces of José Ferrer, Rita Moreno, Chita Rivera, and José Feliciano are familiar to moviegoers and devotees of the more popular side of music. Recently, the singing group of teenage boys called *Menudo* ("small change") has become an international sensation.

To acquaint the world with the arts and culture of Puerto Rico, "Operation Serenity" was established in 1955. It created a climate in which talent could grow and flourish. The Puerto Rico Symphony Orchestra, a conservatory, and a music school were soon part of the plan. The late Pablo Casals, the famed cellist who adopted Puerto Rico (the birthplace of his mother) as his permanent home, is credited with having sparked this musical renaissance. For many years he was the star of the annual Casals Festival—an ongoing delight and special attraction each year.

"Serenity" also prompted the establishment of the Institute of Puerto Rican Culture, which successfully affected a renaissance of appreciation of the island's creations in folklore, music, sculpture, painting, theater—the last through an annual theater festival. The Institute is bringing back the past—refurbishing old churches and historic landmarks, building museums, and supervising the restoration of Old San Juan's lovely Spanish buildings. At least a dozen professional galleries are now open in the old city, and a dozen or more are dotted in communities around the Puerto Rican countryside. The Areyto Folkloric dancers have been encouraged to learn and perform (in costume) the old dances of Puerto Rico in the *LeLoLai* Festival, a weekly program of folklore, printed in the monthly *Qué Pasa*. At the performances, you'll see the "*cafetal*" (coffee plantation) dances and the dance performed by the Taino Indians at the death of a child. The group does an interesting imitation of the cockfights as well as other typically Puerto Rican events.

Past and Present

The Spanish culture dates to 1508, when Juan Ponce de León (whose remains are entombed in the San Juan Cathedral) established the first settlement. For three centuries thereafter, an international rivalry flared for possession of the island. Sir Francis Drake tried for it in 1595, but was whomped. Peace reigned in the nineteenth century. Luis Muñoz Rivera, the George Washington of Puerto Rico, won from Spain in 1897 the Charter of Autonomy which gave the island dominion status. But the autonomy was short-lived. The Spanish-American war erupted, and U.S. forces landed on the south coast July 25, 1898. Under the Treaty of Paris, proclaimed April 11, 1899, Puerto Rico passed from Spanish to U.S. sovereignty.

Military government prevailed until the Foraker Act of 1900 was passed, reestablishing civil government, but a colonial one under the thumb of Washington. The islanders were Puerto Rican citizens, ruled by a foreign power, until 1917 when the U.S. Congress made them American citizens and gave them some autonomy.

In 1926, under the sugar barons, cane cutters were getting ten cents an hour and eagerly selling their vote for $2 to elect company lawyers to the island legislature. Needlewomen, for hemming a dozen handkerchiefs, earned three cents.

Luis Muñoz Marín, at that time agitating for independence, described his island in 1929 as "a land of beggars and millionaires, of flattering statistics and distressing realities. More and more, it becomes a factory worked by peons, fought over by lawyers, bossed by absent industrialists, and clerked by politicians . . . "

However, in 1938, Muñoz had satisfied himself that independence was not feasible. In groping for something more practical, he formed the Popular Democratic Party and promised land reform and labor laws instead of independence. He was elected to the island Senate. The Popular Party set in motion a plan to industrialize the island and "Operation Bootstrap" was underway.

Although unemployment is high and the island's economy "enfeebled" (according to a 1984 study by the 20th Century Fund, a nonpartisan research foundation), the government remains optimistic and full of plans for the future. Manufacturing remains the island's first industry, but agriculture is still much in evidence throughout the interior, where visitors can see such crops as tobacco, sugar cane, beans, bananas, and citrus fruits. Puerto Rican rum continues to maintain its worldwide reputation, and a number of distilleries are open to visitors on tours.

Crime is reported to be a problem in Puerto Rico, but visitors—especially in tourist areas where facilities are well protected and well patrolled—will probably see no evidence of it. Furthermore, those who take the proper precautions necessary anywhere these days and those who do not tempt fate (like swimming from deserted beaches or flaunting money and jewelry in depressed areas) will have no cause to worry.

EXPLORING PUERTO RICO

Part of Puerto Rico's special charm is the juxtaposition of old and new. Nowhere is this more apparent than in San Juan, where the moss-covered bastions of El Morro and precincts of the now-restored old city contrast with the modern office buildings and high-rises of "new" San Juan.

Old San Juan

Old San Juan was founded in 1521, but centuries have layered their patterns on the buildings in town. Spanish buildings nestle against more modern architecture in this area, still partially encircled by its walls, begun in 1630. The ambitious restoration preserves the atmosphere of seventeenth-century Spain, as it came to the New World in the minds of the immigrants.

Plaza Colón, the starting point for a walking or minibus tour of Old San Juan, is dominated by a statue of Columbus, erected in the Plaza in 1893 to commemorate the 400th anniversary of his discovery of Puerto Rico.

The chief tourist attraction of Old San Juan is El Morro, the great fortress that the Spanish constructed at the northwest tip of the city from 1540 to 1586. Covering more than 200 acres, rising 145 feet above the Atlantic, this great bastion of colonial Spain remained impregnable from the sea even when attached in 1595 by such doughty foes as Drake and Hawkins. It was taken by the English from the land side and held briefly in 1598. The Spanish continued to improve the fortifications, and it wasn't until 1783 that El Morro was completed. The National Park Service retains the castle and part of the grounds, giving conducted tours daily. There's a splendid view from the ramparts, and the labyrinthine tunnels are fascinating. If you look over the sea wall, you'll see the old San Juan Cemetery and its elaborate circular chapel.

San Juan's beautiful harbor, nestled at the foot of the old city on top of the hill, has recently undergone a multi-million-dollar restoration, and parts of the ambitious expansion program are still underway. Trees, flowers and comfortable benches grace the waterfront esplanade, and a modern Tourism Terminal Pier serves both cruise passengers and other tourists. Across the street from the piers is the new Puerto Rican Crafts Plaza, which contains a delightful restaurant (Cafe del Puerto) that overlooks the busy harbor. The enclosed plaza also contains numerous shops selling tasteful souveniers, ceramics, fashions, and hand-carved religious figures called *santos*.

Near the main entrance of El Morro is San José Church, one of the oldest Christian places of worship still in use in the Western Hemisphere. Started by the Dominicans in 1532 the church preserves its vaulted Gothic ceilings, a rare survival of authentic medieval architecture in the New World. Ponce de León lay buried here for three-and-a-half centuries before his mortal remains were transferred to the Cathedral. His family coat of arms still hangs beneath the ceiling of the main altar. Outside on the plaza Ponce himself stands in brazen glory, his statue fashioned from bronze cannons captured from the British in 1797. Next to the church is the old Santo Domingo Convent, built by the Dominican Friars at the same time as San José Church. A handsome example of the sixteenth century Spanish colonial architecture, it was taken over by the government in 1810, when the Dominican order was dissolved. For many years, this was the Army Headquarters for the Antilles Command. Now it has been exquisitely restored by the Institute of Puerto Rican Culture for use as a showplace for island art. Most recently restored are a library and meeting room, with sixteenth and seventeenth century books and furnishings. Concerts are occasionally held in the vast arcaded patio (particularly fun are the Fridaynight, Old World band concerts, complete with shiny tubas and braided uniforms). Here, too, is the Pablo Casals Museum, located in a splendid colonial townhouse. The Maestro's memorabilia, including the famous cellos, which he left to the Puerto Rico people, is all on display. It's open daily except Monday, and well worth a visit.

Casa Blanca, a beautiful house at the foot of Calle San Sebastián near the ramparts of El Morro, was begun in 1521 to be the residence of the first govenor, Ponce de León. Seeking the Fountain of Youth in Florida, Ponce did not live to move in, but it remained the property of his family for two-and-a-half centuries. In 1773, the Ponce family sold the house to the Spanish Government. It became the home of the Spanish military commander, and subsequently the official residence of the U.S. Army's top brass. Now Commonwealth government property, it has been restored for use as a museum and cultural center.

La Fortaleza, the official residence of the Governor of Puerto Rico, is open to the public. It's just a short two-block walk to the left of Casa Blanca as you face the bay. En route you will pass the San Juan Gate, opened in 1635, and once the main entrance to the walled city of San Juan. The view of the bay, of Casa Blanca, and the massive ramparts of the town is most impressive from here. Just up the street is a small plaza, donated to the city in honor of its 450th anniversary, dominated by an impressive sculpture, La Rogativa, commemorating a legend that the flaming torches of a religious procession *(rogativa)* were what caused British troops to abandon their seige of San Juan in 1797.

Begun in 1533 as a fort, La Fortaleza, which is a remarkable building, half-palace, half-fortress, was burned by the Dutch in 1625, rebuilt in 1640, enlarged and restored to its present state in 1846. The oldest executive mansion in the Western Hemisphere, it has been the residence of 170 governors and the seat of Puerto Rico's government for more than four centuries. Its two sixteenth century towers are among the oldest military constructions in the New World.

You will probably not see the dining room, but you can pass the wrought-iron gates, see the lovely terraced gardens, the magnificent mahogany stairway, the marble floors of the reception rooms, the mosaic-studded chapel, the room once used by the Puerto Rican treasury for the storage of gold, and other rooms of this fine executive mansion. Special aides conduct tours of the mansion weekdays between 9:00 and 4:00 P.M.

Walk down Calle del Cristo with its blue ballast stones, past the Cathedral to Cristo Chapel, which was built to mark the spot where a horse and rider in 1753 leaped over the seventy-foot bluff on which it is built. (Legend had it that the young rider survived, but unfortunately his death was later substantiated by researchers.) Next to the Cristo chapel is the cool little Parque de las Palomas, with benches and an unobstructed view of the harbor. From the old city wall you'll see the courtyard of La Princesa Prisión, at the end of what was once a landscaped promenade. Bastión de la Palmas, another pleasant park, is at the harbor end of San José Street. Go back up Calle del Cristo to the corner of Calle Luna and the great Catholic shrine of Puerto Rico, the Cathedral of San Juan Bautista. Begun as early as 1521, the Cathedral has risen several times like a phoenix from its ashes. The present building dates from 1802 but conserves Gothic details dating from 1540. In it you will find the tomb of Juan Ponce de León; numerous mementos of *los reyes Católicos,* Ferdinand and Isabella; in a glass case opposite Ponce's tomb, the remains of a converted, martyred Roman centurion, St. Pio, once buried in the catacombs of Rome, is now seen in the light of the New World. Ask to see the Renaissance madonna and the sixteenth-century chalices.

Following the streets of Old San Juan as they wind up and down hills is good for the ankles and the stomach muscles. Halfway between the Cathedral and San Juan Gate, you will find one of the original staircase streets that has not succumbed to cars. This is the Callejón de Las Monjas, and if you climb it to the next street, you'll see another, the Caleta del Hospital, rising another steep block.

Visit the Museum of Colonial Architecture, La Casa del Callejón, at 319 Fortaleza Street, a restored eighteenth-century building, which has displays of four centuries of Puerto Rico's Spanish colonial architecture. There are scale models of some of the important structures you will have already visited, and a collection of antique tiles. Upstairs is the Museum of the Puerto Rico Family, furnished in the manner of a typical nineteenth-century urban household. In the first floor courtyard and small rooms, a restaurant features traditional Puerto Rican food and drink. You'll be ready, by this time, for one or both.

At 101 San Sebastian, adjacent to San José Plaza, is the Casa de los Contrafuertes, or Buttress House, built in the early eighteenth century —one of the oldest colonial buildings still standing in San Juan. It has been restored by the Institute of Culture, and houses the Museum of Puerto Rican Santos, with fine examples of the small religious figures carved from wood, some 200 years old, and the Pharmacy Museum. Upstairs is a graphic arts museum.

La Casa del Libro at 255 Cristo Street is a superb museum of rare books in an eighteenth-century house, beautifully restored and furnished, open to the public from 11:00 A.M. to 5:00 P.M., Monday through Friday. Next to La Casa del Libro is the Institute of Culture's Museum of Puerto Rican Art with a permanent exhibition of works by old masters and modernists. The façade of the City Hall, *La Alcaldia,* on the north side of the Plaza de Armas, is an exact copy of the municipal building in Madrid, built here in the seventeenth century. It houses a small museum of San Juan's history.

Casa Don Q. on Cristo, is an eighteenth-century Spanish colonial townhouse, meticulously restored by the rum-producing Serrales family as an oasis for visitors. The upstairs veranda houses a bar, replica of one in La Mancha where complimentary rum drinks are offered.

If you are an addict of military architecture, you will want to visit the Fort San Critóbal, begun in the seventeenth century to protect San Juan from any land attack from the east. It is very much larger than the El Morro fort, though with fewer levels. There are magnificent views from its ramparts and gun emplacements. The National Park Service conducts daily tours. South of the Plaza de Colón are the harbor piers and the colorful waterfront of Old San Juan. From here you can take a ferry ride (10 cents) to Cataño across the bay, an excursion whose chief rewards are refreshing breezes and a splendid view of the Old City. On Sundays and holidays there are special one-

and-a-half-hour cruises around the Bay, departing at 2:30 and 4:30 from the ferry terminal (adults, $1.50; children under 12, $1).

Facing the Plaza Colón on the south side is the municipal Tapia Theater, built about 1832 and remodeled in 1949, and named after the nineteenth-century playwright Alejandro Tapia y Rivera. Plays and ballets are often staged here. Behind the theater is the old stone public baths building, restored for use as a small museum of pre-Colombian art.

East of Plaza de Colón the island becomes an isthmus. Two major thoroughfares, Avenida Ponce de León and Avenida Fernández Juncos, lead out of Old San Juan to the booming business and tourist sections of Santurce.

"New" San Juan

Once east of Plaza de Colón, distances are too great and sights too decentralized to warrant further exploration afoot. You can go by bus, taxi or *público* to places of interest along Ponce de León Avenue. They include El Capitolio, Puerto Rico's imposing white Georgia marble capital. Although construction on the neo-Renaissance building was begun in 1925, the impressive rotunda was not completed until a few years ago. A booklet is available from the House secretariat on the second floor describing the extensive mosaics and marble friezes executed in Italy from sketches by Puerto Rican artists. The two modern buildings flanking the Capitolio house are the Senate and the House of Representatives. On the sea side of El Capitolio is a cliff-top observation plaza with a bird's eye view of the surf and, to the east, of the tourist towers of the Condado. Steps lead from the plaza down to the popular surfing beach below. The Condado area, once *the* place to go for elegant resorts, fell from grace for a while, but with recent refurbishings, the area is again San Juan's leading beachfront playground.

There's no doubt that while exploring this coastal area, you'll want to visit and photograph old Fort San Jerónimo, whose crumbling, sun-mellowed texture provides such a striking contrast with the spit-and-polish façade of the Caribe Hilton Hotel immediately to the west. Built in 1788, San Jerónimo staved off a major English attack in 1797. It has been restored and now houses a museum of Spanish military armor and weapons.

Well frequented by travelers is Boca de Cangrejos, a rocky point of land east of booming Santurce near the International Airport. On lagoon and sea, it is a good place for fishing and snorkeling; the reef is above water at low tide so walk far out to the best places for sighting the coral caves through which swim schools or brilliant tropical fish. The center of activity in Boca is the Cangrejos Yacht Club, whose members keep power boats moored in the lagoon near the club house. *La Paseadora,* a thirty-passenger launch, tours the tranquil lagoon and goes out into the Atlantic for a brief view of the hotels along the beach. The one-hour excursions begin at 11:00 A.M. daily except Monday (adults, $2.50; children up to 10 years, $1.50).

Santurce and Río Piedras

If you're looking for those technicolor local markets, shining with all the rich produce of the tropics, you'll find two in Santurce and Río Piedras. The first district, with its shiny shops and office buildings, you

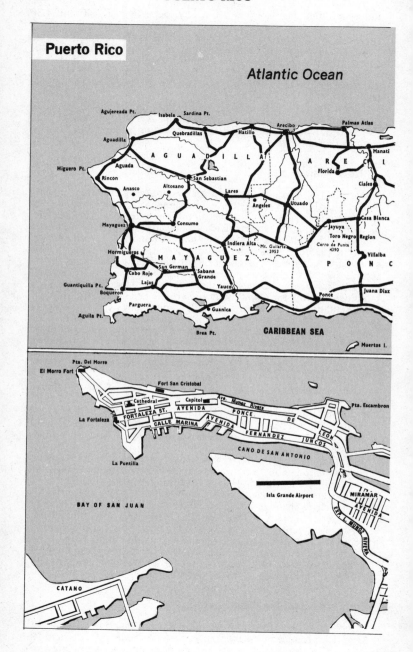

Puerto Rico

Atlantic Ocean

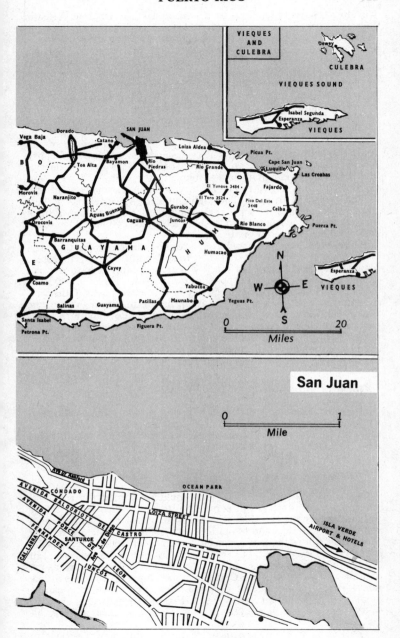

will already have passed through, driving down the main drag, Avenida Ponce de León. Santurce's "progress" from tranquil suburb to booming metropolis is the story of twentieth-century San Juan. Away from the traffic of Ponce de León Avenue, you'll still find a few old Spanish estates, vestiges of a quieter day, but most of them have been subdivided. Smart modern houses are the mark of residential Santurce today.

Heading south toward Río Peidras from Santurce you pass through what has become the city's new hub—Hato Rey. Once a no-man's land, it is now marked by a towering concentration of handsome office buildings that house almost all the major banks, corporations, and professionals.

Río Piedras, once a quiet town, is now a southern suburb of San Juan. The University of Puerto Rico is here. Its campus is a landscaped beauty and the site of the annual Casals Festival, as well as concerts and theatrical productions held throughout the year. Visit their Museum of Anthropology, Art, and History, which has a small but intriguing collection of artifacts. The highlight here, however, is the vast Botanical Garden, with a network of paths that cut through a thick forest, past a lotus lagoon, and through a bamboo promenade to reach their spectacular orchid garden.

Before extending your explorations "out on the island," as the Puerto Ricans say, perhaps you will want to see another industrial process in action, the distillation of rum. If you are planning to go to Arecibo or Ponce, you can save this experience for the Ron Rico or Don Q Rum distilleries, which operate respectively in those two towns. Otherwise drive to the little town of Palo Seco on the southwestern shore of the Bay of San Juan, where the Bacardi people will show you how sugar is transformed into rum and ply you with copious draughts of same, after which the view across the bay to El Morro and San Juan seems even more romantic than usual. A 50¢ bus ride will carry you between the distilleries and the Cataño-San Juan ferry dock.

Out on the Island

Puerto Rico has about 400 miles of good roads, and you could spend weeks exploring the island. The short tour below you can drive yourself, arrange through one of the agencies indicated in the monthly *Qué Pasa,* or take your own group in a *público.*

Pineapple Country

Our short tour, an all-day affair, could be termed the rum and pineapple route, since it will permit you to visit a distillery and tour the pineapple country. Take Route 2 west out of San Juan through Bayamón, Vega Baja, and Manatí. Branch right on Route 681 beyond Manatí and follow the coastal road to Arecibo. Settled in 1556, Arecibo is one Puerto Rico's oldest towns. Four miles east of the town you can visit an Indian cave, used a place of worship before the Spaniards came, its walls decorated with pre-Columbian drawings and carvings in low relief. Arecibo is a center for deep-sea fishermen. Information can be obtained at the Club de Caza y Pesca. Freshwater fishermen also like to try their luck near here in the lakes made by Dos Bocas and Caonillas dams.

The Public Works Department operates a free launch service to points around man-made Dos Bocas Lake. Launches leave from the

Embarcadero (Route 10, Km. 63) for two-hour roundtrips at 7:00 and 10:00 A.M. and 2:00 and 5:00 P.M., and for a one-hour trip at 12:30 P.M. Near Dos Bocas is the teak-filled, 5800-acre Río Abajo State Forest, with a ranger's office, sawmill, and brookside picnic area. A small swimming pool is open weekends.

There are also dozens of mountain caves and ruined sugar mills to explore and the world's largest radar-radio telescope, open Sundays from 2:00 to 4:30 P.M.

The Ron Rico rum distillery at Arecibo welcomes visitors. Have lunch, visit the sugar mills; then take Route 2 back to Manatí, heart of the pineapple country. If you turn left here on Route 685 you come to grotto-like Mar Chiquita Beach, where the sea plunges in through an opening in the rock cliffs to a lovely crescent beach.

Heading back to San Juan on Route 2, a short detour on Route 165 will take you past Cataño to the Bacardi distillery and to the causeway leading to Cabras Island, a popular picnic area with snack bar and thatched huts, a seventeenth-century Spanish fort, El Cañuelo, in picturesque ruins, lovely views of the bay and the Old City.

Scenic Stretches

If it's simply fabulous scenery you crave, you should include any (or all) of the following particularly scenic stretches of road to be found in Puerto Rico; in the western half of the island, (1) Route 149 from Villalbra to Ciales; (2) Route 143 from Barranquitas through the Toro Negro forest to Route 10; (3) Route 105 from Mayagüez to Maricao, south on Route 120 through the Maricao State Forest to Sabana Grande; (4) Route 10 from Arecibo to Utuado, right on 111 to Aguadilla. In the eastern half of the island (in addition to El Yunque rain forest) you can travel: (1) the completed segments of the long-awaited Panoramic Route, eventually to stretch all the way from Yabucao in the southeast corner to Mayagüez on the west coast, by taking Route 1 to Caguas, Route 30 to Humacao, south on 901 to Maunabo and circling back north again on Route 3; (2) Route 181 from Trujillo Alto to Gurabo; (3) Route 181 from Trujillo Alto to left turn on 858, then right on 852, then follow signs on small unnumbered roads to 853, where you turn right then left on 185, then right on 186 to Río Grande; (4) Route 1 south from Caguas, left on 765, then right on 763 until it merges with 184, south on 184 to Patillas, (5) Route 15 from Cayey to Guayama, another section of the Panoramic Route, passing Jájome, the Governor's summer residence.

Most spectacular of all is the San Juan-Ponce toll road, which cuts a wide and wonderful swathe through the rugged mountains of the Cordillera Central making driving time between the two cities an hour and a half.

When organizing your trips, here are some places of more than ordinary tourist interest to include: Aguada and Aguadilla. On the northwest coast, Aguada, settled in 1590, claims to be the place where Columbus first set foot on Puerto Rican soil and marks the spot, at the end of Calle Colón, where the Admiral's foot presumably stepped. Aguadilla, a few miles to the north, disputes the foregoing claim and has its own monument. Aguadilla is a center of the island's straw-hat industry. The former Ramey Air Force Base is a few miles north of town and, as Borinquén Field, is open to civilian air traffic. Now operated as a resort complex, Punta Borinquen, the former officers homes (solid three-bedroom houses) are rented to vacationers for a modest $60 per day. Las Playuelas beach is nearby.

Aguas Buenas is half an hour from San Juan up into the cool mountains. The towering antennae that mark the town from afar belong to the government-operated radio and television stations, WIPR. A pleasant, typical town built around a plaza.

Barranquitas, a charming mountain town almost in the center of Puerto Rico and between San Juan and Ponce, is a popular year-round resort because of its cool climate. It is the birth and burial place of the great statesman Luis Muñoz Rivera (1859–1916), father of the former governor, whose home is a library and museum, open to public. One Sunday in mid-July, the Institute of Culture sponsors a craft show in the town plaza. Artisans come from all over the island to commemorate Muñoz Rivera's birthday.

Boquerón, a lovely public beach on the west coast, rivals Luquillo.

Cabo Rojo, once the lair of the pirate Roberto Cofresí, is a quiet town on the dry southwestern coast, known by the Puerto Ricans as the "desert" country. About eight miles south of Cabo Rojo are the marine salt beds with a commercial production of some 12,000 tons of salt annually. At the southwesternmost tip of the island is El Faro de Punta Jagüey, a lighthouse standing sentinel over the rugged cliffs. En route, at El Combate, there is a ramshackle fishing village set at one end of a long beach of incredible tranquility and beauty, and a fresh fish and lobster are prepared in the one or two small cafés by the pier.

Camuy, west of Arecibo, is the site of an extensive cave system, hailed by the National Speleological Society as unique and awe inspiring.

Caparra, on Route 2, a few minutes south of San Juan, is historically interesting as the site of the first settlement in Puerto Rico. You can still see the foundations of Ponce de León's first house, built in 1508. Excavated and restored by the Institute of Culture, they stand in a small park. A small museum contains Indian relics, charts, and ornaments uncovered during excavation.

Dorado Beach, twenty miles west of San Juan, is the locale of the Caribbean project started by Laurance Rockefeller interests. Visitors can stop for lunch, a swim, tennis or golf at secluded Dorado Beach or the 503-room Cerromar Beach Hotel. The town of Dorado is small, rural Puerto Rican and, except for those residents who work at the hotels, little affected by tourism.

A few minutes past the entrance to Dorado Beach is the seaside village of Cerro Gordo, where many Sanjuaneros weekend. The beach here is one of the area's best, and the small inn in the heart of the weekend community serves Puerto Rican specialties.

Fajardo, on the northeast coast of the island, is a fishing and sailing center that changed hands three times during the Spanish-American War. The Isleta Marina yachting center is nearby, but in Fajardo itself, you'll find Las Croabas with its array of fishing boats; the Puerto Chico marina, and the Villa Marina Yacht Harbor. The beautiful uninhabited island called Icacos is not far offshore. You can negotiate with one of the fishermen to take you over for a swim, or make a full day of it by signing aboard the *Spread Eagle* cantamaran for a quiet sail that includes snorkeling the reef, swimming, sunbathing, and a buffet lunch for $25 per person. Ferries also leave from Fajardo for the offshore islands of Culebra and Vieques ($2.25 one-way). Culebra has white sand crescent beaches, reefs to explore, and a few small inns. Vieques is similar, with a fine beach on Sun Bay, which has lockers, showers, a snack bar, and the small inn, La Casa del Francés.

Guánica was the site of the American landing on the south coast in 1898. The Copamarina Hotel is here, near an inviting beach, and there's a picturesque old Spanish lighthouse. Nearby, the strange scrub and cactus landscape of the Guánica State Forest extends to the edge of the sea. Special attraction here is the population of Puerto Rican whippoorwills, believed to be extinct but rediscovered in 1961.

Hormigueros, a southwestern village a few miles south of Mayagüez, is famous for its Shrine of Our Lady of Monserrat, who, in the seventeenth century, responded to a peasant's call for help and saved him from the charge of a mad bull. An annual pilgrimage takes place every September 8.

Humacao is a bustling industrial town on the eastern coast of the island, producing tons of sugar in the most up-to-date refineries, and providing a dramatic contrast to sleepier, undeveloped neighboring villages. There's a magnificent public beach north of town, with lockers, changing facilities, and restaurants.

Just to the south of Humacao, in an area of extraordinary beauty, is 2800-acre Palmas del Mar resort and leisure community that includes residential, resort, and commercial facilities as well as botanical gardens, marinas, beaches, restaurants, villages for golf or tennis, a special inn, and a brand-new hotel in the center of it all.

Jájome, the attractive summer residence of the Governor of Puerto Rico, is located right on Highway 151 between Cayey and Guayama, an old south coast Puerto Rican city, founded in 1790. Now enlarged, the main stone structure was originally built by the Spaniards to house *camineros* (highway maintenance men). Cordillera Central, in superbly graded serpentine style, is admired by engineers, and the scenery makes it a top flight favorite. Near the Governor's residence is a replica of the Grotto of Lourdes.

Mayagüez, with a population well over 100,000 is the third city of Puerto Rico, smack in the center of the western coast. Long the needle-work center of the island, it is still a good place to pick up lovely embroidery and drawn-thread work. Just north of the city is the Mayagüez Institute of Tropical Agriculture with splendidly landscaped grounds replete with exotic trees: cacao, ilang ilang, cinnamon, and bamboo. And don't miss a trip to the zoo nearby, where more than 500 birds and animals, both indigenous and imported, roam 45 acres.

Parguera is a fishing village on the southwestern coast, popular with visitors, but still "unspoiled." You can rent fishing boats and tackle here, fill your scuba tanks, eat seafood at the Villa Parguera Hotel or in a number of unpretentious local restaurants where they know how to grill lobster and fry *pescado*. The great attraction, though, is Phosphorescent Bay. Draw your arm through the water and you describe an arc of darting quick silver flame. Impressive on any night, the phosphorescent effects are most striking during the dark of the moon. You can arrange for a motor boat tour of the bay at the Villa Parguera.

Luquillo and El Yunque

Perhaps the most popular side trip out of San Juan is a day's visit to lovely Luquillo Beach and the nearby El Yunque rain forest, both less than an hour's drive to the island's northeast section. (Take Route 3 east from San Juan.)

Luquillo, which was once a thriving coconut plantation, is a graceful, crescent-shaped, white-sand beach. Its calm, crystal-clear lagoon, protected by barrier reefs, is perfect for swimming. Its hard-packed sands make beach strolls a delight. Bring a picnic lunch or pick up native treats, including slices from whole roasted pigs, at the numerous roadside stands. Luquillo charges a small entrance fee (25¢), and parking is $1. Closed on Mondays and crowded on weekends.

El Yunque rain forest encompasses 28,000 acres and reaches an elevation of 3,526 feet, so its climate is pleasantly cool. Some 100 *billion* gallons of rain fall each year—in brief, tropical showers—so the flora is lush, to say the least. At least 240 different tree species grow here, along with such flowers as long—stem white tuberoses, masses of pink impatiens and white ginger, and clusters of tiny orchids. El Yunque is also a notable bird refuge (the striking Puerto Rican parrot is in residence here), and millions of inch-long tree frogs called *coquis* chirp amid the dense foliage.

The rain forest is vast, so by all means join a tour or arrange a guide. One "must" stop is the 95-step concrete observation tower that affords breathtaking views of the surrounding forest and the sea far away. El Yunque is named for the good Indian spirit Yuquiyú—the Luquillo Mountain Range (El Yunque is also the name of the highest peak) sheltered the ferocious Carib Indians for over 200 years.

Ponce

Ponce, the "Pearl of the South," is the second city of Puerto Rico, but is still little known to most visitors to the island. It is just a one-and-a-half-hour drive from San Juan and, with a population close to 150,000, hopes to become an important port and tourist center. Take the time to walk through this charming provincial capital and to enjoy its main plaza where fountains play and gardens flourish in front of Our Lady of Guadalupe Cathedral, which dominates the square. The 1883 Parque de Bombas, Ponce's colorful firehouse, is the single most photographed object in Puerto Rico. It's painted red and black, the city's colors, and its trucks are painted a bright yellow. Walk on and note the *rejas,* balconies and other wrought-iron details on the old Spanish houses. The local market and waterfront are exceptionally colorful. El Tuque Beach, two miles southwest of Ponce, is a first-rate beach and recreational area. There are picnic tables, lockers, a swimming pool, and a coffee shop. It's closed on Mondays. If you still haven't seen the process that turns sugar cane into demon rum, here's another chance at Ponce's Don Q Rum Distillery.

The Ponce museum, designed by Edward Durrell Stone, is across from the Catholic University on Las Américas Avenida. It has hexagonal art galleries, a circular pool, and graceful, curving stairways leading to the second floor. Works on view in this Museo de Arte de Ponce include paintings from major European schools from the fourteenth to twentieth centuries, as well as those of Puerto Rican artists.

Las Américas Expressway, known as route 52 and opened officially in late '75, makes it possible to race from San Juan to Ponce in an hour and a half. The sixty-three mile road weaves around some of Puerto Rico's highest mountain peaks, once you've mastered the traffic and confusion of Río Piedras in the San Juan orbit. Explore Ponce, have lunch in town or at the Holiday Inn pool, and drive back, or fly Prinair to San Juan (20 minutes) from the Ponce Airport.

San Germán, in the southwest sector of the island, is one of the most attractive towns in Puerto Rico and in the West Indies. Founded on its present site in 1573, it keeps the look of a little Spanish town, the special ambience of Mediterranean civilization. Although its population is under 20,000, San Germán was once the rival of San Juan. Until the second half of the seventeenth century, San Juan and San Germán were the only two towns on the island; the rest were merely hamlets.

But today, while San Juan is exploding, San Germán remains relatively untouched by the innovations of a newer time, in spite of being headquarters for the 8,000-student Inter-American University. This only tends to give a more cultural air to this charming town.

The Porta Coeli (Gate of Heaven) Church takes you back to the days of Spanish colonialism. Built in 1606, Porta Coeli is the oldest church under the U.S. flag to remain intact. Its altar, its carved wooden pillars, and its heavy entrance doors are just as they were nearly five centuries ago. It houses a colonial religious art collection.

Vieques, off the eastern coast, is one of Puerto Rico's three island "possessions." The other two are its neighbor Culebra, notable for its crescent beaches and underwater sea life on its reefs, and Mona, a barren plateau off the western coast. Vieques is easily reached by ferry from Fajardo. Horses can be rented at La Casa del Francés, a lovely old plantation house, now a guesthouse. There are several gorgeous beaches. Another, even brighter, phosphorescent bay has been discovered here and is expected to add greatly to the island's tourist potential.

PRACTICAL INFORMATION FOR PUERTO RICO

FACTS AND FIGURES. The island of Puerto Rico encompasses 3500 square miles; it is 100 miles long by 35 miles wide. Three coasts are lapped by the Atlantic, one by the Caribbean. Nearest neighbors are St. Thomas (40 miles east) and the Dominican Republic (54 miles west). The Commonwealth of Puerto Rico also includes four small offshore islands: Culebra, Vieques, Icacos, and Mona, plus various uninhabited islets and cays. Total population is approaching 3.5 million, with 1 million of these people in the metropolitan area of capital, San Juan.

Puerto Rico's annual average temperature is 77 degrees F. The north coast averaged 90 inches of rainfall a year, the south coast about 45. In the rain forest as much as 200 inches may fall in the course of a year. Winter temperatures in San Juan range from the low 70s to the low 80s; it's about five degrees warmer in the summer. Mountain climate is about 5 to 10 degrees colder. The driest season is March–April, the wettest May–December.

WHEN TO GO. Because millions of Puerto Ricans have migrated to the mainland United States, particularly to the East Coast, holidays mean mass homecomings. The Thanksgiving, Christmas, New Year's, and Easter vacation periods—which coincide with the island's most popular tourist months (November–April)—can be crowded periods. Airline, cruise-ship, and hotel reservations are advised as far in advance as possible, although this may mean missing out on last-minute airfare fluctuations or special package plans.

Puerto Rico's weather has been called one of the most equitable climates in the world, and the average islandwide annual temperature is in the upper 70s, with only a six-degree difference between the warmest and coolest months. No wonder the Puerto Ricans boast about their "twelve months of summer," and no wonder the island is an attractive vacation spot all year long. This salubrious climate results from Puerto Rico's tropical location (between the equator and the Tropic of Cancer), the ocean currents that surround the island, and the cooling breezes that keep humidity under control, especially in the coastal areas. Puerto Rico's central mountain range, where some of the most attractive country inns *(paradores)* are located, registers considerably cooler temperatures throughout the year, and this factor also helps to regulate the island's climate.

Still, summer temperatures often reach into the 80s and 90s; if you are away from the beaches—or on a dusty country back road—you will know you are in the tropics. Consequently, the fall, winter, and spring months remain the most popular. If you do visit in summer, stick to the beaches, stay in one of the self-contained coastal resorts, or head for the hills.

 HOW TO GET THERE. By Air. Puerto Rico's San Juan International airport is a gigantic web of activity that serves as the gateway to the Caribbean. There are dozens of flights from major U.S. cities via *American Airlines, Capital Airways, Delta, Eastern,* and *Pan American; Air France, British Caledonian, Iberia, Lufthansa,* and *Pan American* fly in from Europe; and *Avianca, Mexicana,* and *Viasa* connect Puerto Rico to the larger cities in Mexico and South America.

Puerto Rico is the northern terminal, as Barbados/Trinidad is the southern, for inter-island flights. *Prinair,* the "national" airline of Puerto Rico, serves the islands between Puerto Rico and Gaudeloupe. Their services are supplemented by an expanding network of small charter planes. It is possible to get to all islands, even the smallest, out of Puerto Rico and often at the height of the season. This is the best way to get south.

By Sea. There is no passenger service direct from New York to San Juan or Miami to San Juan, although most cruise lines do stop here on their journeys through the Caribbean. In recent seasons, San Juan has become home port for several ships that set out from here on journeys farther south. *Cunard, Chandris, Costa, Princess Cruises, Sitmar Cruises,* and *Sun Line* operate more than a dozen ships from San Juan's harbor.

PASSPORTS AND VISAS. None needed for U.S. citizens. Canadian citizens need proof (a passport is best). British citizens need a passport and visa.

MONEY. U.S. dollars.

TAXES AND OTHER CHARGES. There is a 6% government tax on hotel rooms. Some of the hotels add a service charge of 10% on top of that, but most do not. There are no airport departure taxes.

WHAT WILL IT COST?

A typical day in winter for two persons in San Juan will run:

	U.S.$
Accommodations in the Condado/Isla Verde area (moderate hotel)	$80
Breakfast at the hotel coffee shop	10
Luncheon at a moderate restaurant	20
Dinner at an "in town" restaurant	30
Taxes, tips, and service charges	15
Car rental or one-day sightseeing	25
	$180

TELEPHONES AND EMERGENCY NUMBERS. The area code for Puerto Rico is 809. Some useful phone numbers: Fire, 343–2330; Police, 343–2020; Ambulance, 343–2550; Emergency Medical Services, 754–3535; Travelers' Aid, 791–1054, ASSIST (Assistance to Stricken Travelers), 724–2160; Ashford Community Hospital, Ashford Avenue in the Condado area, has an emergency station.

HOTELS. Puerto Rico offers accommodations to suit every budget and every type of vacation: luxurious, self-contained resorts (for gracious, relaxing visits); high-rise hotels and casinos on San Juan's Condado/Isla Verde beachfront (for excitement, night and day); guesthouses and country inns called *paradores* (for warmth and charm); fine, modern hotels "out on the island" in Puerto Rico's other cities like Ponce and Mayagüez (for all the conveniences, but away from the hustle and bustle); and, in a class by itself, El Convento Hotel, a former 17th-century Carmelite convent, in Old San Juan (for those who want to steep themselves in the comfort of today while soaking up the romance of yesterday).

High season for Puerto Rico comes when chilly weather hits the Northern Hemisphere: roughly November–April. Within this peak period, holidays like Thanksgiving, Chanukah/Christmas/New Year's, midterm school vacations, and Passover/Easter are especially busy. Although Puerto Rico prides itself on a wealth of accommodations—and encourages last-minute, impulse trips—it's always wise to book rooms as far in advance as possible. Plans made at least two weeks to a month ahead should guarantee the rates and reservations you seek.

Daily rates range from about $40–65 a double room in the government-operated *paradores* to about $200 in the luxury resorts. Weekly rates at resorts run $700–1,500, and special rates and package plans can produce bargains everywhere. Price ranges for double occupancy in season are: *Deluxe,* $150–200; *Expensive,* $100–150; *Moderate,* $50–100; and *Inexpensive,* under $50.

Luxury Resorts

Cerromar Beach Hotel. Route 693. Tel. (800) 545–4000 or 796–1010. 508 air-conditioned rooms and suites in an eight-story luxury hotel run by Hyatt Corporation. Cerromar caters to meetings as well as individuals. Rooms, each with a sea-facing balcony, offer spectacular views. Plant-filled lobby, greenhouse cocktail lounge, *El Yunque Bar, El Bucanero* informal dining room, more formal *Surf Room and Supper Club Cerromar.* All-weather tennis courts (14), two 18-hole Robert Trent Jones golf courses (with guest privileges at sister resort Dorado), free summer and holiday Camp Coquin for kids, bike paths. Dancing and nightclub entertainment at Club Cerromar; gambling at the casino.

Dorado Beach Hotel, Hyatt Corporation, Route 693 (Cerromar's sister resort, less than 30 minutes west of San Juan). Tel. (800) 545–4000 or 796–1600. 308 air-conditioned rooms and elegant casitas. A private, 1,000-acre beachfront plantation estate with two pools, wading pool, two 18-hole Robert Trent Jones golf courses, tennis courts, full recreation and sports facilities and reef-sheltered crescent beaches. Beautifully planted grounds, lavish meals in the candlelit *Surf Room,* plus dining and dancing in the original hacienda *Su Casa.* Small casino.

Hilton International Mayagüez. Mayagüez. Tel. (800) 223–1146. 150 air-conditioned rooms, overlooking the deep-water harbor on the island's west coast. This luxury resort hotel is a 25-acre paradise offering a pool, three night-lighted tennis courts, a new fitness center, attractive cocktail lounge, and fine dining room. Just minutes away from two golf courses, Puerto Rico's famed Boquerón Swimming Beach, Punta Higuera surfing beach, the Mayagüez Marina for deep-sea fishing, and seven prime beachfront fishing spots.

Palmas del Mar. Humacao, Route 923 (about an hour from San Juan on southwest coast). Tel. 852–3450. 102 rooms, 88 beach villas and 88 harborside villas. Once a 2,700-acre cocoanut plantation, this still-developing resort village (begun in 1972) now has two hotels (Palmas Inn and Candelero Hotel), villas and townhouses, private homes and two-story condos. Golden-sand, crescent beaches face the Caribbean but the currents are usually too strong for swimming. An 18-hole Gary Player golf course, tennis courts (20), freshwater pools (four), sailing, windsurfing, snorkeling, scuba diving, deep-sea fishing, jogging, biking, horseback riding. Continental, Caribbean, and American cuisine, including freshly caught seafood. Family plans, honeymoon, anniversary, and sports packages.

SAN JUAN BEACHFRONT

Expensive

Caribe Hilton International. Puerta de Tierra. Tel. (800) 223–1146 or 721–0303. 707 air-conditioned rooms and suites. The grande dame of the Hilton International chain (built in 1949) occupies 17 acres and includes tropical gardens and historic Fort San Jeronimo. A private, palm-lined swimming cove, two swimming pools, tennis courts, putting green, water-sports headquarters, skytop health club and solarium, dance lessons, craft classes, and a lobby lined with shops. Fine restaurants, the island's most exclusive disco, and a casino.

Condado Beach Hotel. Ashford Ave., Condado. Tel. 721–6090. 252 air-conditioned rooms and suites. Built in 1919 by Cornelius Vanderbilt and now beautifully refurbished, this peaches-and-cream Spanish beauty adjoins the Convention Center (meeting facilities for 4000) and La Concha Hotel, recently reopened. Speak-easy parties, silent movies, and fashion shows recreate the Great Gatsby ambience. Third-floor pool surrounded by palms and waterfalls; *El Gobernador* dining room overlooks the ocean; *Grand Ballroom* hosts the island's most extravagant social events. Monte Carlo Casino.

Condado Plaza Hotel & Casino (formerly the Condado Holiday Inn). 999 Ashford. Tel. 721–1000. 587 air-conditioned rooms and suites. Wildly successful, this large luxury hotel incorporates the former Flamboyan. A shop-filled tropical lobby, three pools, two tennis courts, beautiful beach, four restaurants, *Casanova's* (a nightclub with Las Vegas floorshows), *Isadora's* disco, and Puerto Rico's largest casino.

Dupont Plaza San Juan. 1309 Ashford, Condado. Tel. 724–6161. 450 air-conditioned rooms and suites. Lively and convivial, with a popular piano bar *(Zanzibar),* a top-floor *Steak Penthouse* for dining and dancing, and an action-packed casino.

Isla Verde Holiday Beach Resort. Route 187. Tel. 791–2300. 410 air-conditioned rooms and suites. A warm, homey, on-the-beach hotel with water sports, three tennis courts, swimming pool, coffee shops, and familiar foods. Casino.

The Palace. Route 187, Isla Verde. Tel. 791–2020. 450 air-conditioned rooms and suites. A tropical garden by the sea with six restaurants, two nightclubs, six lounges, water sports, tennis, casino.

Ramada San Juan, 1045 Ashford, Condado. Tel. 724–5657. 96 air-conditioned rooms, Oceanfront views, pool, restaurant, casino.

Moderate

Carib-Inn. Route 187. Isla Verde. Tel. 791–3535. 225 air-conditioned rooms and suites. Formerly the Racquet Club, this place teems with youthful action. Health club, eight tennis courts, racquet-shaped pool, five minutes from beach by foot or beach buggy. *Cousin Ho's* Restaurant, *La Tinaja Cafe, El Intimo Club,* casino.

Dutch Inn & Towers, 55 Condado. Tel. 721–0810. 144 air-conditioned rooms and apartment suites. Freshwater pool, excellent *Greenhouse* restaurant, sidewalk café.

Excelsior Hotel. 801 Ponce de León, Miramar. Tel. 721–7400. 140 air-conditioned rooms and suites (many with kitchenettes). Dining room, cocktail lounge, pool, free transportation to nearby beach.

Howard Johnson's Nabori Lodge. 1369 Ashford, Condado. Tel. 721–7300. 150 air-conditioned rooms and suites. Simplicity, comfort, and good value—the HJ trademarks—with Puerto Rican touches. A family place—no charge for children.

Inexpensive

Arcade Inn, 8 Taft, Ocean Park. Tel. 728–7524. 19 air-conditioned rooms and efficiency units. Owned by Aurelio Cinque, this stucco home is near Condado. Breakfast and light lunch only; close to beach.

El Canario Guesthouse. 1317 Ashford, Condado. Tel. 724–2793. 25 air-conditioned rooms in a former Condado house turned into an inn. Homelike feeling with many regulars. Small pool, sundeck, laundry facilities, near beach.

Tres Palmas Guesthouse. 2212 Park Blvd., Punta Las Marias. Tel. 727–4617. Eight air-conditioned rooms. Right on the beach, this 50-year-old Spanish house treats guests as family. Rooftop sundeck, luncheon with a sea view, a spa/pool, reading and game room.

OLD SAN JUAN

El Convento, 100 Cristo. Tel. (800) 468–2779. 100 air-conditioned rooms and suites. A first-class property of moderate to expensive prices. An aristocratic, architectural, historic gem. Once a 17th-century Carmelite convent, it has been thoroughly modernized with every creative comfort. Rooms on each of five floors open onto galleries that overlook the inner courtyard, where meals are served and entertainment is staged. There is also a small pool and free transportation to the beach. Across from the cathedral, near all historic area shops, galleries, restaurants, and historic sites.

OUT ON THE ISLAND

For Dorado, Humacao, and Mayagüez, see *Luxury Resorts.*

Aguadilla

Parador Montemar, *Inexpensive.* Route 2, 891–4383. 40 rooms. Each room in this hillside inn has a small balcony for superb ocean and sunset views. Fine fishing and beach swimming. Terrace dining on Puerto Rican specialties; small pool; near fascinating 16th-century Taino Indian Ball Park, which was used for religious ceremonies as well as ball games.

Cabo Rojo

Boquemar Hotel. *Inexpensive.* Route 101. Tel. 851–2158. 41 air-conditioned rooms. Unpretentious fishing-village place—one of Puerto Rico's best buys. Swimming, boating—and the restaurant is noted for the freshest fish.

Coamo

Parador Baños de Coamo. *Inexpensive.* Route 546. Tel. 825–2186. 48 air-conditioned rooms. Northeast of Ponce and two hours from San Juan, this modern mountain inn (built on the ruins of Puerto Rico's oldest resort) is located at the hot sulphur Coamo Springs known to earliest Taino Indians. Some say it's the Fountain of Youth Ponce de León was seeking, and among the famous visitors it once welcomed were Franklin Roosevelt, Thomas Edison, Alexander Graham Bell, and Frank Lloyd Wright. Closed since the late 1950s, it reopened in 1977 with two-story buildings surrounding a center courtyard. Puerto Rican food served in the elegant main house. A quiet and peaceful place.

Fajardo

Delicias Hotel. *Inexpensive.* Puerta Real Beach. Tel. 863–1818. 20 air-conditioned rooms. Overlooks the ferry landing for boats to the offshore islands of Culebra and Vieques (and the picnic spots on uninhabited Icacos Island). A modern façade masks a charming, plant-filled courtyard. Neat, well-furnished rooms with shower and modern plumbing. Fine seafood.

Jayuya

Parador Hacienda Gripiñas. *Inexpensive.* Route 527. Tel. 721–2884. 19 rooms. Most visitors' favorite parador, Gripiñas began as a mid-19th-century coffee plantation in the cool, breezy, central mountains north of Ponce. Beautifully tended gardens; a large swimming pool; rooms with Puerto Rican polished woods, crafts, and art works; and fine traditional food and drink. A very special place—perfect for families, poets, and other romantics.

La Parguera

Villa Parguera. *Inexpensive.* Route 304. Tel. 899–3975. 51 rooms (most air-conditioned). Here you arrange deep-sea fishing trips and nighttime cruises of shimmering Phosphorescent Bay. A small, fishing-village hotel with saltwater pool, restaurant, and cocktail lounge.

Maricao

Parador Hacienda Juanita. *Inexpensive.* Route 105 Tel. 838–2550. 21 rooms. Another former coffee plantation in the cool central mountains. Simple rooms in a U-shaped wood-frame building open on a delightful courtyard with splashing fountain. Foliage is abundant, the *coquis* (tiny tree frogs) chirp, and birds sing. A small pool; horses for riding; and bowered lanes for strolling.

Ponce

Holiday Inn. *Moderate.* Route 2. Tel. 844–1200. 120 air-conditioned rooms. Tucked into the mountainside and overlooking the sea, this modern hotel has tennis courts, two pools (one for children), two double beds in each room, color TV, a game room for the entire family, and nightly entertainment in the lounge. Steaks are charcoaled on an open hearth. Babysitting services.

Melia Hotel. *Inexpensive.* 2 Cristina St. Tel. 842–0261. 80 air-conditioned rooms, just off the famous colonial plaza. The Melia is a long-established, distinguished address with a charming, memorabilia-filled lobby, a popular dining room, and a delightful rooftop terrace.

Quebradillas

Parador El Guajataca. *Moderate.* Route 2. Tel. 895–2204. 38 air-conditioned rooms. A family-run neighborhood hub on the northwest coast—an ideal spot for those interested in village events and local life. Motel-style rooms, lively bar, occasional evening entertainment, Puerto Rican country food, swimming pool, tennis court.

Rincón

Villa Cofresi. *Moderate.* Route 115. Tel. 823–2681. Named for the legendary pirate, Roberto Cofresi (a local Robin Hood), this surfers' haven on Puerto Rico's westernmost tip is also for families who love both pool and beach vacations. The flora—including sugarcane fields, mangos, pineapples, and coconuts—is profuse, and the sunsets are spectacular. A casual, family-run hotel.

San Germán

Hotel Oasis Parador. *Moderate.* Luna St. Tel. 892–1345. 22 air-conditioned rooms. Puerto Rico's newest parador was once a 200-year-old family mansion and winery in this delightful and historic "little Spanish town," whose 16th-century charm remains relatively untouched.

OFFSHORE ISLANDS

Culebra

Culebra Island Resort Associates. *Inexpensive.* Punta Aloe. Tel. 742–3575. Four fully-equipped houses (for up to six occupants). Snorkeling and windsurfing equipment; jeeps available. A get-away-from-it-all place for the self-sufficient adventurer.

Seafarer's Inn. *Inexpensive.* 6 Pedro Márquez, Dewey. Tel. 742–3171. 11 rooms and two apartments (for up to six occupants). A casual, roadside, oceanfront haven for barefoot boat and water-sport fans.

Vieques

La Casa del Francés. *Inexpensive.* Barrio Esperanza. Tel. 741–3751. 19 air-conditioned rooms. Once the home of a French West Indies planter, this informal inn offers horseback riding, beach strolling, snorkeling, scuba diving, sailing, and pool swimming.

 HOME AND APARTMENT RENTALS/TIMESHARING. There is, unfortunately, no centralized service handling private rentals of homes or apartments. Similarly, timesharing has not hit Puerto Rico in a big way. However, if you prefer a housekeeping vacation, you're not out of luck. Posh condominiums and villas are available at Palmas del Mar ($180–$400 for a double in high season; less than half that the rest of the year). ESJ Towers, in Isla Verde, are condominium apartments with hotel management and a beachfront location; average $200 in high season, $80 low season. Various hotels and motels offer an apartment option, including the Beach House and the Dutch Inn Towers. For any long-term rental, your best bet is to allow yourself a few nights in a hotel while you shop the classified ads in the *San Juan Star*. Apartments with kitchen facilities can be rented from Heidi Steiger, 2019 Cacique St., Santurce, Puerto Rico 00911 (tel. 727–6248) or Roberto Maldonado, Box 386, Luquillo, Puerto Rico 00673 (tel. 889–3425). Rates run $250–700 per week.

 HOW TO GET AROUND. The Airport Limousine Service serves hotels in Old San Juan, Isla Verde, and Condado. Price is $1 to $1.75 per person, depending upon distance—but don't be surprised if you're asked to pay a bit more, especially if the limo isn't filled. Taxis are also numerous in San Juan, at the airport, and at the major hotels; all those authorized by the Public Service Commission are metered, with an $.80 initial charge, $.10 for each additional mile, and $.50 for every suitcase. Waiting time is $8 per hour. If you are heading for Dorado Beach or Palmas del Mar, you can take their own limousine services or make a ten-minute hop via Crownair's small aircraft.

Transportation by buses or *guaguas* in the San Juan area is good. Buses operate on exclusive lanes along the major thoroughfares (although the fact that the bus lanes go against normal traffic can be disconcerting; this is something to watch for if you do any driving yourself in San Juan). Main terminals downtown are at Plaza Colón and the Cataño Ferry Terminal. Other bus stops throughout the city are marked by yellow obelisks, or by signs reading *Parada* or *Parada de Guaguas*. Fare on these buses is $.25. For information on routes or schedules, you can call the *Metropolitan Bus Authority* at 767–7679.

For public transportation outside San Juan, use the well-known *públicos*. These are five-passenger cars that run on frequent schedules to all the island's towns. Their license-plate numbers show the letters P or PD at the end. *Públicos* are required to be insured, and their routes and rates are fixed by the Public Service Commission. Main terminuses are the airport and along the waterfront in Old San Juan, as well as the plazas of towns throughout the island. Drivers of *públicos* are not noted for fluency in English, though, so don't expect a sightseeing tour.

The *Puerto Rico Motor Coach Co.* has daily scheduled service between San Juan and Mayagüez, with stops at Arecibo and Aguadilla. Fare is $6; runs every two hours, from 6:00 A.M. to 6:00 P.M.; reserve a seat by calling 725–2460.

Your U.S. driver's license is honored in Puerto Rico for up to three months. You can rent cars from all the major car-rental firms, including *Avis, Budget, Hertz, National,* and *Thrifty,* plus many local outfits. Rental desks can be found at the airport (lower level) and along Ashford Avenue in the Condado district, as well as at many of the major hotels.

Ferry service is another option for getting around in a more leisurely fashion. Ferries run from Old San Juan to Cataño and back every half-hour from 5:15 A.M. to midnight daily, for $.10 each way. The 400-passenger ferries of the Puerto Rico Ports authority leave Fajardo twice daily for the offshore island of Vieques, with less-frequent connecting service to Culebra. One-way fare is $2 for adults, $1 for children.

Many small planes are available for charter; in addition, there is ample local air service within Puerto Rico and to nearby islands, including *Vieques Air-Link* to Vieques and Culebra, *Crown Air* to Dorado and Palmas del Mar, *Aero Virgin*

Islands to the U.S. Virgin Islands, *Air BVI* to Tortola and Virgin Gorda. *Prinair* is the best of the lot in terms of frequency, service, and extent of routes; one of the top Caribbean airlines, it is based in Puerto Rico and serves many other islands, as well as offering regular service to Ponce and Mayagüez.

TOURIST INFORMATION SERVICES. The government-sponsored Puerto Rico Tourism Company is responsible for the island's tourism programs. It runs a Tourist Information Center at the airport which offers literature, accommodations assistance, and free local drinks (and it's one of the few air-conditioned areas in the airport). The head office is at 301 San Justo in Old San Juan, tel. 721–2400. Out on the island, each town's city hall (invariably located across from the *plaza,* or central square) can provide tourist information. The Tourism Company also maintains an office at City Hall in Old San Juan, tel. 724–7171. For information closer to home, see the "Tourist Information Services" section in the *Facts at Your Fingertips* chapter.

SPECIAL EVENTS. Puerto Rico has more than its share of special events and holidays. *LeLoLai* is a year-round festival that celebrates Puerto Rican dance and folklore. Sponsored by the Tourism Company and major San Juan hotels, it is a weekly revolving program offering something different every night: Afro-Caribbean *bomba y plena* music and dance, folklore dance sketches, a musical welcome, historical perspective, audiovisual presentations. Headquarters for the festival is at the Condado Convention Center. Program sites move from hotel to hotel, and reservations are recommended; call the office, tel. 723–3135.

Every town has a patron saint, and every patron saint gets honored once a year, in a local festival centering around the town's *plaza* that can run anywhere from one to ten days. Monthly listings are included in the front of *Qué Pasa.* Other major holidays and festivals:

Three Kings Day (January 6) is the traditional gift-giving day in Puerto Rico.

From January through May, *Sugar Harvest Festivals* are celebrated all across the island.

The *Vieques Cultural Festival* in mid-February fills the town plaza with arts and crafts, folkloric dances, native food and music. Additional ferry services to Vieques is added during this period.

March 22, *Emancipation Day,* is an island-wide holiday celebrating the day in 1873 when slavery was abolished.

The *Annual Puerto Rican Music Festival* (May–June) offers folk, popular, and classical music by Puerto Rican composers, performed by leading native singers, dance groups, and musicians. In the courtyard of the Dominican Convent, Old San Juan.

At the *Festival Casals* (during June) soloists and conductors from all over the world perform at University of Puerto Rico, San Juan.

The *St. James Festival,* held in late July in Loíza Aldea, is possibly the most colorful and authentic folk festival in Puerto Rico.

The *Summer Arts Festival,* mid-August through early October, is a mixed bag of events from dancing and crafts to kite-flying competitions. Held on the grounds of El Morro fortress in Old San Juan.

Jayuya Indian Festival takes place in mid-November and celebrates Taino Indian heritage in Jayuya. Crafts shows, Indian ceremonies, and dances.

Bomba y Plena Festival takes place in Ponce in mid-November with folk dancing and music.

The Puerto Rican Food Show takes place at Luquillo Beach in mid-November.

TOURS. Each San Juan hotel has a tour desk that makes reservations for half-and full-day tours of the city and countryside. Passengers are picked up at their hotels by tour-company buses and minibuses, which make a loop of leading hotels in the Condado/Isla Verde/Old San Juan areas. Group members are then returned to the hotels at the end of the tour.

Leading sightseeing tour operators include: *Borinquen Tours, Inc.,* 725–4990 or 722–1745; *Normandie Tours, Inc.* 725–6990 or 725–7133; *Gray Line Sightseeing Tours of Puerto Rico,* 727–8080; *Reliable Tours,* 723–3812 or 721–0810 (ext. 1515) or 786–6959 (evenings); *Rico Tours,* 722–2080 or 721–4605; and *United Tour Guides,* 723–5578 or 721–3000 (ext. 2597). *Cordero Sightseeing Tours* offers limousine service to different parts of the island, and rates are by the hour—tel. 780–2442 or 728–1100.

The most popular half-day tours, which cost $10–15, are: Old and New San Juan, Old San Juan and the Bacardi's Rum Distillery, Luquillo Beach and El Yunque rain forest. (Although some Luquillo/Rain forest tours give you time for swimming, many buses just stop for sightseeing. Most visitors who want a day at Luquillo simply rent a car and drive the short distance—about an hour—from San Juan.)

All-day tours ($15–30) include: a drive to Ponce on the island's southern coast, a day at El Comandante Racetrack, and a combined City Tour and El Yunque rain forest.

If you select a Ponce tour, it is recommended that you ask for a bus that takes the rugged route over the central mountains going down from San Juan—then returning via the superhighway. The backwoods route, though marvelously scenic and educational (you really feel as if you're seeing the "real" Puerto Rico and its people), is full of twists and turns, with many a *curva peligrosa.* By all means, sit up front with the driver if you're prone to carsickness. Because the drivers are very friendly and love to talk, you'll also learn a great deal about the countryside.

Half-day tours last approximately four hours, run mornings and afternoons, and are easily arranged. Full-day tours last about eight hours, and bus companies are reluctant to leave with less than ten passengers.

Although guided tours of Old San Juan and El Morro fortress are helpful to a certain extent, these areas are compact, well-marked, and are best done on foot with guidebook in hand. Guided tours *should* be taken to "difficult" places like El Yunque rain forest (which is vast and where guidance to the most interesting vantage points is essential) and to cities like Ponce and Mayagüez, where museum hours, the times of park concerts, and restaurant selections will be problems worked out by your driver/guide. Meals and drinks are not included in day-long trips, but you will be directed to reasonable, reliable places.

Additional help in arranging tours is cheerfully given by the charming, English speaking staff of the *Tourist Information Center,* 301 San Justo St., Old San Juan, tel. 721–2400.

Sailing charters and special cruises contribute to recreational sightseeing. These range from the do-it-yourself "cruises" on ferries from the port of San Juan to Cataño, Vieques, and Culebra, to private charters of deluxe yachts for sails to neighboring islands. Hotel water-sports desks generally have information on day sails. A combination of sightseeing, cruises, picnic, and snorkeling is common; among the major cruise operators of this sort are Condado Plaza Hotel Watersports and Captain Jack.

In addition to evening cruises of Phosphorescent Bay on Puerto Rico's southwest coast, many small boats offer casual meanderings to nearby beaches and cays from the main dock in La Parguera fishing village; the most popular offshore destination for picnickers and sunbathers is Mada de la Gata, two miles out. One-hour boat trips of Phosphorescent Bay (so called because of its millions of luminescent microorganisms) leave between 7:30 P.M. and midnight. Inquire at La Parguera Hotel.

Puerto Rico's only navigable river, the Espíritu Santu, flows from the Luquillo Mountains to the Atlantic Ocean outside Río Grande, 24-passenger launches offer 1½-hour cruises on this pleasant, jungle-like river.

PARKS AND GARDENS. The *Botanical Garden* is on the grounds of the University of Puerto Rico, off Avenue Ponce de León in San Juan's Río Piedras section. Part of the University's Agricultural Experimental Station, the garden has paths leading through a dense tropical garden and through a bamboo promenade, past a lotus lagoon, to an orchid garden and palm garden. Open 9:00 A.M. to 4:00 P.M. daily.

Muñoz Marín Park is a handsome new recreation area (find it by going west on Jesús T. Piñero Avenue). Wide walks, shaded by numerous trees, wind among gardens and small lakes. Recreational facilities include picnic areas, children's playground facilities and games, a minitrain, boats, and bicycle paths.

In the western coast city of Mayagüez, the *Tropical Agriculture Research Station* of the U.S. Department of Agriculture offers self-guided tours of their lush tropical gardens. Once a 19th-century plantation, the gardens contain such exotic flora as pink torch ginger, cannonball trees, Ceylon cinnamon, Panama canoe trees, and a shower of orchids. The gardens are on Route 65, between Route 108 and Post Street, next to the large Mayagüez campus of the University of Puerto Rico. Open free, 7:30 A.M.–noon and 1:00–4:30 P.M. weekdays.

There are also several large forest reserves that offer undeveloped tranquility. Best are Río Abajo Forest, south of Arecibo, and Toro Negro Forest, east of Adjuntas. The latter offers spectacular island views, and experienced climbers can attempt the heights of Inabon Falls. Most points of interest and trails are unmarked, but each reserve has a ranger station that can give you a brief orientation. Picnic facilities are available.

BEACHES. There are a dozen public beaches, or *balnearios,* ringing the island. These government-run facilities offer lockers, showers, and picnic tables. The beaches around the island are normally white or tan sand. Swimming is a bit rougher on the Atlantic than Caribbean side, but all public beaches are generally usable. (An exception is the beach at Palmas del Mar on the east coast; here the undertow is extremely strong and dangerous, as posted signs indicate.) Beaches in or near metropolitan areas—Isla Verde in San Juan, El Tuque in Ponce, even lovely Luquillo about an hour's drive east of San Juan—tend to be crowded on weekends and holidays, when the Puerto Ricans are at play. So if you crave peace and quiet on the sands, go on a weekday—but never on a Monday (or Tuesday, if Monday is a holiday), Election Day, or Good Friday—they're closed then. Parking (costing about $.25) is available at all public beaches. The major *balnearios* are:

Isla Verde Beach, in metropolitan San Juan. Borders many hotels. Wide in spots but narrow near the oceanfront highway.

Luquillo Beach, 30 miles east of San Juan on the north coast. Long and lovely—the site of a former coconut plantation—this crescent-shaped beach boasts hard-packed sands and a crystal lagoon protected by coral reefs.

El Tuque Beach, on Route 2 four miles west of Ponce, is the newest in terms of public facilities; a lovely Caribbean beach with some nice seafood restaurants nearby.

Boquerón Beach, off Route 101 on the southwest coast, is in the protected area of Boquerón Bay a popular local swimming and yachting area. A great place to watch the sun set.

Other attractive beaches include the long, palm-lined stretch at *Joyuda* on the west coast, south of Mayagüez—again with many seafood restaurants nearby, although they don't spoil the peaceful ambience—and the smooth sand at *Quebradillas* near Parador Guajataca on the northwest coast.

Many hotels have attractive swimming beaches. Along the nicest are those at *Dorado Beach* and *Cerromar Beach.*

There are also surfing beaches (not meant for swimmers). The major surfing area is at *Rincón,* home of the annual Professional Surfing Contest and once used for the World Surfing Championships. Best surf times: October thru April. *Aviones* and *La Concha* beaches in San Juan are good for summer surfing. *Pine Grove* for winter. *Casa de Pesca* in Arecibo is a summer surfing spot.

Puerto Rico's coral reefs and keys are perfect habitats for snorkelers and scuba divers. But unless you're an expert—or have a seasoned guide—you should avoid poking around unsupervised reef waters and mangrove areas, no matter how enticing they are. Stick to the water-sports centers of major hotels like the Caribe Hilton in San Juan (which offers snorkeling and scuba-diving lessons in an enclosed reef with caves) or the Mayagüez Hilton (which takes expert divers on tours of islands off the west coast). On Culebra Island, scuba diving and snorkeling are available through Exotic Dives of San Juan, an outfit that operates a 36-ft. diving boat.

PARTICIPANT SPORTS. Deep-sea fishing is booming in Puerto Rico, and some 30 world records have been broken in the island's numerous tournaments. The chances for blue marlin are superb—better than 50-50 for a trophy fish—and sailfish, wahoo, tarpon, bonefish, mackerel, snook tuna, dolphinfish, and yellowfish are all worthy sport. May to November are the very best months but year-round opportunities abound. Captain Mike Benitez, who charters the *Sea Born* out of San Juan Yacht Club, is a famous fisherman in his own right and generally is booked up well in advance for his half-day or split charter cruises, particularly in the heavy summer marlin season (contact Club Náutico de San Juan, Stop 9½, Fernández Juncos Avenue, Miramar, tel. 723–2292). The Castillo Fishing Fleet is another professional operation, with offices at the Dupont Plaza Hotel (Condado, tel. 724–6161, ext. 1317). Or try a pick-up charter at San Juan Fishing Center in Miramar (Stop 10, Fernández Juncos Avenue, tel. 725–0139). Rates average $50 to $70 per angler for a full-day trip. Outside San Juan, you can often bargain for a trip with local fishermen for substantially lower prices; there are, for example, many small charters available out of Parguera on the south coast.

Snorkeling and **scuba diving** can usually be arranged through your hotel. These can be from off-beach or as part of offshore cruises. Most major resorts have water-sports directors who give scuba-diving instruction. You can also arrange dive excursions out of La Parguera; air fills are available, but you're better off bringing your own equipment. (Also see "Beaches" section.)

Sailing. Small-boat rental is widely available along the hotel strips of San Juan Condado and Isle Verde sections. For example, the Condado Plaza Hotel Watersports Center (tel. 721–1000, ext. 1361) rents everything from windsurfers and Sunfish to paddle boats and water-skiing equipment. Other resort areas, such as Dorado and Plamas del Mar, have their own water-sports concessions.

Tennis may be played at hotel courts or public facilities. Among the court-equipped hotels are Caribe Hilton, Carib Inn, Condado Beach, Condado Plaza Hotel and Dupont Plaza in San Juan; also at Cerromar Beach, Dorado Beach, Mayagüez Hilton, Palmas del Mar, and Parador Guajataca. There are 17 public courts, all lit, in San Juan Central Park on Cerra Street (tel. 722–1646), open Tues.–Sat. 8:00 A.M.–10:00 P.M., 2:00–10:00 P.M. on Mon., and 10:00 A.M. to 6:00 P.M. on Sun. Use of a public court costs $1.

For **golf**, there are courses at Cerromar Beach, Dorado Beach, Palmas del Mar, and Punta Borinquén in Aguadilla. The four 18-hole courses shared by Dorado and Cerromar are the island's best. Other clubs through which golfing privileges may be arranged include the Berwind Country Club (Río Grande), Camp Chico (Caguas), and Mayagüez Hilton. Greens fees for the public courses run $10–$25 for 18 holes.

Horseback riding is available at Palmas del Mar Equestrian Center; instruction also available. Parador Guajataca in Quebradillas can also arrange trail and beach riding. Average rates: $8–$12 per hour.

SPECTATOR SPORTS. Cockfighting is the national sport in Puerto Rico. Bloodthirsty but exotic, it exerts an inevitable fascination for tourists. The season for cockfighting runs from Nov. 1 through Aug. 31. While there are many *galleras* (cockpits) throughout the island, the best place to observe this unusual sport is at the Club Gallistico in Isla Verde (tel. 791–1557), an air-conditioned arena with restaurant, cocktail lounge, and a ring carpeted

338   PUERTO RICO

in artificial grass. General admission is $8, ringside $15. Fights every Sat. at 2:00 P.M.; additional fight days are scheduled in the winter high season.

Horseracing can be seen at El Comandante Racetrack in Canóvanas (tel. 724–6060), one of the most attractive and modern tracks in this hemisphere. Races are held on Wed., Fri. and Sun.; first race at 2:30 P.M. Grandstand admission $1, clubhouse admission $3, ladies free on Wed.

Baseball is as popular in Puerto Rico as it is on the mainland, but the season is winter, starting in October and lasting five months. There are baseball stadiums in San Juan, Santurce, Ponce, Caguas, Arecibo, and Mayagüez. Many would-be and past big-leaguers play in the winter league here.

Collegiate sports include **baseball, tennis, soccer,** and **track and field.** With 25,000 students at the various locations of the University of Puerto Rico, there is generally some form of intramural sports event occuring during the school year. Listings are given in each month's *Qué Pasa.* Admission charges vary.

 HISTORIC SITES AND HOUSES. The Spanish culture of Puerto Rico dates back to 1508, and Indians preceded them. Consequently, all of Puerto Rico is a history buff's delight.

In Old San Juan: *San Felipe del Morro.* This massive triangular fortress, begun in 1540 and not finished until 1783, is steeped in history and the romance of adventure. Part natural formation, part structural marvel, "El Morro" (or rocky headland) stands on the rugged promontory that juts into the blue-green sea and guards San Juan harbor. You can tour this fascinating fort—its garrisons, batteries, gun emplacements, towers and turrets, prison cells, latrines and steep passageways—daily, 8:00 A.M.–5:00 P.M. with guided tours ($.50) four times a day. A handsome folder and numerous plaques tell El Morro's exciting story. There is also a small air-conditioned museum. Tel. 724–1974.

San José Church, on San José Plaza not far from El Morro, was built by the Dominican fathers beginning in 1532—making it one of the oldest churches in the Western Hemisphere. Originally the chapel for the Dominican monastery, San José contains a collection of ornate processional floats. Open daily 9:00 A.M. to 4:00 P.M., no admission fee.

Casa Blanca, near El Morro, at the harbor edge of Old San Juan, was intended to be Ponce de León's official residence as governor, although he never lived to occupy it. In his family for 250 years, "The White House" later served as the U.S. Army Commander's residence. Now beautifully restored as a museum of 16th-and 17th-century family life. Guided tours daily. Open 9:00 A.M. to 5:00 P.M., closed Mon. Admission free. Tel. 724–4102.

La Fortaleza, two blocks from Casa Blanca, is the official residence of the Governor of Puerto Rico. Originally a fortress and predating El Morro (it was completed in 1540), La Fortaleza is the oldest executive mansion still in use in the Western Hemisphere. Guided tours Mon.–Fri. in English and Spanish. Open 9:00 A.M. to 4:15 P.M. weekdays. Tel. 721–7000.

San Juan Cathedral, 153 Calle Cristo, was begun in 1521, but hurricanes, fires, wars, and lootings have taken their toll, and what you see today is the impressive Spanish structure dating from the early 19th century. The body of Ponce de León lies in an elaborate marble crypt off the left aisle (the remains were brought here from San José Church in 1908).

Plaza de Armas, San Juan's original main square, is a lovely, graceful rectangle surrounded by carefully restored colonial buildings and houses, which now contain businesses, shops, galleries, and restaurants. The 17th-century City Hall, with its attractive inner courtyard, arcades, balconies, and stately public rooms, is here; a Tourist Information Center and art gallery occupy the ground floor. The square is bordered by San Francisco and Fortaleza streets, between San José and Cruz streets.

Casa de los Contrafuertes (Buttress House), 101 San Sebastián, is possibly the oldest house remaining in the city, dating from the early 18th century. A pharmacy museum and *santos* (carved wooden saints) museum are on the first floor; a graphic arts museum is on the second. Open 9:00 A.M. to 5:00 P.M. daily, admission free.

Photo by Barbara A. Currie

Historic spots abound in the Caribbean, including the palace of Sans Souci, south of Cap-Haitien in Haiti. Once the palatial home of King Henri Christophe, Sans Souci still evokes a sense of grandeur though ruined in 1842 by an earthquake. Old mills are left on Barbados from the bygone era when sugar was king.

Photo by V. Puzo

Photo by Barbara A. Currie

An atypical pirate celebrates Grand Cayman's national festival, Pirates Week, which is held each October. Meanwhile, a fire dancer's nightly performance at Cayman Islander Nightclub awes visitors.

Photo by Barbara A. Currie

Photo by Barbara A. Currie

Throughout the Caribbean, natural wonders are almost commonplace. On Montserrat, the Great Alps Waterfall plunges 70 feet into a cool mountain pool. Exotic flowers, such as these native orchids on Cayman and Barbados, bloom everywhere.

Photo by Barbara A. Currie

Courtesy of Caribbean Tourism Association

Locally made straw goods are always an attraction, especially the hats, which offer shade from the Caribbean sun. At sunset, the views are spectacular. Charlotte Amalie, on St. Thomas, is one of the most impressive.

Courtesy of Caribbean Tourism Association

Casa del Libro, 255 Cristo St. Beautifully restored 18th-century house, now a museum and library devoted to printing and bookmaking. Special exhibits on first floor, including fine collection of rare and antique books. Open Monday–Friday, 11:00 A.M.–5:00 P.M. Tel. 723–0354.

Cristo Chapel, Calle Cristo. This tiny chapel with its silver altar commemorates a miracle that supposedly saved a horseback rider when he plunged off the cliff here in 1753. Open Tues. from 9:00 A.M.–5:00 P.M. and on most Catholic holidays.

In Ponce: the 1883 *Parque de Bombas* is a colorful black-and-red striped firehouse on the busy town square, which is famous for its large, artfully rounded banyan trees. The square also holds the stunning Cathedral of Our Lady of Guadalupe.

Just outside Ponce, *Tibes Indian Ceremonial Center* on Route 503 has a modern visitor's center with exhibits and film, plus spacious grounds. This is the site of the oldest cemetery yet uncovered in the Antilles, with some excavated human skeletons that date back to 300 A.D. Seven ceremonial ballparks; recreated Taino Indian village. Exhibits and films in Spanish, but English-speaking tour guides are available. Open 9:00 A.M.–4:30 P.M. daily; admission $1.50 for adults, $.50 for children. Tel. 844–5575.

In San Germán: *Porta Coeli* (Gate of Heaven) *Church* on Route 119 overlooks one of the town's plazas. Dating back to 1606, it is the oldest intact church under the American flag; it is now a museum of religious art. Open 9:00 A.M.–noon and 1:00 P.M.–4:30 P.M. daily; guided tours Wed.–Sun. Admission $.50. Tel. 892–5845.

 MUSEUMS AND GALLERIES. As can be seen above, historic sites and museums can often overlap. The following facilities are museums first and foremost.

In Old San Juan: *San Juan Museum of Art and History,* Norzagaray St. Exhibitions of Puerto Rican art; audiovisual history of San Juan. Occasional concerts on interior plaza. Open Mon.–Fri., 9:00 A.M.–noon, 1:00 P.M.–4:00 P.M. Suggested donation, $1 adults, $.50 children. Tel. 724–1875.

Pablo Casals Museum, at Plaza San José. Memorabilia of the master, including tapes of performances, manuscripts, photographs—all collected in a lovingly restored townhouse. Open Mon.–Sat., 9:00 A.M.–5:00 P.M. Sun., 1:00 P.M.–5:00 P.M. Tel. 723–9185.

Fine Arts Museum. Calle Cristo. Institute of Puerto Rican Culture's collection of paintings and sculptures from 18th century to present. Open Tues.–Sat., 9:00 A.M.–4:30 P.M.; Sun., 9:00 A.M.–noon and 1:00–4:30 P.M. Guided tours Tues.–Sat. Tel. 723–2320.

Out on the Island: *Museum of the Conquest and Colonization of Puerto Rico,* at the Caparra Ruins on Rte. 2 outside Bayamón. Remains of fort, plus small museum documenting the 16th-century colonial period. Open Mon.–Fri., 8:00 A.M.–noon and 1:00–4:30 P.M. Tel. 781–4795.

Ponce Museum of Art, on Las Américas Ave. in Ponce, is an impressive modern structure designed by Edward Durell Stone. Collection includes more than 1,000 paintings and 400 sculptures, ranging from ancient to contemporary. Open Mon.–Fri. 10:00 A.M.–noon and 1:00–4:00 P.M.; Sat. 10:00 A.M.–4:00 P.M.; Sun. 10:00 A.M.–5:00 P.M. Admission $1.50 for adults, $.75 for children. Tel. 842–6215.

 MUSIC, DANCE, AND STAGE. Cultural events and musical entertainment are generally plentiful in San Juan, less so out on the island. *Qué Pasa* and *San Juan Star* are the best sources of current information as to live performances.

LeLoLai Festival occurs throughout San Juan on a weekly basis (see also "Seasonal Events"). The festivities are free to visitors staying at participating hotels for at least five nights. Admission to individual events can be purchased through the LeLoLai office at the Convention Center; $7 for performances, $11–$20 for performances including dinner.

Symphony Orchestra of Puerto Rico, founded by Pablo Casals, plays for 44 weeks a year at the Fine Arts Center Festival Hall in San Juan. Ticket prices vary according to performance and artist.

Concerts (both soloists and groups), youth series, folkloric and religious festivals, fairs, and photo exhibits are often held at the *Institute of Puerto Rican Culture Theater* in San Juan. Tel. 723–2628.

Tapia Theater, on O'Donnel St., is a municipal theater constructed in 1832 and recently restored. Spanish plays, operettas, and ballet are presented year-round. Tickets cost $5–$25. Tel. 721–0180.

Civic theater of the amateur variety is active. Often held in the auditorium of the convention center, on Ashford Ave. In Spanish.

Poetry readings and other dramatic presentations are held every Sunday afternoon at the Santo Domingo convent in Old San Juan. Tel. 725–5584.

SHOPPING. San Juan is not a free port, so put aside any ideas about picking up bargains on electronics, perfume, or similar duty-free delights. If you're a determined shopper, you can take a shopping-spree flight to St. Thomas or St. Croix (half an hour by air). There is one shop, at the tourist pier, where cruise-ship passengers heading for a foreign port can buy cigarettes, perfume, jewelry, and porcelains at prices competitive with the free ports.

There are many attractive shops along Fortaleza and San Francisco streets in Old San Juan; jewelry stores dominate. In an escalating battle, they advertise anywhere from 50% to 75% "off"; but generally the reduced price winds up equalling the going rates stateside. Nevertheless, the jewelry—gold the specialty —is high caliber overall. Feel free to browse. You can get a free *piña colada* to browse with at *Jewels of the World,* on Fortaleza St. near San José St., which also does a booming business in "knockoffs"—acknowledged copies of famous (and expensive) wristwatches.

If you're a dedicated mall shopper or have a long list, head for the huge mall at Plaza las Américas, just off the expressway in Hato Rey. This has over 190 stores, restaurants, and movie theatres on three levels; it's open Mon. to Sat. 9:30 A.M.–6:00 P.M. (to 9:30 P.M. on Fri.).

The most fun in Puerto Rico shopping is in the search for unusual local handicrafts. Most typical are the small carved religious figures called *santos* (antiques should carry a document as to their authenticity), cigars rolled to order, hammocks, imaginative masks (many made from coconut husks), embroidered clothing, woven straw, papier-maché fruits and vegetables, and ceramics. Painting and sculpture in Puerto Rico are generally quite accomplished and are beginning to be noted in the art world; galleries can be found along Ashford Avenue and in Old San Juan.

Among the top galleries are *Galería Botello* and *Galería Palomas* on Cristo St. in Old San Juan; *Galería Eugenio* on Caleta de San Juan, and *Galería San Juan* on Norzagaray. *The Butterfly People,* on Fortaleza St., has unusual and charming collections of butterflies under glass that can be had inexpensively.

Lace, both new and old, is found on San Francisco St. in Old San Juan, and handmade tablecloths are another distinctive buy. Hand-painted T-shirts and T-dresses are a rather new wrinkle, and those fancy men's shirts called *guayaberas* are perennial favorites. Guava jellies and jams, *piña colada* mixes and, of course, Puerto Rico's rums (perhaps the world's finest) are among the classic taste treats.

For native crafts, the most enjoyable shopping experience can be the *El Centro Market* held each weekend at the Condado Convention Center on Ashford Ave. Craftsmen from all over the country come to show their wares. You can also find a good variety of individual artisans at the *Plazoleta del Puerto,* across from cruise-ship Pier 3 in Old San Juan: 28 stalls and booths on an interior courtyard. The shop at the *Folk Arts Center* at the Dominican Convent, next to San Jose Cathedral in Old San Juan, is open daily; here you can also get a list of local artisans who welcome visitors to their workshops.

RESTAURANTS. The local cuisine, not surprisingly, has a strong Spanish accent, and includes such basic hispanic dishes as *arroz y habichuelas* (rice and beans). *Arroz con pollo* (chicken with rice) is a popular dish, and its more complicated relative, *paella* (rice with a melange of shellfish and Spanish sausages, colored with saffron) is also available in better restaurants. The local version (*jíbaro* cuisine) includes such items as *asopao* (a slightly soupy rice dish made with chicken or seafood). *Empanadillas,* which are rather like turnovers, are a local fast-food bargain with a variety of sealed-in fillings. *Pescado* simply refers to any fish caught; it's particularly good fresh-caught in the little villages along the Caribbean coast. *Jueyes* are delicious land crabs, but you should be careful to eat them only in recommended restaurants.

Puerto Rican coffee is strong, black, and wonderful everywhere, although it seems to taste best at a small roadside inn or *parador* in the mountains overlooking the coffee plantations.

The national drink of Puerto Rico is rum, with 14 brands made here. Some like *Barralito,* are made in such small quantities they are not exported. Not surprisingly, an amazing variety of rum recipes is available—some delicious, some obnoxious. The *piña colada,* it is generally conceded, was invented in Puerto Rico, although several bars dispute the claim of its invention.

Some of the major hotels have as many restaurants as some of the smaller Caribbean islands, and hotel fare tends to be of generally high caliber in the top restaurants. Nevertheless, you'll enjoy your visit more if you venture off the hotel premises at least some of the time to sample the fine variety of local restaurants.

Price categories are based on an average three-course meal for one person, excluding beverage and tip. We call $16 and above *Expensive,* $7–$15 *Moderate,* anything below $7 *Inexpensive.*

Puerto Rico's restaurants can be grouped into three main categories: traditional Spanish/Hispanic places serving specialties based on basics like fish, chicken, pork, beans and rice; modern "international" dining rooms in hotels and self-contained resorts; and those restaurants (comparatively few in number) specializing in such exotic cuisines as Chinese, French, Italian, and German. The finest restaurants are, not surprisingly, located in the San Juan area, but there are notable places in other cities—Ponce, Mayagüez, Aguadilla, and Arecibo. Also not to be overlooked are the charming, out-of-the-way, scenic places found along the southern coast, in one of the countryside *paradores,* or on a terrace up in the central mountain range.

OLD SAN JUAN

Expensive

La Chaumiere. 367 Tetuán. Tel. 722–3330. Fine French cuisine near the harbor and the old walls. AE, DC, MC.

Los Galanes, 65 San Francisco, Tel. 722–4008. Handsome, quiet, dignified, Spanish-style restaurant with arches, ceiling fans, inner courtyard, and massive wood furnishings. Local and international specialties. AE, CB, DC.

El Patio de Convento. 100 Cristo, tel. 723–9020. Located in the graceful inner courtyard of El Convento Hotel (once a 17th-century Carmelite convent), El Patio features continental cuisine with a variety of entertainment (flamenco, piano, fashion shows, even water ballets in the small pool). A moderately priced buffet luncheon is served, and there is a handsome bar. AE, CB, DC, MC, V.

La Zaragozana. 356 San Francisco, Tel. 723–5103. A dark, romantic, elegant hacienda with splashing fountains, gleaming murals, hanging lanterns, and strolling guitarists. Classic Cuban, Puerto Rican, and Spanish dishes: black and white bean soups, *asopao* (a wet rice stew with fish or meat), pork dishes, steaks, heavenly custards, and fine wines. A favorite with natives and visitors alike. AE, CB, DC, MC, V.

Moderate.

Café del Puerto. Across from Pier 3, Port of San Juan. Tel. 725–1500. The second floor of the new Puerto Rican Crafts Plaza is rigged up like a ship's deck overlooking the harbor. Open to the public at lunch (rum drinks, salad plates, burgers, ice cream dishes), it is technically a private club/disco at night (but your hotel may be able to arrange a dinner reservation). AE, CB, DC, MC, V.

El Callejón de la Capilla. 317 Fortaleza. Tel. 725–8529. Puerto Rican fare served inside the antique house or on its patio. AE, CB, DC, MC, V.

La Mallorquina. 207 San Justo. Tel. 722–3261. Local specialties served in an enclosed patio-style dining room with high ceilings and revolving fans. AE, CB, DC, MC, V.

El Mesón Vasco. 47 Cristo. Tel. 725–7819. A Basque restaurant in an old building at the top of Cristo St. across from San José Plaza. AE, DC, MC, CB.

El Patio de Sam. 102 San Sebastián, Tel. 723–1149. Informal, relaxing and friendly. The rustic bar featuring tropical fruit drinks, leads to a delightful inner patio filled with plants. Have the hearts-of-palm salad, broiled steak or fish (*dorado* is a local favorite), key lime pie. AE, CB, DC, MC, V.

Tiffany's. 213 Cristo. Tel. 725–0380. Dark, trendy pub in a neighborhood filled with galleries and shops. Exotic drinks, beers, wines, sandwiches, burgers, hot and cold platters. AE, MC, V.

NEW SAN JUAN

The following restaurants are found in the San Juan beach areas (Puerta de Tierra, Condado, and Isla Verde) and in the inland neighborhoods of Miramar, Santurce, and Hato Rey.

Expensive

La Posada. 999 Ashford, Condado Plaza Hotel. Tel. 721–1000, ext. 1950. A candlelit steak and seafood house with a panoramic view of the ocean. The hotel also boasts a Chinese restaurant (Lotus Flower) and a pasta place (Capriccio). AE, CB, DC, MC, V.

El Cid. Joffre (off Ashford Ave. on the lagoon in Condado). Tel. 723–5894. Spanish and international specialties in a rather formal setting. AE, CB DC, MC, V.

L'Escargot. 1106 Magdalena, Condado. Tel. 722–2436. As the name implies, French cuisine—in a cool, serene atmosphere off the main Condado strip. AE, DC, MC.

Gran Segovia. 1005 Ashford, Condado. Tel. 721–0820. Known as one of the best restaurants on the island. Superior international cuisine and fine wines served in a graceful, softly lighted atmosphere. AE, CB, DC, MC, V.

La Rotisserie. Caribe Hilton International Hotel, Puerta de Tierra. Tel. 721–0303. French and continental specialties in an elegant and formal setting (men must have jacket and tie for dinner). AE, CB, DC, MC.

Swiss Chalet. 105 De Diego, Santurce. Tel. 721–2233. Swiss and continental cuisine served amid Swiss decor. Piano music and dancing after 7:00. Informal, but men asked to wear long-sleeved shirts in the evening. AE, CB, DC, MC, V.

Moderate

La Fragua. 800 Ponce de León, Miramar. Tel. 722–4699. A small find serving Spanish and international specialties (the fish dishes are especially recommended). AE, DC, V.

Green House. 1200 Ashford, Dutch Inn & Towers, Condado. Tel. 725–4036. An enclosed café with a pleasant, parklike indoor setting. Seafood, omelettes, international dishes served 11:30 A.M.–4:30 A.M. CB, DC, MC, V.

Heidelberg Haus. 361 De Diego, Santurce. Tel. 723–0803. German and international cuisine. Lively music each night after 7:00. AE, CB, DC, MC.

Scotch & Sirloin, 1020 Ashford, La Rada Hotel, Condado. Tel. 722–3640. Limited but superior menu of steaks and seafood, with good salad bar. AE, DC, MC, V.

La Tasca. 54 Muñoz Rivera, Puerta de Tierra (near Caribe Hilton). Tel. 722–2410. Unpretentious but pleasant atmosphere for excellent seafood. AE, CB, DC, MC, V.

Inexpensive.

Los Chavales. 253 Roosevelt, Hato Rey, 767–5017. Nicely presented Spanish specialties. AE, CB, DC, MC, V.

Tropical Caparra Heights. Borinquen Tower complex, Caparra area. Tel. 781–1528. Informal, family-neighborhood place, few tourists. Basic local favorites: *sopa de carne* (thick soup with meat, noodles, potatoes), broiled fish and steaks, beans and rice, flan custard. AE.

OUT ON THE ISLAND
Moderate

Anchor's Inn. Route 987, Fajardo. Tel. 863–7200. Steaks and seafood are the things to order in this attractive, across-from-the-beach place with nautical decor. AE, MC, V.

Bolo's Place. Route 102, Mayagüez. Tel. 832–8512. On the ocean outside Mayagüez, Bolo's specializes, of course, in seafood. AE, CB, DC, MC, V.

El Conquistador. 263 Llorens Torres, Arecibo. Tel. 878–5615. Puerto Rican specialties are the menu in this pleasant, informal spot. MC, V.

Cross Road. Route 987, Fajardo. Tel. 863–0690. A simple, casual, pleasant seafood place. AE, CB, DC, MC, V.

Jajome Terrace. Route 15, Cayey. Tel. 738–4016. A lovely, simple, open-air hilltop setting. Drive out from San Juan (about 45 minutes) and arrive about dusk for the spectacular sunset. The views are breathtaking, and the New Orleans specialties are delicious. AE, DC, MC.

Mayagüez Hilton Hotel. Route 104, Mayagüez. Tel. 832–7575. International specialties are featured in this comfortable, dependable dining room. AE, CB, DC, MC, V.

Parador Hacienda Gripiñas. Route 527, Jayuya. Tel. 721–2400. Three tiny, airy dining rooms and a pretty atrium area in this off-the-beaten-track country inn—that serves Puerto Rican and international specialties. MC, V.

Parador Hacienda Juanita. Route 105, Maricao. Tel. 838–2550. The attractive restaurant in the antique main building of this country inn (once part of a coffee plantation) specializes in *jíbaro* cuisine, which flourishes in the central mountains. MC, V.

Parguera. Villa Parguera Hotel, Route 304, Paraguera. Tel. 899–3975. Puerto Rican and international specialties served in a nice place to eat (and stay) if you're in town to see Phosphorescent Bay. AE, CB, DC, MC, V.

La Posada. Route 110 Aguadilla. Tel. 891–5182. Steaks and seafood, along with traditional Puerto Rican dishes. DC, MC, V.

Restaurante Tito. Hotel Melia, 2 Cristina, Ponce. Tel. 842–0260. Just off Ponce's famous main square, this popular local spot serves Puerto Rican meat and seafood dishes (the Creole or breaded butterfly shrimp are very good). AE, DC, MC.

 NIGHT LIFE AND BARS. Night life in exuberant, fun-loving Puerto Rico is as various as the island's culture and customs, and an evening's entertainment can range from timelessly traditional festivals to 20th-century-chic discos. The island's bars, which vary in size and type from a few stools in a country inn to the plush comfort of a beachside hotel's piano lounge, are as lively as the native rums that fuel their famous *piña coladas.*

Basically, Puerto Rican night life can be separated into several major categories: gambling casinos (all located, by government decree, in large hotels), trendy discos and Las Vegas–style supper clubs (most of which are also in hotels), and the performing arts—theater, classical and modern ballet, opera, orchestra concerts, and folklore performances that express in music and dance Puerto Rico's Indian/African/Caribbean/Spanish heritage. Throughout the year—and throughout the island—there are also a number of annual festivals (celebrating everything from fish to flowers), saint's day feasts, street fairs, and national holidays that are marked by parading, singing, dancing, and, of course, eating. (Ask the Puerto Rican tourist offices for up-to-date events lists.)

Needless to say, most of the modern night life is centered in cosmopolitan San Juan. Out on the island, bars, discos, and nightclubs tend to be found in the leading hotels and *paradores,* in luxury resorts like Dorado Beach and Cerromar Beach, and in self-contained vacation villages like Palmas del Mar.

In San Juan's glittering Condado Beach area, the Caribe Hilton International Hotel features name entertainers like Tony-award winner Chita Rivera, plus an elaborate dinner show, at its *Club Caribe. Juliana's* is the Caribe's "elegantly casual" disco, and there is music and dancing till 3:00 A.M. in the hotel's *Caribar Lounge.* At the Condado Plaza Hotel, which has the largest casino in Puerto Rico, you can catch classical Spanish flamenco—a "fiesta fantástica"—in the hotel's *Royal Theatre,* and you can dance till dawn in *Isadora's Discotheque.* The recently restored Condado Beach Hotel, with its stunning Art Deco facade, offers a piano bar on weekdays and live entertainment on weekends in the delightful *"1919" Lounge.*

In the Isla Verde beachfront section, a Las Vegas–style revue (a recent version, "B'Dazzled," was a lavish ice show) is presented nightly (except Sun.) at the *Palace Hotel Showplace Supper Club.* The Palace's *Kum Kum Room* offers Latin dance music nightly, Wed.–Sun.

Charming, small bars that open directly onto the street are found everywhere in the colonial quarter of Old San Juan. One of the most inviting is the *1897 Café-Bar,* near the Cathedral de San Juan and El Convento Hotel. At El Convento itself, which was once a 17th-century Carmelite convent, you can dine in the open-air patio and watch a flamenco show, or perhaps you'll be on hand for one of the hotel's special events, such as a water ballet in the patio's pool.

Along the esplanade down by the Old San Juan docks—an area that is undergoing a multi-million-dollar renaissance—you'll find the delightful *Café del Puerto,* which at night is technically a private club, disco included. Sometimes, however, visitors can be admitted by "prior agreement," and your hotel can check the possibility by calling 725–1500.

A very romantic—and inexpensive—nighttime activity is to take the ferry from the old San Juan piers to Cataño across the bay. The cruise takes only about 20 minutes each way, costs a mere dime per crossing, and gives all passengers the most glorious view of the San Juan skyline. (Remember that the ferries stop at midnight, so give yourself time to get back.)

CASINOS. By law, all casinos are in hotels, primarily in San Juan. The government keeps a close eye on them. Alcoholic drinks are not permitted at the gaming tables, although free soft drinks, coffee, and sandwiches are available. Dress for casinos tends to be on the formal side and the atmosphere is refined. The law permits casinos to operate from noon to 4:00 A.M., but individual casinos set their own hours which change with the seasons.

Casinos are located in the following hotels: *Condado Plaza Hotel, Condado Beach Hotel, Dupont Plaza, Caribe Hilton, Carib-Inn, Palace, Isla Verde, Ramada,* all in San Juan. Elsewhere on the island, there are casinos at the *Cerromar Beach* and *Dorado Beach Hotels,* at *Palmas del Mar,* and at the *Hilton International Mayagüez.*

POSTAGE. Puerto Rico uses U.S. postage stamps and mail rates: 14¢ for a postcard, 22¢ for a first-class letter. Puerto Rico post offices also offer Express Mail next-day service from major cities to the U.S. mainland and to other Puerto Rico destinations. A tip: save time and effort by bringing stamps with you.

ELECTRICAL CURRENT. Electrical current in Puerto Rico is 110 volts, 60 cycles.

SECURITY. Puerto Rico has its share of poverty and a high unemployment rate, but crime is not rampant. However, as in many major resorts, there are always those ready to prey on unsuspecting tourists. Guard your wallet or pocketbook when you walk on city streets, and leave nothing unattended on the beaches. Be sure to place all valuables in your hotel safe. If driving around the island, lock your car doors and stash valuables and luggage out of sight.

Even the hotel beaches are nominally public in Puerto Rico, and unfortunately muggings do occur, especially at night along the beaches outside Condado and Isla Verde hotels. Although you may find it unpleasant to see the fenced-in beach areas around some hotels, these are the only safe places to take a moonlight stroll along the water.

Out on the island, muggings are less a potential hazard than in the city, but back streets and alleys, country lanes and deserted beaches should be avoided both day and night. In some of the more touristed areas, such as La Parguera, you can feel safe strolling at night if accompanied.

SABA

by
CLAIRE DEVENER

"Once upon a fairy tale island there were Hansel and Gretel houses, a vertical highway built by hand, and The Bottom was always up!" So begins the blurb of the Saba Tourist Bureau. When you're at "The Bottom" here, you're not walking on the ocean floor, but strolling through the capital at the top of a hill. There's just one road, few shops, even fewer hotels, and just about 1,050 residents. Saba, St. Maarten's best excursion, is well adapted to the day tourist but even better for a longer stay.

Past and Present

Columbus first saw Saba in 1493, but the island remained uninhabited until a small group of Dutch settlers arrived from Statia in 1640. In 1665 the notorious English captain Morgan captured Saba and deported all the Dutch and their slaves to St. Maarten, leaving behind just fifty-four settlers with roots in the British Isles. Although the island passed back and forth between the Dutch, English, French, and Spanish many times, Saba's white population basically descended from British stock. These intrepid settlers founded an agricultural economy that endured until 1850, when sugar and indigo declined in world importance.

As a member of the Netherlands Antilles since 1816, the islanders by tradition looked to Holland for education and technology. But it was Josephus Lambert Hassell who decided in the 1940s that Saba had to have a road, so he took a correspondence course to build one. Dutch advisors had pooh-poohed the Saban's roadbuilding desires, but Mr. Hassell was determined. He'd been a carpenter and was a practical man. With a team of ten to twenty men, he built a well-graded concrete road wiggling from village to village. It took him twenty years!

Since then, the road has been extended up to the farmlands to transport Saba's bountiful produce to the docks for export to St. Maarten. Jasmine, carnations, and roses are also grown in Saba's soil, so fertile that plants seem to spring up almost as soon as the seeds are sown. Agriculture and fishing are the mainstays of the island's economy. A local rum-based liqueur, Saba Spice, brewed with secret herbs and spices, is also produced. The island has no taxes, no crime, and little litigation. Disputes are settled by the lieutenant governor, who, assisted by a five-member local council, oversees the island's 50% black and 50% white population.

EXPLORING SABA

Although highlights can be covered on a day tour, Saba is really worth much more time. People here are friendly, yet shy and reserved in their own way. Once they discover that you are not going to be just a day-tripper, you'll often find yourself invited into their homes and to parties and celebrations. This is probably the easiest place in the world to hitchhike.

Passengers arriving by air, as most do, will wing onto a minute airstrip pasted like a Band-Aid on the island's only level stretch, Flat Point. It may not look long enough, but the STOL (Short Takeoff and Landing) aircraft are built for just this kind of area and don't even need half of Saba's 1300-foot runway! There's never been an accident either.

Visitors spending only the day should organize an island tour with one of the taxi drivers and be sure that he arranges luncheon reservations immediately. Dining places and spaces are limited.

You won't get lost touring Saba. Its one hand-laid stone road skirts the island, winding like a long snake up, down, and around the hills. There are only four villages—The Bottom, Hell's Gate, St. John's, and Windwardside. Until the arrival of the first jeep in 1947, islanders made their way between them by foot—and on sturdy leg, we imagine, because before the road was built the villages were connected by hundreds of steps chiseled out of the volcanic rock.

After twenty serpentine curves that have you reflexively braking right along with your driver and dizzying views over the sheer drop to the sea, you'll enter Hell's Gate. What could be more appropriate?

Hell's Gate to Windwardside

Despite its name, this is a storybook village nestled in the shadow of the island's largest church. Though it existed long before the airport, it is now the last sight when departing. Sabans love to tell you "what better name for the last place you'll see when leaving heaven!" For to

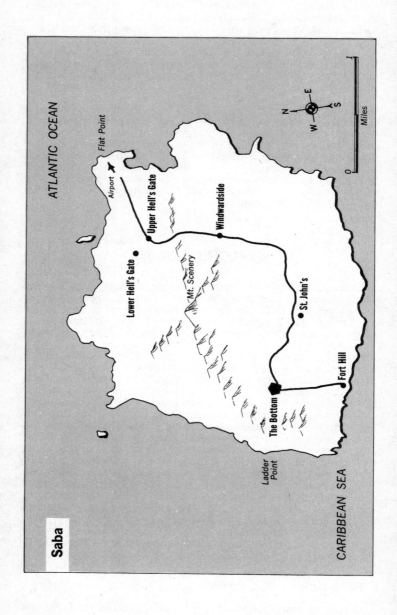

them, leaving Saba is the same thing. The road spirals upward past terraced banana plantations to a village called Windwardside.

Tiny white houses frilled with gingerbread and sporting green-and-white shutters cling to the hillsides. The never-failing trade winds make it cool here on top of the world, making agreeable a wander up and down the narrow lanes between flower-covered stone walls that enclose tiny yards. This is the location of two of Saba's charming inns—The Captain's Quarters and Scout's Place—where you will most certainly be lunching if not staying over. The 1,060 stone and concrete steps that ascend to the top of Mount Scenery begin on the outskirts of this town. The climb up the 3,000-foot extinct volcano is best begun in the morning, and you'll need a half-day for the round-trip excursion. Your hotel will be happy to pack a box lunch and even lend you a walking staff should you feel so inclined—pardon the pun. A sweater should be taken and sturdy, comfortable shoes worn. It may be misty as you make your way up through the tropical rain forest where giant elephant ears, ferns, and orchids grow in profusion. But don't fret, the view from the top is always spectacular; Mount Scenery is aptly named.

Once off the mountain, stop by the tourist office (next to the post office) for a chat with its colorful chairman, Will Johnson, who has become Saba's unofficial historian. Pick up some island lore and literature, like his book, "Tales from My Grandmother's Pipe," filled with fascinating stories and old pictures of Saba down through the years. You should have plenty of time to visit the Saba Museum in a hundred-year-old sea captain's cottage just behind the Captain's Quarters; browse the shops tucked in and around the cottages; even take a dip in the hotel's small pool that seems to hang out over the sea. After a leisurely lunch, it's off again to wind through more spectacular scenery to The Bottom.

The Bottom

The tiny, gable-roofed houses and immaculately groomed gardens of this miniscule capital are not in a crater, but plunked down on an eight hundred-foot-high plateau surrounded by craggy green hills. Take a look at The Ladder, 524 rough-hewn steps that boat passengers often had to use to get to and from The Bottom. Now the corkscrew road ends at Fort Bay, where a 277-foot deep-water pier, opened in 1972, handles tenders from the windjammers and private yachts that call here. It's also the departure point for Saba Deep's scuba excursions. Their dive shop is in the small building at the road's end and one of the owners is usually there during the day to fill in future customers about the many fabulous dive sites they've found off Saba.

If you're leaving the island by boat, you'll be departing from Fort Bay. Winair day-trippers from St. Maarten will ride the roller coaster in reverse back to Flat Point. If you're lucky, you'll be one of the clever travelers who wave goodby to these new-found friends because you're staying on to savor Saba's many charms.

PRACTICAL INFORMATION FOR SABA

FACTS AND FIGURES. Topographically, Saba is the most unusual island in the entire Caribbean. The whole place is an extinct volcano that rises abruptly up 3,000 feet from the sea. It lies 150 miles east of Puerto Rico, 28 miles south of St. Maarten and 17 miles northwest of Statia. The smallest of the Netherlands Antilles, it measures just five square miles. There were 1046 inhabitants as of the last census. Dutch is the offical language, but very few Sabans speak it; everyone speaks English.

WHEN TO GO. Daytime temperatures range from 75 to 82 degrees year-round. Nights tend to be cool, especially as you go higher. Annual average rainfall is 42 in. Hotel prices, which are already low, are the same year-round except at The Captain's Quarters, the island's best accommodations. Here there is a reduction of 20% during the summer season (Apr. 16–Dec. 14). Saba is a bargain at any time of the year.

PASSPORTS AND VISAS. Proof of citizenship is required. A passport is best, but a birth certificate or voter's registration card will do—a driver's license will not. In addition, all visitors must hold a return or ongoing ticket. British citizens must have a"British Visitor's" passport.

MONEY. The official currency is the Netherlands Antilles florin, or guilder. The exchange fluctuates but the rate is about NAF 1.79 = U.S. $1. U.S. dollars are accepted everywhere; credit cards nowhere.

WHAT WILL IT COST?

A typical day on Saba for two persons in the winter season will run:

	U.S.$
The best hotel accommodations including breakfast and dinner	$114
Lunch	20
Tax and service charges	26
Full day sightseeing by taxi or rental car	25
Total	$185

HOW TO GET THERE. By air. *Windward Islands Airways* links Saba with St. Maarten three times a day. Round-trip fare is $40 and the short, twenty-minute flight is perfect for a day trip.
By sea. The deep-water pier at Fort Bay accommodates tenders from the *Polynesia* and *Sea Cloud* that call weekly. The catamaran *Eagle* makes the trip from St. Maarten's Great Bay marina every Friday ($70 all-inclusive for the day).

AIRPORT TAX AND OTHER CHARGES. There is a 5% government tax on hotel rooms, plus a 10–15% service charge. There is no airport departure tax from Saba to St. Maarten or St. Eustatius.

TELEPHONE AND EMERGENCY NUMBERS. The M.A. Edwards Medical Center in The Bottom is a 15-bed hospital with full-time licensed physician, various clinics, and dental services once a month. Tel. 3288/89. The police number is 2237. To telephone from the U.S., dial 011–599–4 and the local number. Telephone communications are excellent here, with direct international dialing available.

HOTELS. The hotels on Saba are as small as the island itself, and if you plan to stay the best bet is to take advantage of their meal plans, since restaurants are few. We call $114 for two people per day, including breakfast and dinner *Moderate;* $50 and below *Inexpensive.*

Captain's Quarters. *Moderate.* Windwardside. Telephone: 2201. A small inn nestled among hibiscus, poinsettia, orange, lime, and papaya trees. Ten spacious rooms located in two turn-of-the-century buildings. Each is individually decorated—some with four-poster beds; all with ingenuity and interesting antique touches. Both air conditioning and keys are unnecessary. Good meals are served on the shaded porch and garden dining pavilion next to the inn's office, library, and sitting room. A fresh-water pool perched 1500 feet above the sea, with a large sunning area and small gazebo bar, completes the picture.

Cranston's Antique Inn. *Inexpensive.* The Bottom. Tel. 5259. Once the government guesthouse, the six rooms (one with private bath) all have wonderful antique four-poster beds, polished hardwood floors, and lots of potential. Unfortunately, Mr. J.C. Cranston, the long-term lease holder and manager of this 130-year-old home, seems to have little interest in improving or preserving his property. Last winter we found a new assistant manager, Statian Kenneth Cuvelay, and his Dutch wife Mona, working hard to upgrade both accommodations and service. If they're still there, try it. If not, even slightly persnickity travelers will probably be happier elsewhere.

Scout's Place. *Inexpensive.* Windwardside. Tel. 2205. Retired owner Scout Thirkield has turned his "Bed'n'Board, Cheap'n'Cheerful" pride and joy over to his longtime cook, Diana Medero. Scout, a native Ohioan who fled St. Maarten over 20 years ago because he found it getting crowded, is still very much in evidence, however. The "4½" rooms are small, spotless, eclectically decorated and usually occupied, though still without hot water. Diana is contemplating ten additional accommodations with hot water and a small pool. Warm, informal atmosphere and always stimulating conversation with Scout's longtime friends, younger newcomers, and locals.

HOME AND APARTMENT RENTALS. 18 very inexpensive ($100–$280 per week) apartments and traditional Saban-style wooden cottages with hot water and modern conveniences are available to rent in Hell's Gate and Windwardside. Write Glen Holm, Director of Tourism, Windwardside, Saba, N.A. for a list of what's available.

HOW TO GET AROUND. Taxis are available at the airport and on request. Fares are $25 for a one- to five-person island tour. A couple of rental cars are available through Scout's (Tel. 2205). But really this island is one where you will be happier to leave the driving to someone else and focus on the breathtaking views at each curve in the road.

TOURIST INFORMATION SERVICES. The local *Tourist Office* is in Windwardside next to the Post Office; tel. 2231. For sources closer to home, see the Tourist Information Services section in the *Facts at Your Fingertips* chapter.

SPECIAL EVENTS. The two big events are Saba Carnival in July, replete with street dancing and costume parades, and Saba Days in early December, featuring island-wide competitions and sporting events.

TOURS. The ten taxi drivers meet all plane and boat arrivals and double as tour guides. Rates for a day tour run $25 per car (one to five people).

BEACHES. Saba has one black sand beach at Well's Bay, but it's a wandering beach and that means it's only there a few months of the year. Tides, winds, currents, and storms at sea all affect the amount of sand that is deposited on the shore as well as the shoreline itself. Work has been started on an access path to take advantage of the sandy stretch when it is around, but this project will take several years.

PARTICIPANT SPORTS. Hiking and mountain climbing are very popular, although strenuous. Climbing to the top of Mt. Scenery (3,000 feet) is a half-day excursion. Include a picnic for a break in the journey. Bring a sweater or a jacket because the higher you go, the cooler it gets. The rain forest and the views from the summit make it all worthwhile. The Tourist Office can fill you in on several other interesting trails.

There is a macadam **tennis** court in The Bottom that few people use or even know about. If there is no net, just ask next door.

Saba has some of the best **diving** in the Caribbean, with excellent visibility, caves, caverns, submerged mountains, ledges, and reefs resplendent with every variety of tropical coral, sponges, and fish. The waters are still new to scuba, and fish are easily hand-fed, including the island mascot, Sabina, a 25-lb. Nassau grouper which escorts divers through his territory in return for a snack. A minimum of 25 dive sites are close to shore with boat trips never longer than 20 minutes. *Saba Deep, NV,* operated by enthusiastic Rhode Islander, Ed "Tat" Arnold, has a well-equipped dive shop (tel. 3347) at Fort Bay. Single-tank dives are $40; double, $70 with reduced rates for multiple dives. Full 5-day scuba certification courses are offered ($200) as well as a one-day introductory course ($80), which includes one dive.

MUSEUMS. The *Saba Museum* is set in a field of flowers just behind The Captain's Quarters to the left. There are small signs marking the way. Open Mon. through Friday from 10:00 A.M.–noon; 1:00 P.M.–3:30 P.M. There is a small admission fee of U.S. $1 which goes for upkeep. This hundred-year-old cottage has been set up just as it probably was when it was a sea captain's home. The kitchen, with its massive brick hearth, old water jugs, and cooking implements is fascinating. Have a good look at the guest book when you sign it— you'll be surprised at some of Saba's famous visitors.

SHOPPING. Saba Spice, a special, locally brewed rum liqueur, is a good inexpensive gift that is found everywhere. Saba lace, also called Spanish Work, is also well known. Gertrude Johnson learned this intricate way of drawing the threads through fine linen during her convent school days in Venezuela, and introduced it to other Saban ladies upon her return home in the 1870s. Large tablecloths, sheets, and clothing made of the finest linen can be expensive, but lovely tea towels, handkerchiefs, napkins, and other small items are within everyone's price range. In Windwardside, the *Saba Shop* and *Island Craft Shop* have the best selections; but you'll also see pieces displayed on people's porches that are for sale as well. The *Captain's Store,* next to the Bar at Captain's Quarters, opens from 9:00 A.M.–3:00 P.M. and has some nice gift items, T-shirts, and hand-screened clothing and fabric designed by the *Saba Artisans Foundation.* The foundation's workrooms and main boutique are in The Bottom. Here you'll find a fairly large selection of unusual cotton prints with colorful motifs. Available by the yard or already made up into clothing for men, women, and children. Saban shop hours are generally 8:00 A.M.–noon; 2:00 P.M.–5:00 P.M. Credit cards are not accepted anywhere.

RESTAURANTS. Since the island was first settled, Saba men have always taken to the sea and fishing is still the major industry, so fresh-caught seafood is the specialty here. Menus are somewhat limited and in some cases offer no choice at all, so call to see what's being served before making a reservation. We call $20 per person *Moderate;* below that *Inexpensive.* Credit cards are not accepted anywhere.

Captain's Quarters. *Moderate.* Windwardside. Tel. 2201. The dining porch is cool and comfortable with big, well-spaced wooden tables and lots of greenery and fresh flowers. Fish, lobster, and steak are always available and there's usually a continental or West Indian recipe as well. *Polynesia* passengers picnic by the pool twice a month at noon, so if it's peace and quiet you're seeking, ask the hotel to pack up a sandwich and head on up to Mt. Scenery that day. If you're after activity, stick around and enjoy the always-lively crowd.

Kate's Red Rock. *Moderate.* Windwardside. Tel. 2230. For sale our last visit, so the name may change. But the small dining room in a pretty Saban cottage is cozy and romantic. The large patio and bar attracts local dart buffs during the week and dancers on Saturday night when the music may go on until after midnight. Nice for lunch too. Fish, chicken, and steak are the menu mainstays.

Cranston's Antique Inn. *Inexpensive.* The Bottom. Tel. 3203. Out back in the garden of this 100-plus-year-old house, you'll find a shaded patio, surrounded by a white picket fence. It's the outdoor bar and restaurant. Open for lunch and dinner, it serves spicy fish cakes, authentic West Indian curries, fresh local vegetables, and other treats savored by locals and visitors alike.

Saba Chinese Restaurant. *Inexpensive.* Tel. 2268. The island's largest menu with a choice of over 50 Cantonese dishes. Not much atmosphere but usually well patronized at both lunch and dinner.

Scout's Place. *Inexpensive.* Windwardside. Tel. 2205. Bring a good appetite along here as servings are plentiful and Diana Medero's cooking is excellent. There's a set menu at both lunch and dinner that can range from West Indian goat curry to whatever. If you like spicy food ask for the special homemade hot sauce but proceed with caution. The large dining porch is a popular luncheon stop with groups visiting Saba for the day.

NIGHT LIFE AND BARS. Just about everybody on the island eventually ends up at *Scout's Place* or *Captain's Quarters* for before- or after-dinner drinks (or both) and conversation. Even visitors staying in The Bottom hitchhike on up to Windwardside, especially during the week. Sometimes there is a Saturday-night dance at the community center in The Bottom, but don't count on it; *Kate's Red Rock,* however, was planning to continue Saturday night entertainment and dancing. Once you get to know Sabans, you'll be invited to dinner and parties in their homes and that's about all there is as far as evening activities are concerned.

POSTAGE. An airmail letter to the U.S. is NAF 1.30; postcard NAF .60.

ELECTRIC CURRENT. Current on Saba is 110 volts, 60 cycles, so there's no need for converters for American appliances.

ST. BARTHELEMY

by
CLAIRE DEVENER

It is said that rainbows are rather common here. Rainbow chasers may not find the fabled pot of gold at the end of this arc but some will discover that St. Barts is itself the treasure. This small island received just over 100,000 visitors last year. Many come just for the day from St. Maarten and find the island too quiet—no big hotels, no casinos or nightclubs, and no organized activity. But others discover the rolling hills, peaceful coves, and lack of entertainment just to their liking. Having found their treasures they come back to it again and again.

Past and Present

As Columbus sailed by in 1493, he named the island for his brother, Barthelemeo. In 1648, a group of sixty Frenchmen arrived to found a colony under the patronage of the governor of the Compagnie de St. Christophe (St. Kitts). Eight years later, the Carib Indians massacred everyone and St. Barthelemy was abandoned. Though the island's resources were meager, its large, well-protected harbor and ideal location were just too tempting. The St. Kitts group decided to try again, and in 1674 sent over a new, hardy group of French Huguenots from Normandy and Brittany. This time the colony prospered slowly but surely—with lots of help, no doubt from French buccaneers who were attracted by the island's strategic position for somewhat different rea-

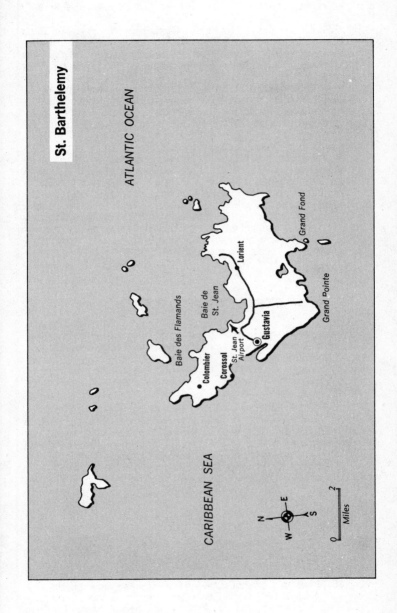

sons. These pirates brought with them vast wealth and priceless plunder taken from ambushed Spanish galleons.

In 1784, King Louis VI traded St. Barthelemy to his friend, King Gustaf III of Sweden, in exchange for French free-port rights in Gothenburg. The Swedes, delighted at last to have property in the New World, renamed the capital Gustavia in honor of their king. New streets were laid out and paved; pastures walled off; a town hall, three forts, and comfortable houses with gardens fenced in stone constructed.

In the nineteenth century the once-prosperous capital and healthy economy went into a decline. One calamity followed another. Commerce plunged, and people left for new islands of opportunity. St. Barthelemy became a drain on the Swedish budget. Finally, in 1878, France agreed to repurchase her former colony.

St. Barts has been blissfully quiet and stable since then. A dependency of Guadeloupe, and thus part of an overseas department of France, the island is administrated by a France-appointed sous-préfet. A mayor and a municipal council oversee things on a local level. French is the official language, but much of the older population speaks a quaint Norman dialect handed down over the centuries. Now that tourism is becoming such an important part of the island's economy and the number of U.S. visitors increases every year, English is far more prevalent, especially in hotels, restaurants, and shops.

EXPLORING ST. BARTS

With only eight square miles to cover, St. Barts is a breeze to tour. You can rent a Gurgel—Volkswagen's version of a Jeep—and head up, down, and around St. Barts.

Gustavia

For a good introduction to island life, head for St. Barts' capital, Gustavia. Stop in any of the several portside cafés around rue de la France and rue de la République for coffee and croissants and just watch the passing parade of people, cars, and boats. Around eleven o'clock the catamarans start arriving with day-trippers from St. Maarten. The few streets and shops will start getting crowded.

If it's Tuesday or Thursday, there will be a small market in progress on the quai at the foot of rue de la France. It's not big compared to what you'll see on some other islands—everything is small scale here—but nonetheless it is worthwhile. Then stroll through the little streets whose plaques sometimes spell out their names in both French and Swedish. Small shops feature French perfumes, resortwear, crystal, gold jewelry, and other luxury items, as well as a few locally made products. The selections are limited but there are some good buys.

Walk up to the tourist office on rue August Nyman in the *Mairie* (city hall). Pick up a map of the island and maybe the excellent 126-page guide "Bonjour St. Barth," sold there for fifty francs. If you have any questions, Elise Magras, the director, will be able to answer them as well as recommend some special spots to visit.

You might also want to stop by La Rotisserie to pick up the makings for a picnic. This local "deli," just down the street near the post office,

turns out some marvelous delicacies that Craig Claiborne, a frequent
St. Barts visitor, has given his stamp of approval.

If you feel like a swim, drive around the end of the harbor to Petit
Anse de Galet. This quiet little *plage* is also known as Shell Beach
because myriads of shells—all shapes, varieties, sizes, and colors—are
heaped up ankle deep in some places.

Then head back the way you came and turn right on the road marked
Lurin. You'll pass the carefully restored Swedish structure that is now
the sous-préfecture and a clock tower you've probably noticed from
town. It's the belfry and all that's left of a long-demolished Swedish
church; but the clock now works perfectly and was recently given a new
face. The views up the winding road overlooking the harbor, Fort Karl,
Fort Oscar and even the airport, are quite spectacular. A small, rocky
road off to the right will take you bumping and grinding down a steep
incline to Anse du Gouverneur, one of St. Barts most beautiful beaches,
where it is said pirate's treasure may be buried. If it's a clear day, the
far-off islands of Saba, Statia, and St. Kitts will appear to be right next
door. More than likely you'll decide to make it a day of sunning and
swimming in this sublime spot. On the way back home, stop by the
Santa Fé restaurant for a "sundowner." You'll be amused by the chickens taking to the trees for their nighttime roost and amazed by the
spectacular view from the terrace. A fine way to end another wonderfully relaxing day.

Corossol

Another morning visit the fishing village of Corossol. This spot
where time has stopped still shows vestiges of the French provincial
origins of St. Barts' population. Not only do most residents on this part
of the island speak an old Norman dialect; but the everyday garb of the
older women—modest, high-necked, long-sleeved, ankle-length dresses
and starched white, shoulder-length sunbonnets—is akin to what their
ancestors wore in the seventeenth century. Here, however, the women
are likely to be barefoot! These hats, called *quichenottes,* designed for
protection from the strong sun, were once considered equally good
protection against the unwanted amorous advances of English and
Swedish suitors, who named them "kiss-me-nots". The women are very
shy and do not like to be photographed. They do like, however, to invite
visitors up to their porches and sometimes into their homes, to see their
straw work—handbags, baskets, broadbrimmed hats, and delicate
strings of birds—which is for sale. You'll often be able to watch them
weaving and braiding threads taken from lantania palms, trees that
were introduced to the island in the late 1800s and that grow nearby.
Women in similar dress but slightly different bonnets may also be seen
in the neighboring village of Colombier.

Continue down from Corossol on the main road to Baie des Flamands, another beautiful and usually very unpopulated beach with two
small hotels, some attractive villas and bungalows, and a couple of good
lunch spots. From here you can hike up to the top of what is believed
to be the volcano that gave birth to St. Barts. It's an easy walk, and
the view from the top over the uninhabited offshore islands in the
north, and off to Pointe Milou in the east, is pure picture postcard.

St. Jean and the Eastern Side

As you leave Gustavia, you'll climb up a big hill with a white cross at its crest. As the road banks sharply to the right, if your timing is good, a Twin Otter airplane will silently skim overhead in a controlled stall, plunge into an abyss, and gently alight on the runway of "La Plaine de la Tourmente" (the plain of torment). If you've arrived by plane yourself, you'll know exactly how the passengers are feeling at this moment. The location of this airport is aptly, though diabolically, named.

Farther down the hill, St. Jean's hotels, villas, and shops blend into the hilly landscape or cluster on the half-mile crescent of sand. This is the hub of twentieth-century, tourist-oriented St. Barts, where beguiling beauties in monokinis soak up the sun, gourmets gather in beachside bistros, and the colorful sails of windsurfers (practicing St. Barts' most popular sport) billow in the breeze. Some St. Barts' fans of long standing now find this area becoming too congested and too commercial. We tend to agree, but there's still much natural beauty to savor.

Continue on the main road past the St. Jean Commercial Center in the direction of Lorient. You'll pass the beginning of a long beach bordered by royal palms, a favorite with surfers for its long rolling waves. At Lorient, considered one of two island crossroads, are an interesting new museum housed in an original 19th-century Norman farmhouse, an old church, rectory and historic headstones, a school, and the only post office and gas station outside of Gustavia. Though it may seem much farther because of the hills, Lorient is less than two miles from Gustavia. If you choose the fork in the road that heads south, the road will dead-end at Grande Saline, where the salt ponds are no longer worked. It doesn't look like much, but get out of the car and walk a minute or two up over the rocky hillock for a pleasant surprise—Anse de Grande Saline, a long arc of pristine white sand without hotels, restaurants, or even houses to spoil the effect. This is one of St. Barts' most popular swimming and sunning places, though it can be very windy.

If you choose the left fork at Lorient, your route rolls around the coast with views out to the Ile de la Tortue and down on the windward coves. Pointe Milou is a new and quite elegant residential colony; and at Marigot, a shop called La Cave caters to discriminating palates with an astonishing collection of fine wines stored under strict temperature control. Grand Cul de Sac has some lovely old stone and wooden houses, ponds, mangroves, and a beach known for its fine water-sports facilities. Grand Fond, where the surf pounds rocky coastlines, again reminds one of Normandy with its low stone fences laid out patchwork fashion on the grassy slopes. Here the road leaves the coast and turns inland and back to the crossroads of Lorient, St. Jean, and Gustavia.

PRACTICAL INFORMATION FOR
ST. BARTHELEMY

FACTS AND FIGURES. St.Barts lies 125 miles north-west of Guadeloupe; 15 miles southeast of St. Maarten. Everything on this eight-mile-square island is small scale, and the 3,050 St. Bartians are doing their best to keep it that way. The biggest hotel—and there are only 20—has just 50 rooms scattered over a hillside; 19-passenger STOL (Short Take-Off and Landing) planes are the largest aircraft that can land on the tiny airfield; VW bugs, mini-mokes and mini-buses are the most common vehicles to ply the nine-foot-wide roads. Gustavia, the capital, has been a free port since 1786 but big cruise ships rarely call here, though the harbor's idyllic anchorage is a favorite among Caribbean yachtsmen.

WHEN TO GO. St. Barts is a dry, sunny island tempered by trade winds year-round. Temperatures average 72 to 86 degrees F. and when rain does fall it's at night and of short duration. Since it's now a very "in" destination with sophisticated travelers fed up with mass tourism, the season here is getting longer each year. Reservations must be made well ahead of time; particularly in winter when some hotels are booked a year in advance. Prices are about 35% less from April 15–December 15. Some hotels and many restaurants close down for refurbishing or their own vacations in September and October.

PASSPORTS AND VISAS. For visits of three months or less, US and Canadian visitors need a valid passport, *or* one expired not longer than five years *or* a proof of citizenship, in the form of a notarized birth certificate with a raised seal or voter's registration card, *both accompanied* by a government-authorized identification with photo. Check with your airline to know exactly what is acceptable.

HOW TO GET THERE. By air. From St. Martin/St. Maarten: *Windward Islands Airways* makes the ten-minute hop from Juliana Airport on the Dutch side; *Air Guadeloupe* from Esperance Airport on the French side. There are also direct flights to St. Barts from Guadeloupe and Antigua aboard *Air Guadeloupe* and from St. Thomas and San Juan aboard *Virgin Air.*

Air St. Barthelemy (tel. 27–61–90)—has two 9-passenger, twin-engine aircraft for charter. They make pick-ups almost anywhere and do day-long or overnight excursions to nearby islands as well. No after-dark landings or take-offs.

By boat. Half a dozen catamarans sail over from St. Maarten every morning except Sun. Arrival in St. Barts is around 11:00 A.M.; departure 3:30 P.M. If there is room, all will accept one-way passengers ($25). Dany and Patrick Siau run regular motorboat excursions for shopping in St. Maarten. Departure is 8:30 A.M., return at 4:30 P.M. Fare is $25 round trip; space should be booked the day before by calling 27–61–33 (9–12:30, 3:30–5) or through the El Sereno Hotel, tel. 27–64–10.

TAXES AND OTHER CHARGES. Most hotels and restaurants add a 10–15% service charge to bills. There is no airport departure tax.

MONEY. The French franc is legal tender. Figure 10 francs to U.S.$1; Dollars are accepted everywhere; credit cards rarely.

WHAT WILL IT COST?

A typical day for two persons in season on St. Barts:

	U.S.$
Hotel with full American breakfast at a top property on the beach	$135
Lunch at a moderate restaurant	40
Dinner at a moderate to expensive restaurant	60
Tips and service charges	25
One-day car rental	35
Total	$295

TELEPHONE AND EMERGENCY NUMBERS. To phone St. Barts from the U.S., dial 011–596 + the local number. Few hotel rooms have telephones but calls can be made from the front desk. There are also automatic telephone booths around the island. These require 5F, 1F or 0.50F French coins. The number for local information is 12. To call collect or with a credit card dial 10. To call the U.S. from St. Barts, dial 19–1 + area code + local number. Gustavia Hospital is located at the corner of rue Jean Bart and rue Sadi Carnot. Tel. 27–60–35. Police emergency number is 27–60–12.

HOTELS. St. Barts has just 20 small hotels that range from a homey half a dozen rooms up to 50. All are located on or near a beach. For a double room with breakfast in season we call $150 and up *Deluxe;* $100–149 *Expensive;* $75–99 *Moderate;* and below $75 *Inexpensive.*

Castelets. *Deluxe.* Mt. Lurin. Tel. 27–61–73. A spectacular spot on a hill above Gustavia. This elegant yet informal enclave has just six rooms and two private duplex villas, each with two bedrooms. All are beautifully furnished with antiques, have marvelous views over St. Jean Bay and the offshore islands, and are *very* much in demand. You'll need a car for the beach but there is a mini pool and excellent French restaurant. Mme. Geneviève Jouany is the very charming and very capable lady in command.

Hotel Manapany Cottages. *Deluxe.* Anse des Cayes. Tel. 27–66–55. The name of this brand-new hotel is a combination of its owners' initials, but also means little paradise, and that it is. 20 cottages containing 1 suite with living room/dining area, kitchen/bar and terrace, and 1 deluxe double room, are terraced up the hillside from the beach. Secluded and serene, each is well-appointed and has a sea view. The pool is the island's largest, and the tennis court St. Barts' only lighted facility. There's a very pleasant seaside grill for lunch and an elegant plant-filled gourmet dining room for evening meals. Closed-circuit TV, 24-hour room service, boutique, morning calisthenics classes by the pool, and a small beach (beware, however, of sometimes strong undertow) round out the amenities of this elegant hideaway.

Taiwana. *Deluxe.* Anse des Flamands. Tel. 27–63–82. The only way to secure accommodations in this top-drawer retreat is to know the owner, a Frenchman who insists on following this protocol. Nine rooms furnished with antique four-posters are clustered in 4 pastel-painted gingerbread cottages. There's a large pool, tennis court, and popular lunchtime beachclub.

Eden Rock. *Expensive.* St. Jean. No tel. The island's first hotel is built on a huge rock that juts out right in the middle of St. Jean Beach. The status of this once-popular place was very iffy on our last visit. Check thoroughly before booking.

Filao Beach. *Expensive.* St. Jean. Tel. 27–64–84 or 27–62–24. 30 bungalows are grouped in a crescent around a flower-filled garden. The spacious, carpeted rooms are decorated in bright contemporary style and well furnished with double beds, seating area with rattan divan, coffee table, and two chairs. Each has a terrace, direct-dial telephone, radio (TV on request), air conditioning, refrigerator, wall safe in the closet, even a built-in hair dryer in the bathroom. Freshwater pool, water sports; a pool restaurant whose menu includes pheasant paté and cheeseburgers as well as the ubiquitous grilled fish and lobster. Often booked up a year in advance.

L'Hibiscus. *Expensive.* Rue Thiers, Gustavia. Tel. 27–64–82. Eleven pretty rooms in individual bungalows set among masses of flaming hibiscus on a small hill overlooking the harbor. All are air conditioned, rush matted, and decorated in soft tones with printed French linens and drapes hand-screened locally by Jean Yves Froment. A well-equipped kitchenette is on the terrace. There's a small pool and a good restaurant. Shopping and Shell Beach are within walking distance.

PLM Jean Bart. *Expensive.* St. Jean. Tel. 27–63–37. The island's largest resort, this property has 50 rooms, 30 with kitchenettes, in cottages terraced up the hillside from St. Jean Bay. There's a freshwater swimming pool, snack bar, breakfast terrace restaurant. We found this hotel somewhat frayed at the edges on our last visit and service had dwindled drastically.

El Sereno Beach. *Expensive.* Grand Cul de Sac. Tel. 27–64–80. Built around a deep main garden, the twenty compact, cathedral-ceilinged rooms are decorated in fresh blue and white. Each is air conditioned and has a small refrigerator, individual wall safe, telephone, and TV/video. There's also a very private, walled-in patio garden where hot croissants and coffee are brought every morning. The angular pool is constructed around islands of flowers, palms, and greenery; a small swimming cove and main beach water sports are just a few steps away. The restaurant here is probably the island's best. Managers Christine and Marc Llepez are gracious and caring; guests are mostly repeats who like the elegant, easy life here.

Autour du Rocher. *Moderate.* Lorient. Tel. 27–60–73. Very casual 6-room inn built on and around a big rock overlooking the surf and sand of Anse de Lorient. The bar and lounge here is one of the few lively places on the island after 10, when everyone who's in the mood to dance and socialize stops by.

Baie des Flamands. *Moderate.* Anse de Flamands. Tel 27–64–85 and 27–64–76. Solange Gréaux' modern, two-story structure faces a long, breezy, and always uncrowded expanse of white sand. The 24 functional rooms are all good sized, carpeted, air conditioned, and have sea views from their balconies. There's a large saltwater pool, and a commendable restaurant. This hotel is especially popular with American families and French Canadians.

Emeraude Plage. *Moderate.* St. Jean. Tel. 27–64–78. This quiet, well-located beachside bungalow hotel recently added ten new rooms to bring the total count up to 30. Accommodations include 24 studios; two two-bedroom, one-bath cottages; and the Villa Emeraude, with two bedrooms and two baths right on the sea. All have air conditioning and ceiling fans, new direct-dial telephones; kitchenettes with large refrigerators; and patios or sundecks. For those who don't care to cook, a breakfast room and bar (that doubles as a video/TV room and library) was added last spring. Several good restaurants are less than a five-minute walk away and the young manager, Geneviève Nouy, provides the kind of service that brings her guests back year after year.

Grand Cul de Sac Beach Hotel and **St. Barts Beach Hotel.** *Moderate.* Grand Cul de Sac. Tel. 27–60–70 and 27–62–73. These two hotels, both under the ownership of Guy Turbé, are situated side by side on a narrow peninsula between a lagoon and the sea. Both are very popular with French and Canadian tour groups as well as individual U.S. travelers. The Cul de Sac's 16 rustic rooms include kitchenettes. Its sister property has 36 simple accommodations. Among the shared facilities are a large freshwater pool, a tennis court, a beach snack bar and an indoor dining room with a view. The well-protected waters here are perfect for swimming, snorkeling, and windsurfing.

Tropical Hotel. *Moderate.* St. Jean. Tel. 27–64–87. A pretty, gingerbread-frilled 20-room complex arranged around a cloister-like garden. Nine rooms have balconies with sea views; the rest, porches that open onto the garden. All have air conditioning, tropical fans, telephones, and small refrigerators. There's a reception bungalow with bar, music, reading lounge, and video room, and breakfast is served on the terrace that girds the small pool. Restaurants, shops, and the beach are just 50 yards down the hill.

Village St. Jean. *Moderate.* St. Jean. Tel. 27–61–39. The view is fine from these comfortable stone and redwood chalets terraced up the hillside above St. Jean Beach. There's a wide variety of air-conditioned accommodations in this 25-room village—balconied rooms, studios, one- and two-bedroom villas—and the best are booked up a year in advance. Some have refrigerators, others complete outdoor kitchens on their spacious decks. There's a game and reading room; breezy restaurant serving breakfast and Italian cuisine at dinner; a boutique and small grocery store on the premises.

Hotel Normandie. *Inexpensive.* Lorient. Tel. 27–61–66. There are just eight simple spotless rooms, all with private bath. The garden holds a small pool and the beach is within walking distance. A good three-course dinner may also be enjoyed on the pleasant garden terrace for around $10.

Le P'Tit Morne. *Inexpensive.* Colombier. Tel. 27–61–02 and 27–62–64. A charming "mini hotel" whose eight attractively decorated studio apartments each have a fully equipped kitchen. There's air conditioning, but you'll probably prefer the naturally cooling Atlantic breezes. The mountaintop pool overlooks St. Barts' northern offshore islands and the beach is only five minutes away by car.

Presqu'ile. *Inexpensive.* Place de la Parade, Gustavia. Tel. 27–64–60. 12 basic rooms are right on the harbor in town. Air conditioning is available if you feel you need it, and the restaurant since Mme. Jacqua, a popular chef from Martinique, took over the kitchen has excellent Creole fare.

Tom Beach. *Inexpensive.* St. Jean. Tel. 27–60–43. 12 attractively decorated rooms in unusual wooden shingled cottages with high-pitched roofs right on St. Jean Beach. Each has a kitchenette and the grocery is nearby. For inexpensive, casual living in a perfect location. Joe Ledée's special three-night summer package that includes transfers, windsurf and house boutique discounts, and a bottle of chilled wine in your fridge, can't be beat at $130 for two.

 HOME RENTALS. Brook and Roger Lacour (she's American, he's from Guadeloupe) have a long list of about 100 possibilities—villas, apartments, and new condominiums—all around the island. Call their U.S. representative: WIMCO, (800) 932–3222, or write SIBARTH, B.P. 55, 97133 Gustavia; tel. 27–62–38, but keep in mind that mail is very slow here. Joe Ledée's *Villas St. Barthelemy* (tel. 27–60–43) handles a dozen or so other properties; and Claude Andrès and Bernard Robert's *St. Barth's House* in the Villa Creole complex in St. Jean (tel. 27–62–49) represent some 20 villas for rent as well as real estate sales. Count on spending an average of $1,000 per week for a one bedroom villa; $1,500 for two bedrooms; $2,000 for three bedrooms.

 HOW TO GET AROUND. Taxis are available at the airport and cost U.S. $2–5, depending on the location of your hotel. Prices increase by 33% from 9:00 P.M.–6:00 A.M. If you don't plan to rent a car, get the list of drivers and their telephone numbers from the tourist office in Mairie on rue August Nyman. You'll need it as you can't just hail a cab, and taxi stands are nonexistent. You can rent VW Beetles, Gurgels (a Volkswagen jeep) and Mini Mokes—all with stick shift only—for $35 per day with unlimited mileage and free delivery and pickup. You must be 25 years old and, in season, there may be a three-day minimum. Motorbikes rent for $13–$15 per day and there is a $100 deposit. Tel. 27–61–63 in Gustavia.

 TOURIST INFORMATION SERVICES. You can obtain information about St. Barts on the spot at the new *Office Municipale du Tourisme,* in the Mairie (city hall) on the rue August Nyman in Gustavia, tel. 27–60–08. Hours: Mon., Tues., Thurs., Fri. 8:00 A.M.–noon, 2:30 P.M.–6:00 P.M.; Wed. and Sat. 8:00 A.M. to 12:30. For sources closer to home, see Tourist Information Services section in the *Facts at Your Fingertips* chapter.

SPECIAL EVENTS. The highlight is the three-day celebration at the end of August to Honor St. Barthelemy, the island's patron saint. It has all the makings of a French country fair, with booths and wining, dining, and dancing in the evening. There are small Carnival celebrations just before Mardi Gras and Bastille Day fireworks.

TOURS. An island tour runs $6 per person in a minibus for 8; $15 for 2 in a private taxi.

 BEACHES. There are over 20 beaches around the island; all public and free. Some—Anse de Colombier in the northwest and Maréchal near Cul de Sac in the northeast—are only accessible by boat. Some of the best include Baie des Flamands, Baie St. Jean, Anse de Lorient, and Anse du Grand Cul de Sac in the north; Anse de Grande Saline; Anse du Gouverneur, and Petite Anse de Galet in the south. Nudism is forbidden; toplessness common.

 PARTICIPANT SPORTS. If a full array of sports is your preference, St. Barts is not the answer. There is no golf and just three **tennis** courts (at St. Barts Beach Hotel, Manapany Hotel, and Taiwana), but the best times are usually reserved by their guests. **Swimming** at over 20 beaches is one favorite pastime and there's good surf at Lorient in the northeast, Anse du Gouverneur, Grande Saline, Grand Fond, and Toiny in the South.

Facilities for water sports have greatly improved. The French are fanatical **windsurfers,** and boards are available to rent on the beach at Anse des Flamands, Bay St. Jean, and Grand Cul de Sac at about $10 per hour. Lessons may be arranged (approx. $30) through St. Bart's Wind School or Mistral on St. Jean Beach and Wind Wave Power at the St. Barts Beach Hotel. The instructor at the latter, Pascal, is tough but one of the best in the business and you'll find him in Westhampton in the summer, in case you feel the need for more lessons.

Sailing enthusiasts will find Sunfish and Hobie Cats available at St. Jean Beach and Grand Cul de Sac. The *Zavijava,* a 42 ft. ketch captained by Dany or Patrick Siau, does a nice day sail to Ile Fourchue for snorkeling and swimming. Cocktails and an excellent lunch are served aboard and then sails are set for Colombier, one of St. Barts' best beaches, accessible only by boat. Maximum 8 passengers, departs 9:30 A.M., returns 5:30 P.M. $50 per person. For reservations contact Dominique's Boutique between 9 A.M. and 12:30 P.M. or 3:30 P.M. and 5:30 P.M., or the El Sereno Hotel. The Siau's will also do overnight or day charters to other destinations. St. Barts Water Sports, on rue du Roi Oscar II (tel. 27–66–16), in Gustavia conducts a licensed, fully accredited dive school for those interested in **scuba. Snorkeling** is good off of any of the calmer beaches such as Gouverneur, St. Jean, or Cul de Sac; fins and masks may be rented at most of the larger beach hotels or purchased at Loulou's Marine, on rue de la Republique in Gustavia.

For those interested in **fishing,** the waters around St. Barts abound in game fish such as tazard, wahoo, dolphin, bonito, barracuda, even marlin. The bulletin boards at the BNP bank and Loulou's Marine have notices of captains who are willing to do charters. The motorboat *Diana* will take up to 6 on fishing trips at $30 per person including breakfast. Departure 5:30 A.M., return 10 A.M. Tel. 27–62–34 between 9 A.M. and noon, 3 P.M.–6 P.M.

Hunting and camping are not allowed on the island.

 SHOPPING. Though limited, the duty-free goods on sale are definitely of interest. Luxury items—cosmetics, perfumes, china, crystal, watches, and jewelry—are all good buys, as is the always chic French resortwear. The largest number of shops is in Gustavia and they are open 8:00 A.M.–noon; 2:00 P.M.–4:00 P.M. On Wednesday and Saturday, all shutter up at noon for the rest of the day. Along rue de la Republique you'll find:

Loulou's Marine. Everything remotely connected to sailing and the sea. *Alma Confection.* Hand-embroidered linens, lacy-white crocheted tablecloths, and some luxury items. *La Fonda.* Hermes beachtowels and other unusual creations from this elegant Parisian purveyor of luxury leathergoods and accessories. *La Boutique sur le Quai.* Bikinis, coverups, and stylish sportswear. *Stephane and Bernard.* Deluxe designer wear for both men and women. *Vestibule.* Soleiado's print provençale table linens and Sevres crystal. Around the corner on rue de la France are: *Le Bastrimgue.* Fiorucci's wild designs. *Privilege.* Cosmetics, watches, and more leathergoods.

Rue du Général De Gaulle houses several more boutiques including: *Smoke & Booze,* fine wines, liquors, liqueurs, toys, and souvenirs; *Le Comptoir* gourmet shop; *La Caleche,* Brook and Roger Lacour's large store stocked with attractive fashions for men and women, shoes, and some unusual accessory and gift items; and *Jean Yves Froment,* the town's prettiest shop crammed with bright colored, hand-painted and hand-blocked tropical fashions—dresses from mini to long, T-shirts and T-shirt dresses, shorts, slacks, bikinis, pareos, and fabric by the yard.

Go out Froment's upstairs door and you're on rue du Roi Oscar II. Here is the original branch (number 2 is in St. Jean, a third in Pte. Milou) of *La Rotisserie.* Pierre and Evelyne L'Hermite came here on vacation back in the 70's and never left. Now their deluxe deli is a gourmet's delight that has been praised by such luminaries of the food world as Craig Claiborne. Not to mention the legions of customers who place their orders each morning for tuna in Chartreuse, Chinese-style pork, curries, paella, Basque-style chicken, nems, patés, and other delicacies on the frequently changing menu, and pick them up, ready to pop into the oven, in the late afternoon. *La Boulangerie,* across the street, is one of the island's two much-praised bakeries, well known not only for their delicious fresh baked breads, but for stuffed turnovers and pastries as well.

Outside of town there's *St. Barth's Pottery,* located opposite the dispensary on the road to St. Jean. Hand-turned in their on-premises atelier, this traditional pottery is meant for everyday use—it's dishwasher-safe and ovenproof. St. Jean itself now has over 30 boutiques ranging from a Haitian art gallery to a perfumer selling exotic scents and essential oils. Names and owners here change frequently so it's best just to stop by and have a look for yourself.

Wine lovers should not miss *La Cave* in Marigot. Here wine merchant Julian Courtois has assembled an incredible collection of France's best vintages and keeps them carefully stored in a large, temperature-controlled building.

Across from the new airport terminal is *La Savane* commercial center, an attractive grouping of little shops in St. Barts-style cottages and *Mammouth,* a much-needed new supermarket.

 RESTAURANTS. Dining on St. Barts is a joy. There are about three dozen small restaurants that serve pure classical French, French with a West Indian touch, or home-style Creole cuisine. Reservations are in order everywhere, both in and out of season. For a three-course meal for *one* person, we call $25 and up *Expensive;* $15–25 *Moderate;* and under $15 *Inexpensive.*

Expensive

L'Ananas. Rue Sadi Carnot, Gustavia. Tel. 27–63–77. Two porches hold just 12 tables in this lovely old house set on a flowering hillside. The menu is small but includes such choices as sashimi, turbot braised in cider, *magret de canard,* and filet mignon with green peppercorns. Open dinner only. No credit cards.

Le Ballahou. Hotel Manapany, Anse des Cayes. Tel. 27–66–55. Brand new last season and reviews were mixed. But we're confident that accomplished young chef Dominique Allegre has the know-how and enthusiasm to make this exceptionally pretty dining room one of St. Barts' best. Candlelight dinner here is a relaxed affair with guests lingering over coffee and cognac while enjoying the piano bar. The Oualanao grill is also a lovely luncheon place by the sea that's just steps from the island's largest pool. AE, MC, V.

Le Brigantin. Rue Jeanne d'Arc, Gustavia. Tel. 27–60–89. This 19th-century stone building on the quai had been in Dantes Magras' family for years, but he and his wife, Maria, recently transformed it into one of St. Barts' prettiest and most fashionable restaurants. Apéritifs are taken at the bar, or in the lounge while soft music plays in the background. There's a choice of dining inside at one of eight candlelit tables covered in white lace, or on the less formal (and quieter) covered patio that has seven more tables. The menu changes monthly but cuisine is always creative and beautifully presented. Scallop mousse with sea urchin cream and fresh salmon served with blinis were standouts last year. The wine list is extensive and reasonably priced. Closed Wed. No credit cards.

Castelets. Morne Lorin, a mile above Gustavia. Tel. 27–61–73. An elegant country auberge dramatically set atop a mountain peak. Marseille-born Michel Viali changes his menu each season but some of his favored, oft-repeated specialties include brioche stuffed with foie gras; warm goose giblet salad; rack of lamb in garlic sauce; Camembert served warm and runny in a puff pastry. Tables are few and *very* much in demand since the cuisine is first class, wines exceptional, and service soigné. Open lunch and dinner but closed all day Tuesday and Wednesday lunch. Yachtsmen call on their radio for reservations long before arriving in port, so plan well ahead if you wish to enjoy one of the island's best spots.

Hostellerie des Trois Forces. Vitet. Tel. 27–61–25. A very special spot, this rustic country inn has much charm, a well thought-out menu and a young owner who really makes an effort to please. Hubert de la Motte has the island's only chimney, and here chef Pierre Thazet turns out excellent wood-grilled shrimp, lobster in basil butter, fish with fennel, and an interesting mixed grill. In the kitchen his wife Christine might be preparing a fish soufflé, curried escargots in a cream sauce, or one of her fabulous desserts such as profiterolles in the form of swans or a light and airy orange bavarois with raspberry sauce. Soft French music plays in the background and the whole feeling is one of total relaxation. AE, MC, V.

Lafayette. Grand Cul de Sac. Tel. 27–62–51. Open only for lunch and very "in" last season. Right on the beach *and* with its own pool, it's the perfect place to spend the day. Swim, sun, sip a drink on the shady terrace, and be sure you've reserved your table for grilled fish, lobster, big creative salads, and some very tempting desserts. No credit cards.

Au Port. Rue Sadi Carnot, Gustavia. Tel. 27–62–36. Gérard Balageas is a serious restaurateur who is also an innovator. His popular upstairs dinner spot has a harbor view from its terrace tables and a lively crowd. Count on a wide variety of fresh seafood; beef filet with green peppercorns, mustard sauce, or shallots; roast lamb with garlic cream; and an extensive dessert list. Closed Sun. D, V.

La Toque Lyonnaise. El Sereno Beach Hotel, Grant Cul de Sac. Tel. 27–64–80. This 50-seat restaurant draws an elegant, international crowd from all over the island at both the dinner seatings. The owners and managers are from Lyon. Twice a year, young Lyonnaise chefs with only the best training and credentials are given a special invitation to become *chef de cuisine* here for six months. Cuisine will always be haute but on the light side. No heavy sauces are used just top-quality ingredients. Foie gras is made on the premises as are the pastries, and the fabulous double-decker dessert cart presents a true dilemma to dieters. A superb but pricey wine list also includes nine champagnes. This is a class operation and without a doubt one of the island's best choices for dinner. AE, MC, V.

Expensive to Moderate

La Cremaillere. Rue General De Gaulle, Gustavia. Tel. 27–63–89. Michel Brunet's traditional, classic French cuisine may be enjoyed in the garden or in his small, elegant country-style dining room. Lobster bisque, onion soup, frog's legs, lobster thermidor, and airy souffléed potatoes are just a sampling of the house specialties. Dinner only. No credit cards.

La Louisiane. St. Jean commercial center. No tel. A big, St. Barts-style house set up on a hill, where dining takes place on the garden terrace. Michel Bonis and his staff are gracious and the menu (dinner only) extensive. Choose from scallops with wild mushrooms flambéed in cognac, lobster in white wine with artichoke hearts, thinly sliced duck breast with grapefruit, and some scrumptious homemade desserts. AE.

Le Pélican. St. Jean Beach. Tel. 27–64–64. Light lunches on the terrace; gourmet dinners prepared by Japanese chef Shigeo Torigai served in a pretty, air-conditioned dining room whose decor is transplanted French provincial.

Specialties here are mainly "nouvelle" with some interesting Oriental and Creole touches. Off-season visitors take note: Torigai moves to Brittany during the summer, where he is also in charge of the well-known Moulin du Duc. AE, D, V.

Restaurant du Vieux Clocher. L'Hibiscus Hotel, rue Thiers, Gustavia. Tel. 27–64–82. Baskets of hanging flowers, greenery, and wooden ceiling fans decorate this 12-table terrace restaurant. The menu is small but usually includes a cold and hot soup, grilled lobster and chicken, shrimp and steaks, as well as daily specials. There's piano music at cocktail hour, a popular time for both visitors and islanders to enjoy the view. AE, V.

Taiwana. Anse des Flamands. Tel. 27–65–01. Another lunchtime-only favorite on the sea with a big pool for adults, wading pool for the kids, and one of the island's three tennis courts. Soups, salads, grilled fish, brochettes, and lobster are the bill of fare of this casual, "loll away the day" beachclub. No credit cards.

Moderate

Chez Francine. St. Jean Beach. Tel. 27–60–49. Very popular with day-trippers. You can order, go for a swim, and return to eat in your bathing suit on the beachside terrace or one of the tables set up on the sand. Lunch only and the menu is listed on a blackboard, but usual specialties are grilled chicken, steak, lobster or shish kebob, all served with crispy *pommes frites.* No credit cards.

Chez Maya. Public. Tel. 27–63–99. Maya, an absolutely charming young Frenchwoman born in Martinique, has put together one of our favorite menus. The rather sophisticated Creole offerings change daily but we can especially recommend her pumpkin soup, conch brochette, shrimp in cocoanut milk, and *rougail de mangue vert,* a delicious mixture of green mango, hommos, and tahini. The appetizers are all so good that you might like to request a tasting. They will gladly oblige with a nicely arranged assortment. Vegetable purees, pigeon peas, rondelles of banana with shredded cocoanut, and a spicy *sauce chien* accompany all the well-executed dishes. Fresh fruit sherbets and pies are all homemade. AE, MC, V.

Chez Tatie. Public. Tel. 27–61–61. Mme. Tatie Bourgeois is the island's only Creole caterer but you can also come to her small six-table restaurant and enjoy her well-known accras, boudin, stuffed crab and christophine, curries, crayfish, and even pigs' tails or tripe and bananas. No car? They'll provide transport to and from Gustavia or St. Jean. No credit cards.

Coté Jardin. Gustavia. No tel. A dozen or so tables on a pretty flower-surrounded terrace that's open nonstop to midnight. The menu is small but well prepared and presented. There's always a *suprise du jour* and if it's the mussels don't miss them. AE.

Le Flore. Anse des Cayes. No telephone. Despite the French name, the *entrecote* (steak) here is all-American—6 oz., 9 oz., or 17 oz., of the best, aged Iowa beef served on a wooden platter. The seven terrace tables and five more in the open-sided dining room may be reserved for lunch but are far more romantic in the evening for dinner. Spotlights illuminate the waves and there's soft background music. Hard to find, so drive out on a test run during the day or get explicit directions from your hotel. No credit cards.

La Langouste. Rue du Roi Oscar II, Gustavia. Tel. 27–66–40. Annie Ange's small, popular restaurant is the 100-year-old Swedish home right next door to the *gendarmerie.* Lobster of course is the specialty, but there's also well-prepared French cuisine, authentic Creole dishes, good salads, and Annie's wonderful coconut flan. Open for lunch and dinner. No credit cards.

Marigot Bay Club. Marigot. No telephone. Jean-Michel Ledée lived in the States for over four years. Now he's back serving up fresh seafood provided by his old fisherman pals. The 16 butcher-block tables on his selfbuilt terrace overlooking the bay are usually filled by nearby villa owners at both lunch and dinner. Closed Sun. eve. and Mon. No credit cards.

Le Tamarin. Saline. No telephone. Open-air restaurant in the countryside with a dozen tables set out under a big tamarind tree. Open every day for lunch. Steak tartare, ribeye with parsley butter, honey and prune chicken, and grilled fish are the specialties. Open also on Saturday nights and for two special theme evenings every month—the young, very popular owners have had Brazilian, Mexican and cowboy nights. No credit cards.

Le Virginien. Carenage St. Jean. No tel. Old-fashioned, refined French cooking by Richard Berthier. His charming partner Chantal Fuchs is your very cordial hostess on the garden-side patio. There's a pretty tea salon next door that plays classical music from 4 to 7 P.M. for before-dinner relaxation and conversation. V.

Inexpensive

Au Bon Coin. Lorient. No tel. Remy Brin's tiny, hillside terrace is down a long, rough road that skirts the sea, then climbs up to his small house. It doesn't look like much, but this is one of St. Bart's best values. Excellent Creole specialties, fresh grilled fish, and meat at a price that's right keep the seven tables filled each evening. Dinner only. No credit cards.

Brasserie La Creole. Villa Creole shopping center. No tel. Pretty terrace opens at 7 A.M. for fresh-pressed fruit juices and hot croissants. Salads and sandwiches at lunch, light meals and snacks served until 11 P.M. AE.

Le Flamboyant. Grand Cul de Sac. Tel. 27–60–57. Ten tables on the terrace, three more inside Albert Balayn's wooden house perched on a hill. Good French cooking any evening but Sunday. The menu is small but there's always an extra Creole *plat du jour.* A full meal with wine will run about $15. No credit cards.

Le Marine. Rue Jeanne d'Arc, Gustavia. No telephone. A small terrace with 12 wooden, picnic-style tables overlook the quai. Seafood is the specialty and you've probably never heard of many of the fish. An 80F menu includes appetizer, main course, dessert, coffee, and a pitcher of red wine, two beers or sodas. Closed Mon. No credit cards.

Presqu'ile. Place de la Parade, Gustavia. Tel. 27–64–60. Mme. Jacqua is now head chef in this very plain and unpretentious little restaurant of the quai-side hotel of the same name. Best to call and see what's cooking or order in advance from the extensive French/Creole menu including those with cheese, fish, and *fines herbes* soufflés for which this Martiniquaise is well known on the island. The daily 80–150F menu is always an excellent value. No credit cards.

Topolino. St. Jean. Attractive, roomy terrace set back from the road. Lively, fun, and open late by island standards. Salads, barbecued fish and steaks, and Italian dishes are featured on the menu. AE.

 NIGHT LIFE AND BARS. Cocktail hour finds the barefoot boating set gathered for beer and small talk in the garden of Gustavia's *Le Select;* the more sophisticated up at *Hibiscus'* pretty bar. Sunset watchers should head up to *Santa Fe* in Lurin or over to *Chez Maya's* terrace in Public for a sweeping view. Then it's a long leisurely meal perhaps followed by an after-dinner drink on a breezy terrace—maybe your own. That's the general pattern of night life here. There is only one discothèque on the island—*Le Must,* in Gustavia, but its name, hours, and days of operation change often. The young and hip gather to "cool out" at *Autour du Rocher* in Lorient, where a game of backgammon, billiards, and dancing all may be enjoyed after 10. But mostly this is an early-to-bed, early-to-rise island and that's one of the reasons people come here.

POSTAGE. Airmail letters to the U.S.: 3.60F; postcards: 2.60F. Canada: 2F postcard; 2.70F letter.

ELECTRICAL CURRENT. 220 volts, 50 cycles. American appliances require French plugs and converter or transformer.

SECURITY. You can drive, walk, or visit anywhere on this small, quiet island at any time of the day or night. St. Bartians are trusting, upstanding, and religious people who have had very little exposure to crime as we know it. You may encounter vehicles with keys dangling in their ignitions, bags full of purchases in open cars, and houses without keys; *BUT* as anywhere, continue the good habit of not leaving cameras and other valuables unattended and use your key, if you have one. There's just no point in inviting problems.

ST. EUSTATIUS

by
CLAIRE DEVENER

Quiet, unspoiled little St. Eustatius, or Statia, as she is more commonly called, once held a role so prominent in eighteenth-century international commerce that she was called "Emporium of the Western World" and "The Golden Rock." Oranjestad is the island's two-level capital and only village. Vestiges of bygone days are clustered in the Upper Town, perched on a 120-foot cliff overlooking the Caribbean. Here civic, commercial, domestic, ecclesiastical, and military structures are mostly silent shells of their former glory. However, a small and very active Historical Foundation founded by Statian, Dutch, and American members, is putting lots of love, effort and money into preserving and restoring the graceful old buildings to return the village to her former charm. Lower Town's old cotton mill was recently transformed into Statia's best restaurant, but ramshackle warehouses and fragments of walls only hint at what was once a prosperous mile-long marketplace where polyglot merchants, sailors, slaves, traders, and adventurers brawled and bartered. Exploration of these ruins and total relaxation are the highlights of Statia's leisurely lifestyle. Only about 14,000 visitors came to Statia last year; and most of them just for the day. Undeveloped Statia is not set up for mass tourism and its limited facilities do not appeal to everyone.

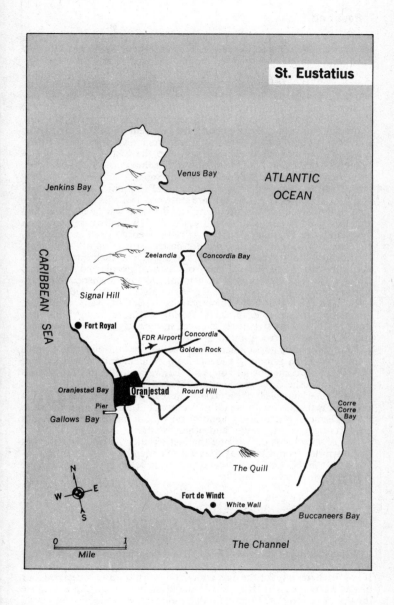

St. Eustatius

ATLANTIC OCEAN

Venus Bay

Jenkins Bay

CARIBBEAN SEA

Zeelandia

Concordia Bay

Signal Hill

● Fort Royal

FDR Airport

Concordia

Golden Rock

Oranjestad Bay

Oranjestad

Round Hill

Pier

Corre
Corre
Bay

Gallows Bay

The Quill

N
W E
S

Fort de Windt
● White Wall

Buccaneers Bay

0   1
Mile

The Channel

Past and Present

Sighted by Columbus in 1493 but not colonized until 1636, when a small group of Dutch settlers arrived from Zeeland, Statia has a history filled with tumult and turmoil, having changed hands between Holland, England, and France twenty-two times before finally becoming Dutch in 1816. In the mid-eighteenth century, the island was at its height of prosperity. As many as eighty to one hundred ships a day anchored off the duty-free harbor waiting to board goods from the bulging warehouses that stretched two deep for a mile along the bay.

Neutral Statia was also a major transshipment point for food, arms, and other supplies for the beleagured American revolutionaries fighting England's colonial blockade. She was also the first foreign power to acknowledge the new American flag and has thus earned the nickname, "America's Childhood Friend." On November 16, 1776, the *Andrew Doria,* a brig-of-war under the command of Captain Isaiah Robinson of the Continental Navy, sailed into port and was saluted by the cannons of Fort Oranje. Soon after, England declared war on Holland, and long provoked by Statia's neutrality, the British finally came down on the island. On February 3, 1781, Admiral George Rodney captured, but (contrary to some stories) did not destroy, the town of Oranjestad. He did close shops; seal warehouses; and auction off their goods, as well as the personal possessions of many of the townspeople and merchants. Dutch flags were kept flying for a month to lure unsuspecting ships whose cargos were then confiscated. After Rodney departed less than a year later (and some five million pounds richer), the island flourished for another ten years despite undergoing six more occupations. But trade routes and tax structures changed in the early nineteenth century and Statia's commerce ground to a halt.

Today not much goes on here except active restoration of the island's landmarks. Each summer, students from William and Mary's College of Archeology come down to dig, and they've been able to trace Statia's history up to the early nineteenth century. The University of Leyden in the Netherlands also has a pre-Columbian program to study Indian sites and artifacts. Statia is still a free port but there is no trade. The Statia Terminal is a large oil blending depot, but major island activities are farming, lobster, conch, and other fishing.

One of six islands comprising the Netherlands Antilles (whose seat of government is in Curaçao), Statia is overseen by a lieutenant governor sent from Holland, two local deputies elected every four years, and a five-member island council.

EXPLORING ST. EUSTATIUS

When landing at Franklin Delano Roosevelt Airport, Statia's six taxi drivers will be out front in various vehicles waiting to transport you. If you are here only for the day, choose one with the audio-cassette tour produced by the local Historical Foundation in five languages, or have the driver stop by the Foundation's headquarters in the new Museum, where they are available free on loan. You may, however, need to provide your own tape player. If you are planning to spend a few days, ask for your driver's card, which will advertise "Peace and Love;"

"Punctuality and Courtesy;" or maybe "Courtesy, Dependability and a Broad Smile"—and keep in mind that these all have cars to rent as well.

Oranjestad

Fort Oranje, in the Upper Town of the capital, Oranjestad, should be your first stop. Visit the tourist office located just across the street and purchase the Historical Foundation's 8-page Walking Tour Map (50¢). Then go out to the bastions to get the lay of the land and an excellent sea view. If it's calm, you'll be able to pick out a few outlines of the old Dutch seawall and building foundations that storms slowly returned to the sea from the reclaimed land on which they were constructed. There's a copper plaque in the parade ground that was presented to Statia by President Franklin Delano Roosevelt in 1939 in commemoration of the fort's salute to the U.S. flag in 1776. This old fortress is the scene, each November 16, of a reenactment of this historic event on Statia and America Day.

Exit by the arched gate and turn right on Fort Oranjestraat (Fort Orange Street) and you'll pass the two story, verandahed Gertrude Judson Library. Since a new modern library was recently completed, this rare example of brick construction in Upper Town has reverted to private ownership. By the way, street signs are written in both Dutch and English.

At #4 Fort Oranjestraat at the corner of Kerkweg (Church Way) is a fine example of traditional turn-of-the-century West Indian architecture—a big yellow house with a stone foundation, shingled walls, and a "gingerbread" frill along the edge of the roof. Behind it is Three Widows Corner, a pleasant tropical courtyard, where an eighteenth-century townhouse and another gingerbread structure show off more of Statia's past. Head west down Kerkweg to the Dutch Reformed Church. Rising at the edge of the cliff, its square tower was once a ship's landmark and its weatherbeaten eighteenth-century gravestones each tell their own story. Continue on Kerkweg and take the next two lefts onto Synagogepad (Synagogue Path) to Honen Dalim—"She Who is Charitable to the Poor"—the second-oldest Jewish house of worship in the Caribbean.

Head back to the main square down Prinsesweg (Princess Way) and you'll pass the Government Guest House. The original purpose of this building is unknown. In the 1920s it was converted into a guesthouse, but is no longer used.

Continue down Van Tonningen Weg to #12, the Simon Doncker mansion. This is the most important intact eighteenth-century dwelling on Statia. The Historical Foundation acquired this house, which is considered to be the island's most beautiful residence, in mid-1983. Preservation was completed last year, and the Foundation's headquarters as well as its museum are now located here. There is an interesting general exhibit room and the original rooms of the house are furnished in the 18th century manner. You might want to purchase a copy of the well-documented book "St. Eustatius—A Short History," by Ypie Attema. Do also consider joining the Historical Foundation to share in encouraging Statia's future by ensuring the survival of her past.

Follow Prinsesweg back to the main square and zig-zag down the cobblestone Fort Road to Lower Town. Here at water's edge, Foundation members have planted palms and flowering shrubs and installed benches in the shade of a towering almond tree. Warehouses and shops that once were piled high with European imports are now abandoned or simply used to store local fishermen's equipment. But the restoration of the eighteenth-century cotton mill on the land side of Bay Road is impressive. It's now called Mooshay Bay Publick House and is the very special bar and dinnertime restaurant of the multi-building Old Gin Hotel complex, a favorite of Statia habitués. If it's lunchtime, by all means stop in the seaside half of the hotel for a pleasant repast on the patio. If not, drop in anyway to make a reservation for dinner.

The best place to end your day or begin your afternoon might just be Crooks Castle, a ten-minute walk along the beach. These ruins of a merchant's house are reportedly the best area to sift sand in search of Statia's increasingly hard to find—but must-have—blue glass trade beads. Found only on this island, these beads were manufactured by the Dutch West Indies Trading Company in Leyden, Holland in the seventeenth century and were traded for rum, sisal, cotton, tobacco, and slaves. One theory suggests that the beads may have been the same currency used to purchase Manhattan from the Indians.

Around the Island

Follow the main road south out of town for about three miles. The 1800-foot-high extinct volcano, called the Quill, is a must, as is a look at the lush tropical rain forest at the crater's bottom. Be sure to wear non-slip shoes. At least climb up to the rim if you don't care to descend and explore the tangle of vines and wild orchids wound among giant mahogany trees. Statians hunt land crabs on the bottom when the moon is full, and whenever these spicy stuffed creatures appear on menus the demand far surpasses the supply. At the southernmost point of the island, is Fort de Windt, where there is positively the very best view of the moon rising over Mount Liamuiga on St. Kitts, seven miles across the channel.

If you head northeast out of Oranjestad, you'll find long gray sand beaches where the Atlantic surf crashes and pounds, especially when the wind is up on Concordia Bay. La Maison sur la Plage, is a nice place to drink or dine after shell-hunting on the broad stretch of sand. If you want to swim, don't go in alone as the undertow can be very dangerous and there are no lifeguards. You will probably prefer to linger awhile by the pleasant pool, then head back to town or to the airport.

PRACTICAL INFORMATION FOR ST. EUSTATIUS

 FACTS AND FIGURES. St. Eustatius is located in the southeastern corner of the Dutch Windward Triangle—38 miles south of St. Maarten, 17 miles southeast of Saba. The topography of 11.8-square-mile Statia features a flat central plain that separates two extinct volcanoes. "The Quill," 1800 feet high with a crater measuring 900 feet across, dominates the southern end; "Little Mountains," the northwest. The capital, and the island's only town, is Oranjestad, on the western edge of the plain facing the Caribbean Sea. The island has 1,600 people—give or take a few—and just 300 automobiles, including 16 rental cars and 6 taxis.

WHEN TO GO. Daytime temperatures average 70 to 82 degrees F year-round and Statia is dry (in fact, periods of drought are not uncommon), with an annual rainfall of just 45 inches. Hotel and restaurant owners often take advantage of the quiet month—September, when Caribbean storms are most likely to brew—to spruce up for the coming season, so it's always a good idea to make sure your favorite is open at this time. U.S. visitors might particularly enjoy scheduling a visit in mid-November, when Statia and America Day (Nov. 16) offers colorful celebrations to commemorate old ties of friendship. Summer tends to be quite lively here with the arrival of American and Dutch students to do archeological diggings.

PASSPORTS AND VISAS. Proof of citizenship is required of all visitors. A passport is best, but a birth certificate or voter's registration card will do—a driver's license will not. In addition, you must have a return ticket. British citizens need a "British Visitor's" passport.

MONEY. The official currency on Statia is the Netherland Antilles florin (or guilder). The exchange rate fluctuates slightly, but the generally accepted rate is 1.79 NAf = U.S. $1. U.S. dollars are accepted everywhere.

WHAT WILL IT COST?

Projected daily estimate for two persons in season

	U.S.$
The best accommodations with 2 meals	$160
Luncheon	20
Service charge and hotel tax	32
One-day sightseeing by taxi or rental car	30
Total	$242

HOW TO GET THERE. By air. *Windward Islands Airways* flies over from St. Maarten four times a day ($40 RT) in about 20 minutes; daily from Saba (10 min., $16 OW) and St. Kitts (15 min., $27 OW). From St. Maarten connections are easy to other islands.

TAXES AND OTHER CHARGES. There is a 10% surcharge (5% government tax, 5% electricity charge) on accommodations, plus a 15% service charge. No airport departure tax is required.

TELEPHONE AND EMERGENCY NUMBERS. Statia has microwave telephone service to all parts of the world. Prinses Beatrix Hospital is located at 25 Prinsesweg (tel. 2211). Police: tel. 2333. To dial Statia long distance from the U.S., dial 011–599–4 + local number.

HOTELS. This is an island with only six guesthouses. Each is small, quiet, and has its own personality. The three listed below are the only formal hotels with services. The others (unlisted) offer only basic rooms. For a double room with breakfast and dinner included, we call $120–160 *Moderate.*
Golden Era Hotel. *Moderate.* Lower Town Oranjestad. Tel. 2345. The 20 small rooms are neat, modern, carpeted, and have telephone and air conditioning. But any kind of tropical atmosphere or ambiance is totally absent ... as were such simple amenities as towel racks and ashtrays. The price is high

($80–85 + 25% service and tax) considering that half the rooms' tiny terraces face the wall or roof of the enclosed, coffee shop-style restaurant. Ten do, however, have partial sea views from their balconies. The reception desk was frequently left unmanned and the manager commuted to St. Maarten during the week. The place had only been open one month when we visited and there's still a pool and seaside terrace to come. Perhaps things will improve, but for now we honestly can't recommend this new Statian-owned property.

La Maison sur la Plage. *Moderate.* Zeelandia on the Atlantic Coast. Tel. 2256. This delightful property is now under the management of Michele Greca, who came from Nice via St. Barths. Ten rooms in eight cottages have been nicely refurbished and plumbing updated. Good French cuisine, a comfortable lounge with a color TV and long, friendly bar, pleasant pool facing the surf, and a two-mile-long gray sand beach backed by wave-sculpted cliffs to explore are just a few of the pleasures that this quiet seaside inn has to offer.

Old Gin House. *Moderate.* Lower Town Oranjestad. Tel. 2319. 14 spacious, modern rooms face a small freshwater pool in the garden of a former 18th-century cotton mill. This part of the complex also contains the *Mooshay Bay Publick House,* a romantic dining room, loft library, comfortable lounge, and beamed pub with a rare "Act of Parliament" Bristol timepiece made in England in 1770. Across the street is the hotel's reception area, shaded terrace, second bar, six more stylishly decorated rooms and a "walking beach," whose gray sand shifts semi-annually. (Wind shifts, current variations, and storms at sea affect how far up the shore the water reaches at various times of the year.) This special island hideaway is the creation of Marty Scofield, ex-Madison Avenue exec, and John May, formerly a Connecticut art teacher. Their flair for decoration and innkeeping is evident in the charming blend of antiques, West Indian arts and crafts, flowers and greenery, and guests who are often old friends who first met here. Not just a winter resort, but also a great summer spot for rest and relaxation, and prices are reduced 15%.

 HOME AND APARTMENT RENTALS. There are just a handful of places and the Tourist Office at 13 Emmaweg (tel. 2219 ext. 15) can fill you in on what's available.

 HOW TO GET AROUND. Taxis are always available at the airport. The fare is about U.S. $3 into town. Should you want a tour, discuss one with your driver en route to the hotel. There is enough to see to warrant a half-day excursion. Cars are available for rental for about $30 per day through any of the taxi drivers or *Maduro's Car Rental* (tel. 2225). *Donny Hook* (tel. 2272) has 3 mopeds to rent at $20 per day and bicycles are available at *The Old Gin House.*

 TOURIST INFORMATION SERVICES. On the island, the *Tourist Bureau* is at 13 Emmaweg, across from the Fort (tel. 2219 ext. 15) in the Government House. Hours: Mon.–Fri. 8 A.M.–noon; 1–5 P.M. For sources closer to home, see Tourist Information Services section in the *Facts at Your Fingertips* chapter.

 SPECIAL EVENTS. The highlight of the year here is *Statia and America Day* (Nov. 16). It's a festival island holiday that begins when Statians and visitors gather at the old fort to celebrate the first salute to the American flag by a foreign government. After the formal ceremonies, parades, picnics, and beach parties. *Carnival* takes place the middle two weeks of July with shows, Calypso contests, parades, and street dances.

TOURS. Let one of Statia's six taxi drivers be your guide and you won't miss a thing in the way of attractions or in island legends and lore, which they'll weave as you go. A half-day tour should be sufficient and will cost about $25 for up to four people.

An audio-cassette tape is available on loan free from the Historical Foundation at the new museum on Tonningen Weg. They've also published a well-designed Walking Tour map that is at the museum or the Tourist Bureau.

 BEACHES. Statia is rimmed by gray sand beaches, coves, and bays. The Caribbean side has small stretches of volcanic sand on the calm waters of the bay off Lower Town. Beaches on the Atlantic side, especially around Concordia Bay tend to have rough surf and a sometimes treacherous undertow. Corre Corre Bay is a nice golden sand cover that is about a 30-minute hike down an easy, marked trail off Mountain Rd.

 PARTICIPANT SPORTS. Swimming is popular off Lower Town Beach. **Snorkeling** is good here as well as at Jenkins Bay and Corre Corre Bay. There's a lighted macadam **tennis** court at Statia's Community Center in Upper Town that residents and visitors may use for 5 guilders per hr. **Hiking** is excellent up The Quill and down into its crater and along a total of twelve marked trails around the island. The Tourist Bureau and The Old Gin House have detailed printed explanations to follow. The proposed Gallows Bay Dive Shop and Sports Activities Center at The Old Gin House should finally bring Statia some much needed, organized **diving** activity. Under the direction of John Noland, former U.S. Coast Guard PADI-certified instructor, the new center will offer photo excursions for divers and snorkelers in the artifact-rich harbor, which was the Caribbean's busiest port in the 18th century. It's a treasure trove of cannons, ballast, anchors, and remnants of the great trading ships of the past. Resort packages, certification courses, and half-day one-tank dives were planned, along with the availability of **windsurfers.** Charter **fishing** excursions should also be offered.

 HISTORIC SITES AND HOUSES. Once referred to as "The Golden Rock," St. Eustatius gained historical fame by acting as the major link between the U.S. and Europe. But a century before that, *Fort Oranje* in Upper Town was built to guard the harbor and now, completely restored, it is one of the most impressive bastions in the Caribbean. The cobbled walks along the seafront show the cannons still at the ready.

Just a short walk away, there is a typical "gingerbread house" dating to the 19th century, and an 18th-century town house. Both are in a tropical courtyard called *Three Widows Corner.*

The *Dutch Reformed Church* was constructed in 1775 on the edge of the cliffs overlooking the sea. Over the years it fell into disrepair and only recently has been restored to its former beauty.

Next on the list for restoration is the *Honen Dalim Synagogue,* a venerable building erected in 1738.

 MUSEUMS. There's only one, the *Historical Foundation Museum,* now in Statia's most majestic mansion, the Simon Doncker House on Tonningen Weg in Upper Town. It's a little treasure trove of engravings, photographs, and prints of Statia's historic past. Especially intriguing is the island's first telephone switchboard. Open Mon.–Fri., 8:00 A.M.–noon; 1:00 P.M.–4:00 P.M. There is no charge but contributions are welcome. The *Dutch Reform Church* also exhibits pre-Columbian pieces in the tower.

SHOPPING. There is very little to buy here, and even island crafts are at a premium. For souvenirs, there is *Mazinga Gift Shop,* in the hardware store of the same name on Prinsesweg. *The Sign of the Goobie,* a small boutique at The Old Gin House in Lower Town, stocks pareus, T-shirts, local prints, dresses, and household items from other islands. The *Golden Rock Artisans Foundation,* at the head of Bay Path in Upper Town, has mahogany wine racks and lamps as well as pine furniture, frames, trays, napkin holders, and trowels fashioned in the foundation's workrooms. Shop hours are 8:00 A.M. to noon, 1:30 P.M. to 5:00 P.M. If it appears closed, go around back and the secretary will let you in.

RESTAURANTS. Lobster, fresh-caught fish, pepper steak, West Indian and French specialties are all part of the fare here. We call $20 and above per person *Expensive;* $10–$20 *Moderate;* below that *Inexpensive.*

The Old Gin House. Lower Town Oranjestad. Tel. 2319. Breakfast and lunch daily on the hotel's seaside terrace is *Moderate.* Special crêpes and pasta daily, cold soups, sandwiches, and salads of every description. In the evening there is only one dinner seating at 7:30 P.M. in the **Mooshay Bay Publick House,** *(Expensive),* still part of the complex but across the street. Reservations must be made in advance and priority goes to guests. Co-owner Marty Scofield's talents definitely extend to his kitchen, which produces imaginative classic cuisine with a tropical touch. His interesting recipes have been praised by *Gourmet Magazine.* The elegant candlelit dining room is furnished with antiques and some excellent reproductions, including a faithful rendition of a late 17th century Hunt Table made by one of the woodworkers of the local Artisans Foundation. AE, D, MC, V.

Maison sur la Plage. *Expensive.* Zeelandia. Tel. 2256. The French chef of this pretty garden restaurant by the sea specializes in fresh seafood—fish soup Mediterranean-style, fish terrine with a tasty tomato sauce, lime fricassee of grouper, lobster in vermouth, butter, and shallots or grilled with olive oil and sweet peppers—but there's also a nice chicken in orange sauce and a tender filet of beef with a choice of roquefort, green peppercorn, or mustard sauce at dinner. Lunch on the terrace features lobster salad, omelettes, and other good light fare. No credit cards.

Golden Era Hotel. Lower Oranjestad. Tel. 2345. *Moderate* to *Expensive.* Coffee shop atmosphere until the seaside terrace is completed but the cook, from Surinam, turns out a tasty conch chowder with dumplings as well as other excellent West Indian specialties. The menu was limited but this is a new endeavor that could become very popular. Occasional live entertainment in season. AE.

The Stone Oven. *Moderate.* 16A Feaschweg, Upper Town Oranjestad. Tel. 2272. Young owner–chef Anastacia Hook's attractive restaurant is situated behind her home at the edge of town. As many fresh local ingredients as possible are used. We especially liked the marinated conch, chicken cutlet with peanut sauce, and when they're available, the stuffed land crabs. Lunch and dinner are served on the back patio under an almond tree where there's a view of the Quill or in an attractively decorated small dining room. No credit cards.

Talk of the Town. *Moderate.* Near the Airport. Tel. 2236. You'll sit on benches at one of six oilcloth-covered tables at this cozy spot. Mrs. Nais, an accomplished cook, will prepare whatever you want—continental, Dutch, West Indian, even oriental dishes—as long as you call before. Otherwise you may be faced with a six-page menu with only four items available. No credit cards.

L'Etoile. *Inexpensive.* Prinsesweg, Upper Town Oranjestad. Tel. 2299. Caren Henriquez is well known for her spicy, stuffed land crab, deep-fried meat-stuffed turnovers, and other West Indian specialties. Her simple, upstairs bar/restaurant is best at lunch. No credit cards.

Inexpensive light lunches—hot dogs, eggburgers, hamburgers, sloppy Joes, and salads—will be found at **Ellis Tea House, Kool Korner,** and **Skells** in Upper Town Oranjestad. None of these have telephones or take credit cards. **Charlie's Bar,** in the same area, offers "Florida's Best Ice Cream" and good stories proffered by colorful 80-plus-year-old Charlie Arnaud, one of Statia's last whalers.

NIGHT LIFE AND BARS. Everyone gathers for after-work drinks at *The Kool Korner,* located at the top of Fort Road in Upper Town. This is the place to meet interesting island people from fishermen to the two local deputies and Statia's only airline pilot. Sometimes there's a Saturday night dance at *Charlie's Bar* or the *Dance Tavern* on Kerkweg. Check to see if the local steel band, led by Ms. Elva Arnaud, is performing. If so, don't miss them—their repertoire is quite diverse and the whole island will be there.

POSTAGE. Airmail: NAf 1.30 letters; NAf .60 postcards.

ELECTRIC CURRENT. 110 volts, 60 cycles. No converters needed.

SECURITY. Statia may be one of the few corners of the world left where crime is virtually nonexistent. Everyone leaves everything wide open, keys in their cars, and there is never any problem. You can walk anywhere alone at night, some of the ruins by moonlight are even more beautiful than they are in the day, but you may well be the only person out on this go-to-bed-early island.

ST. KITTS

by
BARBARA A. CURRIE

Princess Margaret was so enchanted by this northeastern Caribbean island that she dubbed St. Kitts "The Flower Garden of the Caribbean" during her visit there some years ago.

As rich in history as it is fertile and lush with tropical flora, St. Kitts is just beginning to develop its tourism industry, and this quiet member of the Leeward group has that rare combination of fascinating natural and historical attractions, and superb sailing, island-hopping, and water sports options offshore.

St. Kitts is officially St. Christopher, but few, if any, of its 35,000 inhabitants or 30,000 annual visitors call it that. In fact, its name was shortened by English settlers more than 350 years ago.

St. Kitts is roughly oval shaped, 23 miles long, five miles wide, and heavily planted with sugar cane, the island's foremost crop. The central part consists of a rugged mountain range whose highest point is Mount Liamuiga (formerly called Mount Misery) at 3,792 feet. A branch of the range encloses a spacious and fertile valley, on the seaboard of which lies Basseterre, the capital city, which hasn't changed in appearance in about forty years (with the exception of the addition of a few new bank buildings).

The valley and the circle of land formed by the skirts and lower slopes of the mountain range constitute most of the arable and cultivated portion of the island. The higher slopes are covered with short grass, which makes for excellent pastures, and the summits of the range are crowned with forest. Everywhere trees and shrubs hang with brightly colored blossoms and fruits as if nature had suddenly upturned its bountiful basket on this small area of rich earth. The early Carib Indians, in fact, called the island Liamuiga, or "the fertile land."

One main road—called "Main Road"—circles the island. The center of the island is almost unpenetrated by roads, left to cultivation and longtime inhabitants who flouted government efforts to move them nearer public transportation.

St. Kitts is a quiet island, and Kittitians, as the locals like to call themselves, and guests who discovered its unspoiled nature before tourism began to sprout would like to keep it that way.

Past and Present

Columbus discovered the island on his second voyage in 1493, naming it St. Christopher after his patron saint. The English anglicized that almost as soon as they arrived on January 28, 1623 when Sir Thomas Warner established the first English colony in the West Indies.

Oldest of the British West Indian settlements, St. Kitts is proud of its title, "Mother Colony of the West Indies," which it earned by sending out colonizing parties to other islands, most notably to Antigua. Other parties went out to colonize Barbuda, Tortuga, and Montserrat, while the French under the leadership of their governor general, De Poincy, sailed off to claim Guadeloupe, Desirade, Les Saintes, Martinique, St. Barthelemy, St. Martin, and St. Croix.

Intermittent warfare between the British settlers and the French during the seventeenth century ravaged the economy of the island. Ultimately, the two nations reached an agreement which gave the French the north and south portions while the English held the middle. This explains the capital's French name of Basseterre (low land). Another relic of the Anglo-French era is the village of Half-Way Tree, where a big tamarind tree marked the approximate half-way point in English territory on the south side of the island. The English got full title to the island by the 1783 Treaty of Versailles and guided it to full independence in 1983, making St. Kitts–Nevis the newest independent country in the Caribbean.

Its present government, under Prime Minister Kennedy A. Simmonds, is a coalition of two parties—the People's Action Movement (PAM), which was born in 1965, and the Nevis Reformation Party (NRP)—and won reelection in 1984. Government is actively encouraging foreign investment, especially in the area of tourism facilities on St. Kitts. While seeking to improve the quality and diversity of tourist attractions and activities, it wants to move slowly so "imprudent additions won't alter the features of the environment to the extent that it no longer provides the sought-after attractions."

EXPLORING ST. KITTS

The harbor of Basseterre, the capital, has the look of an old print. The pier is where inter-island boats come in, and their produce is sold right on the dock. The "Circus" with its gingerbread clock tower is the hub of in-town activities. Government House is a good example of the

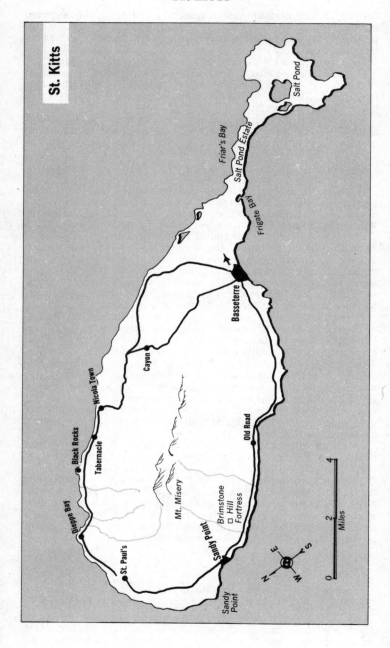

colonial style, as is the nearby Treasury with its domed Victorian stone and cast iron. These are centered in and around Independence Square (renamed from Pall Mall Square after the island gained its independence in 1983).

Around the island's perimeter are a few coves, but nothing spectacular compared to its fellow islands. The area at Black Rocks, where the Guy Fawkes' day picnic is held each year, is dramatic and worth a stop when you drive around the island. The jagged volcanic rocks have been worn to fanciful shapes by pounding Atlantic surf.

At the northern point, the fishing village of Dieppe Bay is worth a stop. A good road follows the coast, almost girdling the island. On any tour, you'll see Brimstone Hill, "The Gibraltar of the West Indies," ten miles from Basseterre. This is one of the most important and impressive historical monuments in the West Indies. The bastion, with its formidable, frowning ramparts, took a century to build, positioned as it is seven hundred feet atop the Gibraltar-like rock. The view encompasses the Dutch islands of St. Eustatius and Saba, St. Martin, and French St. Barts on the west, and Nevis to the southeast, as well as Montserrat on a *very* clear day. It is the high point of an island tour. The area is dotted with places of historic interest: Old Road Village, where Thomas Warner and his intrepid colonists first stepped ashore in 1623; Sandy Point, their first settlement; Middle Island Village, with St. Thomas Church and the tomb of Sir Thomas Warner, who "gave forth large narratives of military worth written with his sword's poynt."

Many ruined forts and battlegrounds bear mute testimony to the ancient enmity between England and France. Bloody Point marks the spot where they combined forces in 1629 to repel with great slaughter a mass attack by the original owners of the island, the Carib Indians. If you or your driver has gotten permission, visit Fountain Estate, long ago the seat of the governors of the French section of St. Kitts.

The southern arm of St. Kitts, by contrast to the lush and mountainous interior, contains the island's tiny "amber coast," the Frigate Bay area which is a developing tourism area with golf course and fine white sand beaches on both the Caribbean and Atlantic sides. Several condominium projects are now open. But tourism is still in the early stages on this island, whose dominant panoramas reflect the main source of the country's economy: sugar. Vast, tall plains of sugarcane line the roads, harvested in February and March. The ruins of sugar mills and plantations dot the hills beyond.

PRACTICAL INFORMATION FOR ST. KITTS

 FACTS AND FIGURES. St. Kitts is in the northern part of the Leeward-Island group of the Lesser Antilles in the eastern Caribbean. It is an oval-shaped landmass with a narrow neck of land extending like a handle from the southeastern end. Its total length is 23 miles. Its area is 65 square miles.

The central part of the island's main body consists of a rugged mountain range whose highest point is Mt. Liamuiga (formerly Mt. Misery) at 3,792 feet.

The island was formed from volcanic eruption and most of its beaches consist of black volcanic sand. White sandy beaches can be found along the peninsula at Frigate Bay and Salt Pond.

The capital city is Basseterre, which has a population of 15,000. Virtually all of the island's inhabitants, called "Kittitians," speak English, the "official" language.

Industry is limited to a few plants that assemble electronic switches for the U.S. market, pocket calculators, and car radios.

 WHEN TO GO. Anytime. But rates are highest in winter (mid-December to mid-April) and cheapest in summer (mid-April to mid-December). Although it is hot year-round, the climate is very pleasant and healthy, with extremes tempered by the breezes from the northeast trade winds. It's never been hotter than 92 degrees F on the island, nor colder than 62 degrees F. There is no rainy season.

 PASSPORTS AND VISAS. U.S. and Canadian citizens need only proof of identity, such as a passport, birth certificate or voter's registration card (a driver's license won't do). British citizens must have passports; visas are not required. In addition, all visitors must hold a return or ongoing ticket.

 MONEY. The East Caribbean dollar (EC) is the local currency, which, as we go to press, is figured at EC $2.56–2.70 = U.S. $1. Exchange facilities are available at banks. Hotels, restaurants, and many shops also accept payment in foreign currency, particularly the U.S. dollar. Major international credit cards are accepted by large hotels, restaurants and shops, but not generally by small inns. Many of these, however, accept personal checks.

WHAT WILL IT COST?

A typical day on St. Kitts in season for two persons will run:

	U.S.
Hotel accommodations, including breakfast and dinner	$135
Lunch at a moderate restaurant	18
Tips/service charges/taxes and other hotel charges	24
One-day sightseeing by taxi or rental car	38
Total	$215

 HOW TO GET THERE. By air. Nonstop service from New York on *Pan American;* on-again, off-again service and charters from U.S. and Canada by *BWIA;* from various other Caribbean islands by *LIAT; Windward Islands Airways International* (Winair), and *Puerto Rico International Airlines* (Prinair). *Pan American* also offers several connecting flights weekly from Miami.

By sea. At least one, sometimes two, round trips (U.S. $7) are offered daily between sister island Nevis by the government-owned *M.V. Caribe Queen* ferry, but never on Thursdays (that's maintenance day) or Sundays. (Confirm schedule with tourist board and arrive in plenty of time; it only has 150 seats.) The crossing takes 45 minutes. St. Kitts' new deep-water port also is increasing cruise-ship traffic.

AIRPORT TAX AND OTHER CHARGES. Hotels all add a 10% service charge and a 7% government tax to your bill. There is an airport departure tax of EC $13 or US $5.

TELEPHONE AND EMERGENCY NUMBERS. The area code for St. Kitts is 809. The prefix when dialing long distance is 465. Police and fire, dial 99; hospital, dial 2551.

 HOTELS. Accommodation in St. Kitts consists of comfortable, modern hotels and several small, owner-managed establishments offering a relaxed and informal atmosphere, all modern amenities and high standards of service. Invariably well located and pleasantly furnished, many such "inns" are converted great houses and sugar mills. Many of these hotels offer meals in their daily rate, and we have noted this in the price range for two persons during the winter season. We call $200 and up *Deluxe;* $150–199 *Expensive;* $90–149 *Moderate;* and $89 and below *Inexpensive.*

The Golden Lemon. *Deluxe.* Box 17, Dieppe Bay. Tel. 7260. Internationally famous, this 21-year-old inn has 17 rooms next to a strikingly beautiful palm-lined, black-sand beach where the Atlantic meets the Caribbean. Furnished with a mixture of West Indian antiques and contemporary articles. A staff of 38 tends to guests' every need. No two rooms are alike—ceiling fans, canopied beds, antique chests. Solar-heated water, so showers are always *hot!* Spacious gardens, secluded pool, free laundry service, tea at 4:00 P.M. Rates include large breakfast (served in your room or on the veranda, if you choose), afternoon tea, and elegant dinners. *Maximum* stay: two weeks. Casual elegance, with a house-party atmosphere and guests get acquainted with host Arthur Leaman and each other during stays. New for 1985 are the **Lemon Court Condominiums,** 2 studios, 2 one-bedroom and 2 two-bedroom two-story units decorated with antiques and Caribbean art. Exteriors luxuriously designed with individual pools and gardens.

Rawlins Plantation. *Deluxe.* Box 340, Mount Pleasant. Tel. 6221. Formerly a thriving sugar plantation, this property now offers eight double rooms in the plantation house and in cottages that are attractively decorated and have all modern facilities. A 17-century windmill has been converted into a split-level honeymoon suite. The hotel is located on 25 acres of hillside pastures and lawns with tropical trees and flowers. Panoramic views of the Caribbean, the Atlantic, and neighboring Dutch islands. Dieppe Bay's fine beach is just a short drive away. Owned and managed by Philip and Frances Walwyn, the property has a swimming pool and new grass tennis court. Horseback riding can be arranged (U.S. $10 an hour). Also offers overnight cruises to Saba onboard luxurious 75' catamaran, *Spirit of St. Christopher,* as well as day sailing for guests around St. Kitts and Nevis. The plantation raises its own beef and grows its own vegetables. Rates include breakfast, dinner with wine, afternoon tea, open bar, and laundry service. Picnic lunches are available for a modest charge. *No credit cards.* Minimum stay is four days in season.

Banana Bay Beach Hotel. *Expensive.* Box 188, Banana Bay. Tel. 2860. Reached only by boat, the 11-room property is nestled between rolling hills and the gentle curve of "sugar-white sand." You'll share snorkeling, sailing, and swimming with less than two dozen fellow guests, two donkeys, and an occasional monkey. Staff picks you up at the airport and drives you to a harbor where you board the *Careebo* for a 45-minute, south-coast cruise to the secluded retreat. A totally relaxed, informal atmosphere with good food. One rate applies year-round and includes all three meals (prepared with native-grown bounty and fresh-from-the-Caribbean seafood). *No credit cards,* no stays of less than a week, and no children under 16.

Frigate Bay Beach Hotel. *Moderate.* Box 137, Frigate Bay. Tel. 8935. This new complex of condominiums has 64 rooms—and more planned—in a cluster of whitewashed buildings with archways, balconies, and peaked roofs. Interiors are furnished like a second home, which many of them really are. Tiled floors, screened porches, pastel color, large rooms, ceiling fans, and air conditioning, understated elegance. Freshwater pool with swim-up bar; beach at the doorstep and 18-hole golf course nearby. Meals are not included, but a new restaurant, like a giant hut, gives guests the opportunity to choose their mealtimes or cook for themselves.

Ocean Terrace Inn. *Moderate.* Box 65, Basseterre. Tel. 2754. One of the most exquisite resorts on the entire island, this hideaway in the center of things has 44 spacious and luxuriously furnished double-bed rooms, some air conditioned, with cooking facilities. Many have paintings by Kittitian Barbara Kassad. Adding 12–16 channels of cable TV. Located on a bay with a commanding view. It is a mile from the main shopping center and less than three miles from the airport. Meticulously maintained tropical grounds with outdoor Jacuzzi, two pools (one with swim-up bar), cocktail lounge in nautical decor, restaurant overlooking the grounds and the bay. Island-wide reputation for hosting one of the best West Indian buffets at its Fisherman's Wharf. Entertainment four nights a week in season. *The Bitter End* disco is used only for special group occasions and for conferences.

Jack Tar Village, St. Kitts. *Moderate.* Box 406, Frigate Bay. Tel. 8651. Formerly the Royal St. Kitts Hotel and Casino, at press time this chain resort operation had planned to be fully operational under new "all inclusive" vacation plan by summer 1985. This 250-acre property has just about everything, including the island's only gaming facilities (blackjack, roulette, craps, and slot machines). 18-hole championship golf course. The new open-air lobby, bar, and breakfast room are exquisite and overlook artificial lakes. The resort also has added 12 new rooms, for a total of 150, including some condominium suites with full kitchens and four channels of cable television. All rooms will have TV in the future. Freshwater swimming pool, three artificial lakes, four tennis courts, dining room with a view. Meals are included in the rates.

Fairview Inn. *Inexpensive.* Box 212, St. Kitts. Tel. 2472. Three miles west of Basseterre on the island's southern shore, this former 18th-century French great house in the country has 30 rooms with comfortable furnishings. Affectionately adopted as the winter roost of many Americans who appreciate the Inn's superb service, friendly staff, and excellent food. Located at the base of a majestic peak, Ottley's Mountain, St. Kitt's original inn remains one of our favorites for its informal charm.

Fort Thomas Hotel. *Inexpensive.* Box 407, Basseterre. Tel. 2695. This 64-room property is on the outskirts of the capital city and set on eight acres overlooking the Caribbean. Olympic-size swimming pool, good restaurant offering fresh-caught fish and West Indian specialties. No meals included in the rate.

 HOME AND APARTMENT RENTALS. Leeward Cove Condominium Hotel. Box 123, Frigate Bay. Tel. 2654. Set in the hills of the Frigate Bay area on a lovely five-acre tract of land between the Atlantic and Caribbean. One- and two-bedroom units that can accommodate two to six persons. Either make use of the fully equipped kitchens or walk to nearby restaurants.

Sun 'n' Sand Beach Village. Box 341, Frigate Bay. Tel. 4037. Very reasonably priced one- and two-bedroom suites in 16 cottages with kitchens; beautifully landscaped beachfront setting on the Atlantic side of Frigate Bay. Freshwater pool, 2 bars, 2 restaurants, and boutique and minimart on premises. Golf course right across street.

Island Paradise Village, Box 139, Frigate Bay. Tel. 8035. New 1- and 2-bedroom luxury beachfront condominiums with fully equipped kitchens; pool, beach. 54 units; located convenient to golf; island's only Pizza Parlour and Wine N Cheese shop.

Guesthouses. St. Kitts has six guesthouses, small, comfortable, with West Indian ambience at very low rates. For information, contact the St. Kitts Tourist Board, Box 132, Basseterre, St. Kitts.

 HOW TO GET AROUND. Taxis are readily available at the airport and in town, but establish the rate and currency (U.S. or EC dollars) in advance or you may find you're paying triple. Cars (mainly Toyotas, Datsuns, and Volkswagens) can be rented through *Avis* (tel. 2631), *Budget* (tel. 4020), *Byrons* (tel. 2165), *Caines Garage* (tel. 2366), *T.D.C.* (tel. 2991), or *Lesmike* (tel. 2193) at rates ranging from U.S. $26 to $38 a day. T.D.C. also has a selection of Yamaha motorcycles. Gasoline is expensive! You'll pay $2 or more a gallon.

You'll need a local driver's license, which can be obtained at the police station (Cayon St.) in Basseterre by showing your normal driver's license and paying a minimal fee. Remember to drive on the left.

Comfortable minibuses, privately owned, also operate around the island. You can circle the entire island for a fare of about U.S. $2.

TOURIST INFORMATION SERVICES. The St. Kitts–Nevis Tourist Board has offices on Church Street in *Basseterre* (tel. 4040). The St. Kitts–Nevis Hotel Association also has offices in the capital city (tel. 2380). For sources closer to home, see the Tourist Information Services section in the *Facts at Your Fingertips* chapter.

SPECIAL EVENTS. The highlight of December—in fact, of the entire year —is Carnival Week, which begins Dec. 26 and continues until Jan. 2.

TOURS. A variety of tours is available from *Liamuiga Tours* (tel. 4080), *Delisle Walwyn* (tel. 2631), or through the major hotel tour desks. Among the possibilities are an island excursion of St. Kitts itself or of such nearby islands as St. Maarten (for shopping), Antigua (a cruise-barbecue) or Barbuda (for water sports). Special-interest activities also can be arranged, including deep-sea fishing (for mackerel, kingfish, wahoo, and yellowtail snapper), snorkeling, waterskiing, scuba diving, horseback riding, horse-and-carriage rides, and moonlight cruises.

PARKS AND GARDENS. Independence Square in Basseterre is a tiny jewel, with plants of the tropics abloom on acreage that once was an 18th-century slave market.

BEACHES. It's difficult to find a spot on St. Kitts that doesn't have a good beach, and the hotels are usually right on them. *Frigate Bay* is the best beach, on both the Atlantic and Caribbean sides. *Conaree* and *Sandy Point* tie for second. The beaches at *Dieppe Bay* are reportedly best for snorkeling and windsurfing. Horseback riders favor the beach of *North Frigate Bay* because it's longer (about four miles). All beaches are open to the public, even those at the hotels whether you're a guest or not.

PARTICIPANT SPORTS. Caribbean Watersports at the Fisherman's Wharf, Pelican Cove (Ocean Terrace Inn) (tel. 2754) can make all the arrangements. **Scuba diving** runs anywhere from U.S. $30–170 depending on the length of the trip. **Fishing** runs U.S. $25 per person for a half-day 'reel-away'. Hobie cat rentals, waterskiing, moonlight cruises, snorkeling trips, and other water sports can also be arranged. Kenneth Samuel is an independent dive operator offering small group trips for certified divers with C cards to nearby reefs. Contact Kenneth's Dive Centre, Bay Rd., Basseterre. Tel. 2235. To see the interior in a great way travel by horse. **Riding** can be arranged (tel. 3226) at U.S. $15 for the first hour; U.S. $5 for every hour thereafter. Play **golf** at the Royal St. Kitts' 18-hole championship course. Call in advance (tel. 2651) to reserve the time and check on greens fees, which keep changing.

Mount Liamuiga (formerly Mount Misery). Climbers should arrange for transportation in advance. After leaving the truck there is a steady climb through virgin forest and wild orchids to the lip of the crater, 2,600 feet high. It is then possible to descend into the crater, holding on to vines and roots. The adjacent mountain peak has an elevation of 3,792 feet. Allow a full day for this exciting excursion.

SPECTATOR SPORTS. Warner Park seems to be hosting one sport or another year-round. **Volleyball, lawn tennis, basketball,** and **squash** take place throughout the year; **cricket** matches from January to July; football **(soccer)** from July to December; **netball** January through August.

HISTORIC SITES AND HOUSES. Black Rocks. Prehistoric lava rocks thrown down to the sea from the crater create turbulent waters and majestic scenery.

Brimstone Hill. History comes alive here at the Caribbean's most impressive fortress. After the routing of the French in 1689, the English erected a battery on the top of Brimstone Hill. Fortifications were erected and in 1736, there were 49 guns on Brimstone Hill. In 1782 occurred the famous siege of Brimstone Hill by the French, when it was defended by 600 regular troops and 350 militia. When the English finally surrendered, the French allowed them to march from the fort in full formation, out of respect for their bravery. The English afforded the French the same honor when they surrendered the fort in 1783. A map shows the construction of the fort in 1791. Take time to wander the ramparts and visit the restoration, especially the bastion officially opened June 1, 1973, by His Royal Highness the Prince of Wales and named for him. Six new mini-museums have been added recently—the Columbia, African, Garrison, American, British, and French rooms.

Carib and other Amerindian remains. There are large stones with Carib inscriptions at Wingfield Estate and West Farm. A fresh site of Amerindian remains was discovered at Pond Pasture in 1961.

Caribelle Batik. Romney Manor, the location of Caribelle Batik Ltd, was a 17th-century great house. Set above the town of Old Road, the residence commands an inspiring view of the surrounding countryside. It is situated on the edge of a tropical rain forest on approximately five acres of gardens that contain terraces, a croquet lawn, exotic flowers, and an old bell tower. The *pièce de resistance* is a huge Saman tree, sometimes called a rain tree, which is said to be 350 years old.

Caribbelle Batik was established by three English people, Sue Dallow, Chris Dallow, and Maurice Widdowson. The aim of the company was to set up a local industry and to provide a workshop for the production of high-quality batik and tie-dyed fabric and goods.

Batik is a 2,500-year-old Indonesian wax-resist process for producing a design on cloth. The sea-island cotton used has been grown on St. Kitts and Nevis; the beeswax is from St. Kitts; the salt is from Anguilla; the paraffin is imported from Trinidad. West Indian sea-island cotton (now with some polyester) was selected as the fabric to use not only because it is locally grown but because of its reputation of being the finest cotton cloth in the world. The dyes used are the latest in dye technology and are color-fast and washable.

Caribelle's designs and colors aim to project the Caribbean feeling, and the finished cloth is used for wall hangings, clothing, and art decor, with every piece an original. The fabric and finished goods are exported all over the Caribbean.

Visiting hours at Romney Manor are 9:00 A.M. to 5:00 P.M. in the week and 9:00 A.M. to 1:00 P.M. on Sat.

Dos d'Anse Pond, Verchilds Mt. Provides beautiful verdant scenery complete with tropical fernery. Accessible from Wingfield, Lambert, or Molineaux Estates.

St. George's Church. Build by the people of one nation and rebuilt by another. Shattered by earthquake and destroyed by fire. Raised again in its present stately form, its history is unique.

Sir Thomas Warner's Tomb. The founder of British possessions in the Caribbean died in St. Kitts in 1648, and was buried in Middle Island churchyard. A fine poem of that date is inscribed on the tombstone.

SHOPPING. *Caribelle Batik,* Romney Manor, Old Rd., offers splendid designs right off the drawing board and has a workshop at Romney Manor near Brimstone Hill and a shop at the Circus right in town. Everything from batik shirts and dresses to wall hangings. (Also see Caribelle Batik under "Historic Sites and Houses.") Other shops for duty-free items, and for browsing through the city are:

Cellar Shop, Princes St. Island clothing, silk-screen and batik fabrics by the yard. Hand-embroidered shirts, blouses, skirts and dresses from sister-island Nevis' well-known *Caribee Clothes.*

Heyliger's Jewellery Store, Central St. The nicest in gold and silver, which is very fine, since this firm is associated with Y. de Lima of Trinidad.

The Kittian Kitchen, Princes St. To enhance your kitchen at home with all the spices and aromas of the West Indies. Everything from home-made jams and jellies to place mats and aprons.

Palm Crafts, Princes St. Sisal rugs, local handicraft, and black coral jewelery make this place worth a stop. Also located at Sun 'n' Sand and Frigate Bay Beach Hotel.

Ram's Duty-Free Shop, Liverpool Row. Cameras, Hummel figurines, watches, perfumes, gold and silver jewelery, and, as they say, "the largest T-shirt assortment in town!"

Slice of the Lemon, Fort St. Gold, silver, crystal, perfumes, porcelain, and a spectacular array of imported watches at duty-free prices, along with its decor make this one of the most attractive shops in the city. Also located near the Golden Lemon at Dieppe Bay.

T.D.C. On the corner of Bank and West Square St. Another duty-free shop where the items include Wedgewood china, Waterford crystal, and imported linens and perfumes.

RESTAURANTS. St. Kitts offers surprising variety and value for dollar, in dining experiences. We call US$25 per person *Expensive;* $15–24 *Moderate;* below that, *Inexpensive.*

The Georgian House. *Expensive.* South Square St., Basseterre. Tel. 4049. Dining out here is a pleasure. The home has been carefully restored and has all the antiques that make it a British manor house in the tropics. Excellent food and its in-town proximity make it one of the most popular places on the island. Accepts credit cards.

The Patio. Frigate Bay Beach. Tel. 8666. *Expensive.* Praised by residents and visitors alike, this small, family-run discovery presents gourmet fare in garden surroundings, with wine included. Owner/chef Peter Mallalieu welcomes you by reservation only. No credit cards.

The Anchorage. *Moderate.* Frigate Bay Beach. No phone. Salads and sandwiches make this informal beach restaurant inexpensive, but the excellent lobster is really king here, which puts it in the moderate category. No credit cards.

Fisherman's Wharf. *Moderate.* Fortlands, Basseterre. Tel. 2754. On the waterfront of the Ocean Terrace Inn, with spectacular views of the capital, this establishment serves up the best Friday-night buffet on the island—West Indian specialties alternating week to week with steak barbecues. Dancing and other entertainment follows. No credit cards.

The Ballahoo. Bay Road, Basseterre. Tel. 4047. Delightful small bistro overlooking the center of Basseterre. Open 11–11 P.M. Mon.–Sat. for delicious daily specials, seafood, sandwiches, and unusual entrees. No credit cards.

The Golden Lemon. *Moderate.* Dieppe Bay. Tel. 7260. West Indian, continental, and American cuisine at its best. Owner Arthur Leaman makes up some of the recipes—like the one for cream of green pepper soup with chicken—and never repeats them more than once in a two-week period. The patio restaurant is particularly popular with Kittitians for Sunday brunch, from U.S. $8.50, which can include such specialties as banana pancakes, rum beef stew, and spaghetti with white clam sauce. Try the house special rum drink (tart rather than sweet!) or the "Bil" (named after a friend). No credit cards.

The Bistro Creole. *Inexpensive.* Cayon St. Tel. 4138. Located in a cute West Indian–style cottage, this cozy restaurant serves good West Indian food, Creole, and continental dishes at very reasonable prices. Open Mon.–Sat. for lunch and dinner. No credit cards.

Cafe de Paris. *Expensive.* Cayon St. Tel. 2228. St. Kitts' new epicurean experience has won high ratings for superb French fare. On the menu: frog leg fritters, lobster soufflé, duck, lamb, and Chateaubriand in addition to fruits de mer. Reservations a must. No credit cards.

The Lighthouse. *Moderate.* Deep Water Port Rd. Tel. 8914. Restaurant, bar, and disco popular with locals and visitors, overlooking Basseterre harbor. Good West Indian dishes and seafood, lobster, and conch specialties as well as sate and steaks. Dine until 10, by reservation, then dance until late. No credit cards.

Paradise Pizza & Deli. *Inexpensive.* Frigate Bay, next to Island Paradise Condominiums. Some of the best pizza you'll eat anywhere, and a surprising find on a Caribbean island. Open daily except Monday for other Italian specialties and sandwiches. No credit cards.

Ocean Terrace Inn. *Moderate.* Basseterre. Tel. 2754. This lovely garden terrace and indoor dining room serves excellent local and continental fare in relaxed but elegant surroundings. Popular with residents and visitors, so reservations are a must. AX, V, MC.

Rawlins Plantation. *Moderate.* Mt. Pleasant. Tel. 6221. Raises its own beef and grows its own vegetables. The buffet, with dessert and coffee, is U.S. $15. Exquisite setting in 17th-century sugar plantation. Accepts credit cards.

Fairview Inn. *Inexpensive.* Boyd's. Tel. 2472. Open for breakfast, but lunch and dinner are the epicurean lures here—superb and imaginative local food with generous portions and courteous service. Dine in a flowerful garden setting by candlelight for a very Caribbean experience. All major credit cards.

Victor's Hideaway Restaurant. *Inexpensive.* 9 Stanfort St., Basseterre. No telephone. Probably the best local food in the capital, with most entrees in the U.S. $4 range and nothing over U.S. $10. Chef Florene Smithen's personal favorite is mutton stew. The 30-seat restaurant gets crowded Wednesdays through Fridays—why, Smithen doesn't know—but reservations are impossible since the eaterie has no phone. If you don't want to wait, tell your taxi to stop by and book before picking you up. Open from 11:30 A.M. to 3:00 P.M. for lunch; 7:00 P.M. till the last patron leaves for dinner. No credit cards.

Jong's Oriental Restaurant. *Inexpensive.* Conaree Beach. Tel. 2062. A rare treat on the island. No matter what you can imagine in Chinese food, this place has it. About a quarter mile off the main road, but it seats about 50 and provides spectacular ocean views. No credit cards.

 NIGHT LIFE AND BARS. A few bars and discos are in operation, but most of the night life is centered in hotels. Many organize cultural shows, steel and brass bands, calypso music, folk dances, and other programs. *The Lighthouse* on Deep Water Port Road has the reputation for being the best disco; *Mr. Z's* at the Royal St. Kitts also has good word-of-mouth. Others to consider include *Night Fever* and *Sea Breeze,* both at Sandy Point.

 CASINOS. The only game in town is at the casino in the Jack Tar Village, which stays open until the last player has gone. Unlike many casinos around the world, dress is casual. You'll find excitement at blackjack tables, roulette wheels, craps tables, and rows of slot machines. The casino lounge is a perfect place to take a break over coffee or your favorite liqueur (try Duke, the local specialty) while watching "Lady Luck" give and take away fortunes on the floor below.

POSTAGE. At press time, airmail postage from St. Kitts to the U.S. or Canada was EC $.35 for postcards and EC $.55 per half ounce for letters. On the average, airmail letters from the island to the U.S. take eight to ten days. St. Kitts and its sister island Nevis have separate stamp-issuing policies, although both honor the other's stamps. Stamps are beautiful, and you may be more interested in collecting them than in sending them home on letters.

 ELECTRIC CURRENT. The current here is 230 volts A.C. However, electricity supply at some hotels is 110 volts. A transformer usually is needed for appliances from the U.S. and Canada.

 SECURITY. St. Kitts probably is as safe as it is beautiful, although Conaree Beach has had a series of petty thefts, and hotel officials caution visitors—particularly women—against jogging on long, lonely roads where tall sugar cane could conceivably conceal dangers.

As in most other places in the world these days, don't leave money and valuables in your hotel room. Carry your funds in traveler's checks—and be sure to record and keep their numbers in a separate and safe place. Never leave your rental car unlocked or valuables in plain sight, even if the vehicle is locked.

ST. LUCIA

by
BRIAN HICKEY

Brian Hickey is a travel writer who has lived for the last five years in New York City. A native of Long Island, he is a graduate of New York University's School of Journalism. He has written for newspapers and magazines on a variety of topics and is a contributing editor for several national travel publications.

Located at the southern end of the crescent formed by the Windward Islands, St. Lucia is an irregularly shaped oval twenty-seven miles long and fourteen miles wide. Its dramatically sculpted topography includes soft, light sandy beaches, a densely lush interior ideal for exploring, a volcano called La Soufrière, sulphur springs, mineral baths dating back to the 1780s, and a warm, industrious people. One of the most awe-inspiring sites on St. Lucia is the twin peaks of Gros Piton and Petit Piton, whose images have come to characterize the island. There are about 125,000 St. Lucians, of whom 50,000 live in Castries, the capital.

Past and Present

History may repeat itself, but it also changes its mind occasionally. Historians today increasingly are questioning whether Columbus (in 1502) actually discovered St. Lucia, named by the Spanish in honor of a virgin martyred in Sicily in 304 A.D. The island presently celebrates

December 13, 1502, as its discovery date. The latest word is that Juan de la Cosa, Columbus's map-maker, sailed by in 1499 and 1501. The French privateer François de Clerc is said to have held out at Pigeon Island, off the northwest coast, around 1550 and there were several accidental landings by the Spanish, French, and English after that. The first official stopover was made by British captain Bartholomew Gilbert, who spent two days on St. Lucia in 1603, before discovering that he was not in Bermuda and nowhere near Virginia.

The friendliness reported extended to Captain Gilbert by natives, however, seems to have been the last act of hospitality by the then-locals—the treacherous Caribs, who had decimated the peaceful Ciboney and Arawak Indians. St. Lucia see-sawed no less than fourteen times between the French and British, until British rule became official after a final assault on the French in June of 1803.

The influence of the French (who tended to settle, whereas the British tended to conquer) is firmly entrenched in St. Lucian culture, most noticeably in the Gallic-influenced patois spoken here and the delectable Creole cooking. St. Lucia became an independant state within the British Commonwealth of Nations on February 22, 1979, and is a member of the United Nations and the Organization of American States.

St. Lucia sent about seventy-five men to Grenada in support of the invasion by the United States in October of 1983. The political scene on St. Lucia, meanwhile, has remained stable, with at least two other political parties balancing out the ideological scale. St. Lucia's government, formed around the precepts of the parliamentary system, has steadily contributed to the island's development as an exporter of bananas (its number-one export), a site for light industry, and a tourist destination.

EXPLORING ST. LUCIA

The island of St. Lucia, shaped something like a leaf, is narrow at the northern tip, broadens in its lower third, then begins to taper again, drawing to the T-shaped peninsula at Moule a Chique at the southernmost tip. St. Lucia's two principal areas are the northern third, which includes the northwest-coast capital city of Castries, and the remaining two-thirds to the south, which is marked by dense forests and mountains.

If you arrive by air, you most likely will land at Hewanorra International Airport in Vieux Fort on the southern tip. Vigie Airport, in Castries, is a regional airport which handles mostly charters from Hewanorra (a Carib Indian word meaning "Land of the Iguana") and surrounding islands. There are two main ports of entry for those who come by sea: Castries or Vieux Fort.

Once you've arrived at Hewanorra, an eager throng of taxi drivers will be waiting for you at the other end of the terminal. Most taxi drivers on St. Lucia are especially proud of their island and take considerable pleasure in showing it off to visitors.

There is a National Council of Taxi Associations and Cooperatives serving the island; nine- and fourteen-seat vans are privately owned. Most drivers are very knowledgable about the sites and scenes on the island, so if you haven't made prior arrangements with your hotel, you

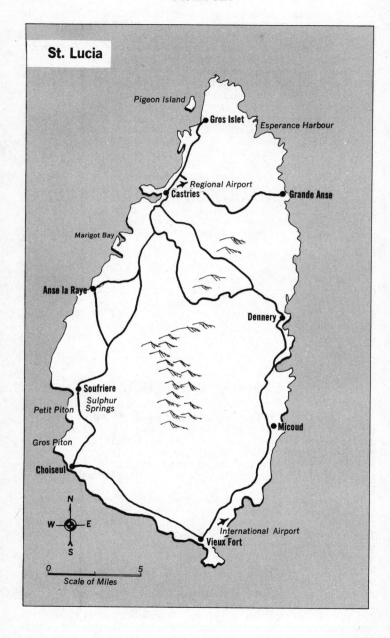

St. Lucia

Pigeon Island

Gros Islet

Esperance Harbour

Regional Airport

Castries

Grande Anse

Marigot Bay

Anse la Raye

Dennery

Soufriere

Sulphur
Springs

Petit Piton

Gros Piton

Micoud

Choiseul

N
W E
S

International Airport

Vieux Fort

0   5
Scale of Miles

shouldn't have any trouble finding a suitable guide at the airport. If you're renting a car, don't forget to drive on the left side of the road.

Castries

The busy port town of Castries is located on the northwest coast of the island, between Choc Bay to the north and Cul de Sac to the south. (It's about an hour-and-a-half drive to town from Hewanorra International.) Castries lies on Castries Harbor and is the site of pleasant Columbus Square plus several streets of shops and restaurants.

Castries itself has no real distinguishing architectural characteristics, since the town was virtually destroyed by fire four times: in 1796, 1813, 1927, and 1948. Hurricanes had also taken their toll long before Hurricane Allan blew into town in 1981. One of the worst was in 1780, when some two thousand St. Lucians were killed and the island devastated. There are, however, a number of places in town worth exploring, and one good place to start is at the Tourist Bureau on Jeremie Street across from the National Bank and next door to the customs office.

In addition to providing information on sites and a small but thorough selection of brochures, they will also tell you how to get around the island (they'll even recommend a taxi if you'd like).

A good place to start out exploring Castries is at Columbus Square, site of a 150-year-old saman tree. Directly across the street, on the corner of Laborie and Micoud streets, is the Cathedral of the Immaculate Conception, begun in 1894 and completed in 1897. The south side of Brazil Street, overlooking Columbus Square, is the site of several nineteenth-century buildings of typical French character which number among the few original buildings in Castries to survive the fires and hurricanes.

Shoppers should head along Bridge Street and William Peter Boulevard, better known as "The Boulevard," and browse in Sea Island Cotton Shop and Y. De Lima Ltd.

One place you won't want to miss is Castries Market, built in 1894 and located on the northeast corner of Jeremie and Peynier streets. Local faramers and small growers come to this hectic place—especially on Saturdays—to offer their week's yield, which ranges from fresh meat and just-caught fish to a cornucopia of local vegetables and fruits. Other items in the market include baskets, chairs, brooms, rugs, and pots and bowls of all sizes.

On the bay are a cluster of fishermen who sell the day's catch from their boats. On the wharf, the banana boat may be loading up next to inter-island schooners taking on provisions, freight, and passengers. When it comes to eating, you'll find a wide range of choices right in downtown Castries. You'll notice that the local cuisine has an East Indian influence; it's another reminder of the island's history. Six hundred indentured East Indian workers were shipwrecked in 1893 off Vigie Point en route to another British island.

Morne Fortune

Leaving Castries via Bridge Street you can head due east to Morne Fortune, which rises above Castries. The drive is pleasant and you'll pass several attractive homes, including Government House (located near the top of the Morne), an expansive, handsome building constructed in 1895. On the way you'll also pass by some of the most beautiful flora you can find in the Caribbean: lilies, poinsettia, bougainvillea, chenille plant, hibiscus, oleander, frangipani, breadfruit, and sea grape.

Over thirty-eight fortifications were built in St. Lucia over the years, with the heaviest concentration found in Vigie, just north of Castries. By the turn of the twentieth century, the English had spent some five million pounds fortifying Vigie, the Morne, and La Toc, north of Vigie. Fort Charlotte, atop the Morne, has been partially restored. The view from the top of Morne Fortune reveals its strategic wartime importance. The view extends from Pigeon Point in the north to the Pitons in the south. Straight ahead is a bird's-eye view of Castries, the harbor, and the Vigie Peninsula, where numerous battles took place between the French and the English.

Also be sure and visit some of the cemeteries in the vicinity for a look at the timeworn tombstones that carry, faintly incised, the names of those veterans who died defending their faraway outpost.

The North End to Gros Islet

Moving north from Castries, you'll find the island's heaviest concentration of hotels—from here to Cap Estate at the northern tip. Heading past Choc Bay and its several archeological sites, you'll eventually come to Gros Islet and Rodney Bay, named after the British admiral responsible for building up the area in late 1700s. There's a new marina that you'll notice on your immediate left as you pass by the Bay. Drive to the very end, Cap Estate, and you will have entered a 2,000-acre estate, open to the public, which includes several secluded beaches (all St. Lucia's beaches are open to the public) and the Cariblue Hotel. Some sixty homes are located at "Cap," the majority of which are used by their owners only part of the year and are rented out to visitors and tenants the rest of the time.

The small town of Gros Islet still lives, in many ways, as it did a hundred years ago. Similar to Anse la Raye halfway down the coast, Gros Islet is a simple seaside town where men gather in their fishing boats during the week, women attend to their chores, and families meet every Sunday in the single church.

Pigeon Island

Named in honor of Admiral Rodney's predilection for raising pigeons, Pigeon Island served an important role in island warfare between England and France and today is the site of Pigeon Island National Park, a historic museum and picnic area for visitors. Pigeon Island is connected to the mainland by a slim isthmus constructed in 1970–71 at a cost of some twenty million pounds. Batteries, soldiers' barracks, garrisons, and other ruins from the days of seafaring battle are sprinkled across Pigeon Island. The museum at Pigeon Island, established thirteen years ago, encloses some of these ruins as well as artifacts from the period.

Grand Anse Beach

Due east of Castries, Grand Anse Beach is an ideal spot for a picnic and stroll. The waters of the rougher Atlantic coast are not recommended for swimming, but Grand Anse Beach is typical of some of the remote, pleasant points worth discovering on the island. You'll want to make provisions for food as there are no eateries on the way. The road there takes you through low land heavily cultivated with banana and coconut estates.

South of Castries

There is no doubt that the drive along the west-coast (Caribbean) highway is the best on the island. Descending from Castries into the first valley south, Cul de Sac, you'll drive past acres of banana plants waving in the sun. Most of the area, as well as several other large estates in St. Lucia, is owned by the Geest family, operating as Geest Industries. The corporation owns a fleet of refrigerated ships that bring the crop to England, and you may spot a bustle of activity around one of the packing sheds if it's shipping day.

Just south of Cul de Sac is the valley of Roseau. One of the first stops is Marigot Bay where the tropical portion of "Dr. Doolittle" was filmed in 1966. On the bay are two hotels: Doolittle's and Hurricane Hole at Marigot Bay. The community itself is comprised of groups of homes and plantations that grow mostly banana. The bay, which offers free docking, is especially popular with yachters. In 1778 it also proved a valuable detour for British admiral Samuel Barrington who evaded the French fleet by taking his boats into Marigot Bay and disguising them as trees by lashing palm fronds to their masts.

Continuing south through Roseau Valley, you may be able to spot one of the island's two rum distilleries. Sugar cane has long been a comparitively minor crop on St. Lucia, and the distilleries make rum from imported molasses. You will also see lots of—you guessed it—bananas. The most common variety here—and on most Caribbean islands—is called Gros Michel, though there were over 127 varieties of banana at last count.

Ahead lies a mountainous region marked by Mount Parasol and, if you look hard enough through the inland mist, Mount Gimie, St. Lucia's highest mountain at 3,117 feet. You'll soon be entering Anse la Raye. Anse la Raye's boatbuilding expertise brings fishermen from as far away as Martinique to buy new boats. Canoes are built the traditional way, by burning out the center of a log and by whooping it up plenty once the work is done. From here, it's through Anse Galet into the town of Canaries, where local ladies gather at the river to pound their clothes clean on the rocks.

Soufrière

The majestic rise of the Pitons will tip you off that you've come upon something out of the ordinary. The town of Soufriére, named for the nearby volcano, was laid out in 1746, and grew into a flourishing district center by 1763. This active, folksy town, with a population of about a thousand, was partly destroyed by a fire in 1955. If you stand at the wharf with your back to the sea, you'll notice that buildings on the left side of town are newer than those on the right side. The church and central square are the focal points, with the rich green of the mountainsides forming a colorful backdrop. You'll probably also see the bright, arresting orange blossoms of the immortelle tree, sparsely sprinkled on the hillsides. Soufrière Harbor, the deepest harbor on the island, accommodates cruise ships that come right up to the wharf to unload passengers.

The Pitons greet you as you approach La Soufrière and its sulphur springs and baths. Gros Piton, on the far side of the little bay, rises 2,619 feet, and its smaller companion rises 2,461 feet. It is believed that the Pitons were formed by an eruption about 15,000 years ago. The next eruption is expected to occur in around 20,000 years.

A short jaunt up into the hills, across the ridge, will bring you into the rain forest, located between Soufrière and Fond St. Jacques. It's a three-hour walk for the complete journey, and you can make arrangements to be picked up by a driver at the other end. You'll see a wide variety of plants and many spectacular tropical birds.

La Soufrière, the volcano, is surrounded by numerous sulphur springs (your nose will notice them before your eyes) and mineral baths, built in 1786 for the troops of Louis XVI to "fortify them against the St. Lucian climate." The baths were destroyed during the Brigand's War, just after the French Revolution, but were restored in 1966. Fed by an underground flow of water coming from the sulphur springs, the baths remain a popular bathing spot for curing whatever ails you.

The volcano and sulphur springs are actually part of three calderas, or collapsed volcanic formations, forming a three-part ring around the island's southwestern region and extending well out into the Caribbean. Recently the underground steam has been capped in at least two locations with an eye toward using it to generate power. Unfortunately, development hasn't passed the capping stage yet, and more funding will be needed to complete the job.

Visitors to La Soufrière actually drive through the volcano and it is from that excellent vantage point that you can see the black sulphur water bubbling up out of the ground and yellow-green sulphur baking in the steamy atmosphere.

South of Soufrière

By this time you will have noticed the slightly cooler temperature as you climb higher into the mountains. Cooling trade winds blow steadily at this altitude. Among the crops you'll see are cocoa and coffee, which do better in the high ground.

From here you'll pass through the charming town of Choiseul, where pots and bowls are made and fired in wood fires. At the turn of the road past the Anglican Church, built in 1846, is the bridge across the River Dorée, so named because the riverbed is covered with iron pyrite, or fool's gold. Next is the fishing village of Laborie, which once had a flourishing industry in bay rum and sugar cane. Beneath Laborie runs an underground passage leading from an old fort at Saphire, up the coast, to an opening at the sea. Its purpose is still a mystery.

If you have time, take a stroll through Laborie and sample the shops offering cheese, bread, fish, and other local goods.

The drive from here into Vieux Fort is particularly smooth because the roads were solidly built for the Vieux Fort air base. Driving out to Moule a Chique you can, on a clear day, see St. Vincent twenty-one miles to the south, and looking at the sea, you'll see where the gray-blue Atlantic mingles with the aquamarine blue of the Caribbean.

The drive north from Vieux Fort along the Atlantic coast will take you past Honeymoon Beach, known officially as Anse l'Islet, a wide, grassy, flat peninsula jutting into the ocean. The warm, quaint, slow-paced towns of Micoud and Dennery, overlooking the restless Atlantic, serve as centers for shopping, residential life, and social goings-on for locals. The drive will take you past a variety of plantations and provide you with a dramatic view of the Atlantic coastline.

In winding your way back to Castries, you'll climb over the Barre de l'Isle Ridge. Here the vegetation is especially dense, and the view from the ridge is superb. The course along the bumpy roads travels through a mini-rain forest where you'll find tree ferns and delicate orchids. Leaving the mountains behind, you soon enter bright, busy Castries.

PRACTICAL INFORMATION FOR ST. LUCIA

FACTS AND FIGURES. St. Lucia is 27 miles long and 14 miles wide, and is located 24 miles south of Martinique and 21 miles north of St. Vincent. It lies about 75 miles west of Barbados and 460 miles southeast of Puerto Rico. The island is covered with lush vegetation. A volcano, La Soufrière, rises from its southern end. The northern third is less vegetated and less hilly. St. Lucia has a population of 125,000 on its 238 square miles. The capital city of Castries, where about 50,000 people live, is located in the northwestern third of the island. Castries is also the main port (there is another in Vieux Fort, at the southern end of the island) and the commercial center.

The leading export is bananas, followed by coconut, cocoa, mace, nutmeg, and citrus fruits. Beaches on the west coast are considered ideal for swimming, and the heaviest concentration of hotels is along the strip from Castries north to Gros Islet. The official language is English, though a French-derived patois is widely spoken. There are two airports: Vigie (near Castries) for charter flights, and Hewanorra International (in the south). St. Lucia is on Atlantic standard time, one hour ahead of eastern standard time.

WHEN TO GO. December through April is the busiest time of year and June through October is the low season, when hotel rates may drop by as much as 50%. Temperatures range from 70 to 90 degrees F, with an average temperature of 78, always tempered by trade winds. The rainy season extends from September through November.

PASSPORTS AND VISAS. Proof of citizenship is required of U.S., British, and Canadian visitors. A passport is best, but a birth certificate or voter's registration card will do—a driver's license will not. All other tourists must have valid passports. A return or ongoing ticket is also required of every visitor.

MONEY. The Eastern Caribbean dollar (EC) is the local currency, which is figured at EC $2.64 = U.S. $1. Be sure which exchange is being used since most places quote in EC dollars.

WHAT WILL IT COST?

A typical day on St. Lucia for two persons during the winter season will run:

	U.S.$
Hotel accommodations, including breakfast and dinner	145
Lunch at a hotel or restaurant	15
Tips, taxes, service charges	25
Car rental or island tour for a full day	40–60
Total	$225–245

HOW TO GET THERE. By air. There are two airports on the island, Hewanorra International on the southern tip, and Vigie just outside Castries on the northwestern shore. *BWIA, British Airways, Eastern Airlines,* and *Pan Am* come into Hewanorra by way of New York, Miami, and San Juan. *LIAT,* the Caribbean's national carrier, links St. Lucia with Barbados, Trinidad, Antigua, and several other islands, using smaller aircraft that land at Vigie Field.

By sea. Cruise ships from New York, Florida, and San Juan offering longer voyages sometimes come into Castries harbor, which is such an occasion that townspeople gather and steel bands provide welcome.

AIRPORT TAXES AND OTHER CHARGES. There is an 8% government tax on hotel rooms, plus a 10% service charge. The airport departure tax is EC $12 (U.S. $5), or EC $6 if you're headed for another Caribbean destination.

TELEPHONE AND EMERGENCY NUMBERS. The area code for St. Lucia is 809. The prefix when dialing long distance is 45 followed by the appropriate 5-digit number. Victoria Hospital in Castries has all medical and surgical facilities as well as a casualty department that operates 24 hours a day. There are district hospitals in Dennery, Soufrière, and Vieux Fort. Dial the operator from anywhere on the island and he or she will connect you with the nearest medical facility, the police or fire department.

HOTELS. Most hotels on St. Lucia are along the strip running north from Castries to Cap Estate at the tip of the island. Others are found south of Castries along the west coast. Accommodations range from folksy West Indian guesthouses and apartments to plush, pampering resorts. Plan on booking at least four months in advance. During the off-season, rates drop at some places by as much as 50%. If you don't mind hot days and deserted beaches, it's worth looking into.

All room rates are subject to a 10% service charge and 8% government tax. The following rates are based on double occupancy, MAP, during the winter (peak) season. Prices quoted are in U.S. dollars. A *Deluxe* designation in St. Lucia means $150 and above; *Expensive,* $100–149; *Moderate,* $50–99; and *Inexpensive,* below $50.

Couples. *Deluxe.* P.O. Box 190, Castries. Tel. 45–24511. 68 rooms and 18 beachfront cottages. Formerly the Malabar Beach Hotel, Couples is just what its name implies—a haven for couples only, no singles or children. The main building is three stories high, and all rooms are air conditioned. Rooms in the main building include king-size beds; the cottages each have one bedroom. Couples covers two miles of beach at Vigie, and is two miles from Castries and one mile from Vigie airport. Hewanorra Airport is 33 miles away—about an hour's drive. Amenities included in the price: transfers, meals, all liquor, cigarettes, all water sports and athletic facilities, including horseback riding, tennis (day and night), scuba diving, and fishing. There's a band seven nights a week and the bar closes when the last person leaves.

Cunard La Toc and Cunard La Toc Villas. *Deluxe.* P.O. Box 399, Castries. Tel. 45–53081. 164 double rooms, 60 villas. Nestled on 106 secluded acres three miles from Castries, the hotel half of this arrangement includes 42 superior rooms, each with a balcony facing the ocean, air conditioning, and king-size bed. Both the hotel and the villas have their own dining rooms. The duplex villas each have a private plunge pool. Tennis and nine-hole golf course. The villas have bright roomy interiors, full kitchen facilities, and views of the Caribbean. The best views are from villas located on "The Point." International mix of guests—British, Italians, Americans, and others.

Anse Chastanet Beach Hotel. *Expensive.* P.O. Box 216, Soufrière. Tel. 45–47354. 20 doubles and a one-bedroom suite. Located 29 miles from Castries on a 400-acre estate, Anse Chastenet's bungalows climb a tropical hillside overlooking a quarter-mile of secluded beach with some of the best snorkeling in the

Caribbean. Simple, hearty island fare is served in the upper restaurant or in the thatched-roof, beachside bar and restaurant. Soufrière and the mineral baths are nearby. Rooms here are clean, neat, and stand in the path of gentle breezes that are especially enjoyable from your own veranda.

Dasheene. *Expensive.* The Kinnebrew Design Collaborative, 13300 Beckwith Dr., Lowell, MI. Tel (616) 897–5938 (collect calls accepted); also Dasheene, Soufriére. Tel. 45–27444. 22 one-, two-, and three-bedroom units. Rumor has it that the Sourfrière region was created by Mother Nature just so Dasheene could take its place a thousand feet above the sparkling Caribbean, within walking distance of major sites, and smack in the middle of the Pitons. Proprietors Joe and Ellen Kinnebrew have established what they call "an environmental design project." The handful of darkwood buildings are made of greenheart wood. While no two buildings are exactly alike, one common feature they share is an open west wall looking out over the Caribbean—no glass, no screen, just space. Full range of recreation possibilities including swimming, short walks to La Soufrière, a canoe ride up the coast to Castries (about 45 minutes), scuba diving, car rental, or just a cool rum punch and an unforgettable view. The restaurant serves delicious food from an ever-changing menu and the Friday night jump-up is one of the best on the island.

Steigenberger Cariblue Hotel. *Expensive.* P.O. Box 437, Castries. Tel. 45–28551/5. 102 double rooms. Nine miles from Castries and situated on the 1,500-acre Cap Estate, Cariblue provides a pleasurable blend of West Indian style and European panache. The 102 air-conditioned rooms and two suites are newly decorated and overlook the bay and beach from private balconies or patios. Swimming, tennis, water sports, horseback riding, squash, and golf on a superb nine-hole course, plus a daily program of scheduled activities from scuba diving to picnics. Cariblue is popular with English, German, and Italian vacationers, and the restaurant and bar area just up from the beach are always busy.

The Moorings Marigot Bay Resort. *Expensive.* Box 101, Castries, St. Lucia (809) 453–4357; 1305 U.S. 19 South, Suite 402, Clearwater, FL 33546 (800) 535–7289. An intimate collection of two hotels and 14 one-, two-, and three-bedroom villas set in an idyllic location. The resort boasts a full range of watersports (free to guests), two restaurants, two bars, two boutiques, and dive shop. All accommodations have cooking facilities. The marina is home to The Moorings' fleet of charter yachts, along with their sailing school. The romantic villas climb the hill behind Doolittle's Restaurant and Bar and there is a small trolley that goes up and down with stops along the way. Each villa is different with a wide plank veranda and dining space. The charming harborside cottages are set in acres of coconut palms with lawns leading down to the water's edge. A fresh water pool, terrace dining room, and bar are nearby.

Smugglers Village. *Moderate* to *Expensive.* Cap Estate. Tel. 45–20551. A 15-minute drive from Castries and 50 yards to the beach, Smugglers is ideal for the independent-minded vacationer. There are 77 one- and two-bedroom units with single beds, either kitchenettes or full kitchens, air conditioning, patios with sitting/dining areas as well as a central restaurant, bar, and minimarket all on the property. There's also a pool, water sports including Sunfish and windsurfing (lessons available), and regular live entertainment. Golf is nearby at Cap Estate, and a variety of sightseeing activities can be arranged.

East Winds Inn. *Moderate.* La Brelotte Bay. Tel. 45–28212. Ten cottages. Six miles north of Castries, East Winds Inn, under new management at this writing, is a quiet, low-key place on six-and-a-half bayside acres of tropical park. Cottages are freshly decorated with carpeting, modern bathrooms with sunken bath and shower, and a covered table in front. The bay is superb for swimming, and arrangements can be made, at extra cost, for other water sports or activities.

Green Parrot. *Moderate.* The Morne, Castries. Tel. 45–23399. What started out as one of the island's premier restaurants has expanded into a beautiful hillside inn. Situated on Morne Fortune, with a view of Castries and the harbor, the Green Parrot has 27 finely furnished double rooms with balconies. Good beaches are ten minutes away by car. A swimming pool, two restaurants, and shops make this a shoe-in for a pleasant, relaxed island experience.

Halcyon Beach Club. *Moderate.* Choc Bay. Tel. 45–25331/4. 98 double rooms. Five miles outside Castries (EC $15 by cab) and convenient to Vigie

Airfield, Halcyon Beach Club features rooms which are clean and simple (most with sea views); a nice, short beach; large freshwater pool; a small batik shop; and two dining areas, including the *Fisherman's Wharf Restaurant* out on the water. There's lively music and dancing six nights a week, with calypso, limbo, and fire eating on Friday nights. One of the prides of Halcyon Beach is its kitchen, which turns out delicious island cuisine. In early 1985 Halcyon had taken over the 47 double rooms at the old Red Lion Hotel at Vigie Beach. This arrangement is only temporary, however, and may change shortly.

St. Lucian Hotel. *Moderate.* Reduit. Tel 45–28351/5. 192 rooms. This expansive, sunny place used to be two separate hotels. Set on Reduit Beach, 15 minutes north of Castries, it is a modern and luxurious complex featuring two restaurants, a night club, the gamut of water sports, and arguably the best beach around. All rooms are air conditioned, set on the beachfront, and include a bath, two queen-size beds, and cheery, colorful interiors. There's buffet breakfast and dinner in one restaurant, or à la carte breakfast, lunch, and candlelight dinner at the poolside restaurant, live music seven nights a week. You can also sign up for a deep-sea-fishing excursion on a 26-foot boat—U.S. $25 per person for a half day. $50 per person for a full day. The crowd here is a mixture of all ages and nationalities. Some water sports are free to guests.

Kimatrai Hotel. *Inexpensive* to *Moderate.* Vieux Fort. Tel. 45–56238. 14 rooms and six apartments. Located five minutes from Hewanorra Airport, above the little town of Vieux Fort, Kimatrai is family-owned and operated. It offers 14 clean, comfortable rooms, each with modern bath and shower, and six self-contained apartments. Food served in the dining room is good and there's also an informal little bar.

Villa Hotel. *Inexpensive* to *Moderate.* The Morne, Castries. Tel. 45–22691. Ten double rooms. Sample local, unadorned West Indian hospitality. Clean, modern facilities, all within walking distance of downtown Castries. All rooms are air conditioned and have private bath or shower. The dining room and bar offer a splendid view of Castries Harbor below. Quiet atmosphere and a good taste of local island life.

 HOME AND APARTMENT RENTALS. For private home rentals your best bet is to contact *Caribbean Home Rentals,* Box 710, Palm Beach, FL 33480, or write *Happy Homes,* Box 12, Castries, St. Lucia. You can also make arrangements with *Cap Estates St. Lucia, Ltd.,* tel. 452–8522.

Islander Apartment Resort. Moderate. Box 907, Castries. Telephone: 45–28757. There are 40 bedroom apartments here, all of which are nicely furnished air-conditioned studios with kitchenettes and a living/dining area. This complex is on the northern end of the island, just a short walk from the St. Lucian Hotel. They have a freshwater swimming pool, nice restaurant, and quiet beach.

Morne Fortune Apartments. Moderate. Box 376, Castries. Telephone: 3603. Just a dozen rooms, but they are in one- and two-bedroom apartments that have fully equipped kitchens and overlook the swimming pool and the sea. There is also a patio where you can dine casually and comfortably.

 HOW TO GET AROUND. Hewanorra International is the jetport on St. Lucia, and Vigie Airport, north of Castries, handles local flights and charters. Taxis will be waiting for you at Hewanorra. Though cabs are not metered, the government has issued a list of fixed rates for point-to-point travel. The drive from Hewanorra to the Castries area (where most hotels are) takes a little over an hour and costs about U.S. $35.

Rental cars are available through *Avis* (located in central Castries; tel. 22700, 22202), *National* (six miles north of Castries; tel. 28721) *Cenac's Car Rental* (half a mile from central Castries; tel. 23295), *Carib Touring Ltd.* (in central Castries; tel. 23184, 22689), and *Hertz* (Castries; tel. 24777). Other companies can be found through the Tourism Bureau in Castries. Most major hotels also have car-rental outlets. A temporary driver's license can be obtained by either presenting your own license to a police officer at either airport, or by going to police headquarters on Bridge St. in Castries. Temporary licenses are valid for three months and cost EC $20 (about U.S. $6). Applicants must be at least 25 years of age.

TOURIST INFORMATION SERVICES. For all you'll need to acquaint you with this island, contact the *St. Lucia Tourist Board* on Sans Soucis Street, in Castries (tel. 25968). It is open from 8:00 A.M. to 4:30 P.M., Monday through Friday.

SPECIAL EVENTS. The biggest celebration of the year is Independence Day, which is celebrated on February 22. Depending upon dates, it comes close on the heels of St. Lucia's pre-Lentan Carnival, making late winter an ongoing festival.

The village of Gros Islet has a hugely successful block party every Friday afternoon, which eclipses anything else. People from around the island come for the music, drinks, and barbecued conch, chicken, and other treats.

TOURS. St. Lucia is surely one of the finest islands for touring the natural wonders of the Caribbean. There are beautiful bays to see as you skirt the island, mountains to admire, and a volcano to enter. Taxi tours cost about U.S. $14 an hour. The *Carib Touring Company* (tel. 3081) offers several options, including full-day, off-island tours. On St. Lucia, they offer the *Soufrière Sea Safari,* which departs at 9:30 A.M. from Castries for a visit to historical Morne Fortune; you then drive through the banana plantations, the fishing villages, and the rain forest en route to the twin peaks and the sulphur springs. You'll cruise along the west coast and enjoy a swimming stop and excursion at Marigot Bay before your 4:00 P.M. return.

Half-day excursions arranged by the Carib Touring Company are the *Taste of St. Lucia Tour,* which is a scenic look at the island's history and beauty, and includes luncheon at the Rain Restaurant. Or select the four-hour *Pigeon Island Picnic,* where you'll have the chance to explore historic ruins, take an adventurous mountain climb, have a leisurely picnic lunch, and swim at one of the island's best beaches.

Barnards Travel offers a complete selection of full- and half-day tours of the island, including trips to Dominica, Martinique, and the Grenadines of St. Vincent. Barnards is on Bridge St. in Castries; tel. 22214/5/7.

PARKS AND GARDENS. Many of the resort hotels and inns are bathed in tropical gardens, but the most verdant of all are the rain forests en route to the Soufrière volcano. St. Lucia's National Park is located on Pigeon Island in the north and connected to the mainland by a causeway. Explore the ruins of Admiral Rodney's Fort to get an idea of how he battled the French invaders, then enjoy swimming or picnicking at any spot you choose along the tranquil western shore.

BEACHES. You won't run out of places to swim here, with beaches, no matter how small, all along the island. *Pigeon Island,* off the northern tip, is secluded and lovely, and *Vigie Beach,* not far from Castries, has beige sands. *La Toc Bay* and *Vieux Fort* in the south boast black-sand beaches that are equally popular.

PARTICIPANT SPORTS. Several of the hotels have **tennis** courts, with some lighted for night play. For **horseback riding,** there are two stables and you'll find this a wonderful way to explore the island. Contact *Sunrise Trekking Center* at Cap Estate.

Golf can be played at either of St. Lucia's two courses: one at Cap Estate, and the other at the La Toc Hotel. Cap Estate has nine holes; La Toc nine plus nine and welcomes guests. The greens fees at both run EC $10, and clubs can be rented at a small additional charge. You'll find **snorkeling, sailing,** and **scuba diving** at most of the resort hotels, but if you want to really explore the ocean floor, contact *Scuba St. Lucia* at the Anse Chastanet Hotel. They offer everything—courses in underwater photography in addition to single-tank, two-tank, and night dives, and courses geared toward certification. In some cases the equipment is provided, in some cases it is not, so figure between $25 to $55, depending upon which option you choose.

SPECTATOR SPORTS. Cricket and **soccer** are national pastimes. The soccer season runs from July through January; cricket games from February through June. Contact the Tourist Office for times. Both cricket and soccer are played at Mindoo Philip Park, located at Marchand, two miles east of Castries.

HISTORIC SITES AND HOUSES. *Fort Charlotte,* at the top of the Morne behind Castreis, has been partially restored so that you can visit the guard rooms and barracks. Built during the 18th century, this historic fort changed hands between the British and French several times. There is no admission charge at Fort Charlotte.

Although some historians say the Empress Josephine was born on Martinique's Trois Islet, others contend that the wife of Napoleon was born on the family plantation at Morne Paix-Bouche, just inland from Castries in the northwest side of the island, and insist she was merely christened in Martinique. The house is now part of a private estate. The historic sulphur springs in Sofriere provide an intriguing natural attraction. There is an admission charge of EC $3.00.

MUSEUMS. *Pigeon Island Museum.* Historic museum from the days of warfare between England and France. Ruins of barracks and artifacts. Open Mon.–Sat. 9:00 A.M.–4:00 P.M. EC $3 admission.

SHOPPING. The most popular place for visitors is *Bagshaw's,* famous for its unique silkscreen designs. Their studio is located at La Toc, where you can buy ready-made fashions or fabric by the yard. Shopping here isn't what it is on the other islands, but there are straw goods, wood carvings, and pottery, all crafted by St. Lucians, in some of the unusual small shops in Castries and at the hotel boutiques. Sisal rugs and shirts made from flour sacking are available at the *Home Industries* store on Jeremie St.; some crystal and china at *Y. de Lima* on William Peter Blvd. and at the *Danish House* on Mongiraud St. *Sea Island Cotton Shop* on Bridge St. sells hand-made batik items.

RESTAURANTS. Besides ruined fortresses and hulking cannons, the French also left St. Lucia a few things for which it is rightfully grateful, especially in the food department. The Creole influence in cooking shows up in many memorable specialties. Fish Creole (try the flying fish) appears in every corner, but meats are almost all imported—beef from Argentina and Iowa, and lamb from New Zealand. Langoustine is the local variety of lobster, which shows up in both garlic and lime butter; vegetables like christophene, green figs, yam, dasheen, and calaloo are boiled, pan-fried, deep-fried, baked, stuffed, served raw, mixed with meat, cheese, spices, and even paupau (payaya), which can also be served as a vegetable when green. It is sometimes mixed with cheese and spices or sautéed.

Most restaurants on the island are informal and casual, with the Green Parrot being the only notable exception. The price classifications are based on the cost of an average three-course dinner for one person *for food alone;* beverages, tax, and tip would be extra. Prices quoted in U.S. dollars. *Expensive* means $15–20; *Moderate,* $10–14; *Inexpensive,* below $10.

The Coal Pot. *Expensive.* Lunar Park, Ganter's Bay. Tel. 25643. A breezy, bayside setting for very good food served on the porch. The menu offers a limited selection of West Indian and continental food. The piña coladas do the trick. Dress is casual and reservations are helpful. AE, MC, V.

Capone's. *Moderate* to *Expensive.* Reduit (across from the St. Lucian Hotel). Tel. 45–20284. This stunning art deco restaurant and bar has been painstakingly decorated in the style of the notorious gangster's era: wall sconces, terraced ceiling, player piano, and well-outfitted bartender and waiters meld to create a uniquely satisfying dining experience. Menu features a good range of Italian cuisine—don't miss the pizza parlor next door—from basic pasta to Ossobucco Alla Milanese, fresh fish, chicken, and steak. The delicious rum drinks give Trader Vic's a run for their money, especially the Mafia Mai Tai and St. Valentine's Day Massacre. Fountain and gardens outside add a nice touch. Restaurant open from five to midnight. Closed Mondays. AE, Barclay, MC, V.

The Charthouse. *Moderate* to *Expensive.* Reduit (next to the St. Lucian Hotel). Tel. 45–28115. This 2-year-old restaurant and bar is located right on the water, and its romantic, woody interior makes for a delightful setting. Foods are fresh and meals are delicious, especially the flying fish, garlic bread, and local soups. The view of Rodney Bay adds a nice open feeling, complemented by hanging plants and fine jazz on the stereo. Open seven days. AE, MC, V.

St. Antoine's. *Moderate* to *Expensive.* Morne Fortune. Tel. 45–24660. Originally the St. Antoine Hotel, a mid-1800s greathouse destroyed by fire in 1970, the restored St. Antoine's is an attractive, airy restaurant and bar perched high on the Morne affording sweeping views of Castries and Martinique in the distance. Cuisine is French, with local dishes as well. There's also a daunting wine list. Additionally, there's a meandering nature trail through a bamboo forest and some 6,500 plants. Closed Sundays. AE, V.

Doolittle's. *Moderate.* Marigot de Roseaux on Marigot Bay. Tel. 16246. An open veranda area for dining on Marigot Bay is the setting for very good island fare (try the shrimp and ask for the special of the day). There's ferry service here, but you may not want to leave this little arcadia. AE, MC, V.

The Green Parrot. *Expensive.* Red Tape Lane, Morne Fortune. Tel. 23399. This is *the* exquisite place to dine on the island, with busboys buzzing about, a sommelier, and crisp, attentive waiters. Fine local and continental cuisine is served up elegantly. Reservations are a must. AE, MC, V.

Rain. *Moderate.* On Columbus Square, Castries. Tel. 23022. The scene is out of Somerset Maugham: tin roof, sultry green-and-white island decor. The rum drinks are powerful. Local dishes are cooked up with flair. Dress is casual. AE, MC, V.

The Ruins. *Moderate.* Castries. Tel. 27328. This restaurant, built around a backyard fig tree, is a former French home some 150 years old. Nowadays it serves up specialties like pepper pot and fried plantain. AE.

The Still. *Moderate.* Soufrière. Tel. 27224. Once in a while they serve a buffet lunch made of mouth-watering island dishes. Otherwise it's table service at this former rum distillery. AE, V.

The Calabash. *Inexpensive.* Mongiraud St., near Clarke's Cinema. Tel. 22869. A convenient stop for lunch while you're touring town, the Calabash serves good food in a casual atmosphere. The entrees go from American to Indian. AE.

Le Boucan. *Inexpensive.* Columbus Square, Castries. Tel. 22415. Located right on Columbus Square, Le Boucan has a sidewalk cafe popular with city stollers and morning shoppers. Fresh fish and Thursday night's Folk Food Night give this worthwhile restaurant a Creole accent. No credit cards.

 NIGHT LIFE AND BARS. There are only a couple of clubs in St. Lucia worth trekking to; most of the nightlife takes place at the hotels, which offer a hefty selection of musical arts and dancing, as well as folkloric entertainment like limbo and steel band jump-ups. Most shakin' and jumpin' is north of Castries.

Capone's. Reduit. Tel. 45–20284. This art deco beauty offers enchanting atmosphere and perhaps the most flavorful rum drink selection on the island. Music is vintage flappers from a player piano. There's also a restaurant, gardens, and fountains outside. Open till around midnight. Closed Mondays.

The Charthouse. Reduit (on Rodney Bay). Tel. 45–28115. There's ample room at the bar here for some elbow bending to the strains of vintage jazz over the stereo and live music on Saturdays. Dress is casual.

The Green Parrot. Morne Fortune. Tel. 23399. Nightclub. The floor show here, with Harry Edwards as M.C., will catch you by surprise. This is a sit-down affair, with anthems and local songs and, during the second half, a limbo dancer who will leave you in awe of what the human body can accomplish. Dress is formal.

Lucifer's. The disco in the St. Lucian Hotel. Tel. 28351. Lucifer's interior may have been designed by the emperor Ming—that is, Flash Gordon's nemesis. Plastic volcano and caves aside, the music is good. And loud. The dance floor could be a little bigger. Cover charge of EC $5. Open seven nights a week.

Rain. Columbus Square. Castries. Tel. 3022. The pleasant South Seas decor makes this a nice place to sit and sip some of the no-nonsense rum concoctions stirred up here. Just remember you have to get up and go home eventually. Casual atmosphere. Open seven nights a week, very late if the crowd is there for it.

St. Antoine's. Morne Fortune (overlooking Castries Harbor). Tel. 45–24660. The bar and terrace make for a delightful place for after dinner drinks and small talk. An interesting wine list and pleasant background music add to the enjoyment.

Graffity's. Castries. (No phone). Disco nightclub with minimal charge on weekends.

 POSTAGE. The General Post Office on Bridge St. in Castries is open Mon.–Fri. from 8:30 A.M. to 4:00 P.M., closed on Sat. There are branches of the post office in all main city centers and in towns and villages as well. Rates (in EC dollars) for international mail from St. Lucia are: flat letters to foreign countries, $.65 up to one ounce; postcards, $.15.

 ELECTRIC CURRENT. The electric current here is 220 volts, 50 cycles A.C. Most hotels can supply you with an adaptor, but it wouldn't be a bad idea to bring one along.

 SECURITY. Ask any St. Lucian taxi driver if Castries is safe for strolling around and he'll smile as if to say "You must be from New York." The truth of the matter is, Castries, and the rest of St. Lucia, is safe. Use common sense when walking through particularly deserted areas late at night. In this part of the world, you'll have to make a thief out of someone, so don't. If you're traveling with valuables, such as jewelry or expensive camera equipment, you'll probably feel a little better off having locked it in the hotel safe if you're going to be out for a prolonged period of time.

ST. MARTIN/SINT MAARTEN

by
CLAIRE DEVENER

This half-French (St. Martin), half-Dutch (St. Maarten) island is the smallest territory in the world to be shared by two sovereign states. It also has the world's most unobtrusive boundary—no customs inspectors, no barriers, no formalities—just two hand-painted signs proclaiming "Welkom aan de Nederlanse Kant" and "Bienvenue Partie Française." The island is marked by its "French flair" (easy-paced villages, small inns and guesthouses, and excellent cuisine) and "the Dutch touch" (flower-bedecked streets, courtyards, and alleyways; pastel-colored shops, lively resorts, nightclubs, and casinos). American visitors find all the conveniences of home here; prices are quoted in both U.S. and local currencies and the dollar is accepted everywhere; English is just about everyone's second, or even first, language. This is one island that offers something for everybody and that's why it's now the Caribbean's most popular destination.

Past and Present

Columbus is said to have discovered the island on St. Martin's Day in 1493, claimed it for Spain, named it San Martino, then sailed on having already tasted inhospitable Carib Indian receptions elsewhere. Both French and Dutch settlers arrived during the early 1630s and set about harvesting salt and raising tobacco. But Spain's King Phillip soon sent 53 ships to expel the intruders from his land. With that accomplished, he raised the price of salt, then forgot about the island and its garrison. In 1644, Peter Stuyvesant, then head of the Dutch West Indies Company in Curaçao, attacked the Spanish forces, but lost the battle as well as a leg in the skirmish. Four years later, however, the Spanish decided that the island wasn't "worth its salt" and abandoned it. According to local legend, four French and five Dutch crew members hid themselves on the island until the Spanish fleet departed, then met and decided to divide the land and live in peace. According to the oft-told story, each group picked a representative. The two were placed back to back at Oyster Pond and then set walking along the shore in opposite directions. It's said that the Frenchman walked farther and faster because of the wine he drank; while the heavier Hollander's penchant for Dutch gin slowed him down. The border remains where the walkers met at Cupecoy Bay.

Today, the French half of the island is a subprefecture of Guadeloupe. A town council is elected by the citizens of St. Martin and headed by a mayor; a subprefect acts as administrator and is appointed by the French government in Paris. The Dutch side has a parliamentary democracy and, as part of the Netherlands Antilles, is an autonomous part of the Kingdom of the Netherlands. Its seven-member island council is elected by popular vote and assists the lieutenant governor, who is appointed by the queen.

This small binational island has become a paragon of stability; a thriving, tax-free international marketplace; and a convention center with facilities for up to six hundred participants. Roads, public utilities, power supplies, and international communications continue to improve. The water problem was solved long ago by the construction of a desalinization plant. The airport is now one of the most modern as well as the second busiest in the Caribbean. Development of the island as an important financial center and location for light manufacturing is a high priority. This healthy economic, investment, and social climate has produced a thriving tourism industry that is growing at a rate of 20% yearly.

EXPLORING THE ISLAND

The entire island can be toured in three hours, but we suggest renting a car and making a day of it with a beach stop or two, and a picnic or lunch at one of the restaurants that dot the island.

The Dutch portion is the southern part of the island. Philipsburg, the diminuitive Dutch capital, strings out for a mile or so along a sand bar between Great Bay and Great Salt Pond. The latter once provided the island's main source of income, but now has been largely reclaimed for town expansion and parking. The capital has just two streets, Front and Back; the former is the main shopping thoroughfare. Forget about your car and explore by foot—preferably on a day when there are no cruise ships in port as both streets and shops strain at their seams with wall-to-wall people. Pastel-hued houses with fancy fretwork and shutters house small restaurants and fine boutiques. Alleyways, courtyards, and flowery patios often lead to more shops where you could spend more hours browsing.

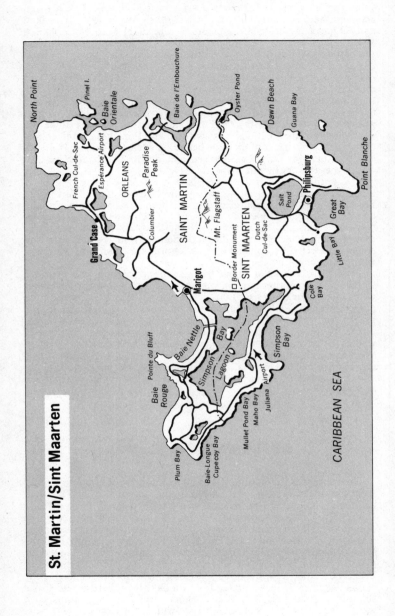

St. Martin/Sint Maarten

You might consider ordering a "Picnic Basket" ($25) in advance from Cafe Royale on Front Street. This gourmet's delight includes a bottle of wine, fresh fruit salad, half a duck or chicken, shrimp-stuffed tomatoes, croissants, a loaf of French bread, cheese, and pastries, plus cutlery, cups, and plates for two. Or choose your own makings from the Food Center at the Bush Road intersection on your way out of town—but be prepared as imported goods are expensive.

Begin your island tour from Philipsburg by heading west along Back Street. You'll pass an eighteenth-century cemetery (the island's oldest) where the grave of John Phillips overlooks the town he founded in 1733. Follow the road up to the ruins of seventeenth-century Fort Amsterdam, whose ramparts offer the first of many spectacular views. Continue west by Cay Bay Hill, where Peter Stuyvesant lost his leg while fighting the Spanish in 1644. Along the way the Caribbean panorama unfolds to display the neighboring islands of Saba, Statia, St. Barts, Anguilla, even St. Kitts and Nevis on a clear day.

Descend to Simpson Bay Lagoon. Once land-locked, this large body of water now opens to the sea by two cuts spanned by drawbridges on both sides of the border. It is a favored anchorage as well as water-sports haven. The right fork of Welfare Road winds around the lagoon's eastern shore through pleasant rolling countryside and leads to Marigot. About a mile and a half from the crossroads is the simple border market constructed by the islanders in 1948 to commemorate three hundred years of living in harmony. If you choose the left fork you'll go by Juliana Airport with popular Maho Bay Beach at the foot of the runway. Bathers here automatically hold their ears as they see the big jets approaching—happily this does not occur too frequently during the day. The road continues on via Mullet Bay and Cupecoy—resorts with nice beaches and a variety of water-sports facilities. At the French border the road becomes dirt; but a mile or so later, the pavement reappears. A small, unmarked road off to the left leads to La Samanna, the luxurious hideaway of the rich and the famous. Farther on, the white sands of Long Beach, Plum Bay, Baie Rouge, and Maho Bay, accessible down bumpy, but short, dirt roads, are perfect for swimming, picnicking, or lazing in the sun.

The road circles horseshoe-shaped Nettle Beach, crosses over a one-lane "turning" bridge, the spit of land called Sandy Ground, and then you're in Marigot, the French capital. Gingerbread houses, wrought-iron balconies, bistros, and tiny boutiques line the streets that cluster around the beautiful harbor. The busy quai is also the location of a colorful market that bustles with shoppers on Saturday mornings. Browse along the rue de la République, rue de la Liberté, and in the fabulous new Port La Royale complex by the marina. Stop in at one of the cafés overlooking the harbor for some French pastry or home-made exotic fruit sherbet. You'll find over a dozen restaurants with menus displayed for future reference. Dinner reservations at these small, popular places should be made in advance in season.

Head up the rue de la République past the *gendarmerie* and follow the signs to Grand Case. Eighteen restaurants serve not only French, but Italian, Indonesian, and Vietnamese fare, and the freshest of seafood. Dubbed the "Restaurant Capital of the Caribbean," the mile-long main street gets so clogged with traffic that there's talk of building a new road around the town to alleviate congestion and provide parking.

Past little Espérance Airport, the road loops south into a series of serpentine curves through lush green hills and past stone fences covered with coralita flowers. Orleans, also called French Quarter, is the oldest

French settlement on the island. It's a sleepy little hamlet where prominent local artist Roland Richardson makes his home. Stop by and take a look at his watercolors, which capture the island feeling.

If you're short on time, you may want to head straight down through Lower Prince's Quarter to Philipsburg, otherwise, take a roller-coaster cut-off just over the border to charming Oyster Pond Hotel for a swim or drink in their attractive bar overlooking the sea.

PRACTICAL INFORMATION FOR
ST. MARTIN/SINT MAARTEN

FACTS AND FIGURES. This two-nation island lies 144 miles east of Puerto Rico and 140 miles northwest of Guadeloupe. The total land area is 37 square miles, with the southern portion of the island, Dutch Sint Maarten, comprising 16 square miles; the northern part, French St. Martin, 21 square miles. The nine-mile distance between the Dutch capital of Philipsburg and the French capital of Marigot can be driven in about 20 minutes, and there are no border or customs formalities between the two sides. The total population is approximately 30,000. Dutch and French are the nations' respective official languages, but English is widely spoken. The terrain is irregular: salt flats in the south, rolling hills in the middle, and a high point of 1,278 ft. at Mt. Paradis farther north. The island is one hour ahead of eastern standard time. Tourism is the principal industry.

WHEN TO GO. Vacation traffic to this island has been on the upswing, not only in winter but year-round. The average temperature is 80 degrees F, annual rainfall just 45 inches. Constant cooling trade winds keep humidity at comfortable levels. In season (early December to mid-April) the island is on the expensive side; however, hotel rates and package prices drop 30–50% after Apr. 15 and some real bargains are available during the off-season.

PASSPORTS AND VISAS. U.S. citizens may stay up to three months with proof of citizenship in the form of a passport (preferably valid, but also acceptable if not more than five years expired); original birth certificate with raised seal or photocopy with notary seal; or voter's registration card. All visitors must have a confirmed room reservation and onward or return ticket. Canadian and British citizens need valid passports.

MONEY. Most prices are given in both Netherlands Antilles florins (guilders) and U.S. dollars. The exchange fluctuates slightly, but the generally accepted rate is about 1.79 NAf to $1. 3.96 NAf = 1£. Although French francs are used on the French side, U.S. dollars are good everywhere. The U.S. dollar is worth about 10 French francs. Credit cards are widely accepted on both sides of the island. Banks on the Dutch side are open from 8:00 A.M.–1:00 P.M. Mon. thru Thur. and Fri. afternoons 4:00 P.M.–5:00 P.M. French banking hours are Mon.–Fri. 8:00 A.M.–noon; 2:00 P.M.–3:30 P.M.

WHAT IT WILL COST?

A typical day on this island for two persons in season will run:

	U.S.$
Standard accommodations at a beachfront resort	$150
Breakfast at the hotel	16
Lunch and dinner at moderate restaurants	90
Tips, service charge, and hotel tax	36
One-day sightseeing by rental car	40
Total	$332

HOW TO GET THERE. By Air: Jumbo jets fly into the Dutch side's Queen Juliana Airport. *American Airlines* has nonstop flights daily from New York; direct flights from Dallas. *Pan Am* flies in daily, nonstop from New York and Miami; *Arrow* twice a week. *BWIA* now serves Toronto, Jamaica, and Trinidad. *Eastern* has service from Miami; *Prinair* from San Juan. *LIAT* flies up from Antigua; *ALM* from Aruba, Bonaire, Curaçao, and the Dominican Republic. *Air Martinique* serves Martinique with ongoing connections to southern islands. *Windward Islands Airways (Winair)*, based on St. Maarten, has daily scheduled service to Saba, St. Eustatius, St. Barts, Anguilla, St. Thomas, and St. Kitts/Nevis. *Air Guadeloupe* flies several times a day to St. Barts and Guadeloupe from l'Espérance Airport on the French side near Grand Case.

By Sea. All the major cruise lines make St. Maarten a regular stop for shopping. There is fast motorboat service several times a day to Marigot, on the French side, from the island of Anguilla.

AIRPORT TAXES AND OTHER CHARGES. All visitors pay a U.S. $5 departure tax from Juliana Airport on the Dutch side; 10 French francs from l'Espérance Airport on the French side. There is a 5% government tax on hotel rooms on the Dutch side, and a *tax de séjour* (maximum $1 per day, per person) on the French side. The latter differs according to each property. A 15% service/energy charge is added to bills by hotels on the Dutch side; a 10–15% service charge on the French side.

TELEPHONES AND EMERGENCY NUMBERS. To call directly from the U.S. to the Dutch side, dial: 011 + 599 + 5 + local number; for the French side, 011 + 596 + local number. To phone from the Dutch side to the French dial 06 + local number; 93 + local number from the French to the Dutch. Police emergency number on the Dutch side is 2222; on the French side, 87–50–10. St. Rose Hospital is located on Front St. in Philipsburg; tel. 2300. Medical emergency number on the French side is 87–50–07.

HOTELS. The larger resort properties and their casinos are all located on the Dutch side. The French side has smaller, Mediterranean-style facilities. Both sides offer a wide range of accommodations in all price ranges. We call above $300 for a double room in season *Deluxe,* $140–299 *Expensive,* $80–139 *Moderate,* and below $80 *Inexpensive.*

DUTCH SIDE

Belair Beach Hotel at Little Bay. *Expensive.* Tel. 3362/3366/3560. 72 large, well-appointed beachfront suites. Each has wall-to-wall carpeting, living and dining room, master bedroom with king-size bed and bath, small guest room with shower, 24-hour color TV, two telephones, and full kitchen with dishwasher, large refrigerator and freezer, and serve-through bar. Guests here have free use of all the facilities of next-door Little Bay Beach Hotel.

The Caravanserai. *Expensive.* Airport Rd. Tel. 2510/2511/4214. A total of 83 units that range from standard rooms facing a lovely courtyard to studios and one-bedroom apartments with balconies and patios overlooking the sea.

Built out on a peninsula at Maho Bay, this inn offers two swimming pools, water sports galore, and tennis. Its only drawback is that it is so close to the airport.

Cupecoy Beach Resort. *Expensive.* Cupecoy Bay. Tel. 4297/4333. This 322-room Mediterranean-style white stucco property offers attractively decorated, spacious one-, two- and three-bedroom suites spread out in hillside or beachside villa complexes. Those by the sea are the most desirable and the most expensive. The fabulous new piazza area should now be completed with formal gardens, gazebo, double-level shops, restaurant, and casino. Three swimming pools each with its own bar, three tennis courts, and beautiful bluff-backed beach complete the well-rounded picture. The guests here tend to be sociable, swinging, and very fashion-conscious, with a heavy repeat package-tour crowd from New York.

Little Bay Beach Hotel. *Expensive.* Little Bay. Tel. 2333/2334. Located on a mile-long white-sand beach, this is the island's oldest and one of the most popular facilities. 120 rooms face the gardens or beach and all are air conditioned and have refrigerator, 24-hour-a-day video/TV, and a balcony or terrace. There's a large freshwater pool, three tennis courts lighted for night play, windsurfing, water-skiing, and sailing. Entertainment ranges from steel bands and beachside barbecues to a piano bar, supper club, and casino. Shops, beauty salon, car rental, and excursion desk complete the list of facilities.

Mullet Bay Resort and Casino. *Expensive.* Mullet Bay. Tel. 2801. A self-contained resort with 622 condominium units spread out over 172 acres that include golf course and lagoon. A $7 million refurbishing has made this resort better than new. The double accommodations, one- and two-bedroom suites, are connected to the resort's many facilities by roving jitney. There are 16 tennis courts, the island's only golf course, 2 pools and a half-mile-long beach, 3 meeting rooms, the island's largest casino, 10 restaurants, every water sport imaginable, shopping arcade, commissary, nightly activities, disco, even a branch of Chase Manhattan Bank.

Oyster Pond. *Expensive.* Oyster Pond Beach. Tel. 2206/3206. This is a favorite for its beautiful setting and sophisticated yet low-key ambience. It's only five miles from Philipsburg, but seemingly all by itself on a peaceful peninsula on the eastern side of the island. The interesting complex of white stucco, red tile, arches, and square stone towers is flanked by two long stretches of sand that overlook the Caribbean and the sheltered harbor. 16 tastefully decorated rooms and four tower suites are built above an open courtyard; most with sea views, all have spacious secluded balconies, white wicker furnishings, and screened louvers for those who prefer sea breezes to air conditioning. There's a comfortable bar/lounge with piano music and an elegant restaurant overseen by a fine French chef. There are also two tennis courts and a complete water-sports center.

Sint Maarten Beach Club Hotel and Casino. *Expensive.* Philipsburg. Tel. 3434/3448/3454/2906. Right in the heart of town, 78 air-conditioned suites with one or two bedrooms, kitchenette, living/dining room, color cable TV, direct international dial telephone, and balconies. Well-planned accommodations attractively decorated; each with sofa bed that can easily accommodate two extra guests. Great Bay Beach is just out the front door with a complete array of water sports; shops are steps away and there's plenty of action in the hotel casino, which opens at 1:00 P.M. Lively tropical *Heartbreak* bar and café is complete with colorful cockatoos and parrots.

Dawn Beach. *Moderate to Expensive.* Oyster Pond. Tel. 2929/2991. 155 good-size rooms, some on the sea (beachside deluxe is closest to the water); others up on the hillside. Each has a combination living/bedroom with king-size bed; complete kitchenette with toaster oven, stove, and refrigerator; closed-circuit color TV, radio, and private patio. Secluded but lively with full water-sports activities, long white-sand beach, big freshwater pool with its own waterfall, two tennis courts. Thursdays there's an open bar followed by a barbecue with steel band. Brunch is popular on Sundays. Other nice touches include bus service to town twice a day, and a small commissary.

Great Bay Beach Hotel and Casino. *Moderate to Expensive.* Western end of Great Bay Beach, Philipsburg. Tel. 2446/7. This 225-room property features large, carpeted accommodations with two double beds, tub, and shower. Three restaurants, two bars, nightly entertainment, full activities program from Happy Hour to Miss Bikini Contest and bingo bashes and a casino. The beach extends a mile down to Philipsburg and there's an angular freshwater pool with town and sea views. Two tennis courts, sailing, waterskiing, jet scooters, and snorkeling complete the sports facilities. Popular with package groups.

Holland House. *Moderate.* Front St., Philipsburg. Tel. 2572. In the middle of town within walking distance of everything. The 42 rooms have a Dutch decor. All rooms are air conditioned and have kitchenettes, radio, and color TV; some face Front St., others Great Bay Beach. There's a terrace restaurant that offers full meal service; a tiny pool; water sports on the beach; a hospitality desk to organize tours, excursions, and car rentals; shops; and an excellent beauty salon. Buffets and barbecues are frequent and happy hour every day features Dutch snacks and guitar music.

Maho Reef and Beach Resort. *Moderate to Expensive.* Maho Bay. Tel. 2115/4202. A fire put everything but the *Studio Seven* disco and 34 tennis cabañas out of commission over a year ago. Plans were to reopen in late '85 with an additional 60 rooms making a total of 250. There should be a new casino, shopping arcade, and 2 to 3 restaurants to keep gamblers and fun seekers happy. Water sports of all kinds, four tennis courts, badminton, and volleyball will again be available, as well as nonstop entertainment, beach parties, barbecues, and floorshows.

Mary's Boon. *Moderate.* Simpson Bay. Tel. 4235. An informal 12-room inn on a big always-deserted beach. The rooms are enormous, furnished with bamboo and rattan pieces and a sprinkling of antiques; each has a kitchenette and seaside patio. Meals are served family style and the fare is as unusual as it is good; the bar is on the honor system so the atmosphere is like a small house party. Unfortunately near to the airport, but repeat guests assure us that you become oblivious to the jet roar very quickly in these pleasant surroundings!

Mary's Fancy. *Moderate.* Dutch Cul de Sac road, half a mile from Philipsburg. Tel. 2665. On the grounds of an 18th-century sugar plantation; four rooms in the old great house, seven cottages hidden among the five acres of tropical foliage. Formerly used as the Governor's Mansion, this imaginative, eclectic, and luxuriously decorated oasis has odds, ends, and collector's items from around the world. A large freshwater pool and beautiful gardens that are a botanist's delight make this unique inn one of the island's nicest getaway places.

Summit Resort Hotel. *Moderate.* Simpson Bay Lagoon. Tel. 2150. One- and two-story, simply constructed chalets cluster on a bluff. The 61 rooms have all been recently redecorated and fitted with new baths. Each has a sitting area and a porch or balcony that runs the full length of the chalet. The property's focal point is its large pool; a shuttle takes guests four times a day to nearby beaches down the hill. Informality is the keynote here, and manager Keith Franca does his utmost to assure personal and friendly service. The Wednesday-night buffet features cuisine from eight different islands. A steel band performs frequently and guests are shuttled to the casinos at 9:00 P.M. every evening.

Pasanggrahan Royal Beach House. *Moderate to Inexpensive.* Front St., Philipsburg. Tel. 3588. Formerly the government's guesthouse, this special, historic inn is set back from the street in a mass of greenery on Great Bay Beach. Oli and Peter DeZela keep adding antiques and the 26 rooms are improving with age; each has air conditioning, a new refrigerator, and colorful, eclectic furnishings. Good West Indian food, personal service, a relaxed and relaxing ambience. There are old bikes for exploring; a courtesy car available on a rotating basis to guests; and tea is served at 4:00 P.M. Some well-known politicians, lawyers, and many just plain folks wouldn't consider staying elsewhere.

Great Bay Marina. *Inexpensive.* Pointe Blanche. Tel. 2167. Seven balconied rooms overlook the busy marina. Each has private bath, ceiling fan, air conditioning, refrigerator, and coffee maker. Three minute walk to town and Great Bay Beach. The lively bar and restaurant is very popular with yachtsmen.

Seaview Hotel. *Inexpensive.* Front St., Philipsburg. Tel. 2323/2324. If you are an early-to-bed person you will be bothered by the music from the *Why Not Nightclub* below; if not, this hotel is an excellent buy for those who want to be in the center of town. The 45 large, cheery rooms have all been redecorated but the 12 on the patio side and four over the sea have the best views, air, and light. All are air conditioned, have private bath, and are immaculately kept.

FRENCH SIDE

La Belle Creole. *Deluxe.* Pointe du Bluff. Tel. 87–59–10. Gemtel, a California developer, plans to have this multimillion-dollar replica of a Mediterranean village ready early in 1986. It is expected to have 150 rooms, 3 beaches, meeting rooms, and gourmet restaurant, and will be managed by Conrad International, a division of the Hilton Hotel Corporation. The spectacular 300-acre property should be a real Caribbean showplace.

Happy Bay. *Deluxe.* La Baie Heureuse, just west of Grand Case. Tel: 87–55–20. The formal opening of this exclusive hilltop property was delayed by financing problems last year, but it should be fully operational for the winter season. The completed accommodations that we visited were luxuriously decorated, have enormous marble baths, three telephones in each suite, bar, radio/TV, and every other modern convenience. 20 oversized and terraced rooms extend from a center, 2-story structure that has the hotel's reception area, offices, bar, and excellent restaurant. 40 extra large one-bedroom apartments with sitting room, cluster in ten units built in a cresent around an oval-shaped pool and natural pond above the white sand beach. Beach restaurant and bar, water sports, gardens, 24-hour room service, a cook for each apartment unit and free cars for guests are just a few of the luxurious amenities planed.

La Samanna. *Deluxe.* Baie Longue. Tel 87–51–22. Exquisite, expensive, and the perfect hideaway. This beautiful, secluded property has a spectacular beach, large pool, three championship tennis courts, water sports, and a dining room that offers the finest haute cuisine on its terrace with a view. The main building has 11 air-conditioned, twin-bedded, terraced rooms; 14 two-story units are spread out along the beach or hillside and house 24 one-bedroom suites and 16 two-bedroom apartments, and there are six three-bedroom villas.

Club Orient. *Moderate to Expensive.* Baie Orientale. Tel. 87–53–85. A clothes-optional resort for naturists. On a secluded peninsula, 61 rooms are housed in wooden chalets imported from Finland. There are 25 one-bedroom accommodations, each with kitchen, living room that can sleep two, private bath, patio with picnic table, barbecue, and outside shower; and 36 studios. The beach is a mile and a half long, snorkeling is excellent, and sailing, windsurfing, and boat excursions are available. A beach bar/restaurant is open from breakfast through dinner and there's a boutique as well as a small grocery stocking basics.

Le Galion. *Moderate to Expensive.* Baie de L'Embouchure, Orleans. Tel. 87–51–77. This 54-room resort offers 26 spacious rooms with sitting area, 20 standard accommodations, and four two-bedroom beach cottages with living rooms and kitchens. There are two beaches here (one shared with Club Orient "naturists"), excellent water-sports facilities, two tennis courts and large open restaurant with a view.

Grand Case Beach Club. *Moderate to Expensive.* Grand Case. Tel. 87–51–87. This informal 76-unit condominium complex is one of the island's most efficiently run hotels as well as one of its best buys. Located at the far end of Grand Case's crescent-shaped beach, the 42 studios, 19 one-bedroom, and 15 two-bedroom suites are large, very attractively appointed, and well maintained. All have balconies or patios and fully equipped kitchens; 62 are oceanfront. A second beach, tennis, water sports of every variety, car rental, land and sea excursion facilities, a congenial bar, and a restaurant with a view are all at hand. Repeat clients here book well in advance; you should as well.

Le Grand St. Martin Hotel and Beach Resort. *Moderate to Expensive.* Marigot. Tel. 87–57–91. This 80-room complex stretches along a cove just four blocks from the harbor. 34 standard studios are in a refurbished hillside building; the 46 accommodations in a new beachfront wing include 20 superior studios; 9 one-bedroom suites; 13 two- and 4 three-bedroom apartments. Some have beamed and vaulted ceilings, others lofts; all have terrace or deck, tasteful decor, air conditioning, and fully equipped kitchens. Two restaurants, a pool bar, nightly entertainment, the island's largest freshwater pool, sailing, windsurfing, and snorkeling are among the many fine new guest facilities and recreational possibilities.

Hotel Marina Royale. *Moderate to Expensive.* Port La Royale, Marigot. Tel. 87–57–28. In a complex of condominiums, boutiques, restaurants, and a marina that's now the "heart" of Marigot. 46 studios; 15 two-room suites, and 11 three-room duplex apartments offer kitchenettes and mountain or lagoon views. Part of the international Novotel French chain, this hotel also offers a lobby bar, restaurant, swimming pool, and excursion and water-sports desks.

PLM St. Tropez. *Moderate.* Marigot. Tel. 87–54–72. This hotel needs a lot of sprucing up and in fact plans were to build 120 new 4-star rooms. But check thoroughly that work has been completed before booking in, as last year's guests had nothing but complaints about accommodations as well as service.

Petite Plage. *Moderate to Inexpensive.* Grand Case. Tel. 87–50–65. John Laurence's motel-style property at the farthest end of Grand Case Beach is always booked solid a year in advance for Dec., Jan., and Feb. The facilities, ideal for families, include 12 one- and two-bedroom apartments with comfortable but simple furnishings, shower, air conditioning, kitchenette, dining area. John's son Roger added six additional spacious, more elaborately decorated apartments. Each has a living room, kitchen, dining area, bedroom, and 30-foot balcony. Laurence Sr. closes from May through Oct. to do some traveling himself, but Laurence Jr.'s highly recommended accommodations are available throughout the year.

La Résidence. *Moderate to Inexpensive.* rue du Général De Gaulle, Marigot. Tel. 87–70–37. 21 very attractive new rooms built around a pretty patio bar and restaurant. Right in the middle of all the activity of Marigot, but this quiet little second floor oasis has a sophisticated cachet, with fountains, well soundproofed rooms, and a special charm all its own. Double rooms, studios with mezzanine loftbeds, large one-level studios and apartments with and without kitchenette are all available.

Beauséjour. *Inexpensive.* Rue de la République, Marigot. Tel. 87–52–18. Ten air-conditioned rooms with showers and refrigerators surround a second-floor courtyard. Breakfast, included in the price of your room, is served on the wrought-iron balcony overlooking Marigot's main street.

Bertine's. *Inexpensive.* Savana, Grand Case. Tel. 87–58–39. Christine and Bernard Piticha's informal guesthouse on a hill has just four simply furnished rooms and a one-bedroom apartment. Guests get together in late afternoon at the treehouse bar for cocktails and good conversation.

Hotel Palm Plaza. *Inexpensive.* Rue de la République, Marigot. Tel. 87–51–96. Upstairs in a pretty building, the 21 rooms are new, modern, compact, air-conditioned, and very comfortable. Three spacious suites (two with kitchenette, one with small refrigerator and terrace) are excellent value for a small family or those who need to set up temporary housekeeping.

 HOME AND APARTMENT RENTALS/TIME SHARING. There's a wide variety of homes, villas, condominiums, and housekeeping apartments available on both sides of the island. U.S. contacts for information on these include: *Caribbean Home Rentals,* P.O. Box 710, Palm Beach, FL 33480; *Jane Condon Corp.,* 211 E. 43rd St., New York, NY 10017; *St. Maarten Assistance Service-Homes,* 1995 New York Ave., Huntington Station, NY 11746; and *Villa Leisure,* 411 Park Ave., Scotch Plains, NJ 07076. On the island, contact *Judith Shepherd,* St. Martin Rentals, Pelican House, Beacon Hill, (tel. 4330); *Carimo,* Land Shops, Marigot (tel. 87–57–58) or *West Indies Immobilier,* La Galiotte, Port La Royale, Marigot (tel. 87–54–97). Some of the more interesting complexes include:

Beachcomber Villas: Burgeaux Bay. Tel. 4228. 24 two- and three-bedroom villas on a secluded beach.

Coral Shore. Pelican Key. Tel. 4363/3429. 17 two-bedroom, two-bath designer-decorated villas on the ocean with two swimming pools on the property.

Horny Toad. Simpson Bay Beach. Tel. 4323. Eight attractive one-bedroom apartments right on the beach near the airport.

The Jetty. Kanaalsteeg, Philipsburg. Tel. 2922/3357. 15 attractive new suites, including a penthouse for four, at the eastern end of Great Bay Beach.

ParcLagon, near Cupecoy on Simpson Bay Lagoon. Tel. 2963. Enter the 3-acre former estate property through its original wrought-iron gate. Studio and flexible one-bedroom apartments are constructed on the ground floor; one-bedroom and duplex apartments on the second story of six clusters of villas. There's a snack bar in a gazebo, pool, jacuzzi, and children's pool down by the beach and a marina. Well laid-out, this complex also offers a Japanese garden with a waterfall and plenty of space for true outdoor living.

The Town Houses. Front St., Philipsburg. Tel. 2898. 11 well-decorated two-bedroom, two-bath, villas set in a lovely garden on Great Bay Beach.

Pelican Resort and Casino. South end of Simpson Bay, 1½ miles from the airport. Tel. 4309/2503. This time-sharing complex should have 160 units completed for 1986. Clustered into nine separate living areas, each with its own pool; a marina, restaurants, and boutiques spread around 12 acres and 1,400 feet of Caribbean shoreline. Each is luxuriously furnished with complete kitchen, 24-hour satellite TV, casette tape player, and other nice touches; all have a good view. There are also two tennis courts (one lighted for night play); a snack bar for breakfast, brunch, and lunch; a convenience store; and a doctor's office. The Casino and Swiss Chalet restaurant offer nightly diversion so this is a lively place.

Sea Palace. Front Street, Philipsburg. Tel. 3108. St. Maarten's tallest building at 7 floors, this new time-sharing property will offer 30 rooms and a bar/restaurant on Great Bay.

Of special mention are **Point Petite** and **Point Piroutte,** a luxurious grouping of four very elegantly decorated, Mediterranean-style villas (one to four bedrooms), each with its own pool and dock; and 12 two- and three-bedroom deluxe villas grouped around a pool. Built on a privately owned peninsula between the Maho Reef and Mullet Bay hotels, this complex also includes a tennis court and facilities for sailing and water- and jet-skiing in the lagoon. The villas are each different, but all very private, decorated with style, and well equipped for gracious entertaining as well as living. Contact Vikii Erato locally at 4207/4332 or Villa Leisure, listed above.

HOW TO GET AROUND. Taxi rates are government regulated; authorized taxis have St. Maarten Taxi Association stickers visible. Fares are 25% higher between 10.00 P.M. and midnight; 50% higher between midnight and 6:00 A.M. The bus, which runs between 7:00 A.M. and 7:00 P.M., is one of the island's best bargains at $.85. Several buses run from Philipsburg through Cole Bay to Marigot. Service between Marigot and Grand Case is hourly. Car rentals can be booked at the airport, but must be delivered to your hotel. You can leave the car at the airport on departure. *Moped Cruising N.V.,* tel. 2330/2520 and *Rent-a-Scoot,* Marigot, tel. 87–58–56 rent mopeds at $15–18 a day including free delivery and pickup and free tank of gas. *Carters* on Bushroad (tel. 2621) or facing the airport (tel. 4251) rents mopeds, scooters, and motorcycles. *St. Maarten Sightseeing Tours* in Philipsburg (tel. 2753) offers island tours Monday through Saturday at $6 per person.

TOURIST INFORMATION SERVICES. On St. Maarten, the *Tourist Office* located on De Ruyterplein in the heart of Philipsburg, tel. 2337, is open every day but Sun. 8:00 A.M.– noon; 1:30 P.M.–5:00 P.M. The French side was planning to open an information office on the port in Marigot last summer. For sources closer to home, see the "Tourist Information Services" section in the *Facts at Your Fingertips* chapter.

SPECIAL EVENTS. Each side of the island has its own holidays, but Concordia Day (Nov. 11), with border ceremonies and island celebrations to mark the amicable agreement that divided the island in 1648 between the Dutch and French (also known as St. Maarten's Day).

Public holidays unique to the Dutch side include Carnival (last two weeks in Apr.), Coronation Day (Apr. 30); and Kingdom Day (Dec. 15). French holidays include Mardi Gras and Ash Wednesday (Feb. 11 and 12 in 1986), and Bastille Day (July 14).

TOURS. Taxis charge approximately $25 for one or two people; $7 per each additional passenger for an island tour. Daylong *excursions to Saba, Statia, Anguilla,* and *St. Barts* may be made via Winair's small island-hopping planes or the catamaran *Eagle* once a week to Saba; fast motorboat several times a day from Marigot to Anguilla; and catamaran from Phillipsburg's pier, Bobby's or Great Bay Marina to St. Barts every day but Sunday. The St. Bart's sail over can be choppy, especially if there is a good wind; queasy sailors should fortify themselves with Triptone, an excellent antiseasickness preparation that does not make you as sleepy as Dramamine.

BEACHES. The island is bordered by over ten miles of powdery white-sand beaches—30 at last count. These range from those used by resort properties with changing facilities and array of water sports available to visitors for a small fee, to hard-to-reach secret coves and long, sandy stretches at *Baie Longue, Plum Beach, Baie Rouge,* and *Friars Beach.* Topless bathing is not unusual at hotel beaches on the French side; *Orient Beach* is the only official nudist beach on the island. *Ilet Pinel,* a lovely palm-fringed, desert-island-type of place just offshore from French Cul de Sac, may be visited by making arrangements with a local fishing boat to take you out *and* pick you up. Bring your own picnic and refreshments—there are no facilities on this uninhabited cay.

PARTICIPANT SPORTS. There is a championship 18-hole **golf** course at the Mullet Bay Resort on the Dutch side. Nonguests are welcome to play when starting times are available for a $32–50 greens fee for 18 holes. Carts and clubs may be rented at the pro shop and lessons are available.

Almost every hotel has at least one **tennis** court, usually lighted for night play at a small extra charge. Mullet Bay offers 16 courts, Maho Reef, 4—both at $5/hour for guests and outsiders. Little Bay Beach Hotel has three courts; Oyster Pond, Caravanserai, Dawn Beach, and Great Bay, two each; and Summit Hotel one court—all available at no charge for guests. These courts may be too busy for outside players, but check in advance. On the French side, La Samanna has three all-weather courts, PLM St. Tropez and Le Galion have two each, and Grand Case Beach Club and Coralita each have one court; all are free for guests. Outsiders should check availability the day they wish to play.

Bicycles may be rented through Mullet Bay Resort for $10 a day.

Horseback riding is available through *Crazy Acres Riding Center* whose stables are at the Wathey Estate in Cole Bay. 3-hour trail rides are $35 and reservations are required 2 days in advance. Tel. 2503 ext. 201 or 4309 ext. 201.

Deep-sea **fishing** for albacore, bonito, dolphin, kingfish, jack, marlin, red snapper, tuna, and wahoo is excellent. Half- and full-day charters are best arranged through *Bobby's Marina* in Philipsburg.

Most hotels lend or rent masks, fins, and snorkels for **snorkeling** and some of the best places to use them on the Dutch side are: around the rocks below Fort Amsterdam off Little Bay Beach, the west end of Maho Bay, Pelican Key and the rocks near the Caravanserai Hotel, and the reefs off Dawn Beach and Oyster Pond. On the French side try Friar's Beach, the west end of Long Bay near Pointe du Canonnier, Baie Rouge, and the western shore of Green Cay, an islet off Orient Beach. **Scuba** lessons and dives may be arranged on the Dutch side through *Maho Watersports* at Mullet Bay Resort; *Watersports Unlimited,* on Great Bay Beach in front of the St. Maarten Beach Club & Casino; and *Beach Bums* at Simpson Bay; Wilson McQueen at *Under The Waves Watersports* at the Grand Case Beach Club.

An unusual and very worthwhile activity is Steve Evans' *Underwater Adventures* located on the beach at Simpson Bay. Participants, even non-swimmers, are personally conducted on an underwater walk near a fish-filled reef actually constructed by Evans himself. Specially made bronze diving helmets are used so eyeglasses may still be worn, and hair does not even get wet.

The calm waters of Simpson Bay Lagoon are perfect for **water-skiing, jet skiing,** and **windsurfing,** but these sports are available all over the island. Check your hotel's activity desk for the nearest location and up-to-date information and prices.

You can take a day-long **picnic sail** to offshore islands or secluded coves aboard the *Gabrielle,* a 45-foot ketch (tel. 2366 after 6:00 P.M.), *Gandalf,* a 61-foot schooner (tel. 2572/2088 evenings) or *Oratava,* the island's only Antillean owned and operated boat, from *Bobby's Marina* in Philipsburg; or *Pretty Penny,* 41-foot ketch (tel. 2167) from *Great Bay Marina* next door. For $50 you get wine, beer, soft drinks, a substantial lunch, the use of snorkeling equipment, and in some cases the use of an underwater camera (bring your own 110 color film). Frik's *Bluebeard II,* a catamaran moored in Marigot, sails down St. Maarten's west coast and around Anguilla's south and northwest coasts to beautiful Sandy Island, where there are some excellent coral reefs for snorkeling and sunning on the powdery white sand that Anguilla is famous for. This trip operates Mon. through Sat. and includes mixed drinks, Heineken, on-board snacks, the use of underwater cameras, and a barbecue of chicken and seafood on this treasure island. Return to Marigot is 5:30 P.M. ($50) tel. 2801 ext. 337. *Lagoon Cruises* at the same telephone number organizes sunset and moonlight sails on Simpson Bay using the catamaran *Marinaut.* The comfortable catamaran *Ninja* spends half its time in Marigot Bay, the other in Anguilla and is available for day sails, picnic cruises, and longer charters. Tel. 2592 in Anguilla or via radio from either the French or Dutch side Channel 16.

 SHOPPING. The entire island is a duty-free port, and as such has some of the Caribbean's best shopping. Credit cards are accepted everywhere and savings can be as much as 50% over U.S. prices. It is always a good idea, however, to do some previsit price comparison homework and this is especially important for New York City—area residents who are considering the purchase of cameras and electronic equipment, as Manhattan's prices are some of the world's lowest.

The shops along Front St. in Philipsburg tend to specialize in cameras and electronic items, fine jewelry and watches, Italian fashions and leather goods, European china, crystal, and silverware, and hand embroideries from China, India, and the Philipines. As you'd expect, in Marigot merchandise is marked *Made in France* and you may find a better selection as well as better prices on French perfume, cosmetics, porcelain, crystal, and resort wear.

Hours on the Dutch side are 8:30 A.M.–noon, and 2:00 P.M.–6:00 P.M.; larger shops are open on Sundays and holidays when cruise ships are in. If there is more than one cruise ship in port, shop another day; the narrow streets and smallish shops get jammed and browsing is next to impossible.

In Marigot, the shops are located along rue de la République, rue de la Liberté, and three galleries; Port Le Royal, Palais Caraibe, and Galerie Périgourdine. Hours here are 9:00 A.M.–noon or 12:30 P.M.; 2:00 P.M.–6:00 P.M.

Dutch Side

The Italians are well represented along Front St. with *Maurella Senesi* for exclusive, one-of-a-kind 18K gold jewelry, Valentino gold designs and accessories, and, for some reason, Louis Vuitton bags and luggage from Paris. *Domnis, Gucci, Maximoflorence,* and *Angelo Pretto* all display fabulous leather goods. *Elle, Bartolemei,* and *La Scala* are best for shoes. *The* place for Italian high fashion is *La Romana,* located in pretty Royal Palm Plaza. Owners Yolanda and Augusto Marini have assembled a stunning collection of creations by Armani, Bottega Veneta, Fendi, Ferre, Krizia, and Gianni Versace, among other well-known names. Shoes and accessories are also included and while not inexpensive, 30% savings are possible. This charming couple has also opened a second shop for European jewelry and watches across the street. Finally, *Leda of Venice* carries designers Missoni, Valentino, and Carrano.

Shops such as *Ashoka, Kings Electronics, Kohinoor, S. Ramchand, Rams, Sonovision,* and *Taj Mahal,* offer a fine selection of cameras, binoculars, projectors, radios, video and tape recorders, and hi-fi equipment of every imaginable Japanese make. *Alberts, Boolchands, Kohinoor,* and *New Amsterdam* are specialists in table linens imported from China, India, and Philippines, and Madeira.

Jewelry is probably St. Maarten's biggest seller. Tops for taste, quality, and selection are *Spritzer and Fuhrmann, La Romana, Oro del Sol, Milles Fleurs, Little Europe, Little Switzerland* and *Colombian Emeralds International. Spritzer and Fuhrmann, Little Switzerland,* and *Provenance Galleries* are our choices for the best in china, crystal, and other elegant gifts from Europe's leading manufacturers.

For a potpourri of local and imported handicrafts, try the *Shipwreck Shop, Coconuts* and *Around the Bend,* a fun little collector's corner in the *Sergio Moorea* boutique. The latter has some very elegant and pricey styles as well as a second Front St. store back in the Marshall's complex. *Flamingo Road,* in a pretty restored gingerbread house, stocks Newman and other French casual wear and *Java Wraps* bright batik dresses, bathing suits, pants, jackets, shorts, and lengths of fabric that can be quickly folded, wound, and turned in many different ways to create almost an entire wardrobe.

French Side

Shopping in the French capital of **Marigot** somehow seems far less frenetic and certainly less crowded. Boutiques are scattered around the streets leading down to the harbor and concentrated around the spectacular new Port La Royale marina complex. While predominantly French, the Italians have also settled in here so the variety and choice of fine quality merchandise is quite astounding.

Start your tour at two old, well-established shops; *Vendome,* where you'll find the best selection of perfumes, cosmetics, accessories, jewelry, fine wines, liqueurs, and champagnes; and *Little Switzerland,* whose tasteful gold and precious-stone jewelry, china, and crystal carry Europe's most prestigious names.

Galerie Périgourdine facing the post office is owned by the Malards, whose seaside restaurant Le Nadaillac is one of the island's best. One of their shops has some lovely things for the home, table, and kitchen; a second, always has a nice selection of designer wear for both ladies and men, including Ted Lapidus' creations.

On rue de la République, *Carat* and *Oro de Sol* proffer fine jewelry; *Samson* has some very chic styles mainly fashioned on Bali; *Guy's Record Shop* carries all the latest calypso, reggae, beguine, and soca songs; *Caribe Cellar* for wines and spirits; the jewelers *Oro de Sol; Claude Chaussures* with some pretty sandals and French evening shoes; *Roberto* for fashions; and *Pomme* for children's things.

In the Jardin Brésilien, *Camaieu Boutique* is open until midnight to offer late-night shoppers Descamps' pretty linens, exotic fabrics, pareos, and original gifts.

The most extensive variety of shops is contained in the two sections of the *Port La Royale* complex. In the older section don't miss *Fiorucci, Boa, Vertiges, O'Lala, Bettina, Marine Marine,* and *La Bastringue* for the latest fashions from the French Riviera; *El Dorado* for its unusual T-shirts; *Lipstick* where designer beauty preparations are sold at big savings over U.S. prices. *Jean Laporte Parfumeur* has lovely gifts, accessories, and jewelry as well as all shapes and sizes of his own special scents. There is also a branch here of *Etna,* the Italian ice-cream maker *extraordinaire.* The newer part of this large shopping complex has many trendy boutiques such as *Ibiza Show, Animale St. Tropez,* and *Raisonnable,* whose clothes are more avant garde than those sold in most of the other boutiques on the island. Such well-established names as *Lancel* for leathergoods and Yves St. Laurent's accessories and Variations clothing will also be found. *Linea Casa* has fascinating objects for the home as does *Mahogani.* Hours in this marina area vary somewhat but use 10 A.M.–1 P.M. and 3–7 P.M. as a general rule of thumb.

K-Dis has now taken over the Gourmet Shop and this supermarket chain is an epicurean's delight offering excellent cheese, wines and liqueurs, fun kitchen gadgets as well as heat-and-serve dishes, patés, salads, and cold cuts.

In **Grand Case** American mystery writer De Forbes has assembled "a few of a kind of attire and sundries" at her charming *Pierre Lapin,* one of this village's first boutiques. Included are Jean Boshoff's soft-sculpture, irresistibly huggable rag dolls dressed in a variety of costumes, hand-crocheted and knitted baby clothes and toy animals, hand-blocked, hand-embroidered and made-to-order clothing. In the back is a small gallery that shows the works of Robert Winkler, and the Lynn family, which include oils, watercolors, and sculpture. French artist Alexandre Minguet's atelier just up the road after the pier is also of interest.

Finally, if you find yourself in **Orleans,** do visit artist Roland Richardson's home, which is open to guests Mon.–Fri., 9:30 A.M.–1:00 P.M. His delightful watercolors and prints of island scenes come in small, medium, and large sizes, and are the perfect reminder of a delightful vacation.

 RESTAURANTS. What St. Martin/Sint Maarten lacks in sightseeing attractions is made up for by the island's fantastic selection of restaurants. Dining has become the favorite visitor pastime and topic of discussion. There are more than 150 small restaurants here, but to dine in this season's most "in" places—and they change from year to year—you must make reservations in advance. We call $40 and above *Expensive;* $25–35 *Moderate;* and under $25, *Inexpensive* for a three-course meal without wine for one person.

DUTCH SIDE

Antoines. *Expensive.* Front St., Philipsburg. Tel. 2964. Dependable Continental specialties in a small, elegant setting overlooking Great Bay. Terrace tables are best and must be reserved ahead. The menu is extensive but some favorite dishes include *gratin St. Antoine* (lobster, scallops, and grouper with a chablis-and-cream sauce, glazed with cheese), veal in port wine, and chocolate mousse pie. AE, MC, V.

Le Bec Fin. *Expensive.* Front St., Philipsburg. Tel. 2976. Part of a French gastronomic complex that operates from 6:30 A.M. until midnight. Included are La Coupole, for croissants, cakes, pastries, and homemade ice creams; a seaside terrace bar/salon, and a second-floor restaurant overlooking the sea. Fourteen tables are set with white linen and lovely Villeroy Boch flowered china, and there's soft classical music in the background. Chef Pascal Petit's award-winning cuisine features light creative dishes and large, luscious desserts. Coffee is served with both macaroons and sugared grapefruit rind. One of the island's top ten. AE.

Le Bilboquet. *Expensive.* Point Blanche. No telephone. Turn left at the VinoMar supermarket in Pointe Blanche, then take the next left up the hill. Make the trip in the daylight to sign up for a table at least 24 hours in advance. Dinner ($35 prix fixe) for a maximum of 20 guests is served in the hillside home of Bob Donn and Bill Ahlstrom. Bob is the chef and his repertoire includes about 35 imaginative recipes culled from around the world. All are listed on a board out in front along with the reservation list; each evening two five-course meals are created from these favorites. A few supplemental ($5) appetizers will also be included—if Caviar Torte Romanoff is among them, don't miss it. Food and ambience are special here. If you seek unusually interesting food in an unusual and interesting atmosphere, this is *the* place. Closed Mon. in season; no credit cards, checks, or parties of more than four.

Elizabeth's. *Expensive.* Mary's Fancy Hotel, Dutch Cul de Sac. Tel. 2665. Everything from the Minestrone Milanese to delicious breads and desserts is homemade by talented Elizabeth Reitz. Dinner is served by candlelight to just 20 guests seated in peacock chairs on the romantic side porch of this old plantation house. Glass tables are set with golden dinnerware and the $40 *prix fixe* Festa Italiana includes 5 rich and copious courses. AE, D, MC, V.

Le Gourmet. *Expensive.* Mullet Bay Hotel Casino. Tel. 2801. This pretty restaurant's menu highlights traditional French dishes with modern touches and a decidedly light hand with sauces and gravies. Dessert offerings are purely classic crepes suzettes, cherries jubilee, and an extensive pastry-cart selection. AE, D, MC, V.

Oyster Pond. *Expensive.* Oyster Pond. Tel. 2206/3206. The romantic dining room is filled with fresh flowers, has a nice sea breeze, a view, and fine French cuisine. Tables are at a premium here and hotel guests have priority so reserve well in advance. To give you some idea of the fare served at both dinner and lunch, there's fresh duck liver terrine, truffle soup, lobster with ginger butter, raspberry mousse cake, and a beautifully presented and prepared chocolate marquise. Excellent wine list as well.

DaLivio. *Moderate to Expensive.* Front St., Philipsburg. Tel. 2690. Classic Italian fare highly praised by locals as well as visitors; there's usually a long list of reservations for Livio Bergamasco's candlelit terrace and elegantly appointed dining room. Major credit cards accepted.

L'Escargot. *Moderate to Expensive.* Front St., Philipsburg. Tel. 2483. One of St. Maarten's oldest restaurants, housed in a lovely red-roofed, verandahed house filled with floor-to-ceiling memorabilia. Stick with snails (Provençale or Burgundy style, in puff pastry or mushroom caps), blinis, pineapple duck, or quail with raisin sauce—all are longstanding and dependably good menu offerings. Lunch and dinner. AE, MC, V.

Félix. *Moderate to Expensive.* Pelican Key. Tel. 5237. Right on the beach enroute to Pelican Resort, this classy little French Restaurant boasts a chef from Cannes' Palm Beach Casino in the winter season. Owners also have a second place in Cannes so cuisine here is a nice mix of tropical and provençale. Salad Félix, an unusual combo of banana, sweet potato, and avocado with a tasty sauce is excellent as are the homemade desserts. Enjoyable at lunch when you can take a swim while waiting, as well as at dinner. AE.

Le Perroquet. *Moderate to Expensive.* Airport Rd., Simpson Bay. Tel. 4339. An immediate success a week after opening last February, this pretty lagoon-side place is decorated in cool green and white with lots of plants and colorful imitation parrots providing the accents. Chef Pierre Castagne's dependably good food and the especially pleasant atmosphere keep tables busy here at both lunch and dinner. We thoroughly enjoyed his mixed seafood coulibiac and special tortellini at mid-day and heard nothing but compliments on the evening fare. Closed Monday. AE, V.

West Indian Tavern. *Moderate to Expensive.* Head of Front St., Philipsburg. Tel. 2965. A typical tropical tavern with ceiling fans, rattan furniture, and backgammon in the bar, and a very vocal parrot. The four garden terraces are always lively. Lobster—broiled, with mayonnaise, thermidor, madras, mornay, or creole style—is one popular choice, but the menu contains many unusual fish, meat, and poultry offerings. Desserts here are very special: "The best key lime pie south of Key West" and a melt-in-your-mouth cold lemon soufflé two favorites. Dinner only. AE, MC, V.

Cafe Royal. *Moderate.* Royal Palm Plaza, Front St., Philipsburg. Tel. 3443. A shady garden where breakfast, lunch, afternoon tea, and candlelit dinner are presided over by gracious René Florijim. Food here is Continental with some nice surprises, especially in the seafood and salad departments. A gourmet deli in the back of the restaurant offers fancy picnic makings and take-out dishes; catering can also be arranged.

Captain Olivers. *Moderate.* Oyster Pond. No tel. Simple seaside terrace with perfect island atmosphere and excellent French-style seafood. The restaurant is built right on the border so the dining terrace and new marina are Dutch but 6 new bungalows and pool planned for 1986 as well as cordial owner, yachtsman Olivier Lange, are French. AE, MC, V.

La Caravelle. *Moderate.* Front St., Philipsburg. Tel. 3011. New last year, this pretty little restaurant with a terrace on the water is open for dinner only. The fare is French; seafood casserole, duck à l'orange, veal dijonnaise, and frog's legs are just a few of José and Jacqueline's treats. AE, D, MC, V.

Chesterfields. *Moderate.* Great Bay Marina, Philipsburg. Tel. 3484. Popular with yachtsmen, who liven up its Mermaid Bar from sunset on. At lunch good hamburgers and salads are the bill of fare; dinner features seafood, steaks, and roast duck served on an indoor/outdoor terrace overlooking the marina and the lights of Philipsburg. AE, MC, V.

Le Pavillon. *Moderate.* Simpson Bay Village. Tel. 4254. A bit difficult to find the first time, this intimate little beachside bistro is located in a village whose main street runs parallel to the airport road. Max Petit (son of the owner of Marigot's popular Chez Max) is an accomplished chef who prepares both Creole and French dishes at dinner only. AE, MC, V.

Callaloo. *Moderate to Inexpensive.* Promenade Front St., Philipsburg. No telephone. Very popular with local residents and visitors in the know, and thus frequently a bit chaotic. Both the *Pizza Piazza* and the small air-conditioned restaurant behind the lively *Gazebo Bar* offer excellent value at both lunch and dinner. Quiche, big burgers, overstuffed sandwiches, barbecued chicken, and charbroiled steaks are the best choices here. No credit cards.

Hemingways. *Moderate to Inexpensive.* Front St., Philipsburg. Tel. 2976. Good but light French fare may be enjoyed before the popular cabaret show which takes place twice a night. This upstairs terrace and bar is open for breakfast at 7:30 A.M. and serves snacks until 2 A.M. AE.

Calypso. *Inexpensive.* Eastern end of airport in Simpson Bay. Tel. 4233. St. Maarten cooking with stuffed crab backs, Creole-style seafood, and other West Indian dishes served from 11 A.M. till midnight. No credit cards.

Asha's. *Inexpensive.* Front St., Philipsburg. No telephone. The island's only Indian restaurant is an authentic one with a diverse menu. Dishes include subtly spiced curries of chicken, lamb, veal, shrimp, lobster, and vegetable; chicken, tenderloin, and lamb chop "sizzlers"; minced beef kebab; and chicken, beef, salmon, or cottage-cheese *tikkas.* AE, MC.

Dragon Phoenix. *Inexpensive.* Back St., Philipsburg. Tel. 2967. East meets West here. An extensive selection of Cantonese, Sichuan, and Mandarin specialties, as well as U.S. steaks, chops, shrimp, and lobster. Open 11:00 A.M.–11:00 P.M.

Fandango. *Inexpensive.* Front St., Philipsburg. Tel. 3434. Coco the cockatoo and Poco the parrot greet customers at breakfast, lunch, and dinner in this pleasant "tropical rain forest" setting on the inland side of the St. Maarten Beach Hotel. A good stop for omelettes, eggs benedict, big sandwiches, burgers, and dogs during the day; steaks and seafood at dinner; and late-night Chicago-style deep-dish pizza and other snacks. AE, D, MC, V.

Pinocchio's. *Inexpensive.* Front St., Philipsburg, Tel. 2166. A lively spot for breakfast, light lunches, a happy hour, pasta, and pizzas until 2:00 A.M. There are games, contests, satellite TV tuned to all major U.S. sporting events, as well as music nightly on the harborside terrace. AE, MC, V.

Rusty Pelican. *Inexpensive.* Front St., Philipsburg. Tel. 2941. Casual spot right on the sands of Great Bay Beach next to Bobby's Marina. The "Paellacan Platter," with lobster, clams, conch, shrimp, chicken, and sausage in a spicy garlic red sauce; and "Hens and Tail," a whole roast Cornish hen and large lobster tail with melted butter and Spanish sauce are two of the more unusual offerings. The bar is lively and opens at 11:00 A.M. for some interesting eye-openers; try a Kahlua Colada, Potted Pelican, Passionate Pelican, or Melon Pelican. The action continues with live entertainment and a usually congenial group of local residents, yachtsmen, and visitors. AE.

Wajang Doll. *Inexpensive.* Front St., Philipsburg. Tel. 2687. In the garden of a pretty West Indian gingerbread house facing the sea. The specialty here is *rijsttafel*—the Indonesian rice table which offers 14 or 19 dishes in a complete dinner. The chef is from Indonesia and his recipes are authentic. Very popular and reservations are a must. AE, MC, V.

Zachary's. *Inexpensive.* Point Blanche. Tel. 2260. Barbecued ribs, chicken, pork chops, and deep fried seafood accompanied by a giant onion ring loaf; attracts a good crowd of both visitors and locals seeking typical American fare at both lunch and dinner. No credit cards.

FRENCH SIDE

L'Aventure. *Expensive.* On the port, Marigot. Tel. via La Vie en Rose 87–54–42. St. Martiner Roger Petit's fine knack of finding talented young chefs continues in this new restaurant, his third in Marigot. Chef Thierry Pultau is a Swiss in his early twenties who has already spent 4 years apprenticing in the kitchens of world-class chef Frédy Girardet. His first menu will surely change as he gets more accustomed to available produce, but his fresh salmon topped with a light mustard seed sauce and poached breast of chicken on a puree of leeks and morel mushrooms were stand-outs last winter. Open lunch except Sun. (high season only) and dinner. AE.

La Calanque. *Expensive.* Blvd. de France, Marigot. Tel. 87–50–82. Jean Claude Coquin's pretty harborside restaurant is a longstanding island favorite that celebrated its twentieth anniversary last winter. People have been coming here for the duck in banana sauce for years but the extensive menu offers a variety of other well-prepared treats every day. Lunch (except Sundays) and dinner may also be taken upstairs on the quiet airy terrace whose bar is also popular. A, MC, V.

Happy Bay. *Expensive.* La Baie Heureuse just outside Grand Case. Tel. 87–55–20. Chef Dominique Dutoya, formerly of *La Vie en Rose,* has now moved over to this elegant enclave. Newly open last spring, but we found service in the first month already impeccable and both his preparation and presentation top rate. As this new hotel gets going, the menu will certainly evolve and expand, but there's no question that Dutoya is one of the island's most talented chefs. AE, D, MC, V.

Hévéa. *Expensive.* Grand Case. Tel. 87–56–85. Sophisticated and romantic. Ten candlelit tables, fine china, crystal, silverware and linens, antique furnishings, and soft piano music. Classic cuisine and Hoa Mai's own personal style and unusual presentations make this a very special dining experience. Dinner only. AE.

La Nacelle. *Expensive.* Grand Case. Tel. 87–53–63. Charles Chevillot (of New York's La Petite Ferme) is proprietor of this small restaurant, once the village *gendarmerie* (police station). Charmingly decorated with a hot-air-balloon motif, it's now one of the island's most delightful dining places. Dinner only. Small, select menu where you can count on perfection. AE.

Le Nadaillac. *Expensive.* Galérie Périgourdine, rue d'Anguille, Marigot. Tel. 87–53–77. Chef Fernand Malard's low-key terrace on the sea offers dependably good French fare. Rich dishes from his homeland of Périgord using truffles and foie gras, as well as a marvelous bouillabaisse for two; a unique red snapper on a bed of fennel branches, flamed in Pernod; duckling with peaches; and a nice choice of meat and fish. Baked Alaska is a very special treat made from a mixture of fruit, and your after-dinner digestif will be served in a brandy snifter on a bed of ice decorated with a fresh hibiscus. Dinner only. AE.

Le Poisson d'Or. *Expensive.* Off rue d'Anguille on the sea, Marigot. Tel. 87–50–33. This attractive 15-table terrace of a restored antique stone house is under the same ownership as *La Vie en Rose* and *l'Aventure.* Island gourmets rave about chef Serge Gouloumes' home-smoked lobster, presented like a sunburst in champagne butter sauce; his medaillons of lobster in a wild mushroom sauce, scallop ravioli, chocolate "indulgence" cake with creme de menthe, and warm oranges in Grand Marnier topped with homemade strawberry sherbet. Lunch (high season only) except Sun., and dinner. Reservations imperative. AE.

Rainbow. *Expensive.* Grand Case. Tel. 87–55–80. A pretty terrace with just six booths for four overlooking the sea, and seven tables set back among lots of healthy greenery. Chic but casual and beautifully run by cordial co-owners Fleur Raad and David Hendrich, this little oasis was probably on most visitors' "must-try" restaurant list last season. Chef John Jackson, a Culinary Institute of America graduate, has a creative menu that features a daily soup such as honeydew melon, scallop chowder, or cream of salmon; a mousse du jour such as chicken, duck, salmon, snapper, or grouper; fresh pasta; and more classic main courses such as roast duckling with brandied bing-cherry sauce, veal medallions with one of seven special sauces, and steak au poivre. The presentation is attractive and wines well priced. Dinner only. Closed June–Oct. No credit cards.

La Rhumerie. *Expensive.* Colombier. No telephone. Fine Creole cooking and traditional French fare are served at lunch and dinner. Francillette Le Moine and her husband Yannick are the former owners of the popular *Chez Lolotte* in Marigot. Now they've moved to a quiet, cool little cottage in the countryside.

Francillette is from Martinique, so her specialties include crab farci, conch, boudin, accras, goat curry, smoked chicken, and crayfish Creole style; but frog's legs, snails, smoked kingfish, red snapper almondine, and duck à l'orange are also on the menu. No credit cards.

La Samanna. *Expensive.* Baie Longue. Tel. 87–51–22. Elegant yet relaxed, the exquisite restaurant of this celebrated hotel is considered by many to be the island's or even the Caribbean's finest. Chef Jean-Pierre Jury is Lyonnaise, and his extensive menu combines gastronomic Gallic fare with imaginative tropical variations. Prices reflect the fact that only the freshest and best-quality ingredients are used in his preparations. Service is attentive; the clientele chic and international. At lunch the view is island-perfect. Candlelight dinner on the tented terrace couldn't be more romantic. Reservations required at both lunch and dinner. AE, D, MC, V.

Le Santal. *Expensive.* Over the bridge just west of Marigot. Tel. 87–53–48. This villa by the sea bills itself as "an exclusive restaurant," but we found the valet parking pretentious, prices somewhat inflated, and our bouillabaisse (mostly frozen ingredients) inedible. This could have been an off night as owners were both absent, but we did receive very mixed reviews on this attractive seaside place. The view will be fine, table settings formal, decor elegant, service excellent, and the clientele very chic, however. Reservations imperative in high season. Dinner only. AE.

La Vie en Rose. *Expensive.* Blvd. de France, Marigot. Tel. 87–54–42. This pretty second-floor restaurant has become one of the island's most popular. If you want one of the small balcony tables you must request it when you make your reservations. Chef Gary Duhr is a talented Luxembourgeois whose unusual menu combinations are always a treat. Desserts are special; chocolate mousse cake with a vanilla sauce and pear shortcake are among the choices. The ground floor tea room and pastry shop serves light meals and snacks noon and night. Lunch (high season only) except Sun., and dinner nightly. AE.

Auberge Gourmande. *Moderate to Expensive.* Grand Case. No telephone. An attractive country-inn setting that is unfortunately marred by the noise and fumes from the nightly traffic jams that have developed on Grand Case's main street. Air conditioning could be one solution. Food is good here, primarily Burgundian specialties: escargots, patés, roquefort filet mignon, frog's legs, and a delicious salad of crisp greens, walnuts, cheese, onion, and ham that's big enough to share. Closed Aug., Sept., and on Wed. No credit cards.

L'Escapade. *Moderate to Expensive.* Grand Case. No telephone. A charming *case Creole* set back from the main street above the beach. Popular Ursula and Michel Bootz two cozy dining rooms have a capacity of just 36. Service is careful and the ambience convivial. Among the house specialties are vegetable terrine, frog's legs soup with lettuce, red snapper with cucumber, sweetbreads with shrimp, and chicken in wine vinegar. Seaside terrace for before- or after-dinner drinks under the stars. Dinner only. No credit cards.

Sebastiano. *Moderate to Expensive.* Grand Case. Tel. 87–51–87 via Grand Case Beach Club. On the seaside at the town's southern outskirts, this modern dining room serves Northern Italian food at its best. Christine and Claudio Gati prepare their pasta fresh daily; their *osso buco primavera* is a nice change of pace; and contented customers keep this place as lively as it is popular. AE.

Le Tastevin. *Moderate to Expensive.* Grand Case. Tel. 87–55–45. Daniel and Martine Passerie of *Auberge Gourmande* opened this, their second Grand Case place last winter. Food is still classic Burgundian with a lighter touch, but the ambiance of the pretty seaside terrace is far more pleasant. The wine list offers over sixty choices, servings are more than generous, and it's difficult to get a table at dinner in season. Open also for lunch. No credit cards.

Waves. *Moderate to Expensive.* Grand Case Beach Club, Grand Case. Tel. 87–53–90. U.S.-style charcoal-broiled steaks, fish, and lobster prepared on an open grill, Italian specialties, and Long Island duckling, all served in a spectacular setting. Built out on a promontory between two curves of white-sand beach, the spacious dining room offers the best view during the day. AE, MC, V.

Les Alizées. *Moderate.* rue de Hollande, Marigot. No tel. A nice selection of Vietnamese specialties served in a quiet, pretty garden behind a typical St. Martin cottage. AE.

Bistrot Nu. *Moderate.* Rue de Hollande, Marigot. No telephone. Look for the sign pointing down a narrow lane across from the public school. Casual, friendly, and patronized by local residents and visitors in the know, this late-night spot serves fish soup, snails, pizza, and seafood until 2 A.M. No credit cards.

Chez Bach Lien. *Moderate.* Waterfront, Port La Royale. Tel. 87–57–74. Bach Lien is a tiny, dynamic bundle of energy who recently moved from her popular restaurant in Guadeloupe to introduce St. Martin visitors to authentic Vietnamese cooking. Her husband André is a true Gallic charmer and together they have created a marina-side restaurant. Open now for both lunch and dinner, but breakfast Oriental style may also be added for 1986. For something unusual, we highly recommend this. AE.

Le Boucanier. *Moderate.* Rue d'Anguille. Tel. 87–59–83. Hidden down an alleyway opposite the post office, this 60-seat terrace restaurant on Marigot Harbor was recently taken over by Canadian Yvonne Remington. Her specialties at lunch and dinner include herbed rack of lamb, duckling in cider-vinegar sauce, frog's legs and veal marengo. Enjoy a game of darts, backgammon, or chess in the garden bar. AE, MC, V.

Cas' Anny. *Moderate.* Rue d'Anguille. Tel. 87–53–38. You'll still see a sign that says Chez Lolotte, but Anne-Marie Boissard has now taken over this seaside terrace restaurant. Creole cooking is her specialty but you'll find typical French fare listed as well. AE, MC, V.

Chateau Charron. *Moderate.* Le Grand St. Martin Hotel, Marigot. Tel. 87–57 –91. This popular hotel's new gastronomic restaurant offers an extensive menu that includes homemade pasta; a ragout of snails with pecans; boneless duck with pears, apples, and kiwis; and charcoal-grilled sirloin, porterhouse, and filet mignon. Open for dinner only, this small, rather sophisticated dining room is decorated like a French country inn. AE, MC, V.

Chez Martine. *Moderate.* Grand Case. Tel. 87–51–59. You dine on the gingerbread-trimmed terrace of this small guesthouse. Charming, homey decor and a dozen or so main courses at lunch and dinner. Quiet and romantic with a nice view of Grand Case Beach. AE, MC, V.

Davids. *Moderate.* Rue d'Anguille, Marigot. Tel. 87–51–58. It's owned by two English yachtsmen named David. The decor is decidedly nautical. This casual, fun place has a lively happy hour from 6:00–7:00 P.M. every evening. The menu is varied—everything from conch fritters, potato skins, and escargots to burgers, wienerschnitzel, steaks, and seafood. Beef Wellington is the house specialty. Open lunch and dinner. AE, MC, V.

Hoa Mai. *Moderate.* Grand Case. No telephone. The best buy here is a $20 dinner that includes Vietnamese or Chinese soup, nems (a special egg roll prepared with chicken, mint, and lettuce leaves), and an assortment of six meat, seafood, and vegetable dishes. Reserve by signing the list posted on the door every afternoon. Dinner only. AE.

Java. *Moderate.* Grand Case. Tel. 87–52–55. Set back from the street at the far end of town, this pretty garden is shaded by coconut palms. Dinners is served from 6:30 P.M.–10:30 P.M. daily and features a 16-course Indonesian rice table *(rijsttafel)* ($20) as well as Creole specialties à la carte. Closed May–Nov. AE.

La Maison Sur Le Port. *Moderate.* On the waterfront, Marigot. Tel. 87–56–38. Christian Verdeau's spacious 18-table terrace in one of Marigot's oldest Creole houses looks out through palm fronds to the port. At sunset the whole place has a kind of rosy glow about it—it's the perfect setting for a memorable St. Martin "sundowner." Lunch is served until 3:00 P.M.: six multi-ingredient salads good for sharing, omelettes, seafood, and meat dishes are among the choices. Dinner is more elaborate, with curried shrimp in puff pastry, filet mignon with foie gras mousse and wild mushrooms, duckling in a brandy or wine sauce, and lobster with caviar. Closed Wednesday in the off-season. AE.

Mini Club. *Moderate.* Rue d'Anguille, Marigot. Tel. 87–50–69. One of the island's oldest restaurants, with a popular upstairs terrace built in the palms. Nice for lunch but the best buy is the bountiful 30-dish buffet that takes place on Wed. and Sat. There's a splendid selection of salads, U.S. beef, roast pork, and lamb, fish, lobster, suckling pig, cheese, and desserts—all for U.S. $30 a person, with wine. AE.

La Rose des Vents. *Moderate.* Grand Case. No telephone. Paul Faure is St. Martin's most accomplished *glacier* (ice-cream maker), known especially for his flower-flavored sherbets. Twenty exotic flavors are available in his new restaurant, which also serves good French cuisine, lobster, steaks, and seafood. No credit cards.

Gianni's. *Moderate to Inexpensive.* Grand Case. No telephone. A cozy little "spaghetteria" with a dozen tables in a black-and-white cottage. The menu lists *penne,* fettuccine, lasagne, veal, fish, chicken, even T-bone steak and filets—all done Florentine style. Desserts are rich and very Italian. Dinner only. AE, MC, V.

Le Ponton. *Moderate to Inexpensive.* Over the Marigot bridge. No telephone. On the water just 20 tables but a 10-page menu. Casual and relaxed atmosphere with a terrace strung with hammocks. No credit cards.

Brasserie Lafayette. *Inexpensive.* Port La Royale. No tel. Eleven tables on a shady terrace facing the marina. The small lunch and dinner menu is simple but well prepared and is popular with U.S. visitors. AE.

Cafe de Paris. *Inexpensive.* Port La Royale. Tel. 87–58–70. Another popular terrace facing the boats at anchor. Typically French fare with an extensive menu and always some unusual daily specialties noon and night. AE.

Chez Max. *Inexpensive.* Rue Felix Eboué, Marigot. No telephone. The decor is eccentric and thrown together; formica tables and an active bar. Food is pure unadulterated island Creole with a bowl of spicy-hot Bello pepper and piquant vinegar on each table to add if you dare. No credit cards.

Mark's Place. *Inexpensive.* French Cul de Sac. No telephone. Very informal and very popular at both lunch and dinner with local residents and visitors. Creole, seafood, and French specialties change daily and are marked on the blackboard; there are à la carte selections as well. No credit cards.

NIGHT LIFE AND BARS. Most of what goes on in the evening centers on the casinos and hotel entertainment. *Hemingways* on Front Street in Philipsburg offers an unusual cabaret show in the style of La Cage aux Folles twice a night. Cleverly done by two talented female impersonators. There are a few discos for late-nighters, including *The Hillside Club* at Mullet Bay Resort. *Studio Seven* at the Maho Beach Hotel. *Flirt* on Front St. in Philipsburg draws more of a young, local crowd. The *Whynot,* a cocktail lounge attached to the Seaview Hotel's Rouge et Noir Casino on Front St. in Philipsburg, has a pianist, band, and singer every night except Mon. The *Heartbreak* at the St. Maarten Beach Club and the bar at *Callaloo,* both on Front St. in Philipsburg, are popular gathering places for local residents and visitors at happy hour and later on after dinner.

On the French side, the *Jardin Brésilien* on Marigot's rue de la République draws a good late-night crowd with its live Brazilian music; *Le Caveau Champenois* next to the Marina Royale Hotel has excellent vintage champagnes to buy as well as try and can be lively late some evenings. The elegant bar of *La Résidence* (near the K-Dis supermarket) draws an attractive international crowd and you can always talk Clément, the gregarious bartender, into a good game of backgammon.

CASINOS. All casinos are on the Dutch side; they are located at the *Great Bay Beach Hotel, Little Bay Beach Hotel, Maho Beach Hotel, Pelican Resort, Mullet Bay Hotel, Seaview Hotel,* and *St. Maarten Beach Club. Cupecoy Beach Hotel* planned to open the island's eighth casino for the 1986 season. All are Las Vegas–style, with craps, blackjack, roulette, and slot machines. You must be 18 years of age to gamble.

POSTAGE. From the Dutch side letters to the U.S. and Canada cost NAf 1.30; NAf .60 for postcards. From the French side postcards need 2.60F; letters up to 20 grams, 3.60F.

ELECTRIC CURRENT. Like the States, the Dutch side uses 110 volts, 60 cycles; but the French side uses 220 volts, 50 cycles, making transformers and French plug converters necessary for those staying on this side. The best solution is to travel with dual-voltage hair dryers, electric razors, irons, etc.

 SECURITY. There is no "wrong" part of the island on either side or in either capital. Few people lock cars and some even leave houses open; but it's always better to follow the same precautions that you would follow at home. Use the safety-deposit boxes provided by your hotel and don't leave valuables unattended anywhere.

ST. VINCENT AND THE GRENADINES

by
BRIAN HICKEY

St. Vincent and the Grenadines are among the last of the world's secret places. St. Vincent, with a population of about 117,000 is a roughly oval-shaped island eighteen miles long and eleven miles wide. It is marked by thickly cultivated valleys and mountainsides and, in the northernmost third, La Soufriere, an active volcano which last erupted on Friday, the 13th of April, 1979. St. Vincent was nicknamed "The Breadfruit Isle" after Captain Bligh brought the tree to St. Vincent from Tahiti, following the mutiny on the *Bounty.*

To the south of St. Vincent lie the Grenadines, a string of thirty-two islands and cays resting like lush green gems in settings of soft, coral sand.

Past and Present

St. Vincent's history dates back to at least 4300 B.C., when it is believed the Cibone Indians lived on the islands, before moving to Cuba and Haiti where the last of them were found by the Spaniards in the early 1500s. The island was then inhabited by the Arawaks. By the early 1500s, the bellicose Caribs had defeated the comparatively docile

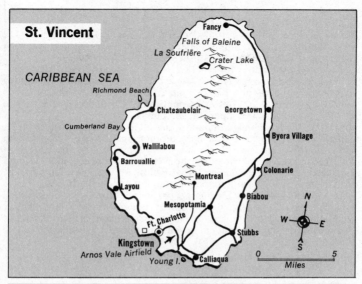

St. Vincent

Fancy
Falls of Baleine
La Soufrière
Crater Lake

CARIBBEAN SEA

Richmond Beach
Chateaubelair
Georgetown
Cumberland Bay
Byera Village
Wallilabou
Barrouallie
Colonarie
Layou
Montreal
Biabou
Mesopotamia
Ft. Charlotte
Stubbs
Kingstown
Arnos Vale Airfield
Young I.
Calliaqua

N
W E
S

0   5
Miles

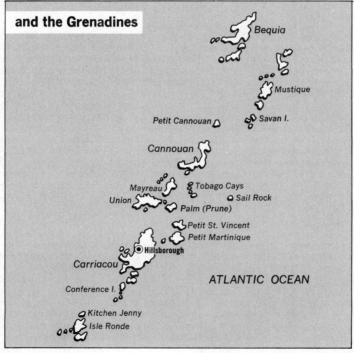

and the Grenadines

Bequia

Mustique

Savan I.

Petit Cannouan

Cannouan

Mayreau
Tobago Cays
Union
Sail Rock
Palm (Prune)

Petit St. Vincent
Petit Martinique

Hillsborough

Carriacou

ATLANTIC OCEAN

Conference I.

Kitchen Jenny
Isle Ronde

Arawaks and taken over St. Vincent. The Caribs retained possession of the island until around 1627.

The African influence in St. Vincent is considerable as well. Black slaves, brought to the islands to harvest sugar cane, intermarried with the Caribs. Their descendants now inhabit St. Vincent.

Recent controversy over whether Columbus did in fact "discover" St. Vincent on January 22, 1498 has led to the suspension of Columbus Day there while history is re-examined. It is expected that Columbus Day will be reinstated, but in recognition of Columbus's first voyage in 1492, when he came upon the Bahamas.

St. Vincent has changed hands some fifteen times, starting with its being declared a neutral island by French and British agreement in 1748. Ceded to the British in 1763, it was captured by the French in 1779, restored to the British by the Treaty of Versailles in 1783, and gained full independence from Great Britain on October 27, 1979. The British influence is still apparent throughout the islands.

In July 1984, the New Democrats party under James "Son" Mitchell replaced the Labor Party government under Milton Cato. (Today Mitchell, with his wife Pat, manages Frangipani on the island of Bequia.) The island's political scene has remained essentially stable throughout this period.

EXPLORING ST. VINCENT

The nucleus of activity on St. Vincent is Kingstown, the island's capital and cruise port, located in the southeastern end of the island about two miles from Arnos Vale Airport. Most of the hotels and good beaches on St. Vincent are concentrated in the southern end of the island as well. St. Vincent's volcanic origins have endowed it with a ring of black-sand beaches with light sand in the south. The placid west or leeward coast is well-suited to swimming, snorkeling, and other water sports. The exposed Atlantic or windward coast offers dramatic vistas, though the water is considered too rough for anyone but very experienced swimmers. Of St. Vincent's 400 miles of roads, only about 200 miles are paved and these run mainly along the island's edge.

The interior of the island is mountainous and heavily cultivated. The northern end of the island is dominated by the volcano La Soufriere (French for "sulphur mine"), the top of which is just visible under a ghost of clouds.

Kingstown

Kingstown, with a population of about 10,000, is St. Vincent's central business district and a busy harbor for cruise ships and commercial vessels. Bananas are the leading export, followed by other agricultural and industrial goods. Boat-building is also practiced on the Kingstown waterfront. The design of locally used motor launches is virtually identical to that of the earliest canoes of the Arawaks.

Kingstown is small enough to see in half a day. Getting to town, and just about anywhere on the island, is easy using the steady stream of mini-buses continually buzzing down the road. The mini-buses, with brightly colored names such as "Uncle D" and "Sweet Dreams" stenciled on the front, cost EC $1 per person regardless of destination.

If you want to see the island through the eyes of an islander, ask your hotel to recommend a driver. Failing that, you'll be met by a swarm of taxis when you arrive at Arnos Vale Airport. Just look for the Taxi Drivers' Association decal on the windshield and look forward to a stimulating, informed tour. You can also rent a car for about U.S. $35 per day. Most car-rental companies provide the first fifty miles free.

Kingstown's three principal streets are Back, Middle, and Bay streets. The fish market on Bay Street is a hectic, lively place, particularly on Saturdays. Get there by 11:00 A.M. to watch itinerant fishermen and local merchants hawk their goods. Kingstown offers twelve blocks of shops featuring local crafts, cameras, Swiss watches and clocks, perfumes, crystal and bone china, gold and silver jewelry, and brilliant local cotton batiks. The St. Vincent Craftsmen Center, in the northwest end of Kingstown, sells grass floor mats, baskets, macrame, black coral pendants and bracelets, leather sandals, locally made silver jewelry, and other useful and attractive items.

Follow Back Street west past the Fish Net restaurant and the Methodist Church and look for St. George's Cathedral, an Anglican church built in the early nineteenth century. Walk inside and notice the simple wooden pews and ornate candelabra hanging over the center aisle, the stained-glass windows and proud Georgian architecture.

Just across the street is St. Mary's Roman Catholic Cathedral, started in 1823, enlarged in 1877 and 1891, and again renovated in the early '30s. The result, so far, is a weirdly appealing blend of Moorish, Georgian, Romanesque, and other architectural styles. The cathedral can be explored with the permission of the priests in charge.

Kingstown is also a good point from which to visit nearby Fort Charlotte, situated 636 feet above sea level on a promonotory overlooking Kingstown and the Grenadines to the south and Lowman's Beach and the placid east coast to the north. Completed in 1806, the fort still has three of its cannons in place, though the only action ever seen there was the assassination in 1824 of Major John Champion of the Royal Scots Fusiliers by a sentry. In later years, Fort Charlotte was used to house paupers, lepers, and "sufferers from the yaws" (a contagious skin disease associated with syphilis).

All of this is prelude to St. Vincent's chief attraction, the Botanic Gardens, east of Fort Charlotte in northern Kingstown. Founded in 1765, the Botanic Gardens are the oldest in the Western Hemisphere. Friendly, well-informed guides will show you a wondrous collection of exotic flowers, plants, and trees, including a descendant of the original breadfruit tree brought by Captain Bligh in 1793. A full tour takes about an hour and is a must.

There are plenty of climbing and hiking opportunities for the explorer. Dorsetshire Hill, about three miles from Kingstown, affords a sweeping view of the city and harbor. Picturesque Queen's Drive is nearby. Mount St. Andrew, on the outskirts of the city, makes for a pleasant climb on a well-marked trail through a rain forest. La Soufriere is approached by way of the windward coast.

The Leeward Coast

Heading north on the narrow, winding leeward coast road you'll soon come to the rustic town of Layou, one of many small, bustling fishing villages that swing into motion each morning as the sun leaks into the untroubled Caribbean sky.

Here villagers can take you to one of several petroglyphs carved by Carib Indians over thirteen centuries ago. Further north is Barrouallie, a base for local whaling. The adventurous may wish to press further north to the Falls of Baleine. You have to take a boat to get there, but it's worth it to see the beautiful sixty-foot cascade of the falls. A trip this far consumes a whole day. You'll want to bring a picnic lunch and get an early start.

The Windward Coast

The gentle bays and relaxing beaches of the leeward coast have a perfect complement in the gray, wave-lashed windward coast. Here St. Vincent lies exposed to the churn of the Atlantic. The scenery may even remind you of the British Isles or the coast of New England.

Take a drive through Belvedere to the government-owned radio station at the top of the hill. The view here is inspiring. Tobacco grows at the foot of the hill, and beyond it corn and sweet potato sweep into the tree-lined coast and the restless Atlantic—with a view of an unnamed islet offshore.

Marriqua Valley

Just south of the Argyle, take the Yambou Pass (or Frenchman's Pass) through the Marriaqua Valley into Mesopotamia, a region of dense forests, freshwater streams and heavy cultivation. Some 300 miles of interior roads are under construction so getting around isn't very tricky. Here farmers grow coconut, dasheen, sweet corn, peanuts, arrowroot (St. Vincent is the world's leading producer of the starch-filled plant), and bananas on hillsides whose volcanic soil is so fertile that the dark ground seems to hiss with richness. The nearby Montreal Gardens perfume the air with the aromas of cocoa and nutmeg.

Once you leave the Marriaqua Valley you can follow the Eastern Highway up the jagged coast road in the direction of Georgetown, St. Vincent's second-largest city (twenty-two miles from Kingstown). On the way you'll pass through Argyle and various small, rambling towns —really just large villages. The soil appears blacker as the road continues north—in La Soufriere's last eruption homes and the surrounding land were blackened by volcanic dust.

The road out of Colonarie includes one and a half miles of straight roadway—the longest uncurving stretch of road on the island.

Watch on the right for Ferdie's Foot Steps Restaurant and Bar. It's a great place to stop for a sandwich and Ferdie's special peanut punch. It's delicious.

Continue through Georgetown past coconut groves, through long, broad tines of elephant grass straining over the roadside, and past the Mount Bentinck Sugar Factory on your left. Pretty soon you'll reach Langley Park and Rabacca Dry River, a rocky gulch carved out by the lava flow from the 1902 eruption of La Soufriere.

La Soufriere

Hearty types regularly climbed La Soufriere until April of 1979, when the volcano blew its stack—spewing steam 20,000 feet into the air and chasing some 17,000 people from their homes.

The last activity before that was in 1972, when a mild eruption produced a 324-foot-long island of lava rock called Crater Lake. A major eruption in 1902 killed 2,000 people.

A climb up La Soufriere can be arranged through your hotel. This is definitely a full day's journey and you'll want to allow a couple of days for arrangements to be made. If you do go, you'll be taking a four-wheel-drive vehicle past Rabacca Dry River and through the Bamboo Forest. From there it's a two-hour hike to the summit—4,048 feet, or three-fourths of a mile high.

North of La Soufriere

Once you've reached this neck of the woods, you may want to stop in for an afternoon cooler at Waterloo House, a converted plantation house built in 1935. The estate is called Orange Hill Plantation, and its 2,800 square miles are covered with bananas, coconuts, eggplants, tobacco, mangos, lime trees, and sweet potatoes. From here it's an eleven-mile ride—via four-wheel drive vehicle—to Fancy, the remote town at the northernmost tip of the island. The beach at Fancy isn't the greatest but its location makes it a nice, quiet spot for a picnic. The playground equipment is a gift to the local children from an American businessman.

EXPLORING THE GRENADINES

The thirty-two islands and cays that make up the Grenadines have long been considered some of the Caribbean's most beautiful. "Informal" is the key word here and you can expect to mingle with an eclectic crowd—Londoners on holiday, travelers mixing business with pleasure, members of the yachting set. In fact, a growing number of amateur sailors are chartering crewed or bare boats for a week of sunning and bobbing in the crystal-clear waters of the Grenadines.

Chartering a yacht is one way of seeing the Grenadines. Contact CSY Marina. Ferry and commercial vessels leave St. Vincent for the Grenadines on regular schedules. Three ferry boats, the *M.V. Grenadines Star, My Edwina,* and *Friendship Rose,* sail on a regular basis from Kingstown, though you may have to share your passage with a tractor and several cases of beer. You can simply arrive at the dock in Kingstown from 6 A.M. to 8:00 A.M. and book passage at the last minute. This is definitely a dress-down affair and you'll want to travel light if you're only making a day trip or short visit to the islands. If you're staying on one of the Grenadines, arrangements will have been made for you to fly to an airstrip on or near your island. Mustique, Canouan, Union, and Palm islands each have airstrips.

Young Island

Young Island, site of Young Island Resort, is considered an elite extension of St. Vincent as well as an island in its own right. Young Island is a thirty-five-acre woody atoll located two hundred yards from St. Vincent, and is accessible from the mainland via a small motor launch. Perched in the thatch-roofed bar sipping a tropical aperitif, you can watch the fragile light of sunset on the lush hills of St. Vincent. You may be treated to the sounds of a local group of musicians—the music of the Windward Islands is an enchanting blend of calypso and reggae —who perform regularly at the resort.

Bequia

When you talk about the Grenadines, you're really speaking of the chain of islands starting with Bequia (pronounced BECK-wee), nine miles from St. Vincent or about an hour's sail. Bequia, the largest of the Grenadines, has about 5,000 residents on its seven square miles. The harbor town is Port Elizabeth, situated on Admiralty Bay.

Unless you're staying at one of the hotels on the island, make sure your first stop is the Tourist Information Center, located right at the port. There you can get any local information you need, as well as hire a driver to take you around the island for the afternoon.

Port Elizabeth is charming and bustling—in its own laid-back way. Along the beach in town you can watch boat builders at work using the same techniques their great-grandfathers used. Whaling is still practiced here; March through June is the season. Locals head out in small boats using hand-held harpoons and the catch is brought to Petit Nevis to be sectioned. Princess Margaret Beach is worth a visit. There's a trail, but save yourself considerable effort and go by dinghy. On the other side of the island is Friendship Bay, where Captain Kydd is said to have laid in wait during the corsair's heyday. (Today, there are several families on the island with the Kydd surname.)

There are also boutiques and shops selling batiks and other gift items. Lulley's Bequia at Front Street sells gifts as well as diving, boating, and fishing supplies; Noah's Arkade sells woodcarvings and swim and resort wear; and Crab Hole, run by Carolyn Porter, sells locally designed hand-screened fabrics.

On the other side of the island from Port Elizabeth are Paget, a small whaling town, and Industry Estates, where you can have lunch. The Whaleboner is a nice place to grab a bite, as is Mac's Bake Shop and Pizzeria. Moonhole is an exotic, extraordinary private community built into the cliffs along the southern coast. You can get a sweeping view of St. Vincent and the Grenadines from atop "the mountain," an eight-hundred-foot peak reached by way of a foot trail. Of course, there's superb snorkeling and swimming and, with a little diligence, you can arrange a sail on one of several charter yachts. Contact CSY Marina in St. Vincent.

Mustique

An hour-and-a-half sail from Bequia, the next principal landfall is Mustique (whose name comes from the French word for mosquito). Mustique, fifteen miles south of St. Vincent, has a small airstrip that accommodates charter flights from St. Vincent and Barbados. Scheduled flights on Mustique Airways and inter-island ferries make Mustique very accessible. More arid and less lush than Bequia and some of the other islands, Mustique has nevertheless become famous over the years because of the celebrities who have homes there: Princess Margaret, Mick Jagger (whose private beach is disappearing as fans continue to snatch jars of sand for souvenirs), Raquel Welch, Cheryl Tiegs, and Kenny Rogers just for starters. Cotton House is the only resort on the island, though Charlie Tennant, son of Colin Tennant, who originally owned the island, now operates a small guesthouse on the island. Visitors can radio ahead for dinner at Cotton House.

The anchorage at Mustique is not very well sheltered, so an overnight aboard a boat can be a rocky experience. The island offers isolated sandy coves and two appealing beaches, Macaroni and the Lagoon. There's good snorkeling along a reef just offshore. The wreck of the *French Angilles* lies on the north reef of the island where it ran aground in 1971. Don't be surprised if you happen upon a model shoot at the beach for *Italian Bazaar* or some other fashion magazine.

A visit to Mustique would not be complete without a stop at the breezy Basil's Beach Bar, the thatch-roofed party place on the water in the harbor. As usual, you can radio ahead for dinner reservations. Proprietor Basil Charles is a gregarious Vincentian who, when he isn't traveling between the islands or house-sitting for "Mick," is usually on hand to join in the tropical revelry. Check out Batik Carib, next door to Basil's, for attractive souvenir shirts and colorful resort wear. There's also a small boutique at Cotton House.

There's a well-stocked general store (which Basil runs) that has an assortment of boating supplies and food which may come in handy for the three-hour sail to Canouan.

Canouan

Canouan, popular with the yachting set, has an airstrip and a superb anchorage in Grand Bay. Crystal Sands Beach Hotel and Canouan Beach Hotel are the two hotels on the three-and-a-half by one-and-a-quarter-mile island. As do establishments on the other Grenadines, both will welcome you for an afternoon bite or a cooling drink at the bar. Credit cards aren't accepted on the island. Camping is permitted and the island is surrounded by some outstanding beaches for swimming, particularly in Grand Bay. There's a local "disco" in the works, Michelle's and Roland's, which should be open as a guesthouse by 1986. If you need to stock up on a few things, there are local shops. If you want to be alone, this is the place for it.

Tobago Cays

Just south of Canouan and east of Mayreau, uninhabited and accessible only by charter boat, the lonely and beautiful Tobago Cays (pronounced "keys") hold a rich reward for anyone who dons a snorkel, mask, and fins. Ringed with reefs of astounding variety, the Cays offer some of the best hard and soft coral formations you'll find outside of the Pacific Ocean. Even if you're not a die-hard snorkeler, it's worth the trouble to see this underwater city. (Try to time your visit to coincide with low tide, otherwise the tug of the current is a little distracting.) Take a picnic lunch ashore to one of the pristine, desolate islets and spend an afternoon beyond the reach of time and troubles.

Mayreau

Paradise continues at Mayreau, a half-hour sail from the Cays. This small island (one-and-a-half square miles), is privately owned and sparsely populated (about 150 locals). Mayreau is reached by ferry from Kingstown on Monday and Thursday mornings and on Tuesday and Friday mornings from Union Island. You can also fly to Union and hire a boat (it's a thirty-minute ride) or, if you're a guest at Salt Whistle Bay Resort, proprietors Tom and Undina Potter will arrange to have you brought over by private launch.

Salt Whistle Bay is one of the smoothest anchorages in the Grenadines, and is ideal for swimming. There's good snorkeling on the Atlantic side of the island. The resort's amenities ensure a fine, relaxed time, though Tom Potter is fond of saying, "If you want absolutely nothing, come here."

Union

Union Island, considered the "Gateway Island" of the Grenadines, is a port of entry for St. Vincent, so you'll be required to go through customs upon arrival. You can reach Union, one of the southernmost Grenadines, by air, or by charter or cargo boat. Clifton Harbor is the main town; tiny Ashton is on the other side of the island. Union's distinguishing characteristic is Mount Parnassus, a nine-hundred-foot peak which is a landmark for yachters for miles around. A well-known port of call for yachts, the 2,100-acre island has clean sandy beaches.

There are three places to stay on the island, or where you can stop for lunch or refreshments. Accommodations are basic island informal.

Palm

Palm Island is not really Palm Island. It's Prune Island—but one visit here and you'll see why it was unofficially renamed and the 110-acre island has a history as romantic as the island is beautiful.

The best way to get to the island is by boat, but you can also fly to Union and have Palm Island Resort pick you up for the five-minute boat ride. Yachters usually spend the day playing on Palm, then head over to Union, where the anchorage is far smoother, for the night.

Palm Island Resort was the brainchild of John and Mary Caldwell, whose story has become enshrined in local island lore. (Treat yourself to a copy of John's book, *Desperate Voyage* in the boutique.) After an ordinary family life in California, the two set off on a world cruise aboard the *Outward Bound,* a cutter of their own design. They found Palm Island when it was a swamp-infested, mango-covered island. Seventeen years and 8,000 palm trees later, Palm Island glistens as a refreshing, easygoing resort catering to young and old. Swimming is superb, there are some interesting coral reefs just offshore around the bend from the dive shop, and scuba devotees can dive at a nearby wreck.

Petit St. Vincent (PSV)

From Palm (or Prune, you decide) it's an hour-and-a-half sail to PSV, where celebrities such as TV newsman Harry Reasoner go to get away from it all. You can also reach PSV by flying to Union and boating over from there. If you're staying on the island, the PSV resort will pick you up at Union. If you're just passing through, the beaches are, naturally, exquisite and there are several coral reefs to explore on the windward side. There's also a jogging path winding through picturesque woods. PSV is the sole resort on the island.

PRACTICAL INFORMATION FOR ST. VINCENT
AND THE GRENADINES

FACTS AND FIGURES. St. Vincent, roughly 18 miles long and 11 miles wide with an area of 133 square miles, is located 100 miles west of Barbados, 21 miles south of St. Lucia, and 75 miles north of Grenada. The population of St. Vincent is approximately 117,000. The interior is mountainous and thickly cultivated with banana and coconut plantations and other crops. Bananas are St. Vincent's leading export. The northern end of the island is marked by La Soufriere, an active 4,048-foot volcano. Black-, gold-, and light-sand beaches ring the island.

Kingstown, the island's capital city, is located in the southwest corner of the island on a bustling, scenic harbor. Arnos Vale Airport is a few miles to the south.

The official language is English; a local dialect is also spoken. St. Vincent and the Grenadines are on Atlantic standard time, one hour ahead of eastern standard time.

The Grenadines. A lush string of over 100 islands sprinkled just south of St. Vincent, the Grenadines have been known to yachters for years as some of the best islands for sailing in the Caribbean. The major islands of the Grenadines are Bequia, Mustique, Canouan, Mayreau, Union, Palm, and Petit St. Vincent. Bequia, with about 5,000 residents, has the largest population.

Mustique, Canouan, Union, and Palm islands have airstrips. Transportation to the other islands is either by charter yacht or pick-up by hotel launch. There are many uninhabited islets and rocks including the renowned Tobago Cays, beloved by yachtsmen all over the world. The Grenadines are variably lush with isolated soft white coral and sand beaches and, in some cases, hilly interiors.

WHEN TO GO. December through May is the busiest time of year and June through September is the low season. The temperature ranges from 64 to 90 degrees F, with an average temperature of 78. The rainy season extends from June to December.

PASSPORTS AND VISAS. U.S. and Canadian citizens need only proof of identity, such as a passport, birth certificate or voter's registration card. A driver's license won't do! In addition, all visitors to these islands must hold a return or ongoing ticket. British citizens must have passports; visas are not required.

MONEY. The Eastern Caribbean dollar (EC$) is the local currency. At this writing the exchange rate is U.S. $1 = EC $2.64. The EC dollar is pegged to the U.S. dollar and so varies proportionately against other currencies. U.S. and Canadian dollars are also accepted here. Be sure which currency is being quoted since most, but not all, places quote in EC dollars.

WHAT WILL IT COST?

A typical day in St. Vincent and in the Grenadines for two persons will run:

	U.S.$
Accommodations at a moderate hotel, including breakfast and dinner	$80
Lunch at a moderate restaurant	10

Tips or service charges at restaurants; taxes and hotel charges	20
One day sightseeing by taxi or rental car	60–65
Total	$170–175

 HOW TO GET THERE. *LIAT,* the Caribbean airline, provides daily scheduled flights from Barbados, St. Lucia, Martinique, Mustique, and Trinidad. There are connecting flights via *BWIA, British Airways, Eastern, American, Air Canada, VIASA, Air France, Pan Am,* and *Caribbean Airways* from North America, South America, and Europe. Airports are located on St. Vincent, Mustique, Canouan, and Union Island. There is a St. Vincent and the Grenadines information desk in the arrival section of Grantley Adams International Airport in Barbados.

WINLINK provides both scheduled and charter service between St. Lucia, St. Vincent, and Union Island and plans to include Mustique soon. *Tropicair* and *Aero Services* provide charter service to and from St. Vincent, Mustique, Canouan, and Union Island. *Inter-Island Air Services* offer scheduled and charter services between St. Lucia, St. Vincent, and the Grenadines. *Mustique Airways* flies between St. Vincent and Mustique. *Air Martinique* operates between Martinique, St. Lucia, St. Vincent, and Union Island.

By sea. There is daily ferry service between Bequia and Kingstown aboard the *Friendship Rose, My Edwina,* and the *M.V. Grenadines Star,* all of which charge EC $5 one way and make the run in 1½ hours. The ships also service Canouan (EC $10); Mayreau (EC $12); and Union Island (EC $15) from Kingstown on Mon. through Sat.'s. Ships from several of the major cruise lines call on St. Vincent all year round.

AIRPORT TAX AND OTHER CHARGES. All room rates are subject to a 5% government tax. Hotels also add either a 10% or 15% service charge. The airport departure tax is EC $10 per person.

 TELEPHONE AND EMERGENCY NUMBERS. The area code for St. Vincent is 809. When dialing long distance, the prefix is 45 followed by the appropriate 5-digit number. Work is in progress on direct-dialing service to countries outside St. Vincent and the Grenadines. There is a 5% government tax on all international telephone calls. All intra-island calls go through the operator. Dial "0" for information, 61185 for medical emergencies.

 HOTELS. There are at least a dozen hotels, an equal number of apartments, and a dozen guesthouses on St. Vincent. On the Grenadines there are a dozen hotels. The peak tourist season runs from mid-December to mid-April; off-season rates are 25–50% lower than peak season rates. You should allow at least six months advance notice when making reservations for the high season at the exclusive resorts. On relatively untrammeled St. Vincent you may get away with a month's notice at certain hotels and guesthouses.

The atmosphere at most hotels on St. Vincent and the Grenadines warmly echoes the casual West Indies lifestyle. Each property has some unique characteristics that in some way set it apart. The following rates are based on double occupancy, MAP (since there are few restaurants on the island), during the winter (peak) season. Prices quoted are in U.S. dollars. A *Deluxe* designation means $210–420 per day; *Expensive* is $118–200, *Moderate* is $60–100, *Inexpensive* below $60 per day.

ST. VINCENT

Waterloo House. *Deluxe.* Orange Hill. Tel. 86330. The only things that will get to you at this hideaway in a 2,800-acre working plantation are the clean aromatic breezes and the enchanting seclusion. Waterloo House, built in 1935, is the former great house of the Orange Hill Plantation, just north of George-town on the windward coast, about an hour's drive from the airport. Cyril and Hazel Barnard, owners of Waterloo House, also own Heron Hotel in Kingstown. Rates include afternoon tea, laundry (not dry cleaning), and transfers to and from the airport. The hotel will also arrange for roundtrip transportation to Georgetown and the leeward coast. Overnight guests can arrange to climb La Soufriere for U.S. $50, which includes a picnic lunch. There are five charming, airy rooms here, all of which are brightly carpeted and have antique bedsteads—a nice touch of England in the Caribbean. Below the terrace overlooking the coconut groves and, beyond, the Atlantic, are a lawn and swimming pool.

Young Island Resort. *Deluxe.* P.O. Box 211, St. Vincent. Tel. 84826. Located on its own island, a 37-acre woody atoll 200 yards from St. Vincent, Young Island Resort covers 25 acres and shuttles its guests to and from the mainland via two small launches. Its 29 rustic cottages (24 superior, 2 deluxe, 3 luxury), all double, are carefully arranged around the northeastern side of the island, each tucked into a bouquet of tropical plants, almond, papaya, and mango trees. Interiors are tropical, nice: queen-sized beds, ceiling fans, and modern bathrooms with one delightful exception—showers are located outside the cottage, discreetly hidden from outside view. Luxury cottages have full kitchen facilities. There's a saltwater pool, a short beach (on Young Island Channel, where boats anchor), tennis court lit for night play ($5 extra; electricity is scarce down here), and trails for ambling over the small island. Cottages 24 and 17 afford the best view from the top of the hill, though it's a good climb up the stone steps. Expect to be met with a cold rum punch at the dock when you arrive here. Live entertainment is featured on Tuesday, Wednesday, Friday, and Saturday nights. A torchlit cocktail party is held at Fort Durvenette, behind Young Island, every Friday night. Guests are mostly couples of all ages from the U.S. and elsewhere; Meals vary in quality but the setting is nothing less than lovely and service is commendable. Ask about the resort's 46-foot yacht, *Windsong*, which sails to Bequia, Mustique, and covers the coast of St. Vincent. *Windsong* departs early and costs about U.S. $40. You can windsurf, snorkel, sail a Sunfish, water ski. You can also sip a tropical drink at the offshore Coconut Bar.

Grand View Beach Hotel. *Expensive.* P.O. Box 173, Villa Point. Tel. 84811. This was originally a plantation house of the Sardine family, who still owns it. The hotel, covering eight acres, is five minutes from the airport and is situated off the main road at the end of Villa Point. It has a spectacular panoramic view east toward Young Island, Fort Durvenette, and Calliaqua Bay beyond. To the south is the smokey outline of Bequia, nine miles away. West is Arnos Vale Bay. The hotel offers 12 bright rooms (23 beds) and, on the west side of the hotel where the trade winds don't reach, air conditioning. The swimming pool is beyond the hotel on the point and there are trails down to the beach where you can snorkel, scuba dive, swim, and fish. Indian Bay is the site of a great scuba dive, a "sheer wall" coral formation. Sunfish and windsurfing is available through a local dive and water sports shop. There are also tennis and squash courts. Dining is in a basic, unadorned dining room and food is superior.

Rawacou. *Expensive.* Stubbs P.O., Mt. Pleasant. Tel. 84459. Ten cottage-style apartments with fully equipped kitchens. The open-sided dining room overlooks the swimming pool and a lovely black-sand beach on the Atlantic coast. To reach Rawacou, take the northernmost exit off the Windward Highway—it's a little longer but very pretty. Manager Pete Mickles says his clientele is mostly the "young adventurous type." Mickles will take you to a good snorkeling site and he keeps four horses available for riding. Most guests rent a car here. Food is fresh and good.

Coconut Beach Motel. *Moderate.* P.O. Box 355, Indian Bay Head. Tel. 84231. On the beach, down the road from Grand View and Villa Lodge, this ten-room inn has a casual, nautical decor. There is a deck on the water, a beach for swimming, and an array of water sports—snorkeling, windsurfing, scuba diving.

CSY Yacht Club. *Moderate.* P.O. Box 133, Ratho Mill, Tel. 84031. This basic but nice 19-room inn, ten minutes from Arnos Vale Airport, is a favorite with the sailing crowd. CSY is located right on the water's edge. Each of the large, appealing rooms have two double beds and a balcony overlooking Blue Lagoon.

The pool is at the end of a circuitous walk up the rise toward the main road and there's a beach, though boats are anchored very close by. The restaurant, which was recently redone (there's also a new conference room), serves good food and the bar is popular with sailors passing through.

Heron Hotel. *Moderate.* P.O. Box 226, Kingstown, Tel. 71631. This informal 15-room inn located in Kingstown, about a five-minute walk from the main shopping center and two miles from the airport, is especially popular with businessmen from Europe, the U.S., and the Caribbean. Heron is next to the Wayfarer's Bookstore and across the street from the loading docks. This is an unpretentious inn operating the traditional West Indian way. Air conditioning is one of the few modern allowances. There's no beach and no scheduled entertainment. The kitchen turns out fresh fish, local vegetables, salads, and soups, and there's steady business from local shopkeepers.

Mariner's Inn. *Moderate.* P.O. Box 868, Villa Beach. Tel. 84287. Mack Inniss manages this quiet, 14-year-old, 15-room inn on the beach. The colonial design includes rooms that are seafarer solid, some with antique four-posters. Outside is the bar, once one of the lifeboats of the *Antilles,* which sank nearby in the early '70s. The Mariner's Inn draws a mixture of young and old (and some children) mostly from the U.S., Trinidad, and Europe. There's always plenty of fresh seafood on the menu. Access to good snorkeling at a coral reef on the eastern tip of Young Island, across the channel; a small spit of beach. Evenings include frequent barbecues and a steel band.

Sunset Shores. *Moderate.* P.O. Box 849, Villa Beach. Tel. 84411. Due west of Young Island, Sunset Shores has 19 rooms, all with air conditioning, and modern bath; deluxe rooms also have patios. Rooms are arranged in a "U" around the swimming pool. Young Island Channel is beyond, affording swimming, Sunfish sailing, snorkeling, and scuba diving at the eastern tip of Young Island. Sunset Shores draws a combination of couples (all ages) and businessmen. A clipboard in the central sitting area carries daily Caribbean, financial, sports, and international news from the wire services. The dining room, outfitted in attractive cane furnishings, is bright. During the busy season you can expect a buffet dinner and steel band once a week. There are plans to add eight rooms soon.

Villa Lodge Hotel. *Moderate.* P.O. Box 222, Indian Point. Tel. 84641. Nestled in a lush, tropical hillside overlooking Indian Bay, Village Lodge is a casual holiday spot aiming for the business traveler. There are ten rooms, furnished with double beds, showers, private patios, and air-conditioning. Some with sea views. A pool with bar, restaurant serving locally inspired cuisine, and the beach (a short walk away) make this popular with businessmen and vacationers who want to be near town and the beach.

Cobblestone Inn. *Inexpensive.* P.O. Box 867, Kingstown. Tel. 61937. This converted sugar warehouse, dating from at least 1814, has been restored to its original Georgian look. Located on the waterfront on Kingstown's Bay Street, this inn is very popular with businessmen who like to be in the center of things and with overnighters headed for the Grenadines. The beach is about a three-mile drive away. Open-air dining area on the roof; downstairs is the air-conditioned bar and restaurant where you can choose from a hefty menu of good West Indian fare.

Haddon Hotel. *Inexpensive.* P.O. Box 144, Kingstown. Tel. 61897. In the suburbs of Kingstown, at the eastern end of town, this 16-room inn managed by Brian Brereton is a little out of the way. The hotel provides transportation to nearby beaches, though the Kingstown tennis club is right across the street. Rooms here are plain; those on the second floor are much brighter. Popular with businessmen. The Haddon has an open-sided restaurant and bar—really basic here—on the top floor.

THE GRENADINES

Bequia

Friendship Bay Hotel. *Expensive.* Friendship Bay, Bequia, Tel. 83222; (800) 223-6764. The new owners here are giving Friendship Bay a desperately needed facelift. All 30 double rooms are attractively decorated with bright, colorful bedspreads and curtains. There are roomy patios, providing views of Friendship Bay and Mustique in the distance. The restaurant offers a barbecue and buffet, Italian cuisine, and steaks from the states. Look for the jump-up on Saturday nights at the Mau Mau Beach Bar. There's a full range of water sports, a 45-foot yawl used for local excursions, and good snorkeling nearby.

Bequia Beach Club. *Inexpensive.* Friendship Bay, Bequia. Tel. 458–3248. The newest kid on the block, Bequia Beach Hotel features 10 neat, modern units with two single beds, a mini-fridge, clock radio, and modern baths with showers. Owner Bruno Fink is offering local as well as German cookery, including wurst and cheeses. Live music is provided regularly. There's a pool as well as skiing and other water sports, including windsurfing and overnight jaunts to the stunning Tobago Cays for excellent snorkeling.

Spring on Bequia. *Expensive.* Write Box 19251, Minneapolis, MN 55419 or, on Bequia, tel. 83414. Set in a lush hillside overlooking Spring Bay, this hotel provides a view from the highest cabins that you'll never forget. Guests here, according to the manager, Candy Leslie, are well-travelled types in search of solitude—with some nice amenities. There are three detached stone-and-shingle hideaways (11 rooms with twin beds, shower, and patio), an open-air dining room and bar, freshwater pool and a tennis court. Ten minutes by taxi (EC $10–12) from Port Elizabeth, Spring features barbecue chicken and shish kebab every Tuesday night and live music on certain nights of the week. Spring not only grows its own vegetables but also boasts the best cook on the island, Elfie Grant.

Frangipani. *Moderate.* Port Elizabeth, Bequia. Tel. 83255. This is the former family home of James "Son" Mitchell, prime minister of St. Vincent. Son, with his wife Pat, operates this sunny establishment popular with yachting people. The new garden cottages on the hill are of stone and hardwood construction, with louvered windows, private baths, dressing rooms and large sundecks. The older rooms are built atop the original house. They feature a corridor bath and each room has a sink. The terrace affords a lovely view of the harbor. Meals in the waterfront, open-sided dining area are exquisite and there's a terrific steel band jump-up (the best on the island) every Thursday night.

Sunny Caribee. *Moderate.* P.O. Box 16, Admiralty Bay, Bequia. Tel. 83425. Eight rooms in the colonial-style main house (built from the timbers of a shipwreck), and 17 bright, modern cabanas, each with its own private veranda and bath. The dining room, bar, and sitting area in the main house are on a wide open veranda extending around the sides of the building. The hotel overlooks Admiralty Bay and has about 700 feet of beachfront. Guests enjoy a full range of water sports. A charter boat, the *Pteropus,* travels to any of the islands, with prices ranging from U.S. $20–60 per person (four persons minimum). There are other charters available, including a locally built schooner, the *Callipygian.* Breakfast includes juice, fresh fruits, and grilled items and lunch and dinner consist of seafood, meats, and fresh vegetables.

Julie's and Isola Guest House. *Inexpensive.* Port Elizabth, Bequia. Tel. 83304, 83323, 83220. This simple, neat property, a five-minute walk from Port Elizabeth, has 20 rooms, all smartly decorated doubles except for two singles at Isola. The inns are across a narrow street from each other. Isola features hot and cold showers, Julie's only cold (not uncommon down here, and you get used to it). The restaurant serves up lobster, conch, fish, hearty local soups, and fresh-baked bread daily. Mornings there's fresh papaya, bananas, and grapefruit. The inn attracts mostly young British guests.

Mustique

Cotton House. *Deluxe.* Mustique. Tel. (809) 458–4621 or (212) 980–3810 or, on Mustique, 84621. This 18th-century stone and coral building has 19 rooms. The hotel was "re-created" by the late Oliver Messel. Everything here is intended to make you feel relaxed, pampered, special—the pristine, restored Georgian house which accommodates half the guests, the three guest cottages near the "Roman ruin" pool, the new two-story, eight-room wing, and the large, sedate sitting room in the main building. Cottage rooms have custom bedspreads and drapes, rush mats, ceiling fans, and breezy balconies and patios. The hotel's cuisine is outstanding—French with a West Indies accent. There is a full array of water sports for guests; also tennis and horseback riding. On the grounds is

Anita's Affeer boutique, which sells chic resort wear from a charming converted sugar mill, and down at the pier you'll find Basil's Beach Bar.

Charlie's Guest House. *Inexpensive.* Mustique. Tel. 458–4621. This is a nice, quiet guesthouse nestled up on the hill across from Cotton House. Its owner, Charlie Tennant, is the son of the former owner of the island, Colin Tennant. There are six rooms—three singles and three doubles. The restaurant serves breakfast only.

Canouan

Canouan Beach Hotel. *Moderate.* Canouan. Tel. 84413. There are 10 clean, nicely furnished rooms here, all doubles, at this seafront location. The restaurant serves tasty local cuisine and is also a nice place for an afternoon cooler.

Crystal Sands Beach Hotel. *Moderate.* Canouan. Tel. 71077. Co-managers Philius and Annella De Roche have a quiet little place in the sun here, on an island 3½ × 1¼ miles in size. Just walk through the gate—you either land by charter flight or arrive by yacht—to the open veranda where the bar and dining area is located. You can call (809) 458–4739 to arrange your air pickup in St. Vincent. There are five double apartments (20 beds), each with its own bathroom and small patio. Cottages share a connecting door for larger groups. This island is ringed by superior beaches. No pool, tennis, or phones here. A good part of the business is from yachters. Fishing and sailing excursions can be arranged and there's excellent snorkeling in the area.

Palm Island

Palm Island Beach Club. *Deluxe.* Prune Island. Tel. 84804. In the U.S., contact Robert Reid Associates, 1270 Avenue of the Americas, New York, NY 10020. Tel. (212) 757–2444. By now, John and Mary Caldwell, owners of Palm Island Beach Club, have become more than local folk heroes. The palm trees offer just the right amount of cooling shade for 24 stone cottages, an al fresco dining patio, and open-walled bar. Rooms here are large with crisp floral prints covering attractive furnishings. Mini-fridge, modern bath, and king-size beds. No air conditioning is needed here as there's always a good steady breeze. Each cottage is actually two adjacent rooms, each with its own patio and table with umbrella. Tea is served at 4:00 P.M.; a hostess leaves everything on your table outside. There's great swimming, snorkeling at Tobago Cays and, at the green dive shack on the beach, Terry Lampert can outfit you for a scuba dive in the area. Instruction is also available. Windsurfing, sailing, and offshore fishing round out the selection of seaside activities. Additionally, a 47-foot sloop, *Angelica,* is available for sailing parties to the Tobago Cays. Sailing vacations are also available: Days Ashore/Days Afloat, bare boats and yacht charters, and Learn-to-Sail Cruises. Fifteen recently built French yachts, operated by Sunsea Marina of Paris, are based at Palm. Guests can charter yachts from Palm to Martinique or other nearby islands, or book a round-robin cruise of the Grenadines. Supplies can be purchased at a grocery store on Palm.

Union

Anchorage Yacht Club. *Expensive.* Union Island. Tel. 88244. The anchorage closed in 1980 and reopened in February, 1984. The new and improved Anchorage has five units (four doubles, one quad) and two apartments (a double and a triple). This is a popular spot for—you guessed it—the yachting set, but guests can also enjoy scuba diving, snorkeling, picnics in the surrounding coves and, on Friday nights, a reggae steel band. The restaurant benefits from a French chef who has many inventive ways of preparing fish.

Clifton Beach Guest House. *Moderate.* Union Island. Tel. 88254. Four small neatly furnished rooms here make it a cozy place for a stopover. There are no dining facilities, so guests use the restaurant at the Clifton Beach Hotel.

Clifton Beach Hotel. *Moderate.* Clifton, Union Island. Tel. 88254. Located on the beach, also on the north end, Clifton Beach Hotel is a simple place to escape to if you're not up for the international hobnobbing that goes on at Anchorage. Furnishings are basic and guests are truly left to themselves.

Sunny Grenadines. *Moderate.* Clifton, Union Island. Tel. 88327. A pleasant, small inn with basic amenities, the Sunny Grenadines is located at the shore not far from the airstrip. Established by Frenchman Andre Beaufrand, who also sponsored the first airstrip on the island.

Petit St. Vincent

Petit St. Vincent Resort. *Deluxe.* Petit St. Vincent. Tel. 84801. In the U.S., write Box 12506, Cincinnati, OH 45212. Tel. (513) 242–1333. 22 luxurious, secluded cottages of bluebitch stone and purple-heart wood, each with a large patio and a glorious view, set on a 113-acre island ringed by soft golden beaches and covered with grassy woods. Room service is provided via a roving jeep—which you'll only see if you hoist the yellow flag in front of your cottage. Hoist the red one and not a soul will come near you. If it's okay with you, coffee will be dropped off in the morning outside your cottage (guests can check off items on a daily menu sheet and leave it for pickup the day before). You can walk from your cottage to *The Pavillion* restaurant and bar, with its sheltered tables. Sunfish, windsurfers, Hobie Cats, and snorkeling equipment are all made available at no extra charge. Guests may also climb aboard PSV's trimaran for a sail to the Tobago Cays, saunter off to the tennis courts, lit for night play, or try their hand at volleyball, horseshoes, ping pong, or darts. Friday nights are a special time when the dining room (and the piano) is moved down to the water's edge for a barbecue buffet. Wednesday nights feature a steel band jump-up.

 TIME-SHARING CONDOMINIUMS. An ambitious time-sharing program is underway on Mayreau, one of the southernmost Grenadines, which covers 1½ square miles and has about 150 local residents. **Salt Whistle Bay Resort** presently has 16 furnished rooms (with expansion to 27 rooms planned) and a restaurant and bar set amid palm and almond trees. There is no airstrip on Mayreau but it can be reached in 30 minutes by boat from Union Island. Contact Thomas Potter, Salt Whistle Bay, Mayreau, Grenadines, W.I. for further information.

 HOME AND APARTMENT RENTALS. Caribbean Home Rentals, Box 710, Palm Beach, FL 33480, carries listings on St. Vincent and the Grenadines, plus exclusive home listings on Mustique. Rates for Mustique are at the top of the scale starting at roughly U.S. $1,800 per week, which includes a car, maid, and cook.

There are about a dozen establishments offering apartments on St. Vincent. Following are some standouts:

Breezeville Apartments. *Moderate.* Box 222, Villa Point. Tel. 84641. Eight air-conditioned apartments (12 beds total) located at Indian Bay on a lush, tropical hillside. There is a swimming pool perched at the top of the hill with a poolside bar and restaurant.

Indian Bay Beach Apartments. *Moderate.* Box 538, Indian Bay Beach. Tel. 84001. Eight units, all with full kitchens, right on the beach for a splendid do-it-yourself vacation. A new restaurant here serves up good local cuisine at inexpensive prices.

Tropic Breeze Hotel. *Moderate.* Box 761, Can Hall. Tel. 84631. Three miles from Kingstown. 12 spacious and neat apartments, each with kitchenette, bath, shower, air conditioning, and large balcony/patios. Swimming pool and fine food if you want a break.

Emerald Isle Casino. *Inexpensive.* Penniston. Tel. 71235. 12 modern, roomy, and very attractive chalets set in a green valley adjacent to the former golf course make this a great getaway. Only a half-hour drive from the beach. Two sparkling swimming pools; dining and bar facilities. Rooms in the dark plank chalets include full kitchen facilities. A gurgling stream runs behind them. There is also a small casino, with blackjack and roulette, which is regaining popularity.

Umbrella Beach Apartments. *Inexpensive.* Villa Beach. Tel. 84651. Opposite luxurious Young Island, this is a basic, no-frills, self-catering 10-unit complex offering small rooms and not a lot of atmosphere.

Yvonette Beach Apartments. *Inexpensive.* P.O. Box 71, Indian Bay Beach. Tel. 84021. Seven housekeeping apartments linked in one meandering building. All have kitchen units and overlook Young Island.

HOW TO GET AROUND. Although many visitors to St. Vincent and the Grenadines arrive by sea, there are open-air buses painted in bright colors, mini-buses (costing EC $1), taxis, and rental cars for the landrovers. Arnos Vale airport is about two miles from Kingstown, St. Vincent's capital city, and taxis make the run for EC $12 per car. Expect to pay about U.S. $15 per hour traveling around the island by taxi.

Rental cars are available at approximately U.S. $35 per day. If you don't have an International Driver's License, you'll need a temporary Vincentian license, which costs EC $10. Remember to drive on the left! Among the rental firms to consider are *Johnson's U-Drive* at the airport (tel. 84864); *Car Rentals, Ltd.* on Halifax Street (tel. 61862). All offer 50 free miles in the daily rate.

To the Grenadines. There are at least two ferry boats that ply the waters between St. Vincent and the Grenadines, the *M.V. Grenadine Star* and the *Friendship Rose.* Prices quoted are in EC dollars. The *M.V. Grenadine Star* departs Kingstown at about 9 A.M. on Mondays and Thursdays for the Grenadines. Stops are Bequia, $5; Canouan, $10; Mayreau, $12; and Union Island, $15. Tuesdays and Fridays it leaves Union Island at about 7:00 A.M. for Mayreau, Canouan, Bequia, and Kingstown. Saturdays, at about 1:00 P.M. it departs for Bequia. The *Friendship Rose* departs Bequia Mon.–Fri. at 6:30 A.M. for Kingstown ($5) and makes the trip back to Bequia at 1:45 P.M. Contact A.C. Hillocks, Sharpes Street, Kingstown. Tel. 61242. *My Edwina* runs between St. Vincent and Bequia Mon. through Sat. leaving Bequia at 6:30 A.M. (the journey takes an hour) for St. Vincent, and leaves St. Vincent at 12:30 P.M.

TOURIST INFORMATION. In Kingstown on St. Vincent, contact the Department of Tourism, located at the end of Egmont, up the block from Back Street (walk away from the waterfront) in a light pink building on the right-hand corner. The mailing address is P.O. Box 834, St. Vincent, W.I. Tel. 71502. For sources closer to home, see the Tourist Information Services section in the *Facts at Your Fingertips* chapter.

SPECIAL EVENTS. Carnival time! The festivities are in full swing by the end of June. Among the events: steel-band and calypso competitions, kiddies carnival, king and queen of the bands contest, and queen of the carnival selection. On the 26th, events gather momentum for Carnival Tuesday on the first Tuesday of July.

The Skippers Regatta, held the third weekend in September, is sponsored by the St. Vincent Hotel Association and CSY.

The preparations go on all year for Independence Day (Oct. 27th) and Tourism Week in early November when Vincentians host barbecues, fashion shows, and tourism-awareness programs.

The highlight of November is the Petit St. Vincent Race. Boats race among the Grenadines, using PSV as their home port. There are games, barbecues, and music at night. It's a major event for tourists. It usually precedes American Thanksgiving.

TOURS. At present there are no officially sponsored, organized tours of St. Vincent or the Grenadines. Plans to establish the Taxi Drivers' Association under the government umbrella have gotten no further than the distribution of stickers saying "St. Vincent Official Taxi" to dedicated drivers. Don't let the dearth of official sponsorship fool you, though. You can ask your hotel to recommend a driver, but even if you just take your pick of drivers displaying the sticker, chances are you'll get a well-informed, friendly, and surprisingly professional driver. Expect to pay about U.S. $15 per hour.

 PARKS AND GARDENS. *The Botanic Gardens,* founded in 1765, are reportedly the oldest botanical gardens in the Western Hemisphere. They contain a wondrous collection of exotic trees and flowering plants, including the main attraction, a descendant of the original breadfruit tree brought to the island in 1763 by Captain Bligh. The gardens are east of Fort Charlotte, in northeastern Kingstown. Follow the headland to Kingstown General Hospital, turn right, and follow the road to the gardens.

Montreal Gardens, located in the Marriaqua Valley in the south central region of St. Vincent, is a delicate retreat well off the beaten track, where the aromas of cocoa and nutmeg mingle with those of exotic flowers. There's a natural spring and a cozy "honeymoon" cottage available for rent.

 BEACHES. The beaches of **St. Vincent,** a volcanic island, are composed of black sand in the north and light coral sand in the south. The best swimming is on the leeward (Caribbean) side. The water is calm and warmer than on the windward (Atlantic) side of the island. There's great snorkeling off the eastern side of *Young Island* and elsewhere in *Indian Bay. Lowman's Beach,* easily visible immediately north of Fort Charlotte (a wrecked tugboat rests near the surface a few hundred feet offshore), is a relatively secluded beach popular with the handful of vacationing businessmen who know of it. Also recommended is *Cumberland Bay,* located halfway up the coast about a mile north of Wallialbou.

The windward side of the island bears the brunt of the Atlantic and, though this coast is a dramatic sight, even strong swimmers will have a tricky time with the strong tides. There is interesting and somewhat sheltered snorkeling at *Rawacou* in Stubbs, just south of Argyle. Chances are you'll be located at the south end of the island if you're staying on St. Vincent and the beaches there are perfect for swimming, snorkeling, windsurfing, or just floating around.

The Grenadines. If white and beige sandy beaches are what you're after, you'll have to try the Grenadines. Here the islands are surrounded by superb fine sand and crushed coral beaches. Most of the Grenadines have an Atlantic coast but some, particularly further south, share the waters with numerous coral reefs, which help to dispel the big breakers. Palm and Union are good jumping-off spots to super scuba diving, and snorkeling is especially good at Mayreau and PSV.

 PARTICIPANT SPORTS. Sailing comes more naturally than breathing down here, followed by all the water sports you can think of. Contact *Caribbean Sailing Yachts* (CSY) on St. Vincent (tel. 84031), or write ahead c/o P.O. Box 491, Tenafly, NJ 07670 (800–631–1593).

There's **tennis** at the *Kingstown Tennis Club* (two lit, hard-surface courts) and at several hotels on St. Vincent and on the Grenadines.

Horseback riding is available at *Rawacou* (about U.S. $5 per hour) on St. Vincent and at *Cotton House* on Mustique (about U.S. $8 per hour).

Snorkeling and **scuba diving** arrangements can be made through *Dive St. Vincent* (tel. 84714), P.O. Box 864, St. Vincent, and *Mariner's Yachts and Dive Center* in Villa (tel. 84645).

Play **squash** at the *Grand View Beach Hotel* (tel. 84811) and at *Prospect Squash Courts* (tel. 84866). **Windsurfing** has also really caught on down here and is available at most hotels. Lessons run about U.S. $10 per hour including equipment, and boards can be rented for about U.S. $10 per hour or U.S. $20 per day.

SPECTATOR SPORTS. Cricket and **soccer** (they call it football) are popular sports, as well as **basketball** and a variation called **netball.** Arnos Vale Playing Field (a couple of minutes from the airport) is the site of both cricket and soccer matches, while Queen Victoria Park in Kingstown holds cricket matches regularly. Contact the Department of Tourism (tel. 71502) for times and venues.

HISTORIC SITES AND HOUSES. St. Vincent. *Fort Charlotte.* This bastion is almost 200 years old and occupies Johnson Point, a prominent ridge that forms the northern lip of Kingstown Harbor. The fort still has three of the 34 original cannons in place. Admission is U.S. $.60 and the fort is open daily 6:00 A.M.–6:00 P.M.

Fort Durvenette. This fort, located 193 feet above sea level on an outcropping adjoining Young Island, was built around 1800 to defend Calliaqua Bay, when it was an important anchorage. The fort is open weekdays, until dark and admission can be arranged through Young Island Resort.

St. George's Cathedral. Built more than 150 years ago, this church is one of Kingstown's major attractions. It can be found on Back Street at the corner of Grenvillle Street. Georgian architecture, a galleried interior, and brilliant stained glass-windows make a visit here worthwhile.

St. Mary's Roman Catholic Cathedral. This century-old church with its melange of architectural styles is located across the street from St. George's.

Layou Petroglyphs and Rock Carvings. Several interesting petroglyphs and rock carvings by pre-Columbian peoples, most probably Ciboneys, Arawaks, and Caribs. The best-known and most easily accessible site is north of Layous, near the river. Here the main surface of a 20-foot rock has been incised with a triangular face and smaller circular faces as well as other marks. There are other petroglyphs at Indian Bay Point, Barrouallie, Petit Bordel, near the Yambou River in Argyle, and at Colonaire. There are also interesting rock carvings at Buccament Bay. They are all open throughout the week.

MUSEUMS AND GALLERIES. *St. Vincent Archeological Museum.* A great collection of artifacts here in a small building in the Botanic Gardens close to Kingstown's Leeward Highway. Artifacts date from 5 or 6 B.C. to 1797.

MUSIC, DANCE, AND STAGE. Steel band jump-ups are the chief musical attraction during the year and musical groups usually hold forth at the hotels. Carnival in June is the time of the year when the islands come to life with folkloric dancing, a variety of bands, and days of celebration.

SHOPPING. St. Vincent. There are about 12 blocks of shops around Bay St. *Batik Caribe,* the name of the Stevensons' screen designs on sea island cotton, has an attractive shop next to Noah's Arkade on Kingstown's main street. Be sure to inquire about having clothes made—they can be ready in two or three days. Crystal, china, silver, gold, Swiss watches, and leather goods can all be found at *Stretcher's.*

St. Vincent Craftsmen Center is located in the northwest end of Kingstown where French's Gate meets Richmond Hill (tel. 71288). It's a craft cooperative offering an attractive assortment of hand-made items including extensive straw work, ceramics, wood carvings, locally made silver jewelry, and highly polished black coral bracelets and pendants. The center also has a branch at Arnos Vale Airport and is open during regularly scheduled flight times. The Kingstown Center is open Mon.–Fri. 8:00 A.M.-noon and 1:00 P.M.–4:00 P.M.; Sat. 8:00 A.M. -noon. Closed Sun. There are other craft centers in Barrouallie, Spring Village, Troumaca, Petit Bordel, and Chateaubelair on the leeward coast; and Biabou,

New Grounds, and Georgetown on the windward coast. There's also Noah's Arkade on Bay Street (tel. 71513; and one on Bequia, tel. 83424) which sells a large array of clothing, including colorful sports clothes, as well as arts and crafts.

Bequia. *Crab Hole* in Port Elizabeth, on Bequia, is a good place to visit for silk-screened items and attractive resort wear. You can watch the entire silk-screening process being done between 8:30 A.M. and 4:30 P.M.

 RESTAURANTS. There is hearty West Indian cooking down here and the absence of a great variety of restaurants is made up for by the hotels, some of which are outstanding. There are a couple of restaurants, though, and both they and the hotel kitchens turn out memorable meals.

The price following classifications (quoted in U.S. dollars) are based on the cost of an average three-course dinner for one person *for food alone;* beverages, tax, and tip would be extra. *Expensive* means $15–20; *Moderate,* $10–14; *Inexpensive,* below $10.

ST. VINCENT

Cobblestone Inn. *Moderate.* Bay St., Kingstown. Tel. 61937. This is a busy spot—one taste of the food and you'll know why—so reservations are recommended. The steamed red snapper is outstanding, as is the fresh vegetable salad. Romantic, candlelit atmosphere. Dress casual. AE, MC.

Emerald Isle Casino. *Moderate.* Penniston. Tel. 71325. Chef Irwin McIntosh has been named St. Vincent's Chef of the Year for the last three years running, and that's all the reason you need to sample this establishment. McIntosh has a variety of ways to serve zucchini, and the lobster thermidor will bring the most reticent epicurian out of his shell. AE.

Grand View. *Moderate.* Villa Point. Tel. 84811. The food portions are ample though there's a nouvelle cuisine touch to the presentation. Try the creamy callaloo soup and the broiled red snapper. AE.

Harbor View. *Moderate.* Villa. Tel. 84922. Basic, good, French cuisine, at the island's sharpest dining spot, located just across from Young Island. Their specialties include escargot, fresh lobster, and steamed fish. Atmosphere is a notch above casual. AE.

Juliette's. *Moderate.* Middle St., Kingstown. Tel. 71645. Hearty local cuisine —vegetable dishes and good seafood. No credit cards.

French Restaurant. *Expensive.* Villa Beach. Tel. 84972. The place to find crepe, lobster bisque, and frogs' legs, plus a full menu of French cuisine from grilled lamb chops to shrimp sauté. There's also a decent wine list and lunch menu (the same as dinner along with quiches and sandwiches). MC, V.

Dolphin. *Moderate.* Villa Beach. Tel. 84238. A warm, straightforward, pub-style restaurant and bar, located directly across from Young Island, offering a mouth-watering selection of grilled items, fish and chicken with chips, burgers, soups, salads, and most important of all, scrumptious pizzas, with at least eight garnishes. You can even specify your own pizza, then wash it down with a draft beer. No credit cards.

J. Bees Restaurant. *Inexpensive.* Grenville St. Most people who have spent more than a couple of weeks here have discovered J. Bees (all the local residents recommend it). Good simple burgers, hearty island dishes for a quick eat-and-run or to linger over. No credit cards.

Chicken Roost. *Inexpensive.* Bedford Street, Kingstown. Tel. 71032. Island "fast food" including local dishes plus burgers, fish, chicken, and that great pizza found at the Dolphin restaurant (the same owner). Plans call for some tables outside for al fresco people-watching. No credit cards.

THE GRENADINES

Bequia

Mac's Bake Shop & Pizzeria. *Moderate.* Port Elizabeth. No tel. Freshly baked goodies here everyday including cookies, muffins, breads, pies, quiches, cakes, and pita bread. The main menu includes sandwiches, salads, pizza with lots of toppings, and other daily specials. Pleasant covered dining on a porch with good music on the stereo and a relaxed come-as-you-are atmosphere. No credit cards.

Frangipani. *Moderate.* Tel. 83255. Outstanding food at the barbecue buffet—try everything, then have seconds. Dinner served on the airy open-walled veranda. Background music provided by a superb steel-drum band. Dress casual. V, MC.

The Harpoon. *Inexpensive* to *Moderate.* Bequia Slip, Port Elizabeth. Tel. 83272. Owners Bill and Barbara Little run a quiet (usually) bar and restaurant out on the water of Admiralty Bay, where you can sit and watch the Caribbean drink up the sun before continuing with your own fate. The menu covers lunch and dinner and runs from lobster salad sandwiches to lamb, lobster, and chicken. The conversation among visiting yachtsmen and others is friendly and easy-going. No credit cards.

Whaleboner. *Moderate.* Port Elizabeth. Tel. 83304. House specialties are fresh fish and chips and a fresh lime pie. The bar here is carved from the jawbone of a whale; stools made from vertebrae. No credit cards.

Mustique

Basil's Beach Bar. *Expensive.* Tel. 84621. The husky, gregarious Basil Charles runs "the" place on the island. Breakfast, lunch, and dinner are served here. The dinner menu has a mouth-watering selection of fresh lobster, fish, barbecue or roast chicken, roast beef, thick soups, and fresh vegetables. Order the banana flambé for dessert. Dining is in the thatch-roofed structure on stilts over the water. Dress casual. The music in the background and the moon above make this an excellent choice. Barbecue ("Leh-Go" jump-up) on Wednesday night. AE, MC, V.

Palm

Palm Island Beach Club. *Expensive.* Tel. 84804. This is the only resort on the island. Fresh fish, lobster, conch, locally grown vegetables, rich callaloo and pumpkin soup. AE, V.

Petit St. Vincent

Petit St. Vincent Resort. *Expensive.* Tel. 84801. Grouper, kingfish, and lobster head up the seafood offerings here. There's also prime ribs and chicken (meats are shipped down fresh each week by Julia Child's butcher in Massachusetts). Dress is island casual. Delicious drinks, too. AE, V.

 NIGHT LIFE AND BARS. St. Vincent. *Aquatic Club,* Villa. Tel. 84205. Disco. Located next door to the Young Island landing pier. This is a very popular nightspot with locals and visitors. There's usually an admission charge of a few EC dollars. Dress casual.

Emerald Isle Casino, Penniston. Tel. 87421. Music/supper. Beautiful setting for an evening of fine food and great music. There's a DJ on Wednesday nights and weekends. The Casino offers blackjack and roulette. This is poolside partying at its casual best.

Wheel Beach Bar, Ratho Mill. Disco. The music is loud, the bar is busy, and there's room to stroll and cool out between songs spun by a DJ who plays all disco, loud. Casual dress and busy most weeknights and weekends. A small admission charge on Wednesday nights.

The Grenadines: Bequia. *Frangipani,* Port Elizabeth. Tel. 83255. The best steel band jump-up on the island and a friendly, packed bar make this the island hot spot, especially on Thursday nights. No charge for music or dancing.

Also check out *Sunny Caribbee* (tel. 84325) and *Friendship Bay Hotel* (tel. 83222) for jump-ups on Friday and Saturday nights.

Mustique. *Basil's Beach Bar.* Tel. 84621. There's live music here two or three times a week including a barbecue and "Leh Go" jump-up every Wednesday night (adults EC $35, children under 12 EC $20). The crystal ball is always spinning at this place.

Petit St. Vincent. *Petit St. Vincent Resort.* Tel. 84801. The local steel band arrives on Wednesday nights for a jump-up and guests enjoy a cocktail party each week given by Hazen and Jennifer Richardson. The revelry lasts into the wee hours on this sparkling island of wealthy vacationers.

POSTAGE. Airmail rates (in EC dollars) for international mail from St. Vincent and the Grenadines: flat letters to North America, EC $.45; to Europe, $.60. Postcards to North America, $.35; to Europe, $.35.

ELECTRIC CURRENT. The current here is 220–240 volts, 50 cycles A.C.

SECURITY. Almost all of St. Vincent is safe for travelers, even the most remote regions along the coast or inland. If there's any place worth avoiding it's the central portion of the Middle St. section of Kingstown. There's no real danger of bodily harm here, but there are a few locals selling marijuana and it makes for a less-than-savory stroll. The Grenadines are quite safe. Of course, common sense prevails in any settings: Don't leave money out in your hotel room where it can too easily make a thief of someone, and if you're carrying expensive jewelry or camera equipment, you may find it worth the peace of mind to have the hotel hold it in their safe for you.

TRINIDAD AND TOBAGO

by
CLAIRE DEVENER

Most southerly of the West Indies, the two sister islands that comprise the independent Republic of Trinidad and Tobago couldn't be more different.

Dynamic and vibrant Trinidad is the seat of government. The Caribbean's most prosperous and industrialized island, it's the home of calypso, steel bands, and one of the world's most spectacular Carnival celebrations. The capital, Port of Spain, is a cosmopolitan city complete with traffic jams, a busy port, eclectic architecture, multilevel shopping centers, modern hotels, and an active night life. The diversity of racial ancestry and cultures has left a unique mark on Trinidad and gives a richness to its national life that no other island has.

Tranquil Tobago basks in the sun just twenty-two miles off Trinidad's northeastern tip. This is Crusoe's desert island—an enchanted land of swaying palms, deserted beaches, and secluded half-moon bays sheltered by coral reefs and underwater gardens. Scattered fishing villages, pastel-hued houses, small and special hotels, easygoing people, and a feeling of total peace and quiet belie its turbulent past as the most fought-over island in the West Indies.

Two different worlds, but Trinidad and Tobago balance and complement one another. Their polyglot people are bound together by the common denominator of pride in their homeland and confidence in their future.

Past and Present

Iere, land of hummingbirds—was the Amerindian name for Trinidad; Tobago probably originates from their word for tobacco. Columbus reached Iere in 1498 on his third voyage. Three prominent peaks around the southern bay where he anchored inspired him to call it La Trinidad, after the Holy Trinity. Somehow he missed Tobago, unmentioned in his log. Credit for its discovery goes to the British who landed there in 1508. The fierce Caribs, by then well known for their particularly ungracious welcomes, inhabited both islands so no European colonization took place until the mid-1500s. At that time, Spain used Trinidad mainly as a stepping stone while searching for the fabled gold of El Dorado. English, Dutch, French, and Courlanders (from what was later Latvia) all started small settlements on Tobago in the 1600s.

In 1783, a royal proclamation from Madrid offered land grants to Roman Catholics of all nations who would settle in Trinidad. The result was a major increase in population and a big influx of French settlers who were fleeing from their own country's revolution. They introduced sugar cane and African slaves to cultivate it, and Trinidad soon developed into a very important colony. Following the war between Britain and Spain that broke out in 1797, Trinidad was formally ceded to England by the Treaty of Amiens in 1802, thus ending three hundred years of Spanish domination. When slavery was abolished in 1834, the local blacks and freed slaves from other islands began cultivating the soil in small holdings, and the colonists brought in laborers from Portugal, China, and India. It was at this point that the great wave of Hindu, Moslem, and Parsee immigration began; East Indians now account for nearly half of Trinidad's population.

Tobago has a far more tumultuous history, having been tossed back and forth thirty-one times in two centuries of battles among the Spanish, Dutch, French, and British. It was finally declared neutral territory in 1684, but that attracted so many pirates and privateers that Britain stepped in to drive them away. In the eighteenth century, when sugar was king of the Caribbean, Tobago raised cane with the best of them, and produced as much as half a million gallons of rum in 1793. The French were awarded the island under the terms of the Treaty of Amiens in 1802, but the English took it back again the following year. In 1814 Tobago was ceded to England under the Treaty of Paris. In 1889 the sugar industry collapsed, and Tobago was annexed to Trinidad for the sum of $19,200. The two islands remained in British hands until they achieved independence within the Commonwealth in 1962; then went on to become a republic in 1976.

Trinidad is one of the oldest petroleum producers in the world; today it is the third-largest oil exporter in the Western Hemisphere. With rapid development of her bountiful natural resources and a stable government (the People's National Movement [PNM] party has been in power for 30 years) the country has become the most prosperous and industrialized nation in the Caribbean. Trinidad and Tobago is a land of opportunity with a high standard of living. There's a 98% literacy rate and education is free from primary school to university. Future progress seems assured through the development of Point Lisas, an industrial estate already producing steel, fertilizer, ammonia, methanol, and other hydrocarbon biproducts.

Lately declining petrodollars are forcing the government to look for other sources of foreign exchange and tourism is making an increasingly significant contribution to the economy. Agriculture and small-industry development are other sources. Trinidad is upgrading roads, communications, public housing, transportation and expanding its tourist facilities such as hotels, entertainment programs and other attractions. Similar developments are taking place in Tobago.

"We're almost there" is the T & T Telephone Company's slogan, but it's valid for the whole country—Trinidad and Tobago is on the move.

EXPLORING TRINIDAD

Port of Spain is a big city, spread out between high hills and the curving shoreline of the Gulf of Paria. The view from the hills embraces a checkerboard of red and white roofs, one of the busiest harbors in the Caribbean, and the shore of South America, clearly visible across the Bocas or the Dragon's Mouths. At night, from some vantage points, you can see the lights of Venezuela. During the day, Port of Spain hums with activity; it is best explored by foot as the main thoroughfares are clogged with cars during the morning, noon, and evening rush hours and parking is next to impossible. Schedule your walking tour early as the city center gets hot and quite uncomfortable as the sun gets higher.

A good place to begin is Independence Square, which is not really a square at all but a long street with a multitude of shopping stalls set up in the middle. On the eastern side is the Roman Catholic Cathedral of the Immaculate Conception, dating back to 1816. It is laid out in the shape of a Latin cross and took sixteen years to complete.

Head up Frederick Street and you can't miss the big domed brick neo-Renaissance building known as Red House. It's on the western side of Woodford Square, Port of Spain's version of Hyde Park. After the building was twice destroyed by fire, the present structure was built in 1907 and is the seat of Trinidad and Tobago's government. The new Hall of Justice is on the north side of the square; on the south, the Anglican Cathedral, an 1818-vintage Gothic building with a beautifully carved altar and choir stalls.

Walk over to the Angostura Bitters Factory three blocks east of Woodford Square. This landmark has a fabulous butterfly collection that may be visited, but call first as it is sometimes on loan. Established in 1824, Angostura is made using a secret formula that has never been totally divulged. This mysterious aromatic is frequently an important ingredient in cocktails as well as a good stomach settler.

Frederick Street itself is a fine place for people-watching as well as browsing in small shops piled high with Indian silks and saris or well-organized department stores with "in-bond" luxury European imports. Stop off at the Tourist Board at #122–24 and pick up some of their colorful brochures as you may not be visiting this part of town a second time.

While central Port of Spain is not particularly pretty, each turn brings a new architectural surprise and this conglomeration of old and new, weatherbeaten and whitewashed, mosque and minaret, Gothic and gingerbread, give the city its own special, offbeat charm.

Continue north up Frederick Street to Queen's Park Savannah, a 200-acre open expanse of grass with a racetrack in the center, shaded by African tulip trees, royal palms, pouis, and flamboyants. Its edges are bordered by vendors proffering tiny mangrove oysters, roti, roasted corn, oranges, bananas, and coconut water. It's a wonderful place to sit and relax and watch the world of Trinidad jog, ride, walk, picnic, practice tai chi, yoga, soccer and cricket. Early in the morning there will be racehorses exercising; later in the day maybe a steel-band concert; and during Carnival competitions take place here.

In the southwest corner of the park is the National Museum and Art Gallery, a small museum guarded by Spanish cannons that date back to the eighteenth century. Turn left on Queen's Park West (confusing, as it is actually the Savannah's southern boundary) and you'll pass Knowsley, the first of a group of mansions that, along with the Red House downtown in Woodford Square, comprise what is called "The Magnificent Nine." This "sandwich of blue stone and brick" has a predominantly Italian and German flavor and now houses several ministries. At the intersection of Maraval Road and St. Clair Avenue, on the Savannah's western side, is Queens Royal College, a boys' secondary school that has been the country's most prestigious since 1902. This H-shaped German Renaissance structure has broad galleries and a chiming clock on a tower, whose four faces are illuminated at night. As you continue up Maraval Road, you'll see six mansions lined up one after the other, ranging architecturally from a French/English country house to a rather foreboding turreted fortress. Among these six are the Corsican white wedding cake, Whitehall, housing the offices of the Prime Minister; a French Provincial mansion; a complicated Baroque Colonial house with domes, cupolas, columns, and wrought-iron filigree; and the Archbishop's House, described as a semioriental, Romanesque, Byzantine, and early Renaissance. In fact, its Irish architect managed to incorporate a bit of each of these styles in the massive structure. These six mansions were built in the early 1900s by cocoa magnates, three ex-mayors, and other men of great wealth, all of whom seemed to compete with each other for architectural grandeur. The mansions are used now as offices though the government has taken over several to try to preserve and restore them.

North of the Savannah are the beautifully landscaped President's House, whose gardens are often used for picnics and wedding-party photos; and the Royal Botanic Gardens, which date from 1820 and cover some sixty-five acres. Licensed guides will take you around and you'll find them indispensable. The variety of trees and flowers includes lotus lilies sacred to the Egyptians; the holy fig tree of the Buddhists; the bleeding "raw beef" tree, monkey pods, monkey puzzles, Indian and Chinese banyans; Ceylon willows; an orchid house, fernery, and nutmeg ravine; plus the spectacular tropical blooms that have never failed to please. Next door, the Emperor Valley Zoo, with some of the island's unusual wildlife, is a good place to get to know some of Trinidad's younger generation since it's a popular spot for school excursions.

By then, footsore and certainly weary, you'll have discovered much of Port of Spain by day, so head for your hotel for a rest. The city by night is a spectacle of its own and you won't want to miss it.

Set aside a day to explore Fort George and environs by taxi tour. Fort George is an old bastion that was recently restored. A fine spot for a picnic, it sits atop a 1,100-foot hill on the western edge of town and commands an impressive panoramic view. Stop at the temples and mosques of the St. James district. From Lady Young Road, near the Hilton, go to Lady Young Lookout for the best view of the city and its harbor activities. If you have more time, a drive out to Chaguaramus

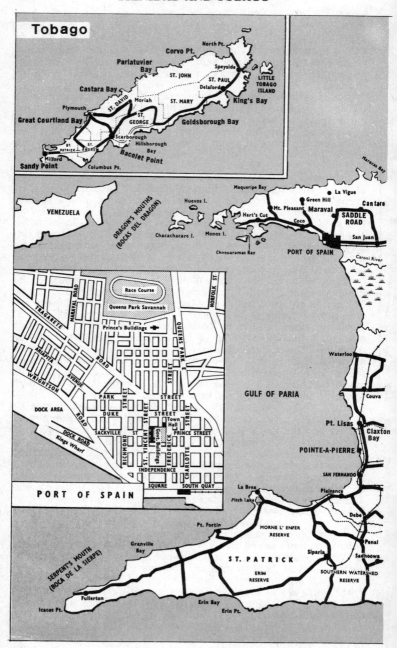

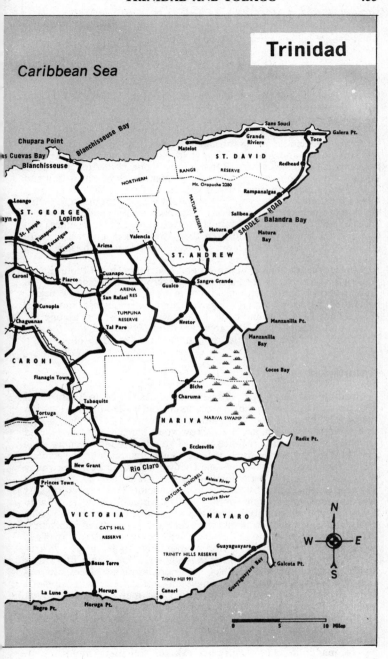

Trinidad

Caribbean Sea

Peninsula for a look at some of Port of Spain's prettiest residential areas, the former U.S. military installations, and a close-up of some of the offshore islands might also be of interest.

The North

The most popular excursion for visitors is to the North Coast beaches, about thirty-four miles from Port of Spain and reached by what is known as the "Skyline Highway." You'll drive through the exclusive residential areas of St. Clair and Maraval, past the Moka Golf Course, and over The Saddle, a pass through the ridge that separates the valleys of Santa Cruz and Maraval. The road winds through the luxuriant vegetation of the Northern Range even at one point under vaulted arches of bamboo—the views are spectacular. Both Maracas Bay and Las Cuevas Bay are long curved stretches of white sand fringed by green hills and coconut palms. You could walk for hours here or try surfing in the long rolling waves, or just relax with a picnic. Undertow can be tricky, especially at Maracas, so you shouldn't bathe unless you are a strong swimmer—and even then, don't do it alone. There are changing facilities and small open-air restaurants serving fresh seafood and local dishes at both beaches.

Continue on to Blanchisseuse, a small colorful French Creole village. Its Victorian cottages are laden with gingerbread trim and there is a little wooden church with primitive paintings and a narrow bridge spanning the Arima River where villagers sometimes fish and bathe. The foliage here is brilliant; the little town is almost lost among the palms and banana trees. This area can also be combined with the Asa Wright Nature Centre located inland, seven miles north of Arima.

Northeast

Heading east out of Port of Spain on the Eastern Main Road, you'll pass through St. Joseph, the former capital, and Tunapuna, the location of the University of the West Indies. In the town of Arouca, a sign points north to Lopinot. The narrow road hairpins up, down, and around precipice after precipice and—if you dare to look—offers some breathtaking views over the Northern Range and down on the Arouca River, farmlands, forests, and small villages. Nestled in a lush valley is Lopinot, originally a predominantly French settlement founded in the nineteenth century by the Count de Lopinot. This French royalist was awarded these lands for his service with the British in Santo Domingo and he literally hacked out of the thick forest a prosperous coffee and cocoa plantation on terrain everyone considered impenetrable. His lovely estate house has been well restored and now displays some interesting furniture, period memorabilia, tools, musical instruments of the area, and photographs showing the estate in various stages. The grounds and gardens, both popular picnic places, are lovingly tended by Martin Gomez, whose ancestors date back to Lopinot's time. He will explain a bit of the history and may also entertain you with a Parang, a typical song of the valley that has become Trinidad's traditional Christmas music. The villagers are a mixture of French, Spanish, Amerindian, and African, and their rhythmic, toe-tapping songs, sung in a French/Spanish patois, are accompanied by guitar, cuatro, mandolin, chac-chac (maracas), and sometimes violin.

Also in this village is a "moved over" church, brought stone by stone from nearby Caura, whose residents were resettled in Lopinot when a dam was constructed in their valley; and a maze of five caves, all with stalactites of varying ages. A colony of white cockroaches has been discovered in one of these caves—it's the only place in the world that this species has so far been sighted.

Another excellent all-day excursion is the Asa Wright Nature Centre, seven miles north of Arima. Both serious naturalists and those even mildly interested will enjoy walking, looking, investigating, or just relaxing among the variety of exotic fauna and brilliant flora of the rain forest. Situated at 1200 feet of elevation in the Northern Range, this former private estate was purchased from the Wright family in 1967 and set up under a trust administration by the Bank of Nova Scotia and an international management board. The Centre was a coffee, cocoa, and citrus plantation and, because its previous owners shared an interest in nature with the public, has long been a favorite for birdwatchers. So rich is the fauna here that serious watchers may add over a hundred varieties to their "lifelong list," many exclusive to Trinidad. One of these is the nocturnal oilbird or *guacharo,* whose breeding colony on the grounds in Dunston Cave is the only accessible place to see these rare creatures. The trail down to the cave is moderately difficult and at one point you'll need to wade through shallow water over slippery rocks and walk *over* a metal ladder to gain access to the cave, where these fat brown birds nest in the crevices and on ledges.

You may look here, but don't touch or pick. If you do discover something special, record it in the Centre's nature log to share with those who follow.

The nearby Simla Research Station, owned and operated by the Asa Wright Centre, offers fine scientific facilities for bona fide local and foreign researchers who wish to conduct tropical biological studies.

Return to Port of Spain via Arima, or if it is still early in the afternoon, wind through some spectacular mountain scenery to the coastal village of Blanchisseuse; turn west along the coast and go over The Saddle to reach the capital.

The Southwest

To visit the southwest you might want to head directly for Pitch Lake and work your way back up the west coast to be at Coroni Wildlife Sanctuary to view the return of the Scarlet Ibis at sunset; or start with Caroni at sunrise to see the birds take off en masse.

While Pitch Lake is certainly a geological curiosity, the trip is long, hot, and tiring with few really interesting sights for the average visitor. The southwest is for those who have a full day to kill and want another perspective of the island. On the other hand, petroleum-oriented business travelers will be fascinated by the huge refineries, vast oil fields, and supermodern industrial complexes.

The eighty-six-mile round trip to Pitch Lake from Port of Spain will take you on Uriah Butler Highway, which runs along the coast to San Fernando, Trinidad's second-largest city. Along the way visit Chaguanas, a good place to buy handmade East Indian jewelry. Stop in at the colorful market if it's Saturday. Pointe-à-Pierre is home to a Texaco refinery that is one of the world's largest. On the coast between California and Pointe-à-Pierre is Point Lisas, the Caribbean's most modern industrial complex. This 1500-acre estate has its own deep-water harbor and oxygen/nitrogen plant and the eastern Caribbean's largest power station. This year, when the complex is complete, facilities will be operational for the manufacture of steel, ammonia, fertilizers, liquefied natural gas, methanol, and other important byproducts of Trinidad's abundant oil and natural gas resources. A short film and scale models of the different aspects of the project, as well as a tour of the complex, may be arranged at the reception center.

Not too far south of San Fernando is La Brea, the location of Pitch Lake. As you approach this town the road dips and becomes pocked by what seem to be the world's largest potholes. You'll begin to notice houses leaning at crazy angles due to the pitch that bubbles up unexpectedly, then subsides just as quickly. It can happen anywhere—in a garden or a garage—as this town is built on a foundation of pitch. The lake itself is 130 feet below sea level and encompasses over one hundred acres of thick, warm, viscuous pitch, which the Trinidad and Tobago Tourist Board has likened to "a magnified elephant skin." You can walk on this tough hide if you want to; the experience may remind you of your childhood when you couldn't resist taking a few gumshoe steps in fresh tar. The lake, which is 285 feet deep at the center, has supplied millions of tons of asphalt to the four corners of the world over the past seventy years and apparently will continue doing so—where blocks of pitch are removed by bulldozers one day, the hole fills up again with the semiliquid the next.

About half an hour from Port of Spain on the Uriah Butler Highway is the Caroni Wildlife Sanctuary, 494 acres set aside especially to protect thousands of Scarlet Ibis who roost there. Visitors are taken by flat-bottom motor boat through crisscrossing canals, mangroves, and lagoons, the feeding grounds of over 150 species of birds, 27 of which are not known to nest elsewhere on the island. The real attraction here is the spectacle of clouds of flaming-pink Scarlet Ibis returning home to roost just before sunset, or taking off at dawn. You will not see many in March, April, or May as it is the nesting season. January and February are good; June through December spectacular.

East and Southeast

The Eastern Main Road from Port of Spain will take you to Valencia, where you can take a side trip through the beautiful countryside that surrounds Hollis Reservoir. Or you can continue east, then north on the Valencia–Toco Road, which passes a series of lovely beaches and secluded coves linked by rugged headlands plunging down to the Atlantic. Horseshoe-shaped Balandra Bay is the best place for a swim. You'll pass an assortment of towns with odd names such as Matura, Salybia, Rampanalgas, and Redhead. At Toco turn off to Galera Point, the easternmost tip of Trinidad.

From Valencia you can also continue south on the Eastern Main Road. Sagre Grande, an important market town, is followed by Cocoa Bay, a succession of immense beaches edged with miles of coconut palms. These are said to be the result of the wreck of a ship from Brazil carrying a cargo of coconuts. At low tide these beaches become a superhighway of sand stretching over thirty miles from Manzanilla down to Guayaguayare, another important petroleum-producing area. For those with more than a few days on the island, a leisurely tour through this, "the other side" of Trinidad, is definitely worthwhile.

PRACTICAL INFORMATION FOR TRINIDAD

FACTS AND FIGURES. Rectangular-shaped Trinidad measures 50 miles by 37 miles and has a surface of 1,864 square miles. Its rough, jagged outline resembles a jigsaw puzzle piece and you can almost see where it should fit into Venezuela, just seven miles away. Geologists are certain that it was once attached to South America and broke away from the continent around 10,000 B.C. Rich in continental fauna and flora, similar to those of Venezuela, Trinidad is home to over 400 kinds of birds, 700 varieties of orchids, 617 butterflies, 55 different reptiles, 108 mammals, and 25 amphibians. The island's tree-covered Northern Range, an extension of South America's coastal Andes, sweeps abruptly down to the indented coastline; the two highest peaks are Cerro del Aripo, 3,085 feet, and El Tuchche, 3,072 feet. A lower range of hills cuts through the center of the island, an important farming area as well as the location of the principal towns. The south is vast and almost flat with sugar cane, marshes, tropical forest, oil fields, and the world's largest pitch lake. Port of Spain is the capital and, with its suburbs, is home to about 400,000 of the island's total population of 1.2 million. English is the official language, spoken with a very particular Trinidadian lilt; Urdu and Hindi are also spoken by the large East Indian population. Trinidad is one hour ahead of eastern standard time.

WHEN TO GO. Trinidad and Tobago have two seasons: dry from January–May; wet from June–December. There is a short dry spell, a sort of Indian summer, called "Petit Carême" in September and October, but even in the height of the wet season rain may be heavy but of short duration and is soon followed by sun. There is an average of eight hours of sunshine every day and 80 to 84 degrees F is the average daytime temperature; it drops into the mid-70s in the evening, cooler in the mountains. This tropical warmth is tempered by year-round cooling trade winds. Tobago is slightly cooler and less humid than Trinidad. Carnival is an exciting time to be in Trinidad (main festivities the two days before Ash Wednesday) and especially in Port of Spain, where the action goes on day and night; it is important to note that hotels have a five-day minimum and higher rates during this period. While most Trinidad hotels do not lower their rates after April 15, all the Tobago resorts take as much as 40% off their tariffs until the high season starts on December 15. At this time there are also some excellent packages from the States that provide economy-minded travelers the opportunity to visit this relatively expensive destination for a price that is far below the usual airfare alone.

PASSPORTS AND VISAS. Valid passports are required of all U.S., Canadian, and British visitors, and validity must extend a minimum of six months beyond your entry date, even if you're only staying a few days. Visas are required for U.S. citizens who plan to stay more than two months and for business travelers to Trinidad and Tobago.

MONEY. Trinidad and Tobago use TT dollars, which equal U.S. $.42. A U.S. dollar = TT $2.40. It is advisable to exchange money for local currency since purchases will cost you less in local currency. Banks give the best rate. Be sure to keep your receipts for changing money back before departure. Major hotels have banks on their premises.

WHAT WILL IT COST:

A typical day on Trinidad for two persons will run:

	U.S.$
Hilton Hotel with breakfast	$ 140
Luncheon at an in-town restaurant	30
Dinner at a moderate in-town spot	50
Tips or service charges at the restaurants: taxes and service charges at the hotels	30
Car rental or sightseeing for one day	50
Total	$ 300

HOW TO GET THERE. By Air. *American Airlines, BWIA,* and *Pan Am* fly direct from New York; *BWIA,* and *Eastern* from Miami. From Canada: *Air Canada* and *BWIA* fly in from Toronto; *Air Canada* from Montreal. From London: *British Airways* and *BWIA.*

Within the West Indies, regular and frequent service is provided by *BWIA,* Eastern, *LIAT,* and a number of small airlines.

By Sea. Several cruise ships include Trinidad in their itineraries.

From Trinidad to Tobago. *By Air.* BWIA's Airbridge shuttles over every half hour starting at 6:30 A.M.; extra flights on weekends. Flight time is 15–20 minutes; return airfare TT $75. Visitors flying to Trinidad from the U.S. and Canada may have a round-trip Tobago ticket included for no extra fare; be sure your travel agent is aware of this.

By Sea. There is ferry service twice a day aboard the *M.F. Gelting* and *M.F. Tobago.* Both ships carry vehicles as well as passengers. The 90-mile trip takes about 4½ hours. Cost: TT $26 tourist class; TT $40 cabin class round trip.

AIRPORT TAX AND OTHER CHARGES. There is a 3% government tax on hotel accommodations, as well as a 10% service charge. The international airport departure tax is TT $20.

TELEPHONE AND EMERGENCY NUMBERS. Police: 999; fire: 990; ambulance: 990. Port of Spain General Hospital is located on Charlotte St., near the southern border of The Savannah, tel: 625–7869. To call Trinidad directly from the U.S., dial 1 + 809 + five-digit local number. International direct dialing is possible but you must go through the operator at all hotels; a handling fee will be charged, usually 20%.

HOTELS. There are just a handful of hotels on Trinidad, so reserve well in advance, especially at Carnival. We call $120–150 *Expensive;* $70–95 *Moderate;* $28–60 *Inexpensive* for a double room.

Farrell House. *Expensive.* Southern Main Rd., Claxton Bay. Tel. 659–2271/2230/2272. Perfect for those with business in the south, this modern hotel is spread out on a hill and offers 50 air-conditioned spacious rooms and nine suites—including a Royal Suite with four-poster bed and Victorian trappings. All have wall-to-wall carpeting, good-size balconies with a sea view, telephone but no television. There's a pleasant pool as well as facilities for meetings and banquets.

Hilton International-Trinidad. *Expensive.* Lady Young Rd., Port of Spain. Tel. 624–3211/3111. The 12th floor is at ground level, and taxis swirl in the *portecochere* at the lobby on the top of the hotel. Interesting "upside-down" idea that we still find appealing. The 442 rooms and 16 suites are large, nicely appointed, and have balconies with a view, minibar, radio, and TV. The North Wing contains 57 deluxe rooms on three Vista Executive floors and offers such special features as full secretarial services, interpreters, photocopy machine, international courier service, and other helpful timesavers for business travelers. This is the island's liveliest and best facility with a large pool on the seventh floor; two tennis courts lighted for night play; shopping arcade; health club, sauna, and beauty salon; the city's best restaurant with nightly entertainment; and a steel-band brunch by the pool on Sundays.

Chaconia Inn. *Moderate.* 106 Saddle Rd., Maraval. Tel. 623–2354/2101. Located in a quiet residential area a few miles north of Port of Spain, this 48-room property has well-decorated, air-conditioned accommodations that include 22 standard rooms; 16 deluxe rooms with hot plates, refrigerators and TVs; and ten two-bedroom suites, each with a full kitchen, in a separate building across the road. There's a small pool, nightly disco, good dining room with entertainment Wednesday through Sunday, and a roof garden with three-times-a-week barbecues (TT $40–50). A comfortable, well-run alternative to the larger hotels, with the Moka Golf Course just minutes away and the Maxi Taxi route running right by the front door.

Holiday Inn. *Expensive.* Wrightson Rd., Port of Spain. Tel. 625–3361/4531. Set in a tropical garden in a not very attractive commercial area in downtown Port of Spain. The 249 rooms include nine junior suites and two executive suites, each with typical Holiday Inn amenities: air conditioning, balcony overlooking the pool or harbor, two double beds, radio and TV, telephone, and wall-to-wall carpeting. The facilities are excellent with everything from free room service to Monopoly games to borrow; an Olympic-size swimming pool and a children's pool, beauty salon, shopping arcade, meeting rooms, cocktail lounge with nightly entertainment, and two restaurants, one the revolving rooftop *La Ronde,* with fine food and views to match.

Kapok Hotel. *Moderate.* 16–18 Cotton Hill, St. Clair. Tel. 622–6441/4. The enterprising Chan family has constructed a convenient small complex consisting of a seven-story hotel, two of Port of Spain's best restaurants, a conference room for 50, a swimming pool, and a shop or two. The 71 rooms have all been redecorated completely, with new carpeting, wicker furniture, upholstery, and curtains, and more modern plumbing. All are spacious and have air conditioning and radio, but only 12 come with TV. There are six well-appointed suites with full kitchens and nine efficiency studios. Hard to beat for price, convenience and location right off the Savannah.

Asa Wright Nature Centre. *Inexpensive.* G.P.O. Bag 10, Port of Spain. Tel. (212) 840–5961 for reservations. Seven miles north of Arima, about an hour from Port of Spain. Naturalists and bird watchers might be interested in the rustic cottages here in the middle of a wildlife preserve. Two meals are included in the $60 per person fee charged for the 14 very simply furnished rooms. Come equipped with slacks, long-sleeved shirts, sturdy nonslip walking shoes, and your favorite insect repellent for hiking the Centre's fascinating trails. No children under 14.

Hotel Normandie. *Inexpensive.* 10 Nook Ave., St. Ann's. Tel. 624–1181/5. A small hillside hotel in a cool green suburb, just a few minute's drive from downtown Port of Spain. The 45 air-conditioned rooms have been newly redecorated and feature modern furniture, radio, telephone, shower, and bath. Twin beds in the 25 standard rooms; two double beds and TV in the 20 superior. Rooms are located in the three wings or in the main building around a courtyard with swimming pool. There's a bar/lounge for evening entertainment, a good restaurant, and three meeting rooms.

Monique's. *Inexpensive.* 114 Saddle Rd., Maraval. Tel. 629–2233. Mike and Monica Charbonné's very popular little guesthouse has just seven rooms; all with private bath, most with air conditioning. This is a real at-home atmosphere and the Charbonnés couldn't be more helpful. Mike is the former sales promotion officer for Angostura—a man who knows his rums, local history, and how to tell a good story. There's TV on the back porch and good home-cooked meals available if you give the Charbonnés advance notice. A U.S. $5 full American breakfast and $10 dinner featuring West Indian specialties are both bargains that can't be beat. Guests have full run of the house.

HOME AND APARTMENT RENTALS. While there are a few homes and apartments for rent in Trinidad, most visitors prefer the hotels, most of which have suites with kitchen facilities for long-term stays.

HOW TO GET AROUND. If you are only staying a short time in Port of Spain, we do not recommend renting a car. The time and energy wasted sitting in Port of Spain's traffic jams could be far better utilized. But if you insist, reserve well in advance and be prepared to pay the Caribbean's highest rate (U.S. $50 per day and up, unlimited mileage) for rental cars. Know also that a deposit of about TT $1,000 will be required as will an International Driving License. Gas is no longer the bargain it once was. Recent price rises have brought it up to almost U.S. $1.50 per gallon. And remember to drive on the left and use your horn in the mountains.

Taxis are unionized and have set fares, though the driver's quotations are not always what they should be. Official rates are posted on a board as you exit customs; the Tourist Board also provides rate sheets, so ask for one—it will be useful. A typical fare would be TT $50 from the airport to the Hilton or Holiday Inn. Driving from and to Piarco Airport is about 45 minutes; *much* longer during rush hours.

An excellent new airport minibus service makes scheduled trips to Piarco from major hotels for just TT $17 and is allowed to use the quicker "priority route" during congested hours. There is also a public bus that runs every half-hour from 5:00 A.M.–11:00 P.M. and goes from the airport to Tunapuna for TT 50¢; then you transfer to a regular bus to your destination for another TT 50¢. Tickets for this bus must be purchased in advance at the priority bus route stations in Port of Spain and Tunapuna.

To get around Port of Spain, try the route taxis which take on and let off passengers as they travel. The route taxis are regular cars with the letter "H" on their license plates and two colored vans called Maxi Taxis. There is a set fare for each route; route taxis may be hailed along the road as they pass, and they do pass frequently.

TOURIST INFORMATION SERVICES. The on-island head office is the *Trinidad and Tobago Tourist Board*, 122–24 Frederick St., Port of Spain. Tel. 623–7405; hours: 8:30 A.M.–4:30 P.M. Mon.–Fri.; and at Piarco Airport. For sources closer to home, see "Tourist Information Services" section in the *Facts at Your Fingertips* chapter.

SPECIAL EVENTS. Carnival (Carnival Monday and Tuesday are Feb. 10, and 11 in 1986). For color, rhythm, and sheer flamboyance, Trinidad's Carnival is unsurpassed. Preparations begin almost as soon as the previous year's celebration is over, with various group leaders laboring over their next theme's elaborate costume designs before setting them into production in various "mas' camps"—mas' is short for masquerade. Right after New Year's, the *fetes* (public parties with several orchestras to dance away the night), calypso shows, steel-band rehearsals, and preliminary judgings begin and enthusiasm starts building. For those with an urge to really join in a "mas' band" (parade group), places can be purchased (long in advance) for fees that vary according to the prestige of the group and the intricacy of the costumes.

Parades take place in San Fernando, Arima, and Tobago, but Port of Spain is the real center of action. The city starts bubbling with excitement the week before Ash Wednesday, when The Savannah offers a treat for ears and eyes with steel-band and King and Queen semifinals. Kiddies Carnival has thousands of minimasqueraders in regalia any adult would be proud of, parading through the streets before their Junior King and Queen are chosen. Saturday the Steelband Panorama Finals take place when the top ten survivors of two days of preliminaries strut their stuff, playing everything from the latest calypso to Tchaikovsky's 1812 Overture. The following day is the great spectacular of *Dimanche Gras,* when eight top calypsonians compete for the Monarch crown and the finalists for most outstanding costumes again parade on stage for the election of the King and Queen of Carnival. It's an exciting evening of music, song, and dance with the most spectacular of all the costumes spotlighted onstage in The Savannah. At dawn on Monday, it's *J'ouvert* (or "Joovay," as it is locally called), which means "the day begins" and the official start of Carnival is underway. The whole town starts jumping up, literally leaping into the air to the compelling beat of thousands of steel drums rolling down the streets. The celebration progresses from mere abandon on Monday to overwhelming rapture on Tuesday morning and reaches a throbbing, ecstatic climax on Tuesday night, when pandemonium reigns and everybody tries to get in the "las lap." Suddenly the clock strikes midnight and Carnival collapses like a punctured balloon until the following year.

Phaguah. This Hindu festival is usually observed on a Sunday in March or April and celebrates the triumph of good over evil. Prayer and fasting take place, but there is also a day-long celebration of singing, dancing, drumming, and the dousing of everyone with *aheer,* a vermillion dye.

Hosein. A three-day winter celebration in the Moslem holy month of Muharram. The highlight is a long procession of wood-and-paper, temple-shaped Tadjahs which are set afire when they reach the sea.

Santa Rosa. A month-long festivity observed by the Carib community of Arima paying tribute to the Peruvian saint, Rosa de Lima. High mass is celebrated but the fiesta revolves around the selection of an annual Carib Queen, which takes place late in August.

Best Village. Begun by Trinidad and Tobago's first prime minister, the late Dr. Eric Williams, in 1962. This annual series of competitions provides the opportunity for villages from all over Trinidad and Tobago to show off their talents in song, drama, and dance as well as arts and crafts and cooking. The selection of a Queen assures that beauty is not forgotten. Concerts and folk fairs take place from mid-August to early November; handicraft and food fairs usually between Independence Day and Republic Day.

 TOURS. While renting a car may be cheaper, we feel that you'll be much better off with an organized tour operator or knowledgeable taxi driver. Two of Port of Spain's most reliable operators are *Hub Travel Ltd.,* 68–72 Maraval Rd., tel. 622–0936/37 with branch offices at the Hilton, Bel Air Hotel, and Piarco Airport; and *Rolly Fun Tours,* 48A Perseverance Rd., Maraval, tel. 629–8023. Prices range from U.S. $20–30 for a city tour to $100 for a seven-hour island circular tour. You can cruise in the Gulf of Paria off Trinidad's northwest peninsula to five offshore islands, where many residents have weekend homes, aboard the *Jolly Roger* a motor sailboat fitted out like a pirate ship. It makes sunset trips during the week, daytime excursions on weekends (TT $25). There's usually a band on board and a cash bar for drinks or snacks. Tel. 622–8941 or 622–9055 for their schedule. The *M.V. Flamingo* is a 39 foot motorboat that makes four-hour day trips (TT $120) that include a swim at Grand Fond Bay, buffet lunch, and open bar. Tel. 632–0044. Boat tours of the Caroni Wildlife Sanctuary are conducted by two authorized operators. Mr. Nanan at #1 Bamboo Grove Settlement, tel. 638–3033; and Mr. Ramsahai at #2 Bamboo Grove Settlement, tel. 638–3162. Be sure you get one of these gentlemen in person for the most rewarding visit with full explanation of this ecologically fascinating swamp area, which covers over 48 miles of water and is home to hundreds of species of birds, including the Scarlet Ibis.

 PARKS AND GARDENS. *Royal Botanic Gardens and Emperor Valley Zoo.* Circular Rd. on the northern boundary of The Savannah. Open daily 9:30 A.M.–6:30 P.M. Botanic gardens are free; the zoo has a TT $2 entry fee for adults; TT $1 for children. These tropical gardens stretch across 65 acres right in the heart of the city. There are licensed guides to help you identify trees, flowers, and plants from all over the world that have been planted here since

1820. Next door, the zoo offers a good look at some of Trinidad's usual and more exotic species as well as other animals such as bison, lions, and tigers.

Queen's Park Savannah. A 200-acre expanse with a racetrack in the center, beautiful trees and flowers, and *the* place for jogging, soccer and cricket games, and picnics. Food vendors line its borders and some of the city's most interesting architecture is found along Trinidad's biggest "round-about."

Cleaver Woods Recreation Park. 30 acres of verdant natural forest extending north and south on the road to Arima, east of the capital. There is a forestry guide on hand to accompany visitors, a small museum, and a 200-year-old water wheel that is being restored. Picnic facilities and a playground for children.

 BEACHES. Trinidad is not as known for its beaches as Tobago, but you might consider *Maracas* and *Las Cuevas,* about an hour's drive north of Port of Spain. Both offer long curved stretches of white bordered by shady palms, rolling surf (with sometimes treacherous undertow), picnic and changing facilities, and small restaurants. In the north near *Toco* is a series of lovely beaches and secluded coves linked by rugged headlands plunging down to blue waters; no facilities. In the southeast the beach stretches from Manzanilla to Guayaguayare Bay, but this is the Atlantic and the surf can be rough; the water is often cloudy due to nearby oil fields and the confluence of South America's Orinoco River which sends out quite a lot of silt and mud. No facilities but the sight of this "superhighway of sand" at low tide is spectacular.

 PARTICIPANT SPORTS. **Surfing** is good at Maracas Bay and Las Cuevas, especially during the winter months. The Trinidad Hilton has two **tennis** courts lighted for night play. **Golf** is best at the 18-hole championship Moka Golf Course in Maraval. It was designed in the late 19th century and modeled after St. Andrews in Scotland. There is a second course in Chaguaramus, west of the city. This is a public course with pro shop and pull carts. Tel. 625–1021, ext. 738 for further information. **Squash** may be played on the courts of the Pelican Inn, near the Hilton, open 6:00 A.M.–10:30 P.M. daily. 40-minute sessions may be reserved by calling 624–2486. Contact the Tourist Board, tel. 623–7405, for up-to-date information on deep-sea **fishing, hunting,** and **sailing. Bird watchers** should not miss the Asa Wright Centre north of Arima and the Caroni Wildlife Sanctuary, ten miles south of Port of Spain.

 SPECTATOR SPORTS. **Cricket** matches are held at the Queen's Park Oval on St. Clair Ave. in Port of Spain and Guaracara Park in San Fernando from January to June; the most important meets are on weekends. Informal matches may be viewed almost any day in Queen's Park Savannah. **Horseracing** is held at Queen's Park Savannah, the Arima Race Club, and Union Park Turf Club in San Fernando almost every Saturday. Main races are run Christmas, Easter, and in May, June, August, October, and November.

The National Stadium and Jean Pierre Sports Complex on Wrightson Road Extension, in the western part of Port of Spain, provides facilities for track and field events and all major sports from wrestling, boxing, netball, soccer, and lawn tennis to karate exhibitions.

 HISTORIC SITES AND HOUSES. **Fort George.** Fort Rd., about three miles northwest of Port of Spain. Hours: 10:00 A.M.–6:00 P.M., no fee. This bastion, 1,100 feet above sea level, was built in 1805 by Sir Thomas Hislop, Governor of Trinidad from 1803 until 1811. There are some interesting 18th-century cannons, a small museum, a signal station that was once used to monitor and report the movement of sailing ships, and a series of uninterrupted views—the one to the west over Chaguaramus Peninsula, the offshore islands, and Dragons' Mouths to Venezuela is especially impressive.

Lopinot. Lopinot Rd., Arouca District, 22 miles northeast of Port of Spain. Hours: 8:00 A.M.–4:00 P.M., no fee. Founded in the 19th century by the royalist Charles Josephe Count de Lopinot, a Frenchman who was awarded this land for services rendered the English against the rebels of Toussaint l'Ouverture in Santo Domingo. Mostly impenetrable forest, but the Count managed to literally hack out a prosperous coffee and cocoa plantation whose estate house—"La Reconnaissance"—jail, barracks, stone oven, and cocoa-house church have been preserved. His grave is also on the property, and at the northern boundary are five caves which may be explored.

The Magnificent Nine. A group of historic buildings built in the early 1900s, each with its own unique touches of European-influenced architecture. Included are two solid and ornate German Renaissance structures: *The Red House,* Woodford Sq., used as the seat of Trinidad and Tobago's government; and *Queen's Royal College,* Maraval Rd., a prestigious boys' secondary school. The official residence of Port of Spains' Roman Catholic archbishop is an elaborate Romanesque/Renaissance/oriental palace that simply goes by the name of the *Archbishop's House.* Next door to it on Maraval Road is the Anglican bishop's home, *Hayes Court,* a French/English country manor house. The rest of the Magnificent Nine were built as private residences, four of them side-by-side on Maraval Rd.: *Stollmeyer's Castle,* a German, Romantic, Rhenish, Scotch, and French fortress built by a Philadelphian; *Whitehall,* Corsican/Moorish with both French and Venetian influences, used as U.S. Army headquarters in 1941–44; now the offices of the prime minister; *Ambard House* or *Roomer,* a complicated French Baroque building and the only one of the group that is still privately owned and occupied; *Mille Fleurs,* a charming French provincial house built by a Venezuelan as a present for her husband; and *Knowsley,* on Queen's Park West, a large German/Italian-style structure built originally by a Scotsman, now used by several ministries.

 MUSEUMS AND GALLERIES. National Museum and Art Gallery. 117 Frederick St., Port of Spain. Hours: 10:00 A.M.–6:00 P.M., Tues.–Sat., no fee, Tel. 623–6419. A small museum guarded by Spanish cannon dating from England's capture of the island in 1791. Revolving historical exhibits.

Art Creators. Flat 402, 7 St. Ann's Rd., Port of Spain. Call for hours. Tel: 624–4369. Changing shows by local artists and sculptors.

 MUSIC, DANCE, AND STAGE. It is impossible to date the emergence of *calypso* as a folk art, but its melodies in 2/4 and 4/4 time have spread throughout the Caribbean. Its wellsprings are in the melodies of France and Spain and the tribal rhythms of Africa. Even the origins of the name is obscure. One theory is that calypso is an Anglicized corruption of the African word *kai-so,* meaning bravo. The important thing is that calypso is the living expression of a very lively people; its vitality and rhythm are the essence of Trinidad.

The calypso singers adopt high-sounding names: Blue Boy, Lord Melody, and Mighty Sparrow. The singer is also generally the composer, and he will improvise on any theme: politics, sports, personalities, scandal, graft, the high cost of living, love and marriage, love without marriage, and every event of human life. The lyrics are frequently charged with sarcasm, double entendres, and innuendo. More than one politician has been defeated at the polls because his short-comings have been dinned into the electorate's ears by the satire of calypso.

You'll hear calypso singers and bands at Carnival, the four public halls of Port of Spain, in clubs, on beaches, in hotels, and at private parties.

No less ubiquitous in the Land of Calypso are the *steel bands.* It took the Trinidadians to add the fourth dimension of steel to the conventional orchestral categories of strings, woodwinds, and brass. With an intuitive skill and taste that still amaze musicologists, they contrived new instruments out of oil drums, gas tanks, pots, pans, and biscuit tins. The vibrant percussive effects coaxed from these steel instruments have been compared to "melted gold and molten lava, the cross between the melody of a harpsichord, organ and a Hawaiian guitar." The steel bands have their origins in the Shango drums of slaves from the

Yoruba and Mandingo tribes of Africa, drums whose music was forbidden by the planters. As always in the rich cultural melting pot of Trinidad, there were other influences in the development of this musical phenomenon, notably the percussion instruments brought in by East Indian immigrants.

Whatever its ancestry, the steel band as we know it today became public on V-E Day, 1945, when the population of Trinidad grabbed garbage pail lids, empty cans, and anything they could lay their hands on to beat out a victory march in the streets of Port of Spain. It wasn't long before the resonance of metal containers was being controlled by marking their surfaces into segments that would produce the notes of the scale. An uncanny sense of rhythm and tone guided the "untutored" ears of the steel band tuners. Within a year, there were ensembles of "ping pongs," "piano pans," "second pans," "tenor kittles," and "tune booms." Within a decade, steel bands had carried a new and fascinating musical art to the United States and Europe. With calypso, steel bands have become a symbol of the irrepressible vitality of Trinidad. You'll hear a broad spectrum of music ranging from the traditional calypso to concert arrangements of Bach, Rossini, etc. The best time is after New Year, when all the island musicians tune up for the spectacle that is Trinidad's Carnival.

Another special music is *Parang,* Trinidad's traditional Christmas music that has its origin in Venezuelan folk songs. This is a rhythmic, infectous, toe-tapping music sung in a mixture of French and Spanish and accompanied by cuatro, *chac-chac* (maracas), guitar, and sometimes violin. The people who live in the Arouca Valley and especially around Lopinot are best known for this.

There are folkloric shows, plays, and dance recitals at the *Little Carib Theatre,* at the corner of Roberts and White Sts. in Woodbrook, tel. 622–4644; and concerts at *Queen's Hall,* 1–3 St. Ann's Rd., St. Ann's, tel. 624–1284/3194. *Anancy House* (formerly the Astor Cinema) at 37 French St., tel. 625–2650, is a newly converted theater named after a character in many West Indian folk tales. Touchstone Productions, a group of Trinidad's most talented and well-known performers puts on plays here. Your hotel guest relations officer should have detailed information about what is going on at these places.

 SHOPPING. Port of Spain is one of the big bazaars of the West Indies, with all the expected items from India, the Orient, and Europe. Be very sure you are buying what you think you are: All that glitters is not gold here. Many shops offer the "in-bond" system, whereby you pick out and pay for your purchases, which are then delivered to the airport or pier for you to pick up just prior to leaving the country.

Among the duty-free shops at the airport are *Stecher's* for perfume and some luxury items; *Y. DeLima* for watches, cameras, and local jewelry; and a shop for local rum and imported liquors. All shops in the airport are located before you go through immigration.

Island souvenirs that will delight both child and adult are the many dolls that reflect Trinidad's cosmopolitan culture. Steel-band players, native limbo dancers, calypso characters, Moslem Hosein dolls, and sari-draped Hindu dolls are just a few of the colorful miniature personalities that you can take with you.

The main shopping streets in Port of Spain are Independence Sq. and Frederick St.; but the huge shopping malls spread out around the city and its environs are far more comfortable places to browse.

The best "in-bond" shops are *Stecher's* and *Y. deLima.* Both have branches that sell china, crystal, jewelry, perfumes, silver, watches, and cameras. Branches are located at Long Circular Mall on Long Circular Rd. in St. James; West Mall in West Moorings Cocorite; Kirpalani's Round About and ValPark on the way to Piarco Airport; and in the Caribbean's largest mall, Gulf City, south of San Fernando.

If you are looking for English bone china, Limoges porcelain, or Lalique and hand-cut English crystal, try *Stephens and Johnson,* a large department store at 10 Frederick St.

The Trinidad Hilton had an excellent selection of shops including both *Stecher's* and *Y. deLima; Boutique Cybele* and *Begum Boutique* for ladies' apparel; *Kacal's* for wood carvings, wall hangings, furniture, and local handicrafts; *Les Artisans* for leather goods, copper, and semiprecious jewelry; *McLeod's,* with an extensive collection of European, oriental, and local antiques; and *Meilling,* whose exotic and expensive designs are the favorite of Trinidad and Tobago's most fashionable women.

For art, the pretty multiroom gallery *Art Creators,* at #7 St. Ann's Rd., has work of the country's best artists and sculptors on exhibition and also offers some nice inexpensive note cards with watercolor and line drawings of Trinidad and Tobago's architectural gems.

Shopping hours downtown are 8:00 or 8:30 A.M.–4:00 P.M. Mon.–Fri.; 8:00 A.M.–noon on Sat. The malls are open 10:00 A.M.–7:00 P.M. daily including Sun. And, so you will be sure to have enough dollars for shopping, bank hours are Mon.–Thurs. 9:00 A.M.–2:00 P.M.; Fri. 9:00 A.M.–noon and 3:00 P.M.–5:00 P.M.

 RESTAURANTS. Trinidad is famous for its international specialties. You'll find good Chinese, Indian, Creole, French, Italian, Arabic, and West Indian restaurants in Port of Spain and environs. Typical of West Indian fare are "the King and Queen of Creole soups," *sans coche* and *callaloo.* The former is a fabulous ragout of fat pork, salted beef, pig tail, a couple of pounds of meat, onions, chives, split peas, butter, yams, dasheen, *cush-cush* (couscous), cassava, sweet potato, Irish potato, green plantain, coconut milk, and green pepper—topped with dumplings. All *callaloo* requires three bunches of dasheen leaves, a spinach-like leaf, two crabs, twelve okras, two onions, a bunch of chives, a clove of garlic, and a couple of ounces of fat pork and salt beef. Try peppery pigeon pea soup if you see it on a menu; it's also a local specialty, as is pork souse, made with pigs' feet, lots of spices (both aromatic and hot), and garnished with cucumber, lime, and onions.

Try *pastelles,* a concoction of minced meat mixed with corn flour and wrapped in a banana leaf. Crab *matete* is crabmeat and farina. Crab backs are crab meat highly seasoned, then put back in the shell.

Among the Indian contributions are red hot curries and something called *roti,* which is like a king-size crêpe, rolled around a filling of chicken, fish, or meat and seasoned to the palate-burning point. You'll see roti carts all around Port of Spain, particularly along Frederick Street and around The Savannah. Or at night they are sold from stalls and vans in Independence Square.

Delicious bean-size oysters are another specialty. They grow on mangrove roots and have far more flavor than their big brothers from the sea. There is also *chip-chip,* a tiny shellfish that tastes a bit like a clam. From freshwater streams comes the *casadou* or *cascadura,* a fish that is especially good when stuffed—some say it's an aphrodisiac, others say if you eat it you are guaranteed to return to the island.

Rum is the national drink of Trinidad, and there's nothing better than a rum punch flavored with Angostura Bitters, another local product. The joys of rum and Coca Cola and gin and coconut water have been recorded in calypso verses. Carib and Stag are both locally brewed and very good beers.

On special occasions and holidays you may have a chance to taste some of Trinidad's exotic game; armadillo (*tatoo*), whose tender, succulent meat bears no resemblance to its armorlike exterior; wild boar (*quenk*); *lappe* (a large rabbit); fried iguana; or possum (*manicou*) stew. But don't expect these to appear on any menu. There are hunting seasons for each—and all are extremely difficult to catch, thus very, very expensive! Dining out tends to be rather pricey in Trinidad; we call $30 and up *Expensive;* $15–25 *Moderate;* and under $15 *Inexpensive* for a three-course dinner for one person (excluding beverages). Imported wines and liquors are expensive because there is so much duty on them; stick with the good local rum unless you don't mind shelling out over U.S. $6 for something like a Campari and soda; $21 a bottle for a Beaujolais; $13 for a bottle of Gallo Rosé.

La Boucan. *Expensive.* Trinidad Hilton, Lady Young Rd., Port of Spain. Tel. 624–4211. The atmosphere, entertainment, and fine food together make this Trinidad's best and most popular restaurant. Geoffrey Holder's nostalgic, impressionistic mural dominates one wall; the room is large and tables well spaced and "Sugar Fingers" Roach plays a sweet piano nightly. "Boucan" literally means smoke oven in old French patois, and "buccaneers" got their name because they used these ovens to prepare and preserve meats for long voyages. Here, the modern boucan is a red-brick oven fired with tropical guava wood; some of the specialties that come out of it are unusual. There's also a good choice of continental dishes; steaks and seafood; a nightly Chinese dish, and some interesting old Trinidadian recipes such as Creole fish stew. If you still have room, the dessert tray is famous. Monday through Friday there's an "executive buffet" lunch; dinner is served Tuesday through Saturday; an international buffet on Thursdays highlights dishes from a different country each week. Major credit cards accepted.

Café Savanna. *Expensive.* Kapok Hotel, 16–18 Cotton Hill, St. Clair. Tel. 622–6441. Chef Wilfried Martina is Dutch but his menu is as international as the cuisine of Trinidad is diverse. This is a pretty and very popular place with just 16 tables accommodating a maximum of 75 diners on the ground floor of a small hotel on the outskirts of town. The selection changes every three or four months but good Dover sole, lobster, and excellent steak are always available. Then there might be such tempting treats as seafood mousse in aspic or veal scallopini stuffed with smoked salmon and served with hollandaise. Closed Sat. lunch and all day Sun. Major credit cards accepted.

Le Cocrico. *Expensive.* 117–A Henry St., Port of Spain. Tel. 623–8249. Unfortunately the upstairs dining room of this pretty old house has been closed; lunch and dinner are now served downstairs in the wine bar. With just ten tables, it's small, intimate and cozy at dinner; very busy at lunch with local businessmen. The luncheon fare tends to be an eclectic mixture of everything from hamburgers to seafood; dinner is far more interesting and predominantly French with Creole touches. Claude Homeward, known better as Soly, has taken over the kitchen from Francis Pau. He's from Tobago, his father was a chef, and he had been training with Pau for several years. Apparently he learned his lessons well. Desserts are worth saving room for. Lunch is served Mon.–Fri.; dinner Wed., Thurs., and Fri. only. No credit cards.

Le Petit Bourg. *Expensive.* Farrell House Hotel, Southern Main Rd., Claxton Bay. Tel. 659–2271/2230/2272. The one and only place for a good lunch or dinner when touring the south, unless you want authentic East Indian food. The menu here features local dishes such as stuffed crab backs and callaloo, as well as steaks with seafood, French duck à l'orange or coq au vin; even a "cuisine minceur" dish built on classic principals without the classic calories—there is no butter, cream, or flour in the preparation. Call in advance to make sure a conference group has not booked the entire dining room for both lunch and dinner, which is sometimes the case.

La Ronde. *Expensive.* Holiday Inn, Wrightson Rd., Port of Spain. Tel. 625–4521, ext. 7. Dinner only in this romantic setting, a revolving glass-windowed restaurant with fantastic views of the city lights, soft guitar music, and careful, attentive service. The menu is elaborate. The emphasis is definitely continental though stuffed crab back and callaloo are offered as first courses. This is a nice place to sit back, savor the view and enjoy the music—but don't expect haute cuisine. Dinner only, closed Sun. and Mon. evenings. Major credit cards accepted.

J.B.'s. *Moderate to Expensive.* Valpark Plaza, Valsayn Park. Tel. 662–5837. Well-established and popular second-floor place in the middle of a shopping center about half an hour out of town on the way to Piarco Airport. The bar is frequented by this affluent suburb's residents and we've been told that J.B.'s steaks are the best in town. Seafood is another house specialty but the menu is varied and mainly continental. After dinner go downstairs and next door where J.B.'s disco swings until the wee hours; it really gets jammed with a very young crowd on Saturday night. Major credit cards accepted.

The Waterfront. *Moderate to Expensive.* West Mall Shopping Ctr., West Moorings. Tel. 632–0834. Another good place in another shopping center, this one on the western side of Port of Spain. This place really cries out for a seaside setting but decorators have done their best to set the right atmosphere with sunken aquariums placed in the wooden bar, sea-oriented murals, and nautical touches. The menu is heavy on seafood prepared in a variety of ways. For meat eaters there's charbroiled filet mignon, New York strip sirloin, and prime rib as well as "Reef and Beef" and "Surf and Turf" platters for those who want the best of both worlds. Open Mon.–Sat., 10:00 A.M.–midnight. Major credit cards accepted.

Alfie's. *Moderate.* 6–A Warner St., Port of Spain. Tel. 625–6800. Lunch or dinner is a delight in this unique old rum house just off The Savannah, with its authentic brick walls and hand-hewn ceilings. The menu is an eclectic mixture of Arabic appetizers—*sleeh bi burghul* (steamed spinach, wheat, black-eyed peas, and onions), *tabouleh,* beef and patchoi pies, *hummos,* and *kibbe;* and seafood, barbecued chicken, charbroiled steaks, escargots, and quiche lorraine. Closed Sat. lunch, all day Sun., and Mon. evenings. Major credit cards.

The Copper Kettle. *Moderate.* Earl J. Lau Hotel, 66 Edward St., Port of Spain. Tel. 625–4381/3. This cozy downtown restaurant takes its name from the 200-year-old "slave kettle" on display that doubled as cooking pot and "creole safe" where valuables were stored. There are just 13 tables and they are usually filled by businessmen at lunch, so do reserve. Grilled meat is the specialty, but callaloo soup, a vegetable plate, and a fisherman's platter with lobster tail thermidor and shrimp are also featured; all are served with corn on the cob. The lunch and dinner menus are the same, but prices go up in the evening. Closed all day Sun. and dinner Mon. No credit cards.

Il Giardino. *Moderate.* 6 Nook Ave., St. Ann's. Tel. 624–1181/5. Small, romantic spot with soft lights, a garden setting, and guitar music. Luciano has finally settled into this new spot in a pretty suburban house, his third locale over the years. The highlight here is a set five-course (TT $40) prix fixe "Gourmet Tour of France, Italy, or Spain," offered at dinner only. Though we haven't tried it yet, this popular Italian restaurant has a good reputation. No credit cards.

Mangal's. *Moderate.* 13 Queens Park East, Port of Spain. Tel. 624–1201. A beautiful gingerbread mansion. The Mangal family uses the top floors as living quarters and lunch and dinner are served at eight big tables off the *Rooster Bar and Lounge* on the ground floor. The TT $45 East Indian buffet is a lot of good spicy food at a very reasonable price—shrimp cocktail; *dal purri* or *paratha roti;* Mulligatawny soup; curried beef, chicken, or goat (lobster or shrimp available at a supplement); vegetables; *dal;* dessert, and coffee or tea. Also order à la carte T-bone steaks, lamb chops, or chicken platters. Closed Sun. No credit cards.

Normandie. *Moderate.* 10 Nook Ave., St. Ann's. Tel. 624–1181/5. Mrs. Haglin, the chef here, is Scandinavian, so her stuffed crabbacks are seasoned with Swedish spices; her pea soup and pork chops prepared Danish style; and smoked salmon à la Norwegian west coast. But she also does wienerschnitzel, tournedos Rossini, barbecued chicken, baked red snapper, lobster tail, and creme caramel with equal flair. There's a smorgasbord buffet lunch on Wednesday and Friday (TT $35) and a Saturday-night steak barbecue at TT $40. Major credit cards.

Tiki Village. *Moderate.* Kapok Hotel, 16–18 Cotton Hill, St. Clair. Tel. 622–6441/4. Chef Fong is Cantonese but his extensive menu lists everything from egg rolls and fried wontons to corn soup and Mongolian hot pot, Szechuan spiced shrimp, Hawaiian Luau fish, and steak Samoa to crispy fried chicken—and over 100 other choices in between. The decor is Polynesian, and was just redone last summer; the view of Port of Spain from the eighth floor at night is the perfect backdrop for a fine meal in a relaxed atmosphere. Major credit cards.

Veni Mange. *Moderate.* 13 Lucknow St., St. James. No telephone. Do not miss this place! Two Creole beauties, Cordon Bleu–trained Allyson Hennessy and her sister Rosemary Hezekiah, offer the most interesting food in town. Under Allyson's supervision, the kitchen of this little Victorian house is capable of producing perfect beef bourguignon, chili con carne, Hungarian goulash, leg of lamb Milanese, and paella. But more interesting are local specialties such as the island's best calalloo soup; a coconut cakebread called "bake"; stewed beef with eggplant fritters; or just mussels and shrimp; Trinidad hot pot—oxtail pork and beef; and *Oildown,* a classic West Indian dish made with breadfruit, pigs' tails, salted beef, and coconut. The menu changes daily, but there's always a choice of fish, meat, or vegetarian main course. Portions are plentiful but desserts most tempting—fresh fruit crumbles or chocolate sherry tarte are just two in Allyson's large repertoire. Open lunch only, Mon.–Fri. 11:30 A.M.–2:30 P.M. No credit cards.

New Shay Shay Tien. *Moderate to Inexpensive.* 81 Cipriani Blvd. Tel. 622–6294/5592/5123. Chinese dishes plus some with a decidedly tropical touch. The

50-seat upstairs dining room is rather ordinary, but the food is reputed to be the best of its kind. Open lunch and dinner. Closed Sun. No credit cards.

The Outhouse. *Moderate to Inexpensive.* 82–B Woodford St. Tel. 622–5737. We're sure you will agree that the new owners of what was formerly Goddard's could have found a better name for this small, frilled Victorian cottage. The food is unchanged, however, with the accent on vegetarian dishes, seafood, and exotic ice creams. Lunch Mon.–Fri.; dinner Wed.–Fri. No credit cards.

The Verandah. *Moderate to Inexpensive.* Marli St., corner of Woodford. Tel. 622–6583. It's hard to find because there is no sign, but this shady porch on a charming residential street looks most inviting. We can't tell you much more than that this is a popular gathering place for local radio and television people who work nearby. Lunch only.

 NIGHTLIFE AND BARS. Evenings here begin when most people are ready to go to bed in other places. Clubs throb with pulsating bands, disco rocks on, and the major hotels offer everything from limbo to quiet guitar music. For those who want it, Trinidad offers a bit of everything every night of the week.

Mondays is the barbecue with steel band, show, and limbo contest at the *Hilton;* Wednesday is Carnival Night with calypsos and more steel bands, Friday poolside steel band concerts. "Sugar Fingers" Roach and his trio provide music for dancing at *La Boucan* Tuesday through Saturday with Calypsonians contributing songs on Saturdays; a guitarist appears on Tuesday, Thursday, and Friday.

The Calypso Lounge at the Holiday Inn features live music with a view on Wednesday, Friday, and Saturday; a guitarist provides soft music in *La Ronde.*

The Chaconia Inn's Wednesday happy hours with live music from 5:00 P.M. to 8:00 P.M. draw a good crowd, as does their barbecue on the roof garden on Wednesday and Friday. Denise Plummer and Formula perform from 9:30 P.M. on Thursday, Friday, and Saturday in the newly refurbished, indoor restaurant.

The preferred disco keeps changing, but it could be one of the following: *Heritage 67* out in Chaguaramus or *J.B.'s* in the Valpark Center, both on weekends; *Atlantis* in West Mall.

If you are lucky enough to catch The Mighty Sparrow in town, his *Sparrow's Hideaway* in Petit Valley, Diego Martin, about nine miles from Port of Spain, is a great place to meet local residents on the weekend and to really get into the best of calypso.

POSTAGE. From Trinidad and Tobago postage for letters for the U.S. and Canada is TT $.55; TT $.30 for postcards.

ELECTRICAL CURRENT. Trinidad and Tobago use both 110 and 220 volts A.C. Be sure to check which it is before plugging in appliances.

 SECURITY. Trinidad's Port of Spain is a big, cosmopolitan city, so visitors should do here as they would in New York, Toronto, or London—lock cars and doors; not leave valuables around unattended. Women should not walk unescorted downtown or in The Savannah at night.

Tobago is a quiet place with not much activity except at the hotels or The Donkey Cart in the evening so there's no reason to wander in town at night. Most people don't bother to lock cars here, but do it anyway, especially if there is anything at all of value inside. Pigeon Point is a popular beach with cruise-ship excursions, so belongings should not be left unattended.

EXPLORING TOBAGO

Scarborough, a town of 17,000, is one of the quietest places under the sun. Its official sights are few. There is a colorful fruit and vegetable market daily that's liveliest on Wednesday and Saturday mornings. You can drive up the hill to Old Fort King George. From this height, 430 feet, you will have a view of town, bay, countryside and the great sweep of the Atlantic stretching twenty-one miles southwest to Trinidad, clearly visible like a ship on the horizon. Nothing remains of the old French fort, but you can see the ruins of the old barracks, a domed structure under which is a freshwater well, and an old mortar near the lighthouse, a silent reminder of Tobago's days of violence. The impression of past history is deepened as you descend the hill past a row of silent cannon trained toward the sea and enemies long forgotten. Below the General Hospital you will see another relic of the past, the old prison. Here, in 1801, after a revolt of the slaves, the ringleader and thirty-eight of his associates were imprisoned. To terrorize the blacks into submission, the governor pretended to hang all thirty-nine of the prisoners from a gibbet on the prison walls. The townspeople watched thirty-nine hangings; the slaves were terrified into submission, the planters appalled at such reckless destruction of their property. But only one man, the ringleader, was really executed, his body being strung up again and again from the gallows.

Using Scarborough as a starting point, excursions can be made to all parts of the island. Allow a full day for the trip to the northern coast. This run will take you on the Windward Road along the Atlantic coast, through lovely valleys, up steep hills, through groves of coconut and cocoa, and along mountain ridges affording matchless views over the beaches, bays, and reefs until you come to Speyside. This is a delightful fishing village, set on the crescent of Speyside Bay. Behind it, the green profile of Pigeon Peak, at 1800 feet Tobago's highest mountain, dominates the northern end of the island.

Speyside is the jumping-off place for a star-shaped island with three names: Little Tobago, Ingram Island, and Bird-of-Paradise. The last is the least official but the most firmly established. It was here that Sir William Ingram brought those Greater Birds of Paradise from New Guinea in 1909, and it's here alone in the Western Hemisphere that you may be lucky enough to catch a glimpse of one of these extraordinary cockerels flashing about with their sprays of golden plummage. The island is now a 258-acre bird sanctuary. It's just a mile and a half offshore and is easily reached by small boat from Speyside. Guides will meet you on the island and conduct small tours along the trails. Unfortunately Hurricane Flora did a great deal of damage here in 1963, and most of the birds were lost or perhaps flew off elsewhere. Anyway sightings have become rarer and rarer. Admission to the sanctuary is free. Go in the early morning or late afternoon.

From Speyside, drive uphill northwest across a narrows to Charlotteville and Man o'War Bay, one of the finest natural deep-water harbors in the Caribbean. It is 1¾ miles long by 1¼ wide; forty fathoms deep at its mouth, ten fathoms right offshore. The south side of the bay is a long sandy beach. Above it on the hillside, the white houses of Charlotteville nestle like pigeons come home to roost. Pigeon

Peak rises grandly behind the whole scene, verdant, majestic, silent. A Government Rest House is situated on the palm-fringed beach at Man o'War Bay—a perfect setting for a swim and a picnic.

Store Bay is the base for a difficult mile-and-a-half hike to Robinson Crusoe's Cave. It can be reached only on foot. "A local descendant will take you there," writes Commander Alford, author of *The Island of Tobago*, "but it is only fair to warn you that there is not very much to see!" This advice, coming from a staunch exponent of the theory that Robinson Crusoe slept here, is still valid today. Head instead for the lovely little horseshoe beach, Miss Esmee's roti stand, or the pleasant patio bar of the Crown Reef Hotel for a Crusoe Cocktail.

Another day should be spent visiting Buccoo Reef and taking a swim in the Nylon Pool two miles offshore. This quiet, warm natural pool has a white-sand bottom that gives it the clear, bright blue color of a nylon fishing line. Also go by Pigeon Point, a long promontory of white sand shaded by coconut palms—an idyllic place to do nothing but relax, swim, and sun. Take a late-afternoon drive up to Plymouth, just six miles north, to visit the historic sights of Fort James, built by the British in 1777, the Courlander's monument to the brave settlers who came from what is now Latvia, and the grave of Betty Stivens, who died in 1783 and whose epitaph reading "She was a Mother without knowing it and a Wife without letting her Husband know it, Except by her kind indulgences to him" still remains a mystery.

PRACTICAL INFORMATION FOR TOBAGO

Note: Please see *Practical Information for Trinidad* for the following information: When to Go, Passports and Visas, Money, How to Get There, Airport Taxes and other Charges, Postage, Security, and Electricity.

 FACTS AND FIGURES. Tobago measures 26 miles long by seven miles wide and has a total area of 116 square miles. The population is 42,000, half of whom live in the capital of Scarborough. A range of volcanic hills runs the length of the island, descending in the South to a narrow plain whose origins are coral. Pigeon Point near Speyside is the highest peak at 1800 feet. Torrents flowing down from the hills have formed pretty valleys perpendicular to the coastline. The island's soil is fertile and there are many forests in the uplands comprised of rare woods; there are sugar, cocoa, pineapple, citrus, and copra plantations in the valleys. The beaches are powdery white sand fringed with coconut palms. There are more exotic birds here per acre than on any other West Indian island, including seven species of hummingbird native to Trinidad alone. There are no buildings higher than two stories; cars may not exceed 35 mph and roads are more like narrow country lanes, with the exception of a seven-mile stretch of superhighway around Scarborough.

WHAT WILL IT COST

A typical day on Tobago for two persons in season, will run:

	U.S. $
Beachside hotel accommodations including breakfast and dinner	$150
Luncheon at an in-town restaurant	30

Tips or service charges at restaurants; taxes and service charges at hotels	27
Car rental or sightseeing for one day	45

$252

TELEPHONE AND EMERGENCY NUMBERS. Police: 639–2512; hospital: 639–2407. To call Tobago directly from the U.S. dial 1 + 809 + 5-digit local number. From Tobago to the States you must go through the operator; hotels will charge a 20% international handling fee.

HOTELS. Hotel development on Tobago has been toward small, tastefully designed retreats, none of them high-rise, and all nestled into the coves that brought the visitors and developers in the first place. All hotels are beach oriented; most convey an intimate, homey atmosphere. We call $155–200 *Expensive;* $110–150 *Moderate;* and below that *Inexpensive* for a double room with breakfast and dinner in season.

Arnos Vale Hotel. *Expensive.* Arnos Vale. Tel. 639–2881/2. Red tile roofs, white stucco and natural stone give this special hotel a Mediterranean air. The 400-acre property is both a botanist's and bird watcher's delight with lush tropical greenery and brilliant blooms that vie for attention with the brightly colored birds that flock to strategically placed feeders, especially at teatime. This perfect little hideaway has three suites and 28 rooms—three on beach level; the rest in four cottages reached by stone steps that wind up the hillside from the rustic main house. Dinner is served on the terrace; drinks in the lounge where a magnificent handpainted Playel piano built for the 1851 Paris exhibition graces one corner, and a Murano glass chandelier brightens the room. Down more stairs, a pool overlooks a nice sweep of sand; snorkeling is excellent just a few yards offshore—a gift shop rents masks and fins—and a tennis court is hidden among the flowers.

Crown Reef Hotel. *Expensive.* Store Bay. Tel. 639–8571. This property is beauty stretched out on 2½ acres fronting the bay. 110 deluxe rooms and seven suites are fully carpeted; attractively decorated and *large.* Some have TV, all have telephone, radio, and air conditioning. Each suite is different; all are luxurious. There's a sheltered pool in a courtyard overlooking the sea. Shopping arcade, tour and National car-rental desk, two bars, an excellent indoor restaurant called *The Captain's Table,* the lively *Reef Terrace,* roof garden for parties, a ballroom, and meeting facilities complete the well-rounded picture. Congenial manager Charles Solomon is quick with a smile and a joke, but he was trained in Switzerland at Lausanne's prestigious hotel school, so count on everything running like clockwork here.

Mt. Irvine Bay Hotel. *Expensive.* Mt. Irvine Bay. Tel. 639–8871. A modern 150-acre resort built around one of the Caribbean's finest 18-hole championship golf courses. There are 64 standard and superior rooms, all air conditioned and with balconies or patios overlooking the pool and tropical gardens. 23 cottages, each with two units; enormous private patios with outdoor bar and refrigerator face the sea or more tropical gardens. A small beach is just across the road with showers, changing facilities, and a snack bar; several larger stretches of sand are within easy walking distance. Guests have golfing privileges and there are also two tennis courts lighted for night play. There are three bars: the air-conditioned *Cocrico,* one poolside with underwater seats, and one in the base of the 200-year-old sugar mill that forms the nucleus of the outdoor dining room. The pool patio has frequent entertainment that might be a combo, calypso singer, steel band, or limbo dancers. The *Shamrock and Palm* cellar pub is open late for disco dancing every night but Sunday. A shopping arcade, car-rental and tour desk, hairdresser, meeting rooms, and health club with sauna are among the excellent facilities that draw repeat guests, who are about half golfers, half vacationers.

Crown Point on the Bay. *Moderate.* Store Bay. Tel. 639–8781. Sprawled over seven landscaped acres with lawns, flowering bushes and lots of greenery. It's not luxurious, but the 109 suites are comfortable and functional; each has a fully equipped kitchenette. Choose from studios, cottage cabanas, or one- or two-bedroom apartments; those in the new wing added last summer should be the nicest. There's a TV room, small market, two tennis courts, pool, terrace restaurant, and the beach is one of the island's best.

Sandy Point Beach Club. *Moderate.* Tel. 639–8533/8534. A triangular-shaped, two-story condominium complex with 22 air-conditioned studio apartments and 20 duplex suites—those facing the sea have the best views and breezes. Attractive decor is tropical Scandinavian (perhaps in deference to their many guests from that part of the world)—angular, modern, and somewhat stark blond wooden furniture accented by colorful throw pillows, wall hangings, curtains, and bedspreads. Each unit has a large, well-equipped kitchen, patio or gallery, color TV for nightly closed-circuit films, and piped-in music. There's a sauna, freshwater pool that just might be bigger than the beach at high tide, a terrace pool table, and a good, lively restaurant and bar by the sea. Mike Small is the cordial manager here and he and his accommodating staff really go out of their way to assure their guests enjoyment. Note: Although the hotel is located at the end of the airport runway, there are no night flights here—yet—so at least for the moment sleep is not disturbed by the din of jet engines.

Turtle Beach. *Moderate.* Great Courland Bay. Tel. 639–2851. Mike and Monica Charbonné's modern two-story hotel. The 50 rooms are spacious, colorfully decorated, tile floored, and air conditioned. Those on the second floor have beamed cathedral ceilings and glass doors that can be left open for natural cooling by Caribbean breezes. There's a nice pool with a view, two tennis courts, shuffleboard, and a watersports center that also rents bicycles—a great way to explore this part of the island. The main house contains the reception area, lounge, bar, and an open dining room. At sunset, the beachside bar is one of the island's nicest places to watch the sun sink into the sea and the fishermen bring in their day's catch just in front of the hotel.

Blue Waters. *Inexpensive.* Batteaux Bay, Speyside. Tel. 639–4341. This little inn has 11 very simple rooms set on a golden sand beach that faces Little Tobago Island, perhaps better known as Bird of Paradise Island. Excellent offshore diving nearby. Peter and Rose Fernandez are your congenial hosts. Rose looks after the day-to-day operations, while Peter mans the often-lively bar and restaurant. This is a supercasual, relaxed, barefoot kind of place where bird watching, fishing, tennis, snorkeling, scuba, and boat excursions are all available if and when you garner up the energy to move from the beach. The phone is known not to work very often so don't get discouraged if you call and no one picks up—it's just not ringing on the other side.

Cocrico Inn. *Inexpensive.* North & Commissioner Sts., Plymouth. Tel. 639–2961. Named after the brown-and-red national bird of Tobago, this friendly little inn is just a five-minute stroll up or down the street to two good beaches; ten minutes from Plymouth's three historic monuments. There's a pool; a popular restaurant with good local home cooking; the *Village* bar, known for its whipped fruit concoctions; a trendy boutique; and 16 simple spotless rooms and one suite whose second-floor balconies all overlook the sea. Ten of the rooms are air conditioned; only two have kitchenettes. Always-innovative owner Ida Boyke Jacke, (a well-respected cook herself) has solved the problem of guests asking her to fry up their freshly caught fish by building three "floating kitchens" available for rent by the hour. Ida and her husband Russell couldn't be more charming, thoughtful, and caring; through them you'll really get to know the wonders of Tobago and the Tobagonians.

Della Mira Guest House. *Inexpensive.* Windward Rd., Scarborough. Tel. 639–2531. Another homey spot ably and charmingly run by Neville Miranda and his wife Angela, who also operates a beauty salon and barbershop on the grounds. This island guesthouse has just 14 rooms; not fancy but comfortable and neat as a pin. The well-kept property has a breezy location overlooking the sea about a half-mile from town. There's a nice pool on the lawn with ample space for sunbathing, a small terrace restaurant popular with islanders, and set off to the side is the Miranda's *Club La Tropicale,* Tobago's only nightclub.

Kariwak Village. *Inexpensive.* Crown Point. Tel. 639–8545. 18 attractive rooms in nine octagonal cottages surround the swimming pool of this relatively new property. Store Bay Beach is a short walk down the road, an even shorter hike across the town playground shared with grazing cows. The airport is just around the corner. Allan and Cynthia Clovis, your affable hosts, designed and supervised every step of the construction of their intimate little village. Service and staff here were the friendliest we encountered on the entire island; the West Indian dishes and homemade ice cream superb; and the Saturday-night buffet with live entertainment popular with local residents as well as hotel guests.

HOME AND APARTMENT RENTALS. *Tobago Villas Agency*, P.O. Box 301, Scarborough, tel. 639–8737, represents nine attractive properties overlooking the Mt. Irvine Golf Course and two more in Charlottesville on the north coast. Most sleep six and have private swimming pools; a couple are on the beach. In-season rental is $250–325 per day with a five-night minimum. These are homes owned mainly by well-to-do Trinidadians and are tastefully decorated, well maintained and have reliable maids; cooks are also available at an extra charge. *Ida Boyke Jack* of Cocrico Inn also has four simple apartments with one to four bedrooms in the Plymouth area for $12–15 per day per person.

HOW TO GET AROUND. Public buses, surprisingly modern and very inexpensive, make several daily trips from one end of the island to the other, with stops in almost everyone's backyard. We don't recommend this for expediency, but for an interesting excursion at a very low fare. There are 220 miles of good roads and rental cars are available through your hotel desk for U.S. $45–50 per day with unlimited mileage. An international driving license is necessary. Remember to drive on the left! Bicycles can be rented, but are practical only for riding around the hotel grounds or to Pigeon Point Beach from hotels located in the Store Bay and Crown Point area. There is a bus that runs every 30 minutes from Crown Point Airport to Scarborough and vice versa; fare is TT $.50, hours of operation 6:00 A.M.–8:30 P.M. Taxis have set fares, but often a bargain may be struck, especially if business is slow.

TOURIST INFORMATION SERVICES. There's a small Tourist Bureau in Scarborough (tel. 639–2125).

TOURS. Tours on Tobago are on both land and on sea. *Tobago Travel, Ltd.* on Milford Rd., Store Bay (tel. 639–8778) offers several options. Among them are: an all-day sightseeing on-island tour, to include Scarborough and environs, old Fort George, Pigeon Point on the northwestern shore, Charlotteville, Craig Hill Falls, and the town of Plymouth, in addition to a scenic and lovely drive around the island. (U.S. $42 per person); and Buccoo Reef all-day tour, which includes snorkeling the underwater coral reef gardens and then lunch and swimming at Pigeon Point Beach (U.S. $42 per person).

BEACHES. The beaches and bays which ring this island are ideal for swimming, sunbathing, and picnicking. Pigeon Point, Courland Bay, Store Bay, and in the north, Man O' War Bay are among the loveliest. You'll also find many coves so solitary that you'll feel just like Robinson Crusoe.

PARTICIPANT SPORTS. Snorkeling is the highlight on Tobago, especially over the famous Buccoo Reef, an underwater wonderland. Your hotel will arrange your visit to the reef, which must be timed to coincide with low tide. A boat takes you out and you can explore the submarine gardens through its glass bottom or with snorkel or diving mask, supplied by the boatmen, along with rubber shoes. Even nonswimmers can enjoy this experience, wading knee deep in water of incredible clarity—convenient yes, but unfortunately detrimental to the already worn-down coral! You'll become so absorbed in gazing at these exotic coral gardens and their schools of multicolored fish that you'll forget about time. The only danger here is overexposure to the blazing sun, which is amplified by the reflection. It is imperative to wear a shirt and something to protect your feet from the razor-sharp coral. Snorkeling is also excellent just off the beach at the Arnos Vale Hotel—and far less crowded. On the Buccoo Reef trip, a stop is also made at the Nylon Pool, a three-acre area of crystal-clear water the color of a nylon fishing line, calm and shallow with a white-sand bottom—it's about a mile offshore.

The Mount Irvine **Golf** Club draws visitors for that sport alone. This par-72, 18-hole championship course, 6,800 yards long, has palm-lined fairways and a view of the sea at every hole. Greens fees run TT $40 a day; electric carts may be rented at TT $40 for 18 holes, TT $28 for nine holes. Lessons are available at TT $20 per half hour.

There are **tennis** courts each at the Arnos Vale, Crown Point, Turtle Beach, and Mount Irvine hotels.

Bird watching is another favorite pastime with the best areas being Arnos Vale, Blue Waters Hotel grounds, Hillsborough Reservoir, and along the Old Castara Road. There may well be no Birds of Paradise left on Little Tobago Island but looking for them is an adventure.

Scuba enthusiasts will find shallow dives, caves, reefs, drifts, a wreck or two, and spectacular wall dives with visibility of over 100 feet in Tobago's warm clear waters. Skin Diver Magazine called it "the garden spot of the Caribbean." Check the Tourist Board or your hotel for information on certified divers and excursions.

Deep-sea fishing is best arranged by contacting Stanley Dillon at Milford Bay, tel. 639–8765. A four-hour trip in his 31-foot twin outboard equipped with four lines, outriggers, and fighting chairs is TT $320.

SPECTATOR SPORTS. Goat racing is a one-day-only event that takes place at Buccoo Point on Easter Tuesday. Here, too, on this day, there's **crab racing,** which is a delight to watch.

HISTORIC SITES AND HOUSES. *Fort George.* The ruins of this old bastion, which was built by the British in 1777, stand on top of a 452-foot hill overlooking Scarborough and afford a grand view of the harbor.

Fort James. Overlooking Great Courland Bay. This fort, built by the French in 1666, was Tobago's first.

The Tomb of Betty Stivens. Located in the town of Plymouth. What's fascinating and provocative here is the inscription on the tombstone.

MUSEUMS AND GALLERIES. *The Museum of Tobago History,* located on the grounds of the Mount Irvine Bay Hotel next to the tennis courts. Here are artifacts, implements, and pottery of the Caribs and Arawaks as well as geological and marine exhibits; maps, coins, and other memorabilia illustrate Tobago's archeological and historic past. The museum is open on Tues. and Thurs. 5:30 P.M.–8:30 P.M.; Sun. 4:30 P.M.–7:30 P.M. Admission is TT $2 for adults; TT $.25 for children.

SHOPPING. You won't find the myriad shops of Trinidad here, but what there is is similar. Crown Reef and Mt. Irvine Hotels have several interesting shops in their arcades, while the small stores around Scarborough's A.P.T. James Park and the Handicraft Center on Bacolet Street are best for baskets, straw goods, and other handmade local products.

RESTAURANTS. Most Tobago hotels offer the MAP plan (breakfast and dinner) and their dining rooms have set menus with a maximum of two or three choices; a few offer no choice at all. A "Dine Around" scheme was recently devised to give visitors the chance to get to know hotels and restaurants other than their own and to try a maximum variety of cooking styles. It's best to give a call to see what's cooking the day you plan to take advantage of this plan, so as not to be disappointed. All hotel and outside restaurants we have recommended fall into the *Moderate* category, at U.S. $15–25 for a three-course dinner for one person. If lobster is ordered, count on paying anywhere from U.S. $23–30 for that course alone. All major credit cards are accepted by the larger hotels; none by small guesthouses and inns.

We recommend the **Arnos Vale's** Sunday buffet brunch featuring West Indian dishes; Crown Reef's indoor, air-conditioned **Captain's Table** anytime, as their accomplished chef turns out fine continental cuisine as well as interesting local dishes. **Mt. Irvine Hotel** has an atmospheric dining terrace built around an old sugar mill, though frankly the food could be improved upon; **Cocrico Inn** and **Della Mira Guest House** serve excellent island dishes. **Turtle Beach's** special Wednesday-night barbecue has a spectacular steel band; **Kariwak Village's** menu is limited though creative, their homemade ice cream fabulous, and the Saturday-night buffet with live music is an always-interesting blend of local and international cuisine.

Hotel and outside restaurants with à la carte menus include:

John Grant's Place. Store Bay. No telephone. A small roadhouse kind of place across the street from the Crown Reef Hotel. Tasty fried shrimp, chicken, fish, and hamburgers, all served with crispy "chips"—French fries to Americans. Open lunch and dinner, a good place to have pack a picnic lunch for the beach. In the evening, this becomes a gathering spot for local residents for dancing and socializing to the sounds of soca, reggae, and calypso. No credit cards.

Old Donkey Cart House. Bacolet St., two miles north of Scarborough. Tel. 639–3551. Casual and friendly, this cozy wine bistro is located in a nicely restored French colonial house that was Tobago's first guesthouse. There are comfortable booths inside and tables on the front porch as well as out under the light-strung trees in the garden overlooking the bay. Gloria Jones Schoen, a stunning local model, her striking daughter Samantha Mackey, and Kurt Henschel have a small but growing menu that includes good salads, omelettes, seafood, a varied imported cheese board, open-faced sandwiches on delicious homemade bread, even frankfurters and corn on the cob. Definitely not to be missed are the elegant, flaming desserts, which many residents stop by for after their own dinners at home. The wine cellar is extensive and highlights unusual German vintages selected by Gloria and Kurt on annual vineyard visits. On special holidays, this is the place to try armadillo and possum (*manicou*) stew prepared especially by cooks who know how to prepare this exotic and expensive game. Open Mon.–Fri., noon–2:00 A.M.; weekends and public holidays 6:30 P.M. –2:00 A.M. No credit cards.

The Steak Hut. Sandy Point Beach Club, Crown Point. Tel. 639–8533. A pretty little covered seaside terrace with just a dozen tables. The specialty here is U.S. steak—T-bone, striploin and tenderloin, sirloin kebabs, and seafood—flying fish, shrimp, dolphin, kingfish, and lobster. There's a complete curry dinner on Wednesday nights for TT $30 and Friday's three-course fish (TT $35) or steak (TT $45) dinners include all the rum you can drink. All major credit cards.

Voodoo Nest. Main & Bacolet Sts., Scarborough. No telephone. Tiny wooden shack with real local atmosphere. You'll have to stop by in the morning to check out the menu, which could offer callaloo, crab backs, crayfish, conch, lobster, or grilled flying fish. The owner will also consider a special request if what you crave can be found fresh in the market. Reservations needed. No credit cards.

The island's best roti may be found at **Miss Esmée's** stand across from Store Bay Beach, along with good crab and dumplings, tamarind and sesame balls, and coconut muffins.

NIGHT LIFE AND BARS. All hotels offer local entertainment—steel bands, calypsonians, and limbo dancers—several nights a week. One event not to miss is the Buccoo Folk and Cultural Group Theatre performances, but check your hotel desk to see when and where these take place. A new discothèque called *CMB's,* at the Sunset Inn next to Pigeon Point, opened last spring. Owned by Michael Baker, lifeguard supervisor and Tobagonian calypsonian, this was planned as a nightly operation. Mt. Irvine Hotel's *Shamrock and Palm* dj plays all the latest hits; it's liveliest on weekends. *La Tropicale,* next to the Della Mira Guesthouse and under the same ownership, has excellent shows and is the best place to meet local residents. *John Grant's Place,* across from the Crown Reef Hotel, has a lively crowd and dancing to soca, reggae, and calypso records almost any evening.

TURKS AND CAICOS ISLANDS

by
BARBARA A. CURRIE

For too many years, the 8,000 people of the Turks and Caicos Islands were the only ones who had ever heard of these specks in the Atlantic Ocean. There are eight main islands and over forty smaller cays, stretching over an area about seventy-five miles wide by fifty miles north to south, southeast from the Bahamas. Today, however, those in search of quiet, peaceful, sandy shores head to the inns and resorts of the Turks and Caicos for sea- and sun-oriented holidays.

Past and Present

The two groups of islands, separated by the Turks Island Passage, a twenty-two-mile deepwater channel, were officially sighted by Ponce de Leon in 1515. Some historians believe that it would have been impossible for the ubiquitous Christopher Columbus to have sailed from San Salvador in the Bahamas to Cuba, even with stronger-than-usual winds over the stern of the *Santa Maria,* without touching near Jacksonville on East Caicos. There's no official record of this visit. These islands—at least the Turks Islands—got their names, according to one local legend, from the scarlet blossoms on the local cactus, which reminded some early settler of the Turkish fez! As for the Caicos Islands, the name probably is a derivative of the word *cayos,* Spanish for cays or small islands.

The English were the first (and about the only) people to bother with the Turks and Caicos Islands in the early years. Bermudians moved south to rake salt from the flats as early as 1678, spending several months here and returning to the Bermuda islands to sell their crop. In 1766, one Andrew Symmers settled here to hold the islands for Her Majesty the Queen of England. Georgia Loyalists obtained land grants in the Caicos Islands and began plantation life with imported slaves.

Turks and Caicos were governed by the Bahamas for a time after 1799, and, following the dissolution of that charter in 1848, under the watchful eye of the government of Jamaica. Today these islands are a British Crown Colony, whose main source of revenue comes from vacationers' dollars.

The government functions under a ministerial system. The Governor, appointed by England, acts as the Queen's representative and is responsible for internal security, external affairs, defense, and certain judicial matters. The Legislative Council consists of eleven elected members. The Executive Council consists of the Governor, Attorney General, Chief Secretary, Financial Secretary, and the Chief Minister and his cabinet of three appointed ministers selected from the elected members of the Legislative Council.

Most of the population lives on Grand Turk; South Caicos, North Caicos, and Provo have the bulk of the remaining population, with small settlements on Middle Caicos and Salt Cay.

When tourism was first touted as a means for increasing the standard of living in the islands—and creating some source of income for the islanders—the Turks and Caicos Islands subscribed to a long-term development plan designed by Shankland Cox, an English firm. The program is being followed today, allowing for residential and hotel properties.

The Turks and Caicos islands are hoping to develop not only their tourism infrastructure—particularly on the island of Provo, considered by many to be the sleeping beauty of the archipelago—but also the offshore financial industry of banking, companies registration, and captive insurance. Casino legislation was passed several years ago, and by the end of 1986, the island of Provo will have at least one casino resort, at the planned Sheraton on Grace Bay.

EXPLORING TURKS AND CAICOS ISLANDS

Twice-daily interisland flights connect all inhabited islands in the archipelago. If you have the interest and the energy, you could see them all. Where you go depends on your interests and your taste in accommodations. If you spend your entire stay on one island, you won't really understand *what* the Turks and Caicos Islands are. But, the most important thing is that you find the particular blend of accesibility and isolation that pleases you most in these islands—and there are a variety of them.

Grand Turk

Cockburn Town, the colony's capital, is in Grand Turk making it the seat of government and the financial and business center of the islands.

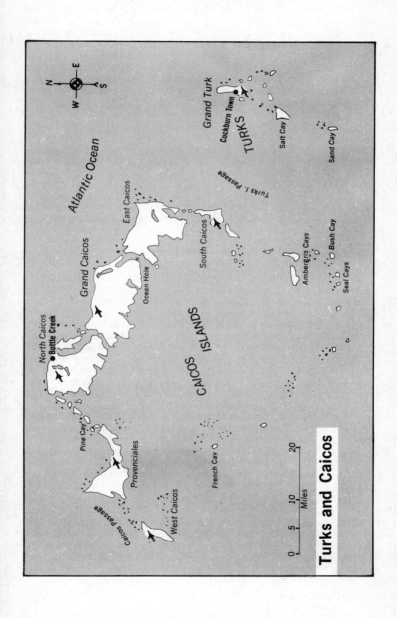

Turks and Caicos

The island has many buildings which reflect the Bermudian style of architecture dating back to the last century. Narrow streets are confined by stone walls; old street lamps, now illuminated by electric power, still stand along Front Street, the "Main Street" of Grand Turk. Donkey carts still clatter through the streets occasionally, carrying a load of water or freight. Grand Turk is an island which seems to meld the cable and wireless era with the age of Pony Express.

The main attractions are the excellent scuba-diving opportunities and other water sports.

Salt Cay

Tiny Salt Cay is probably the cleanest and friendliest of the islands—as well as the least populated, with fewer than four hundred people. Balfour Town boasts old Bermudian-style buildings and interesting examples of industrial archaeology dating back to the days when the island was a leading producer of salt. Old windmills and salt sheds still stand, and salt ponds have an "ice skating rink" appearance in the sun.

There are only a few small stores here—and one phone serves the entire island.

South Caicos

South Caicos has the best natural harbor in the Caicos chain and the oldest hotel in the Turks and Caicos Islands, the Admiral's Arms Inn, established in 1963. Once an important salt-producing island, South Caicos has become the busiest industrial center in the archipelago at the heart of the fishing industry. The shallow Caicos bank to the west is the home of the spiny lobster and queen conch harvested for export by local plants. South Caicos also offers sport fishermen access to some of the finest bonefishing in the West Indies; the elusive gamefish is prized as a local delicacy and islanders eat it as casually as Americans eat cod. South Caicos also has examples of old Bermudian architecture, and is the home of the annual Commonwealth Regatta, held each year at the end of May in Cockburn Harbour.

A herd of wild horses roams the eastern ridge, usually eluding visitors' cameras, around Highlands, a nineteenth-century house which overlooks Cockburn Harbour.

The south coast offers fine scuba diving along the drop-off, and good snorkeling exists on the windward (east) side, where large stands of elkhorn and staghorn coral shelter a variety of small tropicals.

East Caicos

Once the site of a major sisal-growing industry and range for a herd of cattle, East Caicos is now uninhabited—except for a few wild cattle and many species of birds. The north coast boasts a magnificent seventeen-mile beach with a peacock-tail pattern of coral heads offshore—all inaccessible except by boat from neighboring islands.

Middle Caicos

Largest of the Turks and Caicos Islands, Middle Caicos has the most dramatic coastline of all: towering limestone cliffs which carve into the sea along the north coast, scalloped with secluded beaches. Only one small guesthouse, run by the government, exists in Conch Bar settlement. Middle Caicos has approximately five hundred residents and is the least developed of the inhabited islands, lacking both telephone communications or centrally generated power in any of its three settlements (Conch Bar, Bambarra, and Lorimers).

Conch Bar offers visitors a fascinating attraction: cathedral-sized caves which have yielded Lucayan artifacts in recent years, and, in the 1880s, were the site of a thriving guano-export industry. You can explore the caves with a local guide. Nearby, wild cotton plants are evidence of the plantocracy that Loyalists from the southern U.S. colonies established in the eighteenth century.

North Caicos

North Caicos could become the garden center of the Turks and Caicos Islands. If you believe the myth that nothing can grow in these islands, you should arrange a taxi tour of Kew and Sandy Point, where fruit trees sag beneath the weight of a variety of tropical treats, including limes, papaya, and custard apples, as proof of this island's fertility. Some small-scale kitchen farming of vegetables exists here, but none of North Caicos' riches ever reach markets on other islands.

You might like to take a taxi tour of the local settlements and visit the ruins of the old loyalist plantations. The beaches offer good shelling and beachcombing for glass floats, as well as snorkeling, scuba diving, swimming, and fishing.

Pine Cay

Pine Cay is one of a chain of small cays connecting North Caicos and Provo. A privately owned eight-hundred-acre island, it is under development as a planned community. It has what may be the most beautiful 2½ miles of beach in the Turks and Caicos Islands plus its own 3,800-foot airstrip and the Meridian Club resort, famous for its appeal to blue-chip clientele from the U.S. Transportation around the island is by electric cart.

Providenciales

Most developed in terms of tourism, "Provo," as it is called, is considered by many to be the most beautiful of the islands, with its rolling hills and twelve-mile beach along the northeast coast.

Serious development began fifteen years ago, when a group of U.S. investors, including DuPonts, Ludingtons, and Roosevelts, began to open up this island for visitors and those looking for homesites in the Caribbean. Today, a considerable number of its 1,100-member population are U.S. and Canadian citizens in varying stages of retirement. Other are active members of a sizeable resident expatriate community.

A three-hundred-room Club Mediterranee opened in December 1984 on a 70-acre tract of superb beachfront land at Grace Bay. The newest addition to Club Med's roster of resorts has been dubbed the "Tahiti of the Caribbean."

Provo offers visitors the most extensive variety of quality accommodations, and is the most popular island with yachtsmen, offering two modern marinas with complete services and accommodations ashore.

Visitors staying in any of a dozen rental villas will find excellent stocks of groceries and sundries in either Island Pride or B.W.I. Trading stores near Ludington International Airport. Liquor, liqueurs, beer, and wine are available from the islands' best-stocked package store, Carib West, also located near the airport. Provo also has a modern Health and Medical Centre.

Among the activities on Provo are excellent scuba diving and bonefishing. You can explore Cheshire Hall, the ruins of an old cotton plantation. There are also boat trips to nearby Ft. George Cay, Dellis Cay, Parrot Cay, Pine Cay, and West Caicos. An island tour by taxi can be arranged for about $25 per hour.

Provo is now the home of PRIDE (Protect Our Islands and Reefs from Degradation and Exploitation) and the Caicos Conch Farm, where conch mariculture achieved a major milestone in 1984 and the operation is now farming the mollusc commercially in these waters. Located at Leeward Going Through, the Farm facilities and geodesic dome are open to visitors each afternoon.

West Caicos

Now uninhabited, West Caicos was once home for pirate ships and later sisal plantations and a number of proposed projects which failed to materialize—including a luxury marina, dive resort, and condominium complex.

The island is rugged and untamed, similar in geology to Grand Turk except for its large Lake Catherine, a saltwater lake which rises and falls with the tides and shelters nesting flamingos at certain times of the year. Its northwest point has a beautiful mile-long beach trimmed with thatch palms and offshore the diving is possibly the most exotic in the islands. A wall inhabited by every kind of large marine life begins a quarter-mile offshore and the Northwest Reef offers great stands of elkhorn coral and acres of staghorn brambles. But this area is only for experienced divers—currents exist and the wall starts deep. And there are sharks in the area.

The area between West Caicos and Provo was the scene of numerous wrecks in the past few centuries and has lured a number of treasure hunters, including author Peter Benchley, to seek exploration licenses. To the south, the Molasses Reef area is now a restricted area being surveyed by an underwater marine archaeology group who believe they may have located the wreck of the *Pinta*.

West Caicos can be reached by charter plane (there is a 3,000-foot dirt airstrip) but there are no facilities at all there, and explorers should know in advance that mosquitoes, deer flies, and sand flies are sadistic at certain times of day, and the interior is overgrown with dense shrubs including machineal, which causes painful scarring blisters.

PRACTICAL INFORMATION FOR TURKS AND CAICOS ISLANDS

FACTS AND FIGURES. The Turks & Caicos Islands are an archipelago of eight large islands and over 40 small cays which occupy a total land mass of 193 square miles, form a necklace of coral specks spreading for 50 miles, beginning 575 miles southeast of Miami and extending to within 90 miles of the north coast of Hispaniola (Haita and the Dominican Republic).

One of the few remaining British Crown Colonies, this little-known destination consists of two island groups. The Turks Islands include Grand Turk, the capital and seat of government, and most populous island with just under half the country's population of 8,000 living on its seven square miles; Salt Cay, only 2½ square miles with a resident population of 400; and a sprinkling of uninhabited cays.

To the west, 22 miles across the 7,000-foot depths of the Turks Island Passage, are the Caicos Islands: South Caicos (8½ square miles), East Caicos (18 square miles), Middle Caicos (48 square miles), North Caicos (41 square miles), Providenciales (37½ square miles), and West Caicos (9 square miles), with the remaining land mass occupied by the Caicos Cays. Within the Caicos group, South Caicos, Middle Caicos, North Caicos, and Providenciales are the only inhabited islands, and Pine Cay and Parrot Cay the only inhabited cays.

These islands resemble the Bahamas out islands in topography, climate, and vegetation: low-lying and primarily arid, with a maximum elevation of 163 ft. on uninhabited East Caicos. Like the Bahamas, the Turks and Caicos Islands are not volcanic, but have a base of oolitic limestone.

Despite their lack of lush tropical vegetation and dramatic mountainous panoramas, these islands have some striking natural attractions. Almost 100 miles of pure white-sand beaches burnish their coastline. But the most spectacular attractions these little-developed islands offer are the fringing reefs off the shore of each island and the dramatic coral drop-offs. Sheer coral walls begin as shallow as 40 ft., often just a few hundred yards from shore, offering encounters with huge sea turtles, sharks, manta rays, and a variety of prized saltwater gamefish. During spring months humpback whales migrate north through the Turks Island Passage and are occasionally sighted by yachtsmen and low-flying pilots.

The country's citizens are called Turks Islanders or "Belongers," and about 98% are black. English is the national language.

Only a handful of resorts and guesthouses provide accommodations to visitors (who numbered approximately 12,000 during 1985). Each island in this archipelago is a separate destination. They share a common heritage and geography, but differ in ambience and vacation offerings.

The Turks and Caicos Islands operate on eastern standard time, changing to daylight savings time in accordance with the eastern U.S.

WHEN TO GO. These islands enjoy year-round sunshine. As suggested by the once-flourishing salt industry, there is abundant sunshine and scant rainfall in the southern islands, with easterly trade winds to cool the warmer summer months. The average winter temperature is 77 degrees F, with daytime fluctuations reaching the mid-80s. Temperatures rarely go below 60 or above 90. Summer temperatures average 88 degrees, but daytime temperatures can reach as high as 100 in the salt islands during the hottest days.

You can enjoy these islands any time of year. Grand Turk, South Caicos, and Salt Cay have low humidity, but water can also be in short supply during the dry summer months. The northern Caicos Islands have denser vegetation and significantly more rainfall, as much as 44–50 inches compared with 22 in the salt islands.

While there is no "rainy season" like that of some Caribbean islands to the south, the wettest months are May through Nov.

For the budget-minded, May 1-Dec. 1 is low season, hotel and airlines rates are 25–50% lower than winter-season rates.

PASSPORTS AND VISAS. Some proof of citizenship is required. A passport—even if it's expired—is the best proof (and a current one is required for British citizens); your driver's license is not sufficient. All visitors must have a return ticket.

MONEY. U.S. dollars are legal tender. Credit cards are not usually accepted.

WHAT WILL IT COST?

A typical day in the Turks and Caicos Islands for two persons during winter season (Dec. 1-May 1) will run:

	U.S.$
Hotel accommodations:	$80
Breakfast and dinner at hotel	55
Lunch at hotel	15
Tips or service charge at restaurant; tax and service charge at hotel	10
One-day rental car	25
Total:	$185

HOW TO GET THERE. By air. *Cayman Airways* offers several weekly flights via 727 jets between Miami and Providenciales and Miami and Grand Turk. *Bahamasair* offers turbo-prop service from Nassau to South Caicos weekly.

Arrival on Provo is at Luddington International Airport; on Grand Turk, at Grand Turk International Airport; and on South Caicos, at South Caicos International Airport.

Interisland air service is available via *Turks and Caicos National Airlines (TCNA)* Islanders and Trislanders on a daily schedule.

By sea. Charter boats cruise around the islands and an occasional cruise ship anchors off one of the sandy bays for a "day at the beach," but the islands are definitely off the beaten path for the usual cruises.

AIRPORT TAXES AND OTHER CHARGES. There is a U.S. $5 departure tax, payable upon departure from the islands. There is also a government tax of 5% and in lieu of gratuities, resorts add a 10% service charge. Normal tipping is 15% at restaurants and bars.

TELEPHONES AND EMERGENCY NUMBERS. The islands of Grand Turk, South Caicos, and Providenciales are connected by telephone and telex to the continental U.S., Canada, and Europe, but the volume of commercial activity in the business capital of Grand Turk creates often lengthy delays during weekday office hours for incoming or outgoing calls. Some countries can dial direct into the exchange, but operator assistance is required for others. Ask for "160 plus 105" if you require operator assistance calling in; otherwise, dial area code 809, then 946, plus the four-digit number.

Emergency Numbers: Police: Grand Turk, 2299; South Caicos, 3299; Provo, 4259. **Hospital:** Grand Turk, 2333. **Clinics:** South Caicos, 3216; Provo, 4228.

HOTELS AND APARTMENTS. In less than ten years, tourism has become the main source of income (and the main industry) for the Turks and Caicos Islands.

Hotels offer accommodations on the islands of Grand Turk, Pine Cay, Providenciales and South Caicos; there are small guesthouses on Salt Cay. Additional hotels and hotel/condominiums are *planned* for Grand Caicos and North Caicos.

Resort accommodations in the Turks and Caicos Islands vary dramatically in style and rates; emphasis has been on small guesthouses and resorts. However, on Provo, with the opening of the "Club Med Turkoise" and plans for a 145-room Sheraton now underway, this island will offer visitors the option of small, intimate resorts or large, full-service hotels.

We call *Expensive* U.S. $95–140; *Moderate* $55–80 and below that, *Inexpensive*. Rates are for two people, EP, during winter season.

GRAND TURK

Island Reef. *Expensive.* Tel. 2055 or (800) 243–4954. Grand Turk's newest resort and only self-catering complex is a lovely ridgetop cluster of 21 attractively decorated and furnished apartments, each with complete electric kitchen, overlooking the scenic eastern coastline. The restaurant and bar are popular gathering spots for the small professional crowd on Grand Turk, and the hotel attracts a large following of visiting businessmen. Tennis, pool, and boutique on the premises. Water sports can be arranged with local dive operations.

Hotel Kittina. *Moderate.* Tel. (305) 667–0966. Long the roost of visiting businessmen, located directly across from the beach and Caribbean sea on Grand Turk's main street, Front St. This 54-room hotel opened its new beachfront units in spring 1985 and its superb rooms rival the finest of resort offerings in the Caribbean. Lovely restaurant; boutiques and gourmet shop; special dive packages through Turks Islands Divers Ltd. Another plus is an on-site travel agency, TAC. What began as a small businessman's inn is now a fine small hotel on the beach.

Salt Raker Inn. *Moderate.* Box 1, Grand Turk. Tel. (305) 946–2260. This charming ten-room inn on Grand Turk's Front St. was the home of a Bermudian shipwright 150 years ago, and its confined main building and "courtyard" beyond are a kind of colorful oasis on this arid island. Year-round cascades of brilliant bougainvillea shade the patio bar and dining area, and hibiscus, scarlet cordia, yellow elder, and flame trees grow on the grounds. The beach is directly across the street, offering fine sunbathing and swimming; scuba diving can be arranged through the hotel's operation. Owners/hosts Angela and Doug Gordon are long-time Turks tourism folk with a repertoire of island tales. The food is some of the island's best, emphasizing local seafood. The bar is a popular watering hole for a fascinating cast of island characters.

Turks Head Inn. *Moderate.* Tel. 2466. This once-grand home turned nine-room "inn" has suffered from benign neglect over the years and will not be many vacationers' choice, as it can best be described as "rustic." The atmosphere has become too laid back to make for a carefree vacation at any price.

Evans Inn. *Moderate.* Tel. 946–2098; 16 rooms, some with air-conditioning, all nicely furnished, situated on a ridge overlooking the ocean inlet of North Creek. Nice view, good food, terrace, patio, and saltwater pool. Apartments also available.

PINE CAY

The Meridian Club. *Expensive.* Tel. (305) 523–3134. Located on a privately owned eight-hundred-acre island, this 12-room exclusive club rates among the polished gems of small Caribbean resorts. A substantial portion of the club's charm is the island itself, a completely unspoiled cay with 2½ miles of pure white-sand beach used only by club guests, occasional drop-in day-trippers, and the resident population of 40. There are 200 acres reserved for vacation homesites, with 20 cottages completed to date; clubhouse/resort, and amenities including a small electric power plant, commissary, private airstrip, and dock. The remaining 500 acres are preserved as a tropical landscape sprinkled with freshwater ponds and nature trails of special interest to bird watchers and botanists. The only nonpedestrian form of transportation is electric golf cart.

The resort itself features an attractive clubhouse and dining room and office overlooking a large pool and deck area and beach beyond. The 12 casual seaside units are furnished with twin beds and each has a private patio.

Beachcombing, snorkeling, sailing, windsurfing, bonefishing, and tennis are recreation offerings for those who don't wish to explore the underwater world with Meridian Divers, or take a boat trip to nearby uninhabited cays.

Smith Cottages. *Expensive.* Tel. (617) 227–1877. These lovely island-style apartments offer an idyllic lost-island holiday for would-be Crusoes who want self-catering conveniences and privacy, with the option of socializing with Meridian Club guests and sharing club facilities. Definitely some of the nicest vacation villa accommodations to be found on an unspoiled and undeveloped Caribbean island.

PROVIDENCIALES

Third Turtle Inn. *Expensive.* Tel. 4230 or (800) 323–7600. On and off during the past decade, this 15-unit resort has been the legendary exclusive haunt of jet-setters and a host of celebrities who come to let down their hair in out-island informality while enjoying the unusual ambience and unspoiled aquatic offerings of this resort island. This lovely small hotel clings to the side of a small ridge overlooking a man-made marina, Sellars Pond, and its airy, nicely appointed island-style decorated rooms shelter pilots, divers, treasure hunters, and a traditionally upscale clientele who comes for the company as much as for the climate. The famous *Seven Dwarfs Bar* is a popular swap shop for island gossip and spontaneous entertainment by the expatriate population of Provo.

Restaurant, boutique and tennis court on premises, as well as the Third Turtle Divers headquarters. Ideal for water-sports afficionados of all kinds, from yachtsmen to professional divers, with scuba trips and courses available; underwater photography; windsurfing, sailing, and deep-sea or bonefishing on request. Five minutes from Provo airport.

Treasure Beach Apartments. *Expensive.* Tel. 4325 or (800) 243–4954. These four attractive units are located on Provo's exquisite 12-mile beach, and are perfect for a self-catering vacation centering around lots of sunbathing, beach-combing, and snorkeling. Each with fully equipped kitchen and furnished with everything except food. Pool, tennis court on the grounds, located ten minutes from the airport.

Nautilus Apartments. *Expensive.* Tel. 946–4385. This resort offers 18 rooms in a combination of one-bedroom, fully furnished villas and more spacious two-bedroom units easily shared by two couples or a family. Each has private sun deck. Located in Sapodilla Village, about ten minutes from airport.

Island Princess Hotel. *Moderate.* Tel. (800) 243–4954 or 4260. This fun, friendly 57-room beachfront hotel is one of our favorites, due to the "mom and pop" atmosphere the Piper family creates. Another wing is under construction, and pool and conference rooms are pluses. Their restaurant offers a superb menu featuring seafood and weekly barbecues. Scuba, windsurfing, and other water sports easily arranged. Rooms are nicely furnished, each with private patio or balcony.

Mariner's Hotel. *Moderate.* Tel. (305) 871–4207. A Caribbean discovery with a view of sea and coral cliffs that rivals anything in Antigua or the Eastern Caribbean. 25 rooms, beach access, dive shop, and bakery on premises. Truly, a gem of an inn worth finding.

Erebus at Latitude 22. *Moderate.* Tel. 4240. Just up the road from the Third Turtle Inn, this 12-room resort offers one of the islands' finest ocean views and comfortable, breeze-cooled locations. Divers are easily accommodated with Provo Turtle Divers nearby; other water sports can be arranged. The bar serves some of the islands' most exotic concoctions and the hotel restaurant offers good continental and French fare. Purchased in 1984 by a French operation, who plan to make this a health spa during the next two years, appealing to an international clientele.

SALT CAY

Club Med Turkoise. *Expensive.* This lavish $23-million resort village, opened in December 1984, is the vacation firm's showpiece, reputedly the most elegant of their 100 Club Med villages. It boasts 246 rooms, a mile of isolated beach, and all the unusual luxuries Club Med sells. You must book through Club Med (or a travel agent).

The Windmills at Salt Cay. *Expensive.* Tel. (301) 822–6306. Located on the island's north beach, these new cottages, rooms, and suites were constructed using traditional designs and materials reminiscent of those used by early Bermudian settlers. Suites have private courtyards and Jacuzzis; all rates include three meals daily in the restaurant specializing in island-style cuisine. An unusual experience on an undeveloped island with a 19th-century atmosphere.

SOUTH CAICOS

Admiral's Arms. *Moderate.* Once a fine small inn, now an "iffy" vacation venture due to an unpredictable quality of accommodations and cuisine. Rumors of the Arms being sold and restored to a fine divers' resort have not come true yet. Best to check with the Tourist Board before booking.

Harbour View Guest House. *Moderate.* Tel. 946–3251. A twelve-room, locally planned and constructed resort situated overlooking Cockburn Harbour and the fishing district. Spacious restaurant, bar, and simply appointed rooms within walking distance of the township.

PROVO

Skyways Motel. *Inexpensive.* Tel. 4251. A small, simple, 8-unit air-conditioned businessman's rest and roost, owned and operated by a former airline figure named Ed Hegner. Convenient, clean, and economical for an overnight stay if a room is all you need. Bar and rental car agency adjacent. A minute from Provo's airport.

Chalk Sound Villas. *Moderate.* Tel. (404) 237–1581. Unusual and nicely furnished wooden "island houses" with a beautiful view of Chalk Sound, an inland saltwater lake known for fine bonefishing. A perfect self-catering opportunity on Provo, about 10 minutes from the airport.

Turtle Cove Yacht Club. This 1.5-acre recreation complex offers tennis, pool, two bars, restaurant, and accommodations nearby in marina-front condo units. Although not itself a resort, Provo's new recreation complex is worth seeing, especially if you're a tennis buff. Private club, but visitors can get guest passes for use of facilities.

NORTH CAICOS

At press time, the only resort open is listed below. The once dependably luxurious **Prospect of Whitby** resort has changed hands and closed, but may reopen late in 1985.

Pelican Beach Hotel. *Moderate.* Tel. 4448 or 4296. This isolated 6-unit beachfront resort is owned and operated by North Caicos enterpreneur Clifford Gardiner, who also owns his own charter air service. If you love peace, quiet, and a remote location on miles of unspoiled beach, this is your place.

 HOW TO GET AROUND. The easiest way to explore the townships on Grand Turk, South Caicos, and Salt Cay is on foot, but island tours require hiring local taxis or, on Grand Turk and Provo, renting a car. There is a *Hertz* representative on Grand Turk at the Island Reef Hotel (Tel. 2055) and on Provo, in BCP Plaza (tel. 4475), and rates average U.S. $25–35 per day. To rent cars on South Caicos, check with your hotel manager for rates and information.

Island tours will run about $20 per hour, with tips expected.

Interisland travel is on small aircraft via Grand Turk-based TCNA (Turks and Caicos National Airlines) which links all inhabited islands with daily service. Airfares range from $20 to $90, round trip from Grand Turk, depending on the island.

TOURIST INFORMATION. The government maintains Tourist Board offices in Miami and Grand Turk, and there is a Visitors Bureau, operated by residents of Provo, which has a representative at the international airport. The Tourist Board office on Grand Turk is located in the Government Office Building on Front St.; in Miami: P.O. Box 592617, Miami, FL 33159. Tel. (305) 871–4207.

SPECIAL EVENTS. *The Annual South Caicos Regatta,* featuring local catboat and powerboat races, dances, and low-key folkfair atmosphere takes place on South Caicos at the end of May each year, commemorating the visit of Queen Elizabeth II and HRH the Duke of Edinburgh to these islands in 1967.

TOURS. The best way to see the islands is by small aircraft, and charter services specializing in this personalized service operate from Grand Turk, South Caicos, North Caicos, and Providenciales. These local pilots are experienced in flying this area, and can also organize day or overnight trips to Haiti, the Dominican Republic, and the Bahamas: *Flamingo Air Services,* Tel. 2109, Grand Turk; *Blue Hills Aviation Services,* Tel. 4226, Provo; *Gardiner Air Services,* Tel. 4250, North Caicos; *TCNA,* Tel. 2350, Grand Turk.

BEACHES. You'll find stretches of white-sand beaches spread along the coasts of every island and almost every cay in this archipelago. One of the most memorable day trips in these islands involves meeting a local fisherman, boatman, or dive operator and arranging a boat trip to the numerous isolated beaches on uninhabited cays close by.

In all, over 100 miles of beaches trim the Turks and Caicos coasts, and all of them are public. The variety is staggering, with clean leeward beaches stretching for miles in the Caicos Islands, and east-coast windward beaches collecting the flotsam and jetsam of the south Atlantic and Caribbean currents. Cove beaches decorate some islands, protected and dominated by wind-sculptured limestone cliffs, while, in other areas, flat sandy expanses extend into vast bonefish flats. The best advice is to ask the islanders where to go and how to reach the beach areas.

PARTICIPANT SPORTS. Limited, and not necessarily championship quality, **tennis** courts exist on Grand Turk, South Caicos, North Caicos, Provo, and Pine Cay. Most activities focus on the sea; **windsurfing** is popular on Provo and arranged through the hotels.

Sailing is available through the Third Turtle Inn or the Island Princess Hotel on Provo, and **deep-sea fishing** for sailfish, marlin, and tuna can be arranged through Provo hotels or the Banana Boat Restaurant.

Scuba diving is the main sporting reason for visiting these islands, and this archipelago promises to become a premier diving destination during this decade. Miles of shallow fringing reefs, gardenlike patch reefs, breathtaking walls, and gradual drop-offs skirt all these islands, and the marine life here is both varied and abundant. You're likely to see anything here, from dolphin to occasional sharks. Each island offers a different kind of diving experience, and visitors dedicated to diving should visit every island with an established dive operation to make their vacation a memorable event.

Special mention here should be given to PRIDE (the Society to Protect our Reefs and Islands from Degradation and Exploitation), founded in 1976 to preserve and protect the marine resources of the archipelago. Based on the island of Provo, at Leeward Going Through, PRIDE encourages not only strict conservation by islanders and visitors, but also safe and conscientious scuba exploration of the region.

"Dive with PRIDE" dive vacation packages including hotel and diving plus all meals prove an excellent value at the Meridian Club (Pine Cay), Island Princess (Provo), Hotel Kittina (Grand Turk), and Salt Raker Inn (Grand Turk). Tel. (305) 279–3315 or write 8770 Sunset Dr., Miami, FL 33172 for information.

Third Turtle Divers also offers excellent dive holidays on Provo at the Third Turtle Inn. Tel. (800) 323–7600.

Bonefishing can be arranged on South Caicos, Middle Caicos, and North Caicos, but many claim it's best in Provo and Pine Cay. Information is available through hotels.

SPECTATOR SPORTS. Cricket is played in season (June–Nov.) but on a low-key local level. No other organized sports exist.

HISTORIC SITES AND HOUSES. In the Turks and Caicos there is little signposted history. The sites and houses exist but to date little effort has been made to turn them into tourist attractions. On the **Salt Islands** (Grand Turk, Salt Cay, and South Caicos) the old churches and homes are well worth examining. The architectural detail of century-old wrought-iron hardware, the "kneed" shipwright-built sturdy timber homes, the cut Bermudian stone, the drystone walls, the windmills and sluices, the old salt sheds and the harbor machinery, all bear witness to the economic activity of earlier times and to the skill, wealth, and sophisticated lifestyle of the early settlers.

In the **Caicos Islands** one can trace the old plantation walls, some of them fortified against pirates and invaders. The Lucayan Caves of Grand Caicos are a must for those interested in pre-Columbian artifacts, though most of these are on display in the Smithsonian in Washington, D.C. Recent marine salvage work has produced an interesting variety of cannons, slave hardware (leg and neck shackles), and marine bric-a-brac. At Fort St. George (close to Pine Cay) the stone footings of the old palisade fort can still be seen and the unusual vegetation is probably caused by the concentration of pips and seeds discarded by the soldiers based here in 1798. The cannons that protected the Fort George Cut still lie, somnolent and barnacle-encrusted, within easy snorkeling distance of the shore.

MUSEUMS AND GALLERIES. The Victoria Library on Front St. in Grand Turk is the nearest thing to a museum in the islands. The most interesting collection of genuine antique furniture is preserved in its original setting at The White House on Salt Cay. This is still a private residence but the owners are happy to show appreciative visitors around. The old salt proprieter's home, sitting on top of his warehouse full of ground salt, contains samples of Bermudian- and Jamaican-built furniture.

MUSIC, DANCE, AND STAGE. Nearly every island in the group has its favorite "ripsaw" band and local musicians, who migrate around the islands playing for various functions and on most weekends. Some are good, others are loud, but several do contain some highly proficient entertainers, songwriters, and musicians. If one of these is playing locally it is well worth visiting. The dances are well organized, friendly, and fun, and visitors are always welcome. The music is a blend of the traditional Caribbean, calypso, and Bahamian beats, combined with the latest reggae from Jamaica and socca from Trinidad, traditional Caicos tunes (which appear to have more of the Haitian/African beat), and renderings of the latest hits from the U.S. top forty.

Both schools and churches provide regular drama and choral performances and the Grand Turk Checkerboard Players put on cabaret shows, musicals, and pantomimes, mainly for local resident amusement—but fun if you enjoy amateur theatricals.

SHOPPING. With only 12,000 tourists arriving each year, and no cruise ships, no duty-free shopping exists here yet. There are very few "tourist" shops and even fewer with shop-window displays. Ask at your hotel or your taxi driver who stocks what, and don't be surprised if a store apparently specializing in auto parts is the only place you can locate suntan oil or the best T-shirts. There are the island equivalent of supermarkets and the variety and quality of food is good. Remember however that most of the fresh and frozen goods come by air and it is vital to know what day the plane arrives on your particular island. The perishables sell out quickly and most residents buy for a week at a time.

The best selection of small boutiques and shopping opportunities is found on Provo. We recommend the *Conch Closet* at Provo Plaza for fine gold jewelry, original tropical fashions, and interesting shell gift items.

 RESTAURANTS. We must warn you that due to the high cost of importing all edibles, dining out is not cheap anyplace in these islands. At hotels and restaurants you should be prepared for typical entree tariffs as high as $18 per person, à la carte. With few exceptions, the only restaurants you'll find are at the guesthouses and hotels on Grand Turk, South Caicos, Provo, Salt Cay, and Pine Cay.

On *Grand Turk,* try **Amanda's** on Hibiscus Hill for good seafood, specialty drinks, and draft beer (a first in these islands). While you dine you can watch wide-screen cable TV—another unusual twist on this tiny island.

The tiny seaside **Papillon** specializes in French cuisine, a surprising find on this tiny isle and a favorite roost of the expatriate community. For local dishes, excellent conch fritters, and lobster, souse, shark, and other island delicacies, you should find your way back salina on Grand Turk to **The Pepper Pot,** a favorite local spot run by Peanuts Butterfield—a fabulous and well-known local character who plays a variety of local instruments (like the grater and saw) to entertain her guests.

On *Provo,* the **Banana Boat Restaurant** at Turtle Cove Marina is a popular dining spot and watering hole and a good place to meet the cast of characters on that island.

Henry's Road Runner in *Blue Hills* is a popular local native restaurant, and the restaurants at all resorts on this island are predictably good for seafood.

 NIGHT LIFE. Strictly local discos exist on all inhabited islands, and you can ask about them from any taxi driver. Local bands play at jump-ups or island dances from time to time—again your local cabbies can tell you what's happening on weekends.

The first real nightclub opened in Provo in 1984: *Disco Elite* on the Airport Road. The restaurant is open for breakfast and lunch, and the disco opens at 8:00 P.M. nightly except Sun. Again, this is not the sophisticated kind of establishment you'd find in Paradise Island, but it is a real disco with strobe lights, elevated dance floor, and other previously unheard-of things in these islands.

CASINOS. Although casino legislation has been passed, none exists yet.

 POSTAGE. Postal rates for letters to the U.S., Bahamas, and Caribbean are $.25 per half oz.; postcards, $.15; letters to the U.K. and Europe, $.40 per half oz.; postcards, $.20; letters to Canada, Puerto Rico, and South America, $.30; postcards, $.15.

In addition to regular postal services, the government operates a Philatelic Bureau on Grand Turk and South Caicos. The postage stamps of these islands have become popular collectors' items during the past seven years, and rank among the most colorful and unusual issues in the world. They make delightful souvenirs and can be obtained at cost or as a variety of souvenirs from the Grand Turk Philatelic Bureau on Front St., open weekdays 8:30 A.M.–4:30 P.M.

ELECTRICAL CURRENT. Electricity is 110 volts/60 cycles, as in the U.S.

SECURITY. Visitors are strongly advised to be very careful in preventing unfortunate situations in these islands. The people, as mentioned earlier, are friendly, if somewhat reserved, but some tend to be friendlier than others for the wrong reasons. Despite what you may be led to believe, drugs—marijuana, cocaine, and other illegal substances—are prohibited in these islands and you are subject to immediate imprisonment if you are apprehended with any of these substances. You buy and use at your own foolish risk as a foreigner and the consequences can be very serious.

All hotel and guest house managers advise that you secure valuables and keep room doors locked; petty crime does occur from time to time and the prevention of such incidents can save you from a ruined holiday.

WATER. Because of scant rainfall in Grand Turk, Salt Cay, and South Caicos, water is in short supply in those islands which lack any fresh water supply other than rainwater collected in cisterns. Visitors are urged to be as conservative as possible in their consumption of water on those islands, and all vacationers should follow the advice of their hotel manager regarding drinking tap water in their individual accommodations to avoid any unpleasant gastrointestinal problems.

MOSQUITOES. It would be an injustice to visitors not to mention that mosquitoes *do* exist—sometimes in quantity at dusk and dawn—in these islands, more so in the northern Caicos Islands than in the salt islands. A strong repellent is an important part of your vacation planning.

THE U.S. VIRGIN ISLANDS

by
MARGARET ENOS KEARNS
and JANET E. BIGHAM

Margaret Enos Kearns is a freelance writer/editor living on St. Thomas. She is the Associated Press stringer for the U.S. Virgin Islands and contributes to a number of local and national publications. Janet Bigham is a television news reporter living on St. Thomas.

The U.S. Virgin Islands lie about forty miles east of Puerto Rico, in an inverted triangle, with St. Croix at a point forty miles south of St. Thomas and the British Virgins off to the right—all of them jewels that rest on the hilt of the Antillean scimitar that curves southward to the Spanish Main.

What makes these islands a special place for travelers is that each is different—St. Thomas, the most gregarious and lively; St. Croix, slower-paced with a quiet charm; and St. John, the lush, sleepy little brother of the trio. Another factor is that all three can be visited easily and inexpensively by seaplane or ferry.

Past and Present

Columbus first sighted St. Croix in 1493, christened it "Santa Cruz," and then sailed north to discover the other sand-fringed isles and cays, which he named in memory of St. Ursula's 11,000 virgins who died in

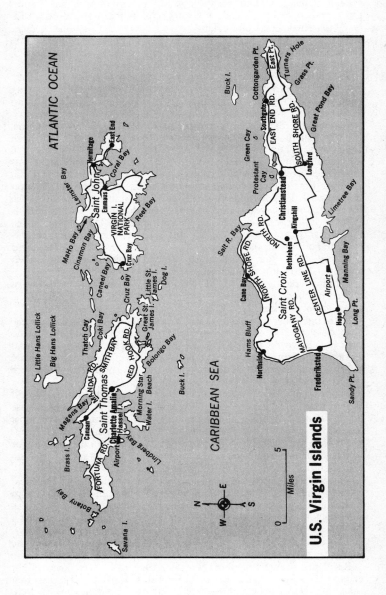

U.S. Virgin Islands

an epic defense of their chastity. A less pious admiral, Sir Francis Drake, rebaptized the islands a century later in honor of a more worldly virgin, Elizabeth I of England.

The largest of the islands, St. Croix was to fly seven flags—Dutch, French, Danish, and Knights of Malta among them—before the U.S. purchased the entire chain from Denmark in 1917.

St. Thomas was settled by the Danes in 1666. Once on shore, they divided it up into plantations of 125 acres each. Eventually shipping and commerce replaced agriculture on the island, and Charlotte Amalie, the capital, became an official port in 1724.

Historically, St. John followed the path of its larger fellow-Virgins. It has known the tread of Dutch, English, Spanish, French, and Danish adventurers. The Danes didn't settle St. John until 1717, and by 1726 all available land had been taken over by plantations and sugar was king. The slaves, ill-treated by their Danish masters, revolted in 1733, at which time many of the planters took refuge at Caneel Bay Plantation. It took French soldiers imported from Martinique to quell the rebellion. Some slaves are said to have leaped off the cliff at Mary's Point in preference to capture and its consequences. The islanders insist that the ghosts of these ancestors still haunt this lofty promontory.

The abolition of slavery in 1848 dealt a death blow to the sugar economy of St. John. The planters left; the tropical jungle took over; and the island returned to bush.

Administered by the U.S. Navy from 1917 to 1931, the islands—an unincorporated U.S. territory—are now under the jurisdiction of the Interior Department. Residents were granted U.S. citizenship in 1927, and, though federal taxpayers, still cannot vote in national elections. They do elect their own governor and one delegate to Congress—who does not, however, have a vote on the floor of the House. The local territorial government (roughtly the equivalent of mainland-style state governments) is headed by the governor and his administration. There is a fifteen-member locally elected legislature.

Major federal development of the islands took place during World War II when the military built roads and a submarine base and airbase on St. Thomas. Today, the development of tourism, attracts most federal funds. Both airports—one on St. Thomas (the Cyril E. King) and one on St. Croix (the Alexander Hamilton)—are undergoing major construction and expansion to accommodate larger jets and new cruiseship facilities are planned for St. Thomas and St. Croix.

Residents recognize the importance of tourist dollars to the local economy and annually welcome more than a million visitors from throughout the world.

Politically, the islands, with nearby Puerto Rico, are viewed as a stronghold for democracy in the Caribbean basin and many local politicians would like to see the U.S. government make greater use of the islands as a liaison with other Caribbean island nations.

Residents, though proud of their allegiance to the U.S., keep a tight grip on their West Indian heritage. English is spoken, but more often than not it is English Creole—a poetic mix of English, Spanish, Dutch, and French with an African syntex. Dollars, too, are American but often what they buy is quite foreign—unusual and exotic fruits and vegetables, admission to folk shows, or woven goods based on native Carib or Arawak Indian designs with African accents.

EXPLORING ST. CROIX

St. Croix is forty miles south of St. Thomas, just twenty minutes away by the amphibian planes that sweep into and out of Charlotte Amalie and Christiansted several times daily.

The island's name is pronounced "Saint Croy" by the local people and everyone else "in the know" (no one uses the French form) and is the largest of the U.S. Virgin Islands: encompassing eighty-four square miles of rolling land that used to be covered with waving carpets of sugar cane. The ruins of great plantation houses recall the days when St. Croix rivaled Barbados as the greatest producer of sugar in the West Indies.

Those days are long gone, but the island's heritage remains. Its capital, Christiansted, is a beautifully restored old Danish port on a coral-bound bay on the northeastern shore. The red-roofed, eighteenth-century buildings are pale yellow, pink, and ochre, resplendent with bright blazes of bougainvillea and hibiscus.

Both Christiansted and St. Croix's other gracious town, Frederiksted, are a treat for pedestrians and lovers of distinctive, graceful architecture. The prosperous Danes built well, using imported yellow brick or blocks cut from coral, fashioning covered sidewalks (called "galleries" here) and stately colonnades, leaving an eduring cosmopolitan atmosphere unique in the Caribbean.

Christiansted

The best place to begin your exploration of St. Croix is in Christiansted. Its town square and waterfront area at the foot of King Street have, for the past thirty years, been officially classified as a National Historic Site. Outstanding here are the Dutch Fort, Christiansvaern; the Danish Post Office; the original Customs House; the old church known as the Steeple Building; and the splendid and imposing Government House. The National Park Service operates these five buildings.

Fort Christiansvaern was built in 1734. This elaborate stronghold never saw battle—but it does have a number of dungeons, kitchens, battlements, and so on.

Visit the Steeple Building, which houses the St. Croix Museum (not the big, exhausting type, but a fine collection of pre-Columbian artifacts, plus a number of historically interesting relics of Danish plantation days). You will be able to obtain self-guiding leaflets at the National Park Service office in the Fort.

The West India and Guinea Company Warehouse, occupying a full block at the corner of Company and Church streets, holds the U.S. Post Office. Upstairs is U.S. Customs. Built in 1749, the building contains a guard shelter (and public restrooms) at the outer north corner of the courtyard.

Explore Government House, which was the original seat of government for the nearby Danish West Indies. Its ballroom is decorated with replicas of the original Danish furnishings, a gift from Denmark to the U.S.

The Christiansted shopping center is cheek by jowl with the National Historic Site. Centering on Company Street and King Street, it's smaller than the one at Charlotte Amalie, St. Thomas, but has the same free-port advantages and offers similar temptations.

Along the North Shore to Frederiksted

Frederiksted, St. Croix's "other town," lies seventeen miles to the west. You can get there by heading out on North Side Road which forks north to become North Shore Road or southwest to Midland Road/Mahogany Road. Either way you'll find that in between are old sugar plantations, some in picturesque ruins; one or two are still in use and have been restored as guesthouses. Their names are haunting: Peter's Rest, Upper Love, Jealousy, Lower Love, Morning Star. They are fascinating with their round sugar mills, their noble double stairways, their mute and melancholy testimony to past grandeur.

Palatial Judith's Fancy, just northwest of Christiansted, was once the residence of the Governor of the Knights of Malta. It is a romantic ruin set in the midst of an estate of several hundred scenic acres, long since developed as a residential community. No one with a feeling for history can remain insensible to the experience of seeing where Columbus anchored at Salt River in 1493. He called it El Cabo de las Flechas, or Cape of the Arrow, in memory of the reception he got! You'll get a fine view of it from the hill beyond Judith's Fancy.

From the North Shore Road, you'll get quite a view of this tropical island and its steep hills rising to over 1,000 feet. Their cool heights offer a rich forest of palms, ferns, fruit trees, mahogany, and enormous vines that shade the roads. There are a number of scenic rides branching off the main road (a four-wheel-drive vehicle is best for these) that will take you through lush forest and along beaches to places such as Ham's Bluff.

Frederiksted

Frederiksted charms the visitor with wide, tree-shaded streets, a lovely waterfront distinguished by several blocks of arcaded sidewalks, and picturesque architecture. Taking advantage of the sheltered sea on the west coast as an anchorage, the town still handles the larger freighters that land on the island.

Frederiksted was ravaged by a fire in 1878. When the houses were rebuilt, Victorian architecture was the rage, so you have the pastel-colored Danish-type houses plus lacy galleries of iron and wood, cupolas, curlicues, and enough gingerbread details to illustrate all the fairy tales of Hans Christian Andersen. Some of the nearby homes hold small duty-free shops.

The old and famous Fort Frederik, at the harbor's edge, has been completely restored and stands as it did when the Danes built it in 1760. Visit the cells, the non-commissioned officer's quarters, the canteen, and the arsenal on the ground floor and the Commandant's Quarters upstairs. There is also a small museum with changing exhibits. Don't miss the Customs House (now also the Visitor's Bureau) on the waterfront, Apothecary Hall at Queen and King Cross streets, and the enormous banyan tree on Fisher Street at the south end of King Street, one of the biggest banyans in the West Indies.

Heading east again out of Frederiksted, stop at the Whim Great House, just off Centerline Road, one of the island's great showplaces. This house has been converted to a museum and personifies the high life of the sugar planters in the late 1700s at the peak of St. Croix's prosperity. Its great windmill has been rebuilt, and is one of the most photographed sites on the island.

One mile east of Whim, visit St. George's Botanical Gardens, which are set on sixteen verdant acres of land that was once an Indian settlement. An arcade of royal palms marks the entryway, then leads to the rare and exotic plantings which have been developed around the ruins of the old village homes and work buildings. There's also a tropical garden with papaya, avocado, limes, grapefruit, and tangerines growing in color and profusion, along with such brilliant tropical plants as frangipani, bougainvillea, poinsettia and hibiscus.

East End

If you go east of Christiansted, you'll find yourself at the rocky tip of the East End—the easternmost point of the United States. The dry terrain of this part of the island offers rolling hills covered with flowering cactus and a shoreline scalloped with sheltered coves. Many of the island's beaches are here, including public Cramer Park, a long sandy beach with good protected swimming. It's a very popular beach on weekends and provides restrooms and a snack bar.

Excursions from St. Croix

One offshore aspect of St. Croix that should not be missed is Buck Island National Monument. Plan to devote a full day to this adventure, with a leisurely morning sail (cold beer provided on board, but better ask your hotel to pack a picnic lunch). Buck Island itself has a glorious border of beach, but its principal attraction is the underwater snorkeling trail. Swimmers are able to follow a sequence of labels that identify the different types of coral, underwater growth, and brightly hued tropical fish. A late-afternoon sail back to Christiansted Harbor completes the day.

EXPLORING ST. JOHN

About twenty minutes by ferry, three miles east of St. Thomas across Pillsbury Sound from Red Hook, St. Thomas, St. John comes close to realizing that travel-folder dream, "an unspoiled tropical paradise." Two-thirds of St. John's twenty-one square miles officially became the Virgin Islands National Park in 1956. St. John's restrained and tasteful development to date and its presentation to the American people are the work of Laurance S. Rockefeller, founder of Caneel Bay Plantation, an attractive luxury resort.

Beautiful and seemingly undisturbed, St. John is covered with tropical vegetation, including a bay-tree forest that once supplied St. Thomas with the raw material of its fragrant bay rum. Clean, gleaming white-sand beaches fringe the many bays scalloped out along the northern shore, and the iridescent water is perfect for swimming, fishing, snorkeling, and underwater photography. At Trunk Bay, one of the loveliest of all, there is an underwater trail with flora and coral formations signposted along the way, and just off the Cinnamon Bay camping area is a small undisturbed islet with an extraordinary marine population.

Today, there are only about 3,000 permanent residents on St. John, most of them native Virgin Islanders. Most continentals are in the tourist business or are permanent residents who've chosen the island for retirement. Cruz Bay, the administrative capital, is still a small West Indian village, even with the advent of the National Park Service and two small shopping arcades. Mongoose Junction, a mini-mall, has eight intriguing shops, with the emphasis on local crafts, a restaurant, and a great deli for eat-in and take-out. Lemon Tree Center nearby is fun for browsing.

St. John is for the traveler who wants to escape from the pressures of twentieth-century life for a day, a week, or perhaps forever. Sightseeing is done by jeeps which, with or without a driver/guide, can be hired on the island. Guides are useful—sometimes indispensable—in exploring the scenic mountain trails and the sobering bush-covered ruins of old forts and palatial plantation houses. At Annaberg Ruins, the vast estate has been well cleared and partially restored. A Park Service pamphlet available at the site explains the workings of the old sugar plantation and points out ruins of particular interest. The warlike Caribs were here as well as the peaceful Arawaks, whose language survives them in two of our adopted words, a reflection of amenities bequeathed to the white man: tobacco, hammock. Both tribes are gone. The land remains, the beaches, the forests, the mountains, the lagoons and the sea.

Cruz Bay

This pint-sized port town, with its sleepy, tropical charm, can be seen in an hour or less—but for some, captured by its magic, a lifetime wouldn't provide enough time. To slip into "St. John time," begin your day at Cruz Bay Park. Absorb the sights and sounds of the island coming alive in the early morning hours. Islanders gather here to "lime" (hang out and relax), catch up on local gossip, and people-watch. Located just off the park is the island's tourist information office (island maps, brochures, and hotel/camping info provided here). Historic buildings in town include the Battery and St. John Library. The Battery, built in 1735, provides good views of Cruz Bay Harbor and now houses the island's administrative offices. The library, located just behind Sprauve School about four blocks up from Cruz Bay Park, is housed in a beautifully restored Danish estate house. The tiny St. John Museum is located in the same building. Walk back through town to the Virgin Islands National Park Visitor Center for an introduction to various park hikes, walks, tours, and programs (maps and brochures available here). Directly across from the Park Visitor Center is Mongoose Junction, an environmentally designed, multi-level complex of working art studios, boutiques, restaurants, and bars. Everything from practical canvas handmade totes to whimsical, hand-painted designer clothing can be found here. For more shops, be sure to visit Boulon Center and the Lime Tree Center (both in the heart of town). Charming shops also line many Cruz Bay streets.

The North Shore

Get an early start from Cruz Bay in your rental jeep (available in town) and drive the length of Northshore Road to spend the morning at the Annaberg Ruins (about six miles from Cruz Bay). Set your beach-resistance level high, since you'll be passing some of the world's most beautiful white-sand crescent bays while en route—but don't worry, you can beach-hop all the way back to town!

The National Park–restored and maintained Annaberg Ruins provide visitors with the best glimpse of Danish plantation life during the eighteenth century on the island today. Built in 1780, the plantation operated through the mid-1800s. The park provides on-site brochures to ease visitors along the quarter-mile self-guided loop trail. From Annaberg's Sugar Mill, the British Virgin Islands look close enough to touch (at this point the deep-water Sir Francis Drake Channel separates St. John from Tortola, BVI, by just about one mile). The park also sponsors cultural demonstrations about three times weekly—check at the visitor center in Cruz Bay for the schedule.

When you've had your fill of culture and history for the day, set a leisurely pace back to Cruz Bay, backtracking on scenic Northshore Road. Take time to stop at any or all of those fabulous beaches you eyed on your way out of town. Don't miss Cinnamon Bay, Trunk Bay (the park's underwater snorkel trail is located here), or Hawksnest. If you're not staying at the world-famous Rock Resort at Caneel Bay, now is the time to stop in for a refreshing Plantation Punch or even a late lunch (they serve until 3:00 P.M.) at the resort's Sugar Mill Restaurant. The tariff is high but worth it—the food is delicious and the ambience is relaxed-chic.

Coral Bay and the East End

For an even more tranquil piece of St. John, take Centerline Road from downtown Cruz Bay about nine miles east over the central spine of the island to Coral Bay, the island's second city. The area was established by the Danes in 1718 as the island's first sugar plantation and, with its immense, protected natural bay, was considered the most obvious site for the establishment of a capital city. Cruz Bay, with its proximity to St. Thomas, soon outgrew this more isolated area. It's a thirty-minute drive from town to town over a sometimes bumpy but scenic road. There are spectacular views of St. John's mountains and valleys en route, and once at the East End you'll enjoy panoramic vistas of the British Virgin Islands. Continue east past Coral Bay for some of the best snorkeling the island has to offer—Haulover Bay is short on beach (small and rocky) but has one of the most active, near-shore reefs in the U.S. Virgin Islands. Vie's Snack Shack, just down the road from Haulover, dishes up some of the island's best native cooking. Garlic chicken, johnny cakes, fruit tarts, and tropical juices are among the selections. Other lunch stops in the area include Redbeard's Saloon in Coral Bay and Shipwreck Landing on Route 107, about ten minutes south of Coral Bay proper. Located further south on Route 107 are secluded Salt Pond and Lameshur bays—beautiful beaches at both locations—take your pick for an afternoon swim before the drive back to Cruz Bay.

EXPLORING ST. THOMAS

Thirteen miles long, less than three miles wide, the island of St. Thomas rises abruptly from the sea to an altitude of 1500 feet. Roads festoon the hillsides like Christmas tinsel, bending and weaving their narrow paths to new residential villages. The Atlantic cuts its sprawling shores on the north, the Caribbean indents it on the south into a series of jagged, spectacular bays. One of these forms the deep-water harbor of the Virgin Islands' superbly situated capital, Charlotte Amalie.

This historic port, more commonly known as St. Thomas harbor, was the nearest thing to home port for such cutthroats as Captain Kidd and Edward Teach (Blackbeard the Pirate). From this lair, Sir Francis Drake launched his attacks on Spanish galleons laden with New World gold, lumbering through the Anegada passage on their way home to Spain.

Today the harbor bustles with yachts, ships, and the constant buzzing of the Virgin Islands Seaplane Shuttle's amphibians that provide commuter service between the Virgins. Container ships and a few island sloops bring meat, vegetables, and fish to markets of St. Thomas, but the prize product today is tourists. At the height of the season, you will see as many as five major cruise ships tied up in a row at the West India Company pier, while two more ride at anchor outside the harbor.

Charlotte Amalie climbs as high as it can up the hillside without the benefit of terraces. Its only similarity to the town the pirates knew is the three hills that sailors still compare to the foretop, main, and mizzenmast of a ship.

The Danes, who moved quietly into St. Thomas in the seventeenth century amidst the colonial squabbles of England, Spain, and France, built this town and named it after the consort of King Christian V. The governor divided the islands into "states" and soon there were over 170 thriving sugar plantations—and a slave trade that supplied the plantations of America and made St. Thomas the biggest slave market in the world.

Charlotte Amalie, already famous as a free port and a protected harbor, welcomed all comers: New England sea captains, Civil War blockade runners, religious refugees from Europe, even pirates who came to buy supplies and sell their loot in this busy trading post with no holds barred, no questions asked. On two occasions, the pirates actually captured the place. On two others, the British seized St. Thomas in protest against the toleration of so much illegal piracy. St. Thomas, accustomed to receiving visitors of every stamp, took everything in stride. The visitors in their turn stamped the port of Charlotte Amalie indelibly with all the color and excitement of a busy waterfront town.

Charlotte Amalie

Charlotte Amalie is a town to be explored by walking. If you're staying a short time, you may prefer to pay a driver for an island tour which will take about two hours. If you're staying for a few days, consider renting a car to allow you greater flexibility for beachhopping and exploring. Should you start your tour at the top of the island, you'll find the vista from Skyline Drive overlooking the town and harbor, one of the most memorable views of the Caribbean. Beginning at the bottom, you can (and most will) dart into and out of the warehouses that once housed pirate treasure and now store the imports that tourists gather to the full duty-free quota and more.

Most visitors are surprised to learn that the great impressionist painter Camille Pissaro was born in the heart of the shopping center, and that his parents are buried in the Jewish cemetery of St. Thomas.

While supermarkets have taken over most of the shopping baskets from the local markets, it is still possible to catch an island schooner at the waterfront with its pile of coconuts or fish from nearby sources, or the local ladies selling produce at the open market on the far end of Main Street.

Over half the buildings of St. Thomas are more than a century old—something of a record for an American community. Most venerable of all is Old Fort Christian, built by the first Danish settlers more than 300 years ago and named for King Christian V. A striking example of seventeenth-century military architecture, this fort served as jail, church, vicarage, courthouse, and governor's residence all rolled into one massive pile of masonry. Numerous pirates were hanged at Fort Christian. Now its cells have been set aside for a small collection of Arawak and Carib relics and remnants of the early Danish settlements.

Two old churches are worth a visit: the Dutch Reformed Church, one of the first of this faith in the New World outside of New Amsterdam–New York, and the eighteenth-century Lutheran Church, second oldest in the Western Hemisphere and still using its two-centuries-old ecclesiastical silver. Both churches are an easy five-minute walk from the old fort. The Lutheran Church is at Eastern end of Main Street (just west of the shopping district) and the Reform Church is two blocks from the Lutheran church off Back Street.

The Jewish synagogue, the second oldest in the Caribbean, long thought to be the first, is the only one on American soil to maintain the old tradition of keeping clean sand on its floor to commemorate the flight of the Jews from Egypt through the desert. This place of worship and the interesting Jewish cemetery are another reminder of the rich cultural heritage and the tradition of tolerance that have shaped the Virgin Islands. The Synagogue is on Crystal Gade, 2 blocks from the Reform Church.

Charlotte Amalie's Grand Hotel, which opened in 1841, is a fascinating relic of nineteenth-century luxury. Its original third story was blown off in a hurricane, and the rest of it was destroyed by fire years ago. Now fully restored, but not as a hotel, the Grand houses several shops on the main floor and the pleasant Mandarin Restaurant upstairs. Swing around the corner to the Hospitality Lounge for full information on the island.

You'll probably want to take a taxi from town to Bluebeards Tower at the Bluebeard Castle Hotel. It sits high on a hill on the eastern edge of Charlotte Amalie. You can walk there but it's a very steep climb.

The Seventeenth-century Nisky Moravian Mission is located on the western edge of town near Frenchtown. From the waterfront, it's a twenty-minute stroll or a short taxi ride. Frenchtown is also a good spot to stop for lunch.

Other buildings of more than usual interest include the handsome Government House, built in 1867 for meetings of the Danish Colonial Council and now the center of political life and the official residence of the governor. Nearby is one of the few remaining stair-streets of the old town, this one called the "Ninety-Nine Steps" although there are not 99 steps today. Two-centuries-old Crown House, the former residence of early Danish officials, is in this area and open to the public. Atop the Ninety-Nine Steps on Government Hill, it's a fine example of how the rich lived here in the early eighteenth century. Hotel 1829, built as Lavalette House by a French sea captain, opens onto a Spanish-style courtyard draped with colorful bougainvillea. Also note the Lutheran Parsonage and the Danish Consulate, dominating the whole bay from Denmark Hill, both typical of nineteenth-century Danish architecture; and "Quarters B," once the German consulate, now a government office building famous for its unusual staircase, which was transplanted from a ship. The character of the whole municipal area is protected by a watchful government commission which is supposed to check all construction plans before issuing building permits.

If you have prowled around the waterfront and the shopping district, climbed the Ninety-Nine Steps, and seen more than one of these historic buildings, you will be ready for some refreshment. Take a cab up to the Mountain Top Restaurant, which is world famous for its banana daiquiris and spectacular view. Stay for lunch and enjoy tropical salads, sandwiches from the grill, or local specialties.

Frenchtown and Environs

Just ten minutes west of Charlotte Amalie (by taxi or rental car) the mood is decidedly tricolor—Frenchtown encompasses only a few blocks on the westernmost fringe of greater Charlotte Amalie Harbor but is big on charm. A number of French and Italian restaurants line the narrow streets, including many outdoor cafes. Wander about this tiny fishing village (its inhabitants are directly descended from the Bretons and Normans who settled the French island of St. Barts) and then take time out for an espresso or Pernod at one of the many cafés. Continue west from Frenchtown on Route 30 (the main waterfront highway) to visit the St. Thomas campus of the College of the Virgin Islands and adjoining Reichhold Center of the Arts (perhaps a performance will be scheduled during your stay). College buildings are situated on rolling green hills and reflect typical West Indian architecture. Tours of the performing arts center—a stunning open-air ampitheater carved from a rocky hillside and opening into a natural valley—are available Monday through Friday from 9:00 A.M. to 4:00 P.M.; phone for an appointment before you go: 774–8475. Return to town via the same route—if time allows enjoy a refreshing swim at Brewers Bay Beach located on the Campus of the Virgin Islands.

A View from the North Side

Having explored Charlotte Amalie, it is time to cross the mountain range that cuts St. Thomas in two and visit the north side of the island, far more beautiful, the northsiders will tell you, than anything on the Caribbean side. Here are the splendid panoramic views over the Atlantic, Magens Bay, which many call the most beautiful beach in the world, and the whole eastern sweep of American and British Virgins, green in the opalescent sea. The north side has more rain, lusher vegetation, more tranquility, better beaches.

Of special interest in this area are: Drake's Seat, where that old sea dog surely never sat, but from which you will have a grand view of the waters in which he operated and which are now named in his honor; Venus Pillar, the astronomical obelisk on Magnolia Hill; and Mafolie, the quaint French refugee settlement with its pretty little church.

From Mafolie, follow Route 35 to Mahogany Run Golf and Tennis Resort. The resort encompasses more than 320 acres of wooded hills, green valleys, and dramatic northshore cliffs overlooking the Atlantic (spectacular down-island views of St. John and the British Virgin Islands). The eighteen-hole championship golf course is considered by many to be the most challenging—and beautiful—in the Caribbean. The clubhouse bar and restaurant welcome outside guests for drinks, breakfast, lunch, and dinner.

East End—Gateway to St. John

Plan to spend at least one full day on this delightfully casual and active end of the island. From town follow Waterfront Drive east to the Yacht Haven Hotel, turn left at the junction and follow Route 38 about five miles to the Coki Point turnoff (taxi shuttles provide regular service from town, but rental cars, at about $40 per day, provide much more flexibility). Before turning left be sure to stop for goodies at the Sweetlife Bakery (located about half a block from the intersection). Sinfully delicious, individual-size cheesecakes with a variety of tropical toppings are gold-star menu items. Also topping the menu hit list: the best vegieburgers this side of San Francisco. Perfect fare for a picnic at Coki Beach (excellent snorkeling) following your visit to Coral World Marine Park located just off the beach on Coki Point. Don't miss the daily 11:00 A.M. fish feeding—sharks, barracudas, and even moray eels eat from the hands of Coral World–employed scuba divers at the underwater observatory, the only underwater tower in the Western Hemisphere. The marine complex provides a fish's-eye view of St. Thomas' fascinating undersea world.

From Coki Point, return to Route 38 and turn left to make your way to Red Hook Harbor at the very easternmost end of the island. The St. John Ferry ($2 per person, fifteen minutes each way) departs on the hour from Red Hook for Cruz Bay, St. John. Try to reserve a full day—preferably longer—to visit this tropical gem (nearly two-thirds of the island is National Park, so development has been minimal and controlled). Continue on Red Hook Road (Route 32) to the junction of Route 30 (Antilles Road) for a view of the island's south side before returning to town. The road, though hilly and somewhat steep in places, provides breathtaking panoramas of the Caribbean and surrounding cays (St. Croix, located about thirty-five miles south, is often visible from these vantage points on a clear day).

PRACTICAL INFORMATION FOR
THE U.S. VIRGIN ISLANDS

FACTS AND FIGURES. The U.S. Virgin Islands are comprised of three major landfalls—St. Thomas, St. Croix, and St. John—with more than 50 small cays and islets completing the group. Situated in the eastern Caribbean, the islands have shores facing both the Atlantic Ocean and Caribbean Sea. The islands form part of the Leeward Islands in the Lesser Antilles chain and are 70 miles east of Puerto Rico and about 1,000 miles south of Florida. St. Thomas is a 32-square-mile island—12 miles long and only three miles wide, with its tiny neighbor, St. John, just five miles east across Pillsbury Sound. St. John is only nine miles long and five miles wide, and nearly two-thirds of it is protected by the National Park Service. Largest of the three, St. Croix is 84 square miles (28 miles long and seven miles wide) and lies about 40 miles south of the other two Virgins. St. Croix also boasts the highest population at just about 50,000, with St. Thomas (by far the most active of the three and also home to Charlotte Amalie, capital city of the Virgin Islands) just behind it with 46,000, and tiny St. John checking in at latest count with just under 3,000 permanent residents. Tourism is the number one island industry, and Virgin Islanders welcome more than a million visitors annually.

 WHEN TO GO. High season has traditionally been from about December 15 through April 15—or, as one tourism official put it, "the crowds start with the first snow up north." Temperature varies little between winter and summer (average is a pleasing 79 degrees F); winter lows rarely dip to 65 and summer highs rarely reach 98. July through November can be considerably more humid, however, and those are also the months when hurricanes are most likely to strike. Rainfall averages about 40 inches per year, mostly in brief night or morning showers. May is traditionally a rainy month—the first after usually dry winter months. Prices and crowds drop after April 15; some hotel rates can be as much as 50% lower in summer. Unlike some smaller Caribbean islands, most resorts and restaurants remain open year-round.

 PASSPORTS AND VISAS. Proof of citizenship is required for U.S. citizens. Reentry regulations must be complied with by those coming from foreign ports. Non-U.S. citizens must have passports and clear Immigration when coming from their own country or from the U.S. British citizens must have both passports and visas.

MONEY. These are U.S. islands, and the dollar is good everywhere. U.S. $1.55 = 1£

WHAT WILL IT COST?

A typical day in the U.S. Virgin Islands for two persons during the winter season will run:

	US$
Hotel accommodations (overall average)	$110
Full breakfast at the hotel	10
Lunch at a moderate restaurant	15
Dinner at one of the top restaurants	70
Tips, taxes, and service charges	25
One-day sightseeing by rental car or taxi	40
Total	$270

 HOW TO GET THERE. By Air. *American* and *Pan Am* offer daily direct flights from New York to St. Thomas and St. Croix, while *Eastern, Midway Express,* and *Pan Am* fly daily from Miami. *American* also offers direct flights, weekends only, from Dallas. Out of San Juan, the half-hour flight to St. Thomas and St. Croix is made by *Prinair, Aero Virgin Islands* and *Ocean Air. Virgin Islands Seaplane Shuttle* and the *Sea-Jet*, inter-island amphibians, make several daily commuter runs between St. Thomas and St. Croix.

By sea. St. Thomas has been the number-one cruise port for the past several seasons, some days seeing as many as seven large ships in Charlotte Amalie harbor at a time! More than 21 cruise lines include St. Thomas as a port, sailing out of New York; Norfolk, Virginia; and Florida (Port Everglades and Miami), as well as out of other east-coast ports and from the west coast. In addition, the cruises that start in Puerto Rico stop in St. Thomas and sometimes in St. Croix.

Boat service to St. John is out of St. Thomas, from East End's Red Hook Landing. *Caneel Bay* operates its own boat for its guests from the National Park dock, also at Red Hook Harbor.

There is regular boat service, leaving from the St. Thomas waterfront, to the British Virgin Islands, stopping at West End and Road Town, Tortola.

Frederiksted, the smaller of the two towns on St. Croix, has a deep-water pier that is touched by some of the short cruises out of San Juan and Miami. Although the same customs exemption applies for St. Croix ($800 duty free for U.S. citizens) and there are many excellent shops, this island has never been able to draw the cruise ships the way St. Thomas has.

TAXES AND OTHER CHARGES. All room rates are subject to a 6% government tax. Some hotels add a 10% service charge. Be sure to check in advance. There is no airport departure tax from these islands.

TELEPHONES AND EMERGENCY NUMBERS. The area code for the Virgin Islands is 809. Calls between the Virgin Islands are local. Within the U.S. Virgin Islands, local calls at public telephones require a 25-cent deposit and you only need to dial the last five digits of the number and not the 77 prefix. Dial 913 for directory assistance and "0" for operator for assistance on long-distance calls. The emergency number throughout the Virgin Islands for police is 915; fire, 921; and ambulance, 922. For scuba-diving emergencies dial 8–1608.

HOTELS. The Virgin Islands win the numbers game. They have more hotels per square inch than any other area in the Caribbean. The concentration is at Charlotte Amalie, St. Thomas, and Christiansted, St. Croix, but almost every beach has its hotel as well. The government rate sheet, published twice yearly (for low summer and high winter rates) lists about 100 choices, with 50 on St. Thomas, 40 on St. Croix, and ten on St. John. Places range from luxury hotels to small guesthouses and include apartments, cottages, private homes, villas, and campsites.

St. Thomas leads in the guest house field, with more personality inns than any other island in the Caribbean; St. Croix has beach resorts and places scattered around the countryside to bring the "good life" to the vacationer; St. John has Caneel Bay, in a class by itself for elegance and comfort in peace and quiet, and the campsites at the 29th U.S. National Park.

High-season rates are in effect generally from Dec. 15 to April 15. Rates are from 25–50% lower the rest of the year. A 5% hotel tax is added to all bills. The following price categories are based on daily double-occupancy rates during peak season, EP unless otherwise noted. *Super Deluxe,* $200 and up per night; *Deluxe,* $140–199; *Expensive,* $100–139; *Moderate,* $65–99; *Inexpensive,* under $65.

ST. CROIX

Christiansted

Buccaneer Hotel. *Deluxe.* P.O. Box 218, Christiansted, USVI 00820. tel. 773–2100. St. Croix's top resort. Grand tropical setting, with hilltop, hillside, and beachfront rooms. All 146 of them are neatly arranged and spread out in mini-complexes to avoid making the property seem overpowering. 18-hole golf course, several excellent tennis courts, four restaurants, all water sports, and a long and lovely powdery white-sand beach. This was formerly the enclave of the

Knights of Malta in 1653, and, though they have long since given up their island rule, the treatment you'll receive is still royal.

Mill Harbour. *Deluxe.* Estate Golden Rock, Christiansted, USVI 00820. Tel. 773–3800. A condominium hotel on a good white-sand beach. Five minutes' drive out of Christiansted. There's a choice of good-looking tropical or Spanish decor in the fully equipped two- and three-bedroom apartments, Freshwater swimming pool, tennis, poolside bar for lunch, drinks. Maid service.

Queen's Quarter. *Deluxe.* P.O. Box 770, Christiansted, USVI 00820. Tel. 778–3784. Small, comfortable, private place on a bluff in the center of St. Croix's hills. The 50 rooms, in studios, villas, and suites, all have kitchen facilities and maid services. Lovely setting in acres of lush foliage. Tennis courts, pool, and outstanding *Queen's Court Restaurant.*

Hotel on the Cay. *Expensive.* P.O. Box 4020, Christiansted, USVI 00820. Tel. 773–2035. 55 air-conditioned rooms in a modern stucco building that sits on its own island in Christiansted Harbor. Hilltop restaurant, beach snack bar. Beach barbecues and entertainment on special nights each week. New all-weather tennis courts; olympic-size pool. Just a few minutes to town by small boat, which is on the run constantly from early morning until midnight.

Anchor Inn. *Moderate.* 58A King St., Christiansted, USVI 00820. Tel. 773–4000. 30 air-conditioned rooms in a space you wouldn't believe could hold even ten. The rooms are attractive, if short on sunlight, and right in the middle of town. Most rooms have balconies overlooking the harbor. Small pool, restaurant concession on the premises (and plenty of places to eat within walking distance).

Caravelle Hotel. *Moderate.* Queen Cross St., Christiansted, USVI 00820. Tel. toll free (800) 773–0687. On the waterfront in Christiansted. 46 air-conditioned rooms with bath and dressing room, most overlooking the harbor. Nice location; small swimming pool; excellent restaurant called *The Binnacle* on premises for indoor and outdoor dining.

Club Comanche. *Moderate.* 1 Strand St., Christiansted, USVI 00820. Tel. 773–0210. A long-time favorite with lots of atmosphere. One of the first hotels on the island, it has grown, expanded, burned, and been rebuilt. Some great antiques in the "old" building. The 42-room hotel appeals to repeaters, commercial visitors, and those who have friends in the islands and want to be in the heart of Christiansted boating life. The old-timers gather at Dick Boehm's excellent *Comanche Restaurant* on premises. Pool, no beach. Two steps from all shops.

Holger Danske. *Moderate.* 1 King Cross St., Christiansted, USVI 00820. Tel. 773–3600. Right in the heart of town, not too far from the seaplane ramp. Three stories with 44 small efficiency units. Most popular with the young at heart who want reasonable to low prices and don't demand a lot of fancy service. Convenient to shops and other restaurants. Small pool.

King Christian Hotel. *Moderate.* P.O. Box 3619, Christiansted, USVI 00820. Tel. 773–2285. 40 air-conditioned rooms with private bath and balcony, in a completely rebuilt and redecorated old Danish building on the waterfront. Small swimming pool, sun deck. Shops nearby. *Chart House Restaurant* has adjoining lounge and indoor and outdoor waterfront dining and nightly entertainment. All balconies overlook the harbor.

King's Alley Hotel. *Moderate.* 55 King St., Christiansted, USVI 00820. Tel. 773–0103. A modern hotel right at the water's edge in Christiansted with a view of the harbor and hotel on the cay. All 22 rooms are air conditioned, nicely furnished, and have baths and sliding-glass doors opening onto private balconies. In a tropical garden. Breakfast and drinks on the terrace. Swimming pool, evening entertainment poolside, several fine restaurants nearby.

The Lodge. *Inexpensive.* 43A Queen Cross St., Christiansted, USVI 00820. Tel. 773–1535. 17 simple rooms with private bath on Queen St. in the heart of Christiansted. Casual and comfortable. Swimming-pool privileges at the nearby Caravelle Hotel. Continental breakfast.

East End

Grapetree Beach Hotel. *Expensive.* P.O. Box Z, Christiansted, USVI 00820. Tel. 773–0430. Almost secluded at the east end of the island, the hotel aims to offer enough to keep you from going back and forth to Christiansted. 86 air-conditioned rooms, some beachfront units with patios. All water sports, boutiques, large pool, and two restaurants, all a few steps from broad Grapetree Beach. Full- and half-day sailboat excursions to Buck Island.

Frederiksted

Arawak Cottages. *Expensive.* P.O. Box 695, Frederiksted, USVI 00840. Tel. 772–0305. Located north of Frederiksted, in a secluded, grassy setting, on the grounds of Sprat Hall. There are one-bedroom duplex housekeeping units, some with air conditioning, and two-bedroom cottages that are fine and reasonable for families. All are brightly furnished in rattan, have louvered porches ideal for lounging. Swimming just down the road at Arawak Beach; scuba-diving excursions and horseback riding available.

Frederiksted Hotel. *Moderate.* 20 Strand St., Frederiksted, USVI 00840. Tel. 772–0500. 38 pleasant efficiency rooms surrounding a large swimming pool, each with two double beds and balconies. Close to the waterfront in Frederiksted; complimentary transportation to a nearby beach. Local entertainment some evenings; breakfast served on poolside patio.

King Frederik Beach. *Moderate.* P.O. Box 1908, Frederiksted, USVI 00840. Tel. 772–1205. 20 rooms, most air conditioned, each with kitchen facilities. Tastefully furnished and sedate accommodations on a small but beautiful beach near Frederiksted, at opposite end of island from livelier Christiansted. Some rooms have private galleries overlooking tropical gardens. Pool, bar, patio.

North Shore

Cane Bay Plantation. *Expensive.* P.O. Box G, Kingshill, North Shore, USVI 00850. Tel. 778–0410. Offers 16 apartments with balconies overlooking the beach, plus five completely furnished housekeeping cottages with private baths, on the north shore drive between Christiansted and Frederiksted (about 40 minutes; drive from each). Beach, pool, two restaurants. Excellent view of bay, Ham's Bluff. The cottages (actually they are old slave quarters, charmingly restored) are set in a 26-acre estate. Informal island-style place not too far from Fountain Valley Golf Course. You'll want a rental car to go anywhere. The brunches and some of the other specialty meals have become a Cruzan tradition. Reservations for meals, if you are not staying there, are essential.

Tamarind Reef Hotel. *Moderate.* P.O. Box 1112, Christiansted, USVI 00820. Tel. 773–0463. 16 one- and two-bedroom suites on the beach on the island's North Shore. As private as you like it. No restaurant here, but there are kitchenettes in each suite. Large swimming pool and sun deck; all water sports available on the beach. Ideal for families.

Waves at Cane Bay. *Inexpensive.* P.O. Box 1749, Kingshill, North Shore, USVI 00850. Tel. 778–1805. Ten nice large efficiencies with separate kitchens. Not air conditioned, but ceiling fans and the trade winds are guaranteed to cool you. Seaside pool. Convenient to Fountain Valley Golf Course; arrangements for snorkeling and scuba diving at Cane Bay Beach.

ST. THOMAS

Airport Area

Carib Beach Hotel. *Moderate.* P.O. Box 340, St. Thomas, USVI 00801. Tel. 774–2525. 92 air-conditioned rooms in a garden setting on the beach, two miles from town just west of the airport. Rooms in newer section are preferable; minimum-rate rooms are small. Can be noisy due to proximity of airport. Situated on beautiful Lindbergh Bay with freshwater pool, cocktail lounge, piano bar, nightly entertainment, and Polynesian dining at the *Tonga Reef.*

Island Beachcomber Hotel. *Moderate.* P.O. Box 1618, St. Thomas, USVI 00801. Tel. 774–5250. 50 air-conditioned rooms on the white-sand beach at Lindbergh Bay. Informal, casual crowd into snorkeling, sailing, and beaching it. All rooms have refrigerators and patios; beach bar for cocktails and beachside restaurant for breakfast, lunch, and dinner. Located directly across from the Cyril E. King Airport.

Charlotte Amalie

Yacht Haven Hotel and Marina. *Expensive.* P.O. Box 7970, St. Thomas, USVI 00801. Tel. 774–9700. Located on waterfront Drive at the eastern end of town, next to the cruise ship dock. 223 rooms ranging from studios to suites, some with kitchenettes. All overlook the harbor and 200-slip Yacht Haven Marina. Active, yachting-type clientele. Shops, cafés, freshwater pool, cocktail lounge, and nightly entertainment.

Harbor View. *Moderate.* P.O. Box 1975, St. Thomas, USVI 00801. Tel. 774–2651. Charming 18th-century manor house, lovingly restored by the current owners. Ten air-conditioned rooms on Frenchman's Hill overlooking Charlotte Amalie and the harbor are simply but attractively furnished. A short but windy taxi ride from the heart of town. Freshwater pool; elegant dining room with special food and ambience to match. Cocktail lounge with pianist. Daily continental breakfast included in room rate.

Hotel 1829. *Moderate.* P.O. Box 1567, St. Thomas, USVI 00801. Tel. 774–1829. Picturesque, historic, European-style inn on Government Hill. Once a private home, it has been restored but retains all of its charm—Spanish tiles, fountain-splashed courtyards. 18 rooms, freshwater pool. Dinner on the patio is one of—if not *the*—best dining experiences on the island. Breakfast is also served in the dining room. 15-minute drive to the nearest beach.

Windward Passage Hotel. *Moderate.* P.O. Box 640, St. Thomas, USVI 00801. Tel. 774–5200. Large, convention-style hotel located on the waterfront. 146 air-conditioned rooms on three floors. Nice view of harbor, but not your typical tropical hotel—much more citified than most on St. Thomas. Convenient location.

East End

Pavilions and Pools. *Deluxe.* Smith Bay Rd., St. Thomas, USVI 00802. Tel. 775–6110. Lovely and secluded at east end of St. Thomas overlooking the Pillsbury Sound and nearby St. John. 25 units, each with its own private pool. Spacious air-conditioned pavilions include sun terrace, living room, bedroom, full kitchen and bath.

Virgin Grand Hotel. *Super Deluxe.* Smith Bay, St. Thomas, USVI 00801. Tel. 775–1510. Located off Smith Bay Rd. at the Coki Beach turnoff. 333 luxury beachfront, hillside, and courtyard units. Three swimming pools, convention facilities, and elegant dining.

Point Pleasant. *Deluxe.* Estate Smith Bay, St. Thomas, USVI 00802. Tel. 775–7200. 85 hillside units overlook St. John and surrounding cays—one of the most dramatic views on the island. Choose from villas to one-room units, each air conditioned with private kitchen and balcony or patio. Expanded terrace lounge and restaurant serves breakfast, lunch, and dinner. The view makes up for somewhat ordinary fare. Rates include use of cars, tennis, small sailboats, and snorkel gear.

Sapphire Beach Resort and Village. *Deluxe.* P.O. Box 8088, St. Thomas, USVI 00801. Tel. 775–6100. Sprawling beachfront complex with marina, hotel, condos, surfside restaurant, freshwater pools, and your choice of on-the-beach hotel rooms or condominiums. One of the most attractive, active beaches on the island—windsurfing, snorkeling, sailing are fantastic. Active, young crowd.

Red Hook Mountain Apartments. *Moderate.* Box 9139, St. Thomas, USVI 00801. Tel. 775–6111. Spacious apartments on the hillside above Red Hook Harbor. Spectacular east-end view. Hot tubs, cable TV, full kitchens.

Frenchtown

Villa Olga Hotel. *Moderate.* P.O. Box 4976, St. Thomas, USVI 00801. Tel. 774–1376. Located in quaint, historic Frenchtown (on Charlotte Amalie Harbor about midway from airport to town). Operated by the St. Thomas Diving Club, this casual, friendly resort emphasizes water sports—specifically scuba diving. Rates include continental breakfast daily; the hotel does not offer lunch or dinner—choose from any number of French, Italian, and even Austrian cafés in the neighborhood. 12 air-conditioned rooms overlook the pool and Charlotte Amalie Harbor.

Northside

Mahogany Run. *Super Deluxe.* P.O. Box 7517, St. Thomas, USVI 00801. Tel. 775–5000. Spectacular 315-acre condominium resort on the island's dramatic north shore. Wooded hills, green valleys, and breathtaking down-island vistas. Features the island's first 18-hole championship golf course, clubhouse, pro shop. Accommodations in one- and two-bedroom villas with fully equipped kitchens. Swimming pools and tennis courts. Superb nouvelle cuisine served at the *Old Stone Farm House* on Mahogany grounds. Breakfast, lunch, and dinner also served at the clubhouse.

Inn at Mandahl. *Expensive.* P.O. Box 2483, St. Thomas, USVI 00801. Tel. 775–2100. A quiet hilltop resort located near Mahogany Run Golf Course on the north shore. Eight spacious, studio-style rooms with terraces offer beautiful down-island views. Relaxed, tropical setting. Rates include continental breakfast (served in your room). Freshwater pool, good restaurant.

Magens Point Hotel. *Expensive.* Magens Bay Rd., St. Thomas, USVI 00801. Tel. 775–5500. An easy drive up and over the mountain to Charlotte Amalie, just minutes away from the island's best-known Beach, Magens Bay, with free transportation provided to and from the beach. The 28 hillside rooms have views of the sea. Dining at *Green Parrot Restaurant.*

South Side

Morningstar Beach Resort. *Expensive.* Box 7100, St. Thomas, USVI 00801. Tel. 776–8500. Completely renovated and recently reopened, this stunning tropical resort offers 96 charming rooms on one of St. Thomas' prettiest beaches.

Frenchman's Reef. *Deluxe.* P.O. Box 7100, St. Thomas, USVI 00801. Tel. 776–8500. Vast, Holiday Inn–affiliated complex at the eastern tip of Charlotte Amalie Harbor. 410 air-conditioned rooms, all with phones and color TV. Huge dining room, three cocktail lounges, freshwater pool, shopping arcade with 24 shops. Full convention facilities. Home away from home for visiting mainlanders. Atmosphere is a bit more plastic and sterile than most Caribbean places.

Limetree Beach Hotel. *Expensive.* P.O. Box 7307, St. Thomas, USVI 00801. Tel. 776–4770. About a 15-minute drive from town on palm-shaded beach at Frenchman's Bay. Luxurious three-level cottage units with 84 rooms; superior accommodations are particularly lovely. Bar, restaurant in hilltop estate have fine food, view, dancing. Good sports facilities—freshwater pool, scuba instruction, sailing tennis.

Secret Harbour Beach Hotel. *Expensive.* P.O. Box 7576, St. Thomas, USVI. Tel. 775–6550. Five miles east of Charlotte Amalie on secluded beach. 85 air-conditioned units from studios to two-bedroom apartments. Elegant seaside dining for breakfast, lunch, and dinner on the *Bird of Paradise* terrace. All water sports, tennis, freshwater pool. Tranquil, relaxed atmosphere.

Watergate Villas. *Expensive.* Estate Bolongo Bay, St. Thomas, USVI 00801. Tel. 775–2270. Hillside and beachfront condominiums. Ultra-modern studio to two-bedroom units overlooking Bolongo Bay just a 15-minute drive from town. All tastefully decorated and air conditioned. Swimming pools, tennis courts, white-sand beach, and all water sports. Cordon Bleu–trained chef serves up some of the island's finest cuisine at the *Fiddle Leaf* and *Little Leaf* restaurants on the property.

ST. JOHN

Cruz Bay Area

Gallows Point. *Deluxe.* P.O. Box 58, Cruz Bay, St. John, USVI 00830. Tel. 776–6434. St. John's new condominium complex overlooking Cruz Bay Harbor and Pillsbury Sound. Super location within walking distance (less than five minutes) from town. Elegantly updated West Indian–style, two-story cottages house four units each—about 28 units total on 4½ acres of beautifully groomed grounds. Beautifully appointed one-bedroom suites include large living rooms, modern kitchens, some loft bedrooms, tropical furnishings with lots of tile, rattan, and designer fabrics.

Carla's Cottages. *Expensive.* P.O. Box 432, Cruz Bay, St. John, USVI 00830. Tel. 776–6133. Nestled in the hills above Cruz Bay, guests enjoy a spectacular 360-degree view from what is best described as a tropical country inn. Three deluxe cottages accommodate two couples each and are fully equipped. Gourmet dinners only in the dining room (not included in room price). Open-air hot tubs.

Serendip Apartments. *Moderate.* P.O. Box 273, Cruz Bay, St. John, USVI 00830. Tel. 776–6646. Up the hill out of Cruz Bay overlooking town and Pillsbury Sound. Ten suites, each with twin bedroom, living room, kitchen, and bath. There's a bar-lounge for mingling with other guests.

Northshore

Caneel Bay Plantation. *Super Deluxe.* P.O. Box 720, Cruz Bay, St. John, USVI 00830. Tel. 776–6111. This super-luxe, sprawling complex pampers guests in true Rockresort fashion. Incredibly beautiful, naturally landscaped grounds—some 170 acres with just 156 guest rooms. Guests have seven postcard-perfect white-sand beaches to choose from. Astronomical rates include three meals a day, tennis, bicycles, snorkel gear, board sailing and small sailboats. Winter daily rates from $225 to $370. Three dining rooms offer cuisine for the most sophisticated palate. Located one mile from town off Northshore Rd.

Cinnamon Bay Campground. *Inexpensive.* P.O. Box 720, Cruz Bay, St. John, USVI 00830. Tel. 776–6330. Off Northshore Rd. in Virgin Islands National Park about three miles from Cruz Bay. Administered by the National Park Service, managed by Rockresorts, Inc. Accommodations include concrete cottages, tents, and bare sites. Equipment for cooking is included in the cottages and tents. High season is booked months in advance—reserve early! Well-stocked commissary is open daily and the beautiful, environmentally designed *Rain Tree Terrace* offers breakfast, lunch, and dinner daily. Good fare and reasonable rates. Dinner specials include barbecues about twice a week and West Indian food about once a week.

Maho Bay Camps Inc. *Inexpensive.* P.O. Box 310, Cruz Bay, St. John USVI 00830. Tel. 776–6240 or toll-free 800–392–9004 (212–472–9453 in New York). Located at the end of Northshore Rd., about six miles from Cruz Bay. 96 units, tucked in and around the foliage on 14 acres that rise from a white-sand beach and overlook Maho and Francis bays. The dwellings are best described as tent cabins—well-furnished, three-room cottages—built on wooden platforms. An interconnecting system of boardwalks links the entire complex together. Breakfast and dinner offered at the outdoor pavilion. A well-stocked store provides an assortment of healthful foods and sundries.

East End

Estate Zootenvaal. *Expensive.* Hurricane Hole, St. John, USVI 00830. Tel. 776–6321. Just a handful of private, waterfront homes are available for rent at Estate Zootenvaal on the island's east end. Located nine miles from Cruz Bay, just about one mile from Coral Bay. The beach houses are designer appointed and offer the ultimate in a private, tranquil tropical hideaway.

 HOME RENTALS. There are dozens of beautiful homes available for rental all over St. Croix throughout the year. Most have private swimming pools and/or beach facilities; all are fully equipped and many offer maid service as well. Those who have discovered how ideal these properties are for families book well in advance. Write well ahead of time to any of the following: *American Rentals,* Hamilton Mews, Christiansted, St. Croix, USVI 00820; *Elaine Bidelspacher Rentals,* Grapetree Bay, Star Route, St. Croix, USVI 00864; *Cram St. Croix Rentals,* c/o 725 Stone House Road, Moorestown, NJ 00857; or *Caribbean Home Rentals,* P.O. Box 710, Palm Beach, FL 33480.

HOW TO GET AROUND. From the airport. *St. Thomas:* to get into town by cab costs about $3.50 or $3.00 per passenger if two or more share. *St. John:* As there is no airport, you must take a taxi from St. Thomas airport to Red Hook Ferry at East End St. Thomas which costs about $8.00, or if two or more share, $4.00 per person. Red Hook Ferry to St. John costs $2 per person one-way. *St. Croix:* to get to Christiansted costs about $8.00 or $4 if two or more share the taxi; to Frederiksted costs $6.50 or $3.25 if two or more share the cab.

If you rent a car, remember they drive on the left-hand side in the Virgin Islands.

St. Croix. *Olympic, Hertz, Avis,* and *Budget* are the car rental leaders. Airport pickup and delivery is no problem with prior notification of your flight.

Taxi rates are posted on a panel near your luggage pickup at the airport. Look before you leap into a cab, and be sure of the fare. Rates are usually per person, even if you are a family of four. It's advisable to negotiate with a cab driver if you are going to want island tours and a lot of transportation. These days, he'll probably give you a good rate.

Buses do travel main routes on the island, the 17 miles between Christiansted and Frederiksted and the 22-mile length of the island. Rates are inexpensive; stops are frequent.

To reach Buck Island, nonsailors prefer the *Reef Queen,* whose glass panel permits seeing the marine gardens without leaving the boat. Swimmers can dive off and snorkel with guide. Rate for a half day (bring a picnic; drinks can be purchased aboard) is $18. The *Queen* leaves from the Fort in Christiansted. Sailors can charter a boat for the day. Sloops, catamarans, etc., take six passengers. Departures from town, from Buccaneer Hotel and from Grapetree Beach. Sailboats cost $25 to $35 per person for a full day.

St. John. Transportation is by jeep, Volkswagen mini-moke or taxi. Shuttle buses make scheduled stops at Cruz, Caneel, Trunk, and Cinnamon bays. The *Red Hook ferry* plies between St. Thomas and Cruz Bay on St. John every hour from 7:00 A.M. to 7:00 P.M., then every other hour until 11:00 P.M.

St. Thomas. *Avis, Hertz, National* and many local agencies are found in St. Thomas (Hertz and Avis at the airport as well as in town). Or rent a scooter from *ABC Auto Rentals* at Yacht Haven Hotel (advisable only if you know the roads well). Taxis are available everywhere. In St. Thomas, the rates are for one person; additional passengers pay extra. Most drivers are courteous and qualified to act as guides.

TOURIST INFORMATION SERVICES. *The Virgin Islands Department of Commerce* operates tourist information offices at Christiansted and Fredricksted, St. Croix; Charlotte Amalie, St. Thomas; and Cruz Bay, St. John. In Cruz Bay the office is located just off Cruz Bay Park across from the ferry dock; tel. 776–6450. In Charlotte Amalie, the office is located on the west side of Emancipation Square; tel. 774–8784. On St. Croix, the Frederiksted office is located in the Custom House Building; tel. 772–0357. There is also an office in downtown Christiansted; tel. 773–0495. For sources closer to home, see the Tourist Information Services section in the *Facts at Your Fingertips* chapter.

SPECIAL EVENTS. Carnival festivities, are the highlight each year, especially on St. Thomas. However, the U.S. Virgin Islands celebrate all the U.S. mainland holidays, along with several of their own.

St. John. *Carnival.* An annual, week-long event co-celebrating island traditions and the Fourth of July. Carnival Village springs up in Cruz Bay in late June and features island food, music and dancing daily. The week, a mix of cultural programs, food fairs, hibiscous shows, and traditional folk dancing, culminates with fireworks and a parade on the Fourth. Watch local media for schedule of events.

St. Thomas. *Carnival.* Celebrated on St. Thomas since 1952, this annual event usually takes place about one week after Easter—late April through early

May. Week-long festivities with Mocko Jumbies (stilt dancers), calypso greats, steel bands, parades, and some of the island's best cooks preparing native specialties. All action takes place in Charlotte Amalie, with Carnival Village set up in the Fort Christian parking lot on the waterfront. The festivities culminate with all-night dancing in the streets—*J'ouvert*—followed by a parade of costumed celebrants, floats, and marching bands the next morning. *The* island event of the year.

St. Croix. *Carnival.* Festival Village opens Christmas week each year and activities culminate with the colorful Three Kings Day Parade on Jan. 6. More than 20,000 spectators jam the streets of Frederiksted or Christiansted (the event alternates between the two towns each year) to watch the gala spectacle. Food booths and local bands blasting the latest calypso hits are the highlights of the Village.

 TOURS. St. Croix. There are very few guided tours of St. Croix's sites, with the exception of the Cruzan Rum Pavilion. Most places, however, do have self-guiding pamphlets, and, as on all three islands, taxi service is readily available for touring. Rates are based on location rather than mileage. The rates are set by Virgin Islands law and a copy of the rates is available from the driver for your inspection.

Cruzan Rum Pavilion. Free tours through the Virgin Islands rum distillery. The new pavilion features a tasting bar with complimentary rum cocktails. On-the-house package contains recipe booklets and island postcards. Specially equipped for the handicapped; groups of ten or more call ahead. Located on West Airport Rd., Open Mon–Fri., 8:30 A.M. to 4:15 P.M.

St. John. National Park–sponsored hikes, walks, and bus tours are offered daily. Check at park visitor center in Cruz Bay or Red Hook, St. Thomas, for schedules (they change with the season). Reservations are required, especially during busy winter months, for many hikes and tours; phone 776–6201 to reserve space. Among the more popular tours: the *historic bus tour*—a passage through time to early Danish days, plus some of the island's most spectacular vistas; the *Reef Bay Hike*—three miles (all downhill) through the interior of the island to the petroglyphs (ancient rock carvings) and the Reef Bay Sugar Factory on Reef Bay Beach (a 20-minute boat ride from there delivers you back to Cruz Bay); and the *Ram's Head hike* over the island's semi-arid east end (cactus and century plants are rampant here) to dramatic Ram's Head Bluff, the oldest continuously exposed point of land on St. John. Other park tours include weekly seashore walks and underwater snorkel tours at Cinnamon Bay.

Island Taxi Tours. Most open-air taxi shuttles on St. John provide round-the-island tours departing directly from the Cruz Bay ferry dock. Most of the drivers are native St. Johnians who are extremely proud of their island and are only too happy to tell you about it. Rates vary, but a good average is about $10 per person for a two- to three-hour tour. The St. John Taxi Association is located one block from the ferry dock, to the left as you make your way off the dock to the street. Tel. 776–6060. Keep an eye out for Lucy Smith—her copper-brown van is adorned with bull's horns and tropical blossoms; her island tour is witty, warm, and full of island charm. Phone her at 776–6804 evenings for reservation.

British Virgin Islands. *Inter-island Boat Services,* Cruz Bay, tel. 776–6282, offers daily service to West End, Tortola; $13 each way. From Cruz Bay to Tortola at 8:30 and 3:30 P.M., Mon.–Sat.; 5:00 P.M. Fri. and Sun. only. From West End, Tortola, to Cruz Bay 9:15 A.M. and 4:15 P.M., Mon.–Sat.; 5:30 P.M. Fri. and Sun. only.

St. Thomas. A number of land, sea, and air tours are availale from Charlotte Amalie. Contact *United Tours Inc.* at the Windward Passage Hotel, tel. 774–6719, or *Virgin Islands Sightseeing and Tours* at the St. Thomas Airport, tel. 774–1556, to arrange various package tours. Most taxi and open-air shuttle drivers are happy to arrange half- and full-day island tours. Ask your hotel or cruise director for recommendations or check with the *Virgin Islands Taxi Association,* tel. 774–4550. A 2½-hour island tour for two by surrey bus or taxi is about $20 and covers most of the important sights.

By air, the *Seaplane Shuttle* offers daily, convenient downtown-to-downtown transportation between Charlotte Amalie and Christiansted, St. Croix (about 20 minutes flying time and about $50 roundtrip) for shopping or touring that island for a day. 15 to 30-minute helicopter tours of St. Thomas and nearby St. John leave from the waterfront several times daily; contact one of the tour companies listed above for more information.

Full- and half-day sails from St. Thomas to St. John for snorkeling and picnic lunches leave from Charlotte Amalie and Red Hook daily. Contact the *Virgin Islands Charter Boat League,* tel. 774–3944 or check with your hotel or cruise director—the list is endless. *St. Thomas This Week* publishes an extensive list as well. Rates (including lunch) vary between $25 and $50 per person.

Day trips to the nearby British Virgin Islands are available via the *Bomba Charger Ferry,* tel. 774–7920. Rates and schedules vary to the islands of Jost Van Dyke, Tortola, and Virgin Gorda, so check before you go.

Not-to-be-missed tours on St. Thomas: *Harbor and cocktail cruise* each Tuesday and Saturday aboard the catamaran *Ho-Tei.* $10 per person for two-hour harbor/sunset cruise; leaves the Charlotte Amalie waterfront at 5:45 P.M., tel. 774–2435. *West Indies Bay Co. bay rum factory* near the airport, phone 774–2166 for appointment. *Coral World Marine Park.* Up-close look at fascinating undersea world—and you needn't get your feet wet. This unique complex at Coki Point, at the east end of St. Thomas, tel. 775–1555, is home to the only underwater observatory tower in the Western Hemisphere. Daily feeding (including sharks, barracudas, and moray eels) at 11:00 A.M. A marine gardens aquarium, duty-free shops, and a bar/restaurant complete this complex. Admission $7 for adults; children $3.50. Taxi shuttles provide transportation several times daily from the Grand Hotel in town, or arrange for a taxi from your hotel.

 PARKS AND GARDENS. St. Croix. *Buck Island National Park and Underwater Trails,* just off St. Croix, is a snorkeler's and scuba diver's delight. The park itself covers over 850 acres, including the island proper, with a sandy beach, picnic tables, and barbecue. The reef has two major underwater trails, Turtle Bay Trail and East End Trail. Ask your hotel for specifics on transportation.

St. George Village Botanical Garden. The gardens cover 16 acres of lush woods and rich land between Christiansted and Frederiksted. Tour ruins of a 19th-century sugar cane village and rum factory. Step back in time with a walk through the workers' homes, manager's house, superintendent's house. View the lime kiln, bake oven, stone dam, foundations of a watermill, and the village cemetery. Truly a historian's delight. Open daily, 8:00 A.M.–3:00 P.M.

St. John. Nearly two-thirds of this pristine island is protected by the National Park Service—9,600 acres on land and another 5,600 acres underwater. *Virgin Islands National Park* has visitor centers located at Red Hook on St. Thomas and Cruz Bay on St. John. The park offers a number of interpretive programs including seashore walks, snorkel tours, inland hikes, and evening programs at the park's one campground, located at Cinnamon Bay. Check at the park-operated visitor centers for program schedule (it changes seasonally). Self-guiding trails are located at Annaberg, Cinnamon Bay, Reef Bay, and Salt Pond Bay. Two favorite tours are the historic bus tour and Reef Bay hike. Both require advance reservations. Pack lunch and comfortable walking shoes for the Reef Bay Hike—you'll trek nearly three miles through the interior of the island and lunch at the petroglyph reflecting pools. The petroglyphs are ancient rock carvings that are still a mystery to experts. The meaning and origin of the symbols are still unknown. Some argue they were carved by native Arawak or Carib Indian tribes, while others say they are the work of early African arrivals to the island. Rangers identify native flora and fauna along the way and leave time for exploring the 18th-century Reef Bay Sugar Factory at the end of the 2½-hour bus tour that traces the island's history. Bring your camera—there are many wonderful vistas. The park's famous underwater trail, whose sunken markers identify a variety of soft and hard corals, and describe the type of fish most likely to be seen in the area, is located at Trunk Bay—it is also self-guided. Park programs concentrate on the island's natural beauty and resources as well as the island's rich cultural history. Cultural demonstrations are sponsored several times a week, at Cinnamon Bay and Annaberg Ruins. Traditional cooking, basketmaking, gardening, and story-telling provide a glimpse of plantation-era life. Reservations are required for many of the hikes and programs, especially during peak season, so be sure to phone (776–6201) or stop by the park visitor centers before you go.

Cruz Bay Park. Adjacent to the ferry dock in the heart of town. This postage-stamp-sized park—more of a town square really—is lazy and relaxed. People-watching is the number one activity. If you sit here long enough you'll see the entire population, visitors and residents alike, parade by. Open-air cafes and shops line its perimeter and with just a moment's notice food fairs or arts-and-crafts displays pop up within the park itself. On Sundays local reggae bands or jazz ensembles frequently stage free performances here. There's rarely a schedule—it's just as the mood strikes!

St. Thomas. *Emancipation Gardens,* Charlotte Amalie's inner-city minipark, encompasses one city block. This is the spot where newly freed slaves, emancipated by the Danes on July 3, 1948, danced and celebrated their independence. Now school children can be found most afternoons trying out the latest dance steps in the park's West Indian–style gazebo. Rare lignum vitae trees shade the park. In bloom, their flowers are a brilliant blue.

Fairchild Park. Perched high in the hills above Charlotte Amalie, this charming, exquisitely landscaped tiny jewel of a park offers views of both the Atlantic and Caribbean to the north and south of the island.

 BEACHES. Powdery, white-sand beaches fringed with coconut palms are scattered throughout the U.S. Virgin Islands. In fact, the beaches and gin-clear turquoise waters score high, along with duty-free shopping, scuba diving, and sailing as top visitor attractions. Most hotels are situated on the waterfront so you won't have far to go to beach it. According to Virgin Islands law, all beaches throughout the territory are open to the public and hotels and individuals cannot prevent access. Nude sunbathing is strictly prohibited. On St. John the National Park Service protects and administers many of the beaches, including many of the most popular along Northshore Road, and has its own set of rules and regulations regarding spear-fishing, water-skiing and other water sports. The park's visitor center in Cruz Bay provides informational brochures. To choose the best beach is to choose among an array of tropical gems—difficult but not impossible. What you want to do once you get there—swim, snorkel, windsurf, or simply soak up the sun—will help determine your destination.

St. Croix. The list of white-sugar sand beaches is endless. The 84-square-mile island is scalloped with tiny coves and beautiful sheltered beaches; most of the hotels are located directly on them. The right of access to any beach in the Virgin Islands is protected by law. In addition to the world-famous Buck Island National Park, St. Croix boasts three surf-free, exceptional public beaches. All have changing facilities and rest rooms, but you must bring your own snacks, etc. In Frederiksted, west of the fort and across from the ball park is a public beach, great for beginning snorkelers. *Cramer Park* lies in a sheltered cove on the east end, and overlooks spectacular Buck Island. *Altonna Lagoon* is right on Christiansted Harbor, a spacious park and beach still under development. For those who like to surf, *La Grande Princesse,* is not a public beach, but certainly a lively one.

St. John. Some of the most photographed and talked-about beaches in the world are located on the north shore of this tiny, pristine island. Start at *Hawksnest* (about one mile from Cruz Bay) and beach-hop, stopping at *Trunk Bay* (hailed as one of the ten most beautiful beaches in the world), *Cinnamon, Maho,* and *Francis.* The park's famous underwater snorkel trail is located at Trunk Bay; concessionaires rent equipment if you don't have your own. No problem with parking or public transportation (via shuttle bus from town) to any of the locations. Changing facilities and snack bars at Trunk and Cinnamon; changing rooms only at Hawksnest. For more seclusion and a look at the island's more primitive east end, rent a jeep in Cruz Bay and head for *Salt Pond* or *Lameshur Beach.* Both park-protected and excellent for sunning, swimming, snorkeling, or a romantic picnic for two (pick up picnic goodies at Moveable Feast's Take-Out Deli in Mongoose Junction, Cruz Bay). Windsurfing equipment and instruction available at Cinnamon and Maho Beach on the north shore; snorkeling equipment available for rent at Cinnamon and Trunk Bay or at local dive shops in Cruz Bay.

St. Thomas. Beaches are scattered around the island and the large resorts are situated on some of the best. While some hotels will restrict use of beach chairs to guests only, all beaches are open to the public. Some of the best and most active hotel beaches include *Sapphire, Morningstar, Secret Harbour,* and *Lindbergh.* Most water sports, from snorkeling to windsurfing available at these locations. Special places (all public beaches): *Hull Bay* on the north shore for wind or body surfing; *Coki Beach* on the east end for snorkeling; *Cowpet Bay* on the east end for windsurfing; and *Magens Bay* for its paradisiacal, picturesque setting, and nearly every water sport. This is St. Thomas' best-known beach and really is breathtakingly beautiful, but it is also incredibly crowded most weekends and holidays. It offers dressing rooms, snack bar, and ample parking. Windsurfing equipment, snorkeling equipment, and small sailboats for rent. Coki Beach has a snack bar and snorkel gear for rent; Hull Bay, snack bar only; Lindbergh, changing rooms; Morningstar, changing rooms and restaurant.

 PARTICIPANT SPORTS. Water sports have it hands down throughout the Virgin Islands, but golf, tennis, and hiking (especially on St. John) are becoming increasingly popular with visitors and residents alike.

St. Croix. On St. Croix, there are public **tennis** courts in Christiansted and courts at the Buccaneer, Gentle Winds, Grapetree Beach, and Queen's Quarter hotels, and at Hotel on the Cay, just a few minutes' water ride from King's Wharf. Additionally, the Caribbean Tennis Club, close to Christiansted, has 12 courts (seven lighted for night play) and a Pro Shop, which are open to visitors.

For **golf,** the 18-hole course at Fountain Valley, St. Croix, is a championship course designed by Robert Trent Jones and created by Rockefeller. It has a pro shop, restaurant, showers, and lockers, and is open to the public. Buccaneer Hotel has 18 holes, pro shop, golf carts on its seaside acreage. There is also a nine-hole course at The Reef.

Water sports are really the highlight here on St. Croix. There's terrific **snorkeling** along its seven-mile reef on the south shore; its marine gardens and underwater trail to the northeast. Should you not arrive with your own mask and fins, you can rent them through most of the major hotels or at any of the island's water-sports centers. A few to consider are: *Caribbean Sea Adventures,* which also specializes in **scuba-diving** safaris and **sportfishing** trips. Contact *Sun Sails* for daily and sunset excursions under sail—both are headquartered on King's Wharf in Christiansted. *The Dive Shop,* which has its office aboard a houseboat in Christiansted harbor, offers rental of scuba gear and underwater photography equipment, as well as special dive charters. In Frederiksted, *West End Boating,* next to the La Grange Beach and Tennis Club, can arrange scenic cruises and sailboat rentals.

The ultimate enjoyment on this island, as we've said previously, is the underwater trail at Buck Island. Don't miss it!

St. John. **Swimming** and **snorkeling** are excellent at literally every beach. Special place: the park's underwater snorkel trail at Trunk Bay. Snorkeling is at its best at Honeymoon Beach and Turtle Bay at the Caneel Bay Resort (watch for sea turtles at that resort's Scott Beach, as well as the beaches at Maho and Francis bays) and at Cinnamon Bay on the north shore. On the island's east end head for Haulover Bay or Salt Pond for excellent snorkeling and fewer people. Dive shops in Cruz Bay and Coral Bay rent equipment; concessions located at the beach at Trunk and Cinnamon.

Scuba diving. Instruction, equipment, and tours available at *St. John Watersports* in Mongoose Junction, tel. 776–6256; *Cruz Bay Watersports, Inc.* in downtown Cruz Bay, tel. 776–6234; and *Coral Bay Water Sports* in Coral Bay, tel. 776–6857. One- and two-tank boat or beach dives offered daily; check with shop owners for rates and schedules.

Sailing. Caneel Bay Resort offers complimentary Sunfish to its guests; fully crewed day-sails with lunch available through *St. John Watersports,* tel. 776–6256; *Cruz Bay Watersports,* tel. 776–6234; *Cinnamon Bay Campground,* tel. 776–6330; and *Maho Bay Campground,* tel. 776–6226. *Trade Wind Charters* on the waterfront in Cruz Bay offers bare-boat charters (small sailboats or power-boats) on a daily basis. No phone—stop by for reservations and rates.

Windsurfing. Instruction and equipment available for rent at Cinnamon Bay and Maho Bay. About $30 per hour. Caneel Bay reserves lessons and equipment for guest use only.

Tennis. Two public courts located in Cruz Bay, just behind Sprauve School, are lit until 10:00 P.M. daily. No reservations. Caneel Bay reserves seven beautifully maintained hard-surface courts for the exclusive use of their hotel guests. The resort offers lessons daily and tournaments weekly. Ball machine also available for use by reservation. Lessons, tournaments, and ball machine for use by hotel guests only.

St. Thomas. **Swimming** is excellent at nearly all St. Thomas beaches and most hotels are located on one or more beaches so you won't have far to go. Among the most calm swimming beaches: Magens Bay, Coki Point, Secret Harbour, Brewers Bay, Lindbergh Bay, and Pineapple Beach.

Snorkeling. Equipment available for rent at local dive shops and some hotel water-sport centers (check the local publication *St. Thomas This Week* for extensive listings or check at your hotel desk). Best snorkeling at Coki Point, Sapphire Beach, Secret Harbour and Magens Bay.

Scuba Diving. Qualified instruction and tours offered by a number of local dive shops and water-sports centers. Among them: the *St. Thomas Diving Club* (with three locations), tel. 774–1376; *Watersports Centers* at Sapphire and Point Pleasant, tel. 775–6755; *Chris Sawyer Diving Center* at Compass Point, tel. 775–7320; *Aqua Action* at Secret Harbour, tel. 775–6285; *Joe Vogel Diving Company* near Mahogany Run, tel. 775–7610; and the *Virgin Islands Diving School,* tel. 774–8687. Most offer complete certification courses, mini-resort courses, and one or two tank dives daily. With underwater visibility often exceeding 100 feet and water temperature an average 78 degrees, the Virgin Islands are heralded worldwide as a mecca for divers. Dives include boat or shore dives to active reefs, as well as extra-special wreck dives that allow you to explore Spanish galleons and modern-day ships, all shrouded in mystery and promising yet-to-be-discovered treasure. Most famous is the wreck of the Rhone, actually located in British Virgin Islands' waters, just off Salt Island. This British steamship sank in 1867 and remains remarkably intact. It's a haven for marine life, and colorful sponges and corals encrust its propeller and hull. Many dive operators offer day-long tours to the Rhone (a two-hour boat ride each way; about $80 per person for two-tank dive).

Windsurfing. The hottest new sport to hit the Caribbean. Equipment and instruction available at the following locations: Cowpet Bay, Sapphire Bay, Pineapple Beach, Secret Harbour, Morningstar, and Magens Beach. Check at your hotel for location nearest you. Rental and instruction about $30 and up per hour.

Sailing. Most hotels and water-sports centers rent small sailboats (some hotels offer complimentary use to guests) such as Sunfish, Lasers, and Hobie Cats. The *Watersports Center* at Sapphire Bay, tel. 775–0755, offers daily rentals of Sunfish as well as larger sloops such as the Ensign 22. Half- and full-day rates available. A number of charter sailboats (complete with crew) make daily excursions to St. John or surrounding cays; half- and full-day trips available at rates ranging from $25 to $50 per person. Check *St. Thomas This Week* or at your hotel for complete listing of charter boats. Term bareboat charters (you sail and provision the boat yourself) are available for a week or more. The concept has proven so popular that the U.S. and British Virgin Islands have become known as the charter-boat capital of the world. Check with the *Charter-yacht League* in Charlotte Amalie's Yacht Haven Hotel, tel. 774–3944, for complete listing.

Deep-Sea Fishing. For big-game sportfishing (blue marlin and sailfish among the fighters) and bottom and reef fishing (yellowtail, snapper, tuna, blue runners, and dolphin among the catches), check with the *American Yacht Harbor* at Red

Hook, tel. 775–6454, or *Fish Hawk Marina* on the East End Lagoon, tel. 775–9058.

Golf. At St. Thomas' spectacular 18-hole championship golf course at Mahogany Run. Rental clubs and lessons available. Greens fees $27; golf cart required at $22 for two people; tel. 775–5678 for reservations.

Tennis. Courts by reservation at the following locations: Bluebeard's Castle Hotel, 774–1600; Frenchman's Reef Tennis Courts, 776–8500; Limetree Tennis Center, 774–8990; Mahogany Run Tennis Club, 775–5678; Virgin Isle Hotel, 774–1500. Public courts are located at Subbase, Long Bay, and Bordeaux; lights on until 10:00 P.M. Courts at Bluebeard's, Frenchman's Limetree, Mahogany, and Virgin Isle Hotel also lit—some by request only, so check before you go. Most courts have hard surfaces; Pineapple has four fast-drying clay courts. Court fees vary.

SPECTATOR SPORTS. St. Croix. Aside from the numerous **sailing** regattas that fill the waters around the Virgin Islands, **tennis** tournaments take place at the Buccaneer Hotel throughout the year. For details, ask at your hotel desk.

St. Thomas/St. John. Informal **tennis** tournaments at the public courts in Cruz Bay; posters around town announce the matches, or just ask around. Slow-pitch **softball**—minor and amateur leagues—comes to Cruz Bay ballpark (at Sprauve School) in the late spring and summer. Most games take place in the early evening; again watch for signs announcing games posted around town. **Yacht racing**, including the annual "Around St. John Race" and the 5-day Rolex Regatta (usually in late winter or early spring; phone St. Thomas Yacht Club, 775–6320, for date and course details) can be viewed from any number of beaches, points, or hilltop vistas.

The annual **Little Switzerland Tennis Tournament** at the St. Thomas Yacht Club—generally in February; entrants are among the islands' best.

HISTORIC SITES AND HOUSES. St. Croix. In Christiansted: *Alexander Hamilton House.* King St. opposite the Government House. The revolutionary statesman was born on the nearby British Island of Nevis, but worked in this building as a youth when it was a hardware store. Open daily 9:00 A.M.–5:00 P.M.

Fort Christiansvaern. End of Company St. on the waterfront. The best-preserved of the five remaining Danish forts in the Virgin Islands. A prime example of 17th- and 18th-century Danish colonial military architecture, the fort was built mainly of hard yellow bricks brought from Denmark as ballast in sailing ships. Largely completed by 1749, it became a police station and courthouse in 1878. Open daily 8:00 A.M.–5:00 P.M.

Government House. The corner of King and Queen Cross Sts. One-time capital of the Danish West Indies, still the headquarters for governor's administration for St. Croix, U.S. District Courts, and other government offices. Incorporates old dwellings dating to 1747. Ceremonial staircase at north end leads to handsome ballroom on second floor. Open daily 9:00 A.M.–5:00 P.M. In Frederiksted: *Fort Frederik.* On the waterfront at the northern end of town. Like the town, the fort was named in honor of King Frederik V of Denmark-Norway. It is the site of the first foreign salute in 1776 to the flag of the new American republic, and at this site on July 3, 1848, Governor General Peter von Scholten freed the slaves in the Danish West Indies.

Victoria House. 1½ blocks south of Customs House. In 1803, it was a residence owned by the Gordon Family. During the uprising called "Fireburn" in 1878, this part of Frederiksted was burned, including Victoria House. Some of the old structure has been preserved in the present building. Open daily 9:00 A.M.–5:00 P.M. In East End. *Whim Great House.* Centerline Rd. Experience the planter's life at the great house at Estate Whim. Built in 1794 at the height of St. Croix's sugar and rum prosperity. There is a formidable moat of native stone and coral plus a famous sugar mill and historical museum. Open seven days a week, 10:00 A.M.–5:00 P.M.

St. John. Virgin Islands National Park has restored and maintains a number of 18th-century Danish ruins, including those on the sites of former plantations such as *Annaberg, Catherineberg, Cinnamon Caneel* and *Reef Bay.*

Annaberg Ruins. The best of the restored 18th-century plantations on the island. The National Park Service has recently provided for handicap access with paved walkways and ramps to the area. Brochures are also available to help visitors along the quarter-mile, self-guided loop trail. One of the many plantations operating on St. John through the mid-1800s, Annaberg is a reminder of the era when sugar was king. Three times weekly, the National Park Service sponsors cultural demonstrations, including traditional cooking techniques and basketmaking. Check at the park's visitor center in Cruz Bay for schedules; days and times vary according to season. The Annaberg Plantation is located about eight miles from Cruz Bay off Northshore Rd. Shuttle buses provide round-trip transportation from town for approximately $6 per person.

Cruz Bay Battery, located on Cruz Bay Harbor. This red-roofed, white structure was completed in 1827 and has housed St. John's administrative offices ever since. Over the years it has also served as a museum and jail.

St. Thomas. The Historical American Building Survey has designated a number of buildings in Charlotte Amalie and on *Hassel Island* in Charlotte Amalie Harbor for architectural beauty and historical significance. They include the 18th-century forts and batteries on Hassel Island (most of that island is now protected by the National Park Service; Sea Adventures provides frequent ferry service from Charlotte Amalie waterfront to Hassel Island, tel. 774–8500) as well as lookout towers of infamous pirates Blackbeard and Bluebeard on the hills above town. *Blackbeard Tower* is now part of a private home and is not accesible to the public. *Bluebeard's Tower* is located in the gardens of Bluebeard's Castle Hotel and is open daily.

Other structures cited by the Historical American Building Survey include: *Fort Christian,* located on Charlotte Amalie's waterfront and completed in 1672, this is the island's oldest standing building. Once it housed the entire village and since then has been used as a jail and municipal court. It is now a museum open Mon.–Fri. 8:00 A.M.–5:00 P.M.; Sat. and Sun. 12:30 to 5:00 P.M.

Government House and the 99 Steps. Government Hill, Charlotte Amalie. The governor's residence and offices for more than 100 years. The second-floor reception rooms open to the public weekdays 8:00 A.M.–noon and again 1:00 P.M.–5:00 P.M.; closed weekends. Bright white with a traditional red roof, this Georgian-style building was built in 1867. 99 steps lead from Government Hill to Little Tower Street, the passage is one of many "long steps" that were part of the original city plan to solve the problem of reaching homes on hilly terrain. Dates to 18th century. A treat for photographers.

The Grand Hotel on Charlotte Amalie's Emancipation Square opened in 1841 as the West Indian Hotel. The hotel closed in 1974; the building now houses restaurants, shops, and a hospitality lounge.

St. Thomas Synagogue. Located in town just two blocks north of Main St. Second-oldest synagogue in the Western Hemisphere. Designed in Spanish-Moorish style, it is one of the most beautiful buildings in Charlotte Amalie. Sand on the floors is symbolic of the exodus from Egypt. Services Friday at 8:00 P.M. Open 9:00 A.M. to 4:30 P.M. Mon.–Fri.; Saturday 8:30 to 11:30 A.M.

Frederick Lutheran Church is on Norre Gade just below Government House. Official church of the Danish Virgin Islands; rebuilt after a fire in 1826. Open Sun. 8:00 A.M.–noon; Mon.–Sat. 8:00 A.M.–5:00 P.M.

MUSEUMS AND GALLERIES. St. Croix. In Christiansted: *Apothecary Hall.* Downtown Christiansted. Inside a large courtyard, this 18th-century structure was the site of a Danish apothecary and pharmacist's residence since 1832. It now houses a restaurant and art gallery. Open daily 9:00 A.M.–4:30 P.M. *Steeple Building.* Company St. The first Danish Lutheran Church, now an informative museum of Indian relics unearthed on St. Croix, and sugar plantation operations. Open 9:00 A.M.–4:30 P.M. daily.

In Frederiksted. *Fort Frederik.* Waterfront. The first foreign salute to the flag of the thirteen U.S. colonies took place at this fort. Now serves as a historical site and museum. New park facilities surround the fort.

St. John. The *St. John Museum,* located in the Elaine Ione Sprauve Library (the former Enighed Estate House from the days of Danish rule, beautifully restored) just off Centerline Rd. behind Julius Sprauve School. Open Mon.–Fri., 9:00 A.M.–5:00 P.M. Small collection of cultural artifacts and displays tracing cultural history from native Indian inhabitants to present. Often features the work of local artists in limited, one-person shows. *Cinnamon Bay Museum,* located on the beach at Cinnamon Bay Campground in old Danish Warehouse. Open daily 8:30 A.M.–4:30 P.M. Small exhibit of cultural artifacts and displays of natural history specimens. Administered by the National Park Service. No admission charge at either museum. *St. John Art Project,* located in Cruz Bay just behind Cruz Bay Park. Open Mon.–Sat. from 10:00 A.M. to 5:00 P.M., this small gallery exhibits and sells the work of many local artists.

St. Thomas. Art galleries line Charlotte Amalie's Main St. and its passages. Most feature Caribbean art and some contemporary graphics (see "Shopping" section for specifics). *Jim Tillet's* art gallery and crafts studios feature hand-screened tropical fabrics and are located at Estate Tutu on the island's east end. St. Thomas' only true museum is located in historic *Fort Christian.* Contains a number of historic artifacts. Traces island history from native Carib and Arawak Indian settlements through Danish rule. Open Mon.–Fri. 8:00 A.M.–5:00 P.M.; Sat. and Sun. 12:30–5:00 P.M.

 MUSIC, DANCE, AND STAGE. St. Croix. Certain folklore specialties of the Virgin Islands are featured. Watch for Africanized quadrilles and Irish jigs, relics of plantation days, danced with tap drum and flute accompaniment. Ask at your hotel about events for visitors. We do *not* recommend walking around the islanders' Carnival Village.

Plays, concerts, and ballet performed from time to time by local and imported professional groups. See local papers for dates and places, or ask your hotel desk. The island center of Peppertree Road, half-a-mile north of the Sunny Isle Shopping Center, has the largest stage in the islands.

St. Thomas. The *Reichhold Center For the Arts,* located on the College of the Virgin Islands campus, attracts world-class performers, dance troupes, theatrical performances, and musical groups specializing in everything from Beethoven to rock. The season runs from October through April, though special performances are booked throughout the year. Tel. 774–8475 for schedule and ticket information. The center is exquisite—an open-air amphitheater carved from a hillside and set in a valley. Guided tours are available Mon.–Fri. 9:00 A.M.–4:00 P.M.; tel. 774–8475 for appointment.

SHOPPING. St. Croix. Just as much of a duty-free selection on this island as on St. Thomas, although not as many shops.

Many of St. Thomas' leading shops have branches: *Continental, Little Switzerland, Bolero, Compass Rose,* and *Patelli.* The latter is in King's Alley, where there is also: *The Gold Shop;* the *Cage of Gold;* the *Perfume Bar; Mahoney Place* for tropical fashions; and *Land of Oz,* with unusual adult games, puzzles, and toys.

Longest of the Christiansted arcades is in the Caravelle Hotel, where you'll find *Betsy Cantrell's,* children's wear by Merry Mites; and *Violette Boutique,* sportswear, accessories, jewelry by Europe's leading designers. *Island Imports* represents *Maison Danoise* with their fine line of china, glass, and silver and in addition have a fine stock of English leather goods, framed old prints and maps, straw hats and bags, and unique shadow-boxes made in St. Croix.

At the Pan Am Pavilion is *Quick Pics* for stereo and camera equipment; *The Jewelry Store; Many Hands,* fine arts and handicrafts exclusively from the V.I.; and *The Spanish Main,* silk-screen originals by Jim Tillett.

Copenhagen, Ltd. has everything in the decorative arts from Scandinavia, including Bing and Grondahl Christmas plates, and Arabia dinnerware. Boda and Kosta glass, plus pewter from Holland, straw rugs from Dominica, perfumes from France, cigars from Jamaica, mahogany crafts from Haiti.

Java Wraps features Balinese fashions; fine gold, crystal, and china at *Heritage House; Sonya's Corner Shop* has beautifully hand-designed gold and silver jewelry.

There are many liquor merchants—*Comanche Liquor Locker, Grog & Spirits, Tradewinds, The Conch Shell,* and *Carib Cellars.* All will pack your five duty-free bottles in a safe carrying carton. At Carib Cellars you can sample Cruzan liqueurs brewed from coconuts, bananas, pineapple, almonds, roses, and hibiscus!

Danish furniture is also available at the *Continental.* They'll take your order and have it delivered to the States from Denmark.

Other shops worth looking into are *The Linen Cupboard* for Madeira work, Saba drawnthread; *The Wadsworth Boutique,* on the waterfront, for straw bags, charms, fanciful jewelry, including a gold lizard pin, scarves, and other accessories.

Nini of Scandinavia has fabrics by the yard from Sweden, fashions (including the Finnish Marimekko dresses), wooden shoes, and jewelry from Denmark.

At *Whim Greathouse* there's a small shop selling locally made jewelry, notepaper, jams, soaps and perfumes. They'll make a planter's chair to order. The *Royal Frederik,* in Frederiksted, has Ballantyne cashmeres, beaded bags and sweaters from the Continent and Hong Kong. Royal Delft china (exclusive here). *A.H. Riise's* gift shop has a branch here, too. *Raine's,* in nearby Victoria House, has a fine selection of designer sports clothes for men and women. *Island Stuff* sells hand-screened Caribbean prints and Indonesian batiks. *Gerdian's,* at #1 Strand St. on the waterfront, has watches, gold jewelry, china, and crystal.

At *Fletcher Pence's* studio in the hills above Frederiksted you can purchase the artist's handsome wood sculptures.

St. John. Though shopping is somewhat more limited—and prices a bit higher—than on the other islands, some unique finds and buys can be made. Extra special is the traditional St. John Basket—quantities are limited so you'll have to scout around. *Wicker, Wood and Shells* in the Mongoose Junction center is a good place to start your search. Mongoose Junction, located in Cruz Bay just across from the Park Service Visitor Center, is a beautifully designed, multi-level center for artists' workshops and boutiques. You'll find everything from custom-made fine jewelry with an emphasis on island motifs to hand-painted clothing to canvas bags and woven baskets. For the best in stained-glass creations, from small fish-shaped window hangings to wall-sized murals and Tiffany lamps, check out *Suncatchers, Inc.* at the Boulon Center. Tropical shells found throughout the Virgin Islands adorn mirrors and containers of all shapes and sizes at the *Cruz Bay Dive Shop.* The proprietors dive for the shells and then hand-decorate the mirrors and containers. The National Park Service Visitor Center carries a number of books on a variety of subjects pertaining to the undersea life, cultural heritage, and natural history of the islands.

St. Thomas. Bring all your keen shopping experience to the fore to spot the bargains. Liquor is one, foreign designer fashions, exotic and rare imports are others. Remember that U.S. residents may take back $800 worth of purchases duty free. These purchases may be carried home with you or declared and shipped ahead. In addition, you may mail home each day a gift worth up to $50 to any friend or relative, as long as no one is sent more than one gift per day.

Once again, we refer you to *Here's How* and *St. Thomas This Week* for suggestions, but here are some of our favorite shops.

Little Switzerland, at the town square near the fort and a few steps away from the hubbub, is housed in an 18th-century Danish building. A treasure-trove of crystal, housewares, jewelry, and watches on just one spacious floor. Just around the corner on Main St., is another fine location with a fine Waterford crystal collection (including lamps and chandeliers). A third, stunning shop featuring only Rosenthal's Studio line is also located on Main St. The artist's contemporary designs in crystal, flatware, china, and art pieces are priced 45–50% below stateside prices.

A. H. Riise, in spectacularly restored private warehouses, with old bricks sandblasted to warm hues, has a variety of counter-boutiques in its gift shops, and endless lines of interesting bottles in its liquor store a few doors down Main St., as Dronningen's Gade is now called. At the gift shop counters, you'll find perfumes and cosmetics, sweaters and blouses, neckties and some menswear;

watches, jewelry, china, and crystal—in fact, a little bit of everything, most of it high-quality merchandise.

Boutique Riviera sells terrific designer fashions. Louis Vuitton luggage and quality name jewelry. They're located in town and have a small branch at Frenchman's Reef Hotel.

Tropicana Perfume Shoppes is so vast that there are two stores on Main St. Best buys are on the French imports, although they have a full line of fragrances from Estee Lauder, Elizabeth Arden, and Revlon.

For watches, check *Boolchand's, Accuracy, Inc.,* and *Sparky's;* for interestingly displayed island-made items, browse through the new shopping area on Mountain Top.

Courreges and *Gucci* each have their own boutiques in town, offering a nice variety at good prices. One of the largest selections of dinnerware, such as Limoge, Spode, and Royal Worcester, can be found at *The English Shop.*

Even if you don't buy, enjoy the glitter of the finest jewelry at *Cardow; Colombian Emeralds; H. Stern;* or at *Irmela's Jewel Studio.*

Equator, at the western end of Main St. near Market Sq., features fine men's resort or wear-at-home fashions by Ralph Lauren, Alexander Julian, Calvin Klein, Henry Grethel, and other designers.

The Tie Rack (just beyond Travel Services, Inc., across from the Grand Hotel at the eastern end of Main St.) offers an assortment of island-made goodies, including ties, of course, but also stuffed animals and West Indian dolls in an array of island prints and fabrics.

Bakery Square, on Charlotte Amalie's Back St. (parallel to Main St. and one block up) houses more than a dozen shops and restaurants in a brick courtyard setting. Down Island Traders specializes in such tropical delicacies as mango chutney, hibiscus tea, Jamaican Blue Mountain Coffee, sea-grape jelly, and specially prepared island seasonings; The Cloth Horse has Marimekko fabric at prices well below stateside, Haitian cottons, mahogany plates, island-made ceramics and baskets.

 RESTAURANTS. It used to be almost impossible to find West Indian cooking in St. Thomas, but that's changed now, with such places as *Daddy's,* near the lagoon, serving delicious local fish specialties and *Victor's Hideaway* in town near Subbase offering a variety of island dishes. The selection of other restaurants runs from steak-and-lobster places to French, Mexican, and Polynesian. In most places dining is casual but neat. Winter vacationers dress up more, especially at places like *Harborview, Secret Harbour,* and the *Old Stone Farmhouse* at Mahogany Run. Almost all hotels in our listing have restaurants, and when they are exceptional we have so noted. The best are featured again in this restaurant roster.

The following price classifications are based on the cost of an average three-course dinner for one person, food only; beverages, tax, and tip are extra. *Deluxe,* over $30.00; *Expensive,* $20–30; *Moderate,* $10–19; *Inexpensive,* less than $10. Traveler's checks are accepted nearly everywhere, but almost no establishments accept off-island, personal checks.

Hours and days of operation change with the season, so it's always best to call before you go. During high season dinner reservations are needed nearly everywhere.

ST. CROIX

You can't go wrong on this island, with more than 40 restaurants serving up everything from asapao to zucchini. Make it your own international gourmet safari and find menus and prices to suit every palate and budget. We surely can't list them all, but some special favorites follow. Be sure to call before you go to find out which, if any, credit cards are accepted.

American

Chart House. *Moderate.* King's Wharf, Christiansted. Tel. 773–7718. Appropriately designed in a nautical theme. Their salad bar seems endless, and their entrées, such as beef kabob and Alaskan king crab, are delectable. Dinner only. AE, V, MC, DC.

Comanche Restaurant. *Moderate.* Christiansted. Tel. 773–2665. Dick Boehm's place in King's Alley has been a tried-and-true favorite for years. With fans spinning overhead, a huge outrigger canoe suspended from the ceiling, and oversized fan chairs commanding the tables, you know you're in the tropics. The curries are superb, and the fresh-caught fish topped with Creole sauce, delectable. Open for lunch and dinner daily except Sunday. All major cards.

Donn's Anchor Inn. *Moderate.* King St., at the Anchor Inn Hotel, Christiansted. Tel. 773–0263. Open-air dining on a terrace overlooking the water. Famous for Sunday brunch, which ranges from an avocado-and-bacon omelette to buttermilk pancakes cooked in beer, all of it accompanied by sparkling champagne. Open seven days a week, breakfast, lunch and dinner. AE, CB, DC, MC, V.

Chinese

Golden China Inn. *Moderate.* King Cross St., Christiansted. Tel. 773–8181. Authentic Chinese cuisine, featuring Szechuan, Mandarin, Cantonese, and Hunan specialties. Sift and sort, sample Chinese wine and enjoy the oriental music in the background. Open for lunch and dinner daily except Sunday. AE, MC, V.

French/Nouvelle Cuisine

1742 Great House. *Expensive.* Christiansted. Tel. 773–3801. One of the old St. Croix homes that has been renovated in the famous Apothecary Hall on Company St. Terrace dining on its second-floor balcony, with the emphasis on fine French cuisine. Dinner only. AE.

Tivoli Gardens. *Moderate.* Christiansted. Tel. 773–6782. Nice layout in a garden setting atop the Pan Am Pavilion. A popourri of dining areas, eclectic menu. All backed by live music, which, depending on where you're seated, can be loud. Open for lunch and dinner daily, except brunch replaces lunch on Sunday. AE, V, MC.

Eccentric Egret. *Moderate.* King St., Christiansted. Tel. 773–7644. This restaurant in the heart of town takes its name from the snowy egret that can be found skimming the surf or strutting the island's shore. Two dining rooms on the second floor of a restored building. Their salad jordan is a master Caesar, with such added treats as artichoke hearts, tomatoes, and olives; and their house specialty, asapao aurora, is a delicious dish of fresh shrimp or lobster served with two kinds of rice, sliced pimento, and a secret hot sauce. Lunch, Monday–Friday; dinner daily. AE.

International

Barbara McConnell's. *Expensive.* Frederiksted. Tel. 772–3309. Off the mainstream, but long a St. Croix institution. Her restaurant is located in a restored home that was the Anglican vicarage in 1760. Imaginative lunches and dinner prepared by reservation only. Expensive, but worth it.

Swashbuckler. *Moderate.* Frederiksted. Tel. 772–1773. Pleasant and attractive spot at the end of Strand St. They specialize in steaks, but also offer seafood and Cruzan cuisine. Lunch and dinner daily except Monday. All major cards.

Italian

Frank's. *Moderate.* Strand and Queen sts., Christiansted. Tel. 773–0090. An Italian feast here any time—either inside in a small dining room or outdoors in the cobblestone courtyard. Extensive menu. Dinners only, daily. V, MC.

ST. JOHN

Eating out on St. John is casual, relaxed, and for the most part al fresco. Since nearly all food is imported to this tiny island, tabs are high whether you order hamburger or filet mignon. Generally, visitors and residents dress for dinner only at ritzy Caneel Bay (jackets required for men); elsewhere almost anything goes.

Caneel Bay—The Terrace or **Sugar Mill.** *Deluxe.* At Caneel Bay Plantation Resort, off Northshore Rd. about one mile from Cruz Bay. Tel. 776–6111. Heavenly American/continental food with sky-high prices to match. Beautiful tropical setting on the grounds of the exquisitely groomed Rockresort. Open daily, lunch and dinner, reservations required. AE, MC, V, DC.

Frank's. *Expensive.* Boulon Center, Cruz Bay. Tel. 776–6848. Innovative gourmet menu featuring American/Continental cuisine prepared with care from the finest, freshest ingredients. Daily seafood specials, veal, fettucine Alfredo, and unique, garden-fresh salads. Lunch and dinner Tues.–Sat.; brunch only on Sun. No credit cards.

Cafe Roma. *Moderate.* Downtown Cruz Bay above Joe's Diner. Tel. 776–6524. Specializing in pizza, pasta, and various chicken and veal dishes. The lasagna is hard to beat. Friendly, relaxed atmosphere in the heart of town. Open daily, dinner only. No credit cards.

Meadas Restaurant. *Moderate.* Just off Cruz Bay Park across from the ferry dock. No phone. Good island cooking with an emphasis on seafood. Grouper yellowtail, shrimp, and "old wife" (trigger fish) are usually on the menu, which fluctuates depending on the day's catch. Conch stew, chicken West Indian style, johnny cakes, and funghi are special island treats. Small, intimate setting in island-style home. Lunch and dinner Mon.–Fri. No credit cards.

Moveable Feast. *Moderate.* Mongoose Junction, Cruz Bay. Tel. 776–6454. Dining in tropical garden setting. Eat-in or take-out deli specials (perfect for the picnic basket), daily specials and luscious home-made soups and salads. Typical American breakfasts. Specializes in frozen bar drinks—kahlua freezes, peach coladas, etc. Breakfast, lunch, and dinner Mon.–Sat.; Sun., brunch only. No credit cards.

Joe's Diner. *Inexpensive.* Downtown Cruz Bay. No phone. If you find yourself craving fast food, eat here—it isn't McDonalds but it's as close as you'll come on St. John. All-American hamburgers, fries, and shakes with some island goodies thrown in at reasonable prices. Breakfast, lunch Mon.–Sat. No credit cards.

Nature's Fruit Stand. *Inexpensive.* Cruz Bay waterfront. No phone. This small fruit stand has some of the best island-grown fruits and vegetables on St. John—perfect for snacking. Depending on the season you'll find such island delights as mango, genips, banana figs, soursop, passion fruit, and pineapples on the usually well-stocked shelves. Open daily; no credit cards.

Vie's Snack Shack. *Inexpensive.* Outside Coral Bay on Route 10 at the easternmost tip of the island. No phone. Best garlic chicken on the island. Or try meat patés with coconut, guava, or pineapple tarts for dessert. Extra special home-made juices ranging from mango to passion fruit to the even more exotic tamarind or soursop. No regular hours or days of operation for this informally run family operation. Take your chances—the food is worth it and the drive is breathtaking.

ST. THOMAS

French/Nouvelle Cuisine

Fiddle Leaf. *Deluxe.* Watergate Villas at Bolongo Bay. Tel. 775–2810. Cordon Bleu-trained chef lovingly prepares new American and French nouvelle cuisine. Sinfully delicious from appetizer through dessert—if you have but one big splurge on St. Thomas, this is the place for it. Dinner only. Tues.–Sat. AE. Reservations required.

Stone Farm House. *Deluxe.* Mahogany Run on the north side. Tel. 775–5000. Elegantly refurbished Danish estate house with gourmet cuisine to match. Jackets preferred for men. Some Caribbean specialties mix with nouvelle French cuisine. Reservations required. Dinner daily (except Tues.); Brunch on Sun. AE, MC, V, DC.

Cafe Normandie. *Expensive.* Rue de St. Bartholomew in Frenchtown. Tel. 774–1622. Intimate, candlelit atmosphere. Specialties of the house: veal, lobster, squab, duckling, and beef Wellington. The chocolate fudge pie is worth the price of the meal alone—*Gourmet* and *Bon Appetit* magazines have thus far been unsuccessful in sweet-talking the owners out of the recipe. Dinner daily; reservations required. AE, V, MC.

L'Escargot. *Expensive.* Two locations: downtown Charlotte Amalie in the Royal Dane Mall off Main St. or outside town in Subbase. Tel. 774–8880 (town) or 774–6565 (Subbase). One of the most popular restaurants on the island for lunch or dinner. Offers superb classic French cuisine with the most extensive wine list on St. Thomas—more than 500 wines to choose from. Extensive menus at both locations with some local specialties. Lunch and dinner Mon.–Sat. AE.

Harborview. *Expensive.* On Frenchman Hill above Charlotte Amalie. Tel. 774–2651. A beautifully restored 19th-century Danish manor house with elegantly prepared and presented gourmet cuisine. Menu is actually a blend of French and Italian dishes with a few island specialties; fish, steaks, and chops included as well. The innovative cuisine has been written about in several publications including *Town and Country* and *Cosmopolitan.* Reservations required. Dinner only; closed Tues. AE, MC, V.

Parkside. *Expensive.* In Charlotte Amalie just off Roosevelt Park. Tel. 774–1695. Delightful garden setting with just a dozen or so tables situated in an old Danish townhouse. The island's only French/Swiss restaurant. Among the house specialties: lamb provençal, dolphin caviar, fondue, frogs' legs. A sumptuous chocolate pie and various ice cream confections top the dessert menu. Limited reservations. Dinner only, closed Tues. AE, MC, V.

Italian

Bartolino's. *Expensive.* Heart of Frenchtown. Tel. 774–8554. Specializes in Northern Italian food. Diners enjoy a spectacular view of the harbor. Choose among a variety of pasta, veal, and seafood dishes—prosciutto and melon is a favorite appetizer. Dinner only; closed Mon. AE, MC, V.

Barbary Coast. *Moderate.* Frenchtown. Tel. 774–8354. Chianti bottles hang from the ceiling in this fun-loving, friendly establishment. A local favorite featuring an authentic Italian menu with island flair—conch parmigiana is among the many delicious offerings. Best veal piccata on the island! Dinner daily, AE, MC, V.

German/Austrian

Alexander's Cafe. *Moderate.* Frenchtown. Tel. 774–4349. Good, hearty food in an upbeat, open-air café. Superb selection of quiches, crepes, soups, and salads for lunch. Dinner specialty is weinerschnitzel. Mouthwatering apple strudel for dessert. Breakfast, lunch, dinner. Closed Sun. No credit cards.

Mexican

For The Birds. *Moderate.* At Compass Pt. on St. Thomas' east end. Check directory for tel. (new). Located on beautiful Scott Beach, the restaurant features a Tex-Mex menu with south-of-the-border and barbecued entrees. Dynamite Margaritas accompany an assortment of appetizers. Best of the bunch: Super nachos and chili con queso. Succulent baby back ribs, fish Vera Cruz, fajitas, and shrimp matzatlán are house specialties. Dinner daily. Reservations accepted only for parties of six or more. MC, V.

El Papagayo. *Moderate.* East end of St. Thomas at Estate Tutu. Tel. 775–1550. Dine in a relaxed, tropical-garden setting. The bar features delicious strawberry margaritas and refreshing sangria. A large menu with everything from tacos to chile colorado and even some standard American fare (some say they offer the best hamburger on St. Thomas). Lunch, dinner Mon.–Sat. No credit cards.

Chinese

China Gardens. *Moderate.* Norre Gade in downtown Charlotte Amalie. Tel. 776–3256. Convenient lunch or dinner spot, specializing in Cantonese-style cooking. More than 150 dishes to choose from. Lunch, dinner Mon.–Sat.; Sun., dinner only. Take-out available, but phone in advance. AE, CB, DC, MC, V.

Chang's Patio. *Inexpensive.* Off Main St. Tel. 774–2141. Great luncheon destination in tranquil courtyard setting just steps from busy Main St. Best spring rolls this side of San Francisco. Daily specials most often include sweet-

and-sour chicken, pork or chicken teriyaki, vegetarian delight, and beef with broccoli. Lunch only, closed Sun. No credit cards.

Vegetarian

Sweetlife Café & Bakery. *Inexpensive.* Coki Beach turnoff on Smith Bay Rd., east end St. Thomas. Tel. 775–2650. Visitors and locals come from miles away for the delicious house specialties: vegieburgers and rich, creamy cheesecakes. Eat here or take out. Open daily, breakfast, lunch, dinner. No credit cards.

Island Food

Daddy's. *Moderate.* On the lagoon near Red Hook on the east end. Tel. 775–6590. Island restaurant well known for consistently good West Indian cuisine. Emphasis is on local seafood specialties: conch, lobster, scampi, and dolphin. Heavenly key-lime pie for dessert. Dinner daily. No credit cards.

Victor's Hide Out. *Moderate.* Subbase. Tel. 776–9379. Relaxed, tropical atmosphere off the beaten path. Native foods at their best. Choose from stewed mutton, curried chicken, conch in butter sauce, and a variety of seafood and daily specials. Lunch and dinner. Dinner only on Sun. No credit cards.

American/Continental

Bird of Paradise. *Expensive.* Secret Harbour Resort, east end of St. Thomas. Tel. 775–6198. Tropical, beachfront dining by candlelight, especially romantic when the moon is full. Innovative menu, daily specials. Ask for the lobster en croute stuffed with spinach and crabmeat, or choose one of the many milk-fed veal entrées. Tempting desserts. Breakfast, lunch, dinner. Reservations required for dinner. No credit cards.

Cafe Amici. *Expensive.* In the scenic A.H. Riise Alley in town—an Italian-style sidewalk cafe with an innovative menu. Breakfast and lunch only, Monday –Friday.

Cafe Blasé. *Inexpensive.* Two blocks up the hill from the heart of Charlotte Amalie's Main St. Tel. 774–6447. Avante-garde, Parisian café atmosphere. Imaginative luncheon menu ranging from tempura fried vegetables to lasagna. The pumpkin soup is out of this world and the key-lime pie arguably the best in the Caribbean! Open Mon.–Sat., Lunch and dinner. No credit cards.

Hotel 1829. *Deluxe.* Government Hill, Charlotte Amalie. Tel. 774–1829. Former 19th-century townhouse, now a National Historic Landmark. Dinner is served on the Spanish-style balcony or in the high-ceilinged dining room. *Gourmet Magazine* has featured several of the dishes, which include rack of lamb, a variety of veal entrées, and seafood specials. Liqueur soufflés and flaming café le Baron provide a delightful finish to the meal. Dinner only, Mon.–Sat. Reservations required. AE, MC, V.

Mountain Top. *Inexpensive.* Top of Crown Mountain Rd.; Tel. 774–5760. Best known for its spectacular down-island view and equally intoxicating banana daiquiris. Lunch is cafeteria style with a different West Indian specialty daily. Lunch only.

Piccolo Marina Cafe. *Moderate.* At Red Hook Marina. Tel. 775–6350. Heavenly pastas with a touch of France, Italy, and even the Orient. Open daily, Sundays for brunch only. AE.

Sparky's Waterfront. *Inexpensive.* Waterfront Dr. in Charlotte Amalie. Tel. 774–8015. Informal and fun. All-American, no-nonsense fare: hamburgers, omelettes, salads, and chili. The piña coladas and Sunday brunch are extra special. Open daily, breakfast, lunch, dinner. No credit cards.

Williams & Daniels, Ltd. *Moderate.* Located on Main Street, upstairs from the Scandinavian Center—the heart of the shopping district. No tel. Intimate, European-style dining room with carefully prepared fare. Exquisite desserts. Luncheon only, 11 A.M. to 3 P.M. AE.

 NIGHT LIFE AND BARS. Throughout the U.S. Virgin Islands night life is low key, since most of the focus is on sunny, daytime activities. After dark most activity takes place at casual pool- or beach-side bars at larger resorts and tourist hotels. During the season, many feature steel bands, guitarists, or pianists during cocktail hour, as do many of the restaurants.

St. Croix. The nightlife on St. Croix takes place mainly in the hotels, most of which have music, dancing, and entertainment. You can dine high in the hills overlooking the breathtaking harbor sites, or take in a show of calypso singers and limbo dancers. Try *The Binnacle* at the Caravelle Hotel (tel. 773–4755) for drinks on an outdoor patio, live music nightly during the winter season. *Buccaneer Hotel,* east of Christiansted (tel. 773–2100) has live entertainment seven nights a week and a limbo show on weekends. The *Cane Bay Plantation,* Kings Hill, North Shore (tel. 778–0410) has a live steel band Thursday nights. The *Excelsior Club,* across from Sunny Isle (tel. 773–5800) boasts live music and disco on Saturday night—be sure to call for the weekly entertainment schedule. *Hotel on the Cay* at Christiansted Harbor (tel. 773–2035) has nightly entertainment featuring reggae, calypso, and steel bands. *Tivoli Gardens,* Strand St. in Christianstad (tel. 773–6782), has a vocalist/guitarist nightly from 7:00 P.M. The *2 Plus 2 Disco* on Northside Road (tel. 773–3710) has live music Tuesday through Sunday. Also try *Seven Flags* in Frederiksted for dancing most nights to a steel band or the *Moonraker Lounge* on the second floor of the Lodge Hotel on Queen Cross St. in Christiansted.

St. John. Most of St. John goes to sleep when the sun goes down—more than St. Thomas and St. Croix, this tiny island moves by day. For the determined, however, some nighttime distractions are available. *Caneel Bay Resort,* during season, features nightly cocktail hour shows at its Terrace Lounge. These include everything from local scratch and steel bands to clubby New York-style entertainers. With the exception of nightly, park-sponsored evening programs at *Cinnamon Bay Campground* (rangers give slide presentations, cultural and natural history talks, or show films on the marine world at 7:30 nightly; check park for schedule) Cruz Bay is the place for night life (what there is of it!). And during off-season, even in town, most action winds down by 10:00 or 11:00 P.M. *The Backyard Bar and Restaurant,* with or without live entertainment, tends to be the town's rowdiest late-night spot—a favorite hangout for sailing types. Friendly, open air, and loud; located just off Cruz Bay Park. *Frank's* has a popular happy hour each Friday from 5:00 P.M. to 7:00 P.M.—locals flock to it. Local bands rotate weekly between two or three local establishments; music starts late (10:00 or 11:00 P.M.) and often goes until 4:00 A.M. Look for signs posted around town or listen for word-of-mouth announcements of who is playing where and when. Most popular late-night bars and dance floors: *Fred's, The Lime Inn,* and *Ric's Hilltop* and the new *Purple Line* (all located within blocks of each other in tiny Cruz Bay—just follow the music). Don't-miss local bands include Prophecy (best reggae in the Virgin Islands), Frontline, and Eddie and the Movements.

St. Thomas. During the season, big hotels such as *Frenchman's Reef, Carib Beach, Limetree Beach Hotel,* and *Bluebeard's Castle* offer specialty shows (limbo, calypso, and broken-bottle dancing) at least once a week; check with your hotel for schedules. The local guide *St. Thomas This Week* also lists schedules. Frenchman's Reef's *Top of the Reef Supper Club* features a Las Vegas-style review every night but Sunday at 9:00 P.M. and 11:00 P.M. Reservations required, tel. 774–8500. Discoteques located at Virgin Isle Hotel's *Studio 54* and *Club Raffles* at Compass Point. Studio 54 open Fri. and Sat. nights only; 10:00 P.M.–2:00 A.M., $7 cover. Club Raffles nightly midnight—4:00 A.M.; no cover or minimum. The "life in the fast lane" set (mostly under 30, with most patrons 18 to 25 years old) gathers weekends at any number of Charlotte Amalie's Backstreet bars and clubs. Bar-hopping is the trend, and the popular spots fluctuate from weekend to weekend depending on which band is playing where. Among the most lively: *Yesterdays, The Ritz* and *Partners* (all on Back Street within one or two blocks of each other). *Safari* (located just off Back Street), with dancing nightly, attracts a gay clientele, although women and couples are welcome: usually a mixed crowd.

POSTAGE. Since the U.S. Virgin Islands is a territory of America, postal rates are the same as on the mainland. First-class mail to the mainland U.S. automatically travels by air. Airmail is recommended to other parts of the world. Current first-class rates are $.22 for one ounce or less (postcards $.14). For foreign rates check at local post offices located on all three islands.

ELECTRICAL CURRENT. The current here is 110 to 120 volts A.C., 60 cycles, just as in the U.S.

SECURITY. Although the U.S. Virgin Islands are touted "America's Paradise," local law officials advise visitors to exercise the same precautions they would at home. The Department of Public Safety makes four suggestions: Make sure doors are locked in car and hotel room; keep valuables in safe-deposit boxes (available at most hotels); don't take valuables to the beach and leave them unattended; stay on well-lit, frequently traveled streets when driving or walking. The back streets of Charlotte Amalie on St. Thomas and Christiansted and Frederiksted on St. Croix are the prime areas for tourist rip-offs—purses, shopping bags, camera equipment, and even jewelry may be taken—day or night. Stick to those routes outlined in visitor publications available on all three islands. Even on sleepy St. John, police and National Park officials warn visitors to be especially cautious of their valuables while enjoying the islands's beautiful beaches. Again, avoid leaving valuables unattended even while you take just a "quick dip."

INDEX

The letter H indicates Hotels & other accommodations.
The letter R indicates Restaurants.

GENERAL INFORMATION

GEOGRAPHICAL & PRACTICAL INFORMATION

544 INDEX

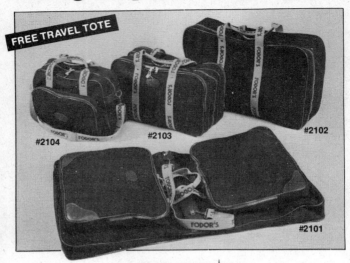